A Probus Guide to World Markets

THE GLOBAL ASSET BACKED SECURITIES MARKET

Structuring, Managing and Allocating Risk

CHARLES STONE
ANNE ZISSU
JESS LEDERMAN

EDITORS

PROBUS PUBLISHING COMPANY
Chicago, Illinois
Cambridge, England

ISBN 1-55738-460-6

Printed in the United States of America

BC

1 2 3 4 5 6 7 8 9 0

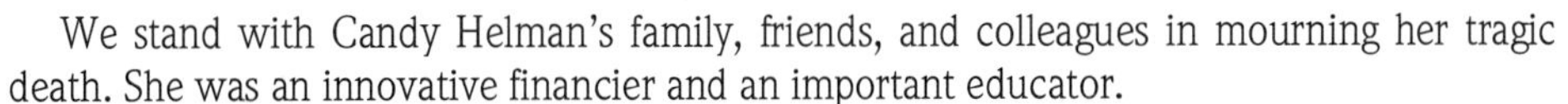

We stand with Candy Helman's family, friends, and colleagues in mourning her tragic death. She was an innovative financier and an important educator.

On behalf of each author and the people at Probus Publishing, we dedicate *The Global Asset Backed Securities Market* to the memory of Candy Helman.

Charles A. Stone
Anne Zissu
Jess Lederman

Table of Contents

Contributors ix
Introduction xi

Part I
Sources of Value

1 The Future of Asset Securitization: The Benefits and Costs of Breaking Up the Bank 3
George J. Benston

2 Elements of Mortgage Securitization 15
Alan C. Hess and Clifford W. Smith, Jr.,

3 Sources of Value Added from Structuring Asset-Backed Securities to Reduce or Reallocate Risk 27
John D. Finnerty

4 An Overview of Techniques in Structured Finance 61
Blaine Roberts

5 International Securitization for the Emerging Economies 71
Alexandre Hayek

6 Financing Opportunities for the Commodities Industry Through Securitization 77
Monique de Zagon

7 Securitization—A European Bank's Introspective View 83
Andy Clapham

Part II
Identifying and Allocating Risk

8 Risks in Securitisation Transactions 99
Jonathan E. Keighley

9 Auto Loan Securitization: A Case Study of the U.S. Auto Finance Industry 109
Gary J. Kopff

10 The Management and Transfer of Credit, Liquidity and Contingency Risks 127
Nicholas Millard

11 Structured Securities: Credit, Cash Flow, and Legal Risks 135
Clifford M. Griep

12 Credit Risks and Their Analysis in Asset Securitization 153
David L. Gold and Julie Schlueter

13 Credit Enhancement 169
Fredrik Månsson

14 The Role of the Monoline Financial Guarantor: How Safe Is Safe? 179
Henry T. Mortimer, Jr.

15 Financial Guaranty Reinsurance: Bridging Global Asset-Backed Securities Markets 189
David A. Smith

Part III
Managing Risk

16 Evaluating Securitisation—The Perspective of a European Financial Institution 199
Jonathan E. Keighley

17 Asset-Backed Finance—Risk Control for Traders in Asset-Backed Securities 217
Paresh Mashru and Mark Rhys

18 Asset-Backed Finance—Accounting Issues 223
Paresh Mashru and Mark Rhys

19 Securitization Trade-Offs—How Deal Structure Can Influence the Future Value of Your Company or Portfolio 227
Kathryn A. Cassidy

Part IV
Structured Finance Within the Law

20 Asset Securitisation in the United Kingdom and Other Jurisdictions—Main Considerations 235
David Bonsall

21 Multi-Country Securitization and Currency Hedging Programs 265
Stephen Oxenbridge and C. Mark Nicolaides

22 Asset-Backed Commercial Paper Programs 277
Barbara Kavanagh, Thomas R. Boemio and Gerald A. Edwards, Jr.

Part V
Mortgage-Backed Securities

23 MAES ECP No. 1 PLC: An Example of the Risks and Rewards of Asset-Backed Euro Commercial Paper 289
Candy Helman

24 Managing Risk in a LIBOR-Plus Fund 299
Paul Derosa and Laurie Goodman

25 Developments in the UK Mortgage Securities Market 305
N.S. Terrington

26 The Risks and Opportunities of the Canadian NHA MBS Market 319
Lori Terry

27 The Australian Mortgage-Backed Securities Market: The Role of Mortgage Insurance in Reducing Credit Risk 337
Brian W. Richardson

28 Mortgage Securitisation in Developed Housing Finance Systems 341
Douglas B. Diamond, Jr. and Michael J. Lea

29 The Hazards of Default 357
Robert Van Order

30 Credit Intensive Mortgage Securities: B Pieces 363
William F. Wallace

31 AAA Senior Mortgage-Backed Securities versus AAA Mortgage-Backed Securities 375
Charles Austin Stone, Anne Zissu, and Jess Lederman

32 CMO Volatility Ratings 383
Stephen W. Joynt, James D. Nadler, and Robert E. Phelan

33 CMO Tranche Risk Revealed 389
James D. Nadler and Brandon H. Einhorn

34 Optional Plays 397
Donald R. Rindler

35 Strategic Options 405
Donald R. Rindler

36 Risk, Return, and Hedging of Fixed-Rate Mortgages 413
Douglas T. Breeden

Part VI
The Securitization of Credit Cards

37 Evaluating the Risk of Credit Card-Backed Securities 449
Gregory C. Raab, Neil Baron and Deborah W. Madden

38 Understanding Credit Card Subordinate Certificates 471
William F. Wallace

Index 491

Contributors

Neil Baron, *Fitch Investors Service, Inc.*

George J. Benston, *Emory University*

Thomas R. Boemio, *Board of Governors of the Federal Reserve System*

David Bonsall, *Freshfields*

Douglas T. Breeden, *Duke University and Smith Breeden Associates*

Kathryn A. Cassidy, *GE Capital*

Andy Clapham, *Natwest Markets*

Paul Derosa, *Eastbridge Capital Inc.*

Douglas B. Diamond, Jr., *Cardiff Consulting Services*

Gerald A. Edwards, Jr., *Board of Govenors of the Federal Reserve System*

Brandon H. Einhorn, *Fitch Investors Service, Inc.*

John D. Finnerty, *Fordham University and McFarland Dewey & Co.*

David L. Gold, *Duff & Phelps Corp.*

Laurie Goodman, *Merrill Lynch*

Clifford M. Griep, *Standard & Poor's*

Alexandre Hayek, *Salomon Brothers Inc.*

Candy Helman, *J.P. Morgan Securities Ltd.*

Alan C. Hess, *University of Washington*

Stephen W. Joynt, *Fitch Investors Services, Inc.*

Barbara Kavanagh, *Federal Reserve Bank of Chicago*

Jonathan E. Keighley, *Gracebury Securitisation Limited*

Gary J. Kopff, *Heritage Management Ltd.*

Michael J. Lea, *Cardiff Consulting Services*

Jess Lederman, *Private Investor*

Deborah W. Madden, *Fitch Investors Service, Inc.*

Fredrik Månsson, *Trygg-Hansa SPP Financial Insurance*

Paresh Mashru, *Arthur Andersen, London*

Nicholas Millard, *Special Risk Services*

Henry T. Mortimer, Jr., *Financial Security Assurance*

James D. Nadler, *Fitch Investors Services, Inc.*

C. Mark Nicolaides, *Mayer, Brown & Platt*

Stephen Oxenbridge, *Morgan Grenfell & Co. Ltd.*

Robert E. Phelan, *Fitch Investors Service, Inc.*

Gregory C. Raab, *Fitch Investors Service, Inc.*

Mark Rhys, *Arthur Andersen, London*

Brian W. Richardson, *MGICA Ltd.*

Donald R. Rindler, *Freddie Mac*

Blaine Roberts, *Bear Stearns*

Julie P. Schlueter, *Duff & Phelps Corp.*

Clifford W. Smith, Jr., *University of Rochester*

David A. Smith, *Capital Reinsurance Company*

Charles Austin Stone, *Université Paris Dauphine*

N.S. Terrington, *National Home Loans Holdings PLC*

Lori Terry, *Burns Fry Limited*

Robert Van Order, *Freddie Mac*

William F. Wallace, *Morgan Stanley & Co.*

Monique de Zagon, *Baker & McKenzie*

Anne Zissu, *Temple University*

INTRODUCTION

Two Boeing 747's (plane X and plane Y) fly between London and New York five times per week. Both planes are always filled to capacity. Both planes have the same operating costs, on time records, safety records, and bad food. Pilots on both planes are "top guns." The planes have the same exact schedules and both leave from gates which are five miles from where passengers check their luggage. Plane (X) is financed with an issue of $20,000,000 of common stock and $10,000,000 of 10-year debt which is collateralized by the value of the plane and an unsecured $10,000,000 five-year bank loan. Plane (Y) is financed with $30,000,000 of common stock and $10,000,000 of debentures. The important point is that the cash flowing out of the operation of each plane is identical and independent of the mixture of claims which have been issued to fund the plane. When the wandering consultant approaches the manager of plane (Y) and suggests that he/she refinance the plane with an issue of asset-backed securities, the manager should reflect on the following excerpt from *Managing Financial Risk* (pages 362–363, Clifford W. Smith Jr., Charles W. Smithson, & D. Sykes Wilford, Harper & Row, Publishers, Ballinger Division, 1990).

> The relation between the real cash flows of a firm and its financial policies was established by Franco Modigliani and Merton Miller in 1958 in what has come to be referred to as the M&M proposition I.[1] In its original version, the M&M proposition stated that:
>
> *If there are no taxes,*
>
> *If there are no transaction costs, and*
>
> *If the investment policy of the firm is fixed,*
>
> *Then the financial policies of the firm are irrelevant.*
>
> Risk management-hedging is one of the firm's financial policies. The M&M proposition indicates that in a world with no taxes, no transaction costs, and fixed investment policies, investors can create their own risk management by holding diversified portfolios (precisely the conclusion we came to in the preceding section). Although the proposition itself is of extreme importance to an academic, the impact of the M&M proposition to a practitioner is most evident when it is inverted:
>
> *If financial policies matter, that is, if risk management policies are going to have an impact on the value of the firm, then it must be that the financial policies impact taxes or transaction costs or the firm's investment policies.*

Securitisation is one of many financial policies which can be utilized by financial and non-financial firms. Securitization has expanded the capital base to which public and private institutions have access. Innovations continue to increase the scope of the market for securitisation and make it a viable funding option to firms throughout the world. The

1 The original M&M proposition was stated in terms of the firm's debt equity ratio: see Franco Modigliani and Merton Miller, "The Cost of Capital, Corporation Finance and the Theory of Investment," *American Economic Review* 48 (June 1958): 197–261. The rationale is that, since individual leverage is possible, an investor will not pay the firm for corporate leverage. The M&M proposition was extended to dividends in 1961: "Dividend Policy, Growth, and the Valuations of Shares," *Journal of Business* 34 (October 1961): 411–433, which argued that "homemade" dividends can be created as the investor sells the firm's stock.

integration of the international money and capital markets, the convergence of regulatory policy governing financial markets and institutions, advances in financial engineering, and the increase in the relative value of liquidity have all been factors which have increased the value of securitization. Securitisation enables risks which are imbedded in individual assets to be extracted and reallocated. Securitisation does not eliminate risks but often enables risks to be allocated more efficiently.

The trend of the increased utilization of securitisation by firms outside the U.S. can be tracked in the *American Bond Buyer/American Banker* newsletter, "The Global Asset Backed Monitor." It is becoming more and more common to read about a company's first foray into the securitisation market or a country adapting its securities laws to encompass the process of securitisation. The company may be a bank in Canada, an industrial company in the mideast, a multinational corporation in Belgium, a mortgage originator in Australia, or a bank in Japan. Securitisation has recently been legalized in Turkey. In Turkey an institution may securitize up to 90 percent of its total portfolio of assets. South American banks, industrial companies, and service firms are actively securitising receivables. Our objective was to edit a book which offered the manager of a financially sound but isolated firm information which would enable him/her to lower the firm's cost of capital. The purpose of this project was to offer people who are currently managing financial institutions and students of business valuable insights into the process of securitisation.

If reading this book offers those people, who are responsible for managing and raising the capital of public and private enterprises, sufficient insight into the process of securitization so that they can lower their company's marginal cost of capital then this book will have added value. This has been our intent.

We would like to thank each author for considering *The Global Asset Backed Securities Market: Structuring, Managing, and Allocating Risk* an appropriate forum for his/her analysis. As students of banking and finance it has been a privilege to edit the research of the people who are at the forefront of the developments taking place in the international money and capital markets.

The expertise of each author is a scarce and valuable resource. Their schedules are always 150 percent full. We are honored that they dedicated their time and resources to writing *The Global Asset Backed Securities Market: Structuring, Managing and Allocating Risk.*

We would like to thank Professors Alan C. Hess and Clifford W. Smith Jr. for permitting us to reprint their article "Elements of Mortgage Securitization" which first appeared in *The Journal of Real Estate Finance and Economics* (Vol. 1, No. 4, December 1988). We would like to thank Professor George J. Benston for allowing us to reprint his article "The Future of Asset Securitization: The Benefits of Breaking up the Bank" which first appeared in *The Continental Bank Journal of Applied Corporate Finance* (Spring 1992, Vol. 5, No. 1) We would like to thank Professor Douglas T. Breeden for granting us permission to reprint his article "Risk, Return, and Hedging of Fixed-Rate Mortgages" which first appeared in *The Journal of Fixed Income* (September 1991).

Special thanks must be given to Maxine Stone who helped us coordinate this project while we traveled between Paris, Philadelphia, and New York. Without her help many of the chapters would have been lost over the Atlantic.

We look forward to sharing the ideas which are analyzed in *The Global Market for Asset Backed Securities: Structuring, Managing, and Allocating Risk* with our students at Temple University and Université Paris Dauphine.

Charles A. Stone   Anne Zissu   Jess Lederman

Part I

Sources of Value

Chapter 1

The Future of Asset Securitization: The Benefits and Costs of Breaking Up the Bank*

by George J. Benston,
Emory University

Securitization is the process of converting bank loans into securities. The essential procedure is straightforward. A bank or thrift[1] in direct contact with borrowers *originates* loans. It then sells the loans to an investment bank or an affiliate of the bank that *pools* and structures them, often together with loans made by other banks, into a security. To make the security more acceptable to investors, another firm (for example, an insurance company) *guarantees* the security against credit losses. The security is then sold to *investors* such as pension funds, insurance companies, and other banks. The originator services the loans for a fee, passing payments to the pooler who distributes the funds to the investors.

In 1988, McKinsey & Co.'s Lowell Bryan published a book entitled, *Breaking Up the Bank: Rethinking an Industry Under Seige.*[2] The fundamental thesis of the book is stated by Bryan as follows:

> *Structured securitized credit is a new technology for lending that has been developed essentially by nonbankers. It is better on all counts than the traditional lending system. It is growing very rapidly precisely because it is a superior technology—one that, in fact, is rendering traditional banking obsolete.* (p. 63)

In the same year, James Rosenthal and Juan Ocampo, Bryan's colleagues at McKinsey, published a book that made similar claims about the future of asset securitization.[3] Parts of both books were published in the Fall 1988 issue of the *Journal of Applied Corporate Finance*, together with other articles explaining and extolling the benefits of asset securitization.

How justified is this enthusiasm about the future of securitized credit? Will securitization grow to the point where traditional banking, as we have known it, becomes largely a relic of the past? I address these issues by analyzing the expected benefits of securitization for financial market participants, institutions, and the economy in general—and then setting them against the expected costs.

THE BENEFITS AND COSTS OF SECURITIZATION

Bryan argues that securitized credit is a "more efficient, effective technology . . . [that] offers great benefits to each participant" (p. 81)—that is, to

1 Hereafter all chartered depository financial institutions are called "banks," except where specifically designated as thrifts (savings and loan associations and savings banks) or commercial banks.

2 Lowell L. Bryan, *Breaking Up the Bank: Rethinking an Industry Under Siege*, (Homewood, IL: Dow Jones-Irwin), 1988. All page references for citations of Bryan throughout this chapter are drawn from this source.

3 James A. Rosenthal and Juan M. Ocampo, *Securitization of Credit: Inside the New Technology of Finance* (1988). All page references for citations of Rosenthal and Ocampo in this article are drawn from this source.

*This chapter benefited from helpful criticism by Don Chew and Peter Stockman.

Reprinted with permission from author from the *Journal of Applied Corporate Finance*, reference, Vol. 5 No.1, Spring 1992, pp. 71–82.

investors, guarantors of credit risk, investment bankers (poolers), issuing institutions (originators), and borrowers. In evaluating this claim, I discuss the benefits to each group, giving the most space to the issuing institutions because the benefits claimed for them are the basis for Bryan's prediction that banking as it has been practiced is on its way out.

Investors

Like other debt instruments, securitized credit sells at a price that reflects credit risk and prepayment (or cash flow) risk.[4] Various measures are usually taken to reduce or virtually eliminate these risks, at least for some investors.

Credit risk for most investors in securitized credit can be virtually eliminated in one of three ways. First, only very high-quality loans can be included in the security. Second, the guarantor can guarantee the payment when due of all loan interest and principal. Investors would then be concerned only with the financial standing and probity of the guarantor.[5] The cost of this remaining uncertainty can be reduced by having securitized loans guaranteed only by firms with very strong reputations for financial strength and probity, or by obtaining the backing of the federal government.[6] Third, the cash flows from a loan pool can be repackaged to shield *some* investors from credit risk. For example, a collateralized mortgage obligation (CMO) may be "cut" into three tranches: fast-paying, medium-paying, and slow-paying (or "residual"). The fast-paying (senior) tranche gets the first payments of principal received; hence, there is usually little risk that these amounts will not be made as promised. The medium-paying tranche bears some, but also usually fairly minimal, risk. Investors in the slow-paying tranche absorb the residual cash flow risk, excluding that portion taken by the guarantor and originator.

Prepayment risk occurs when prepayments are permitted (as is the case with most consumer loans) on loans that are not continuously repriced to the market. Although the timing of cash flows is uncertain, it is predictable (to an extent) because prepayments tend to accelerate when interest rates on similar new loans fall below the rates on the pooled loans. Tranches also serve to segregate prepayment risk, thereby protecting some investors.

Thus, senior securitized loan securities are on a par with U.S. Treasury or agency obligations with the same maturity structure. There are, however, four qualifications. First, investors may not fully trust the credit risk guarantees, resulting in a credit risk premium. Second, loan-backed securities are not as well known to investors as U.S. government obligations, thus giving rise to a potential liquidity or transactions-cost premium. Third, to the extent cash flows remain uncertain because prepayments are not fully predictable, there will likely be a call premium built into the interest rate. Fourth, since interest on the obligations is fully taxable (unlike interest on U.S. government obligations, which is not taxed by state governments), there will be a tax premium. For these four reasons, securitized loans should sell at an interest rate somewhat above the rate paid on a U.S. government obligation with the same maturity.

Guarantors of Credit Risk

Bryan writes, "Guarantors who have the skills to assess credit risks have the opportunity of charging fees greater than expected losses without actually having to extend loans" (p. 85). Like all forms of insurance underwriting, however, providing credit guarantees is subject to the problems of "adverse selection" and "moral hazard." Adverse selection refers to the propensity of originators to securitize riskier loans when they believe guarantors cannot adequately assess loan characteristics, which in turn gives risk to a "moral hazard" faced by guarantors. Like all forms of credit extension, providing credit guarantees is further subject to the

4 Securitized loans also are subject to interest rate risk. However, as is the situation with other financial instruments, investors can offset this risk by holding assets and liabilities with durations that neutralize the risk and with interest rate futures and options.

5 According to Bryan (p. 88), although guarantors of securitized loans can become bankrupt, among the over 1,000 securitized credit issues floated only one (Ticor Mortgage) failed and was liquidated. But its failure resulted in a tangle of lawsuits and losses to investors in the EPIC issue it guaranteed.

6 The federal government guarantees pools of FHA and VA mortgages assembled by the Government National Mortgage Association (GNMA). Similarly, pools of farm mortgages guaranteed by the Federal Agricultural Mortgage Association (Farmer Mac) may be considered as credit-risk free by investors because Farmer Mac can call on a $1.5 billion U.S. Treasury line-of-credit in addition to cash reserves from its initial $23 million issue of common stock. Securities backed by the Federal National Mortgage Association (FNMA) are considered credit-risk free because investors believe that the Congress will bail FNMA out should it take losses sufficient to bankrupt it.

cost and difficulty of assessing the probability that loans will not be repaid as promised.

The severity of these problems will likely differ among the kinds of loans that might be securitized. They are not too severe for home mortgage loans, provided the borrowers have substantial interests in the mortgaged properties and the market values of the properties can be assessed accurately. The value of a house can be determined from sales of reasonably similar properties, and the borrower is usually required to make a 20 percent down-payment (or the mortgage is guaranteed by a government agency (FHA or VA) or private insurer). Furthermore, in the case of home mortgages, the borrower's ability to repay the loan can be fairly readily determined from his or her employment and wealth situation and from much past experience with similar loans.

The repayment risk of most consumer loans is also often not difficult to determine because of their uniformity, small balances, and large number, and the considerable experience of originators. This is particularly true for small consumer loans that are not tied to specific purchases (where higher risks may be accepted in return for higher prices on the goods purchased), and loans collateralized by readily valued and marketable assets, such as automobiles.

But commercial and industrial loans tend not to be so uniform. Borrowers present a wide range of risks that depend on circumstances that are unique and often unstable. True, the risks of non-payment can be reduced or controlled with such devices as collateral and covenants. But such devices frequently require continuous monitoring and expeditious actions by the originating bank to secure repayment or seize control of collateral. Furthermore, unlike mortgage loans, there is no uniformity among banks in the forms on which information about borrowers is recorded. Thus, it often is difficult for guarantors to determine the extent to which they are at risk for a given loan or pool of loans.

Reflecting the "moral hazard" or "adverse selection" problem mentioned above, guarantors may also expect bank originators to sell loans of lesser quality (if for no other reason than the originators expect the guarantors to believe they are getting the lesser quality loans in the portfolio). For this reason, an originator who does not sell lesser quality loans may nevertheless be charged a "lemons" discount by guarantors on the assumption that the loans sold were of lower quality.

Guarantors can deal with the situation, in large part, by dealing only with originators whom they trust to deliver loans of a specified quality. Or, they can hold the originators responsible for most of the potential losses on the loans they sell. Bryan, for example, suggests that "the originator needs to guarantee at least two or three times the expected credit loss on the asset" (pp. 88–89). But even if that is the case, guarantors must still determine the expected loss as well as the amount and probability of catastrophic losses.

It is true, however, that guarantors' risk can be reduced to insurable proportions if they are presented with a pool of loans that is well diversified. This is the task of the pooler, usually an investment banker the guarantor can trust to structure the pool effectively.

Investment Bankers (Poolers)

The investment banking industry, as Bryan notes, has been "the driving force behind this new technology over the last several years" (p. 71). Investment bankers benefit from underwriting fees and trading profits. They typically create trusts or other special purpose vehicles that serve as intermediaries. Such intermediaries pool borrowers' obligations to achieve an adequately diversified portfolio (at least $100 million), structure the pools so they can be rated by an independent rating agency like Moody's or Standard & Poor's or insured by a credit guarantor, and then repackage the cash flows to meet demands by specialized investors.[7]

Poolers also sometimes guarantee a large portion of the securities issued, either because their guarantee is less expensive than shifting the entire burden to a separate credit guarantor or to meet a legal requirement (as is the case with Farmer Mac obligations). For example, Farmer Mac poolers must be responsible for at least the first 10 percent of credit losses on each pool. As a consequence, poolers have considerable incentives to evaluate the loans offered to them by originators and to insist on initial underwriting standards that allow them to assess the probability of borrower defaults.

Issuing Institutions (Originators)

Loan originators might get three important benefits from securitization. The first, and likely the most important, is a reduction of interest rate and credit

7 Trusts may be established by poolers to facilitate the receipt and distribution of funds. However, the interest receipts net of payments then would be subject to corporate tax unless exempted by act of Congress, as has been done for real estate mortgage investment conduits (REMICs).

risks. When banks make and hold loans, they accept both types of risk. Securitization could allow them to specialize in bearing only those risks in which they have a comparative advantage, while shifting other risks to banks and investors better able to handle them. The second benefit follows from an originator's comparative advantage over other banks or financial institutions in making and servicing certain kinds of loans. These other firms (the "buyers") may place a higher value on the loans originated by other banks because such loans allow them to diversify their own portfolios. To the extent the buying banks place a higher value on loans originated by the sellers, the selling banks could benefit from making and servicing but not holding loans. The third possible benefit I discuss below is a reduction in capital costs, which includes the cost of constraints imposed by regulatory agencies as well as the cost of funds.

Risk Reduction

Rosenthal and Ocampo emphasize the risk reducing properties of securitization, which they see as "a very sizable [technological] advance." They say emphatically:

> *Although credit securitization is sensitive to regulatory guidelines and other arbitrary limits, it draws its lifeblood not from regulatory arbitrage but from the way it handles risk. In this respect, it is fundamentally more efficient than conventional lending* (p. 5).

They specify three basic sources of risk reduction: better estimation and control of risk, lower concentration of credit risks, and reduction of interest rate and prepayment risk.

Better Estimation and Control of Risk. Securitization adds additional reviewers—credit guarantors and poolers—to the loan originators' credit review, monitoring, and servicing processes. This benefit is not obtained without cost, however. The personnel of these outside firms must familiarize themselves with the credits they are guaranteeing and evaluating. Furthermore, because they cannot know as much about the loans as do the originators, they face adverse selection and moral hazard risks.[8]

Hence, the charge for external credit review and enhancement includes both operations costs and the cost of expected losses. Once the reviewers' charge for moral hazard is included, securitization probably represents a net cost rather than a benefit from the "estimation and control" source of risk reduction, except in those instances where investors believe an originator is incompetent or dishonest.

Lower Concentration of Credit Risks. Securitization can increase the diversification of assets, thus reducing the impact of credit losses. Banks that serve areas and industries subject to similar risks—such as local housing, farming, and oil and gas production—can serve their customers by originating the loans (for which they have a comparative advantage) and then selling the loans to poolers or investors who can create diversified portfolios. Total risk—that which arises from the variance of cash flows—is reduced when loans are pooled from areas and industries subject to shocks that are not perfectly correlated (or, better yet, negatively correlated). For example, a bank in Houston can sell mortgage loans whose value depends on the financial health of the oil industry to a pooler who combines them with mortgages from many other cities subject to different economic conditions. Farm mortgages from corn-growing areas can be combined with farm mortgages from wheat-growing and vegetable-growing areas, as well as mortgages from cattle ranchers. Total risk not only can be reduced in this manner, but it can be predicted more accurately, thus reducing the cost of investor uncertainty.[9]

Reduction of Interest Rate and Prepayment Risk. When banks hold long-term fixed-interest obligations such as mortgages and fund them with short-term liabilities like demand deposits or CDs, they risk capital losses if interest rates increase unexpectedly. This mistake was responsible for the

8 That is why, as Merrill Lynch's Craig J. Goldberg and Karen Rogers report, "rating agencies assume a worst-case scenario for losses when determining the level of loss coverage necessary to attain a given rating." See Goldberg and Rogers, "An Introduction to Asset Backed Securities," *Journal of Applied Corporate Finance*, 1 (Fall, 1988), pp. 20–31.

9 If the pooler or credit enhancer reduces its moral hazard exposure by holding the originator responsible for two to three times the expected credit losses (as Bryan suggests), this benefit to the originator would be nullified, except for catastrophic losses.

insolvency of hundreds of thrifts during the 1980s.[10]

Reduction of such interest rate risk is perhaps the most important advantage of securitization for thrifts and, to a much lesser extent, for commercial banks. By selling mortgage loans to poolers, banks can meet their customers' demands and earn fees by making and servicing mortgages.[11] Farmer Mac poolers similarly allow lenders to offer and service long-term, fixed-interest, real-estate-secured loans to farmers without exposing themselves to the risk of unexpected increases in interest rate.

Prepayment risk can be reduced by securitization when the obligations are divided into tranches. Holders of junior tranches, as suggested earlier, bear all or most of this risk. Thus, while prepayment risk can be divided among investors, it cannot be reduced in total. In addition, where expected prepayments can be estimated more accurately by the originator (who is likely to know more about individual borrowers and local economic conditions) than by the secondary holder, guarantors or investors are subject to adverse selection.

Comparative Advantages in Making and Servicing Loans

Some banks may be located in areas with heavy loan demand. Their presence and experience is likely to give them a comparative advantage over other lenders in making and servicing local loans. Such banks may also have significant economies of scale in making and servicing such loans. But if these same banks have higher costs of capital than other banks or investors, or if other investors value the obligations securitized by the loans for diversification, originating banks can benefit from making and servicing, but not holding, the loans.

But, again, moral hazard concerns by purchasers of the loans could offset these advantages. Many bankers will continue to recall the Penn Square Bank debacle, where banks purchased outright and in participations billions of dollars of loans that turned out to have been very poorly (even fraudulently) made and serviced.

Commercial loans, in particular, are subject to an additional disadvantage of securitization. Securitization and sale of loans is likely to reduce, even eliminate altogether, the value of the flexibility that banks typically provide their borrowers in responding to changing business conditions. An example is a revolving demand loan, which allows borrowers to increase and decrease their loan balances (within specified limits) without notice to the lender. Borrowers and lenders often want to change the terms of collateralized loans to sell pledged assets or to increase the loan by including additional collateral. The ability to relax restrictive covenants is also likely to be valuable, especially to smaller business borrowers. Securitization eliminates much of this flexibility or, at best, makes it very expensive to regain.

Lower Capital Costs

Banks seeking to expand their lending business have basically two choices. They can expand by originating and holding the loans, financing this investment with deposits and capital (non-government-insured debt and equity). Or they can instead securitize and sell the loans. Bryan and his McKinsey colleagues assert that the latter course is almost always preferable for banks that have relatively low credit ratings. Indeed, Bryan says unequivocally: "For intermediaries who themselves are not at least single-A credits, it will always pay to securitize high-quality assets, because in doing so they can fund themselves more cheaply" (p. 82).

In the analysis that follows, I explain why this conclusion is unlikely to hold—at least in the absence of significant diversification benefits for buying banks and a comparative advantage in origination by selling banks. If Bryan were correct, it is only because the latter benefits for lower-rated issuers systematically outweigh the costs—an assumption I will challenge.

Capital Cost When Loans Are Held. If a bank holds the loans it makes, it can obtain the required financing in the form of government-insured deposit debt, noninsured debt, and equity capital. Depositors' funds are insured up to $100,000 per

10 For details, see my 1985 monograph, *An Analysis of the Causes of Savings and Loan Association Failures*, Monograph Series in Finance and Economics, Salomon Brothers Center for the Study of Financial Institutions, Graduate School of Business Administration, New York University.

11 However, thrifts that hold the mortgage-backed securities to meet the "70 percent of assets thriftness test" required by the Financial Institutions Recovery and Enforcement Act of 1989 (FIRREA) or the 60 percent test required by the Internal Revenue Service to obtain tax benefits, still are subject to interest rate risk, although their liquidity ("fire sale") risk is lower.

account by the funds operated by the Federal Deposit Insurance Corporation (FDIC).[12] The cost of deposits equals the interest rate promised plus the costs of getting the funds, operations required to service the accounts, government insurance charges, and the opportunity costs of required reserves. Because deposit insurance premiums are not properly adjusted for the level of risk assumed by the insurance fund, some banks are penalized and others are subsidized.[13] The lower-rated (more risky) banks are likely to be undercharged for deposit insurance; hence, they would tend to benefit more from holding loans funded with insured deposits to the extent permitted by the supervisory authorities.

Banks that have comparative advantages in obtaining deposit funds—perhaps because their market area includes customers who demand deposit services, have a branch network effective in obtaining and processing deposit funds, or experience significant economies of scope among deposit and other banking services—also tend to benefit from holding or purchasing rather than selling loans. On the other hand, banks that find deposits relatively expensive can fund investments in loans with non-deposit debt or with equity.

It is true, however, as some have argued, that to the extent regulation imposes costs that can be avoided by other, less regulated competitors, non-deposit sources of capital could be more costly for some banks than for other firms. The cost to banks of raising outside capital could also be prohibitively high if regulation causes them to be run less efficiently than their unregulated competitors. As I discuss later, there is considerable evidence to support this argument.

Capital Costs When Loans are Sold. For the sake of argument, assume a bank chooses to sell its loans rather than borrow non-deposit funds. If the loans are sold with recourse, the bank is merely substituting collateralized borrowing for noncollateralized borrowing. It is true that a collateralized loan requires a lower interest rate than a noncollateralized loan, all other things equal (and ignoring the transactions cost of collateralization).

But this is only part of the entire story. The removal of high-quality loans from the pool of assets to which other uncollateralized (and partly collateralized) debt holders can look increases the risk of bankruptcy they face, and thus the interest rate they demand. As Modigliana and Miller demonstrated formally in 1958, holding the proportion of equity constant, the *total* interest paid by an issuer on *all* its debt can be reduced by collateralization of some of the debt as long as the distribution of cash flows expected from the bank's assets is not changed.[14] The conclusion is the same if loans are sold without recourse, assuming the amount received is the same as the present value to the bank of the assets.[15]

In short, unless securitization changes something "real," the sum of the parts cannot be greater than the whole. One such possible change emphasized by Rosenthal and Ocampo is reduction in

12 As established by the FIRREA, the Bank Insurance Fund covers commercial bank deposits formerly directly insured by the FDIC, and the Savings Associations Insurance Fund covers deposits at thrift institutions, formerly insured by the Federal Savings and Loan Insurance Corporation. Although amounts up to $100,000 per account are covered legally, in practice all deposits (and, in some cases, all liabilities) usually have been *de facto* insured.

13 Direct risk-adjusted premiums were not used before January 1, 1993 (the risk-adjusted capital requirements adopted in 1989 very imperfectly reflect the risks undertaken by banks). Indirect risk premiums are imposed in the form of more extensive and restrictive, and hence more costly, examinations and supervision.

14 Franco Modigliana and Merton H. Miller, 1958, "The Cost of Capital, Corporation Finance, and the Theory of Investment," *American Economic Review*, 58 (December), 261–297. The M & M capital structure proposition also assumes that transactions costs are not affected by collateralization, and debtholders' demands for certain types of debt are satisfied entirely by expected risks and returns (or equated by arbitrage).

15 The effect of securitization on the total risk of the originator appears to be recognized by credit evaluators. As representatives of Moody's commented:

An important issue to Moody's is the degree to which the originator's asset quality deteriorates as a result of securitized assets sales and concurrent reinvestment of the proceeds in new assets. In analyzing this issue, Moody's focuses on the specific quality of the assets being sold in relation to that of the entire portfolio, the availability of suitable reinvestment opportunities, and management's plans for the use of securitized asset sales as a continuing financing alternative.

From Harold H. Goldberg, Robert W. Burke, Samuel Gordon, Kenneth J. H. Pinkes, and M. Douglas Watson, Jr., 1988, "Asset Securitization and Corporate Financial Health," *Journal of Applied Corporate Finance*, 1 (Fall), pp. 45–51.

CAPITAL COST EXAMPLE. In their book, Rosenthal and Ocampo (hereafter R & O) present a case study intended to demonstrate how securitization produced savings in the cost of capital for General Motors Acceptance Corporation (GMAC). In 1986 GMAC sold $4 billion in automobile loans to a special purpose entity, Asset-Backed Securities Corporation (ABSC). ABSC issued notes supported by a guarantee by GMAC of up to 5 percent of the losses and equity of $40 million contributed by First Boston Securities, backed additionally by a "back-up" letter of credit issued by Credit Suisse. R & O compared the cost to GMAC of this method of financing with the cost if GMAC had held the loans and issued its own debt.

According to their estimates (p. 40), the cost of the securitized debt was 7.69%, comprised of 6.91 percent for the debt, 0.28 percent for underwriting fees and expenses, and 0.50 percent for credit enhancement. They estimate that traditional financing would have cost GMAC 8.99%—7.01 percent for the debt, 0.20 percent for underwriting fees and expenses, 0.50 percent for loan loss allowance, and 1.28 percent for the equity cost capital. The "savings" of 1.30 percent (8.99–7.69) comes from 0.10 percent more for the cost of debt and 1.28 percent more for the cost of equity less 0.08 percent for the difference between the costs of credit enhancement and underwriting. Thus, most of the benefit from securitization is seen as coming from savings in GMAC's equity cost of capital.

R & O fail to recognize two important capital costs GMAC must have paid when it securitized its debt. One is the cost of First Boston's capital contribution. As the equity holder, First Boston can expect to earn a return on its capital that compensates it for its being a residual risk bearer. This return should be no less than that expected by GMAC's capital providers. Indeed, it is likely to be higher to the extent First Boston is concerned with the possibility that GMAC sold particularly risky automobile loans. For example, to enhance the sale of cars, GMAC (and other captive sales finance companies) have accepted long-maturity loans, the unpaid balance of which are likely to exceed the value of the cars at some future time. The cost of this capital should be reflected in the price at which the receivables were transferred from GMAC to ABSC. (R & O recognize this possibility in a footnote, but do not include the cost in their estimates.)

R & O do point out, however, that GMAC's 5 percent guarantee makes losses to First Boston unlikely, thus reducing the "adverse selection" problem and its associated costs. But GMAC's own guarantee gives rise to a second capital cost ignored by R & O—namely, the increase in GMAC's cost of debt and equity capital from accepting the full credit risk on the loans. They state that GMAC typically chooses to hold equity amounting to 7 percent of its assets, and could therefore reduce its equity by this amount. But GMAC's equity holders are still liable for the 5 percent part of the default risk on the securitized loans. Furthermore, to the extent GMAC sells loans that are of higher-quality than average, the risk to its equity holders has increased. Hence, unless investors in GMAC were fooled by the complexity of the transaction, they will demand a return sufficient to compensate them for the higher risk they now face.

Thus, in the absence of any other effects, the cost of capital to GMAC should not change. The consequences of securitization would likely have been the same if GMAC had instead increased its assets by the $4 billion of securitized loans without reducing its equity, provided the new assets were of the same quality as those securitized.

---

investors' distrust of bank management or in the managers' inability to inform investors. As Rosenthal and Ocampo put it, the "pooling and sale of assets make the loans more transparent and thereby reduce uncertainties for capital market investors. Since the pool is pre-specified, investors know the risk they are absorbing; they are funding only a clearly delineated existing pool of loans . . . [which] facilitates the actuarial analysis of their risks" (p. 34).

Although this conclusion may be correct, it is incomplete. The risk of securitized loans can be determined readily because the securities are guaranteed by the originator and credit enhancer. But these latter firms' capital (equity and debt) holders must in turn assess the risks *they* face, which are greater as a result of securitization. As discussed in the capital cost example above, there is no reason to believe that the *total* cost of risk assessment, and hence the cost of capital, will be reduced as a result.

Securitization as a Means of Expropriating Debt holders. A bank could use collateralized borrowing or sale of assets via securitization of loans to expropriate current debtholders by accepting more risk than the debtholders expected when they first priced their investments in the bank. Ordinarily, one would expect debtholders to protect themselves from this expropriation by including covenants to prevent the bank from increasing its risk. But, to the extent these covenants did not anticipate the possibility of securitization, a bank could take advantage of this oversight to transfer wealth from debt to equity holders.

Such an advantage, however, is likely to be temporary at best. When the bank's debt matures and it seeks to replace it, it will have to pay a higher rate that reflects not only the higher risk, but the expectation by potential debtholders that it will increase the risk they face in the future. Thus, a "one-time" gain will be more than offset by higher rates demanded by future debt providers.

There is reason to expect, however, that an important contingent debt holder, the FDIC, does not act effectively to protect its interests. The premiums charged for deposit insurance are imperfectly related to the costs imposed on the insurance funds, and the supervisory agencies react to changes in banks' risk profile slowly—sometimes not until after some banks clearly have failed.

Banks that choose to play this game of "heads we win, tails the FDIC loses" also could take advantage of the fact that banking agencies do not require market value accounting to measure required capital. Consequently, banks can bolster their recorded capital simply by selling assets that have increased in value while holding those that have gone down because of increases in interest rates. In this way, a bank could meet its regulatory capital requirement even though its economic capital was significantly lower. This procedure appears to have been followed during the 1980s by many economically insolvent or close to insolvent savings and loan associations.

The Amount of Capital and the Cost of Regulation. Bryan concludes that

> *high-quality lenders would reap their greatest savings from securitization in the form of capital cost savings. They would no longer be forced by regulatory capital requirement to hold capital equal to 7 percent of the loan, which is significantly higher than the actual, expected credit losses inherent in many types of high-quality loans* (p. 83).

Bryan overstates the cost of regulatorily mandated capital. Indeed, he overstates the cost of capital in general. For a bank, "capital" simply represents funds not insured by the FDIC.

The returns to capital from a bank's operations can be measured as the amount earned (net of associated expenses) on the assets in which the capital is invested. There is no reason to believe that these yields are lower than those that could be earned on assets employed in other enterprises, with three major exceptions.

First, constraints prevent depository institutions from holding optimal portfolios of assets (such as equities and other direct investments) and from engaging in an optimal set of activities (such as the many securities transactions prohibited by the Glass-Steagall Act).

Second, the regulatory authorities refuse to accept debt subordinated to the claims of the FDIC as fully meeting capital requirements. As a result, banks may be prevented from taking full advantage of the tax laws that treat interest payments but not dividends as expenses deductible against income.

Third, anti-branching and merging laws prevent restructuring and consolidations of banks (including acquisitions by nonbanks) that could reduce redundant facilities and employees and displace incompetent managers.

But even if the amount of capital required by the authorities were higher than the amount banks would hold voluntarily, the regulatory capital requirement would be binding only if the depository institution's *marginal* cost of capital exceeds the *marginal* yield on loans or other investments it wants to make. Such a situation could arise when an institution has a comparative disadvantage in raising capital but an advantage in making and servicing loans. For example, the owners of a closely held bank might not want to invest more capital and would find raising funds from minority investors prohibitively expensive. Mutual thrifts with low relative amounts of equity capital might find the cost of uninsured subordinated debentures high. In these circumstances, the sale of loans via securitization could allow such institutions to make and service a greater volume of loans than they could hold, assuming the loans were sold without recourse. But, in most cases, banks are not prevented from raising capital; they will raise capital or take in more deposits as long as the cost of the additional capital does not exceed the returns they expect to earn from making additional loans or other investments.

Why, then, do some bankers and commentators like Bryan complain that some banks—indeed, the entire banking industry—are overcapitalized and that the authorities' higher capital requirements impose onerous costs on banks? One reason is given above—namely, regulatory restrictions on assets, activities, and mergers. Another reason is derived from the role of the deposit insurance in allowing some depository institutions to take more risks than they would take if their depositors' funds were at risk. As is well known, deposit insurance that is not priced according to the risks faced by the FDIC provides banks with incentives to increase risk-taking. Requiring depository institutions to hold higher levels of capital makes their owners co-insurers of deposits, in effect, thereby reducing and perhaps eliminating the subsidy provided to some banks by underpriced deposit insurance.

The cost to these banks of higher capital requirements is thus the reduction or elimination of the deposit insurance subsidy. Nonsubsidized banks would be damaged by capital requirements if the funds generated by capital could not be invested in positive net present value projects. But such banks would likely benefit their shareholders by shrinking in size, perhaps by selling loans, thereby reducing deposits and equity capital.

It should be noted, however, that if securitized loans were sold *with* recourse, the bank would not be able to avoid the regulatory authorities' capital requirements. The regulators would (and should) count these loans as assets in their calculations of the amount of capital required of the bank, because capital is necessary to absorb losses for which the bank still is liable.

Lower Capital Cost—Conclusions. In short, the cost of capital to a firm cannot be reduced by securitization as such. As long as the risk inherent in the loans has not changed, someone must bear it and will charge for bearing it. Indeed, because of the transactions costs of securitization and the costs arising from moral hazard, the total cost of capital or debt may even be greater for many banks securitizing rather than holding their assets. If there are savings, they would have to come from reductions in risk more from effective diversification and comparative advantages in lending rather than in deposit-taking.

Borrowers

Borrowers' benefits are derived from the enhanced ability of banks to make loans that meet borrowers' demands, but which cannot be held by banks without subjecting them to unacceptable interest rate and credit risks. Borrowers could also benefit from lower borrowing costs to the extent securitization permitted banks to achieve economies in risk reduction.

SUMMARY—BENEFITS AND COSTS TO INDIVIDUAL PARTICIPANTS

Among investors, then, thrift institutions can obtain special benefits from holding mortgage-backed securities because these allow them to meet regulatory "thriftness" tests while diversifying their assets for credit risk. The benefits to other investors appear to be slight, because they already can purchase a wide variety of similar obligations. Guarantors of credit, investment bankers, and lawyers would benefit, of course, as securitization increases the demand for their services.

Issuing institutions (banks) and borrowers can benefit by using the securitization and sale of loans to achieve more effective diversification of credit and interest rate risks. Some banks may also benefit from a greater ability to make use of their comparative advantage in local and otherwise specialized lending areas. These benefits to issuers, together with the investment demand by thrifts, appear to be largely responsible for the great growth in securitized mortgage securities.

However, contrary to the claims of advocates of securitization, with one important exception lower capital cost is not a direct benefit from securitization. Lower funding costs on securitized asset sales result in higher funding costs on the remaining portfolio as risk is merely shifted among investors in the issuing institution. Furthermore, securitization would be costly if the discount due to moral hazard and transaction costs charged by credit guarantors, investment bankers, and lawyers exceeds the benefits just discussed. The exception is lower capital costs to banks from shifting risk to the FDIC by securitizing and selling high-quality assets, assuming that the FDIC is unwilling or unable to recognize and charge for the higher risk imposed on it.

SECURITIZATION AND THE STRUCTURE OF BANKS AND BANKING

Bryan's Assessment of the Problem and His Proposed Solution

In the introduction to his book, Bryan makes the following observation:

> *Today, banks are under siege. The industry's underlying economics are weak and deteriorating. Credit losses are enormous and growing. And if that weren't enough, a new technology for lending—structured securitized credit—threatens the industry's very franchise.* [Securitization has] *undermined* [the franchise as] *the large borrowers and high-quality borrowers who were subsidizing the banking system began to explore the alternatives offered to them by securities firms . . . Large depositors moved in droves to money market mutual funds, while high-quality borrowers moved to commercial paper* (pp. viii).

The banking system, Bryan continues, was supported by subsidies from "large depositors (primarily individuals) who were not paid full value for their deposits . . . and high-quality borrowers (primarily corporations) that paid more for their loans than their risk would justify." "These subsidies," he explains, "were hard to spot because of the cost structure of the banks." The lack of adequate bank cost information and banks' practice of bundling products and operations gave rise to "cross-subsidies" that bankers often did not recognize and that customers could not prevent because of the oligopolistic structure of the industry. This structure allowed banks "to pass on costs to customers, as utilities can." The result was an overcapitalized, oligopolistic industry with overcapacity and high overhead costs that was protected by regulation.

The turning point, Bryan states, was the Garn-St Germain Act of 1982, which "gave depository institutions power to compete for funds based on price." While banks regained much of their deposits that had been lost to money market mutual funds, their costs increased. Bryan believes that monopoly profits from inelastic demanders of credit—consumers, small businesses, and trusts—helped support the "bottom line," until increased competition eroded these gains. But the regulators allowed insolvent institutions to continue operations, which prevented the industry from shrinking as it should have done. Rather than simplifying their integrated operations through spin-offs and mergers, as have other industries experiencing overcapacity and intense competition, he says, banks attempted to reduce costs and took excessive risks.

Bryan proposes the following solution:

> *We must use the new securitized credit technology to unbundle, or break apart, the bank into component functions so that each function can be performed by whichever players are most capable of delivering the best service at the best price. Specifically, this means separating deposit taking from credit risk taking . . . The objective would be to redesign banks so that each customer pays for the full costs of the explicit, discrete service he or she uses without cross-subsidizing others or being cross-subsidized by others . . . All this can be done using credit securitization, because this technology allows for a variety of discrete, functional roles . . .* [pp. 92–93].

> *[Deposit insurance would continue, but] the institution taking deposits . . . would be allowed to invest those funds only in instruments with no significant credit . . . [or] interest-rate risk* [p. 96].

Lending and all other functions would be completely unregulated. Although Bryan does not explicitly say so, presumably banks could own businesses, engage in underwriting and other securities-related transactions—indeed, do anything their owners wished that would be supported by the market. Furthermore, by predicting that "deposit taking functions [would be consolidated] until they reached an economic size," he implies that all restrictions against interstate and intrastate branching would be eliminated.

Critique of the Assessment and Solution

Neither Bryan nor Rosenthal and Ocampo discuss in depth how lenders who securitize their loans might deal with the attendant moral hazard problems and continue to provide flexibility to borrowers who want to change the terms of their loans as unexpected events occur. Nor do they consider loss of economies of scope when lending and deposit operations are separated.

Bryan's analysis of banking's problems suffers additionally from an apparent lack of understanding of some basic facts. While banks have failed in far greater numbers in the 1980s than in the years following the 1930s depression, few if any of these failures can be attributed to inadequate earnings. Rather now, as in years past, they failed because of losses due to unexpected changes in economic conditions, fraud, occasional gross incompetence, and insufficient capital to absorb losses. Banks with undiversified portfolios, such as thrifts and commercial banks that served primarily farm and oil-producing areas, failed now as in the 1920s and 1930s when their capital was insufficient to absorb losses on investments that comprised too large a portion of their assets. Indeed, highly specialized banks and other lenders of the sort proposed by Bryan are and were much more prone to failure. Far from being overcapitalized, these institutions were grossly undercapitalized.

While depositors did remove their funds from banks, the reason was not how banks were structured, but rather legislatively imposed ceilings on time and savings deposits and the prohibition of interest on demand deposits. Money market mutual funds provided a means for small (not large, as Bryan states) depositors to get market rates of interest that previously were available only to purchasers of $100,000 and over CDs, from which interest rate ceilings had been removed. In essence, the funds were a means of circumventing the Reg Q ceiling.

Large and well-known borrowers have, indeed, turned increasingly to commercial paper. But this has little to do with the securitization of loans. Commercial paper is similarly a means of circumventing costly interest-rate regulation through disintermediation. It represents direct borrowers that are not collateralized because there is little doubt about the borrowers' excellent credit standing. Commercial paper thus allows banks, their customers who pose almost no credit risk, and depositors with funds to invest to avoid the cost of required noninterest-bearing reserves and the prohibition of interest payments on demand deposits.[16]

Moreover, Bryan presents no evidence (nor do I know of any) supporting his assertion that banking is supported by subsidies from large depositors and high-quality borrowers. The existence of such subsidies implies either collusive pricing by banks or ignorance of alternatives by their customers.

As Bryan would agree, the securitization of loans has played an important role in maintaining the franchise for some banks. In particular, securitization of mortgages has allowed some thrifts to reduce their exposure to credit risk while continuing to serve their markets and maintain the requirement that they hold 60 percent to 70 percent of their assets in mortgages or mortgage-backed securities to qualify for favorable federal tax treatment and to meet the requirements of the FIRREA. But securitization also may have allowed regulatory-capital-deficient thrifts to increase their measured capital artificially by booking capital gains on sales of higher-than-market-rate loans. (It is important to recognize, however, that such thrifts would thereby reduce their interest-rate risk only if the duration of the securities purchased matched more closely the duration of their liabilities than the mortgages they sold.)

This special role of mortgage securitization is documented by Bryan, who reports that "about 35 percent of home mortgages, 5 percent of auto loans, 1 percent of commercial mortgages, and 2 percent of credit card loans in the United States had been securitized by the end of 1987" (p. 78). By the end of 1987, securitized home mortgages totaled $669 billion, representing 88 percent of all loans that had been securitized. Bryan, along with Rosenthal and Ocampo, admit that relatively small amounts of bank loans other than mortgages had been securitized as of their writing (in 1988), but express their belief that the present amount represents but the beginning of a large-scale change.

I suggest that the basic economics of banking make this development unlikely, particularly for commercial loans.

Many, perhaps most, banks exist primarily because they offer market participants an efficient means to transfer claims over resources, to invest, and to consume in the present rather than in the future. The means is efficient because it reduces the costs users must pay (directly and in the form of inconvenience) to effect these transactions, including the cost of controlling and reducing the cost of risk and uncertainty.

An important aspect of this efficiency is the processing of information and a reduction in the cost to consumers of providing information.[17] These costs are reduced when banks both make loans and take deposits from the same customers. That is why most commercial banks throughout the world almost always were and are both depositories and lenders. These banks and their customers can achieve economies of scope by combining deposit taking and lending. Furthermore, banks are able to reduce the cost of risk by offsetting deposit and loan inflows and outflows to achieve a greatly reduced and more predictable variance of cash flows than could be obtained if banks' activities were separated (as Bryan seems to advocate).

Another very important aspect of banking is evaluating and monitoring the credit risk posed by borrowers who are not well known (which Bryan acknowledges). Such loans are rarely sold and would be expensive to securitize because of the moral hazard problem discussed above. Loans to well-known borrowers, particularly those with shares regularly traded on the exchanges, can be much more readily evaluated. Indeed, that is why many of these companies find it efficient to borrow

16 For a more complete discussion of the growth of money market funds and commercial paper, and supporting empirical analysis, see my article, "Interest on Deposits and the Survival of Chartered Depository Institutions," *Economic Review*, Federal Reserve Bank of Atlanta (October, 1984), pp. 42–56. The growth of money market mutual funds and commercial paper are well described by the level of U.S. Treasury bill rates, which provide a measure of the opportunity cost of intermediation. However, there is reason to believe, as Rosenthal and Ocampo observe (p. 218), that once a new instrument becomes established, it is likely to maintain its market position after the initial impetus for its development has become less important.

17 For a more complete exposition, see George J. Benston and Clifford W. Smith, Jr., "A Transactions Cost Approach to the Theory of Financial Intermediation," *Journal of Finance*, XXXI (May, 1976), pp. 215–231.

directly in the form of commercial paper. But such companies also tend to use bank loans when the credit risk they pose is significant and evaluation and monitoring by banks is less costly than going directly to the securities markets.

Large (and small) borrowers also use bank loans when their fund requirements vary over short periods, because the transactions costs of these funds are less than those required by securities underwriting and sales.[18] As noted above, the advantage of the law of large numbers from banks' processing of many deposits and loans, plus economies of scale and expertise in placing and borrowing funds on the daily and intra-day funds markets, allow full-service banks to offer much lower transactions costs to borrowers than could be achieved with securities.

In short, if full-service banks did not exist, someone would write a book extolling the obvious advantages of combining deposit and loan services, consumer and business accounts, investments and loans, trusts and investment advice, and so forth. Indeed, universal rather than specialized banking tends to dominate the scene where it is permitted.

This is not to deny the partial truth of Bryan's argument that some banks might find some kinds of specialization a more valuable strategy. These are clearly banks that do not have comparative advantages in obtaining deposit funds (such as money center banks without efficient branch networks), but are well placed to make loans for which moral hazard problems are not severe. The cost of funds to these banks might exceed the funding costs of potential buyers of their securitized loans.

Well-capitalized or conservatively managed banks also might find the cost of government-insured deposits exceeding the benefits therefrom. These banks probably would want to earn fees by placing their customers' borrowings or securities (where permitted by the Glass-Steagall Act) directly with investors rather than making direct loans funded by deposits. Indeed, some money-center banks might find it most profitable to their shareholders to give up deposit banking entirely, thereby avoiding the costs and constraints of regulation. Instead, they can operate as facilitators, makers, servicers, and packagers of loans. But, to my knowledge, no bank has chosen to do so, although several have moved in this direction by downsizing.

The increasing cost of deposit insurance, however, could encourage banks to give up deposit banking. Unlike their competitors, banks are subject to the costs of having to hold non-interest-bearing reserves, the regulatory costs of examinations and supervision, and the inefficiencies arising from bylaws prohibiting nationwide and even statewide branching. Such laws also raise costs to banks by preventing optimal product diversification (such as securities and insurance), and blocking mergers with and ownership by nonbanks. Some bank executives undoubtedly prefer that at least the last set of constraints be kept in place, since it affords protection against unfriendly takeovers. But the costs of such regulatory constraints, together with high deposit insurance premiums and the reduced value of a banking franchise as a result of entry by nonbank competitors, could make deposit insurance more expensive than other capital, and chartered banking more expensive than unregulated banking.

THE FUTURE OF SECURITIZATION

While I do not share Bryan's enthusiasm about the future of securitization of bank loans, I do believe that securitization is here to stay because it has an important role to play. I agree with Bryan and his McKinsey colleagues that regulation calling for higher capital requirements will encourage securitization, but not for the reason they profess. Banks will not securitize loans primarily because they are "overcapitalized," but rather because higher capital requirements will give banks a strong incentive to reduce their risk-taking to the level desired by shareholders who have their own (rather than the FDIC's) resources at stake. Consequently, banks will have stronger incentives to reduce their credit and interest-rate risk. This is the major benefit held out by the securitization of loans.

18 The legal problems and attendant costs and underwriters' fees required for securitization of loans are not trivial. For an account of the former, see Richard M. Rosenberg and Jason H. P. Kravit, "Legal Issues in Securitization," *Journal of Applied Corporate Finance*, 1 (Fall, 1988), pp. 61–68.

Chapter 2

Elements of Mortgage Securitization

by Alan C. Hess,
Washington Mutual Professor of Financial Markets,
Graduate School of Business Administration,
University of Washington
and
Clifford W. Smith, Jr.,
Clarey Professor of Finance,
William E. Simon Graduate School of Business Administration,
University of Rochester

ABSTRACT

In this chapter we review the forms of mortgage securitization, analyze the demand for securitization, and demonstrate how securitization meets these demands by reducing intermediation costs. We argue that the increased use of securitization is a response to increased interest rate volatility and represents a contractual innovation that facilitates an efficient allocation of risk-bearing among households and intermediaries.

1. INTRODUCTION

Securitization is a wholesale financial intermediation process which rebundles individual principal and interest payments of existing financial instruments to create new securities. In this chapter we argue that securitization is a cost-effective way for financial intermediaries to manage their interest rate risk exposure. Our analysis of securitization builds on and integrates three extant arguments in the intermediation literature: (1) financial intermediaries exist because they reduce transaction and information costs to borrowers and lenders (Benston and Smith, 1976); (2) the supply of intermediation services by short-funded mortgage lenders exposes them to significant interest rate risk (Hess, 1987); and (3) hedging is a value increasing response to increased interest rate uncertainty (Mayers and Smith, 1982, 1987, and Smith and Stulz, 1985). We accept points one and three, and develop point two: securitization lowers the cost of separating the supply of intermediation services from interest rate risk management. We argue that the gains from securitization are increased by the implicit put option on interest rates embedded in mortgage loans and the implicit call option on interest rates embedded in long-term deposits.

2. INTERMEDIATION SERVICES

Financial intermediaries provide four types of services to financial market participants: they originate financial assets and liabilities, they enforce the rights and obligations of the parties specified in the financial contracts, they make markets in financial instruments, and they manage the risks associated with the contractually generated cash flows. The intermediary's cash flows come from both the supply of intermediation services and capital gains or losses from risk management; the risks include interest rate risk, prepayment risk, and default risk.

2.1 Production of Mortgage Loans

Mortgage lending, a particular type of financial intermediation, can be divided into three separable activities: loan origination, loan servicing, and ownership of the loan's cash flow rights. Intermediation costs are potentially lowest when each of these three activities is produced by its lowest-cost supplier. A local financial institution, a bank or savings and loan association, has geographically specific knowledge that tends to make it the low-

Reprinted from Journal of Real Estate Finance and Economics, 1:331–346 (1988)

est-cost estimator of the creditworthiness of borrowers and the market value of the underlying real property being mortgaged. As a result, it typically has a comparative advantage in mortgage origination. It is also frequently the lowest-cost servicer of mortgages through its local branch network. This comparative advantage in the origination and service components of the lending process generally is enhanced by continuing investments in human and informational capital that help it maintain a cost advantage over other potential originators and servicers.

An intermediary that makes a mortgage loan does not have to hold the mortgage and manage its attendant interest rate risk until it is redeemed (Deshmukh, Greenbaum and Kanatas, 1983). The potentially harmful results of failing to separate interest rate risk management from intermediation service supply were demonstrated in the early 1980s. Approximately 1,200 short-funded, mortgage-lending savings and loan associations ceased to exist as independent economic entities, even though estimates suggest that as a group savings and loans were viable suppliers of intermediation services. For example, Hess (1987) decomposes savings and loan industry income into that due to the supply of intermediation services (defined as income absent capital gains and losses due to unexpected changes in interest rates) and that due to interest rate risk exposure. The industry's intermediation profit margin was positive even though its measured income was negative due to the effect of unexpected increases in market interest rates given their interest rate risk exposure. This evidence suggests that savings and loans could have benefited from separating the supply of intermediation services from interest rate risk management.

Failure to separate the transaction components of mortgage lending from its funding can increase intermediation costs even in periods of stable interest rates because of the local nature of mortgage and deposit markets. Areas with fast-growing populations and consequently a large number of new homes being built have experienced shortages of mortgage lending from deposit intermediaries at permitted interest rates. This has created pressure to find alternative sources of mortgage loan financing. In other areas at different stages of development, local housing construction has been less than local deposit additions at prevailing interest rates. There, pressures have existed to find alternative uses of savings. In addition to lending and saving imbalances, savings and loans traditionally have lacked geographical risk diversification in both their mortgage loans and deposits. Therefore, changes in local economic conditions lead to increases in the risk of supplying intermediation services that could be reduced through geographic diversification.

2.2 Exposure to Interest Rate Changes

Mortgage-lending deposit intermediaries have supplied financial contracts with the maturities demanded by their customers. These have tended to be relatively short-term deposits but long-term loans. Long-term, fixed-rate mortgages reduce households' exposures to interest rate risk as compared to short-term or variable-rate mortgages. With a long-term, fixed-rate mortgage, the duration of a house times its value more closely approximates the duration of its mortgage times its value.[1] This reduces the response of the housing component of household wealth to changes in market interest rates and partially immunizes the household against unexpected changes in interest rates (Hess, 1984).

Deposits also allow households to transfer some of their interest rate risk to deposit intermediaries. Households have a variety of holding periods for their savings. Some savings are held for near-term spending while other savings are held for distant spending such as during retirement. In principle, if deposit intermediaries offered an unlimited array of savings instruments they could attract more long-term savings. This would allow the intermediary to lengthen the duration of its liability portfolio and reduce its interest rate risk exposure. However, partially for regulatory reasons, deposits have tended to be primarily short-term instruments. Moreover, markets for interest rate risk management tools such as forwards, futures, options, and swaps have been fairly illiquid, especially in long maturity contracts. As a result, mortgage-lending deposit intermediaries have been exposed to interest rate risk and have faced substantial costs due to the difference between the effective maturities of their assets and liabilities.

3. EFFECTS OF CHANGES IN INTEREST RATES

Management of interest rate risk exposure becomes increasingly important as interest rate vola-

1 Kendrick (1976) uses a 70-year average life for residential housing in estimating the housing stock. While the duration of a 70-year house is longer than the duration of a 30-year, fixed-rate mortgage, the 30-year mortgage is closer than a variable rate mortgage to the duration of a house.

Figure 2.1—Yields on 3-Month Treasury Bills from 1947 to 1987

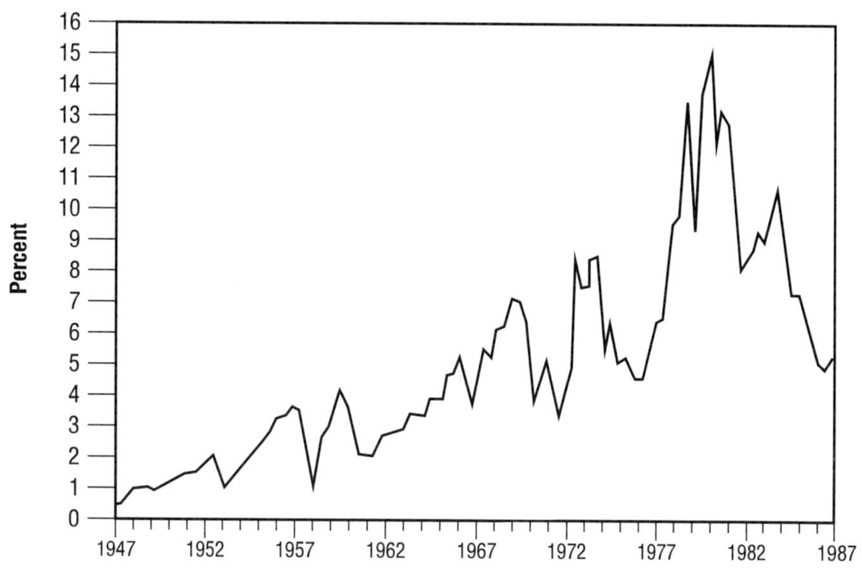

tility increases. Figure 2.1 and Table 2.1 indicate that interest rates (as represented by the secondary market yield on U.S. Treasury bills with three months to maturity) have increased and become more variable since 1947. The variance of the change in interest rates increased by more than a factor of four from the 1960s to the 1970s, and by more than a factor of three in the 1980s over the 1970s.

3.1 Response of Lender Value to Interest-rate Changes

If interest rates rise unexpectedly, market values of short-funded intermediaries fall because the market values of long-term, fixed-rate mortgages fall relative to the market values of short-term deposits. Without prepayment options in the financial contracts the response of value to unexpected interest rate changes is generally symmetric. If interest rates fall unexpectedly, the values of deposit intermediaries rise. Figure 2.2 illustrates the effect of interest rate changes on the value of a deposit intermediary that finances long-term, fixed-rate mortgages with short-term deposits. The horizontal axis records changes in market interest rates (dR) and the vertical axis records the corresponding change in the market value of the intermediary (dV). With no prepayment options in the loan or deposit contracts, Grove (1974) shows that the approximate formula linking dV to dR is

$$dV/dR = (L*DL - A*DA)\ (1 + R) \qquad (1)$$

Here, L is the market value of liabilities.
A is the market value of assets.
DL is the duration of liabilities.
DA is the duration of assets, and
R is the initial market interest rate.

Line *aa* in Figure 2.2 depicts equation (1) for a short-funded mortgage lender. In this case, the market value of liabilities times the duration of liabilities, $L*DL$, is less than the market value of assets times the duration of assets, A*DA, hence the change in the value of the intermediary due to a change in interest rates: dV/dR is negative. If the duration imbalance ($L*DL - A*DA$) is reduced, the line becomes flatter and the response of value to a change in interest rates, dV/dR, falls. Conversely, if the duration imbalance increases, line *aa* becomes steeper and the sensitivity of value to interest rates increases.[2]

2 Convexity, the effect of changes in interest rates on the duration of assets and liabilities, is ignored in this analysis.

Table 2.1—Summary Statistics for the Secondary Market Yield on 3-Month Treasury Bills (% per year)

Variable	*Mean*	*Standard Deviation*	*Minimum*	*Maximum*
		1950s		
R	2.00	0.85	0.79	4.23
dR	0.08	0.41	–1.54	1.01
		1960s		
R	3.98	1.33	2.30	7.35
dR	0.08	0.37	–0.88	0.83
		1970s		
R	6.29	1.87	3.44	11.84
dR	0.11	0.81	–1.61	2.17
		1980s		
R	9.40	2.92	5.35	15.05
dR	–0.21	1.51	–3.74	4.46

R is the level of the yield on 3-month Treasury bills and *dR* is its first difference.

Figure 2.2—The Effect on Lender Value of Interest-Rate Changes for a Short-Funded Intermediary

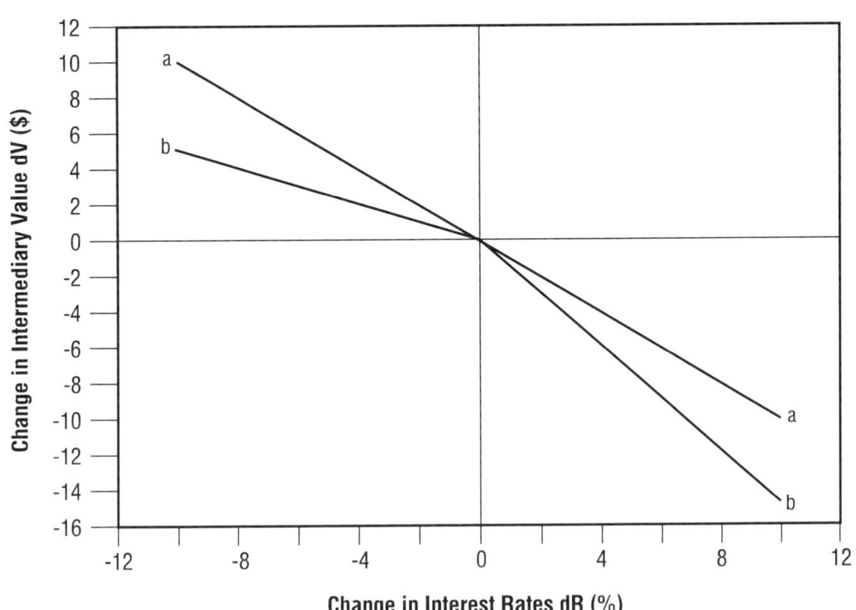

Line *aa* illustrates the negative relation between firm value and interest rates. Line *bb* illustrates the effect of the embedded prepayment options sold loan customers and withdrawal options sold depositors.

3.2 Effects of Embedded Options in Loans and Deposits

Historically, intermediaries have offered loan and deposit contracts which typically have given the customer the option to prepay the loan or withdraw the deposit prior to maturity. Unexpected mortgage prepayments and deposit withdrawals present an important complication to analysis of the effects of interest rate changes on intermediary value. A mortgage consists of an underlying asset, the market value of its remaining principal and interest payments, plus a sequence of call options on these payments. Mortgage lenders have written these call options: generally, each option has an exercise price equal to the book value of the remaining principal payments.

Because of the call options, line *aa* in Figure 2.2 is not appropriate during periods of falling interest rates. If interest rates fall, homeowners can exercise their right to prepay (call) an existing mortgage at its book value. In many cases they refinance at the then prevailing interest rate. Mortgage prepayments and refinancing have two separate effects on the value of short-funded mortgage lenders. First, when a mortgage is prepaid at book, the lender gives up a capital gain equal to the difference between the market and book values of the mortgage. Second, the lender must reinvest the cash in some new financial instrument; for simplicity, assume this is a new mortgage on the same property. The new instrument yields the then prevailing lower market rate and, other market conditions being constant, has a longer duration than the prepaid mortgage.

If mortgage contracts allow prepayment, the mortgage lender receives capital gains only on the mortgages which are not prepaid. Line *bb* to the left of the origin in Figure 2.2 represents these capital gains. Prepayments reduce the response of the value of the intermediary to interest rate changes. To the left of the origin, the vertical distance between lines *aa* and *bb* reflects the difference between the market and book values of prepaid mortgages. It is the intermediary's foregone value increase due to prepayments.[3] Assuming that the prepaid mortgages are refinanced at the then prevailing lower interest rate, the duration of the intermediary's assets increases. In equation (1) the asset duration, *DA*, increases, making the intermediary's value more responsive to interest rate changes.[4]

Since long-term certificates of deposit (CDs) also include early withdrawal provisions, line *aa* in Figure 2.2 is also incorrect for increases in interest rates. With higher rates, holders of long-term CDs will redeem their low-rate CDs and take out new higher-rate CDs. The value of this option is shown in line *bb* to the right of the origin.

Because of the maturity options offered in both loan and deposit instruments, value changes produced by interest rate changes are not symmetric. Unexpected increases in rates lead to reductions in loan prepayments and a lengthening of the effective maturity of the loan portfolio. This increases the fall in the value of the intermediary from the rate rise. At the same time, depositors roll over their long-term deposits at the higher rates, again increasing the fall in the value of the intermediary. These options cause the gains to the mortgage lender from declines in market interest rates to be less than the losses associated with increases in interest rates. *As a result, expected intermediary value is reduced by increases in interest rate volatility.*

3.3 Incentives To Hedge Interest Rate Risk

Securitization is a special case of corporate hedging since it transfers interest rate risk from short-funded mortgage lenders to other parties which have a comparative advantage in managing the risk.[5] Since the typical mortgage lender is a corporation, not an individual, risk aversion does not provide a satisfactory rationale for corporate hedging. We treat hedging by a value-maximizing intermediary as a special case of corporate financial policy. Modigliana and Miller (1958) demonstrate that with fixed investment decisions, no taxes, and no contracting costs, a firm's choice of financing policy does not affect its current market value.

3 In a well functioning market this opportunity cost is reflected in the pricing of the mortgage at origination.

4 This could be shown in Figure 2.2 by increasing the steepness of lines *aa* and *bb*. Subsequent changes in interest rates have larger effects on the intermediary's value than preceding changes. This process repeats itself if interest rates continue to decline.

5 Since life insurance companies and pension funds have long-term commitments, they have a comparative advantage in owning the cash flow rights to long-lived mortgages. However, neither type of institution typically has local knowledge of borrowers or property values nor do they generally have loan servicing facilities. Thus, a useful exchange is made by having mortgage originators and servicers sell the cash flow rights to insurance companies and pension funds.

Thus, hedging policy (as well as the rest of corporate financing policy) can affect a firm's value only if the policy changes the firm's tax liability, its contracting costs, or its incentives regarding current or future real investment. We believe that each of these arguments provides a partial explanation of a short-funded mortgage lender's incentives to hedge.

If there are fixed costs of hedging, intermediaries have a comparative advantage over individuals in hedging. Consequently, the increased variance of changes in interest rates that has occurred in each decade since World War II has increased the benefits of hedging by intermediaries.

Progressivity in the tax code provides opportunity for some lenders to raise their after-tax expected net cash flows through securitization.[6] For example, in a simple tax system with a positive marginal tax rate on profits and a zero rate on losses, the function relating taxes to taxable income resembles a call option on taxable income. The government is long the call, and the firm and its shareholders are short the call. Option pricing theory implies that the value of this call increases with the variance in taxable income. Securitization allows the intermediary to reduce its exposure to interest rate risk, reduce the variation in its taxable income, lower its expected tax liability, raise its expected after-tax cash flows, and thus increase its market value. (Note that carry-backs and carry-forward provisions reduce the convexity of the tax code and thus reduce the firm's incentives to hedge.) The investment tax credit and the alternative minimum tax are other tax code provisions that introduce convexities into the tax schedule and offer profitable hedging opportunities to value-maximizing corporations.

Myers (1977) argues that a firm's investment incentives can be affected by its capital structure. A firm with substantial debt can have incentives to reject positive net present value investment projects if the cost of acquisition falls primarily on the stockholders but the benefits accrue primarily to the bondholders. In the case of insured deposit intermediaries, the major beneficiary is the insuring agency. Mayers and Smith (1987) show that hedging can control a form of the underinvestment problem for a firm which has risky debt outstanding. If the value of the firm's assets falls unexpectedly, the firm's leverage rises unexpectedly, and the underinvestment incentives become potentially severe. By reducing the volatility of firm value, securitization reduces the probability of rejecting profitable projects.

In addition to stockholders and bondholders, a firm has a vast network of contracts among parties with common as well as conflicting interests. Managers, employees, customers, and suppliers are sometimes less able to diversify firm-specific investments than are stockholders and bondholders. Like the owners of a closely held corporation, these claim holders' risk aversion can motivate mortgage loan securitization. However, the specific incentives of corporate managers to engage in securitization depends on the particular form of their compensation package and its relation to firm value. While risk aversion motivates a manager compensated primarily through salary to lobby for securitization, a manager with substantial compensation through stock options or bonus plans has fewer incentives to hedge. This results from the option-like character of the manager's payoffs under both stock option and standard bonus plans (Smith and Watts, 1982).

4. TYPES OF SECURITIZED MORTGAGE INSTRUMENTS

The principal and interest payments on a mortgage pool constitute a cash flow stream of uncertain size, duration, and value. Changes in market interest rates change the market value of a mortgage pool absent any changes in its expected repayments of principal and interest. This exposes mortgage lenders to price risk. In addition, unexpected variation over time in prepayment rates causes actual cash flows to differ from their expected values. Homeowners prepay mortgages both in response to specific factors that affect homeowners differently, as well as in response to economy-wide factors (such as declines in interest rates) that affect many homeowners similarly. This prepayment uncertainty exposes investors in mortgage-backed securities to reinvestment risk. Securitized mortgage instruments are designed to help investors manage both price risk and reinvestment risk.

Strips, senior/subordinated claims, and collateralized mortgage obligations (CMOs) are bonds that are collateralized by an underlying pool of mortgages which is usually guaranteed by one of the federal housing agencies. They are issued by investment banks, home builders, federal mortgage agencies, savings and loan associations, mortgage bankers, insurance companies, and commercial banks. The issuer either originates or purchases a mortgage pool and then issues a set of

6 See Mayers and Smith (1982), Gurel and Pyle (1984), and Smith and Stulz (1985).

new securities that rebundle the principal and interest payments from the pool.

4.1 Strips

A simply way to construct new securities from a mortgage pool is to separate interest payments from principal payments and sell separate rights to each. The rights to the principal only payments are called POs and the rights to the interest only payments are called IOs.

Because of prepayments and the sensitivity of prepayments to interest rates, changes in interest rates have substantially different effects on the cash flows accruing to POs and IOs and thus on their market values. Prepayments do not affect the total cash flow to POs, but they do shorten the duration of this cash flow. On the other hand, prepayments reduce the total cash flow going to the IO. Figure 2.3 shows the responses of the prices of POs and IOs to changes in market interest rates. As market interest rates fall, prepayments increase. These prepayments go to the PO. The value of a PO rises both because its cash flows are received sooner and because the appropriate discount rate is lower. In contrast, the total cash flows going to the IO are reduced. This reduction more than offsets the effect of a lower discount rate. Hence, the value of an IO falls when market interest rates fall.

4.2 Senior and Subordinated Claims

A second way to unbundle mortgages is along their credit dimension. A mortgage originator with a package of loans ready for resale in the secondary market can have valuable inside information on the probability of prepayment and the credit quality of these loans. If a loan pool is more likely to be held to maturity or if its credit quality is above average but the market is unaware of these favorable characteristics, the market will price the loans to reflect the average value of all loans. Thus, it is to the originator's advantage to signal their higher quality to the market so as to reduce their price discount in the secondary market. Senior/subordinated transactions provide a way to do this. The originator sells a senior claim on, say, 90 percent of the cash flows and keeps a subordinated claim on the remaining 10 percent. By issuing a subordinated claim, the senior claim has greater cash flow rights in case of default or delinquency on the underlying pool. The subordinated claim is typically retained by the originator who has a comparative advantage in assessing loan quality.

4.3 Collateralized Mortgage Obligations

CMOs are analogous to a dual-purpose mutual fund. A closed-end fund issues a fixed number of shares, and uses the proceeds of the sale to finance the purchase of a pool of assets (typically equities). Dual-purpose funds have two types of claims: income shares and capital shares. Owners of income shares have the first rights to all the dividends plus a fixed portion of the principal at the specified date when the fund is dissolved. Capital claim holders are the residual claimants; they re-

Figure 2.3—Responses of the Values of Principal Only (PO) and Interest Only (IO) Claims to Changes in Market Interest Rates

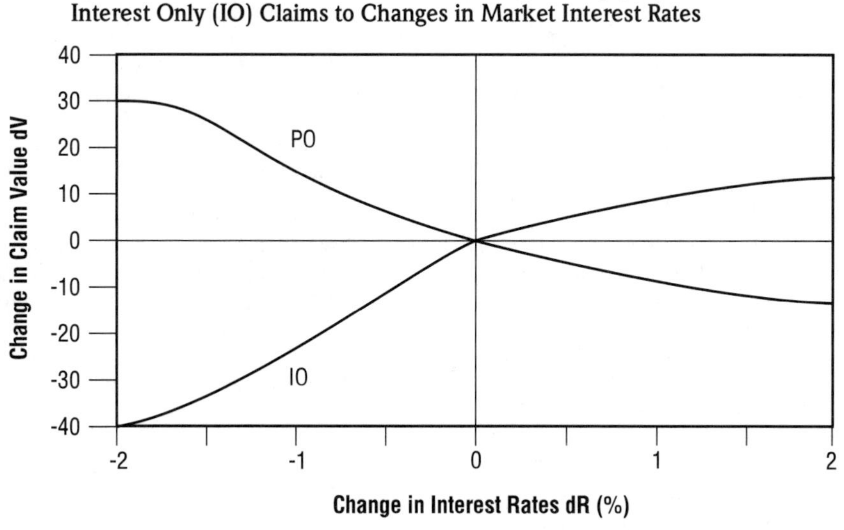

Figure 2.4—The Promised Cash Flows to a Mortgage Pool with Four Classes of Securities Plus a Residual

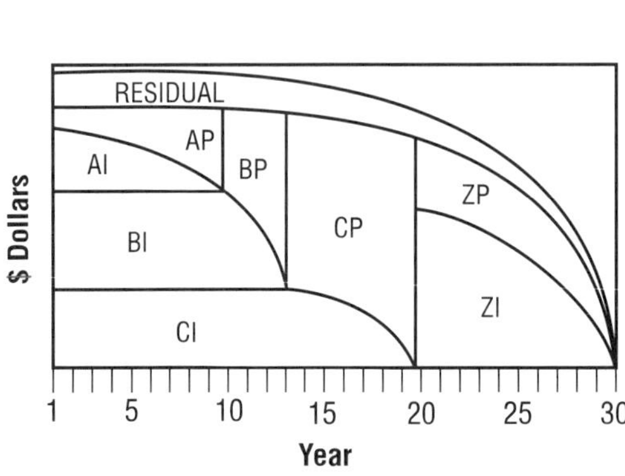

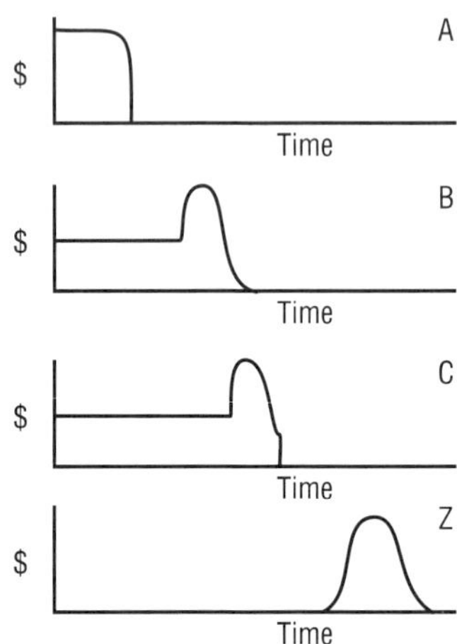

Class *A* receives all the initial principal payments (*AP*) and a portion of the interest payment (*AI*). While the principal payments are going to the class *A* security holders, class *B* and *C* security holders initially receive only interest payments (*BI* and *CI*). Principal repayments go to *B* holders after class *A* is paid (*BP*) and then to class *C* (*CP*). *Z* holders receive interest and principal payments (*ZI* and *ZP*) only after the *A, B,* and *C* claim holders are paid.

ceive everything left over (Ingersoll, 1976). Dual-purpose mutual funds repackage existing cash flows to provide customized cash flows to meet the demands of specific financial market participants. CMOs similarly allow the sale of separate ownership rights to sequential pieces of the principal and interest payments, and the proceeds from the sale of the claims are invested in a pool of mortgages.

Figure 2.4 illustrates a mortgage pool that has four classes of securities plus a residual. Class *A* receives all of the initial principal payments, the section labeled *AP*, and a portion of the interest payments, labeled *AI*. All prepayments up to an amount specified in the contract are paid to class *A* security holders. If prepayments rise because of a fall in market interest rates, the cash flows to class *A* securities rise because principal repayments accelerate. While the principal payments are going to the class *A* security holders, class *B* and *C* security holders initially receive only interest payments. After the class *A* securities are redeemed in full, principal payments flow to the class *B* securities. After the class *B* securities are redeemed in full, principal payments are directed to class *C* securities. The *Z* class of securities, typically called a "modified" zero, receives no payments, neither principal nor interest payments, until the previous three classes have been redeemed.

The four panels along the right-hand side of Figure 2.4 display the time profiles of the cash flows to each security. The class *A* cash flow resembles a short-term mortgage. The cash flows to classes *B* and *C* resemble those on corporate and government bonds, where there are initially level interest payments followed by larger flows from repayment of principal. The class *Z* cash flow is similar to that of a zero coupon security, in that over the early years of its life its cash flow is zero.

The residual is the remaining cash flow arising from a CMO. The cash flows to the residual are similar to the payoffs to the equity holders in a standard corporation. The residual arises in part because credit rating agencies require CMOs to be overcollateralized in order to receive a AAA credit rating. With overcollateralization, non-residual CMO investors have a higher probability of receiving their promised payments.[7]

7 DeAngelo and Masulis (1980) examine the investment tax credit, and Smith, Smithson, and Wakeman (1987) analyze the alternative minimum tax.

5. HEDGING THROUGH SECURITIZATION

5.1 Changing Durations

To reduce the response of firm value to interest rate changes, hedging must reduce the duration of assets or increase the duration of liabilities.[8] Securitization does this by reducing the duration of assets held by deposit intermediaries. For example, a short-funded mortgage lender can use CMOs in three ways to manage its interest rate risk exposure: (1) it can convert its mortgage assets into CMOs and sell them; (2) it can buy or retain class *A* securities and hold them in their portfolios; and (3) it can buy or retain the residual portion. The first two shorten the asset duration and reduce the change in intermediary value caused by a change in market interest rates. The value of the residual, unlike most mortgage market instruments, is constructed to be positively correlated with market interest rates.[9] If market interest rates rise, prepayments decline and cash flows to the residual increase. Thus, its market value increases. This increase in market value can be used to offset the concomitant losses that are incurred on the short-funded mortgage portfolio.

Short-funded mortgage lenders can also use strips to hedge their interest rate risk. They have accentuated convexities. Short-funded mortgage lenders are more likely to be interested in IOs. If interest rates rise, the value of fixed-rate, long-term mortgages declines. Holding IOs offsets the effect of this fall in the value of its whole mortgage loans on the market value of the institution. Its exposure to interest rate risk is reduced. Institutions that service but do not hold long-term, fixed-rate mortgages might be interested in POs. When interest rates decline and mortgages are prepaid, income from servicing mortgage payments declines. The increased value of POs tends to offset this service income decline. This results in less market value sensitivity to interest rate changes.

IOs and POs, senior/subordinated claims, and CMOs help to complete financial markets by unbundling existing instruments and permitting their cash flows to be rebundled in ways that expand hedging and speculating opportunities. For example, strips permit market participants to trade on market interest rate or mortgage prepayment expectations.

5.2 Hedging Volatility Changes

Line *bb* in Figure 2.2 illustrates an important incentive for the mortgage lender to hedge against changes in interest rate volatility. By selling embedded interest rate options in both its loan and deposit customers, the lender is vulnerable to increases in interest rate volatility. The asymmetry in the lender's value profile implies that the firm loses more from a given interest rate increase than it gains from a comparable interest rate reduction. To reduce its exposure to unexpected increases in interest rate volatility, the lender must purchase offsetting interest rate options. Through securitization, the lender resells its position in the prepayment options it originally sold its mortgage loan customers. This makes line *bb* more nearly linear and reduces lender exposure to interest rate volatility.[10]

5.3 Ownership Structure and Bonding

Gains from securitization are limited if the owner of the cash flow rights also bears the default risk. Separating the credit rater from the credit risk bearer tends to induce the credit rater to make too many low-quality loans to receive the origination fee, loans that it would not make if it had to bear the default risk. The simple solution of having the mortgage loan originator retain the default risk is limited by Federal Reserve regulations. If the mortgage originator retains the default risk, it must meet certain reserve requirements and capital adequacy standards. These act as a tax on mortgage origination, causing mortgage costs to be higher and their quantity demanded to be lower. This reduction in loan volume results in a dead weight loss.

A partial solution to this problem of altering credit standards is to have a third party (for example, a private mortgage insurer) bear the default risk. If the mortgage originator and the insurer can negotiate an effective long-term contract, the mortgage originator can be charged on an experience-rated basis. This provides an incentive to the originator to identify good credit risks and package mortgages into pools that have lower than average

8 In the context of equation (1), this will reduce the slope of the line linking firm value changes to interest rate changes.

9 This is true of the typical CMO residual. However, CMO claims can be constructed with other correlations between the residual and market interest rates.

10 Purchasing deposit insurance from the FDIC or FSLIC also helps to make line *bb* less nonlinear. See Brickley and James (1986).

default risks. The saving in insurance fees will offset the increase in the costs required to make accurate ratings. The reserve requirement and capital adequacy taxes will be eliminated and the deadweight loss will be reduced.[11]

5.4 Pricing Securitized Claims

Prepayments complicate the pricing of mortgages and mortgage-backed securities. Most analyses treat the prepayment provision in mortgage loans as a call option written by the lender and owned by the mortgage borrower. Sophisticated models of the optimal exercise of these prepayment options based on changes in the level and structure of interest rates have been derived from modern analysis of the term structure of interest rates (Hendershott and van Order, 1987).

These macroeconomic models of prepayments can be complemented by including microeconomic analyses of demographic factors that affect households differently. Major reasons for mortgage loan prepayments other than interest rate reductions are marriage, divorce, births, promotions, transfers, retirements, and deaths. Since these events are more likely among some identifiable population subgroups than others, actuarial techniques like cohort analysis should be productive in examining how age, income, marital status, and family size affect prepayment probabilities and through them prices of mortgage-backed securities.

Mortgage prepayments should also be related to the provisions of the underlying mortgage. For example, in a given area a 10 percent mortgage with three points may be offered simultaneously with a 10.5 percent mortgage with no points. Individuals choosing the first mortgage are more likely to have a longer expected housing tenure to allow them to amortize the fixed points charge over a longer period of time. Conversely, individuals with shorter expected tenures would choose the second mortgage because it minimizes their expected housing costs. Empirical investigation is necessary to determine the magnitude of the prepayment variation associated with these characteristics of the mortgage. With that information, these factors can be taken into account in pricing mortgage-backed securities more accurately.

6. SUMMARY

Mortgage securitization has grown rapidly in the 1980s. This growth is a combination of (1) an ever present demand by value-maximizing financial intermediaries to hedge changes in their values; (2) a demand by households to have puttable short-term deposits and callable long-term mortgages; and (3) large increases in interest rate volatility. Mortgages have been securitized into CMOs, strips, and senior/subordinated claims. Each of these increases the array of traded financial instruments and reduces the costs of managing the interest rate, credit, and prepayment risks of mortgages and deposits. Hedging can reduce a firm's operating costs by (1) reducing expected taxes if the function linking taxes to taxable income is nonlinear; (2) reducing the compensating differential necessary to induce contracting parties with ill-diversified, firm-specific claims to do business with the firm; (3) reducing the underinvestment problem; and (4) reducing bankruptcy costs.

Deposit intermediaries originate and service mortgages and deposits and manage the cash flow risks associated with these instruments. Prime among these risks is the interest rate risk that results from intermediaries funding long-term mortgages with short-term deposits. Increased interest rate volatility increases the costs of managing these risks and lowers the value of short-funded mortgage lenders. To maintain their cost advantage, intermediaries devise and use new lower cost hedging instruments. Securitization is one instrument in an array of hedging vehicles.

11 Mayers and Smith (1982) provide a similar argument on the comparative advantage of insurers in monitoring.

REFERENCES

Benston, George and Smith, Clifford. "A Transactions Cost Approach to the Theory of Financial Intermediation," *Journal of Finance* 31 (1976), 215–231.

Brickley, James and James, Christopher. "Access to Deposit Insurance, Insolvency Rules, and the Stock Returns of Financial Institutions," *Journal of Financial Economics* 16 (1986), 345–371.

DeAngelo, Harry and Masulis, Ronald. "Optimal Capital Structure Under Corporate and Personal Taxation," *Journal of Financial Economics* 8 (1980), 3–29.

Deshmukh, Sudhakar D., Greenbaum, Stuart I., and Kanatas, George. "Interest Rate Uncertainty and the Financial Intermediary's Choice of Exposure," *Journal of Finance* 38 (1983), 141–147.

Grove, M.A. "On Duration and the Optimal Maturity Structure of the Balance Sheet," *The Bell Journal of Economics and Management Science* 5 (1974), 696–709.

Gurel, Eitan and Pyle, David. "Bank Income Taxes and Interest Rate Risk Management: A Note," *Journal of Finance* 34 (1984), 1199–1206.

Hendershortt, Patric H. and Van Order, Robert. "Pricing Mortgages: An Interpretation of the Models and Results," *Journal of Financial Services Research* 1 (1987), 77–111.

Hess, Alan C. "Variable Rate Mortgages: Confusion of Means and Ends," *Financial Analysts Journal* (January-February 1984), 67–70.

Hess, Alan C. "Could Thrifts be Profitable? Theoretical and Empirical Evidence," *Carnegie-Rochester Conference Series on Public Policy* 26 (1987), 223–282.

Ingersoll, Jonathan. "A Theoretical and Empirical Investigation of the Dual Purpose Funds: An Application of Contingent-Claims Analysis," *Journal of Financial Economics* 3(1976), 83–123.

Kendrick, John. *The Formation and Stocks of Total Capital*, National Bureau of Economic Research, distributed by Columbia University Press, 1976.

Mayers, David and Smith, Clifford. "On the Corporate Demand for Insurance," *Journal of Business* 55 (2)(1982), 281–296.

Mayers, David and Smith, Clifford. "Corporate Insurance and the Underinvestment Problem," *Journal of Risk and Insurance* 54 (1987), 45–54.

Modigliani, Franco and Miller, Merton. "The Cost of Capital, Corporation Finance and the Theory of Investment," *American Economic Review* 48 (1958), 261–297.

Myers, Stewart. "Determinants of Corporate Borrowing," *Journal of Financial Economics* 5 (1977), 147–175.

Smith, Clifford, Smithson, Charles W., and Wakeman, Lee Macdonald. "The Market of Interest Rate Swaps," Unpublished manuscript, University of Rochester (1987).

Smith, Clifford and Stulz, René. "The Determinants of Firms' Hedging Policies," *Journal of Financial and Quantitative Analysis* 20 (1985), 391–405.

Smith, Clifford and Watts, Ross. "Incentive and Tax Effects of U.S. Executive Compensation Plans," *Australian Journal of Management* 7 (1982), 139–157.

Chapter 3

Sources of Value Added from Structuring Asset-Backed Securities to Reduce or Reallocate Risk

by John D. Finnerty,
Professor of Finance, Fordham University
General Partner, McFarland Dewey & Co.

I. INTRODUCTION

Bondholders are exposed to several sources of risk. (1) Interest rates may change in unexpected ways, for example, because of shifts or twists in the term structure caused by unexpected changes in monetary or other macroeconomic factors. (2) The issuer of a corporate bond or the mortgagor under a mortgage contract may prepay the debt obligation prior to the scheduled maturity date. (3) The issuer of a bond or a mortgagor may default on the debt service obligations, in which event the lender may recover but a fraction of the principal amount of the loan. (4) The holder of a debt instrument that is not publicly tradable is subject to liquidity risk.

Holders of asset-backed securities face these same risks, but the risks tend to be more complex than in the case of a conventional corporate bond. An *asset-backed security* is a security that passes through to its holders a portion of the stream of payments of principal and interest received from an underlying portfolio of financial assets, such as a particular pool of residential mortgage loans, automobile receivables, or credit card receivables. The complexity arises because the principal and interest payments are not always simply passed through pro rata but instead, there may be two or more classes of asset-backed securities issued against the underlying portfolio of financial assets. The various classes are prioritized with respect to their right to receive cash payments generated by the underlying portfolio. The number of classes may be large—there exist mortgage-backed securities with 60 classes—and the complexity of the priority rules can become bewildering (perhaps even beyond the comprehension of all but the most sophisticated investors).

A wide variety of financial assets have been securitized. A representative, but by no means complete, list of securitized assets includes:

- residential mortgage loans
- multifamily mortgage loans
- commercial mortgage loans
- computer installment loans
- automobile installment loans
- boat installment loans
- manufactured housing installment loans
- agricultural equipment loans
- truck installment loans
- franchisee payment obligations
- credit card receivables
- equipment leases
- home equity loans
- oil distribution rights
- time share loans
- recreational vehicle installment loans
- commercial bank loans
- dealer floorplan loans
- consumer loans
- foreign sovereign debt

Residential mortgage loans, automobile installment loans, and credit card receivables are the three largest classes of financial assets that have been securitized. As reported in Table 3.1, roughly 41% of the residential mortgage loans, 24% of the credit card receivables, and 10% of the automobile installment loans in the United States have been

Table 3.1—Extent of Asset Securitization in the United States
(billions of US dollars)

	Residential Mortgage Loans (a)	*Automobile Installment Loans (b)*	*Credit Card Receivables (b)*
Total debt outstanding	$2,781	$270	$233
Amount securitized	1,153	27	56
Percentage securitized	41%	10%	24%

(a) Mortgage loans secured by one- to four-family residences. Balances are as of June 30, 1991.
(b) Balances are as of October 31, 1991.

Source: *Federal Reserve Bulletin* (February 1992), pp. A36–A37.

securitized. The US asset-backed security market is maturing. In contrast, only a relatively small percentage of residential mortgage loans have been securitized in Europe, but such securitization is increasing in the United Kingdom, and asset securitization has also taken place in Australia, Canada, France, Germany, Italy, Japan, Spain, and Sweden.

This paper describes the different types of securities issued in the asset-backed securities markets in the United States, Europe, and elsewhere, and identifies the sources of value added from structuring asset-backed securities to reduce or reallocate risk. Section II provides an overview of the sources of value added by securities innovation. Section III discusses the nature of the risks associated with assets that have been securitized. These risks are of four principal types: prepayment risk, default risk, liquidity risk, and interest rate risk. Sections IV, V, VI, and VII review alternative structures for reallocating prepayment risk, reallocating or reducing default risk, reducing liquidity risk, and reallocating interest rate risk. Section VIII provides concluding remarks.

II. THE SOURCES OF VALUE ADDED BY SECURITIES INNOVATION

According to Van Horne (1985), in order for a new financial instrument to be truly innovative, it must enable the capital markets to operate more efficiently or make them less incomplete. (See also Merton (1992) and Ross (1989).) Greater efficiency can be achieved by reducing transaction costs. The capital markets can be made less incomplete by designing a new security whose contingent after-tax returns cannot be replicated by any combination of existing securities. Asset-backed securities are designed to make the capital markets less incomplete by reducing or reallocating certain types of risks to create new risk-after-tax-return combinations.

Finnerty (1988) identifies four principal sources of value added by securities innovations:

1. Tax asymmetries that can be exploited to produce tax savings for the issuer, investors, or both, that are not offset by the added tax liabilities of the other;
2. Reduced transaction costs;
3. Reduced agency costs; and
4. Reductions in risk or reallocations of risk from one market participant to another who is either less risk averse or else willing to bear the risk at a lower cost.

Risk reallocation or reduction represents the principal source of value added by the various types of asset-backed securities.

A. Principal Classes of Risk

Holders of the financial assets underlying asset-backed securities face four principal classes of risk.[1]

Prepayment risk is the risk that the borrower might prepay the loan prior to its scheduled maturity date. In the United States, residential mortgage loan contracts typically extend over 30 years and

1 Standard & Poor's Corporation (1988) discusses the various classes of risk associated with asset securitization, how Standard & Poor's assesses these risks, and how Standard & Poor's evaluates asset-backed securities structures in light of these risks and how the risks are reduced or reallocated through securitization.

permit the mortgagor to prepay the loan, in whole or in part, at any time without prepayment penalty. Sometimes there is a small prepayment penalty during the first few years. Residential mortgage loans can differ significantly from one country to another. For example, residential mortgage loans in the United Kingdom are generally floating-rate loans that do not amortize principal and that exhibit much greater prepayment rates than residential mortgage loans in the United States. The prepayment feature in a fixed-rate mortgage loan is valuable to the mortgagor when interest rates decline because the mortgagor can refinance the loan at a lower interest rate and use the proceeds to pay off the higher-interest loan. But the mortgagor's gain is the mortgagee's loss; the mortgagee suffers an economic loss to the extent of the reduction in interest income when the funds are reinvested in new mortgage loans at the lower interest rate then prevailing.

Default risk is the risk that the borrower might fail to make full payment of principal and interest, for example, because the borrower incurs too much debt or experiences financial adversity and becomes unwilling or unable to make the debt service payments specified in the loan contract. As a result, the lender may suffer a delay in the receipt of these payments, and in the worst case, may fail to recover full principal and accrued interest.

Liquidity risk is the risk that the lender may wish to sell the loan in order to recover the funds invested in it but suffers a loss of principal during the period it takes to effect the sale or must pay larger transaction costs to achieve a quicker sale. For example, residential mortgage loans can be sold to other lenders but transferring all the documentation that supports each loan is time-consuming and expensive. During the time it takes to complete the transaction, the buyer or seller may suffer a loss in value. Trading the claims to the securitized debt service streams is considerably easier and cheaper than trading the underlying financial assets because it is not necessary to transfer the supporting documentation.

Interest rate risk , in the case of a loan, is the risk that an unanticipated increase in the level of interest rates will reduce the value of the loan, and in the case of a financial intermediary, is the risk that an unanticipated change in the level of interest rates will reduce the value of the entity due to a mismatching of the interest rate sensitivities of its assets and its liabilities. In the United States, thrift institutions have historically been the largest lenders in the residential mortgage market. Until the development of adjustable rate and variable rate mortgages, they customarily extended 30-year fixed-rate mortgages and funded those commitments by taking in deposits or selling certificates of deposit maturing in five years or less. The resulting asset-liability mismatch exposed those institutions to substantial interest rate risk, and many of them were rendered insolvent when interest rates rose sharply in the 1970s.

B. Risk Reallocation or Reduction

The development of the asset-backed securities market has enabled financial institutions to reduce or reallocate these four types of risk in the following manner.

Prepayment risk can be reallocated among different classes of investors by creating different classes of securities that prioritize the right to receive prepayments. Investors who have a preference for shorter-dated investments can purchase the highest priority class while investors who prefer longer-dated investments can buy the lowest priority classes. Also, special securities classes can be tailored to suit a particular investor's preferences. Section IV describes different securities structures that have been developed to deal with prepayment risk.

Default risk can be reduced or reallocated by a number of means. In the United States, the Federal Home Loan Mortgage Corporation (FHLMC) and the Federal National Mortgage Association (FNMA) provide payment guarantees, that is, they assume the default risk, for a fee but only for certain classes of residential mortgage loans. A variety of private label insurers are willing to assume the default risk on other classes of financial assets. In addition to default risk transfer, investors and the insurers can benefit from the reduction in exposure to default risk that results from forming a large portfolio of residential mortgage loans in order to diversify away some of this risk. Section V describes mechanisms developed in the asset-backed securities market to reduce or reallocate default risk.

Liquidity risk can be reduced through securitization. Mortgage-backed securities are considerably easier and cheaper to trade than the underlying mortgage loans because the documentation supporting the loans does not have to be transferred. It resides with the mortgage pool servicer. Similarly, the other classes of asset-backed securities are easier and cheaper to trade than the underlying financial assets. Asset-backed securities positions can generally be liquidated at lower overall cost than positions in the underlying assets. Section VI explains in greater detail how asset-backed securities can reduce liquidity risk.

Interest rate risk can be transferred from the originator of the loan to the purchaser of the asset-backed security by securitizing the loans and selling them in the marketplace. The originator earns a fee for generating the loan with minimal interest rate risk exposure. In the United States, FHLMC and FNMA will buy certain qualifying residential mortgage loans on a forward commitment basis so that the loan originator can eliminate its interest rate risk exposure completely by paying the commitment fee, entering into the forward commitment, and then covering its short position by originating a mortgage loan to deliver under the contract. Section VII discusses asset-backed securities structures designed to reduce or reallocate interest rate risk.

C. Evolution of the Asset-Backed Securities Market

Asset securitization represents one of the most significant aspects of the process of financial innovation.[2] The asset-backed securities market began in the United States in 1970 when the Government National Mortgage Association (GNMA) issued the first mortgage pass-through securities (see Hayre and Mohebbi (1989)). A *mortgage pass-through security* simply passes through to each investor that investor's pro rata share of the payments of interest and principal received from a specified pool of mortgages. Prior to the development of mortgage pass-through securities there was a secondary market for whole loans, that is, unsecuritized mortgages, but trading was cumbersome because of the paperwork involved, and as a result, the market for whole loans had little liquidity. Holders of whole loans who wished to sell quickly faced the risk of potentially larger losses. The introduction of mortgage pass-through securities created a means of effectively buying and selling mortgages—actually, buying and selling undivided joint interests in pools of mortgages—that was more convenient and certainly cheaper than the whole loan market. Most of the mortgage pass-through securities have been created and sold by FHLMC, FNMA, and GNMA, the three agencies that were created by the U.S. Congress to provide liquidity in the secondary mortgage market in the United States.

Mortgage pass-through securities simply pass through all cash payments, including principal prepayments. Hence, the pass-throughs also pass through mortgage prepayment risk. Institutional investors, particularly life insurance companies and pension funds, limited their investments in mortgage pass-through securities because of their aversion to prepayment risk. The *collateralized mortgage obligation* (CMO) was developed in 1983 in response to this concern. The earliest CMO, issued by FHLMC, had three classes that receive principal payments sequentially: class A-1 gets all the principal payments from mortgages in the underlying portfolio until it is fully retired; then class A-2 begins receiving principal payments and gets all the principal payments until it is retired; and then class A-3 gets all the remaining principal payments. As a result, the underlying mortgage pool was effectively recharacterized into three classes of securities, one short-term (A-1), one intermediate-term (A-2), and one long-term (A-3). Since that first CMO was developed, the mortgage-backed securities market has experienced a whole host of more complex structures, all designed to reallocate prepayment risk in ways better suited to certain investors' preferences. These newer structures are described in Section IV.

Securities backed by financial assets other than residential mortgages were introduced in 1985 with the sale of computer lease-backed notes by Sperry Lease Finance Corporation. Later that same year securities backed by automobile installment sales contracts were introduced with the sale of undivided interests in a pool of newly originated installment sales agreements on new automobiles and light trucks by a special purpose trust set up by General Motors Acceptance Corporation (GMAC). That issue involved a straight pass-through of principal and interest and was supported by a limited guarantee provided by GMAC. In October 1986, First Boston Corporation created the first CMO-like issue of automobile loan-backed securities, which had the sequential pay structure of the early CMOs and was supported by a limited guarantee from GMAC, a letter of credit from Credit Suisse, and the equity of the special purpose issuer so as to insulate investors from default risk. The first credit card receivable-backed securities

2 See Finnerty (1988, 1992), Marshall and Bansal (1992), and Walmsley (1988) for an overview of the process of financial innovation.

were issued in 1987. The development of the structures for other asset-backed securities has generally followed a pattern very similar to the development of the mortgage-backed securities market.

The first securitization of assets outside the United States occurred in the United Kingdom in 1985.[3] Securitization developed slowly in the United Kingdom because of differences between the US and UK markets. The regulatory environments are markedly different. Also, most residential mortgages in the UK have floating-rate structures as well as other features that required modifications to the securitization techniques that had been used previously in the United States (see Cox (1990)). But a market for sterling floating-rate mortgage-backed securities gradually developed. The first sterling CMO appeared in 1989, six years after CMOs first appeared in the United States (see Gaitskell (1990)). Mortgage-backed securities markets also developed in Canada and Australia during the latter half of the 1980s (see Boyle (1989)).

While commercial mortgages, export-import bank loans, and leases have been securitized in the UK, automobile loans and credit card receivables have not been securitized to any meaningful degree (see Din (1991) and Falconer (1991)). Both markets are very small relative to the UK mortgage market, making economies of scale in securities issuance difficult to achieve (see Cox (1990)). UK stamp duty and UK consumer credit laws are also inhibiting automobile loan securitization. Lack of homogeneity in financial lending methods and UK title law, which is not conducive to transferring and bundling assets, are inhibiting the securitization of credit card receivables as well as automobile loans (see Smallman and Selby (1990)).

Asset securitization could not take place in France until the requisite legal and regulatory framework was put into place with the enactment of "La Loi Titrisation" in December 1988 (see David (1991) and Quéré (1990)).[4] The first French asset securitization occurred in December 1989. Its assets comprised loans extended by the Société des Bourses Françaises to stockbrokers. Other assets that have been securitized in France include automobile loans and consumer loans.[5]

In addition to the countries listed above, there have been occasional issues of securities backed by mortgages or automobile loans or credit card receivables in Italy (see Caputo-Nassetti (1991)), Germany (see Fugel (1991)), Spain (see Llorens and Lanzón (1991)), and Japan. Both Belgium (see Paul, de Zagon, and Scalais (1991)) and Spain are working hard to create a legal environment conducive to asset securitization. The first securitization of automobile receivables in Canada took place in 1991.

D. Illustration of the Potential Benefits from Risk Reallocation

The reallocation of risk from one party to another can be mutually beneficial when the transferee is less averse than the transferor to the risk that is transferred. In such event, it is possible to find a price that the transferor can pay the transferee to assume the risk, and both parties will be mutually better off as a result of the risk-transfer-cum-payment. This fundamental principle underlies the development of futures and options instruments and the existence of all forms of insurance. For example, the guarantees that FHLMC and FNMA provide represent a form of insurance against default risk.[6] On account of their size, diversification and active involvement in the mortgage market, these two agencies can provide default risk insurance to investors at a price that is low enough to make it prudent for them to purchase it and at the same time high enough to compensate FHLMC and FNMA adequately for the default risk they are incurring.

The value of reallocating prepayment risk may be a little more difficult to appreciate. A simple example, which is contained in Table 3.2, will help demonstrate its usefulness. Imagine a security that amortizes fully over three years in three equal annual installments. The level debt service payment stream typifies mortgages and consumer installment contracts in the United States, although monthly payments are usually required. Assuming

3 Roberts (1991) describes the evolution of asset-backed securitization in the international capital markets. Bonsall (1990) and Stone, Zissu, and Lederman (1991) provide an in-depth analysis of asset securitization in Europe.

4 'Titrisation' translates to 'securitization.'

5 Because the French Government did not wish to promote 'credit card mania,' the 1988 law limits asset securitization to those assets that amortize, which excludes credit card receivables.

6 GNMA packages mortgages that are either insured by the FHA or guaranteed by the VA. The FHA/VA programs are designed to promote home ownership by lower income and lower middle income families. The insurance/guarantee is designed to encourage the lender to make the loan rather than to assist in securitizing the loan. The FHLMC\FNMA guarantees are specially intended to promote securitization.

Table 3.2—Illustration of Potential Benefits from Risk Reallocation

I. The Pool

Principal Payments Assuming Prepayment Rate of

Year	*0%*	*5%*	*10%*	*15%*	*20%*	*25%*		
1	$302.11	$337.00	$371.90	$406.79	$441.69	$476.58	μ_{WAL}	= 1.89 yrs
2	332.33	333.08	332.00	329.09	324.35	317.79	σ_{WAL}	= 0.11 yrs
3	365.56	329.92	296.10	264.12	233.96	205.63		
WAL	2.06 yrs	1.99 yrs	1.92 yrs	1.86 yrs	1.79 yrs	1.73 yrs		

II. Class A

Principal Payments Assuming Prepayment Rate of

Year	*0%*	*5%*	*10%*	*15%*	*20%*	*25%*		
1	$302.11	$330.00	$330.00	$330.00	$330.00	$330.00	μ_{WAL}	= 1.01 yrs
2	27.89	–	–	–	–	–	σ_{WAL}	= 0.03 yrs
3	–	–	–	–	–	–		
WAL	1.08 yrs	1.00 yrs	1.00 yrs	1.00 yrs	1.00 yrs	1.00yrs		

III. Class B

Principal Payments Assuming Prepayment Rate of

Year	*0%*	*5%*	*10%*	*15%*	*20%*	*25%*		
1	–	$7.00	$41.90	$76.79	$111.69	$146.58	μ_{WAL}	= 1.82 yrs
2	$304.44	323.00	288.10	253.21	218.31	183.42	σ_{WAL}	= 0.18 yrs
3	25.56	–	–	–	–	–		
WAL	2.08 yrs	1.98 yrs	1.87 yrs	1.77 yrs	1.66 yrs	1.56 yrs		

IV. Class C

Principal Payments Assuming Prepayment Rate of

Year	*0%*	*5%*	*10%*	*15%*	*20%*	*25%*		
1	–	–	–	–	–	–	μ_{WAL}	= 2.82 yrs
2	–	$10.08	$43.90	$75.88	$106.04	$134.37	σ_{WAL}	= 0.14 yrs
3	$340.00	329.92	296.10	264.12	233.96	205.63		
WAL	3.00 yrs	2.97 yrs	2.87 yrs	2.78 yrs	2.69 yrs	2.60 yrs		

three annual payments will keep the example tractable without biasing it. Further assume that the original loan balance is $1,000.00; the interest rate is 10% per annum; and the loan is prepayable, at the option of the borrower, without penalty on any regular payment date. Panel I illustrates the principal payment patterns for the entire pool of financial assets under six prepayment scenarios. The indicated percentage represents the percentage of the remaining principal balance, after the scheduled payment is made, that prepays at the end of year 1 and at the end of year 2. The 0% scenario represents the scheduled amortization amounts.

Panels II, III, and IV show the principal payment patterns for a three-tranche asset-backed security that is backed by the pool of assets represented by panel I. The initial principal balances are $330.00 for Class A, $330.00 for Class B, and $340.00 for Class C. Class A gets all principal payments until it is fully paid. Then Class B gets all principal payments until it is fully paid. Only after Classes A and B are fully paid does Class C receive any principal payments. The same six prepayment scenarios are considered. The mean (μ) and standard deviation (σ) of the weighted average life (WAL) are calculated for the pool and for each security class.

Comparing panels I and II, Class A has a significantly shorter expected WAL than the pool and the standard deviation of its WAL is also less than the standard deviation for the pool. Comparing panels I and IV, Class C has a significantly longer expected WAL than the pool and the standard deviation of its WAL is also greater than the standard deviation for the pool. A substantial amount of prepayment risk has been transferred to Class C from Class A. Finally, comparing panels I and III, the expected WALs are close but the standard deviation of Class B's WAL is greater than the standard deviation of the pool's WAL. Indeed Class B's WAL has the greatest standard deviation.

As the example illustrates, reallocating prepayment risk is really a zero-sum game. Risk is shifted but not reduced: The multiclass structure does not alter the magnitude or timing of the prepayments the pool experiences, but rather, it allocates these prepayments among the three classes of investors. Class A security holders have lower prepayment risk than investors in the pool but Class B and Class C security holders have greater prepayment risk than Class A security holders. As discussed in Section IV, reallocating prepayment risk can benefit investors as a whole because the fixed income markets, in the United States at least, are segmented with regard to maturity preference.

III. SIGNIFICANCE OF THE RISKS ASSOCIATED WITH SECURITIZED ASSETS

This section discusses the significance of each of the four principal classes of risk associated with asset-backed securities. Mortgage-backed securities are not only the oldest class of such securities but they also have the longest final maturity and hence are the most susceptible to prepayment risk, so it is not surprising that most of the risk analysis activity in connection with asset-backed securities has focused on residential mortgage loan prepayment risk.

A. Prepayment Risk

Mortgages. The mortgage market imposes an analytical challenge to fixed income investors because the cash flow patterns are considerably more complex than the cash flow patterns associated with Treasury or corporate securities. The complexity arises out of the mortgagor's right to prepay the mortgage in whole or in part at any time without prepayment penalty. The pattern of prepayments for a pool of mortgages will have a significant impact on the size and timing of the cash flows investors realize. Calculating the expected yield to maturity for a mortgage-backed security requires a projection of the likely prepayment rates, which necessarily introduces an element of subjectivity into the analysis.[7]

In general, there are two primary causes of mortgage prepayments: (1) the property that is mortgaged is sold and either the mortgage contract requires the mortgagor to repay the mortgage out of the sale proceeds or the purchaser of the property decides not to assume the mortgage or (2) the mortgagor decides to refinance the mortgage, for example, because mortgage rates have decreased since the mortgage loan was arranged and the mortgagor wants to take advantage of the drop in mortgage rates.

To facilitate the pricing of CMOs, the securities industry in the United States uses a prepayment benchmark prepared by the Public Securities Association, called the PSA Standard Prepayment Model. Prices or yields for CMO classes are typically quoted based on a stated percentage of the PSA standard, e.g. 50% PSA, 100% PSA, 200% PSA, etc. The PSA standard assumes that mortgages prepay at the annualized rate of 0.2% during the first month the mortgage is outstanding, that the annualized prepayment rate steps up in increments of 0.2% each month until month 30, and remains constant at 6% per annum for all succeeding months. Figure 3.1 presents the prepayment curves for 50% PSA, 100% PSA (the PSA standard), and 200% PSA.

For a pool of fixed-rate mortgages, there are six sets of factors that can affect the future prepayment rate (see Hayre, Lauterbach, and Mohebbi (1989), Richard (1989), and Richard and Roll (1989)):

---

7 Boyle (1989), Davidson and Herskovitz (1989), Dunn and McConnell (1981), Fabozzi (1985), McConnell and Singh (1991), Schwartz and Torous (1989), and Toevs (1985) demonstrate the significant impact that prepayment risk has on the valuation of mortgage-backed securities. Boyle (1989) deals with the valuation of Canadian mortgage-backed securities, and McConnell and Singh (1991) deal with the valuation of adjustable-rate mortgage-backed securities.

Figure 3.1—Prepayment Curves Based on the PSA Standard Prepayment Model

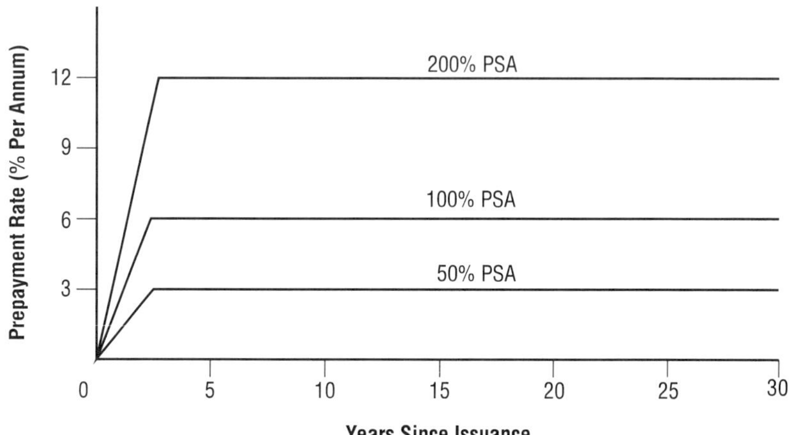

- *Spread between the coupon on the mortgage and the current mortgage rate.* The greater the spread the greater the homeowner's incentive is to refinance the mortgage (provided, of course, the spread is positive). For example, the decline in mortgage interest rates during 1991 caused the prepayment rate on all mortgage-backed securities issued by FNMA to accelerate to an annualized rate of 17.36% in December from an annualized rate of 7.67% in January. The spread appears to be the single most important factor affecting prepayment rates. Because of the out-of-pocket costs associated with refinancing a residential mortgage, a homeowner will generally not find it advantageous to refinance the mortgage unless the spread exceeds 100 basis points, and the rate of refinancing has been found to accelerate very rapidly once the spread exceeds 200 basis points.

  Figure 3.2 illustrates the typical sensitivity of mortgage prepayments to the strength of the refinancing incentive, the coupon rate on the mortgage (C) minus the current mortgage rate (R). The curve has a nonlinear S-shape. When C is less than R, the mortgagor has no incentive to refinance. Nevertheless, there are prepayments due to mortgage retirements that result from property sales. The curve in Figure 3.2 is drawn under the assumption that C=12% so that larger values for C–R correspond to smaller values for R, that is, lower interest rate environments. Even if refinancing is not economically advantageous, lower interest rate environments generally lead to higher home turnover, due to what might be called an affordability factor, so that prepayments will increase slightly as C–R increases. Prepayments begin to accelerate when C–R exceeds 100 basis points and continue accelerating (i.e., the curve steepens) as C–R passes 200 basis points. Eventually though the prepayment curve begins to increase at a slower rate as proportionately greater rate decreases are required to induce homeowners who are less responsive to the favorable refinancing opportunity to take advantage of that opportunity.[8]

- *Seasoning, or age, of the mortgage.* The prepayment data collected by the FHA beginning in 1957 showed that the prepayment rates on new mortgages tended to increase gradually during the first two to three years of the life of the mortgage and to level off thereafter. The PSA Standard Prepayment Model is based on this finding.

8 For example, the mortgagor may no longer meet the income test to qualify for a new mortgage due to a fall in earned income but if mortgage rates fall far enough, the homeowner could again qualify. Put somewhat differently, by the time the current mortgage rate is a few hundred basis points below the coupon rate on the mortgage, a substantial financial incentive already exists to refinance the mortgage. Further mortgage rate decreases will therefore have but a slight incremental impact on the prepayment rate.

Figure 3.2—Sensitivity of Prepayment Rate to the Refinancing Incentive

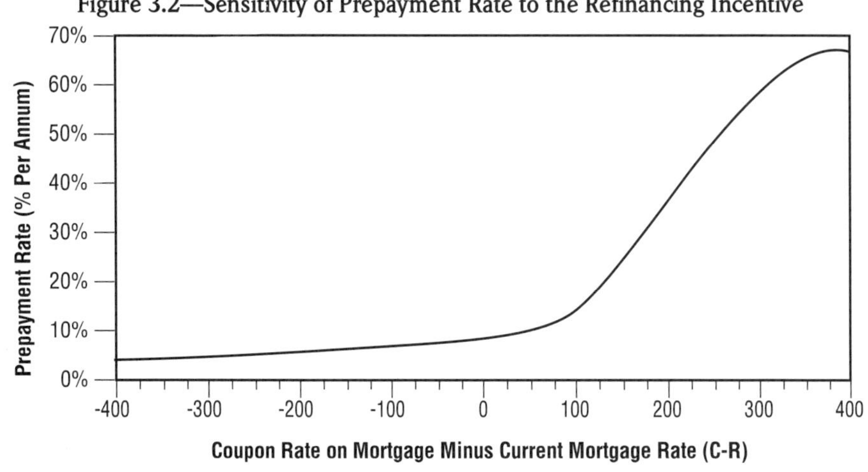

However, mortgage pools often take considerably longer than 30 months to season (Richard (1989)). In general, slight premium pools (i.e., those with an above-market coupon rate) tend to season more quickly than current coupon pools, which in turn tend to season considerably more quickly than discount mortgage pools (i.e., those with a below-market coupon rate).

- *Month of the year.* Prepayments generally exhibit a seasonal pattern, being relatively high in the summer and relatively low in the winter due to the observed seasonal pattern in housing turnover.
- *Characteristics of the mortgage.* The mortgages in GNMA pools are assumable whereas the mortgages in FHLMC and FNMA pools generally are not assumable. Consequently, for any particular coupon rate and current mortgage rate, GNMA pools exhibit lower prepayment rates than FHLMC or FNMA pools. Also, GNMA mortgagors tend to have lower incomes, which may make them less mobile, and the average GNMA mortgage balance tends to be smaller, which creates less of an incentive to refinance. Both factors tend to make GNMA pools prepay more slowly than comparable FHLMC or FNMA pools.
- *Historical prepayment rates for the pool.* Even if a mortgage pool has a very high coupon rate relative to the current mortgage rate, its future prepayment rate may be lower than the prepayment rates of pools with somewhat lower coupons if it has experienced very high prepayment rates already. Premium mortgage pools are subject to a burnout phenomenon: The prepayment rates on premium mortgage pools eventually begin to slow down.
- *General economic factors.* A variety of other factors can affect prepayment rates, including the general state of the economy (e.g., housing turnover tends to slow down during recessions), refinancing incentives offered by financial institutions, the pace of new housing construction activity, regional concentration within a pool, etc.

The aforementioned factors all affect mortgage prepayment rates to varying degrees. Unfortunately, the connection of each factor to future prepayment rates has proven very difficult to quantify, and in view of the 30-year life of most residential mortgage loans in the United States, projecting these factors out over the life of a new mortgage is all but impossible. Consequently, future mortgage prepayment rates are subject to a high degree of uncertainty, which can translate into a considerable degree of investment risk for the mortgage holder. Different securities firms employ different prepayment models—often not disclosing fully to investors the form of the model and the underlying assumptions—which tends to compound the problem posed by prepayment uncertainty.

Other securitized assets. The prepayment patterns for the other types of financial assets that have been securitized have not been studied as intensively as residential mortgage loan prepayment patterns. Nevertheless, during the period prior to their issuance and during the approximately six years they have been in the marketplace, securities dealers who underwrote asset-backed securities and the rating agencies have studied the prepayment patterns and drawn the following conclusions:

- The prepayment patterns, particularly for automobile installment contracts and credit card receivables, are generally more stable than residential mortgage prepayment patterns.
- The prepayments are less sensitive to changes in market interest rates than residential mortgage prepayments. Automobile installment contracts typically do not exceed five years so that the interest component of each payment is substantially smaller than the interest component of each mortgage payment during the first five years the mortgage is outstanding. Consequently, for any given decrease in interest rates, refinancing will have a smaller effect on the size of the monthly automobile payment than on the size of the monthly mortgage payment. Also, the automobile loan payment obligation tends to be a smaller percentage of the borrower's income than the residential mortgage loan payment obligation. In each case, there is less incentive to refinance when interest rates drop.
- While the prepayment patterns of individual credit card accounts vary widely, the weighted average life of a credit card receivables portfolio tends to be relatively stable (see Carron, Olson, and Soares (1989)). However it does depend on the type and the payment terms of the credit card. Table 3.3 reports the monthly average payment rates for three bank and three non-bank issuers of credit cards. Due to these high payment rates, credit card receivable-backed issues are typically structured such that credit card principal payments received during some initial period (typically between 24 and 60 months) are reinvested in newly generated receivables.

B. Default Risk

If a borrower fails to make the required payments on a loan promptly, the loan is classified as delinquent. In most cases, delinquencies are cured promptly. If the delinquency is not cured, then after some period—typically 90 days in the case of home mortgage loans—the lender initiates steps to collect the loan balance and unpaid interest. The collection process is subject to legal restrictions that may affect the timing and amount of any recoveries. Ultimately, the lender may only be able to recover a fraction of the loan and unpaid interest.

Mortgages. In the case of mortgage loans secured by owner-occupied single family homes, the lender may seek to recover funds through foreclosure proceedings. The procedural steps necessary for foreclosure vary from state to state. For example, in California, real estate lenders are unable to obtain a deficiency judgment on a home mortgage loan if they proceed by trustee's sale rather than a lengthy and costly judicial foreclosure. Consequently, in California, if lenders foreclose through a trustee's sale, they are limited to the proceeds from the sale of the real estate securing such loans net of transaction costs. Particularly when real estate values decline, lenders may not recover the full amounts of their loans even though the loans were overcollateralized at the time they were extended.

Table 3.3—Cardholder Monthly Average Payment Rates, by Credit Card Issuer

	1990	*1989*	*1988*	*1987*	*1986*	*1985*	*1984*
Citibank, N.A.	12.76%	13.36%	13.34%	13.35%	12.81%	N/A	N/A
Colonial National Bank USA	15.96	13.60	11.57	9.40	9.57	10.55%	13.44%
First National Bank of Chicago	14.52	13.87	13.31	12.91	12.51	12.46	13.58
Discover RFC	13.22	12.84	13.21	14.30	14.04	N/A	N/A
JC Penney	18.50	19.20	18.70	18.40	16.80	16.90	16.90
Sears, Roebuck	6.74	6.90	8.58	8.69	9.79	9.78	N/A

Source: Joan Barmat, "Effect of Early Termination on Credit Card Receivable Securitization," New York, Bear, Stearns & Co., February 7, 1991.

Figure 3.3—Delinquency and Foreclosure Rates on 1–4 Family U.S. Residential Mortgage Loans, 1960–1990

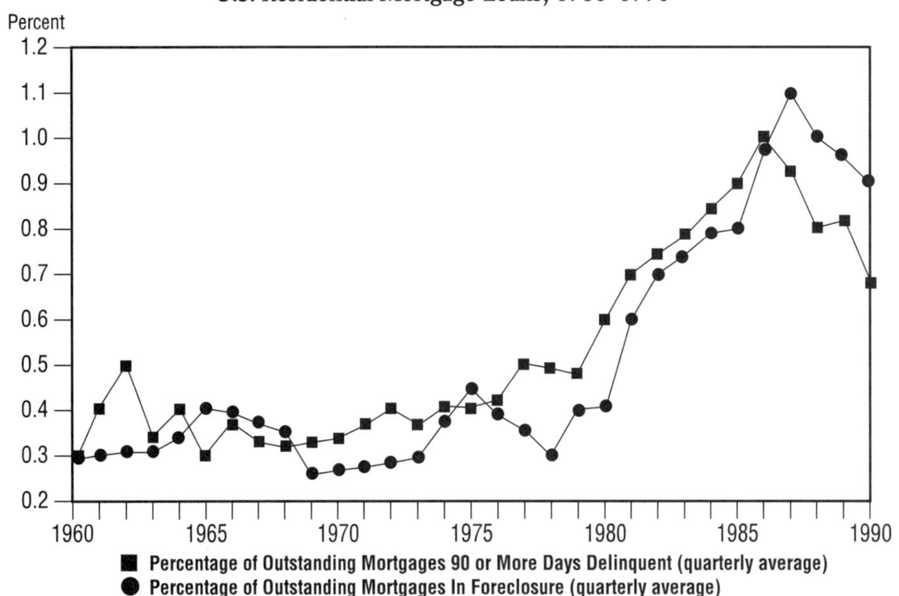

Source: The Mortgage Bankers Association.

The rate of delinquencies and foreclosures, and ultimately the lender's risk of loss of economic value, called default risk, depends on the following principal factors:

- *The general state of the economy.* Delinquency and foreclosure rates tend to increase during recessions. Homeowners who lose their jobs—or who keep them but suffer a reduction in income—may no longer be able to meet their mortgage obligations. Figure 3.3 shows delinquency and foreclosure rates on 1 to 4 family residential mortgage loans in the United States during the period 1960–1990, expressed as a percentage of the loans outstanding. During this period, the percentage of loans 90 days or more delinquent averaged approximately 0.53%, and the foreclosure rate averaged approximately 0.51%, although both rates increased substantially during the 1980s. Interestingly, while delinquencies increased with the onset of recession in 1982, they did not abate when the economy began to recover in 1983. The recession that began in 1990 has once again caused delinquencies to accelerate.
- *The state of particular industries that may be critical to different regions of the country.* In spite of the general economic recovery that began in 1983, the collapse of world oil and commodity prices in the mid-1980s adversely affected the oil-producing and agricultural areas of the United States. Figure 3.4 shows how delinquency rates have varied from region to region in the United States since 1972.
- *The overall level of consumer debt.* The rising level of consumer debt in the United States during the 1980s increased consumers' financial risk exposure. This trend no doubt contributed to the sharp increase in personal bankruptcy filings between 1987 and 1990 and helped keep mortgage delinquency and foreclosure rates from falling as much as one would normally have expected during the 1983-1990 cyclical upswing.

For any particular mortgage loan, default risk will also depend on the loan-to-value ratio, the seasoning of the mortgage, the characteristics of the mortgage, and the state in which the real estate is located. The higher the loan-to-value ratio, the lower the amount of equity the borrower has in the real estate. For example, sharply falling home prices, as occurred in many parts of the United States at different times during the 1980s, can

Figure 3.4—Regional Differences in Delinquency Rates on 1–4 Family U.S. Residential Mortgage Loans, 1972–1990

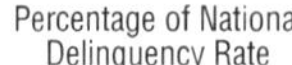

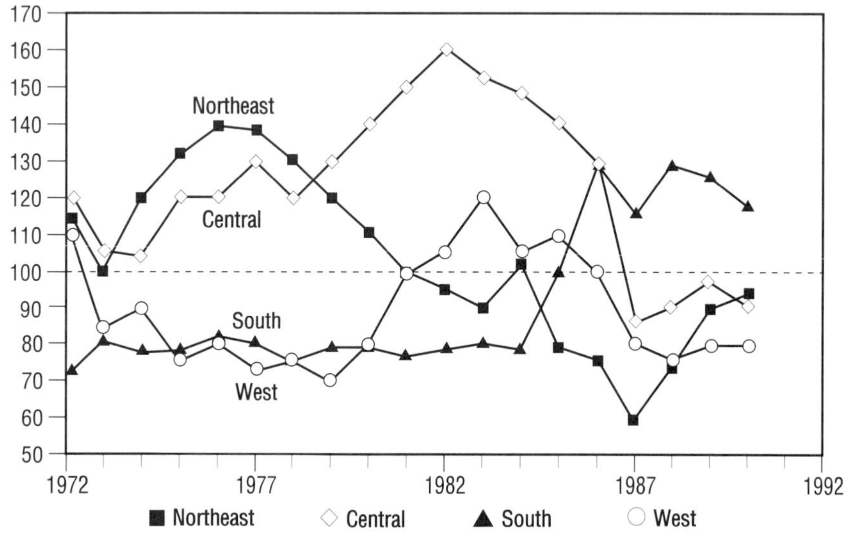

Source: The Mortgage Bankers Association.

wipe out a homeowner's equity in his home. The loan-to-value ratio will be particularly important in states such as California where the lender may be unable to obtain a deficiency judgment against the borrower (possibly, other than through a costly and lengthy judicial process). Second, the more seasoned the mortgage, the less likely the home owner will default and risk losing his home. Third, mortgage characteristics, for example an adjustable-rate mortgage (ARM) in a rising interest rate environment, can also affect the risk of default. For example, a high percentage of the ARMs extended during the latter half of the 1980s had below-market "teaser rates," which ratcheted up to market rates within 2 years. Many borrowers simply could not meet the higher payment obligations.

Automobile Loans. The delinquency rates on automobile loans in the United States have been fairly stable historically, averaging between 1.5% and 2.5% during the past 20 years. The actual losses lenders have realized as a percentage of the outstanding loan balance has been significantly smaller because of the lender's ability to repossess the vehicle and sell it to recover at least a portion of the outstanding loan balance. Also, in many cases, the lender has recourse to the dealer, who must pay off the loan contract if the vehicle is repossessed and returned to the dealer within a specified time period.

Table 3.4 reports the delinquency and net loss rates experienced by GMAC, a leading provider of automobile financing, for the 10-year period 1982–1991. The average daily percentage of automobile loans that were 31 days or more delinquent varied from a low of 1.54% in 1984 to a high of 2.67% in 1991. GMAC's net losses as a percentage of average automobile loan receivables varied from a low of 0.17% in 1984 to a high of 1.06% in 1991. As discussed below, the structures created to securitize automobile loans have included credit enhancement mechanisms designed to withstand default rates and net loss rates several times as great as the rates experienced historically.

Credit card receivables. The delinquency rates and net loss rates tend to be substantially higher on credit card receivables than on automobile loans. These rates can also vary significantly from one credit card lender to another depending upon how stringent are the credit standards the card provider applies. Due to the unsecured nature of credit card lending, recoveries on defaulted receivables tend to be low, in the area of 30%. As a result, the net loss rate on a portfolio of credit card receivables is generally between 3% and 5% (ver-

Table 3.4—Delinquency and Net Loss Rates Experienced by General Motors Acceptance Corporation on New and Used Retail Automobile and Light Truck Receivables, 1982–1991

	1991 (b)	*1990*	*1989*	*1988*	*1987*	*1986*	*1985*	*1984*	*1983*	*1982*
AVERAGE DAILY DELINQUENCY (a)										
31–60 days	2.51%	2.32%	2.14%	1.84%	1.66%	1.63%	1.69%	1.46%	1.56%	1.85%
61–90 days	0.14	0.14	0.13	0.12	0.12	0.12	0.11	0.07	0.08	0.11
More than 90 days	0.02	0.03	0.03	0.02	0.02	0.02	0.02	0.01	0.01	0.02
Total	2.67%	2.49%	2.30%	1.98%	1.80%	1.77%	1.82%	1.54%	1.65%	1.98%
NET LOSSES										
% of liquidations	1.77%	1.94%	1.79%	1.46%	0.97%	0.73%	0.45%	0.30%	0.38%	0.44%
% of average receivables	1.01	1.06	1.03	0.83	0.52	0.37	0.26	0.17	0.22	0.25

(a) As a percentage of the contracts outstanding.
(b) Annualized rate for the period through September 30, 1991.

Source: General Motors Acceptance Corporation

sus 1% or less for secured mortgage and auto loans).

Table 3.5 reports the delinquency and net loss rates experienced by three large providers of bank credit cards since 1984. Average daily delinquencies of 30 days or more for the three banks have averaged between 5.20% and 6.08% since 1986, and average net losses for the three banks have averaged between 4.32% and 5.68% during the same period. The delinquency and net loss rates both increased noticeably in 1991. Note also the significant differences in the banks' delinquency and loan loss experiences, which undoubtedly reflects differing credit standards.

C. Liquidity Risk

Asset securitization involves repackaging illiquid assets into liquid securities. Trading the underlying assets, particularly in the case of residential mortgage loans, requires transferring the entire loan file. This can be a time-consuming and hence expensive process. When secured loans are transferred, the purchaser of the loan must record its lien and perfect its security interest in the asset. As the value of the collateral will affect the value of the loan, the seller will not be able to realize full value for the loan if the purchaser requires a discount to compensate for the risk that the value of the collateral may be impaired, for example, due to falling real estate prices. Or the purchaser of the loan may wish to have another appraisal of the underlying property (in the case of a residential mortgage loan), which takes time and costs money.

An even more important factor is the borrower's capacity to service the loan. The major rating agencies assess the ability of securities issuers to repay their debt obligations. But they do not rate the ability of individuals to repay their loans. There are credit bureaus that provide individual credit histories, but it is still up to the lender to evaluate these credit histories. A purchaser of automobile loans or credit card receivables will have to assess the default risks involved. This will entail making a judgment either about each borrower's ability to pay or about the seller's credit standards. The seller may not be able to realize full value for the asset(s) it is selling if the purchaser requires a discount to compensate for the uncertainty as to the degree of default risk it is incurring or to compensate for the cost of verifying that the degree of default risk is acceptable. Asset securitization involves adding credit enhancement mechanisms to achieve a desired debt rating and then obtaining a major rating agency's confirmation that the desired debt rating (and implied assessment of the issuing vehicle's ability to service the loan) has been achieved.

The degree of liquidity risk the asset holder faces is generally greater when the asset involves a contract that is not standardized. As the securitizers of assets, particularly FHLMC and FNMA in the case of residential mortgage loans, have specified the types of contracts they are willing to purchase for securitization purposes, originators of the underlying assets have conformed the contracts they offer borrowers to the specified forms. This has reduced the degree of liquidity risk they face.

D. Interest Rate Risk

The degree of interest rate risk a financial institution faces depends on the extent of its asset-liability duration mismatch, that is, the difference (called the "asset-liability duration gap") between the duration, or interest rate sensitivity, of its assets and the duration of its liabilities. The degree of interest rate risk an investor faces with respect to a particular financial instrument depends on the duration of the asset, and by implication, whether the financial instrument bears a fixed interest rate or a floating interest rate.

Vehicles that enable financial institutions to close the asset-liability duration gap or enable investors to hedge their exposure to the risk that changes in market interest rates may affect the value of the financial instruments they hold can add value by reallocating interest rate risk to other parties. The potential for adding value is greater the greater is the financial institution's asset-liability duration gap or the investor's interest rate risk exposure.

IV. STRUCTURES FOR REALLOCATING PREPAYMENT RISK

Most multiclass mortgage-backed securities, or CMOs, are designed to reallocate the prepayment risk on the underlying pool of mortgages. CMOs segment the stream of cash flows from a pool of mortgages into various classes and prioritize the classes with respect to their right to receive principal repayments. A CMO converts a pool of long-term mortgages with irregular and uncertain cash flows into high-quality short-term, medium-term, and long-term mortgage-collateralized bonds with a wide variety of risk-return characteristics. CMOs have been created with as many as 60 separate classes.

CMOs are intended to take advantage of the segmentation and incompleteness of the bond market. Money market mutual funds in the United

Table 3.5—Delinquency and Net Loss Rates Experienced by Selected Banks on Credit Card Receivables, 1984–1991

	1991		*1990*	*1989*	*1988*	*1987*	*1986*	*1985*	*1984*
AVERAGE DAILY DELINQUENCY (30–59 days) (a)									
Citibank, N.A. (b)	3.91%	(d)	3.74%	3.51%	3.65%	3.71%	3.82%	N/A	N/A
Colonial National Bank USA	1.97	(e)	2.14	2.21	2.07	2.56	1.96	1.54%	1.84%
First National Bank of Chicago	2.04	(f)	1.93	1.85	1.90	1.74	1.58	1.45	1.17
Average	2.64%		2.60%	2.52%	2.54%	2.67%	2.45%	1.50%	1.51%
AVERAGE DAILY DELINQUENCY (30 days or more) (a)									
Citibank, N.A. (c)	8.63%	(d)	7.64%	7.02%	7.03%	7.01%	7.23%	N/A	N/A
Colonial National Bank USA	5.21	(e)	5.41	5.15	5.45	7.54	5.23	3.86%	4.17%
First National Bank of Chicago	4.41	(f)	3.97	3.66	3.74	3.41	3.15	2.99	2.19
Average	6.08%		5.67%	5.28%	5.41%	5.99%	5.20%	3.43%	3.18%
NET LOSSES AS A % OF AVERAGE RECEIVABLES									
Citibank, N.A.	6.59%	(d)	5.06%	4.65%	4.47%	4.96%	5.14%	N/A	N/A
Colonial National Bank USA	4.40	(e)	3.77	3.87	5.29	5.96	3.86	2.29%	1.57%
First National Bank of Chicago	6.05	(f)	5.00	4.48	4.43	4.19	3.97	3.37	2.07
Average	5.68%		4.61%	4.33%	4.73%	5.04%	4.32%	2.83%	1.82%

(a) As a percentage of the average receivables outstanding.
(b) For a delinquency period of 35–64 days.
(c) For a delinquency period of 35 days or more.
(d) Annualized rate for the period through September 30, 1991.
(e) Annualized rate for the period through June 30, 1991.
(f) Annualized rate for the period through March 31, 1991.

Sources: Citibank, N.A.; Colonial National Bank USA; and The First National Bank of Chicago.

Figure 3.5—Allocation of Principal Among the Classes of the FNMA REMIC Trust 1990–55

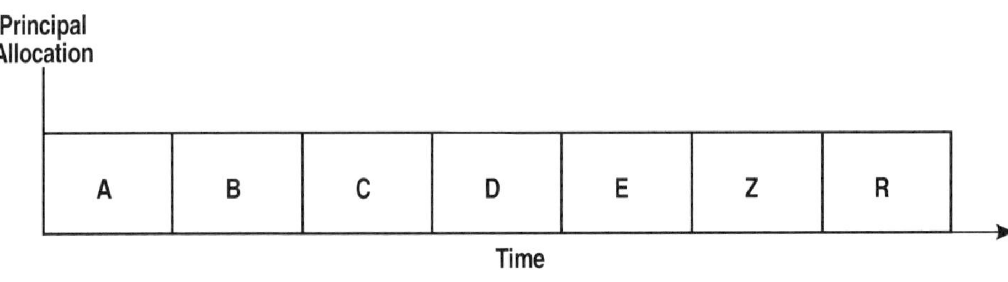

States and other short-term investors are averse to the risk that mortgages may prepay relatively slowly. Pension funds and other long-term investors are averse to the risk that mortgages may prepay relatively rapidly. By carving up the mortgage payment stream, the CMO gives rise to fast-pay class(es) that appeal to short-term investors and slow-pay class(es) that appeal to long-term investors. More complex structures, such as those discussed in this section, make the capital market less incomplete by providing investors risk-return combinations that were not previously available.

The CMO market in the United States was given a major boost in 1986 when the US Congress authorized Real Estate Mortgage Investment Conduits (REMICs) for multiclass mortgage pass-through securities. The new law greatly enhanced issuers' flexibility in structuring multiclass mortgage pass-through securities. Essentially, any corporation, partnership, trust, or segregated pool of mortgages that elects REMIC status becomes transparent for tax purposes. This ensures that the risk reallocation structure does not give rise to tax liabilities that might offset some (or perhaps even all) of the benefits of prepayment risk reallocation.

A. Sequential Pay Securities

The earliest CMOs were of the sequential pay variety (see Spratlin, Vianna, and Guterman (1989)). A more recent example of this type of security is the FNMA Guaranteed REMIC Pass-Through Certificates issued April 24, 1990 (FNMA REMIC Trust 1990-55).[9] The issue consists of seven classes, which are designated A, B, C, D, E, Z (for zero coupon accrual class), and R (for residual class). As illustrated in Figure 3.5, on each distribution date, the principal payments received on the underlying pool of mortgages will be applied, sequentially, to make principal payments on the class A, class B, class C, class D, class E, class Z, and class R REMIC certificates, in that order. No distributions of principal will be made on any class until all prior classes have been repaid in full. In addition, the Z class will accrue interest—with the cash being used to make principal distributions to prior classes—until the class E certificates have been repaid in full. Holders of the class R certificates will be entitled to any assets remaining in the trust after all seven classes have been fully repaid (including the stated principal amount of the class R certificates).

Table 3.6 illustrates the impact of different prepayment speeds, expressed as a percentage of the PSA standard, on the weighted average life of each class. The weighted average life of the underlying mortgage pool is also calculated for different prepayment speeds. Comparing the weighted average lives for each class with those of the pool, it is evident that classes A, B, and C have experienced a reduction in prepayment risk. The weighted average lives are shorter than the pool weighted average life (except for class C at 0% PSA), and the range of weighted average lives (WAL) for classes A and B is narrower than the range of weighted average lives for the pool. Classes D, E, and Z have experienced an increase in prepayment risk. Pool prepayment risk is neither enhanced nor diminished by the CMO structure; it is simply reallocated among the various classes.

Such a reallocation is beneficial when it results in risk-return profiles that better suit investors' risk-return preferences. Money market mutual funds that did not wish to invest in the pool might be interested in investing in class A. Pension funds that might not want to invest in the pool might be interested in investing in class Z. So long as investors can be found for the other classes and the

9 Federal National Mortgage Association, Guaranteed REMIC Pass-Through Certificates, Fannie Mae REMIC Trust 1990-55, prospectus, April 24, 1990.

Table 3.6—Impact of Different Prepayment Speeds on the Average Lives of the Classes of FNMA REMIC Trust 1990–55

	Weighted Average Life Based on Prepayment Speed					
Class	*0% PSA*	*100% PSA*	*185% PSA*	*300% PSA*	*500% PSA*	*Range of WAL*
A	6.7 yrs.	1.9 yrs.	1.4 yrs.	1.1 yrs.	0.8 yrs.	5.9 yrs.
B	14.7	5.5	3.6	2.6	1.9	12.8
C	18.3	8.5	5.6	3.9	2.7	15.6
D	20.2	10.9	7.4	5.2	3.5	16.7
E	22.6	14.8	11.0	8.0	5.4	17.2
Z	27.3	22.9	19.0	14.5	9.8	17.5
R	30.0	29.6	29.6	29.6	27.6	2.4
Pool	17.1	9.2	6.6	4.8	3.3	13.8

Source: Federal National Mortgage Association, REMIC Trust 1990-55, prospectus, April 24, 1990.

aggregate proceeds realized upon the sale of the seven CMO classes exceed (1) the cost of the underlying mortgage portfolio plus (2) the cost of the FNMA guarantees, plus (3) transaction costs, forming the CMO will enhance value.

B. Planned/Targeted Amortization Classes and Companion Classes

Planned amortization class (PAC) bonds and targeted amortization class (TAC) bonds substantially reduce the investor's exposure to prepayment risk (see Perlman (1989)). PAC bonds are designed to make principal payments according to a specified schedule so long as prepayments on the underlying mortgage pool remain within a specified band (e.g., 100% PSA to 300% PSA). Such a CMO class thus gives investors a relatively stable cash flow over a wide range of interest rate scenarios. However, since prepayment risk needs to be reallocated among CMO classes, some of the other CMO classes—called companion classes—issued against the same mortgage pool function as prepayment shock absorbers in absorbing a disproportionate share of the overall prepayment risk. Investors in the companion classes need to understand the degree of prepayment risk to which they are exposed on account of the inclusion of PAC classes in the CMO structure.

Consider for example the FNMA REMIC Trust 1989-57, which has the principal repayment structure illustrated in Figure 3.6.[10] The CMO, issued August 3, 1989, has nine PAC classes (A, B, C, D, E, G, H, J, and K) and one TAC class (L). Companion class M and the accrual class Z act as principal repayment shock absorbers. Distributions of principal are allocated:

1. On each distribution date, class R is allocated .003% of the principal funds available for distribution.
2. Until April 1992, after the allocation to class R, principal payments are next allocated to class L in an amount necessary to reduce the outstanding principal balance to the targeted principal balance specified in the prospectus; thereafter to class M, until the principal balance has been reduced to zero; and thereafter to class Z.
3. Beginning in April 1992, after the allocation to class R, a portion of the available principal is allocated sequentially to classes A, B, C, and D, in alphabetical order, in an amount necessary to reduce the outstanding principal balances to their respective planned principal balances as specified in the prospectus; a portion of the available principal is allocated sequentially to classes E, G, H, J, and K, in alphabetical order, in an amount necessary to reduce the outstanding principal

10 Federal National Mortgage Association, Guaranteed REMIC Pass-Through Certificates, Fannie Mae REMIC Trust 1989-57, prospectus, August 3, 1989.

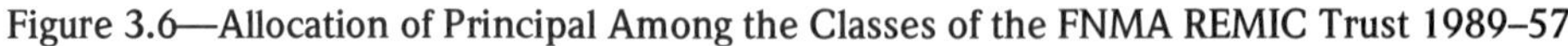

Figure 3.6—Allocation of Principal Among the Classes of the FNMA REMIC Trust 1989–57

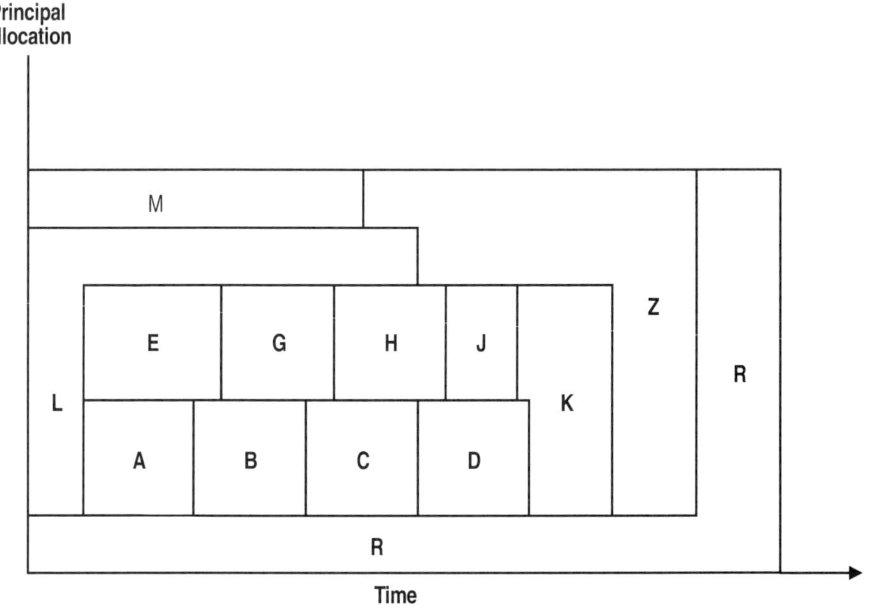

balances to their respective planned principal balances as specified in the prospectus; thereafter to class L in an amount necessary to reduce the outstanding principal balance to the targeted principal balance; thereafter to class M until the principal balance has been reduced to zero; thereafter to class Z until the principal balance has been reduced to zero; thereafter to class L without regard to the targeted balance; and then sequentially to classes E, G, H, J, K, A, B, C, and D, in that order until their respective principal balances have been reduced to zero.

4. Class R gets any amount remaining in the trust.

The principal balances of classes A, B, C, and D will be reduced to their respective planned principal balances on each distribution date if the prepayment speed is constant and falls within the range from 40% PSA to 500% PSA.[11] The principal balances of classes E, G, H, J, and K will be reduced to their respective planned principal balances on each distribution date if the prepayment speed is constant and falls within the range from 75% PSA to 275% PSA. The principal balance of class L, the TAC class, will be reduced to its targeted principal balance on each distribution date if the prepayment speed is constant at 180% PSA.

In general, the amount of accelerated repayment/delayed repayment risk each companion class faces is a function principally of

1. The sensitivity of the underlying mortgage pool to interest rate changes,
2. The width of the PAC band, and
3. The size of the companion class relative to the PAC class.

Delayed repayment results when mortgage prepayments fall below the lower end of the band because principal otherwise due the companion class(es) is allocated to the PAC class. Accelerated repayment results when mortgage prepayments fall above the upper end of the band because principal payments in excess of those required to satisfy the specified sinking fund schedule are allocated to the companion class(es).

It should be noted that a PAC class does not eliminate the investor's exposure to prepayment risk. If prepayment rates fall outside the band, the

11 PAC bonds that protect holders against extreme interest rate movements and extreme variations in prepayment rates are often referred to as VADM (Very Accurately Defined Maturity) bonds.

PAC will not be able to pay according to the specified sinking fund schedule. Also, if the prepayment rate remains within the band but is extremely erratic from month to month, the PAC may not be able to keep to the sinking fund schedule.

TAC bonds evolved from PAC bonds. PAC bonds are designed to maintain a specified sinking fund schedule within a range of prepayment rates above and below the particular prepayment speed (% of PSA) at which the PAC class is priced when offered for sale to investors. TACs are 'targeted' to a narrower range of prepayment rates, and the particular prepayment speed at which the TAC class is priced forms one of the boundaries of the specified range. If the prepayment speed assumed in pricing forms the lower (upper) boundary of the specified TAC range, the sinking fund schedule will be adhered to (assuming prepayments remain within the indicated range and are not too erratic) at prepayment speeds above (below) the pricing speed. Thus, TACs and PACs represent alternative mechanisms for allocating the risk that the actual prepayment speed may differ from the pricing speed.

C. Prepayment Guarantees or Insurance

PAC/TAC classes substantially reduce the certificate holder's exposure to prepayment risk but they do not eliminate it. In the case of automobile and truck loans, where prepayment risk is much lower than in the case of mortgage loans, financial institutions have been willing to bear all the risk of prepayment. For example, the Asset Backed Securities Corporation issued $1,410,840,000 of Asset Backed Obligations Series 4 in July 1987 that included a Minimum Principal Payment Agreement, under which Morgan Guaranty Trust Company of New York agreed to purchase automobile receivables from the issuer when prepayments are too slow or invest funds on behalf of the issuer when prepayments are too fast, to maintain the sinking fund schedule specified in the prospectus.[12] The elimination of prepayment risk reduced the required yield by approximately one-third of a percentage point.[13]

Mack Trucks Receivables Corporation has sold several issues of truck loan-backed securities that lay off the prepayment risk on the letter of credit provider. But due to the relatively greater prepayment risk associated with mortgages, no entity has yet come forward to guarantee mortgage prepayment risk. Nevertheless, the development of PAC/TAC classes represents an important step in the right direction.

D. Interest Only/Principal Only Securities

Interest Only (IO) and Principal Only (PO) CMO classes, called IO STRIPS and PO STRIPS, respectively, are created by dividing the cash flows from a pool of mortgages (or mortgage securities) into two (or in some cases more than two) securities: The IO STRIPS get all the interest and the PO STRIPS get all the principal. Waldman, Gordon, and Person (1989) provide an in-depth analysis of these securities.

IO STRIPS and PO STRIPS have differing exposures to prepayment risk (as well as to interest rate risk). When prepayments accelerate, PO STRIPS, which have large positive durations, increase in value because principal is received sooner. IO STRIPS, which have large negative durations, decrease in value because the faster repayment of mortgage principal means that the aggregate flow of interest payments is reduced. Both types of instruments exhibit great price volatility.[14]

IO/PO STRIPS are ideal securities for investors who wish to make a bet on prepayment rates (speculate) or institutions who wish to transfer prepayment risk to others (hedge). (See Carlson (1989) and Waldman, Gordon, and Person (1989).) For example, a financial institution that is concerned that a slowing of prepayment rates (say, due to an increase in interest rates) will reduce the value of its mortgage portfolio can hedge that risk by buying IO STRIPS. A financial institution that wishes to protect a portfolio of high-coupon mortgages against rising prepayments (say, due to a decrease in interest rates) can purchase high-cou-

12 Asset Backed Securities Corporation, Asset Backed Obligations, Series 4, prospectus, July 29, 1987.

13 "First Boston Unit's Loan-Backed Issue Has New Structure," *Wall Street Journal* (July 29, 1987), p. 25.

14 PO STRIPS are recognized as 'bullish' investments because a decrease in interest rates, which benefits bond prices generally, tends to boost prepayments and hence PO STRIP prices. IO STRIPS are recognized as 'bearish' investments because their prices move in the opposite direction. The riskiness of trading and investing in IO/PO STRIPS has been highlighted by some large financial losses securities firms have experienced trading these instruments. See for example, "Anatomy of a Staggering Loss," *New York Times* (May 11, 1987), p. D1ff, and "J.P. Morgan Had $50 Million in Losses in Trading Mortgage-Backed Securities," *Wall Street Journal* (March 10, 1992), p. A4.

pon PO STRIPS. If prepayments do accelerate, the increase in the value of the PO STRIPS will at least partially offset the loss on the mortgage portfolio. IO/PO STRIPS can also be combined with other types of mortgage-backed securities to alter the prepayment rate (and interest rate) sensitivities of mortgage portfolios. IO/PO STRIPS add value by altering mortgage portfolio risk-return characteristics in ways that investors find valuable.

E. More Complex Risk Reallocation Structures

Efforts to fine tune the risk-return characteristics of CMO classes have resulted in compound structures incorporating multiple PAC/TAC classes, floating rate classes, IO/PO classes, accrual classes, and residual classes. One combination of classes that is often found in multiclass CMOs involves one or more PAC/TAC classes, which lay off prepayment risk, and a PO class, which absorbs it. The greater the size of the PAC/TAC classes, the greater the prepayment sensitivity of the PO class. This creates what is termed a 'Super PO.'[15] The Super PO appeals to PO STRIP investors who want the heightened prepayment sensitivity it provides.

V. STRUCTURES FOR REDUCING OR REALLOCATING DEFAULT RISK

Asset-backed securities, as their name implies, are backed by a diversified portfolio of assets. For example, the GMAC 1991-C Grantor Trust, issued December 10, 1991, is backed by 105,663 contracts with an aggregate initial principal balance of $1,326,372,556.[16] Forming a diversified portfolio reduces the exposure of the asset-backed securities purchasers to default risk through diversification. Large institutions could accomplish much of this risk reduction on their own but achieving similar diversification could be expensive for smaller institutions and certainly for individuals. The formation of asset portfolios by asset-backed securities issuers to diversify away default risk reflects one of the benefits of financial intermediation.

Asset-backed securities structures have been designed to reduce the investor's exposure to default risk further by reallocating it to other parties. There are two basic methods for reallocating default risk:

1. The issuer of the asset-backed security can purchase a guarantee, letter of credit, surety bond, or similar promise of payment from a creditworthy third party, or
2. The issuer can assume a disproportionate share of the default risk by subordinating its right to receive payments from the underlying asset pool to the rights of other investors, by pledging a cash collateral account to cover the cost of defaults, or by undertaking to substitute replacement contracts for defaulted contracts.

Often a combination of these various default-risk-shifting measures is employed.

A. U.S. Agency Guarantees of Mortgage-Backed Securities Payments

In addition to reallocating prepayment risk, the mortgage-backed securities issued by FHLMC, FNMA, and GNMA carry certain payment guarantees, which transfer much of the default risk to the agencies from the holders of the asset-backed securities. FHLMC guarantees the timely payment of interest at the stated interest rate on its Participation Certificates and also guarantees the ultimate payment of principal on the underlying residential mortgage loans by no later than the stated final payment date. FNMA guarantees the timely payment of interest and principal on the residential mortgage loans underlying its Guaranteed Mortgage Pass-Through Securities. The mortgages underlying the GNMA securities are either insured by the Federal Housing Administration (FHA) or guaranteed by the United States Department of Veterans Affairs (VA), and GNMA, whose guarantee carries the full faith and credit of the U.S. government, guarantees the timely payment of principal and interest on GNMA certificates.

Agency guarantees eliminate entirely the investor's exposure to default risk only if the agency guarantees the timely payment of principal and interest, as FNMA and GNMA do. FHLMC guarantees only the timely payment of interest and the ultimate payment of principal. FHLMC may pay the amount due on account of its guarantee of ultimate collection of principal at any time after default on an underlying mortgage, but no later than 30 days following the later of (i) foreclosure sale, (ii) payment of the claim by a mortgage insurer

15 Roberts, Wolf, and Wilt (1989) analyze Super POs. Perlman (1989) describes a variety of compound CMO structures.

16 GMAC 1991-C Grantor Trust, 5.70% Asset Backed Certificates, Class A, prospectus, December 10, 1991.

Figure 3.7—Pass-Through Installment Loan Securitization Structure

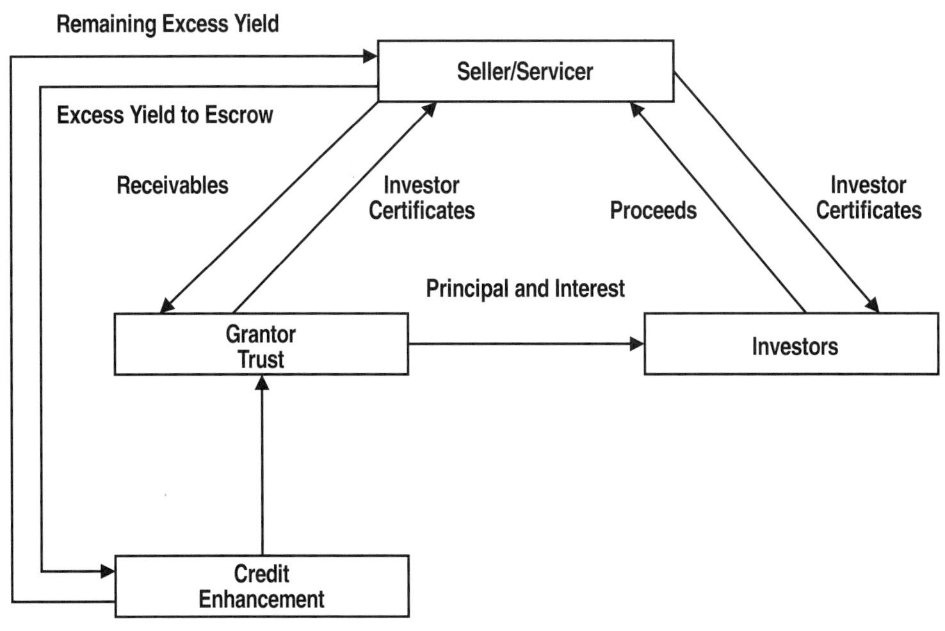

(if applicable), or (iii) the expiration of any right of redemption, and in any event no later than one year after demand has been made upon the mortgagor for accelerated payment of principal or for payment of principal due on the maturity of the mortgage. The payment delay represents a cost to the investor, which will be fully offset only if the interest rate on the PC is no less than the yield the investor could earn on the reinvestment of principal payments that are received in a timely fashion. Nevertheless, as a practical matter, the FHLMC guarantee substantially eliminates any exposure to default risk on the underlying mortgages.

B. Guarantee/Insurance Security Structures

A mortgage, automobile, or credit card lender can retain the bulk of the default risk associated with a specific pool of assets by providing a limited corporate guarantee or by overcollateralizing the asset-backed securities issue or by retaining a subordinated interest in the asset pool. The senior/subordinated structure is described in the next section. Alternatively, the default risk can be transferred to creditworthy third parties by arranging a letter of credit, a pool insurance policy (often used in connection with mortgage pools), or a surety bond. There are two basic structures that are used for this purpose: a pass-through structure and a pay-through structure.

Pass-through structure. Figure 3.7 illustrates a typical pass-through structure. There are a number of variations of the basic structure that all operate similarly. Loans are selected for securitization. The seller/servicer provides a limited guarantee, establishes a reserve fund, arranges a letter of credit, or purchases pool insurance or a surety bond for the benefit of the trust. The loans are transferred to a grantor trust pursuant to a pooling and servicing agreement in exchange for pass-through certificates, which are sold to investors. The pass-through certificates represent fractional undivided interests in the trust that owns the receivables. In some cases, seller/servicers have sold undivided fractional interests in a pool of loans directly to investors and provided credit enhancement by selling interests against only a fraction of the pool in order to overcollateralize the asset-backed securities issue.

All collections of principal and interest are collected in a segregated bank account maintained by the trustee. Interest payments, at the stated pass-through rate, together with principal repayments and prepayments are passed through to investors on the specified payment dates. The

Figure 3.8—Pay-Through Installment Loan Securitization Structure

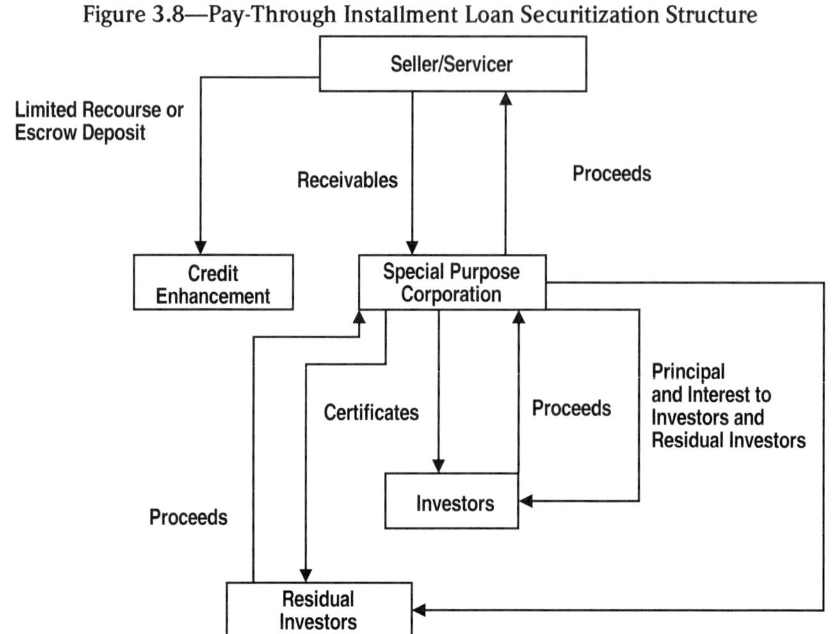

trustee can draw on the credit enhancement mechanism as required to make up for defaults. Normally, the seller/servicer must advance funds, or arrange for a credit line for that purpose, to cover delinquencies that are expected to be recovered.

To insulate certificate holders from bankruptcy risk to the maximum extent possible, title and other documents relating to the securitized assets are held physically by the trustee or a custodian. The grantor trust structure does not permit recharacterization of principal or interest and allows only minor modifications of the cash flow received from the underlying asset pool. This allows the entity to remain free of income tax liability.

The pass-through structure has been used in securitizing residential mortgage loans, commercial mortgage loans, automobile installment loans, credit card receivables, recreational vehicle installment loans, equipment leases, boat installment loans, manufactured housing installment loans, and home equity loans.

Pay-through structure. Figure 3.8 illustrates a typical pay-through structure. The seller transfers assets to a special purpose corporation (SPC), which issues notes collateralized by the assets. The notes are obligations of the SPC. They bear interest at a stated rate. Prior to issuing the notes, the SPC arranges for credit enhancement. Any of the forms of credit enhancement utilized in the pass-through structure can also be used in the pay-through structure.

The pay-through structure permits the seller/servicer to modify the cash flows received on the underlying collateral. Such a structure has been utilized to provide automobile loan- and truck loan-backed securities with fixed sinking fund schedules, which eliminate the certificate holder's exposure to prepayment risk as well as transfer default risk to others. Of course, the cash flows must be sufficient to amortize fully all the SPC's debt by its stated maturity date in order to eliminate default risk. The restructuring of the cash flows is often used when deeply discounted, 'incentive' rate automobile loans are securitized or when a multiclass CMO-like structure is desired (in order to reallocate prepayment risk).

In order for the SPC to be able to deduct its interest payments for tax purposes, the SPC must have some minimal amount of equity. The seller/servicer can contribute this equity, or the equity interest can be sold to (residual) investors.

The pay-through structure has been employed in securitizing automobile installment loans, truck installment loans, and consumer loans.

Shifting of default risk. The amount of credit enhancement is chosen so as to achieve a desired debt rating, typically AA in the case of mortgage-backed securities and AAA in the case of automo-

Table 3.7—Credit Enhancement Levels for Selected Automobile Loan-Backed Issues, by Lender

Sponsor	*Credit Enhancement Level*	*Sponsor*	*Credit Enhancement Level*
Chrysler Finance Corporation	7.00– 9.50%	Chemical Bank	8.50–10.11%
Ford Motor Credit	9.00	Marine Midland Bank	9.00– 9.50
General Motors Acceptance	5.00–24.87	Shawmut National Bank	7.00–10.00

Source: "Asset Credit Evaluations," New York, Moody's Investors Service, September 1990, pp. 38-41.

Table 3.8—Credit Enhancement Levels for Selected Credit Card Receivable-Backed Issues, by Credit Card Issuer

Sponsor	*Credit Enhancement Level*	*Sponsor*	*Credit Enhancement Level*
Bank of America	10.00%	Discover RFC	10.00%
Citibank, N.A.	11.00	General Electric Credit Corporation	15.00
Colonial National Bank USA	18.00	JC Penney	12.00
First National Bank of Chicago	12.00	Sears, Roebuck	8.50
Security Pacific National Bank	10.50	Spiegel, Inc.	30.00

Sources: "Asset Credit Evaluations," New York, Moody's Investors Service, September 1990, pp. 44-47, and Joan Barmat, "Medium Term Credit Card Receivable-Backed Securities," New York, Bear, Stearns & Co., June 6, 1990.

bile loan-backed and credit card receivable-backed securities. Tables 3.7 and 3.8 show the credit enhancement levels in securitization transactions sponsored by selected automobile and credit card lenders, respectively. In many cases, the indicated credit enhancement level reflects (in the aggregate) more than one form of credit enhancement for a particular pool, e.g., a letter of credit supplemented by a limited guarantee.[17]

The amount of credit enhancement determines the allocation of default risk.[18] With asset-backed securities rated AAA, the credit enhancer bears virtually all the default risk associated with the collateral pool. Even with a AA rating, the certificate holder's default risk is slight. Note, however, that the certificate holder is exposed to the risk that the credit enhancer may default. This risk increases if the credit enhancer's financial condition deteriorates while the asset-backed securities are outstanding, as has happened recently in the case of certain credit card receivable-backed issues supported by bank letters of credit.

Credit card receivable-backed trust structure. As indicated in Table 3.3, credit card receivables have such relatively high monthly average payment rates that a credit card receivable-backed issue would mature within approximately one year if all the payments were passed through to investors. In order to create an intermediate-term security, credit card receivable-backed certificates typically pay only interest for a period that normally falls within the range from 24 to 60 months.

17 The relatively wide range of credit enhancement levels for GMAC in Table 3.7 reflects the GMAC 1985-A and GMAC 1986-A issues. More recent issues have required credit enhancement in the 5.00% to 8.64% range.

18 The required amount of credit enhancement also depends on the availability of insurance coverage for specific risks. For example, mortgage-backed securities often have the benefit of a special pool hazard insurance policy, which protects mortgage-backed certificate holders against the risk of loss (i.e., default) associated with events that are not insured under the standard form of homeowner insurance policy. Such events typically include earthquakes, tidal waves, and flooding.

Figure 3.9—Amortization Structure of a Credit Card Receivable-Backed Security

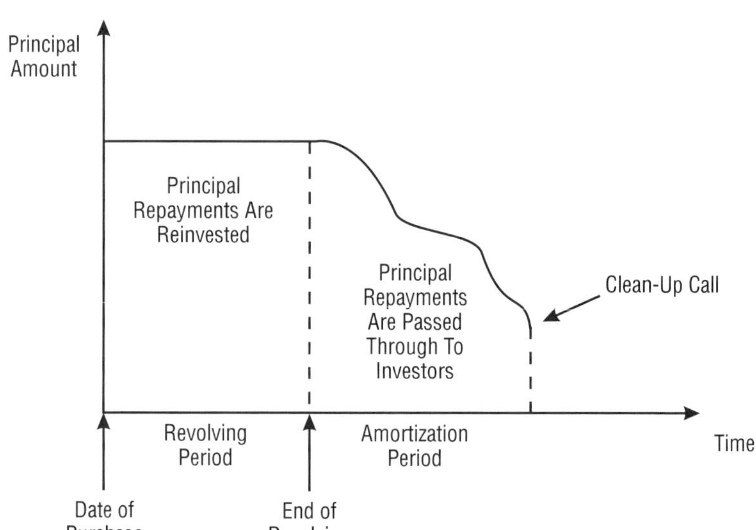

Principal payments received during this 'revolving period' are 'reinvested' in newly generated credit card receivables. Figure 3.9 illustrates how the credit card receivable-backed certificates amortize. When the pool balance falls below a specified level, typically either 5% or 10% of the original pool balance (at which it becomes too expensive to administer the pool), the seller/servicer has the right to redeem the outstanding certificates.

Figure 3.10 illustrates a typical credit card receivable-backed securitization structure. The seller/servicer normally sells an amount of receivables to the trust that is greater than the aggregate value of the certificates sold to investors. The seller interest in the trust represents the excess amount of receivables sold to the trust. It typically starts out at 15%–30% of the total pool and then declines. The seller interest will decline due to cardholder attrition—cardholders closing their accounts and either paying off their balances or defaulting—unless new accounts are added to the pool. The seller/servicer is required to maintain a specified minimum seller interest, typically between 5% and 10% of the pool, in order to avoid having the pool balance fall below the amount of outstanding certificates. The minimum seller interest acts as a buffer against default risk and prepayment risk.

Default risk is reallocated in three ways:

1. The seller/servicer arranges a letter of credit or surety bond for the benefit of the trust or the seller subordinates the seller interest in the pool to the investor interest;[19]
2. Any excess yield (i.e., any funds remaining after interest on the certificates, servicing fees, and credit enhancement fees have been paid) is used to maintain an escrow/reserve account that reimburses the letter of credit or surety bond issuer for any draws made under those facilities; and
3. If the level of loan losses exceeds a specified level, the base yield on the receivables portfolio falls below a specified level, insufficient new receivables are generated to maintain the minimum required seller interest or cer-

19 Credit card receivable-backed issues often take the form of a "mezzanine" structure in which a senior class and one or more subordinated classes (i.e., subordinated to the senior class) are all senior to the seller's interest in the credit card receivables pool.

Figure 3.10—Basic Credit Card Receivable-Backed Securitization Structure

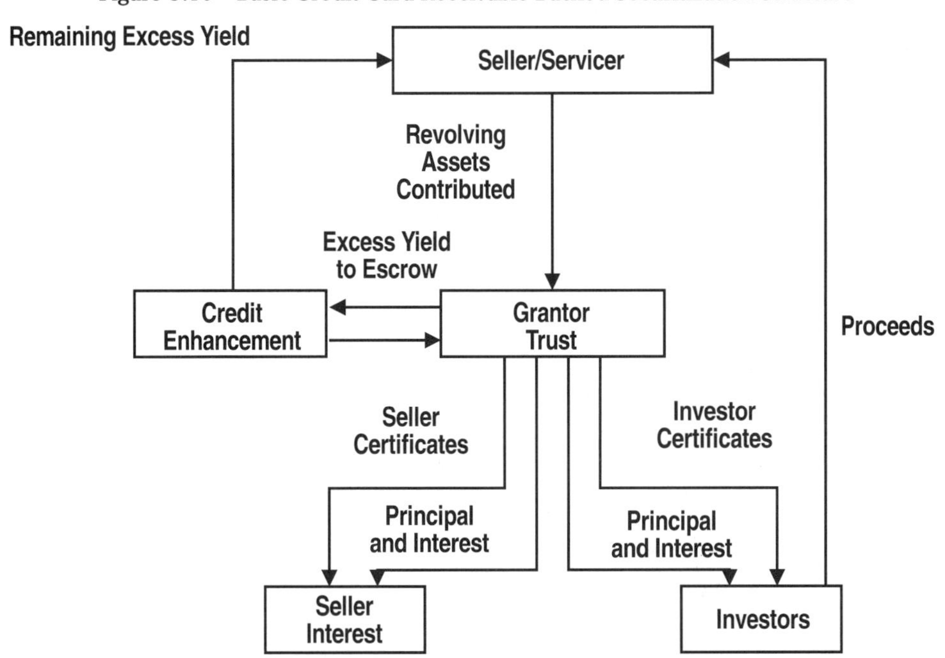

tain other 'pay-out events' occur, an early, accelerated amortization period commences.[20]

The credit enhancement mechanism transfers default risk to the credit enhancer. The escrow/reserve account represents a form of reinsurance provided by the seller/servicer, who will receive the excess yield to the extent it is not required to reimburse letter of credit or surety bond draws. It may also reduce default risk by enhancing the seller/servicer's motivation to achieve the lowest possible loss experience on the collateral pool.

C. Senior/Subordinated Asset-Backed Securities

FHLMC and FNMA are restricted by law to the purchase of mortgage loans whose balance is no greater than a stated maximum and that meet certain other standards. Similarly, there are legal restrictions on the size of mortgage the FHA can insure or the VA can guarantee. Loans that do not meet these tests are called non-conforming loans. Reducing the investors' exposure to default risk associated with non-conforming loans requires non-US agency entities to assume the unwanted default risk. The earliest mortgage pass-through securities backed by non-conforming loans relied on mortgage pool insurance or special hazard insurance for credit enhancement. The uncertainty regarding the availability of satisfactory mortgage pool insurance and the high cost of such enhancements led to the development of a senior/subordinated structure to eliminate the need for pool or hazard insurance (see Bhattacharya and Cannon (1989)). Such a structure can also be used to reallocate default risk for automobile installment

20 Note that this feature, which transfers default risk away from investors, exposes investors to the risk of early pay-out. This risk is certainly not remote. Increased consumer default rates led to at least one early pay-out of a US credit card receivable-backed issue in 1991, and US Congressional consideration of legislation in 1991 that would have capped the interest rate on credit card accounts at 14%, well below the 19% average then prevailing, raised the specter of many additional early pay-outs and severely disrupted the credit card receivable-backed market. See "Early Pay-Back Considered for a Credit Card Security," *Wall Street Journal* (June 20, 1991), p. C1; "Giant Credit Card Securities Market Witnesses First Early Pay-Out on Southeast Bank's Issue," *Wall Street Journal* (July 18, 1991), p. C19; and "Credit Card Issues Face Uncertainty," *Wall Street Journal* (November 18, 1991), p. C1.

Figure 3.11—Senior/Subordinated Structure for Amortizing Loans

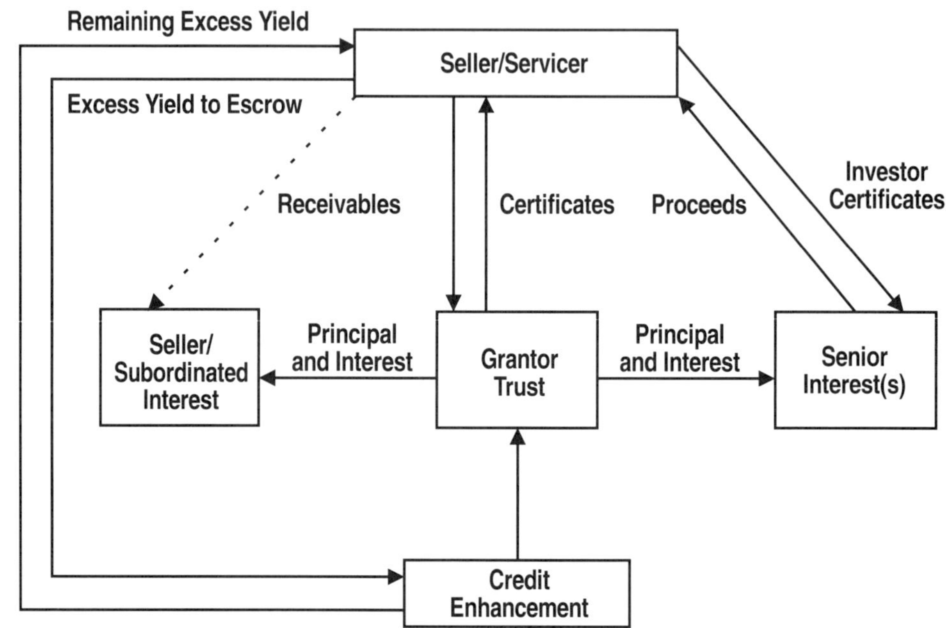

loans, credit card receivables, commercial mortgage loans, manufactured housing installment loans, home equity loans, time share loans, or any other type of installment loan contract.

Basic structure for amortizing loans. Figure 3.11 illustrates the senior/subordinated structure developed for securitizing loans that amortize, such as residential mortgage loans and automobile installment loans. A pool of amortizing loans is formed and contributed to a grantor trust. Alternatively, in the case of mortgages, the loans can be contributed to a corporation or partnership that qualifies as a REMIC. In each case, the structure is designed to pass the tax attributes of the underlying loans through to investors. The financing entity then issues two (or in some cases more) classes of securities. In the typical case, one class (designated the "senior class") represents a 90–95% interest in the trust and receives a prior claim on cash payments by the trust. The other class (designated the "subordinated class") represents the remaining interest and provides credit support for the senior class because of its subordinated position. The subordinated class is normally retained by the financial institution that formed the trust but some institutions have sold the subordinated classes.

The size of the subordinated class depends on the type of collateral, extent of diversification of the collateral, and the experience and capabilities of the servicer. In the case of mortgage loans, the size of the subordinated class required to achieve a AA rating will be greater

1. The less diversified the loan portfolio (i.e., smaller number of "large" loans),
2. The more concentrated the collateral in any single state or geographical region,
3. The greater the proportion of loans with a loan-to-value ratio higher than 80%,
4. The higher the proportion of 2- to 4-family properties or condominiums, and
5. The greater the proportion of investment properties or second/vacation homes in the collateral pool.

Senior/subordinated mortgage-backed securities are generally structured in either of two ways: a reserve fund structure or a shifting interest structure (see Bhattacharya and Cannon (1989)). Senior/subordinated automobile loan-backed securities are generally of the reserve fund structure type.

Reserve fund structure. The subordinated class is supplemented by a reserve fund to ensure the timely payment of principal and interest to senior certificate holders. The sponsoring financial institution establishes a reserve fund with a deposit of between 0.10% and 0.50% of the initial pool balance at the time the trust is formed. The subordinated certificate holder receives no cash flow until the reserve fund builds up to a prespecified level, typically 1%–2% of the pool balance in the case of mortgages, and up to 4%–5%, depending on actual loss experience, in the case of automobile loans. Once the reserve fund reaches the specified level, the senior certificate holders and subordinated certificate holders share pro rata in any payments of principal and interest made by the trust except to the extent

1. Principal and interest otherwise payable to subordinated certificate holders will be paid to senior certificate holders to cover payment shortfalls, and
2. Principal due to subordinated certificate holders will be used to replenish the reserve fund if it falls below a specified level.

The reserve fund is tapped to the extent cash flow due the subordinated certificate holders is inadequate to cover senior certificate payment shortfalls.[21] The specified reserve level may increase or decrease over time depending on the loss experience of the collateral pool. Excess cash in the reserve fund reverts to the subordinated certificate holders.

Shifting interest structure. The ownership percentages of the senior and subordinated certificate holders shift in a way that will compensate senior certificate holders for any payment shortfalls they suffer. The senior certificates have a prior claim on the trusts's cash receipts, and payment shortfalls on the senior certificates are deducted from the subordinated certificate ownership percentage and added to the senior certificate ownership percentage.

Sometimes a reserve fund is included in the shifting interest structure to enhance the ability of the subordinated class to absorb fully any potential losses on a current basis. Alternatively, the rating agencies may require that all prepayments on the underlying pool of mortgages be applied to retire portions of the senior certificates for a period of, say, 5 years, with the subordinated class's share of prepayments gradually increasing thereafter to the subordinated class's ownership percentage. As a result, the senior certificates amortize at a significantly faster rate than the subordinated certificates.

The senior/subordinated shifting interest structure has also been employed outside the United States. Bear Stearns and Credit Lyonnais used it when they securitized unsecured personal loans in the French capital market in 1991 (see Asset Securitization (1991) and Bear Stearns (1991)). The subordinated class initially represented 12.50% of the loan balance of the Fr 2 billion issue.

Comparison of the two structures. Table 3.9 compares the reserve fund and shifting interest structures. The senior certificate's 90% share of scheduled monthly principal and interest amounts to $900,000 and 90% share of defaulted principal amounts to $1,350,000. In the reserve fund structure, the senior certificates are entitled to net liquidation proceeds and principal and interest received from the underlying mortgage pool to the extent required to satisfy these payment obligations. The subordinated certificate's 10% share of the liquidation proceeds, principal, and interest is allocated to the senior certificates to the extent required to cover any cash shortfall. If additional funds are required, they are obtained from the reserve fund.

In the shifting interest structure, the senior and subordinated certificates receive pro rata distributions of net liquidation proceeds, principal, and interest. Any payment shortfall to the senior certificates, in this case $463,500, increases the senior certificate ownership percentage to 90.47% from 90% and reduces the subordinated certificate ownership percentage to 9.53% from 10%.

The two structures involve a critical difference: The reserve fund structure is designed to compensate senior certificate holders immediately for any cash shortfalls that would otherwise occur whereas the shifting interest structure compensates senior certificate holders on a deferred basis by increasing the proportion of future cash flows they will receive. In a perfect capital market the two alternatives would be perfect substitutes. In practice, investors prefer the reserve fund struc-

21 If the reserve fund is exhausted, senior certificate holders are protected by a carryforward account that accrues interest at the senior certificate's pass-through rate. Future principal payments that would otherwise be payable to the subordinated certificate holders are dedicated to paying down the carryforward account balance.

Table 3.9—Comparison of the Reserve Fund and Shifting Interest Structures

Initial Pool Balance	$100,000,000	Outstanding Principal Balance of Foreclosed Loans	$1,500,000
Monthly Principal and Interest	$ 1,000,000	Net Liquidation Proceeds	$1,000,000
Senior Percentage	90%	Principal and Interest Received from Pool	985,000
Subordinated Percentage	10%		

Reserve Fund Structure	
Senior Certificates' share of monthly principal and interest due	$900,000
Senior Certificates' share of defaulted principal	1,350,000
Amount due Senior Certificates	2,250,000
Available from:	
Net liquidation proceeds	1,000,000
Principal and interest received from pool	985,000
Payment to Senior Certificates from the Reserve Fund	$265,000

	Shifting Interest Structure		
	Senior Certificates	Subordinated Certificates	Total
Initial share of pool	90.00%	10.00%	100.00%
Principal and interest due	$900,000	$100,000	$1,000,000
Liquidation proceeds due	1,350,000	150,000	1,500,000
Total due	2,250,000	250,000	2,500,000
Allocation of principal and interest	886,500	98,500	985,000
Allocation of net liquidation proceeds	900,000	100,000	1,000,000
Shortfall	$463,500	$51,500	$515,000
Initial balance	$90,000,000	$10,000,000	$100,000,000
Reduction of principal due to foreclosures	(1,350,000)	(150,000)	(1,500,000)
Allocation to Senior Certificates to cover shortfall	463,500	(463,500)	–
New balance	$89,113,500	$9,386,500	$98,500,000
Share of pool	90.47%	9.53%	100.00%

Figure 3.12—Senior/Subordinated Structure for Revolving Loans

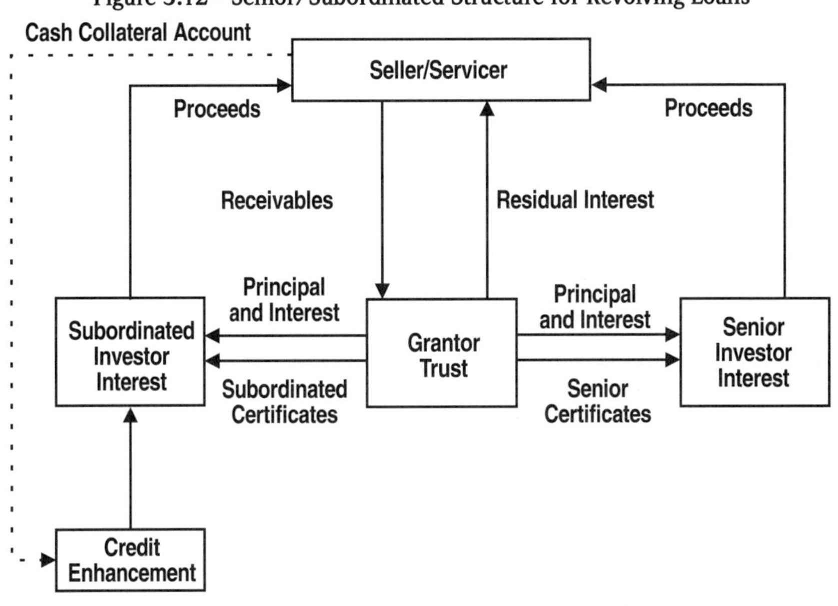

ture, which has consequently accounted for the majority of the senior/subordinated mortgage-backed securities issues sold in recent years.

Basic Structure for Revolving Loans. Senior/subordinated structures are also commonly used to securitize revolving loans, such as credit card receivables. Figure 3.12 illustrates the senior/subordinated structure developed for securitizing revolving loans. A trust is formed to hold the pool of receivables. There is a revolving period and other features that are typically found in credit card receivable-backed guarantee/insurance security structures. The principal difference is that the seller interest in the trust is expressly subordinated to the investor interest, and this subordination replaces the insurance, letter of credit, limited corporate guarantee, or surety bond that is found in the guarantee/insurance structure. In both the senior/subordinated and the guarantee/insurance security structures, the investor certificates are treated as debt of the sponsoring bank for income tax purposes. The same basic structure has also been used to securitize automobile dealer revolving 'wholesale' financing (also referred to as 'floor-plan' loans), as for example, the CARCO Auto Loan Master Trust Asset-Backed Certificates, Series 1991-1.[22]

D. Guarantee/Insurance Supported by Subordinated CMO Class

Certain features of the senior/subordinated structure can be combined with the guarantee/insurance structure to reallocate default risk. For example, the GE Capital Mortgage Services, Inc. Series 1992-3 REMIC provides for five sequential pay classes (A, B, C, D, and E) plus a subordinated class M and a residual class R.[23] Default risk is reallocated through a combination of (i) a mortgage pool insurance policy, (ii) a special pool hazard insurance policy, (iii) a bankruptcy support arrangement, and (iv) the subordination of one CMO class.

Actual losses due to mortgagor default are covered first by the mortgage pool insurance policy except for losses specifically covered under either the special pool hazard insurance policy or the bankruptcy support arrangement. The special pool hazard insurance policy covers certain specified risks not covered under the standard form of home-

22 CARCO Auto Loan Master Trust, Floating Rate Auto Loan Asset-Backed Certificates, Series 1991-1, prospectus, May 16, 1991.

23 GE Capital Mortgage Services, Inc., REMIC Multi-Class Pass-Through Certificates, Series 1992-3, prospectus, March 23, 1992.

owner insurance policy. The bankruptcy support arrangement obligates the CMO issuer, in the event a home mortgagor whose mortgage belongs to the collateral pool declares personal bankruptcy, to deposit funds into a designated account to the extent a bankruptcy court either (i) establishes a value for the mortgaged property that is less than the amount of the loan secured by the property or (ii) reduces the mortgagor's debt service obligations.

If coverage under the mortgage pool insurance policy is exhausted, through either the payment of claims or default by the pool insurer, then losses due to default are allocated to class M (of course, only until its principal balance has been reduced to zero). Thereafter, the sequential pay classes bear default risk proportionately.

The mortgage pool insurance policy is issued by an affiliate of GE Capital Mortgage Services, and the bankruptcy support arrangement is guaranteed by General Electric Capital Corporation, also an affiliate of the issuer. Thus, the guarantee/insurance and the bankruptcy support arrangement allocate default risk primarily to affiliates of the issuer, GE Capital Mortgage Services. Any remaining default risk is allocated next to the holders of the subordinated class M certificates and thereafter to the other CMO classes.

VI. STRUCTURES FOR REDUCING LIQUIDITY RISK

Asset securitization reduces liquidity risk in five principal ways:

- The asset-backed security is easier and cheaper to transfer between investors than the underlying assets. The loan files for the underlying assets reside with the pool servicer and never have to change hands during the entire life of the loan (unless, of course, a new servicer is selected).
- Credit enhancement mechanisms coupled with either debt ratings obtained from nationally recognized rating agencies or a government agency guarantee (e.g., from FNMA or FHLMC) serve to reduce the uncertainty as to the degree of default risk that the investor must bear and to eliminate the need for a lengthy and costly credit review of the underlying assets by the investor.
- The asset-backed securities are either registered for public sale or issued by government agencies that are exempt from registration requirements. As a result, the asset-backed securities are freely tradable among investors.
- The packagers of mortgages, automobile loans, and credit card receivables into asset-backed securities make markets in those securities. Holders who wish to sell can contact the packager/underwriter or any other securities firm that is making a market in the securities for a quotation.
- Asset-backed securities structures are designed to ensure, to the maximum extent practicable, that investors will receive payments of interest and principal on schedule. Temporary payment delinquencies on the underlying loans often occur. Mortgage-backed securities typically require the servicer to advance funds as required to meet the REMIC's temporary liquidity needs. Senior/subordinated structures typically solve the problem through subordination of the seller's interest. Other asset-backed securities structures use a letter of credit facility, reserve fund, or other form of credit enhancement to meet temporary liquidity needs.

VII. STRUCTURES FOR REALLOCATING INTEREST RATE RISK

Asset securitization structures reallocate interest rate risk in three principal ways. First, securitizing a pool of assets can facilitate a closer matching of the interest rate sensitivities of the securitizer's assets and liabilities. Second, there are a variety of securitization structures, such as IO/PO STRIPS and floating-rate/inverse-floating-rate CMO classes, that reallocate the sponsoring entity's interest rate risk among different classes of investors. Third, interest rate swaps have been employed in conjunction with asset securitization to securitize floating-interest-rate assets in the form of fixed-interest-rate obligations and vice versa without exposing the issuing vehicle to unacceptable interest rate risk.

A. Securitization of Assets

The securitization of assets can reduce a financial institution's exposure to interest rate risk. For example, a bank that rolls over 5-year certificates of deposit to fund a 30-year fixed-rate mortgage loan is exposed to the risk that rising interest rates could cause the bank to lose money on the transaction. Securitizing the mortgage can eliminate this risk. In the simplest form of transaction, the financial institution securitizes an entire portfolio of assets on a non-recourse or limited-recourse basis. The cash flow from the pool of assets services the asset-backed securities fully. The financial institution earns a profit equal to the difference between (1) the yield on the assets and (2) the interest cost of the liabilities plus servicing fees plus any fees paid to third parties for credit enhancement.

B. IO/PO STRIPS

IO STRIPS and PO STRIPS were discussed in connection with reallocating prepayment risk. Because of the well-documented sensitivity of prepayment rates to interest rate changes, IO/PO STRIPS also represent vehicles for reallocating the interest rate risk present in a pool of mortgages. As interest rates rise or fall, prepayment rates tend to vary inversely. As interest rates fall (rise), principal payments accelerate (decelerate) and the aggregate flow of interest payments falls (rises). IO STRIP prices tend to fall when interest rates fall, giving IO STRIPS a negative duration. PO STRIP prices tend to rise when interest rates fall, only more rapidly than the prices of the underlying mortgages, giving PO STRIPS a relatively long positive duration. Portfolio managers value IO/PO STRIPS for their duration characteristics.

C. Floating-Rate/Inverse-Floating-Rate Classes

The inverse-floating-rate note has proved to be a very popular mortgage-backed security innovation (see Carron, Hemel, and Golub (1989) and Perlman (1989)). The coupon rate on the note varies inversely to changes in a specified bench mark interest rate. As a result, inverse-floating-rate notes have very long durations, e.g., when interest rates drop, not only does the investor's required rate of return decrease but the coupon increases. The price of an inverse floater will therefore increase much more rapidly than the price of an otherwise identical fixed-interest-rate note. Certain institutions have found inverse floaters very attractive for portfolio hedging purposes.

A fixed-interest-rate CMO tranche can be subdivided into a conventional floating-rate tranche, subject to an interest rate cap, and an inverse-floating-rate tranche, as illustrated in Figure 3.13. One such example is the FHLMC Series 27, issued

Figure 3.13—Allocation of Principal Among the Classes of the FHLMC Multiclass Mortgage Participation Certificates, Series 27

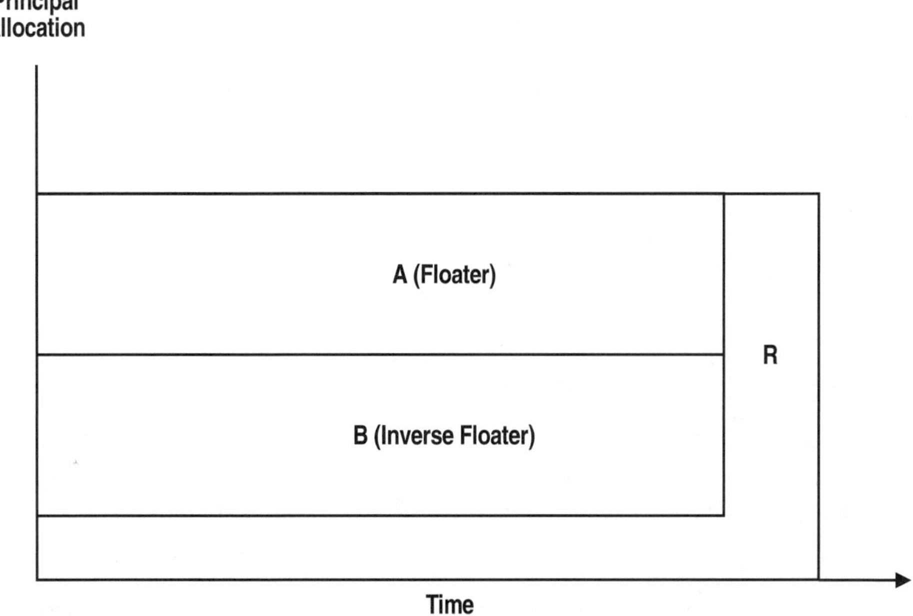

December 12, 1988.[24] The Class A certificates pay interest at the rate of LIBOR (London Interbank Offer Rate) plus 2.50%, subject to a cap of 15%. The Class B certificates pay interest at the rate of 17.26190475%–1.38096 × LIBOR, subject to a floor of zero. The REMIC's aggregate interest payment obligation is the same as it would be for a conventional pass-through structure, but the conventional floating-rate tranche has much less exposure to changing interest rates while the inverse-floating-rate tranche has much greater exposure (which is the source of its appeal). Such a reallocation of interest rate risk can be mutually beneficial to investors, such as money market mutual funds that typically invest in floating-rate instruments, and to financial institutions desiring to include the inverse floater's interest rate sensitivity features in their portfolios.

D. Interest Rate Swaps

Interest rate swaps involve the exchange of interest payment obligations (see Kapner and Marshall (1990)). Financial entities enter into interest rate swaps to convert fixed-interest-rate obligations into floating-interest-rate obligations and vice versa. Accordingly, they reallocate interest rate risk between the counterparties to the swap.

Interest rate swaps have been used in connection with mortgage-backed, automobile loan-backed, and credit card receivable-backed securities. For example, in November 1988, Household Mortgage Corporation PLC, a UK residential mortgage lender, created a special purpose vehicle, HMC 101, to issue fixed-rate sterling notes backed by a portfolio of variable-rate UK mortgages (see Weir (1990)). The nature of the assets and liabilities of the issuing vehicle created a duration mismatch. So the issuing vehicle entered into a pay-floating-receive-fixed interest rate swap in order to hedge the interest rate risk involved. The fixed-interest-rate payments received under the swap offset the vehicle's fixed-interest-rate payment obligations. The floating-interest-rate payments required under the swap contract were paid from the floating-interest-rate payments received from the mortgage portfolio.[25] Because of these arrangements, the HMC 101 issue was indistinguishable to the investor from any other intermediate-term fixed-rate sterling issue with a bullet maturity.

In 1990, Citibank, N.A., wished to create a floating-rate credit card receivable-backed security.[26] The receivables it intended to pledge were fixed-rate obligations. To eliminate the trust's duration mismatch, Citibank arranged for the trustee to enter into a pay-fixed-receive-floating interest rate swap. In 1992, Ford Motor Credit Company wished to securitize automobile dealer floorplan revolving credit facilities, which bear interest at a floating rate.[27] In order to create a fixed-interest-rate asset-backed security, Ford Motor Credit arranged for the trustee to enter into a pay-floating-receive-fixed interest rate swap to eliminate its duration mismatch.

VIII. CONCLUSION

Asset securitization involves converting illiquid assets to marketable securities. In the process, cash flows are redirected through an intermediary vehicle so as to suit better the risk-return preferences of different classes of investors. As a result, new instruments have been crafted to link the sources and users of capital. Asset securitization has not

---

24 Federal Home Loan Mortgage Corporation, Multiclass Mortgage Participation Certificates (Guaranteed), Series 27, prospectus, December 12, 1988.

25 Two other significant risk management problems were also involved. The mortgages would prepay, which would require a callable interest rate swap so that Home Mortgage could reduce the notional principal amount of the swap as the mortgages prepay. Callable swaps can be very expensive. The problem was solved by creating a substitution period equal to the life of the fixed-rate issue sold to investors. During the substitution period, prepayments would be reinvested in new variable-rate mortgages. In order to shift the risk that sufficient new mortgages might not be generated with interest rates equal to or greater than those of the prepaid mortgages, Home Mortgage arranged for a guaranteed investment contract. The second problem concerned HMC 101's 5-year bullet maturity: how to ensure that the fixed-rate investors would be repaid fully at the end of 5 years. The problem was solved by having an entity separate from HMC 101 own the mortgages and issue a conventional mortgage-backed floating-rate note to HMC 101 and having HMC 101 purchase a put option from a creditworthy third party. The put option would obligate the third party to purchase the floating-rate note on the fifth anniversary of its issuance at par.

26 Money Market Credit Card Trust 1989-1, Floating Rate Renewable Credit Card Participation Certificates, prospectus, January 25, 1990.

27 Ford Credit Auto Loan Master Trust Series 1992-1, 6-7/8% Auto Loan Asset-Backed Certificates, prospectus, January 30, 1992.

only led to new products but attracted new classes of investors to the mortgage and consumer receivables markets.

The reallocation of various types of risk, principally prepayment risk, default risk, liquidity risk, and interest rate risk, is one of the principal benefits derived from asset securitization. Just as a butcher adds value to a side of beef by creating various cuts of meat that can be marketed separately, so securitization adds value by unbundling and parceling out the various risks associated with a pool of assets. The key to both processes is determining how to make the specific cuts that will appeal most to customers and hence command the greatest value in the marketplace.

The risk reallocation process—and asset securitization—should be viewed within the broader context of financial engineering. The trend toward securitization reflects the natural evolution of an increasingly sophisticated international capital market. The more efficient allocation of various classes of risk, which asset securitization facilitates, is designed to exploit opportunities to make the capital markets less incomplete.

The pace of asset securitization has accelerated during the past decade. Much of this activity has taken place within the separate domestic capital markets, beginning with the United States and then spreading first to the United Kingdom, then to Canada and Australia, next to France, and then on to other European countries. Legal and regulatory restrictions, tax frictions, and institutional impediments have tended to segment the separate domestic markets for asset-backed securities—as well as slow the process of asset securitization—but the globalization of the capital markets, perhaps to be spurred on by EC 1992, should stimulate the internationalization of this process. This internationalization is likely to take the form of cross border financings, perhaps one day even backed by multinational asset pools, and involve the development of new structures to reallocate currency risk, political risk, and other forms of risk in a manner that achieves greater overall economic efficiency.

REFERENCES

Bear Stearns, "French Franc Asset-Backed Securitization," London, Bear, Stearns International Limited (April 1991).

___, "Asset Securitization in France May Be Set to Arrive Full Force," London, Bear, Stearns International Limited (May 1991).

Anand K. Bhattacharya and Peter J. Cannon, "Senior-Subordinated Mortgage Pass-Throughs," in Frank J. Fabozzi, ed., *Advances & Innovations*, 1989, pp. 473–483.

David C. Bonsall, ed., *Securitisation*, London, Butterworths, 1990.

Phelim P. Boyle, "Valuing Canadian Mortgage-Backed Securities," *Financial Analysts Journal* (May/June 1989), pp. 55–60.

Francesco Caputo-Nassetti, "Development of Securitisation in Italy," in Charles Stone, Anne Zissu, and Jess Lederman, eds., *Asset Securitisation*, 1991, pp. 423–439.

Steven J. Carlson, "Hedging Prepayment Risk with Derivative Mortgage Securities," in Frank J. Fabozzi, ed., *Investment Management*, 1989, pp. 557–563.

Andrew S. Carron, Eric I. Hemel, and Bennett W. Golub, "High Yield Mortgage Securities," in Frank J. Fabozzi, ed., *Investment Management*, 1989, pp. 491–520.

Andrew S. Carron, Wayne Olson, and Nelson F. Soares, "Asset-Backed Securities," in Frank J. Fabozzi, ed., *Advances & Innovations*, 1989, pp. 527–542.

Kenneth Cox, "Introduction and Overview," in David C. Bonsall, ed., *Securitisation*, 1990, pp. 1–12.

Cyrille David, "Securitisation in France," in Charles Stone, Anne Zissu, and Jess Lederman, eds., *Asset Securitisation*, 1991, pp. 257–272.

Andrew S. Davidson and Michael D. Herskovitz, "Analyzing MBS: A Comparison of Methods for Analyzing Mortgage-Backed Securities," in Frank J. Fabozzi, ed., *Advances & Innovations*, 1989, pp. 305–328.

Steve Din, "Commercial Property," in Charles Stone, Anne Zissu, and Jess Lederman, eds., *Asset Securitisation*, 1991, pp. 193–206.

Kenneth B. Dunn and John J. McConnell, "Valuation of GNMA Mortgage-Backed Securities," *Journal of Finance* (June 1981), pp. 599–616.

Frank J. Fabozzi, ed., *The Handbook of Mortgage-Backed Securities*, Chicago, Probus, 1985.

Frank J. Fabozzi, ed., *Advances & Innovations in the Bond and Mortgage Markets*, Chicago, Probus, 1989.

Frank J. Fabozzi, ed., *The Institutional Investor Focus on Investment Management*, Cambridge, MA, Ballinger, 1989.

Ian Falconer, "Asset Securitisation in the United Kingdom," in Charles Stone, Anne Zissu, and Jess Lederman, eds., *Asset Securitisation*, 1991, pp. 493–512.

John D. Finnerty, "Financial Engineering in Corporate Finance: An Overview," *Financial Management* (Winter 1988), pp. 14–33.

John D. Finnerty, "An Overview of Corporate Securities Innovation," *Continental Bank Journal of Applied Corporate Finance* (Winter 1992), pp. 23–39.

Herbert Fugel, "Prospects for Asset-Backed Securitisation in Germany," in Charles Stone, Anne Zissu, and Jess Lederman, eds., *Asset Securitisation*, 1991, pp. 373–377.

Bruce Gaitskell, "What Securitisation Can Mean for a Commercial Bank," in David C. Bonsall, ed., *Securitisation*, 1990, pp. 91–107.

Lakhbir S. Hayre, Kenneth Lauterbach, and Cyrus Mohebbi, "Prepayment Models and Methodologies," in Frank J. Fabozzi, ed., *Advances & Innovations*, 1989, pp. 329– 350.

Lakhbir S. Hayre and Cyrus Mohebbi, "Mortgage Pass-Through Securities," in Frank J. Fabozzi, ed., *Advances & Innovations*, 1989, pp. 259–304.

Kenneth Kapner and John Marshall, *The Swaps Handbook*, New York, New York Institute of Finance, 1990.

Jaime Llorens and Lucía Lanzón, "Asset-Backed Financing in Spain," in Charles Stone, Anne Zissu, and Jess Lederman, eds., *Asset Securitisation*, 1991, pp. 469–475.

John F. Marshall and Vipul K. Bansal, *Financial Engineering*, Boston, Allyn and Bacon, 1992.

John J. McConnell and Manoj K. Singh, "Prepayments and the Valuation of Adjustable-Rate Mortgage-Backed Securities," *Journal of Fixed Income* (June 1991), pp. 21–35.

Robert C. Merton, "Financial Innovation and Economic Performance," *Continental Bank Journal of Applied Corporate Finance* (Winter 1992), pp. 12–22.

Robert C. Paul, Monique de Zagon, and Jean Scalais, "The Legal Aspects of Asset-Backed Securities in Belgium," in Charles Stone, Anne Zissu, and Jess Lederman, eds., *Asset Securitisation*, 1991, pp. 249–255.

Scot D. Perlman, "Collateralized Mortgage Obligations: The Impact of Structure on Value," in Frank J. Fabozzi, ed., *Advances & Innovations*, 1989, pp. 417–436.

Michel Quéré, "Securitisation in France: Titrisation," in David C. Bonsall, ed., *Securitisation*, 1990, pp. 265–287.

Scott F. Richard, "Relative Prepayment Rates on Thirty-Year FNMA, FHLMC and GNMA Fixed Rate Mortgage-Backed Securities," in Frank J. Fabozzi, ed., *Advances & Innovations*, 1989, pp. 351–369.

Scott F. Richard and Richard Roll, "Modeling Prepayments on Fixed Rate Mortgage-Backed Securities," *Journal of Portfolio Management* (Spring 1989), pp. 73–83.

Blaine Roberts, "The Frontiers of Asset Securitization," Bear, Stearns & Co. Inc. (September 30, 1991).

Blaine Roberts, Sarah Keil Wolf, and Nancy Wilt, "Advances and Innovations in the CMO Market," in Frank J. Fabozzi, ed., *Advances & Innovations*, 1989, pp. 437–455.

Stephen A. Ross, "Institutional Markets, Financial Marketing, and Financial Innovation," *Journal of Finance* (July 1989), pp. 541–556.

Eduardo S. Schwartz and Walter N. Torous, "Prepayment and the Valuation of Mortgage-Backed Securities," *Journal of Finance* (June 1989), pp. 375–392.

Joseph D. Smallman and Michael J.P. Selby, "Asset-Backed Securitisation," in David C. Bonsall, ed., *Securitisation*, 1990, pp. 242–264.

Janet Spratlin, Paul Vianna, and Steven Guterman, "An Investor's Guide to CMOs," in Frank J. Fabozzi, ed., *Investment Management*, 1989, pp. 521–555.

Standard & Poor's Corporation, *S&P's Structured Finance Criteria*, New York, Standard & Poor's, 1988.

Charles Stone, Anne Zissu, and Jess Lederman, eds., *Asset Securitisation: Theory and Practice in Europe*, London, Euromoney Books, 1991.

Alden Toevs, "Hedging the Interest Rate Risk of Fixed Rate Mortgages with Prepayment Rights," in Frank J. Fabozzi, ed., *Handbook*, 1985, pp. 447–473.

James C. Van Horne, "Of Financial Innovations and Excesses," *Journal of Finance* (July 1985), pp. 621–631.

Michael Waldman, Mark Gordon, and K. Jeanne Person, "Interest Only and Principal Only STRIPs," in Frank J. Fabozzi, ed., *Advances & Innovations*, 1989, pp. 401–416.

Julian Walmsley, *The New Financial Instruments*, New York, Wiley, 1988.

Robert Weir, "Profile of a Specialist Mortgage Lender," in David C. Bonsall, ed., *Securitisation*, 1990, pp. 71–90.

Chapter 4

An Overview of Techniques in Structured Finance

by Blaine Roberts,
Senior Managing Director
Bear Stearns

I. INTRODUCTION

Structured finance today represents a major change from traditional lending practices of financial institutions. Historically, a bank would evaluate all aspects of a project and decide whether to make a loan. Loans would remain on the balance sheet in unsecured, illiquid form. These assets would be funded by issuing various liabilities to ultimate investors: individuals, money managers, insurance companies, pension funds, and the like. These loans contain many different characteristics: credit of borrower; put and call provisions; exchange rate risk, in some cases; and differing maturity structures. The portfolio manager was limited to liability mix changes as they matured and loan origination mix changes as they matured. If the market price of one particular characteristic were to change, the portfolio manager was severely constrained in terms of what could be done.

Structured finance departs from traditional lending in three major ways. First, structured finance is a securitization of the assets on which traditional loans are made. By definition, structured finance creates a security that is more liquid and can be bought and sold. Second, and more importantly, structured finance slices and dices the various characteristics into different classes. This enables a credit risk, for example, to be sold to the best bid for credit risk. Thereby, structured finance broadens the market and obtains better execution overall. Third, structured financed is a form of disintermediation. The traditional role of the portfolio is bypassed, and the securities are placed directly in the hands of the ultimate investors.

The motivations at work are clearer from a brief review of arbitrage techniques that have been used in the U.S. CMO/REMIC structures in Section II. Section III contains the conceptual structural optimization problem. Section IV contains two examples of recently structured deals.

II. A BRIEF REVIEW OF CMO/ REMIC STRUCTURES

The following summarizes the evolution of CMO/REMIC structuring techniques. Although current structures in the U.S. mortgage market appear to be quite complex, with deals containing as many as 70 classes, there are really only variations on seven basic themes.

1. Yield Curve Arbitrage

The first CMO was issued by Freddie Mac on June 15, 1983. It consisted of three sequential pay classes that were priced 35/3-year, 54/7-year, and 85/20-year backed by collateral trading about 130/10-year. The average lives were slightly longer than the Treasury bench marks.

2. Accrual Bonds from Coupon Paying Collateral

The next innovation was the development of accrual, or Z, bonds that accrue interest until prior classes have been paid down. This allows much greater face amounts in the earlier classes, as initially all interest from the collateral goes to pay the coupon-paying bonds while the Z bonds accrete in principle value. This increases the yield curve arbitrage when the curve is upward sloping.

3. Using Interest to Pay Principal/ Principal to Pay Interest

Because of the uncertainty of prepayments on mortgages, the total principal of bonds issued have to meet the minimum of the par amount of collateral or the present value of the cash flows assuming zero prepayments. Many of the first CMOs used premium collateral and all cash flows were used to pay interest first and then principal (pass-forward structures). The residual, in this case, was the collateral remaining after all bonds had been retired. In the cases where discount collateral was used, principal was used to pay interest. The next innovation was the pass-back structure where excess cash flows were paid to the residual each period, rather than being used to pay down the bonds. In the case of premium collateral, this is equivalent to carving out an IO strip to be paid to the residual holder. In the case of discount collateral, it is equivalent to an excess PO strip from prepayments paid to the residual holder.

4. Creating Floaters and Inverse Floaters from Fixed-Rate Collateral

The next innovation was to increase the yield curve arbitrage by creating floating rate classes. Since the collateral is fixed rate, this requires a cap for the floating rate class and the creation of an inverse floater. Typically, the floating rate class is a fixed spread over LIBOR and the inverse floater is leveraged. For example, if 80 percent of the collateral principal is used for the floater, the inverse floater coupon will move up by four times the amount the floater adjusts down. The cap on the floater is equal to the collateral coupon divided by the percentage of principal associated with the floater when the inverse floater has a floor of zero. Several variations on caps, floors, and leverage are also possible, but less common.

5. Increasing Cash Flow Certainty and Uncertainty

A very major innovation in CMOs was the creation of structures that increase the cash flow certainty of one class and reduce the cash flow certainty of a companion class. (These go under a variety of acronyms: PACs, TACs, VADMs, and guaranteed maturity classes.) This amounts to reallocating the option components of mortgages to different investors rather than a pro rata exposure to the option.

6. Credit Tranching

The first CMOs used agency collateral and the Agencies provided credit enhancement which is better than AAA. However, an increasing share of the market is whole loan collateral. For mortgages there is an asset, the property secured by a mortgage, and an obligor. The sources of losses include: (a) credit losses—where the obligor goes away; (b) special hazards—where the asset goes away; (c) mortgage repurchase or substitution; (d) bankruptcy—where the legal system intervenes, such as cram downs; (e) liquidity—to ensure timely payments; (f) servicing errors, omissions, or bankruptcy; and (g) fraud—where either the asset or obligor is misrepresented.

Initially, all these sources of losses were credit enhanced by outside sources, primarily insurance companies and bank letters of credit. Increasingly, more of the credit enhancement is being provided internally by the collateral. Bonds are structured with subordination to provide credit enhancement to the senior bonds. for example, a CMO may be structured with AAA senior bonds, mezzanine bonds, AA or A, and first loss bonds that are below investment grade or unrated. These subordinate bonds may provide credit support for losses in general or for particular losses, such as special hazard losses. Another form of internal credit enhancement comes from reserve accounts or spread accounts held by the trustee. Further credit enhancement can be provided by such techniques as shifting interest and other structural features. In addition, combinations of internal and external credit enhancement are common.

III. STRUCTURED FINANCE OPTIMIZATION

Structured finance techniques range from ad hoc, simple approaches to more sophisticated mathematical optimization algorithms. The conceptual optimization problem is as follows:

Let:

A(k,t) = the balance of the kth asset at time period t;

s(j,t) = required percentage loss protection for rating levels higher than j;

B(j,t) = bond class j balance at time t;

r(k,t) = revenue (income) from asset class k at time t;

c(j,t) = revenue to bond class j at time t;

F(k,t) = r(k,t)A(k,t-1)+(A(k,t-1)) = cash flow from asset k at time t;

F(t) = Sum_of_all_k:F(k,t) = cash flow from all assets at time t;

D(j,t) = c(j,t)B(j,t-1)+(B(j,t)-B(j,t-1)) = cash flow to bond j at time t;

D(t) = Sum_of_all_j:D(j,t) = cash flow to all bonds at time t; and

P(j,D(j,t);rho,sigma,nu)

= value function for state-contingent cash flow at time t as a function of parameters: rho, the term structure of Treasury interest rates; sigma, the volatility of short rates; and nu, the correlation between sigma and the volatility of longer rates.

The objective is to maximize the proceeds, which is the sum of the value functions over all j and all t less the cost of the assets subject to the following constraints:

I) Sum_of_all_h_less_than_j:D(h,t)>s(j,t)* Sum_of_all_k:F(k,t) for all t and for some rating agency determined set of possible states of the world; and

II) F(t) = D(t).

The choices in the optimization problem are the selection of assets, A(k,0) and the structure of the state-contingent cash flows, D(j,t), for all time periods t.

All of the variables are state-contingent, including the loss protection percentages, s(j,t), which are based on rating agency criteria. That is, the asset balances and income, the bond balances, and income at any time t depend upon what state of the world occurs: the level of interest rates; prepayments; delinquencies; defaults; recoveries; cures; and so forth.

The set of possible assets includes the collateral, such as loans, leases, and other receivables, and "external" forms of credit support, such as letters of credit, insurance policies, and performance guarantees. Sometimes the set of assets is taken as given. In general, however, asset selection should be an integral part of the optimization procedure. The (notional) class k asset balance, A(k,t), gives the trustee, or trustee equivalent, the ownership (for the benefit of the bond holders) of the state-contingent asset cash flows, F(k,x) for all periods x greater than t, that are allocated under the rules of the trust indenture to the various bond classes.

To meet rating agency requirements there must be a percentage of protection for the structured cash flows of the bonds for a set of possible states of the world. For example, for U.S. mortgage collateral, Moody's requires various levels of protection based on loss experience of the Great Depression. The allocated cash flows to subordinated bond classes may be initially set one level and then may be required to increase or allowed to decrease over time as the assets season or depending on the experience of the collateral.

The (notional) class j bond balance, B(j,t), gives the investor the ownership of the state-contingent cash flows, D(j,x) for all periods x greater than t. Some of the bond classes may be "artificial"; that is, not real bonds but claims on cash flows for servicing, trustee fees, or insurance premia.

The most critical component of the optimization problem is the accurate specification of the value function P for all possible values of cash flows D(j,t) under the assumptions represented by the parameters rho, sigma, and nu. As discussed more fully in "Consistent, Fair, and Robust Methods of Valuing Mortgage Securities," by Roberts, Sykes, and Winchell, Bear Stearns, April 24, 1992, the value function must satisfy at least three basic tenets. First, the value function must be consistent with actual markets. The values for structured securities must be where they can be sold in the market. Second, the value function must be fair in the sense that there is no risk-free arbitrage. In particular, this means that the sum of the values of the parts must add up to the value of the whole and that the value of a pure floater earning the riskless rate is par. Third, the value function must be robust in the sense that the valuations are fair and consistent under all possible market conditions.

The conventional option adjusted spread (OAS) model satisfies these tenets when cash flows are strictly a function of interest rates. When other random components are present, such as delinquencies, defaults, prepayments, recoveries, cures, bankruptcies, and fraud, they must be valued using the stochastic process appropriate for each component.

IV. TWO EXAMPLES OF RECENTLY STRUCTURED DEALS

The first example is a case study of a recent deal on which Bear Stearns was the lead underwriter for the Resolution Trust Corporation, called *1992/6*.

Figure 4.1 contains issues that are specific to mortgages. The first issue is the loan-to-value ratio, for purposes of getting the level of subordination, and whether there is primary mortgage insurance (PMI). Also important in the collateral issues are not just the loan-to-value ratios but, in the case where they're first and second mortgages, the total loan amount associated with them. Seasoning is important on the mortgages because there is a statistically identifiable default curve. Mortgages tend to default early and will become seasoned after about five years.

Many people analyze the loan balances. An important characteristic is not just the average, which is what many people look at, but also the largest amount. A particularly bothersome type of loan is one that has a balance below the agency level. Most of the whole loan deals that are done

Figure 4.1—Collateral Issues

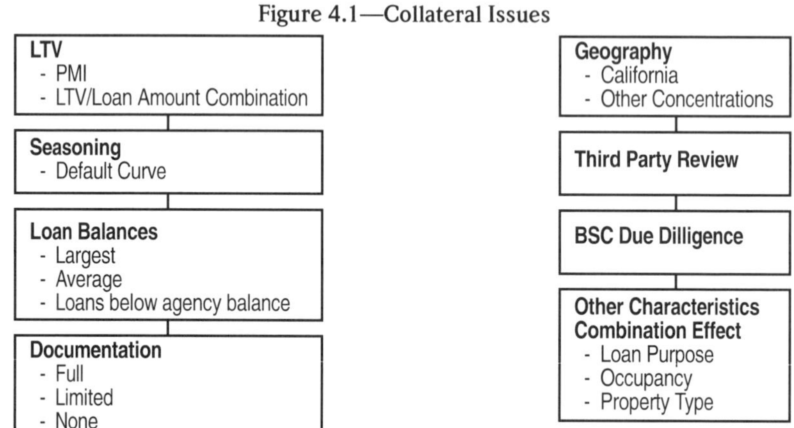

are non-conforming, i.e., they don't conform, for one reason or another, to the agency guidelines; otherwise these loans are just sold to the agencies or swapped with the agencies and then the mortgage-backed security is issued. If a loan would qualify under the agency criteria in terms of the balance but has not yet been sold to an agency, it probably has some significant problems associated with it.

Documentation on mortgages is important. Full documentation is where employment is verified independently by a third party; the deposit is verified independently, so that the loan-to-value ratio is correct; and so on through all the other credit characteristics associated with the origination of the mortgage.

In the United States there have been a number of limited documentations; for example, where a W2 form is sufficient to verify income and employment. One of the binges that many of the S&Ls went on for a while was to have simply no documentation. Anybody who could pass a Breathalyzer test—or even who failed, so long as they were still breathing—was given a loan.

Geography is important of course in terms of concentration.

Among other things that are important is whether there has been a third-party review. As underwriters, we do a great deal of due diligence. In this deal Bear Stearns' due diligence ability was one of the reasons we were selected to do it. We sample not all of the loans but various samples from the loans, to do our own due diligence, and we have a capability that is unique in that respect.

Other characteristics for mortgages are: what the purpose of the loan was; the occupancy (whether owner-occupied or rental); and the property type (whether single-family, multifamily or co-op).

In the schematic Figure 4.2, given all the different risks that have been identified, starts with the mortgage loans, the loan-to-value ratio and the standard hazards,and so on down through the different risks. This feeds into the different types of enhancements that are possible.

In asset securitization, there are two characteristics. Typically there is an asset underlying it—except for the case of credit cards—which has substantive value. Of course in the case of mortgage-backed securities it is the home. Thus, there is the asset and other obligor. Both are important in determining the risk characteristics in mortgage-backed securities.

In the case of standard hazards, i.e., the loan-to-value ratio or credit losses, the mortgagor simply walks away for one reason or another but the house is still there and can be foreclosed and sold, and money is recovered. If the loan-to-value ratio is insufficient, the types of enhancements that are possible are primary mortgage insurance and the standard homeowner's insurance.

In addition, there are all sorts of special hazards that are not covered. This is the case where the asset goes away. The obligor is still there but since the asset is damaged, he is probably not going to make the payments—for example, where there is a flood or an earthquake and the property is destroyed.

Then there is bankruptcy. This is a case where there is some sort of legal intervention. In the United States, for example, there have been instances of what are called "cram down" mortgages, where the interest rate or the face amount on the mortgage has been reduced in the bankruptcy court. You might be left with an asset that

Figure 4.2—An Introduction to Whole Loan Securities

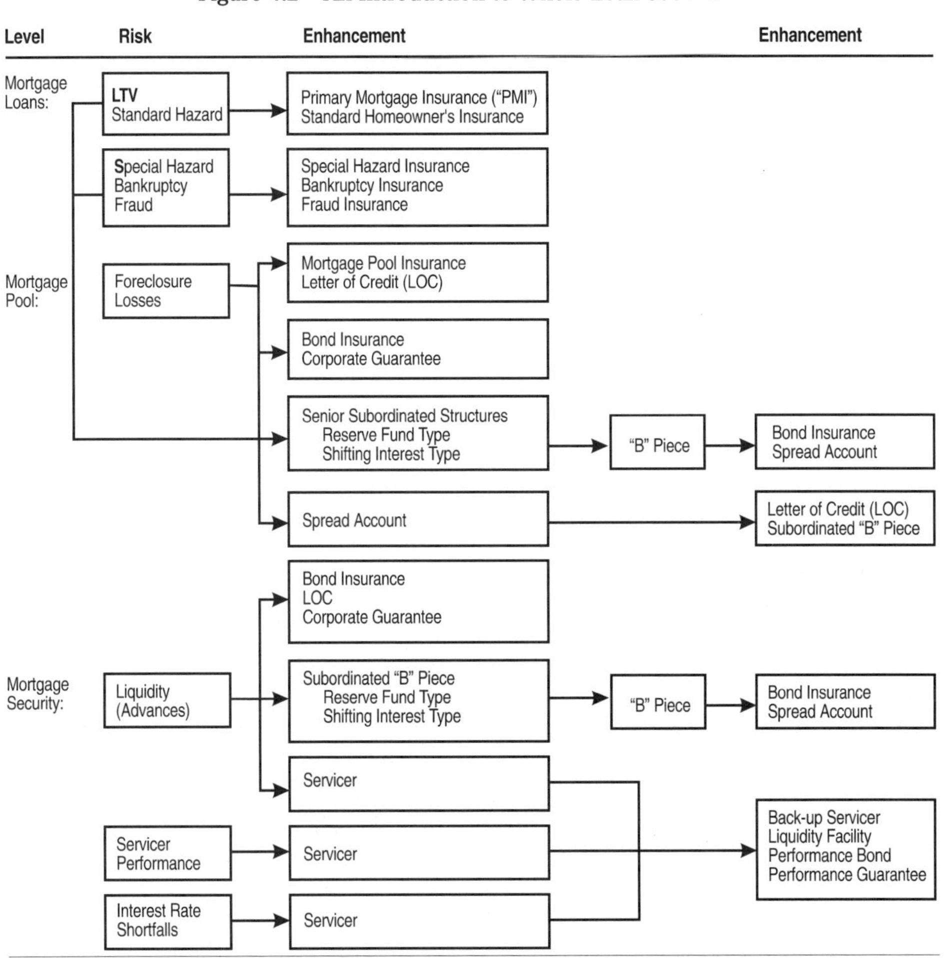

originally had, say, a 12 percent coupon but the judge has reduced it to 8 percent and reduced the par amount from $200,000 to $150,000. There is fraud, which is simply a case where any of the things that were supposed to be done weren't done, on a fraudulent basis. The potential enhancements are special hazard insurance, bankruptcy insurance, and fraud insurance.

Foreclosure losses can be covered from the mortgage pool by having an additional mortgage pool insurance or letters of credit, bond insurance, or corporate guarantees. More recently, most efficient are the senior/subordinated structures, containing either reserve fund types or shifting interest types. In senior subordinated structures, there is a 'B' piece that can be enhanced through either bond insurance or a spread account. The spread account also can be included to support foreclosure losses by itself. That can be enhanced through a letter of credit or simply become a subordinated 'B' piece, in effect.

For the mortgage security itself, there is a need for a liquidity facility to cover delinquencies, when the owner is still there but is not making his payments or when the servicers fails to perform his duties. For liquidity, various kinds of enhancements are possible: contracts with the servicer, back-up servicers, liquidity facilities, performance bonds, performance guarantees, and similar arrangements.

Figure 4.3 illustrates the evolution of these credit structures over time. Initially, virtually everything for a AAA rating was achieved through third-party enhancement. For example, where the rating agencies required an 8 percent pool policy, it came solely from an insurance company.

Figure 4.3—Evolution of Credit Structures

I Third Party Enhancement

AAA

8% Pool Policy

II Senior/Sub

Unrated Sub 8%	Senior 92% (AAA)

8% Sub

III Senior/Carved Sub

Unrated Sub 2%	BBB 1.5%	A 1.5%	AA 3%	AAA 92%

IV Combination

Third Party-Senior/Sub

AAA Credit Cert. 5%	AA 3%	AAA 92%

Event Risk Protection and Third Party Review

The next stage in the evolution was the senior/subordinated, where the 8 percent subordination was created simply by a subordinated piece accounting for 8 percent of the pool, the senior piece of 92 percent getting a AAA rating.

To enhance upon that, going still with the senior piece—after all, the simple structure goes from AAA down to an unrated piece, one could carve up the subordinated piece into different layers. In one example, the sub was carved into an unrated sub at 2 percent, a BBB-rated at 1.5 percent, an A-rated at 1.5 percent, and a AA at 3 percent. Finally other types of enhancements are a combination of the third party enhancement along with the senior and carved subs.

Another innovation is 'super-senior'—to carve up the AAA piece and make a piece of that subordinated. Although both pieces are AAA, one is better than the other because one AAA component is superior.

Figure 4.4 illustrates the RTC 1992/6 deal that consisted of 22,688 loans, the total amount of the

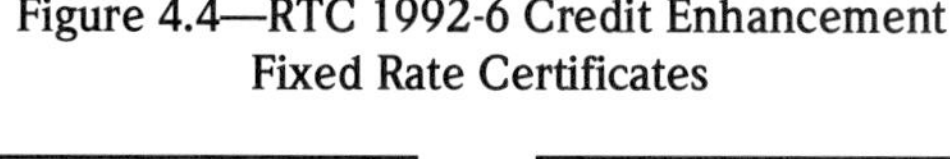

Figure 4.4—RTC 1992-6 Credit Enhancement
Fixed Rate Certificates

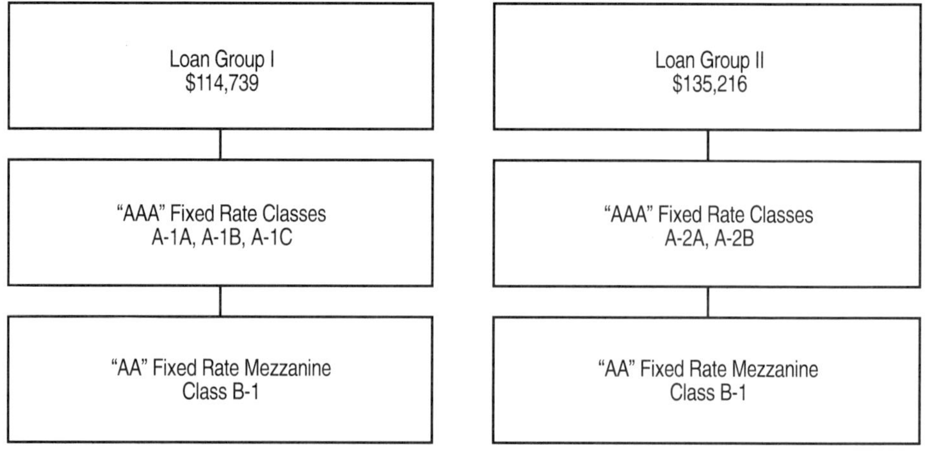

Figure 4.5—RTC 1992–6 Credit Enhancement

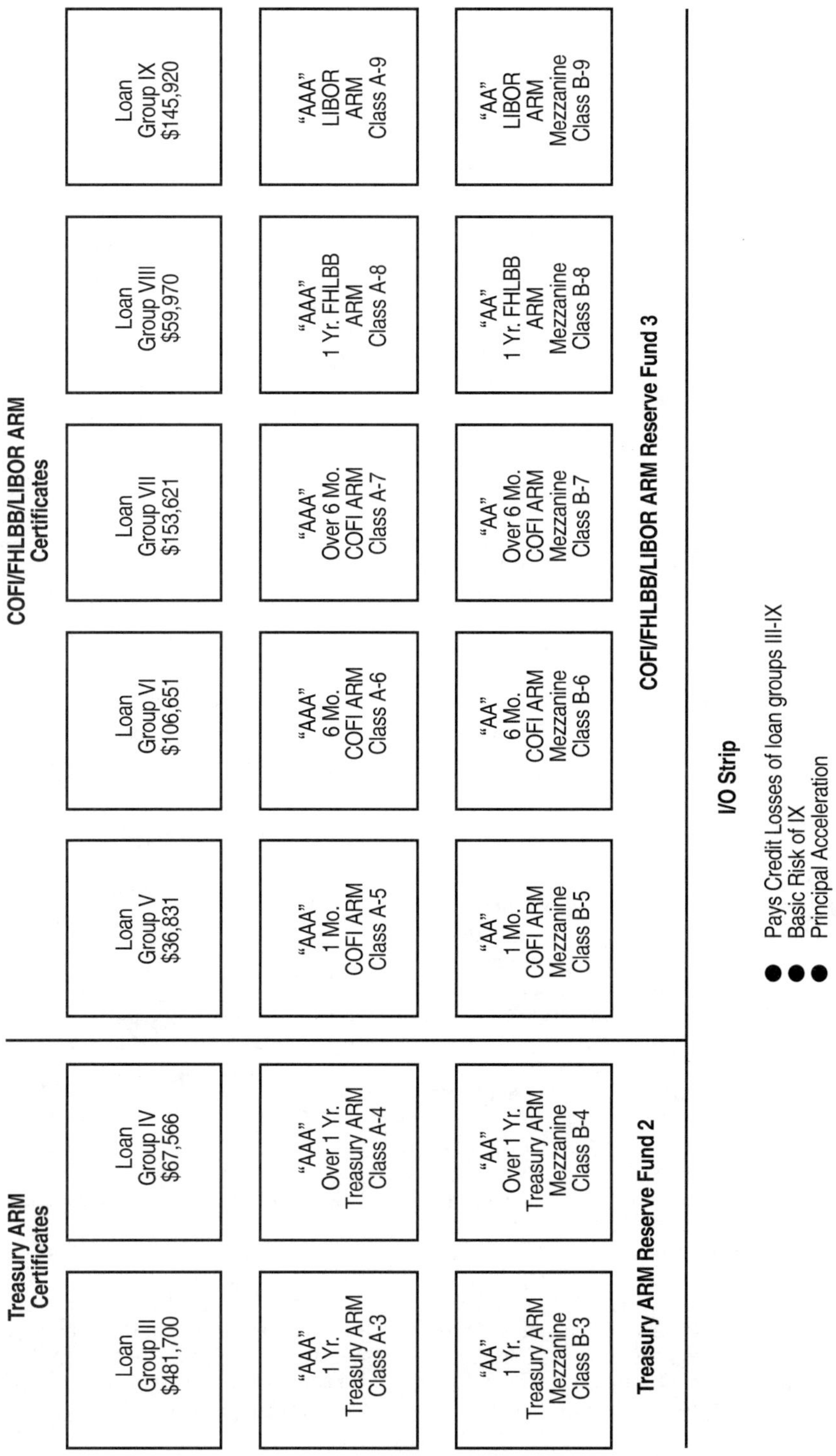

Treasury ARM Certificates

Loan Group III $481,700	Loan Group IV $67,566
"AAA" 1 Yr. Treasury ARM Class A-3	"AAA" Over 1 Yr. Treasury ARM Class A-4
"AA" 1 Yr. Treasury ARM Mezzanine Class B-3	"AA" Over 1 Yr. Treasury ARM Mezzanine Class B-4

Treasury ARM Reserve Fund 2

COFI/FHLBB/LIBOR ARM Certificates

Loan Group V $36,831	Loan Group VI $106,651	Loan Group VII $153,621	Loan Group VIII $59,970	Loan Group IX $145,920
"AAA" 1 Mo. COFI ARM Class A-5	"AAA" 6 Mo. COFI ARM Class A-6	"AAA" Over 6 Mo. COFI ARM Class A-7	"AAA" 1 Yr. FHLBB ARM Class A-8	"AAA" LIBOR ARM Class A-9
"AA" 1 Mo. COFI ARM Mezzanine Class B-5	"AA" 6 Mo. COFI ARM Mezzanine Class B-6	"AA" Over 6 Mo. COFI ARM Mezzanine Class B-7	"AA" 1 Yr. FHLBB ARM Mezzanine Class B-8	"AA" LIBOR ARM Mezzanine Class B-9

COFI/FHLBB/LIBOR ARM Reserve Fund 3

I/O Strip

- Pays Credit Losses of loan groups III-IX
- Basic Risk of IX
- Principal Acceleration

deal being $1.3 billion. It is the Resolution Trust Corporation which is liquidating the remains of a large part of the S&L industry. Among these 22,688 loans there was virtually everything imaginable. There were adjustable-rate mortgages, fixed-rate mortgages, adjustable-rate mortgages with balloons, fixed rate mortgages with balloons. There were all sorts of convertible mortgages, some of which floated and could be converted at the option of the buyer to fixed rate for some period of time, say five years, and after that become floating again. In addition, there were negative amortization, graduated payment mortgages, and so forth.

As the structure evolved, nine different loan groups were created. The first two groups were fixed-rate certificates, backed by fixed-rate mortgages. The first loan group was $114.7 million which was carved into a AAA piece and a AA piece. The AAA piece was again carved into three different tranches for different maturity spectrums, to give different durations and to be priced over the yield curve. The second loan group had a AAA piece in two classes that were maturity tranched, sequential pay, and another AA, fixed-rate, mezzanine class. That was all supported by a fixed-rate reserve fund for the securities which amounted to 1.45 percent.

In the seven other loan categories that were based on the adjustable-rate mortgages in the group, Figure 4.5, there were two classes of Treasury ARM securities which adjusted over the constant maturity Treasury index. There were four classes that adjusted either over the cost of funds index (COFI), the Federal Home Loan Bank Board cost of funds, or LIBOR. Then there was a last class which adjusted over a variety of other things.

For groups three through eight, the ARM certificates pay out to the investors in the different classes a weighted average of the coupons on the mortgages. The last class was converted into a LIBOR-based floating security that adjusted over LIBOR.

Groups three and four have a separate reserve fund. Groups five through nine have a reserve fund. In addition, for loan groups three through nine, there is an "interest only" (IO) strip carved out of the securities. From these various adjustable securities, a piece of interest was stripped and used for credit enhancement. To the extent that the credit enhancement is not needed, the IO cash flows are used to pay down principal. It speeds up the maturity and lowers the duration of the classes under different scenarios. For loan groups three through nine, the IO strip pays credit losses, and it pays the basis risk of loan nine.

A second example is what is typically being done now in the case of credit cards—the super trust, where there are different issues, but as new issues are brought to market, the collateral goes into a single trust which enhances the diversification of the various securities.

A recent Citibank deal is illustrated in Figure 4.6. A super trust has a yield from credit cards of 21.82 percent. The average being paid out to investors is 8.08 percent. Losses, as historically calculated, are 6.36 percent on the pool. Some fees are being paid out of the cash flows which take out another 1.91 percent, leaving excess servicing of 5.47 percent.

Figure 4.6—Allocation of Finance Charges in the Citibank Credit Card Master Trust (Super Trust)

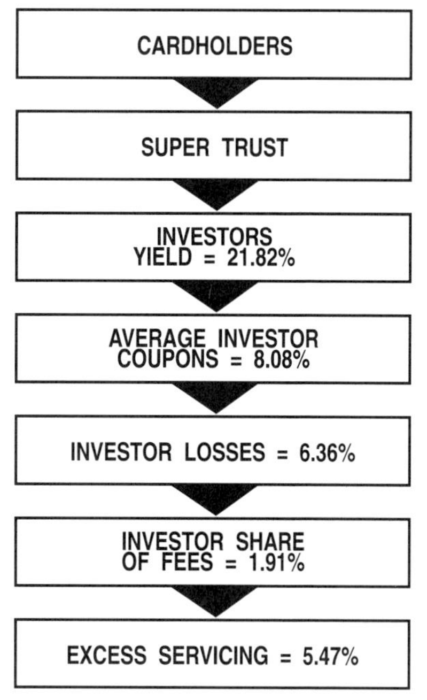

For coverage of losses, it is tranched into a class A and a class B, the B being subordinated (Figure 4.7).

Class A interest shortfall and losses are covered. The first, by the excess finance charge or excess servicing. The second form of protection comes from class B principal in the form of cash that is available. If the losses are such that the interest shortfall on class A cannot be met, then principal is reallocated from B to A. Also, receivables can be

Figure 4.7—Coverage of Losses in Citibank Structures

Class A Interest Shortfall and Losses

First	Excess Finance Charge Collections	
Second	Class B Principal in the form of:	
	Cash	Principal Collections Allocated to Class B reallocated to Class A
	Receivables	Class B's remaining Share of Principal Receivables outstanding reallocated to Class A

Class B Interest Shortfall and Losses

First	Excess Finance Charge Collections not allocated to Class A
Second	Credit Enhancement typically Cash Collateral

taken from B and allocated to A as enhancements for A.

The class B interest shortfall and losses have the excess finance charge collections that are not needed for A, as the first line of defense. Second, it has a credit enhancement which is typically in the form of cash collateral or a cash reserve fund.

This is part of 'financial mining and manufacturing,' and asset securitization is the mining and refining part of it. The manufacturing part takes all these potential building blocks and creates optimal portfolios for different investors: financial Ferraris or financial Mack Trucks.

Chapter 5

International Securitization for the Emerging Economies

by Alexandre Hayek,
Salomon Brothers Inc.

Most securitization literature is US-based and tends to refer to transactions done in other countries such as the UK or France as "International Securitization." They are in fact nothing but domestic securitizations in other countries.

International securitization transactions are the ones that are implemented across international borders. They involve sellers, obligors, investors and arrangers domiciled in different countries. The transactions which have been completed by/for entities in the Emerging Economies have been "International Securitizations."

The familiar concept of securitization presents three different variations when it is considered within the context of the Emerging Economies. To the extent that a nascent capital market exists in a certain country, it is possible to contemplate local currency securitization. Few countries, however, can boast a local capital market. The Emerging Economies remain net importers of capital. Especially when the amount of a certain financing is large, it is imperative that the placement be done offshore. Because of the reluctance of OECD investors to take on the foreign exchange risk associated with a local currency securitization, local entities must use the hard currency receivables on their books to implement a transaction. This is the second version. The third version has been more common to date: it involves the securitization of future (rather than existing) receivables. Typically, entities in Emerging Economies do not have the necessary large volumes of receivables on their books either because of the small size of their operations or because (in an environment where the local currency usually depreciates daily) they collect as quickly as possible and do not extend credit beyond the minimum terms of trade.

It might not be very useful to explore the range of risks associated with the first two versions described above, not because they are rarely implemented—for indeed, they are bound to become more important in the future—but because the third version is the most common and is the one that presents a risk profile different from the ones studied at length in other parts of this book.

Risks associated with the international securitization of future receivables may be grouped in four main categories:

I. Cross-Border Risk
II. Payment Risk
III. Performance Risk
IV. Legal Risk

BACKGROUND

The first securitization of future hard currency (US dollar) receivables was completed by Citibank for the Mexican telephone company, Telmex, in 1987.

The impetus came from Telmex's need to raise large amounts of dollar funding at a time when Mexico was still reeling under the weight of the 1980s' Latin American debt crisis. Banks, trying to collect on past due loans made in the 70s, were in no mood to extend additional financing to a public sector entity of a government already in arrears on its obligations. (Lending into an Emerging Economy is still taboo to most banks, especially given the punitive mandatory reserve requirements applicable.) New sources of financing, therefore, had to be tapped.

MITIGATING CROSS-BORDER RISK

With the newspapers full of articles about the debt crisis, no one was unfamiliar with Mexico's problems. The idea, however, was to convince a group of nonbank institutional investors to tap into Telmex's dollar revenue flow *in the US* before the dollars enter Mexico. Telmex, in effect, exports telecommunication services to AT&T. It does so by helping AT&T complete (in Mexico) telephone calls which originate in the US. AT&T then owes Telmex a portion of what it collects from the US consumer. By giving investors control over this flow so that they may collect payments from AT&T, retain what is owed to them, and then transfer the remainder amounts to Telmex, the financial cross-border risk is effectively mitigated. The Mexican government's debt service capability would no longer be an issue. The Central Bank of Mexico could no longer exercise control over the dollar flow.

The concept is fine, but could it work? Would AT&T agree to pay as directed? How would Telmex deal with the negative pledge clauses in its and the Mexican Government's then existing financing agreements? (Telmex was 100 percent-owned by the government at the time. The most important feature of negative pledge clauses in this context is the prohibition imposed on the Borrower by the Lender(s) against pledging revenues in order to secure indebtedness.)

After diligent study of the negative pledge clauses, it was determined that while a *pledge* of the future receivables was out of the question, nothing in those clauses prohibited the *sale* of those same receivables. A pledge of receivables means that investors consider such receivables as collateral and retain full recourse to the borrower. A sale of receivables, on the other hand, means that investors take the risk of getting paid by the obligor(s) under the receivables and have no recourse to the seller thereof. Consequently, if investors were satisfied to look solely to the receivables for repayment and forego recourse to Telmex, the negative pledge clauses would not apply.

It was further determined that, absent a physical existence of Telmex in the US, perfecting the security interest in the receivables under US regulations (UCC Code) could be achieved by simply serving notice on AT&T. The notice informs AT&T that Telmex's receivables have been sold, and it irrevocably instructs AT&T to make payments from now on to a designated third party (the Trustee). AT&T must comply with the notice.

This combination of several elements, otherwise called a "structure," was perceived by investors as an effective mitigant of the cross-border risk. This type of asset securitization became Mexico's (and, by extension, Latin America's) way to regain access to the international capital markets. It helped reestablish some of the confidence OECD investors lost in 1982.

Figure 5.1 shows a visual depiction of the structure. Figure 5.2 shows how repayment takes place.

Figure 5.1—Basic Structure

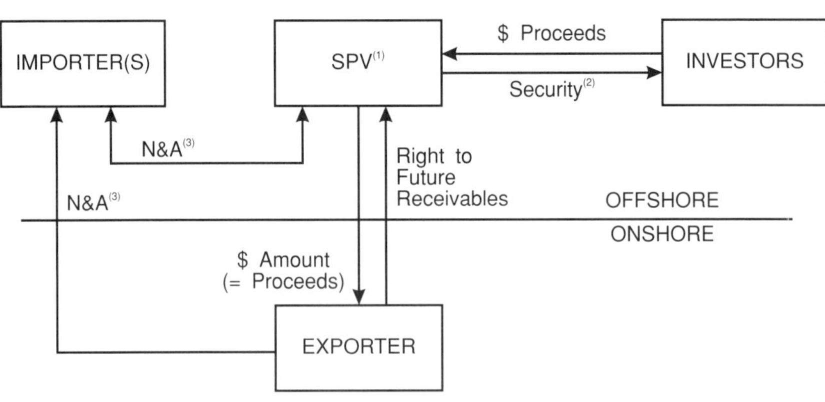

(1) Special purpose vehicle: a trust or special purpose company.

(2) Debt security or trust certificate.

(3) Notice to importer(s) of sale of receivables and acknowledgement by importer(s) of same.

Figure 5.2—Repayment Flows

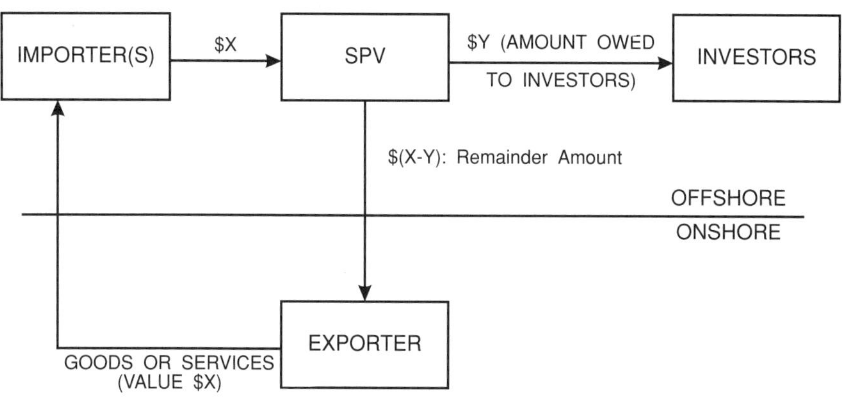

PAYMENT RISK

To a large extent, in a securitization transaction, the seller of receivables is redirecting the focus of the investors' credit analysis toward the obligor(s) and away from itself.

In the US and other OECD countries, securitization transactions enhance the credit of an issue by diversifying the payment risk among thousands, sometimes millions, of obligors. A study of the historic patterns of delinquency, dilution, and other parameters proper to a certain pool of receivables is used to determine an appropriate level of overcollateralization and structural refinements. The exercise leads to a higher rating for the issue than that which the seller would have been able to achieve on its own.

In the context of the Emerging Economies, the above approach would not work. One does not find Emerging Economy organizations which engage in cross-border lending to large numbers of obligors. The entities which generate receivables usually do so as part of their export activities—whether they be exporters of goods or services. They might have one client/obligor or more, but rarely more than, say, 25. Any clients/obligors beyond this level would tend to be less frequent or smaller-sized importers. Further, unless the client is a major one, the exporter typically requests payment through documentary credit and trade finance channels available on a short-term basis from commercial banks. Receivables, which are useful for a securitization, must be available in large amounts and must not be encumbered under trade finance. This description of the commercial activity shows why Emerging Economy securitization transactions do not use a large pool of obligors, and therefore why the payment risk is a lot more concentrated. Indeed, the focus of credit and payment risk analysis is no different from that of a corporate credit. It merely shifts from the seller to the obligor.

If the obligor is, for instance, AT&T (as in the Telmex transactions) or Visa International, investors will be comfortable with the payment risk. If the obligor is a company with a below-investment-grade rating, the transaction is neither advisable nor, in most instances, feasible.

PERFORMANCE RISK

As mentioned previously, entities with dollar receivables are unlikely to have large amounts of receivables outstanding on their books for any useful length of time. If they did, they would be financing OECD entities—not exactly the pattern one would expect. They must, therefore, depend on the sale of *future* receivables.

A sale of existing receivables does not entail performance risk because the activity that is needed to generate the receivable has already taken place. The investor need only worry about collecting from the obligor.

A sale of *future* receivables, on the other hand, entails the risk of the seller continuing to perform as promised and generate receivables in the future. As a matter of fact, the seller sells the *right* to future receivables, not the receivables themselves—since they do not yet exist. The performance risk is multifaceted. Its exact nature varies from transaction to transaction, and it can emanate from within the seller's organization or from without it.

The varying degrees of performance risk can be illustrated by considering three types of transactions: For future telephone receivables, such as in the case of Telmex, millions of callers from the United States will place calls to Mexico without having any knowledge of the existence of a receivables-based financing. All Telmex has to do is keep the switch on. For future credit card receivables, the same is true, except instead of *millions* of calls, the receivables are generated by *thousands* of tourists. The servicing bank need maintain its branch network and its computer processing center. For future trade receivables, however, only *one* entity is generating the receivables and is fully aware of the details of the underlying financing. Its production process tends also to be more complex and difficult to maintain properly.

A sample list of certain performance risk elements is presented below.

Credit and Finance

While the seller is not expected to make the payments to investors, its financial health is very important. A thorough analysis of financial statements and adequate due diligence are always a necessity. A bankrupt company, or one with liquidity problems, might not be able to continue to produce the good or service it is selling abroad. Should that happen, the generation of receivables could slow down or even come to a halt.

Management

A company that is not well-managed could face some of the same problems as a financially weak organization. It might not be able to remain competitive and hold on to its clients or market share, either due to inefficient operations or an inadequate marketing effort.

Labor

Closely related to management quality is the soundness of labor relations. Strikes and unrest could jeopardize the timely performance of export activities and, consequently, have an adverse impact on the generation of receivables. A good labor track record is important.

Operations

A company's operations could be affected by a variety of factors that must be taken into consideration on a case-by-case basis. A credit card processor must have adequate computer systems capable of handling the expected flows; an aluminum producer must have adequate power generation back-up systems; a petrochemical manufacturer must have dependable suppliers of raw materials; etc.

Natural Phenomena

Nature can sometimes affect the generation of receivables: Credit card receivables depend on tourism and could be impacted by an earthquake (Mexico City, 1985) or a hurricane (Jamaica, 1989); a mine could be prone to flooding part of the year; etc.

Political Risk

Political or sovereign risk continues to be a factor to the extent it can affect performance. The mitigation of the financial cross-border risk does not automatically eliminate all political risk. Governments could pass new measures that could adversely impact the generation of receivables. Examples include the imposition of export taxes that render the activity either impossible or financially unattractive (this could affect producers of goods vital for the local economy); the nationalization of a production facility (this could affect oil-related sectors, for instance); the imposition of the government as sole buyer (this could affect agricultural exports); safety concerns of tourists, as in Rio de Janeiro, for example (this could affect credit card receivables); etc.

MITIGANTS

Performance risk is mitigated through structuring techniques that address specific aspects of it. Overcollateralization, or more precisely in this case, "Coverage" (since on Day 1 the existing receivables are not enough to collateralize the security issued, let alone *over*collateralize it) can help with a variety of problems. First, it gives comfort to investors: The receivables they are buying are well within the seller's norm. Not only is the seller capable of generating more than what is needed to service the securities, but it has been doing so for some time. Second, it is possible to establish a minimum acceptable coverage level, referred to as a trigger level, which, once reached, causes an acceleration of the collection process. Acceleration means that all collections are retained and dedicated to servicing the securities until the investors are repaid in full. During this time, the seller must continue to generate receivables, but derives no cash flow. The structure must set the acceleration triggers carefully: It is to no one's advantage that an acceleration take place due to a sudden/drastic/temporary drop in receivable levels. Such a drop could take place in the context of real commercial activity without a long-term effect on the transaction. The triggers must, on the other hand, detect either sudden/drastic/long-term drops or a graduate decrease in receivables volume caused by market or political forces.

Other structuring techniques that mitigate performance risk might include the adjustment of collection periods so as to mitigate the effect of seasonal fluctuations; the establishment of escrow accounts, letters of credit or liquidity lines to allow for set-offs or other events; the linkage of receivable levels to commodity markets variables and the hedging of the same; the provision for a substitution of receivables; etc.

LEGAL *AND REGULATORY* RISK

The structuring that mitigates cross-border and other risks is based, to a large extent, on the applicability of a certain legal and regulatory framework that supports the structure.

The international nature of the subject transactions implies, by definition, that more than one legal framework is involved. The Emerging Economies do not yet possess, within their legal systems, the infrastructure that governs securitization transactions.

The US has the most developed system of legal, regulatory and accounting standards applicable to securitization. It is, therefore, no accident that Emerging Economies securitizations have tended to seek as much US linkage as possible. For instance, a sale of receivables is regarded as an assignment of rights under some Latin American legal systems. The results are adequate, but the legal support ends there. Perfection of the security or ownership interest, therefore, must be done in a second stage under US law, or some other adequate system.

Both New York and English law have been used to govern international securitization transactions. Perfection of security interest is becoming achievable in more jurisdictions, and the trend should continue.

Once an international securitization transaction is closed, the relevant legal risks are not dissimilar from the ones that exist under a domestic deal. They result from changes in the law either by new legislation/regulation or by court interpretation. Were Telmex, for instance, to lose its international communications monopoly overnight—it is now scheduled to lose it in 1996—the receivables flow could be affected. The cramps that gripped the market *in 1991* when Congress toyed with legislation aimed at limiting the interest rates credit card issuers may charge cardholders are a good representation of what legal risks are. The characterizing difference of international securitizations is simply that they can be affected by changes in more than one national legal system.

CONCLUSION

This panoramic examination of risks that may affect international securitizations of future Emerging Economies' receivables was not presented in conjunction with all the benefits that accrue to investors. It might, therefore, seem difficult to imagine that with all the uncertainties surrounding such transactions, enough investors would be willing to participate. Reality is, however, that investors in these transactions are sophisticated international players who possess the capabilities necessary to analyze the various types of risk involved. They often conclude that the risk/return formula in these cases is in their favor. The arrangers of these transactions are also large sophisticated institutions (Citicorp, Goldman Sachs, Salomon Brothers and JP Morgan). The whole concept is based on the premise that the yield to investors is higher than what the underlying risks would otherwise command. It is indeed an arbitrage where both the seller and the investors come out ahead.

We have discussed the Telmex example above. It is one that lends itself to easy understanding. Other examples would have been more complex to examine and analyze. Table 5.1 presents a list of the transactions completed to date (March 1992). These have invariably afforded the Latin American entities concerned with a lower cost of funds than would have been achievable without the asset-backing. Indeed, securitization here, like elsewhere, has meant pricing in line with a credit rating which is higher than that of the seller. Straight debt issuers would normally not obtain a credit rating higher than that of their home country. Due to their international nature and to their structural enhancements, subject transactions have been rated investment grade by the US National Association of Insurance Commissioners (NAIC), by Duff and Phelps, and by Standard & Poors.

Now that the concept has shown viability in Latin America, there is no reason to doubt that, as Eastern European and other emerging economies adopt the free-market path which has prevailed in

Table 5.1—Transactions Done To Date (April 1992)

Issuer	*Country*	*Amount MM (US$)*	*Tenor*
Telmex	Mexico	420.00	5 years
Jamintel	Jamaica	30.00	10 years
Telmex	Mexico	287.00	5 years
Entel	Argentina	17.43	5 years
Jamintel	Jamaica	20.00	10 years
Telmex	Mexico	324.00	5 years
ANTEL	El Salvador	25.00	5 years
CFE	Mexico	235.00	5 years
Embratel	Brazil	50.00	10 years
Telmex	Mexico	0.00	5 years
Banamex	Mexico	130.20	3 years
Bancomer	Mexico	228.72	5 years
ICE	Costa Rica	18.00	7 years
Hondutel	Honduras	11.50	7 years
Sivensa	Venezuela	60.00	5 1/2 years
Telmex	Mexico	567.50	5 years
NCB	Jamaica	30.00	5 years
Banamex	Mexico	181.00	5 years
Varig	Brazil	55.00	5 years
Shell do Brasil	Brazil	152.00	5 years
IBM do Brasil	Brazil	126.00	5 years
Banca Serfin	Mexico	80.00	5 years

Latin America, international securitization will play an important role in enabling those countries to raise funds in the international capital markets at a time when they either have no access to such markets, or have to pay extremely high spreads for the privilege.

Chapter 6

Financing Opportunities for the Commodities Industry Through Securitization

by Monique de Zagon
Partner
Baker & McKenzie

As a consequence of events which happened in the 1980s, the commodities industry will be faced in the 1990s, along with other sectors of the economy, with a shortage of cash available to finance its projects. Those events deeply affected the banking world and its willingness to lend, creating a credit crunch. The most important of these events was the world debt crisis. The legal, political, and socioeconomic ramifications of that crisis permeate the governments of virtually every nation, multinational corporations, financial institutions and individual consumers. The crisis affected American banking institutions very heavily. In the 1970s U.S. banks had been flooded with petrodollars and they invested those petrodollars in less developed countries (which we'll refer to as LDCs). LDCs seemed to be a safe investment since LDCs had an abundance of commodities such as oil and commodity prices were high and going higher still. American banks competed against each other in offering the best rates of interest to LDCs. But, everything was reversed in the 1980s as interest rates rose to combat inflation. The commodities and oil markets were strangled by this increase. The LDC debt crisis followed and American banks basically stopped lending to LDCs.

In Europe the environment also changed during the 1980s. European banks, which had long been protected by an array of regulations that limited competition, saw their profits decline with deregulation. Other banks, including American and Japanese banks, moved into European markets in order to keep their profits and retain and increase worldwide market share. European banks suffered from that competition. Moreover, all banks, including European banks, saw their corporate clients raising money directly in the capital markets and their consumers preferring money market accounts over interest savings accounts. Experiencing declining margins at home, and losses on LDC portfolios, the American and European banking industry looked for new opportunities in the leveraged buyout and real estate fields, taking ever-mounting risks with catastrophic results. Finally, as a result of the adoption of the Cooke ratios, bankers started to look at profitability as a function of capital allocation and they began to move away from the traditional measure of return on assets. Those changes in the global banking environment led to a credit crunch and shortage of available cash. During the late 1980s and beginning of the 1990s, the problem became even more acute because of the capital needs of LDCs such as the Eastern European countries and even countries like Mongolia which are trying desperately to attract badly needed capital by promoting legislation favoring foreign investment in their countries.

It seems that a twin phenomenon of the 1990s will be a shortage of capital and the increase in the availability of commodities at cheaper prices. The price of commodities will continue to drop as more and more LDCs will increase their output of commodities and dump commodities on the world market in an effort to raise foreign currency.

Many commodity producers have now realized that they cannot resort uniquely to traditional bank financing to meet their financial needs. Moreover, for some commodity producers in LDCs, there is no such financing available at all. New financing techniques adapted to the changing world are appearing, even as the capital markets become global, rather than national or regional in scope. Many of the new techniques are be aimed at protecting the financial sector from its past mistakes. For example, one goal of these new techniques is to protect producers and lenders from the volatility in both interest rates and commodity prices that has disrupted the international economy over the past 20 years.

Securitization, which is the process whereby loans and other receivables are packaged, underwritten and sold under the form of securities commonly knows as asset-backed securities, has already been used as a successful financing strategy to meet this goal. American, Canadian, European and even Japanese issuers have issued securities backed by asset cash flows. Companies which have rights to cash flows from intangibles such as contracts can securitize those cash flows. A commodity producer securitizing the cash flow resulting from a commodities production contract would ordinarily enjoy the following benefits as will be illustrated by our example later on:

a. access to capital debt markets at a cost lower than the cost of regular bank financing or senior debt, particularly if the asset-backed securities enjoy higher credit ratings than the producer itself;
b. off-balance sheet treatment;
c. increased liquidity, and new source of funding;
d. non-recourse funding without reliance on the producer's general credit;
e. avoidance of interest-rate and currency exchange risk;
f. transferral of risk of nonpayment by buyer to investors.
g. avoidance of withholding taxes in the producer's country.

Financing strategies using commodity-backed securities were unknown to the commodities industry a few years ago although natural resource financing using structures other than straight bank loans has been in existence since the mid-1970s. Such financing was confined in the beginning to the energy field. The first coal mining financing by Amax Coal was completed in 1974. The transaction involved a three-year sale of output contracts by Amax Coal with utilities in exchange for prepayment for the coal. Since the early 1980s petroleum purchases from Middle Eastern countries have been prepaid for more than one year and many European banks have provided financing on this basis.

An innovative structure, although not a securitization since it was still a financing by a bank syndicate and not by investors through a special purpose vehicle, was developed for the La Caridad Mexican Copper Mine deal. The financing was similar to the Amax Coal deal in that it provided for financing by outside lenders against mine production. This commodity-backed loan in the metals industry was developed in 1989.

The structure of a commodity financing project involving a metal producer generally is as follows: A bank agrees to make a loan to theproducer. The producer previously signed a commercial contract with the consumer to produce a quantity of material over a period of time sufficient to pay down the loan, plus interest. The consumer has agreed to buy the material over that period. Payments by the consumer on the contract are made directly to the lending bank. Thus, the bank's collateral for repayment of the loan to the producer is the proceeds or anticipated proceeds from the commercial contract. These types of contracts are typically called "take or pay" contracts because the consumer is obligated to pay for the commodities, whether it actually needs the commodities or not. Thus, even if the consumer doesn't "take" the commodities, it is obligated to pay for the commodities. A commodity loan produces the following results for each participant: (1) the producer receives the funds necessary to pay down an existing loan or obtain additional funding at an interest rate that will allow positive cash flow from the project; (2) the consumer receives a constant supply of the commodity at favorable terms over an extended time period; and (3) the lender receives an above-market lending rate return, with acceptable security. The concepts of currency risk and delayed payment are converted into production risk and regular payments.

Such commodity loan is frequently coupled with a commodity price swap. A commodity swap is similar to long-term interest rate and currency swaps. An intermediary, usually a financial institution, is used to arrange the swap and provide for clearing of the payments. In the swap, the producer agrees to pay an intermediary the market price it receives for the commodity sold to the consumer and the intermediary pays a fixed price for the commodity for the duration of the loan to the producer. The intermediary makes an agreement with a third party to sell the stream of fluctuating payments to such third party who returns a fixed payment for the term of the loan. The intermediary assumes the performance risk of the seller and buyer which is included in the pricing of the swap. The third party could be a consumer hedging the price of the commodity, a financial institution making a market, or a speculator taking a position.

A floor cap could be used in lieu of a swap because it would be less costly. The price selected at the floor will insure that if the price of the metal drops, there will still be enough monies to repay interest and principal on the loan.

The principal advantages of a commodity indexed loan are as follows:

a. Payment of the loan is denominated in a fixed amount of production rather than fixed currency.

b. Capital raised is secured by a commercial contract and not mortgaged assets. This is important in countries where the taking of a security interest is difficult. Whatever the market condition is, production alone will repay the loan. Minor contract adjustments are easier to make to a commercial contract than a bank loan.

c. A substantial part of the cost of the loan service is measured in local currency since the majority of production costs are denominated in local currency.

The La Caridad transaction was the perfect illustration of a commodity loan coupled with a commodity price swap. Paribas was the lead bank of a bank syndicate and also acted as the intermediary in laying off the risk of fluctuating copper prices against the rise of fluctuating interest rates. Sogem, S.A., a Société Générale de Belgique subsidiary, assisted Mexicana del Cobre, S.A., a Mexican company, in obtaining financing for the La Caridad mine to retire the remaining debt of $210 million due to the Mexican government on the original privatization of the mine. There had been few financing alternatives available for Mexican properties at that time before the restructuring of the Mexican sovereign debt and the subsequent economic success of the Salinas government. Sogem, S.A. acted as the consumer which agreed to buy the cooper from Mexcobre and an unnamed European copper refiner as the third party.

The bank syndicate forwarded the full amount of a $210 million loan to Mexcobre, the miner. The loan carries a fixed interest rate of three-year libor plus 3 percent to be repaid in 12 equal quarterly installments. For three years, Mexcobre agreed to export about 4,000 metric tons of copper a month to Générale at the market price. Paribas and Mexcobre assumed the price to be 90.3 cents a pound.

Proceeds from the sales to Générale, about $7.9 million a month at that price, were to go into an escrow account. The account was to make payments due to the bank syndicate. The remaining amount was to remain in escrow.

The swap was to go into effect if the price of copper strayed from 90.3 cents a pound. If prices fell below that amount, the third party was to pay the difference to Paribas, which was to put the money into the escrow account to make up the shortfall. If copper prices were to rise above that amount, extra money in the escrow account would go through Paribas to a third party.

In either case, the bank syndicate and the miner remain unaffected by the fluctuations in interest rates or copper prices. The consumer could plan on paying 90.3 cents a pound for copper for the full three years of the agreement.

In the La Caridad transaction, lenders were required to deal with four types of risk: (1) copper price risk which was managed through the commodity swap structure; (2) interest rate risk if the lenders funded commodities on a floating rate basis but they could use interest rate swaps to convert the fixed rate paid by the miner into a floating rate to match their funding; (3) payment risk which was mitigated through the agreement with the consumer to make all payments into a collateral account in dollars; and (4) performance risk which remained for the life of the transaction but could have been alleviated through the issuance of guarantees of performance or letters of credit or similar instruments if the lenders had not been convinced of the miner's ability to meet its obligations.

The next step in commodities financing was a bona fide securitization in the oil and gas industry.

In 1990, a special purpose vehicle in the form of a trust was established among Salomon, Phibro Energy Oil, Inc. and Texas Commerce Bank, as trustee.

The assets of the trust consisted primarily of a forward contract, under which the trust agreed to purchase 4 million barrels of oil five years forward from Phibro Energy at $18.60 per barrel, and Salomon's guarantee of all of Phibro's obligations under the forward contract. The contract was thus directly between the trust and the producer with the consumers to be found later on by the trust. This varies significantly from the La Caridad transaction. The forward contract was a direct, unsecured contractual obligation of Phibro, and Salomon's guarantee of Phibro's performance thereunder was a direct, unsecured obligation of Salomon. Each of the trust units offered by the trust evidenced an undivided beneficial ownership interest in the trust which entitled each holder to receive a pro rata share of the distribution amount on the distribution date. The net proceeds from the offering of the trust units were deposited by Salomon in the trust in exchange for the trust units and were used by the trustee on the date of issuance of the trust units (the "closing date") to acquire the forward contract from Phibro. The trustee and Phibro entered into the forward contract which required Phibro to deliver one-quarter of one barrel of crude oil per trust unit to the trust in September 1995 (the "delivery month") at a certain operated facility. The aggregate amount payable to Phibro by the trust under the forward contract was $70,575,840, and was paid to Phibro concurrently with the issuance of the trust units. Delivery of crude oil under the forward contract were to be effected using customary procedures. During the last three trading days of July 1995, a party selected as an advisor to the trustee must solicit bids to purchase all of the crude oil deliverable to the trust under the forward contract in the delivery month, requesting that (i) each such bid be for one-third of the total amount so deliverable, and (ii) the bid price be quoted as a number of cents above or below a certain average price. The parties from whom bids will be solicited will be required to have minimum credit ratings, or to post guarantees or letters of credit from entities with such credit ratings. The trust will be required to sell such crude oil to each of the three highest eligible bidders (or more such bidders, if the third highest bid is received from more than one bidder). Phibro will be obligated, as a standby purchaser, to purchase from the trust, at a slightly discounted price, that portion, if any, of the crude oil deliverable under the forward contract for which the trust is unable to obtain a bid that is at the agreed upon price. In such event, the trust will be obligated to sell such portion to Phibro at such price. A single cash distribution will be made in respect to each trust unit from and to the extent of available funds on November 1, 1995, to the record holder of such trust unit. The aggregate amount to be distributed to trust unit holders on the distribution date will be equal to the excess of (i) the proceeds from the sale of the crude oil delivered under the forward contract during the delivery month, over (ii) the trust expenses.

In December 1990, Enron Corporation filed to establish the Enron Gas Trust to sell 30 billion cubic feet of natural gas forward November 1992 to December 1995 in monthly deliveries at spot market prices. The trust units were to be sold on the New York Stock Exchange. Each unit was equal to 3 million BTUs or 3,000 cubic feet of gas and was to be issued at $5.35 per unit. Market conditions caused postponement of the offering.

Also in December 1990, Citibank securitized $60 million of future payments from Thyssen, the German steel company, to Sidetur, a Venezuelan steel producer. Citibank privately placed 5½-year floating rate Euronotes at six month LIBOR plus 1⅜ percent a savings of 400 points to Sidetur.

In June 1991, Salomon Brothers securitized the gas production flows from the Mesa Limited Partners Hugoton Properties in Kansas and Citibank established a metal trust for the sale of iron ore produced by Companhia Vale do Rio Doce (Brazil) to Thyssen (Germany).

During 1992, the Cerro Colorado Copper Project in Northern Chile was closed by Citibank. Another transaction, also in Chile, was closed by a syndicate led by UBS, Credit Lyonnais and Deutsche Bank. Several other deals are under consideration in Chile and Venezuela.

The La Caridad transaction discussed previously could easily have been refinanced as a securitization, and that several investment banks have made proposals to that effect to the borrower.

In general as illustrated by the foregoing examples, a securitization for a metal producer works out as follows (although many variations are possible).

The first step for the producer is the execution of a forward contract with a consumer, preferably a consumer that enjoys a high credit rating or that is part of a group enjoying such a rating. Because of the securitization process, the credit risk will in general be shifted from the producer's credit to the consumer's credit, making the consumer's credit rating important. Under the terms of the forward contract, the producer agrees to deliver to the consumer a fixed amount of metal over a number of years. The consumer irrevocably agrees to accept the fixed amount of metal from the producer on the agreed dates under this traditional "take or pay" agreement.

A financial institution which will help the producer in the structuring of the transaction (and could make fees as a packager, will arrange for the establishment of a special purpose vehicle (SPV) in a suitable country chosen for tax purposes. The location will depend on the tax jurisdiction of the targeted investors. The SPV will be owned by the financial institution or by a third party (but not by the producer so as to avoid consolidation for tax purposes). The SPV will purchase the forward contract from the producer and will consequently take title to the goods, making the transaction a prepurchase and not a financing, which should avoid withholding tax in the producer's country of residence (and production). Proceeds of the sale of securities issued by the SPV to investors will be used to effect the purchase of the forward contract.

The securities issued by the SPV will be pay-through securities since interest and principal on those securities will be paid to investors based on the cash flow of the forward contract, although not necessarily in the same amount or form received. The securities could bear interest at a fixed or floating rate depending on the producer's funding strategy. The final maturity will match the termination date of the contract. The principal amount of the securities could be repaid in installments matching the delivery dates on the contract. Alternatively principal could be paid on the maturity date in one lump sum.

Payment risks are reduced since payments on the forward contract are paid directly to the SPV by the consumer. Monies secured by the SPV from payments by the consumer under the take or pay contract and not immediately used to pay interest or principal to the investors, will be invested until the maturity date of the securities and will provide additional security for payment.

If the forward commodity purchase contract does not provide a fixed price for the metal for the life of the contract, the SPV will enter into a commodity price swap as described above or alternatively a floor cap.

The SPV's sole purpose will be the purchase of the forward contract from the producer and the issuance of debt securities to the investors. It will be forbidden to issue other debt and will engage in no business other than the transaction at hand. This lessens the risk of a calamitous event occurring to the SPV which could force it into bankruptcy or insolvency. This insulation gives comfort to the rating agencies, if there is a need to rate the deal, allowing them to rate the securities highly and in many cases higher than other debt issues of the producer.

The securities issued by the SPV could be a commercial paper program, bonds or other notes. The SPV will engage a servicer to service the forward contract for an appropriate fee. The servicer will also distribute principal and interest debt payments to the investors, invest available funds, and verify all export documents.

Any monies remaining in the SPV after repayment of the securities could, depending on the terms of the deal, be returned to the producer, kept by the shareholders of the SPV as an additional incentive, or be sold to another class of investors (in which case the SPV would issue several classes of securities).

Additional credit enhancement techniques could be used to cover remaining risks such as:

1. An *insurance policy* which would typically be an insurance policy provided by an insurer to indemnify the SPV against losses arising from sovereign acts hostile to the interests of the investors.
2. A *guarantee of performance* of the producer which would be a guarantee given by the miner's parent. Such guarantor will be contractually obligated to deliver the specified commodity or its equivalent value on behalf of the producer to the consumer in the event that the producer cannot fulfill its obligation under the forward contract to directly deliver its commodity.
3. A *guarantee of performance* of the consumer which would be a guarantee given by the consumer's parent. Such guarantor will be obligated to receive and make payment for the commodity to the SPV on behalf of the consumer in the event that the consumer cannot fulfill its obligation under the forward contract to receive and pay for the commodity.
4. A *reserve fund* which would be a fund established upon the creation of the SPV comprised of a commodity or its cash equivalent (which may include a letter of credit) under the control of the trustee. This reserve fund will be drawn upon by a trustee to satisfy the obligations to the investors.
5. An *irrevocable standby letter of credit* which would be a standby letter of credit issued at the request of the producer, by an acceptable financial institution which could be drawn upon to satisfy the producer's obligations to the SPV in the event of the inability of the producer and its parent guarantor to deliver or cause to have delivered to the consumer metal in compliance with the forward contract.
6. A *performance bond* which would be a bond issued by an insurance company in favor of the SPV at the request of the consumer. Such bond would be drawn upon to satisfy the consumer's obligations to the SPV in the event of the inability of both the consumer to comply with the terms of the forward contract and the consumer's guarantor to comply with its commitments un-

der the terms of the guarantee of performance of the consumer.

Future commodity SPVs could be structured the same as the oil and gas SPVs with forward sales used to pay down the SPV with settlements in either the commodity or cash equivalent.

SPVs could be established in more than one country or currency to diversify the foreign exchange risk. Finally, advances for new projects could be financed with the SPV unit-approach with repayment to be made in three to seven years in commodity equivalent which would provide a parallel market to current futures and options.

Groups interested in commodity financing have changed in the past years. The participants used to be solely commercial banks. Today in addition to commercial banks there are:

- pension funds
- insurance companies
- investment trusts
- commercial finance companies
- investment funds

The 1990s will be an interesting time in commodities markets. Futures markets will continue to expand in volume and duration of contracts.

There are thus many new participants in the financial markets with capital available for project financing. However, with the growing financial problems in the United States and Japan, capital will seek the highest quality investment. Future projects, including those of the commodities industries if this industry wants to share in the global growth of the 1990s, will have to take advantage of the new financing structures to enhance the quality of the debt and provide a future market for the debt instruments.

Chapter 7

Securitization—A European Bank's Introspective View

by Andy Clapham,
Natwest Asset Securitization
Natwest Markets

1. INTRODUCTION

Banks—both commercial and investment—have and continue to have an important role to play in the securitization system for clients. These roles are several and varied. Structuring, the process of actually converting loans or assets into cash flows, and the packaging of them for investors is, and continues to grow into, a major business in which both commercial and investment banks compete. Placing and trading the resulting securities or syndicating out securitized credits into the bank markets is also an important source of income and continues to develop.

Securitization can be very versatile and can also be important in a climate of general credit quality decline and where structuring and analyzing underlying assets and cash flows can improve credit quality and spread/diversify underlying risks. This is also particularly apposite with regard to smaller originators, where it is possible to look through to higher quality assets reducing a bank's credit risk and an originator's underlying cost of funds.

The whole arena of securitization in Europe is becoming an increasingly competitive field as the ballpark is stalked by an ever-increasing number of players and banks, all of which are seeking niches and specializations to obtain and retain market share. In particular there has been recently an increasing number of US players entering into the still relatively embryonic Euro markets.

My own bank has been active in all of the above areas and has participated in the majority of public asset-backed issues that have taken place in the UK over the past 2 years. For example, when there was a relative lack of appetite in the asset-backed floating rate note market and a relatively cost-effective demand in the fixed rate market for mortgage-backed securities, Natwest structured a method whereby the Household Mortgage Corporation could 'tap' both the fixed rate market and simultaneously the floating rate market with a total £225 million issue through two special purpose companies, HMC7 and HMC103. Natwest also participated in the bond distribution and provided certain other unique facilities within the structure itself.

The general growth in the European securitization market has been somewhat slower than initial projections estimated, as in a majority of European countries certain regulatory problems have still to be overcome. Additionally the marketplace continues to develop slowly as legislation is passed to make securitization a more viable option to European banks and corporations. In the UK, the marketplace has been dominated by mortgage-backed issues—the first issue taking place in 1987—although other asset types such as car loans, for example, are now also being securitized.

Securitization for clients continues to be—on an increasing basis—a very important source of fee income for European banks, with these banks being particularly determined to show structuring and placement capabilities on their 'home ground.' However, although originating transactions is important to banks to produce income generation, perhaps an even more important aspect for banks is an introspective view of this business arena with regard to both existing bank assets and future business origination.

One reason for the slower than anticipated European growth has been the lack of origination of suitable assets by corporations together with a reluctance to enter into the sometimes protracted process of securitizing, this being particularly true of indigenous European corporations where there may be certain technology constraints and expensive systems upgrades are required. However,

European banks have ready-made portfolios of mortgages, credit cards, auto loans, revolving loans, etc. with sufficient critical mass to justify up-front expenses which can be amortised over repeat issues. This asset origination 'muscle' together with an increasing will to securitize makes the European banking community a massive source for future issues and the base from which the Euro securitization markets can continue to grow—particularly if the post-global recession period places demands on credit which places pressures on currently strong equity bases.

2. THE ATTRACTIONS OF SECURITIZATION TO A BANK

The attractions to any bank of securitizing assets can be many and can be wide and varied.

2.1 Capital/The Basle Framework

Securitization offers a number of attractions to a banking institution. Perhaps the most relevant to a bank, which falls under the Basle Agreement, is capital freeing or synthetic capital production.

In the period from the end of 1987 to the middle of 1988, the BIS Committee on banking regulations and supervisory practices—'The Basle' Committee—proposed and confirmed the structure of a regulatory framework. The framework is based upon the use of capital as a cushion against losses sustained from investment in assets of different levels of risk. The framework is built around a careful definition of the capital base and a series of asset classes. The outline is as follows:

Tier 1

- equity, disclosed reserves, preferred stock
- deduct goodwill

Tier 2

- perpetual subordinated debt, hybrid debt/equity instruments, general provisions
- lower Tier 2 dated subordinated debt.
- Tier 2 to be no more than 50 percent of capital base
- Lower Tier 2 no more than 1/2 of Tier 1 value
- Dated subordinated debt.

Tier 1 capital must be at least 50 percent of the capital base, and lower Tier 2 can be no more than 1/2 of Tier 1 value.

Assets are 'risk weighted' in accordance with the following weightings:

Risk Weighting (%)	*Asset Type*
0/10	Cash, short-term loans to governments.
20	Long-term Government securities. Loans to OECD group banks. Loans to OECD group public sector entities. Loans to Building Societies.
50	Residential mortgage loans fully secured by property.
100	Everything else.

The risk weightings are applied as follows, assuming, for example, a £1 billion portfolio split equally amongst each risk weighting group:

Risk Weighting	*Asset Amount*	*Risk Weighted Asset*
0	£250m	0
20	£250m	£50m
50	£250m	£125m
100	£250m	£250m
Totals	£1 billion	£425m

The Risk Asset ratio set by the BIS framework is as follows:

$$\frac{\text{Capital base}}{\text{Total risk weighted assets}} \geq \text{ to } 8\%\}$$

Therefore, in the above example a minimum capital base of

£425m × 8%, or £34m, would be required.

Banks governed by The Basle Conversions Agreement have to allocate, for every £100 lent, £8 of Tier 1 and Tier 2 capital as highlighted above. This capital will have its own separate cost, as will the remaining £92 raised from the wholesale markets or funded from retail deposits. Capital is a finite resource and for a bank to expand its asset base it must also be able to expand its capital base, or be in a position to be able to fund assets with no capital requirements.

By packaging assets either directly on origination or after origination and enhancing these assets through liquidity and direct credit support, it is possible to make the assets into a tradeable form suitable, dependant upon the asset type, to be funded through the short-, medium- or long-term wholesale markets.

Through this packaging and enhancement route it becomes possible to statistically analyze precisely what the credit risks are and to segregate these risks. By segregation it then becomes possible to reduce the amount of capital required to allocate against those assets.

Some bankers may feel uncomfortable with the prospect of needing less capital to do business, wondering what to do with the excess capital. However, players with strong capital positions should have real opportunities to reinvest spare capital in other businesses, while weaker capitalised players with perhaps lower returns on capital today will probably find the need for less capital a blessing.

A bank examining the benefits of securitization on the basis of new capital and funding will need to analyze the marginal returns generated by securitizing versus the marginal cost of raising new capital. The cost of this capital would depend upon the relationship between Tier 1 and Tier 2 capital at that time and the respective cost of raising fresh capital in the relevant markets.

2.2 Asset/Liability Management

The added flexibility that securitization gives to the balance sheet can significantly help asset/liability management through:

- The generation of funds from assets that are not achieving an acceptable return in a manner which improves financial performance and enhances market value. An example of this is by being able to reduce the capital cost associated with an asset such that while the income streams are static the costs are reduced and hence there is an increase in performance.
- Maturity Profile Risk. Maturity profiles of some assets can distort a bank's risk portfolio. This is particularly true in certain specialized areas where to get involved in the more lucrative and attractive transactions it is sometimes necessary to take 15 years plus risk. By matching maturities of assets with securities, it can become possible to reduce the maturity profile of a bank's overall book making a bank's funding position shorter and more flexible and taking away any liquidity risks.
- Greater flexibility in the core issues of risk management, including reducing interest rate and currency risk. This can be achieved, for example, by backing fixed rate dollar assets into a fixed rate dollar bond.
- Asset securitization. Asset securitization can represent a new source of diversified funding for an organization. While this may also draw investors away from existing funding instruments it should also help to bring in some new investors.
- Strategic planning. To the extent that asset securitization can help fund a business then the need for capital does not adversely impinge on gross market share objectives, etc. Loan origination economies of scale can be reaped rather than loan volume being a constrained function of available capital.

2.3 Increased Competitiveness

As more and more banks become convinced of the benefits of securitization these institutions should see increased returns as capital is used more efficiently. Part of this cost saving can be passed on to clients to increase the efficiency of asset generation. Institutions without techniques available to reduce capital cost may find themselves at a competitive disadvantage to compete for the most lucrative and attractive business.

3. REGULATORY CONSIDERATIONS

For a UK bank it is vitally important to satisfy the Bank of England's regulatory requirements. Notice BSD/1989/1, which appeared in February 1989, covers the transfer of both a single loan and the transfer of a group or package of loans, the latter being described as securitization.

This notice was further amended and updated in April 1992 through notice BSD/1992/3.

3.1 Loan Transfers and Securitization (BSD/1989/1 February 1989—updated through BSD/1992/3 April 1992)

This notice sets out the Bank's supervisory policy on the treatment of loan transfers involving banks. The notice covers both the sale of single loans and the packaging, securitization and sale of loan pools. It also covers the transfer of risk under sub-participation agreements. The main aims of the policy are to ensure that:

- loan sales and packaging achieve their intended effect of passing rights and obligations from the seller to the buyer;
- all the parties to the transactions fully understand the responsibilities and risks they have assumed or retained; and
- any material risks to buyers or sellers are properly treated in the Bank's supervision of banks.

The Bank considers that the method of transfer of a loan can have an important bearing on the risks assumed by buyer and seller. Below is an outline of the methods of transfer recognized by the Bank of England.

Novation, whereby the rights and obligations of the lender and borrower are discharged and replaced by matching rights and obligations between the purchaser and borrower, is the cleanest method of transfer. It requires the cooperation of the borrower, however, and as a practical matter may be limited to those loan agreements which have incorporated transferability clauses.

Equitable assignment by the lender of his rights under a loan agreement leaves the assignee (purchaser) exposed to the risk of the borrower setting off, against the assigned rights, obligations which arise on the part of the lender in favor of the borrower subsequent to the date of the assignment.

Statutory assignment entails, among other things, the lender giving notice to the borrower of the assignment and thus obviates the set-off risk inherent in an equitable assignment. Neither type of assignment will transfer a bank's obligations on undrawn facilities.

Subparticipation, as a matching non-recourse funding agreement, does not affect the rights or obligations of the borrower and lender as between each other, but does interpose the credit risk of the lender. If a loan agreement restricts the assignment or novation by the lender, subparticipation may prove to be the only method of transferring the loan so as to achieve a zero risk weighting.

Other conditions for zero risk weighting. In addition to the methods of transfer, the Bank of England rules stipulate 15 conditions which must be met in order for a Bank of England regulated entity to achieve a zero risk weighting in respect of a transfer of a pool of packaged assets. Following is a summary of these conditions:

1. **No contravention of the terms and conditions of the underlying loan agreement and all necessary consents to have been obtained.** Usually this will mean it will be necessary to carry out an 'asset sale suitability' audit of the portfolio documentation.
2. **The bank must not retain any residual beneficial interest in the loan or relevant part sold.**
3. **There must be no 'formal recourse' to the bank for losses.** To the extent credit enhancement is required, the bank may not provide it. Similarly, the rule requires the bank to have '**no obligation to repurchase the loan' at any time**. This is subject to the exception that the bank may give warranties about the loans as at the sale date and undertake a repurchase obligation if the warranties are untrue when made. These warranties must be verifiable and must not involve any element of absorption of the credit risk of the borrowers in question.
4. **The bank must give notice in writing to the buyer of the absence of any repurchase obligation or support obligation on the bank's part.** This is a documentation requirement which should not be difficult to comply with, provided the structure of the transaction is consistent with the remainder of the conditions.
5. **It must be the buyer, and not the bank, that is subject to any risk of rescheduling or renegotiation.** This condition is especially important in the context of corporate lending. Many current corporate workouts will capture the original lender of record (especially with respect to new money obligations), rather than the current lender, particularly if a sale has taken place by means of equitable assignment or subparticipation (where the borrower and other banks have no knowledge of the sale).
6. **The bank may not pay monies to the vehicle in advance of their receipt from the borrower.** This may be possible, however, if the bank retains the right to recapture the money from the vehicle afterwards.
7. **Formal confirmation from the bank's lawyers and auditors that there is compliance with the rules as a whole and that the selling bank is protected from liability to investors, save where the bank has been proved to be negligent.**
8. **The bank will have to comply with stipulated notice requirements concerning the transfer of risk.**

9.–
11. **The bank may not own share capital in the special purpose vehicle; the vehicle's name must show no connection with the bank; and the bank's person-**

nel must form no more than a minority of the board of directors of the vehicle.

12. **The bank may not 'bear any of the recurring expenses of the scheme.'** Thus the interest flow from the loan portfolio must support the interest and other continuing costs of any SPC, save to the extent that any shortfall is made good by persons other than the bank. The bank may not pay expenses itself and then recoup them from the cash flows. **The banks may, however, make 'a one-off contribution to enhance the creditworthiness of the vehicle.** This would allow the payment of credit enhancement fees and the provision of 'first loss funds' and 'spread accounts.' However, **any such payment will be deducted from the bank's capital for risk asset ratio purposes** and therefore the size of the contribution, if any, should be carefully limited. **The bank may make a subordinated, long-term loan to the vehicle; any such loan, however, will also be a deduction from capital.** Any such 'contribution' or loan *must* be made *upfront*.
13. **The bank may not 'intentionally bear any losses' arising from the effect of interest rate changes on the transaction. The bank may, however, enter into interest rate swap agreements at market prices with the vehicle.**
14. **The bank may not provide liquidity coverage.** Liquidity coverage must come from a third party.
15. **The bank may not retain an option to repurchase or refinance any loan, save to the extent that the portfolio has fallen to 10 percent of its original size and on condition that the repurchased loans are 'fully performing.'**

Undrawn committed facilities. Of the three methods of transfer discussed, only novation will result in a zero risk weighting for the lender's undrawn commitment to lend money. A transfer of the risk associated with the commitment by way of subparticipation will be treated as a transfer of the lender's exposure from the potential borrower to the buyer.

3.2 Accounting Standards Board (ASB)

In October 1991, the ASB issued a paper covering its proposal for the accounting treatment for companies undertaking a securitization transaction. In the United States—GAAP FASB77—securitization can achieve off balance sheet treatment. Such treatment can also be obtained in most other overseas countries. If the ASB proposals were introduced here, this would make off balance sheet treatment from securitization virtually impossible to achieve for a UK corporation. Not only would this place UK corporations at a distinct disadvantage against global competitors, but importantly would also arguably distort a much greater extent than is currently the case, the 'true and fair view' concept auditors professed to seek.

While assets may be 'on-balance sheet' from an accounting angle the assets can still be 'off-balance sheet' for Basle purposes. At time of writing, further announcements from the ASB are awaited.

4. WHAT TYPE OF ASSET SHOULD BE CONSIDERED FOR SECURITIZING

While the example shows the effects of securitization on part of a mortgage book, this example was chosen because traditionally the majority of asset-backed issues in the UK to date have been mortgage-backed. However, to some banks because of their low risk weighting—50 percent—these will be some of the least attractive securitizable assets.

Where securitization for banks may become a powerful tool is where bank and investor perception of the credit risk are different from those necessarily implied by the BIS framework. For example, a AAA rated loan or a AAA rated package transaction may be perceived to be less risky than a pool of mortgages with no enhancements. However, the former will be 100 percent weighted while the latter is 50 percent weighted. Under this scenario there is a positive weighting advantage to be gained by the banks.

Banks traditionally have a varied portfolio of asset types. The asset side of a bank's balance sheet may comprise Residential Mortgage Loans, Credit Card Receivables, Auto Loans, Revolving Corporate Loans, Term Corporate Loans, HLTs, Revolving Personal Overdrafts, Personal Loans etc, etc. These assets while wide and varied can individually provide attractive cash flows to form the basis of a securitization transaction and supply a critical mass of many £ billion to make a securitization a worthwhile and valuable funding tool.

The reason to securitize one asset type as opposed to another could also be due to several reasons. It could be that the particular bank has an overexposure to one particular asset type or it could be that an asset is chosen—for example,

Table 7.1—Effects of Securitising Assets with Different Margins

	Pre Securitisation	*Post re 25 bp*	*Post re 75 bp*
Assets	£2,000m	£1,500m	£1,500m
Average yield on balance sheet*	50 bp	58 bp	41.67 bp
Total net income**	£10m	£8.7m	£8.7m
Securitisation Costs	–	25 bp	25 bp

* Average yield on assets not securitised.
** Total net income includes income from assets remaining on balance sheet and net income from securitised assets.

Residential Mortgages—because of the tried and tested technology available and hence perhaps the lower inherent developmental costs. Systems considerations are another important factor as the computer system technology for one particular asset may be better than those utilized on another asset type.

Since the aim is for any income generation above the securitization cost to find its way back to the originating bank, in theory it doesn't matter whether the asset being securitized is relatively low yielding or relatively high yielding. This is demonstrated below:

> Taking 2 different assets—one earning 25 bp and one earning 75 bp—and analyzing the book with both assets in return being removed we see the following positions, firstly with the asset earning 25 bps being removed from the balance sheet (post re 25 bps), and secondly with the asset earning 75 bps being removed from the balance sheet (post re 75 bps) (Table 7.1).

Although the average yield of assets remaining on the balance sheet shifts up or down depending on whether the yield on the asset being securitized is above or below the average seen on the book, the total income post-securitization is not a function of the yield on the asset being securitized, but instead is proportionately a function of the securitization cost. Since total income post-securitization is not a function of the yield on the assets being securitized then real yield will not be a function of the yield on the assets being securitized.

This is illustrated in Figure 7.1 below, where it can be seen that although the average yield of the assets left on-balance sheet falls as the return on the assets being securitized rises, the real yield on the asset book remains constant as there is a net income skim from the securitized assets. This 'real asset yield' will fall or rise proportionately with the costs of the securitization.

What is obviously important is that the bank has available some relatively liquid assets such that 'freed' capital can be redeployed relatively quickly to ensure that real returns are enhanced as well as

Figure 7.1—Analysis of Asset Yields

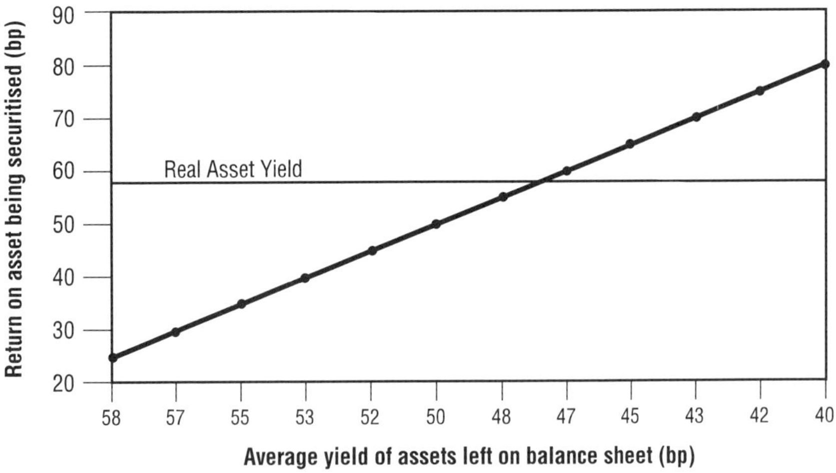

'Return on Capital Employed' (ROCE) and 'Yield on Weighted Risk Assets' (YOWRA)—(please also see Section 5, 'Economics of a Transaction,' for further reference to ROCE, YOWRA and Trading Return On Capital Employed (TROCE)).

What is also important is to look at the overhead and staffing cost and also the bad and doubtful debts associated with the business sector securitizing assets, since unless the funding costs plus the ongoing costs of the securitizing can be achieved at a total cost inside a bank's conventional funding source, there will be a fall in actual income until freed capital is redeployed. Since costs and 'Bad and Doubtful Debts' (B&DDs) will be relatively constant post-securitization relative to those seen pre-securitization, depending upon the size of the cost and B&DDs relative to the original returns, these could have a further impact upon securitizing as the two variables in the TROCE equation,[1] capital and income, are both falling while costs and B&DDs remain relatively constant.

Even with the redeployment of 'freed' capital and the subsequent rise in the income and capital variables depending upon the original effectiveness of usage cost, there may be a need to increase costs and most certainly B&DDs will increase. Improvement in TROCE then becomes dependent upon ROCE increasing faster than in costs as a proportion of capital employed.

The structure a bank decides to adopt will depend to a large degree on the asset type it decides to securitize. For example, if a bank wants to reduce its maturity profile on its book by removing some assets with 15-year terms it is unlikely to adopt a CP-type structure alone. A European bank has a whole plethora of options available when deciding upon the appropriate structure to achieve its aim. The different markets that can, and in some cases have been, used include Euro FRNs, Euro Fixed Rate Bonds, Euro CP, US Domestic CP, Euro MTNs, US MTNs, plus others and combinations of those mentioned.

Several European banks are working on projects whereby assets, for example trade receivables, are assigned directly into special purpose vehicles 'organized' by a European bank, and generally funded through the US $ domestic commercial paper markets where the market depth of circa $600 billion provides sufficient liquidity for ongoing funding requirements.

This type of funding for clients, where capital requirements are generally restricted to low levels of enhancement, or any utilization of liquidity back-up lines, has long been a successful source of business for several US banks.

This type of funding presents European banks with a different set of problems to those confronting an indigenous US bank, since there is both basis and generally foreign currency risks to hedge. For example Figures 7.2, 7.3 and 7.4 show how CP rates compare with LIBOR and where A1/P1 paper generally trades.

If the paper is trading at, let's say, composite 5 bp and composite is at a 5 bp spread below LIBOR then as you can see this effectively produces a source of $ funds sub-LIBOR—to which must be added FX costs—effectively with minimal capital usage.

5. ECONOMICS OF A TRANSACTION—PROFIT VERSUS PROFITABILITY

In the past the margin over funding costs has been used as the reward basis for guiding lending decisions for a banking institution. With the introduction of the BIS framework a single equivalent measure similar to margin has been sought by business management of banking institutions. 'Return on capital employed' (ROCE) or trading return on capital employed (TROCE) were promoted as being such measures. However, except under certain circumstances, ROCE and TROCE do not provide an accurate indication but only part of a larger more complicated equation.

Let's look at a simplistic example.

Table 7.2—A Simple Bank Balance Sheet

Liabilities (£million)	*Against*	*Assets (£million)*
Capital	8	Asset 200
General liabilities	192	
	200	200

Within the process of optimizing the profitability of the bank it is necessary to employ the existing funds in the most profitable manner. Simple ratio analysis tells us that the bank must own a portfolio of assets that has a blended risk weight 50 percent or less to achieve an 8 percent risk asset ratio for BIS assessment (see Table 7.3).

Supposing there are only two assets in which to invest—one zero weighted and one 100 percent weighted. Return on capital employed at first sight

1 Trading Return on Capital Employed =

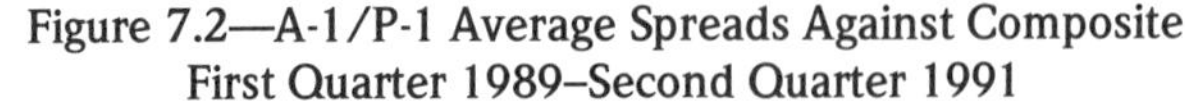

Figure 7.2—A-1/P-1 Average Spreads Against Composite First Quarter 1989–Second Quarter 1991

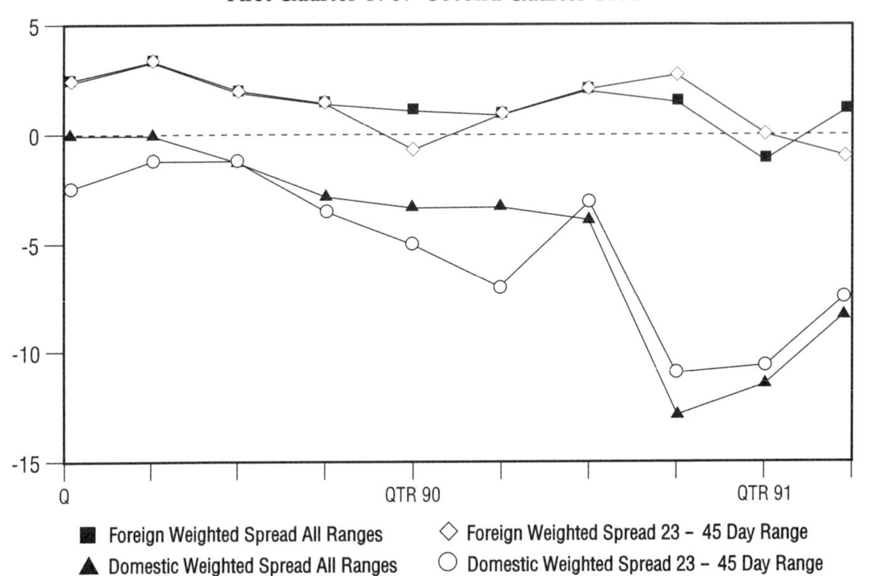

is not a helpful number in this instance. ROCE would suggest that the bank invest everything in the government loan at 12 percent. However this is a constrained situation where the bank only has £200 million to invest and therefore there would be £8 million of capital totally unused. For maximum return given the funds and capital available, the bank will not invest less than £100 million in the corporate loan.

Figure 7.3—Differential Between 30-Day LIBOR and 30-Day Commercial Paper

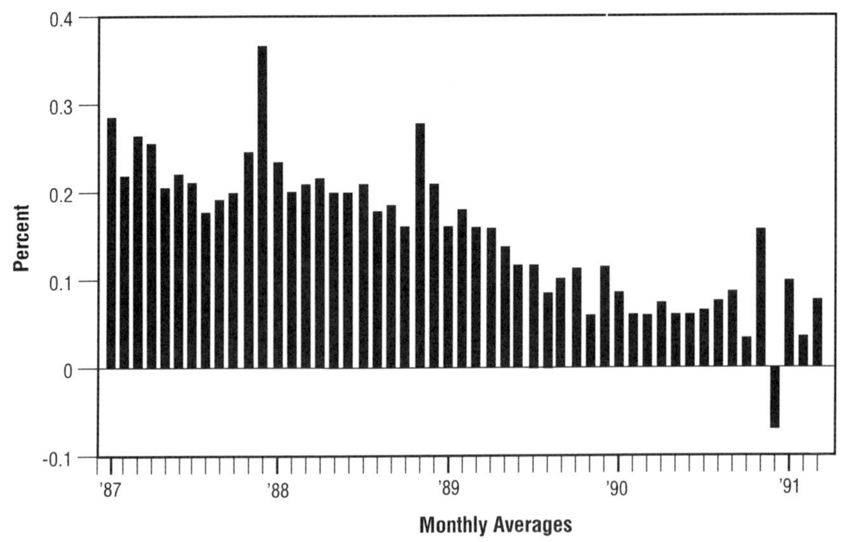

Figure 7.4—Differential Between 90-Day LIBOR and 90-Day Commercial Paper

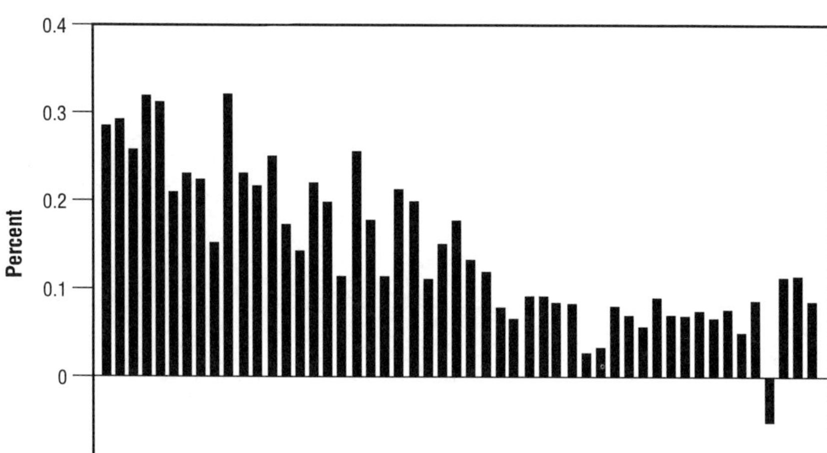

Table 7.3—Assets Available to Invest In

Asset	*Expected Return*	*Risk Weighting*	*ROCE**
Government loan	12%	0%	inf
A-rated corporate loan	15%	100%	53%**

* $\text{Return on Capital Employed} = \dfrac{\text{Income} - \text{Costs}}{\text{Capital Employed}}$

** Assuming 10% cost of funds, 20% capital costs and 8% capital coverage, we see

$$\frac{[15\% - ((8\% \times 20\%) + (92\% \times 10\%))]}{8\%} = 53\%$$

Allocating the other £100 million to the government loan will result in a portfolio with the required risk weighting of 50 percent and offering a return of 13.5 percent. Whilst acknowledging that ROCE and TROCE are important they are only one dimension in a multi-dimensional problem. Within this analysis it is also important to focus on the real return being achieved and within this ensuring that all available capital is being utilised to its maximum efficiency.

Figure 7.5 illustrates the point of optimal capital usage.

Obviously this picture ignores the cost of investing in these assets and the reality that banks can only invest in these assets if they are available, and that prices can become distorted in certain events through the supply and demand equation, or that a bank's investment decision may be limited through credit risk diversification. However, what a bank must do is to continue to buy the best assets until credit limits are reached or the assets are no long available.

High-quality corporate assets (100 percent risk weighted) rarely offer banks adequate reward, even when they offer reasonable spreads above LIBOR. Banks involved in major corporate lending, in bonds or loans, are generally not achieving high returns on capital.

If banks are to remain a dominant source of funds for investment grade corporates then either the cost of bank loans will rise, or equity investors must be prepared to accept low returns on capital for banks lending to corporates in today's market climate. Therefore, any method whereby a bank

Figure 7.5—Optimising Asset Investment (Return versus Weighting)

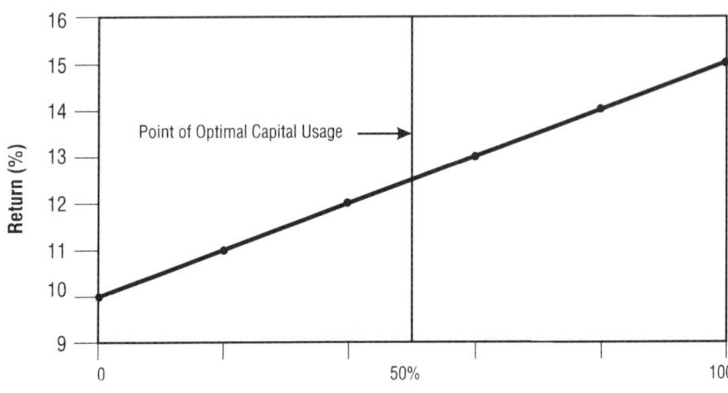

can generate increased returns on capital will be of fundamental importance to a bank's continuing business.

Taking an Example

Let us look at the effects of securitising £500 million out of a bank's £2 billion mortgage book. Let us take a typical structure where the mortgages are backed into floating rate notes. There are inherent upfront costs estimated in Table 7.4.

Table 7.4—Upfront Costs

Legal Costs	
Issuer	£350,000
Trustee	£20,000
Credit enhancer	£65,000
Ancillaries	£25,000
Rating	£115,000
Printing	£30,000
Audit	£40,000
Listing	£10,000
Paying agent	£10,000
Total	£665,000

Taking these in basis point terms against the principal amount of £500 million to be securitised we get 13 bps. Annualised over an average life of 5 years and using a 10 percent discount rate, this gives approximately 3 bps per annum.

Assuming that pre-securitization a bank is achieving a 100 bp return over its funding costs of LIBOR flat at 10 percent, and that post securitization annualized up front costs and ongoing costs such as enhancements and discounted margin gives a funding cost of LIBOR + 87.5 bp we see the following picture (Tables 7.5, 7.6 and 7.7).

Table 7.5—Pre-Securitisation

Assets	£500m
Margin over funding	100 bp
Capital coverage required	£20m (mortgages 50%)
Cost of capital	20%
Funding costs	10%

Total Net Income = £500m × 11% – ([£480m × 10%]
+ [£20m × 20%])
= £55m – (£48m + £4m)
Total Net Income = £3m

Table 7.6—Post-Securitisation

Assets	£500m
Margin over funding	12.5 bp (11 – 10.875)
Capital coverage required	£0m
Cost of capital	20%
Funding costs	10.875%

Total Net Income = £500m × 11% – ([£500m × 10.875%]
= £55m – £54.375m
= £0.625m (i.e., 0.125% on £500m)

Figures 7.6 and 7.7 illustrate how YOWRA on the total book is increasing as more assets are being securitized and also demonstrate how income is reducing as securitization has an inherent built in cost.

Table 7.7

Assuming the assets being securitised, we see the following overall picture:

	Pre-Securitisation	Post-Securitisation
Total assets	£2,000m	£1,500m
Capital cover required	£80m	£60m
Total net income*	£12m	£9.625m
ROCE**	15%	16.04%
YOWRA***	120 bp	128 bp

* Total Net Income Pre-Securitisation, following from Table 7.5 = $£3m \times \frac{£2000m}{£500m} = £12m$

Total Net Income Post-Securitisation, following from Tables 7.5 and 7.6 =

$$\left[£3m \times \frac{£1500m}{£500m} + £0.625m = £9.625m\right]$$

** $ROCE = \frac{\text{Total Net Income}}{\text{Capital Cover}}$

*** $YOWRA = \frac{\text{Total Net Income}}{\text{Total Assets} \times 50\%}$

(since in this case we are deling with lending secured by a first charge over residential property which is risk weighted 50%)

What this shows us is that both ROCE and the yield on the weighted risk asset (YOWRA) have increased while there has also been a freeing of £20 million of capital at an income loss of £2.375 million or effectively 11.875 percent. Under this example, therefore, £20 million of capital could be said to have been created at a cost of 11.875 percent as opposed to an average cost of 20 percent if capital was to be raised through conventional matters.

Since total income has been reduced by £2.375m, what now becomes important is that the 'free' capital is redeployed as quickly and efficiently as possible. Assuming that these assets are reinvested at the same rates as before the overall book now carries the shape as indicated in Table 7.8.

Table 7.8—Pre- and Post-Securitisation with Assets Being Replaced

	Pre-Securitisation	Post-Securitisation
Total assets	£2,000m	£2,000m
Capital cover required	£80m	£80m
Coventional cost of capital	20%	20%
Securitised cost of capital	–	11.875%
Total net income	£12m	£13.625m*
ROCE	15%	17.03%
YOWRA	1.20%	1.36%

* Total Income = [Asset Size × Return on Assets] – [Inter Bank Funding Cost]–[Capital Costs for Capital raised by conventional means]–[Capital Costs with Capital raised through securitization]
= [£2,000m × 11%] – [£1,920m × 10%] – [£60m × 20%] – [£20m × 11.875%]
= £220m – £192m – £12m – £2.375m
= £13.625m

Figure 7.6—Size of Asset versus YOWRA on Book

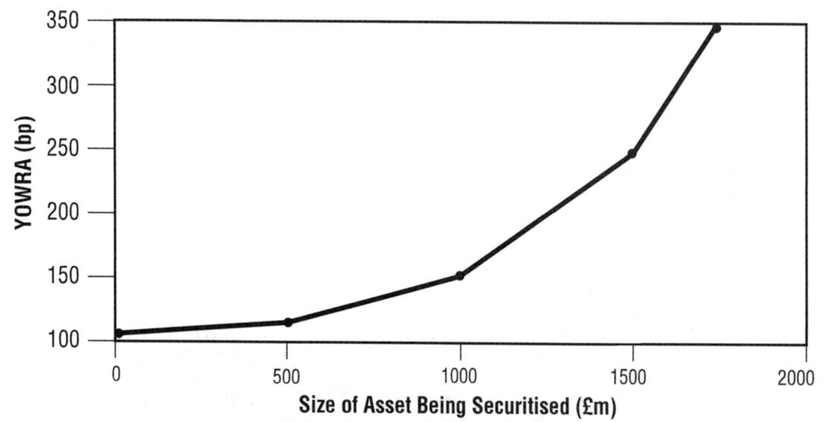

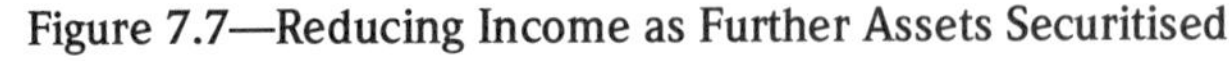

Figure 7.7—Reducing Income as Further Assets Securitised

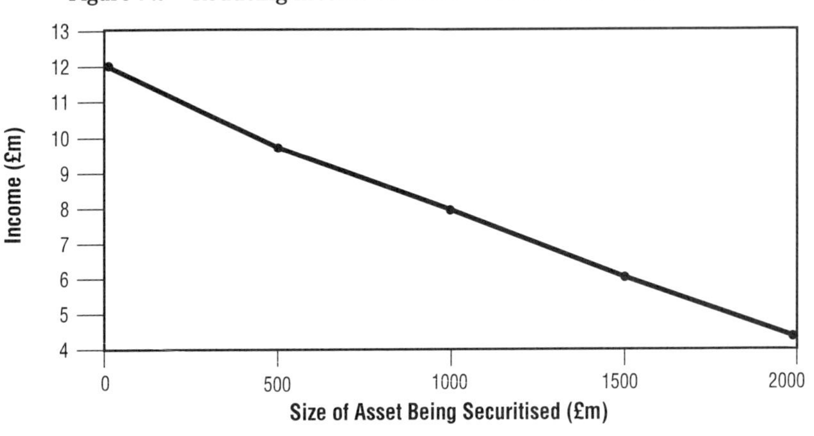

Figure 7.8—YOWRA as Securitised Assets are Replaced

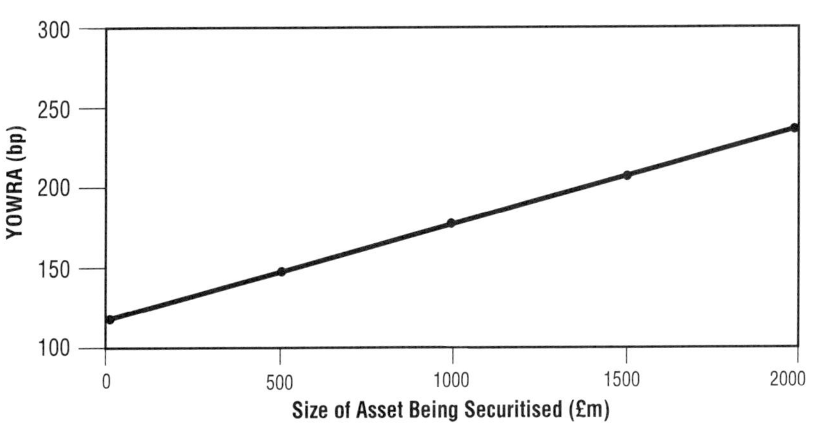

Figure 7.9—Income as Assets Securitised are Replaced

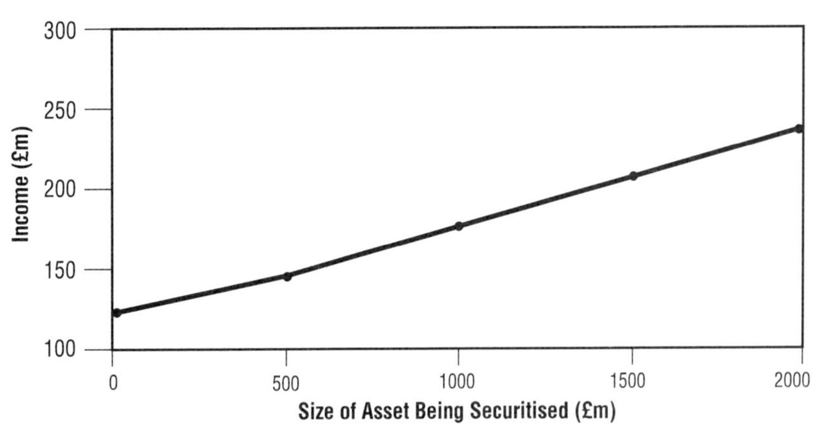

The effects here are to further increase ROCE and YOWRA, and in this instance real return on assets is substantially increased.

Figures 7.8 and 7.9 illustrate how real income and YOWRA are increasing as more assets are being securitized and are being replaced with assets of a similar size and that are earning an identical return.

6. CONCLUSION

What is becoming apparent is that European banks are discovering securitization can be, and in some cases, is, an important part of a bank's short-, medium- and long-term strategies. It is becoming increasingly clear that it is important for a bank to have in-house securitization expertise to remain competitive in certain areas. Those who have not developed such an expertise will find themselves less competitive with their rivals as it becomes difficult to include securitization as part of their strategy when other banks may have that option available. For those banks that have not developed the expertise it may also become necessary to buy in such expertise at a later date which could prove costly, time-consuming and inconvenient.

Rather than permitting total disintermediation by their clients, banks will in part react to BIS regulations by securitizing loans. Banks who might be struggling to take control of their balance sheets in an immensely competitive banking environment will view securitization as a natural route to increase their liquidity since it will continue to reward them for their skills and relationships. To attract more lucrative business or to increase market share in certain key asset areas, banks will need to remain competitive, and securitization provides part of that competitive edge.

While growth in the European markets has to date been slower than anticipated securitization is set to be a valuable tool with which European banks—both commercial and investment—can compete with their US counterparties. Securitization looks set to be a valuable weapon both to european bank treasurers and also deal origination teams to produce lucrative income business well into the next century.

Part II

Identifying and Allocating Risk

Chapter 8

Risks in Securitisation Transactions

by Jonathan E. Keighley,
Managing Director
Gracebury Securitisation Limited

This chapter considers how a manager of a securitisation transaction evaluates the various risks involved, and seeks to demonstrate how he will seek to allocate and manage those risks.

THE RISKS

It is worthwhile to begin by considering the principal steps involved in any securitisation transaction. First, a portfolio which is suitable for securitisation has to be selected. Next a structure has to be devised which is satisfactory from a legal, fiscal and regulatory point of view. The assets then have to be purchased, often on a regular basis, and suitable funding arranged. Finally the special purpose vehicle ("SPV") must be administered throughout the transaction. Each of these functions carries its own risks (Figure 8.1).

There are four major areas of risk in any securitisation. These are:

1. Credit risks relating to the performance of the underlying receivables, which might cause the SPV to experience cash shortfalls.
2. Structuring risks which include the effectiveness of legal transfer of title of the assets, the fiscal neutrality of the transaction and the satisfaction of the requirements of the regulatory authorities.
3. Operational risks of weaknesses in the operation of the SPV, which might increase costs or cause losses.
4. Financial risks deriving from unexpected cash flows, such as pre-payments, delinquencies and interest and currencies mismatches.

In addition, there are further risks which are specific to multi-originator asset securitisation programmes as distinct from transactions involving a single originator.

CREDIT RISKS

The primary objective of the securitiser is to protect the SPV, the investors and the credit enhancement and liquidity providers against losses arising from

Figure 8.1—Functions of an SPV

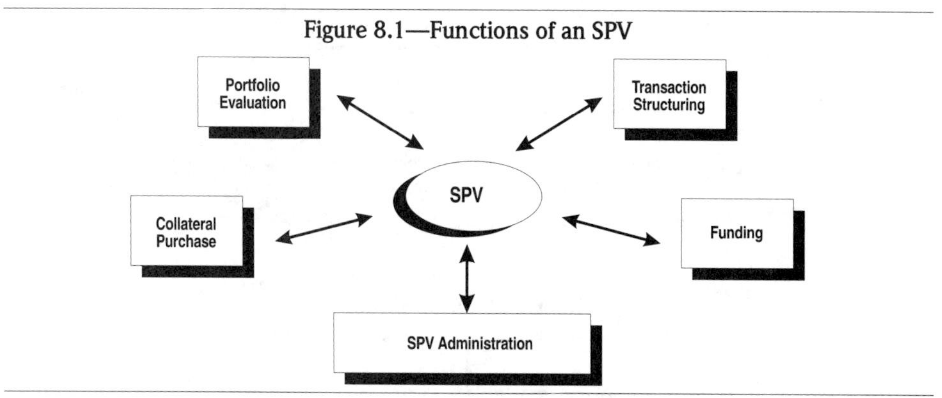

credit risk. Before undertaking the securitisation of a portfolio of assets a securitiser will first examine the historical performance of a potential originator's portfolio. Whilst statistics on defaults, prepayments and recoveries are important for determining the level of credit enhancement and the structure of the transaction, it is also important that the available data on arrears (delinquencies) are carefully considered so as to ensure that adequate provisions are made for liquidity in the structure. If an originator is unable to provide relevant and reliable statistics on his asset pool for a minimum of three years, he cannot hope to complete a successful securitisation (Figure 8.2).

Figure 8.2—Credit Protection Is Multilayered

Receivables Pool Restructuring
Reserves/Recourse
Triggers
External Credit Enhancement

Most securitisations take a multi-layered approach towards obtaining protection from the cash flow risks. The steps taken involve:

- restructuring the pool of receivables to obtain a securitisable portfolio;
- setting levels of reserves or recourse to the originator to absorb a certain level of losses;
- setting triggers which will terminate further asset substitutions if the portfolio performance should deteriorate; and
- determining the appropriate level of external credit enhancement to give the transaction the required credit rating.

Each of these steps is considered in more detail below.

Restructuring the Pool

1) Elimination of undesirable receivables. After analysing the historic data, the securitiser will restructure the originator's pool in order to reduce the SPV's exposure to the riskier receivables. Certain specific receivables will not be purchased because they possess some undesirable characteristic. By screening out such receivables, it is possible to arrange for the SPV to purchase a portfolio which should perform better than the total originating pool (Figure 8.3).

For example, starting with a total pool of £100m, receivables which are overdue will be eliminated first. Then those receivables with a term of greater than (say) 180 days will be excluded; next, those that belong to obligors affiliated with the originator. And so on...

2) Elimination of unwanted concentrations. Receivables from obligors with similar characteristics are likely to be affected by extraneous events in a similar fashion. In order to reduce the SPV's exposure to systematic risk the securitiser will require that the portfolio of receivables being purchased by the SPV is well diversified. The

Figure 8.3—Elimination of Undesirable Receivables

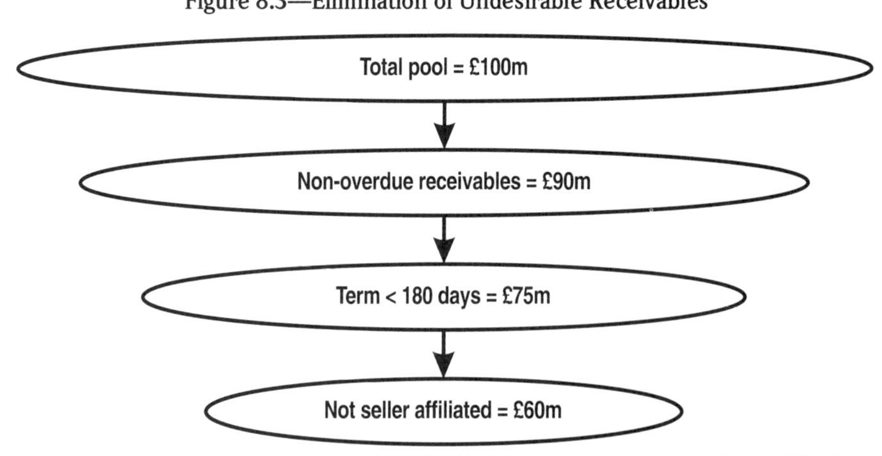

securitiser may therefore limit the percentage of receivables being purchased which emanate from specific industries, geographic regions, or which are associated with specific asset classes or categories of obligors.

Parameters for the portfolio being sold to the SPV might, for instance, be set so that the SPV would not have more than a 10 percent exposure to receivables from a selected industry, or a 3 percent exposure to receivables due from companies in a specific obligor's group. The securitiser will require the originator to eliminate receivables of such categories until the portfolio to be sold to the SPV conforms to the specified concentration requirements.

3) Loss probability reduction. A securitiser will also restructure a pool so that its expected loss characteristics fall within some determined limit. He will eliminate specific receivables with loss probabilities greater than the underwriting standards which he will set for the SPV. In order to do this, the securitiser must first estimate the default probability of each asset and/or obligor category in the pool. Using this data he will then create a loss probability distribution curve for the pool. The mean of this distribution will provide him with the expected loss level for the portfolio. He should also be able to obtain from the distribution a maximum expected loss level for the portfolio, which is the level of losses which he can be 95 percent confident will not be exceeded.

The curves shown in the example below (Figure 8.4) represent the probabilities of a portfolio incurring various levels of losses, before and after restructuring. The mean value of the loss distribution of the initial pool gives an expected loss value of £5m, but there is a 5 percent chance that it will be as high as £10m. The securitiser might decide that such a maximum loss figure is unacceptable and that he needs to be 95 percent confident that the loss on the portfolio to be sold to the SPV will be less than £8m. He will then cause the originator to eliminate those receivables with characteristics giving a maximum risk of loss until the maximum expected loss on the pool is reduced to the acceptable level of £8m.

The maximum expected loss figure is one of the more important factors considered when a securitiser sets the levels of reserves and sizes the credit enhancement.

Setting the Reserves or Level of Originator Recourse

Most transactions provide a mechanism whereby the originator absorbs some level of losses before any third party credit enhancer becomes affected.

In deals involving financial receivables, an originator is typically required to establish a first loss deductible or spread account at the outset by making a cash deposit with, or loan to, the SPV.

In deals involving trade receivables, over-collateralisation is usually the mechanism used. In such deals, the originator will sell more receivables to the SPV than the (discounted) amount for which he is initially compensated, subsequently receiving the excess cash flows only after any losses have been absorbed. Alternatively, the originator may be required to replace defaulting or delinquent receivables sold to the SPV up to a specified level.

Figure 8.4—Loss Probability Reduction

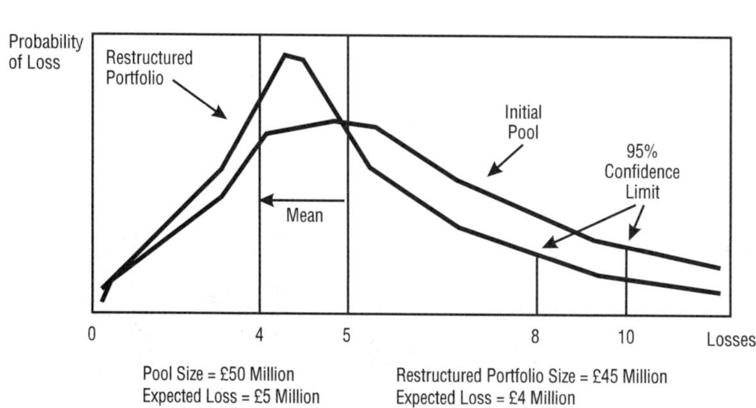

The most obvious source of losses is defaults but there may be other sources of losses of which account needs to be taken when reserves levels are determined. For instance, it may be necessary to build in a dilution reserve in a trade receivables transaction to cater for the small proportion of invoices which are never paid because the underlying goods supplied are returned as defective or damaged, or if the originator offers terms of trade giving a discount for early payment. It may also be necessary to factor in some allowance to cover the carrying cost caused by late payments or delinquencies. Further allowances may also be needed to cover the costs which might be incurred if the SPV were to be forced to perfect its title to the receivables; for instance, the cost of funding the portfolio for perhaps a 180-day period.

In practice, the level of internal reserves is usually based on some historical ratio or absolute figure, typically the greater of three times the highest default rate over the last 12 months, three times the greatest obligor concentration limit, or 5 percent of the face value of the assets.

Setting Termination Triggers

Perhaps the most important protection mechanism used for transactions involving regular asset substitutions is to prevent the SPV from purchasing receivables from the originator if the default rate on the originator's overall portfolio (not necessarily on the part which the SPV purchases) exceeds a certain level. If the originator's pool starts to perform poorly, such a trigger mechanism allows the SPV to restrict any further exposure to a badly performing portfolio before the recourse to the originator or the reserves in the transaction become depleted.

Receivable performance typically does not deteriorate overnight. There are usually observable warning trends: first, a greater percentage becomes overdue, then more receivables default. If the trigger preventing further substitution of assets into the portfolio is set low enough, and the maturity of the receivables is not too long, the SPV should be able to collect all the cash due to it before the performance of the purchased receivables deteriorates to the point where the credit enhancer incurs losses.

In the example below losses on the pool might historically have been at about 0.5 percent per annum. The securitiser would set a trigger restricting further substitution if the annualised loss level were to rise above 1.5 percent. If in Period 4 the losses on the pool exceeded this level, the SPV would cease to purchase further receivables from the originator and the deal would wind down. The example shows the level of internal reserves (primary credit enhancement) as being set at 3 percent of the value of the assets in the portfolio. If portfolio losses were to exceed this level they would have to be absorbed by the credit enhancer (Figure 8.5).

Figure 8.5—Termination Triggers

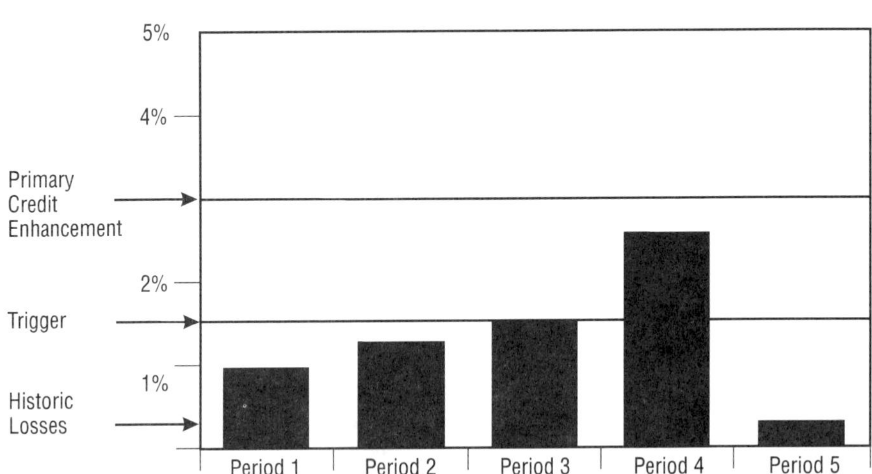

Setting the Level of External Credit Enhancement

In structuring a transaction it is nevertheless necessary to consider scenarios where the internal reserve or recourse provisions may be inadequate to absorb losses. Such circumstances might arise because the originator suffered sudden bankruptcy before any termination trigger was reached, or because a deep recession caused portfolio losses to continue to mount rapidly even after an originator's ability to substitute had been terminated.

A layer of external credit enhancement is typically provided to absorb such risks. Some outside party, usually a bank or an insurance company, will be required to agree that it will carry any losses on the receivables after the originator recourse or reserves have been utilised up to a given level, typically around 10–15 percent of the principal value of the assets. In some transactions, an insurance company, usually a monoline, will insure the entire transaction in preference to providing merely a partial guarantee.

Such third party credit enhancement is often provided by a bank providing an irrevocable letter of credit to the transaction. When called upon, the bank usually obtains rights over all future cash flows in the transaction which would otherwise have returned to the originator. Cash deposits put up by a bank and pledged as collateral have been seen as an alternative to a bank letter of credit as a means of providing credit enhancement to multi-originator programmes. Cash collateral avoids the risk of the credit rating of the programme being downgraded as a consequence of the downgrading of the credit rating of the bank providing the letter of credit support.

Alternatively, credit enhancement can be provided by an insurance company issuing a performance guarantee, whereby it agrees to deliver cash in lieu of defaulted receivables. Unlike credit enhancement provided by a bank, an insurance company will typically only acquire rights over any future cash flows arising from the defaulted receivables.

An alternative structure, which is now being increasingly used, is for the whole transaction to be structured with a layer of subordinated debt effectively replacing the bank or insurer. In such a structure investors in the "B" bonds will only get repaid after the investors in the main securities have been paid off, in return for which they obtain more attractive yields.

The figure below outlines all the processes described above for limiting credit risks and shows the interaction between them. In the bottom right hand corner is written "Ongoing Monitoring," the final and necessary step to ensure that all the structuring has been to good avail. This important protection against operational risk is discussed later (Figure 8.6).

Figure 8.6—Overview of Portfolio Credit Protection Process

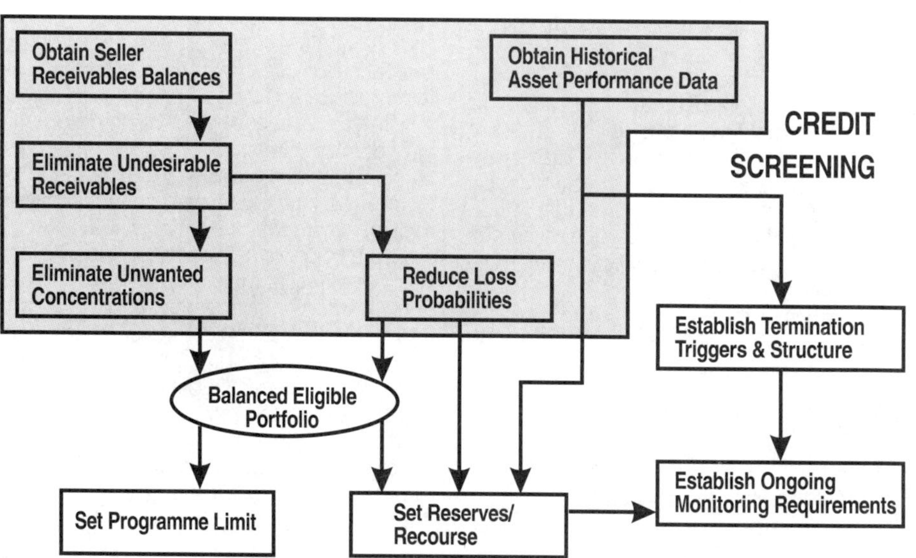

STRUCTURING RISKS

One of the great challenges in any securitisation is to devise a structure which works from a legal, fiscal and regulatory standpoint. This is an immensely complex task and, for a first time securitisation, can prove very costly and time-consuming.

Legal

The legal issues that must be addressed are principally that

- the transaction must reflect a true sale;
- the SPV must be bankruptcy remote;
- the SPV must be able to perfect its security interests in the assets and obtain full control over cash collections in the event of problems arising with the originator;
- any commingling of funds belonging to the SPV with those belonging to the originator must be kept to a minimum;
- any contingent risks relating to the assets, such as potential product liabilities, and the benefit of any insurances obtained by the originator covering such risks must be passed to the SPV and must not remain with the originator; and
- any possibility for an obligor to offset a potential claim relating to the securitised assets against the originator must be eliminated.

Taxation

It is necessary for the securitiser to ensure that the transfer of the assets to the SPV does not attract taxation. Furthermore, it is important that the cash flows from the securitised assets returning to the originator will not have attracted any taxation in the hands of the SPV before it gets back to the originator. Any possible tax incidence must be kept to a minimum both when the transaction is functioning normally, and if the transaction encounters any problems, including the perfection of title and repossession of security.

The structure must be designed to avoid the risk of impact of any of the following taxes carefully:

- corporation taxes (on any profits in the SPV);
- withholding taxes (on any cash flows to or from the SPV);
- capital gains taxes (on any gains or losses on asset realisations by the originator or in the SPV);
- taxes on value added (on asset transfer or on servicing); and
- stamp or transfer duties (on asset transfer).

Ultimately, it will be the rating agencies and the credit enhancer, together with their respective advisers who will be the judges of the efficacy of the structure of the transaction. Any risks which remain in the structure will have to be counterbalanced by an increase in the sizing of the credit enhancement required to give the transaction its required credit rating.

For instance, if, as in the UK, stamp duty of 1 percent is levied on documented on-shore asset transfers and the transaction envisages asset transfer taking place off-shore, the rating agencies will add 1 percent to the required level of credit enhancement to cater for the risk that it may be necessary to bring the assigned assets into a UK court to prove the SPV's title.

Regulatory

Every structure must comply with the regulatory environment in the jurisdiction(s) concerned. Such regulators are likely to include the following:

- government departments;
- the central bank;
- stock exchange/securities industry regulators;
- accountancy bodies; and
- tax authorities.

It is the duty of the securitiser to consult the appropriate regulatory authority for clarification if there are aspects of the proposed transaction which are not fully covered by the rules which have been established.

Normally any securitisation transaction will involve a very large number of professional parties, each of whom will be critically examining the structure from a variety of perspectives. The rating agencies will require that the legal and tax advisers of the transaction manager provide written opinions on the efficacy of the structure, before they in turn will issue any formal or informal credit rating. Furthermore, the credit enhancer, who is primarily at risk in the transaction, and its advisers will also need to be fully satisfied. It is the plethora of interested professionals involved which provides the prime safeguard against the risks of structuring errors.

OPERATIONAL RISKS

While much of the above has focused on credit risk, the risks relating to the operations of the SPV cannot be neglected. The SPV typically remains dependent on the originator for all collections relating to the assets which it acquires, so it is critical that the securitiser pays full attention to the SPV's exposure to the operational procedures of the originator.

If the securitisation being contemplated is a single originator transaction, it is likely that the originator may manage the SPV. In a multi-originator programme the SPV is usually operated by its sponsor.

Management Systems and Controls

Whichever party operates the SPV, its computer systems must carry much of the burden since securitisation calls for the processing of vast amounts of data. Good systems decrease both operating risks and expense. The systems will need to support the following functions:

1. *Portfolio structuring:* automatically eliminating ineligible receivables, calculating concentrations and producing statistical information on the receivables purchased.
2. *Administering the SPV:* managing its debt, interest rate swaps and foreign exchange payments, effecting cash movements, and managing its accounts.
3. *Portfolio monitoring:* regularly providing all relevant parties with details of all the outstanding receivables sold to the SPV and statistical information on their performance.
4. *Financial reporting on all of the functional activities undertaken by the SPV:* permitting proper audit and control.
5. *Treasury management for the SPV:* which is especially important if the SPV is financing its assets by rolling over short-term securities, such as Commercial Paper (CP), and/or operating in markets involving different currencies, funding maturities or interest rate bases.

Regular Audits

All the risks relating to credit are largely evaluated on the strength of information provided by the originator. It is essential, therefore, to protect the SPV from being exposed to the risks relating to the integrity of the information being provided by the originator by ensuring that appropriate monitoring and control procedures have been put in place.

To minimise these risks all SPVs recruit the services of external auditors to check the integrity of the information provided at the initiation of the transaction and to perform the annual audit thereafter. Multi-originator programme managers usually have their own in-house audit team in addition to performing spot checks to ensure that:

- the assets purchased conform with the specified criteria;
- the documentation relating to the assets remains satisfactory and that the terms of trade have not changed; and
- the cash flows from the securitised receivables are being properly handled and accounted for by the originator.

FINANCIAL RISKS

The way in which the financial risks relating to obligor credit are handled have already been discussed. All securitisations structures, though, also have to cope with other important financial risks. These include:

- liquidity risks;
- pre-payment risks;
- interest rate risks;
- foreign exchange risks; and
- cash reinvestment risks.

Each of these areas of risk is considered below.

Liquidity Risks

Typically a bank will provide the SPV with a liquidity line which can be drawn upon to cover the risk of cash flow shortages arising as a result of delinquencies. Its size will be determined by the structurer in liaison with the rating agencies in the light of the historical performance statistics of the portfolio. It will also take into account the structural features of the deal and how rapidly the SPV may be able to realise cash in the event of originator bankruptcy.

In a transaction which is being funded by rolling over uncommitted funding, such as Commercial Paper, the rating agencies will require 100 percent liquidity cover for the assets to provide alternative funding in the event of the SPV being able to access the CP market.

Pre-payment Risk

For transactions involving term financial receivables, such as mortgages or consumer credit, prepayment risk becomes of increasing importance and structuring the debt side of the transaction becomes more critical. Cash flow modeling for such transactions then becomes a significant exercise for the securitiser in determining the structure of the transaction.

Pre-payment risk can be catered for in the earlier years of a transaction by allowing the surplus cash flows to be immediately reinvested in the purchase of further assets from the originator. Once the substitution period is over, pre-payment risk has to be absorbed in the structure of the transaction. Surplus cash from pre-payments must either be reinvested in a guaranteed investment contract (see below), or it must be utilised to retire some of the underlying debt early.

Alternatively several tranches of debt, each with different expected terms, interest rates, levels of subordination and algorithms for principal amortisation can be structured into the transaction. Many structures have now appeared with fast, medium and slow pay tranches of debt. In such structures, usually only one tranche, typically the slow pay (longest maturity) tranche actually carries any significant pre-payment risk, since if assets initially allocated to faster paying tranches pre-pay early they will be substituted by assets from slower paying tranches, thereby transferring all the pre-payment risk to the final tranche. It is this flexibility in debt structuring that can allow a securitiser to spread maturity risk efficiently among various investors for differentials in return, thereby maximising the financial efficiency gain from disintermediation.

Interest Rate Risks

SPV's need to be sheltered from any potential interest exposure rate arising from mismatches between the bases on which interest accrues on the assets and on the associated funding. Such risks may arise because the securitiser decides that in order to obtain the best possible economics for the transaction it is desirable for the SPV to fund fixed rate receivables, for example, by issuing a floating rate note.

The SPV will then need to be protected from interest rate risk by entering into interest rate swap arrangements, either with the originator or with third parties. Interest rate caps and collars have also been successfully used to limit interest rate exposure. It may be necessary for such swaps to have amortising principal balances which are able to be varied to take account of pre-payment experience so as to match perfectly the amortisation of the underlying assets.

The rating agencies require that risk exposure of the SPV to any such mismatches arising from the interest rate exposure be eliminated in the structure to the maximum extent possible, and that the counterparties to any swaps must carry credit ratings of at least the same quality as the debt issued by the SPV, or the arrangements will need to be guaranteed by a suitably rated counterparty. They will also insist that all such arrangements must be uncancelable by the counterparties. If the SPV is left with even the smallest amount of residual exposure to interest rate movements as a result of an imperfect hedge, the rating agencies will require that the sizing of the credit enhancement be increased to fully cover the exposure.

Foreign Exchange Risks

The same principles are applied by the rating agencies to foreign exchange risks, from which they also require that the SPV should be fully sheltered. Potential foreign exchange exposure could arise, for instance, if the structurer were to decide to fund a portfolio of short-term sterling trade receivables, for instance, by the issuance of U.S. dollar denominated CP because of the depth and strength of that market.

If the funding is of a short-term nature, foreign exchange risk can be eliminated by the SPV engaging in spot and forward foreign exchange transactions arranged to match precisely the issuance and maturity of the securities. However, for long-term fundings matching currency swaps will be required to be arranged with suitably rated counterparties. These may need to be specially tailored with amortising principal balances similar to those of the interest rate swaps described above.

Cash Reinvestment Risks

If any cash receipts arising from the receivables are retained by the SPV for any significant period, arrangements will need to be put in place to relieve the SPV of any interest rate exposure relating to its surplus cash balances. Typically, such cash will be put into a guaranteed investment contract ("GIC") provided by a suitably rated bank from the date on which the inflow arose until the next date on which there is due to be interest or principal repaid on the funding. The interest rate paid on the GIC balances will typically be directly linked to, and about 25 to 50 basis points less than, the rate being paid by the SPV on its funding during the period of the deposit.

In circumstances where the funding is being obtained for the SPV by the frequent issuance of short-term paper of varying maturity, the use of a fixed periodicity GIC would not be practical, so cash receipts will need to be invested in interest-earning deposits until they can next be utilised. The mismatch risks so arising would then have to be absorbed by the provision of additional credit enhancement to the transaction.

RISKS IN MULTI-ORIGINATOR PROGRAMMES

Multi-originator programmes usually raise their funds in a way which provides for maximum flexibility to cater for the differing requirements and characteristics of the individual originators and their respective portfolios. Most obtain their funding through the Commercial Paper markets, but some are now being structured so as also to have access to the Medium Term Note markets. Since most of the funding of a programme will thus be of short-term nature, the SPV will require regular access to the markets to refinance its assets. The debt funding obtained by such programmes usually carries a top quality credit rating, which, to a large extent, arises from the credit status of the institution(s) providing the credit enhancement and stand-by liquidity lines, and, to a rather lesser extent, on the underlying assets in, and the structure of, the programme. The larger programmes are able to obtain a marginal reduction in their costs from economies of scale.

There are inevitably some risks to individual originators participating in such programmes. If the relative funding costs incurred by the programme rise, the expected residual cash flows from their securitised assets will diminish. An increase in programme funding costs could be brought about as a result of:

- a downgrading of the credit rating of the institution providing the underlying credit enhancement to the programme;
- market conditions adversely affecting the terms on which funding is regularly being obtained; or
- the performance of other asset portfolios in the programme deteriorating sufficient to cause the rating agencies to downgrade the programme's credit rating.

Because of the continuously revolving and relatively short-term nature of the funding in multi-originator programmes, the residual income stream flowing back to the participants will be directly affected if the cost of the short-term funding being obtained by the programme were to rise relative to market rates.

The most significant risk, therefore, to an originator participating in a programme is that of a downgrading of the credit rating of the programme's credit enhancer. Some programmes seek to avoid this risk by arranging for the programme-wide layer of credit enhancement to be provided either by way of a cash deposit or by the guarantee of a monoline insurance company, or a combination thereof. In other programmes where the credit enhancement is provided by way of a letter of credit drawn on the sponsoring bank, a participating originator has to take the view that the probability of a downgrading of its credit status is insignificant.

The cost of a programme's funding can be affected adversely by market sentiment. In 1991, for instance, the market took fright when legislative changes in the United States were threatened which might have capped interest rate charges on card credit, and accordingly the funding costs of those programmes which were financing credit card assets rose, with immediate adverse consequences for the programmes' participants.

There are also potential contamination risks in multi-originator programmes which are not present in single originator securitisation transactions. An originator participating in a programme needs to be reasonably certain that the potential future income flows arising from his securitised portfolio will not be diminished or jeopardised if problems arise with another portfolio in the programme. Protection against contamination risk is achieved in the more modern structures emerging by ensuring that:

- limited recourse arrangements are built into the programme's legal structure to isolate the assets of each portfolio from any external party enforcing security over other assets in the programme;
- triggers preventing future asset substitutions are in place to limit the SPV incurring further exposure to portfolios which have started to deteriorate;
- each individual portfolio has both internal reserves (or originator recourse) and/or a layer of portfolio-specific credit enhancement provided by a third party which is designed to eradicate virtually the highest expected possible level of losses related to that particular portfolio;
- a layer of programme-wide credit enhancement is provided on which any constituent portfolio may draw if extraordinary losses are incurred beyond the cover provided by its portfolio-specific layer (the provider of

such programme-wide layer of credit enhancement only having recourse to future income streams from the specific portfolio which has incurred the losses); and

- liquidity lines are available to support all the remaining performing receivables in the programme if funding were to become impossible to obtain in the capital markets.

Whilst the above mechanisms go a long way towards limiting the contamination risk, all multi-originator programmes remain exposed to fraud or severe default problems arising from an originator bankruptcy being encountered in one of their constituent portfolios. Such an event could cause the rating agencies to downgrade the credit rating of the programme, with a consequent adverse effect on the availability and cost of its funding. Since originators are not obliged to continue to sell additional assets into a programme, their exposure would be limited to a reduction in, or annihilation of, the anticipated residual future cash flows from assets which they have already sold into the programme. The remaining originators are also always at liberty to negotiate the repurchase of their assets from the programme, so in practice their risk is negligible. It is likely that if such circumstances did occur, the programme's sponsor would very rapidly take action to restructure or wind down the programme.

The recent growth in multi-originator programmes would appear to demonstrate that originators are persuaded that the advantages outweigh the potential risks. Such advantages include:

- significantly lower front-end legal, transaction and systems costs, providing an ability to securitise economically smaller portfolios;
- economies of scale reducing both funding rates and the costs associated with the various supporting financial facilities;
- flexibility regarding the volume and nature of the assets which are able to be sold or substituted into the programme in the future; and
- the anonymity obtained by an originator when securitisation is undertaken in this manner.

SUMMARY

There are many risks in a securitisation transaction. Each risk has to be identified and dealt with in the structure. All this perhaps goes some way to explaining why securitisation transactions, particularly those involving an asset type in a jurisdiction where such a transaction has not been attempted before, take a lot of time to put together and tend to be very expensive to execute.

In spite of the current difficulties that the securitisation industry in Europe is facing from the variety of legal, fiscal and regulatory systems, it has proved possible for the professionals to devise satisfactory structures catering for all the risks for various asset types in most of the major European countries.

As a result, the economic benefits that these techniques can bring to originators, both financial and industrial, are becoming better and more widely known. It is clear now that the securitisation industry in Europe is now beginning to follow the same trends that have been observed in the United States. Securitisation in Europe is about to come into bloom.

Chapter 9

Auto Loan Securitization: A Case Study of the U.S. Auto Finance Industry

by Gary J. Kopff,
President,
Heritage Management Ltd.[1]

"Securitization" is the process through which financial institutions sell or finance assets by transforming them into more liquid securities. Seller/servicers are typically banks, thrifts, finance, and insurance companies. The asset-backed securities, typically AAA or AA rated, are sold by public offerings or private placements into the domestic or global capital markets. Investors are predominately institutions, although a retail market is evolving, and some retail investors do participate through funds in the asset-backed securities market. Over the past 25 years, as the dollar value for securities issued has grown to over $1.400 trillion, securitization has fundamentally transformed the way U.S. financial institutions manage their businesses. Among the businesses transformed by securitization is the financing of automobile loans. Seven years after the initial auto loan securitization, 11 percent of the $258 billion of outstanding auto loans are securitized in at least 212 transactions.[2]

This chapter, will (1) provide the historic context for auto loan securitization; (2) analyze the use of securitization as a strategic tool in the competition between finance companies and banks to finance loans and leases for automobiles, trucks, and recreation vehicles; and (3) examine the underwriters, legal vehicles, debt instruments, credit enhancement, pricing, transaction size, and geographic concentration.

HISTORIC CONTEXT

In the U.S., securitization has evolved over the past 25 years in three stages:

1 Heritage Management Ltd. is a financial advisory firm specializing in securitization. Prior to forming the firm, Mr. Kopff served at Strategic Planning Associates as Partner-in-Charge of the Securitization Practice, which he founded. He also consulted for many years with McKinsey & Company and headed Policy Development at Fannie Mae. Clientele served by Mr. Kopff over the past five years include:

- the largest banks in the U.S., Asia, and France
- 2 of the leading U.S. property and casualty insurance companies
- 1 leading U.S. life insurance company
- 1 of the top 5 U.S. investment banks
- 1 of the top 5 U.S. asset managers
- 1 of the top 5 U.S. finance companies
- 1 of the top 5 U.S. real estate development companies
- 1 of the top 5 U.S. securitization conduits
- 1 of the top 3 U.S. property management/disposition companies
- privately owned banks in the Caribbean and in Pennsylvania

2 Dollar total from Federal Reserve Statistical Release G.19, June 9, 1992; transaction total from Heritage Management, Ltd.

Phase I (1968–85) Mortgage-Backed Securities

Prior to 1968, "conventional" (non-FHA/VA) mortgages were originated by banks and thrifts and funded primarily with consumer deposits insured by the U.S. government. Mortgage bankers also originated mortgages for sale to institutional investors, such as insurance companies, and they originated FHA/VA mortgages which they sold to the Federal National Mortgage Association ("Fannie Mae")—then a part of the U.S. government.

In 1968, Congress restructured Fannie Mae, which had operated since the 1930s, to create a congressional charter for a *private*, shareholder-owned, NYSE-listed company. Concurrently, Congress created a *public* corporation, Government National Mortgage Association ("Ginnie Mae"), within the U.S. Department of Housing and Urban Development.

As a *private* entity, Fannie Mae continued to pursue a *portfolio strategy* throughout the 1970s as if it were a *super*-thrift or *super*-bank. Fannie Mae borrowed funds in the short/intermediate-term capital markets and invested the proceeds by purchasing long-term, fixed rate mortgages. The borrowings, however, were not in the form of consumer deposits, like at banks and thrifts, but were debt raised in a specialized segment of the capital markets known as the agency markets.

As a *public* entity, Ginnie Mae was created to execute a *securitization strategy*—that is, to provide the absolute guarantee of the U.S. government to credit enhance pools of FHA/VA mortgages, which could then be sold into the capital markets. Unable to compete with the AAA-rated securities, portfolio lenders like Fannie Mae, banks, and thrifts gradually withdrew from the FHA/VA market as portfolio investors and served instead as fee participants earning income for *originating* and *servicing* the mortgages, but not *funding* them on their balance sheets. As of March 31, 1992, Ginnie Mae had outstanding guarantees of $421 billion for mortgage-backed securities.

A parallel development emerged in the "conventional" or non-FHA/VA mortgage market as Freddie Mac in 1972 and Fannie Mae in 1982 introduced a form of credit enhanced securitization that was similar to Ginnie Mae mortgage-backed securities, except that it applied to non-FHA/VA mortgages. Both entities provided guarantees that were deemed equal or superior to AAA ratings. Banks and thrifts gradually responded by withdrawing from competition in *funding* long-term, fixed rate mortgages as they and others transformed their business strategies to *originate* and *service* such mortgages while Fannie Mae and Freddie Mac earned fees by providing credit enhancement for the pools that were sold into the capital markets.

In the early 1980s, when I led the Policy Development staff at Fannie Mae, the number one strategic issue for the company was whether to continue to serve as a *portfolio investor*—borrowing short in the agency market and lending long for fixed-rate mortgages—or as a *credit enhancer* for securitized pools, or to perform a combination of both roles. The strategy executed over the past decade was to combine both roles. Initially, Fannie Mae set as a target the achievement of equal amounts of mortgages held on its balance sheet and guaranteed in securitized pools by reducing the portfolio and/or increasing guaranty levels. As of April 30, 1992, Fannie Mae held $136 billion on its balance sheet and had outstanding guarantees of nearly three times that level—$390 billion—for mortgage-backed securities.

Freddie Mac took the opposite approach. For nearly 20 years, it served exclusively as a *credit enhancer* of mortgage-backed securities, which it termed *participation certificates.* Recently, Freddie Mac has expanded its balance sheet holding of mortgage loans. As of March 31, 1992, Freddie Mac had outstanding guarantees for $372 billion of securities and owned $29 billion of mortgages.

Congress has responded to concern by certain private institutions that Fannie Mae and Freddie Mac would dominate the entire mortgage market. Congress has for years set a ceiling on the maximum dollar value of any individual mortgage that the entities could either own or guarantee. Mortgages above this ceiling, which is revised upwards annually, are termed *jumbo* or *super-jumbo* mortgages. These so-called *non-conforming* mortgages (which do not conform to Fannie Mae/Freddie Mac guidelines due to mortgage amount or other terms) constitute about 25 percent of the home mortgage market. Therefore, the final element in the securitization of fixed-rate mortgages was the development of a securitization market for these jumbo mortgages. As of June 30, 1992, the major securitization players in this market included such firms as Prudential Home, Residential Funding Corporation, Citicorp, Ryland Mortgage, Capstead Mortgage, Chase, Sears, Lehman Brothers, and GE Capital.

Collectively, as of June 30, 1992, the market for residential mortgage-backed securities issued by Ginnie Mae, Fannie Mae, Freddie Mac, and other private companies exceeded $1.2 trillion.

Figure 9.1—Asset-Backed Securities Issued Annually, 1985–91
Total = $299 Billion

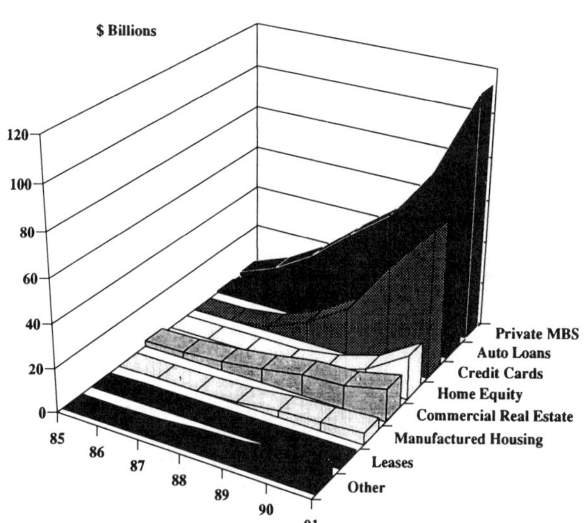

Phase II (1985–90) Asset Diversification

In Phase II, the dominant trend in U.S. securitization was the diversification in asset types from residential home mortgages to various types of consumer and business receivables. After about seven years, over $200 billion has been issued. The market is substantially smaller than the $1.2+ trillion *residential* mortgage-backed securities market for two major reasons. First, credit enhancement is derived from *private* entities and various structuring techniques, rather than from the U.S. government or government-sponsored agencies like Fannie Mae and Freddie Mac. And second, the assets generally lack the standardized terms that characterize U.S. home mortgages.[3]

As of December 31, 1991, the *largest* segment of the asset-backed securities market,—*exclusive* of the Ginnie Mae/Fannie Mae/Freddie Mac government/quasi-government segment—was credit card receivables ($68 billion). The next largest segment was loans/leases for the purchase of automobiles, trucks, and recreation vehicles ($66 billion). However, in early 1992 the order reversed as auto loan transactions surged ahead of credit cards (Figure 9.1).

Securitization was also employed at far lower dollar levels for other types of *consumer* debt—e.g., home equity loans, second mortgages, student loans, and insurance policy loans—as well as *business* debt. The dominant business debt securitized was trade receivables, typically funded with commercial paper and not shown in the illustration above. Additional business assets securitized include commercial real estate mortgages; high-yield ("junk") bonds; equipment leases (computer, health, airplanes); commercial/industrial loans; and health care receivables.

Phase III (1990s) Global Securitization

In the late 1980s and early 1990s, securities issued by Ginnie Mae, Fannie Mae, and Freddie Mac were marketed by investment bankers to institutional investors throughout the world. The guarantee of the U.S. government—or Fannie Mae and Freddie Mac as government-sponsored entities, which are perceived as essentially government—made these securities a higher-yielding alternative to U.S. Treasury bonds for many investors. However, a risk premium was exacted for the fact that the securities were not *precisely* the same as Treasuries and for the uncertainty associated with the maturity of pass-through securities. In a few

3 Moreover, the level of *outstanding* securities is lower than the $200+ billion estimate for *total securities issued* because most of the non-mortgage transaction asset pools have short lives (*e.g.*, 2 years for credit cards, 5 years for auto loans) and, consequently, the transactions in the 1985–90 period were largely or partially paid off by mid-1992.

cases, securities were denominated in currencies other than U.S. dollars to reduce currency risk for the investors.

The second trend in the globalization of securitization was prompted by the Basle Accord affecting required capital for all commercial banks in the OECD nations. Not only were the capital requirements increased, but they were also applied differently among several classes of risk. For example, automobile loans were deemed twice as risky as home mortgages, so twice the amount of capital must be applied to those assets when held in portfolio. In both the U.S., where securitization was already a well-established financing technique, and in other banks throughout the world, asset sales through securitization were being viewed increasingly as an attractive strategic response to the Basle Accord.

ISSUERS OF AUTO LOAN SECURITIES

Financing of automobile loans in the United States prior to 1985 involved the creation of chattel paper primarily by commercial banks and the finance subsidiaries of the "Big Three" U.S. auto manufacturers—General Motors Acceptance Corporation ("GMAC"), Chrysler Finance Corporation ("CFC") and Ford Motor Credit ("Ford Credit"). In addition, loans were made by some thrifts, credit unions, and other financial institutions. The U.S. auto finance business includes three major segments, according to Federal Reserve statistics.[4]

1. Market Share: Banks versus Finance Companies

Banks and finance companies compete to finance auto loans. The finance companies initially may not have viewed themselves in competition. Their primary mission was to support their parent companies—the "Big Three" U.S. auto manufacturers—to sell their own newly built automobiles. The major finance companies still do not compete for loans for all types of automobiles, as do commercial banks, because they focus their capital on the support of the products of their parent companies. However, the *origination* and *servicing* of auto loans can be a profitable business by itself—independent of supporting the parent company sales of vehicles. The profitability is highly dependent on three success factors: (a) careful underwriting to manage losses, (b) effective servicing of delinquent loans, and (c) achieving scale operations in performing the origination/servicing functions.

While Federal Reserve data report banks as the larger of the two primary sources of auto loans, if we allocate the securitized transactions by seller/servicer, estimate the outstanding pool amounts by issuer type, and then reexamine the market share over the past 20 or so years, we observe that banks' market share has declined significantly from 62 percent in 1970 to 44 percent in 1991, while finance companies have increased from 25 percent in 1970 to 32 percent in 1991 (Figure 9.2).[5]

The shift in market share is attributable to a lower rate of growth for banks in the 1985–91 period with no growth in 1990 and an absolute decrease in 1991. This decrease may be due both to the concern with credit quality during a period of recession as well as the requirement for many major banks to achieve higher risk-based capital ratios to meet new regulations. These risk-based capital regulations treat auto loans as a 100 percent risk-weight category, which requires, for example, twice the capital allocation as most home mortgages. At least two major banks that were active as national lenders in the auto loan business—Citicorp and Marine Midland—withdrew from the business.

Finance companies during this same period significantly increased their level of total assets serviced from portfolio and securitized financings, although the level has fallen off in 1990–91. Their growth during this period may be due in large measure both to their mission of supporting the sales of new vehicles manufactured by their parent companies as well as the absence of federal regulations on their capitalization. The decline in the last two years is due to balance sheet reductions, as credit ratings have dropped for the finance companies and their parent automobile manufacturers due to recessionary problems affecting the industry. The securitization levels increased dramatically to offset partially the reduction in portfolios on the balance sheet.

Figure 9.3 illustrates the *rate of growth* since 1985 with 1985 levels = 100. Finance companies grew total assets (portfolio and securitized) at 62 percent compared to 40 percent for banks.

---

4 Federal Reserve Statistical Release G.19, June 9, 1992.

5 The finance company market share in 1990–92 may be understated since the Heritage Management estimates of outstanding auto loan pools assumed a 20 percent paydown per year for all auto loan pools securitized since 1985.

Figure 9.2—Share of Auto Loans (Portfolio and Securitized)

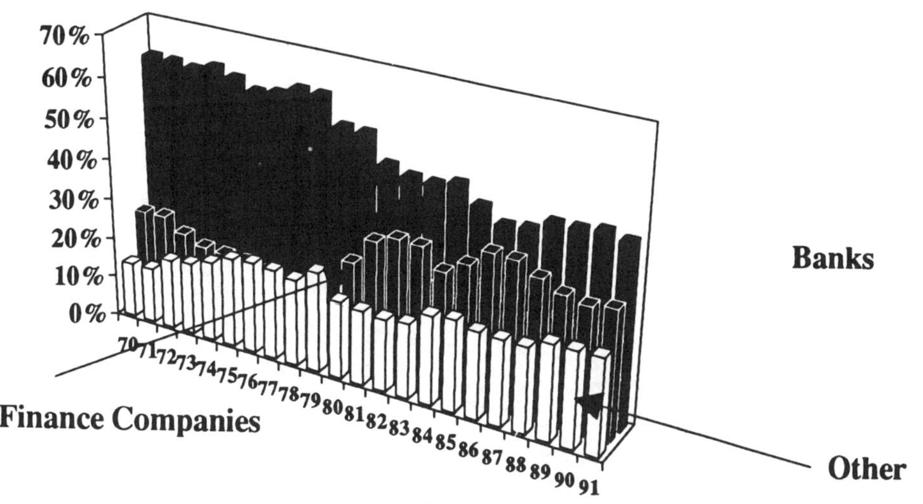

However, the finance companies substantially outpaced the banks in auto loan securitization growth.

Prior to 1985, the auto finance companies funded their purchase of loans from their dealers exclusively by issuing debt. With the backing of their parent companies, the debt was generally rated AA or better. Banks and thrifts, on the other hand, funded their loans with federally insured consumer deposits. After 1985, as the finance subsidiaries of the "Big Three" U.S. auto manufacturers—GMAC, CFC and Ford Credit—and a few other finance companies began to employ securitization to complement balance sheet funded ac-

Figure 9.3—Growth Since 1985 in Total Bank Financings versus Finance Companies

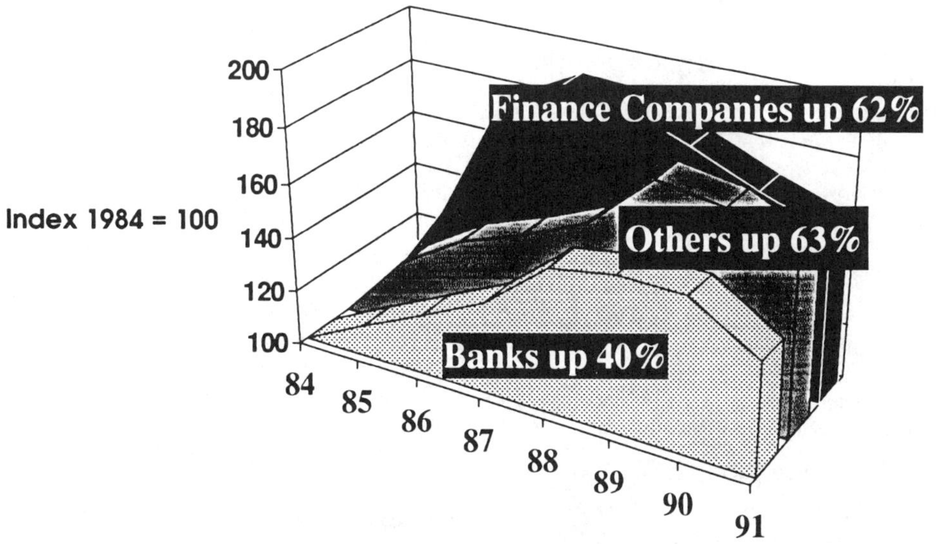

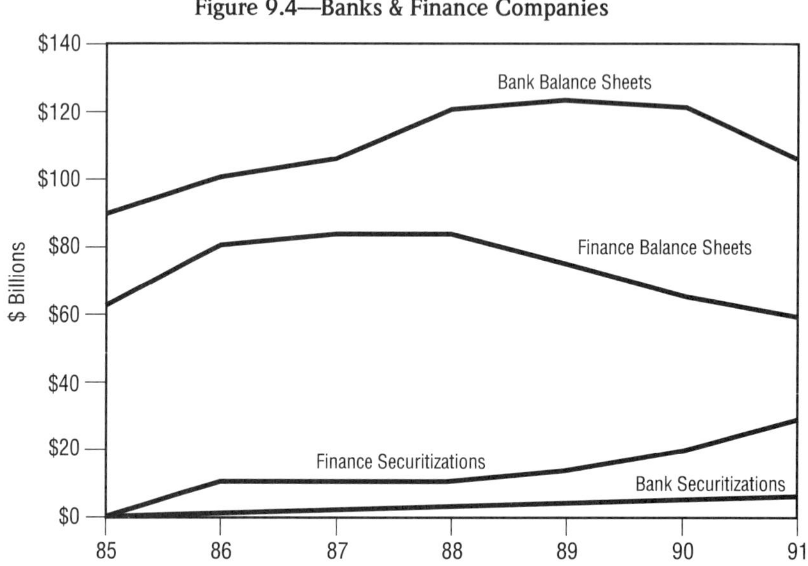

quisitions, their segment of the industry grew faster than commercial banks. As a result of the aggressive securitization strategy employed by finance companies, they have as a group made substantial progress in gaining market share at the expense of the commercial banks (Figure 9.4).

In projecting outstanding balances for auto loan securitization pools, we have assumed that (a) all transactions are executed as of the first of each year, and (b) all pools pay down 20 percent per year for five years. This conservative projection may understate the outstanding pool balances.

In addition to the market share growth by finance companies, at the expense of banks, the other participants in the industry almost doubled their market share from 14 percent in 1970 to 23 percent in 1991. Much of this increase was also due to utilizing a securitization strategy to grow the assets serviced faster than could be supported by the equity base if the assets were funded on the institutions' balance sheets.

In the next section, we analyze why firms that originate and service assets may favor securitization over funding with consumer deposits or issuance of debt. In the following section, we will examine the individual issuers of the 212 auto loan securitizations totaling $78.3 billion that were brought to market from 1985 through mid-1992.

2. Objectives Served by Securitization

In our experience working with banks, thrifts, finance, and insurance companies, securitization becomes a corporate objective when one or more of the goals listed in Figure 9.5 can be met.

The extent to which these objectives pertain varies from issuer to issuer, but some general comments may be useful.

Improve capital ratios. This objective is most pertinent to a few money center and super-regional banks that are sizable participants in the auto finance industry but which are restructuring to comply with the phased-in, risk-based capital regulations. Marine Midland Bank, Citicorp, Chemical, and Security Pacific (now merged with Bank of America) are all within this category. The finance companies do not have regulatory capital ratios; however, the rating agencies perform a similar function. Consequently, the major "captive" auto finance companies have favored securitization because it reduces the leverage that would otherwise contribute adversely to the assessments made by the rating agencies.

Reduce "all-in costs." For some institutions that are highly analytical in measuring profitability—including adjusting for gapping profits/losses and reflecting capital charges and taxes—the "all-in" cost of capital is almost always lower for securitization than funding on the balance sheet. Exceptions might include over-capitalized institutions whose allocated charge is low for equity capital.

Reduce interest rate risk. Most banks do not "match-fund" their auto loans—i.e., the loans are

Figure 9.5

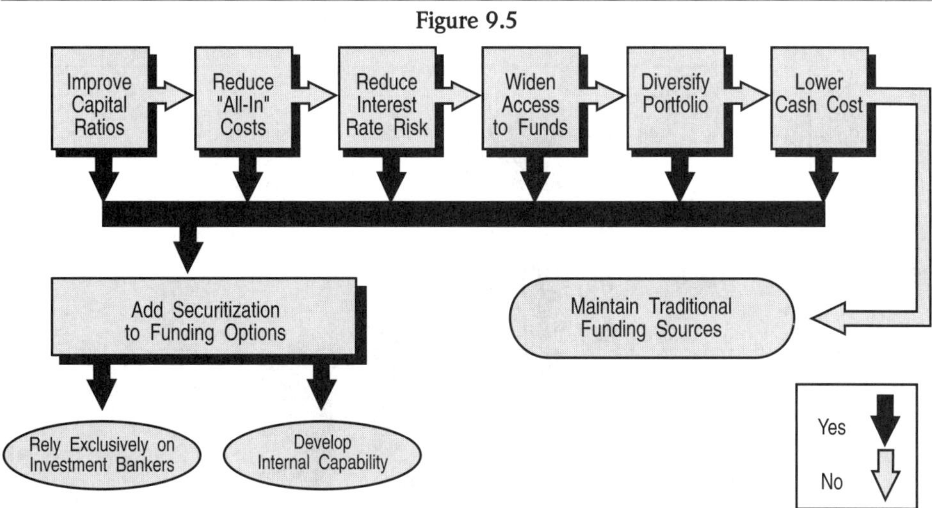

typically fixed rate and five years in maturity, whereas the liabilities are short-term consumer deposits. The resulting maturity mismatch or "gap" can result in "gapping" profits or losses, depending upon how the movement of interest rates affects their liabilities over the life of the loans. These profits or losses are not inherently part of the auto loan business, and an institution seeking to make interest rate "bets" can often do so better with hedge vehicles unrelated to making consumer loans. Accordingly, some banks favor securitization because it eliminates the risk associated with the maturity mismatch for these assets.

Finance companies that would short-fund with commercial paper may favor securitization as a way to secure stable servicing fees and avoid interest rate sensitivities. Others match-fund their loans to eliminate interest rate risk.

Widen access to funds. For Chrysler Financial, the loss of its investment grade rating made it mandatory to widen its access to funds by securitizing auto loan receivables. GMAC may have a similar motivation, although its A-rating still affords them entry to traditional investment grade debt markets. If the A-1 short-term rating were to drop to A-2—as typically would accompany a long-term rating drop to A–, then GMAC would have an even greater imperative to use securitization to widen its access to funds for its auto loan portfolio. Ford sees securitization as a healthy alternative to widen its access to funds, although its ratings are less inhospitable at the present time.

Diversify portfolio. Some of the finance companies diversify as a matter of business strategy, and auto loan securitization enables them to support affiliated auto manufacturers with their sales efforts and earn servicing fees but avoid concentrated risk exposure. Similarly, some banks that have made a major strategic commitment to the auto loan business and are seeking scale in servicing may want to minimize the risk exposure by securitizing some or all of the assets. Marine Midland in the latter half of the 1980s is a good example of this situation.

Lower cash costs. Some institutions ignore the cost of equity capital and measure performance exclusively on a net interest margin basis. In some cases, the securitization may afford lower-cost debt, net of credit enhancement fees and transaction costs.

3. Issuers of Securitized Auto Loans

In the early 1980s, leading investment banks had substantial capacity for home mortgage securitization, including investment bankers, traders, and specialized staff with modeling and other quantitative analysis expertise. These firms were highly motivated to extend the highly successful and profitable techniques of securitization from home mortgages to other asset types, including auto loans.

Marine Midland Bank. Salomon Brothers who, together with First Boston, had dominated the securitization of residential mortgages by Fannie Mae and Freddie Mac, was selected by Marine

Figure 9.6—Marine Midland Securitized Auto Loans

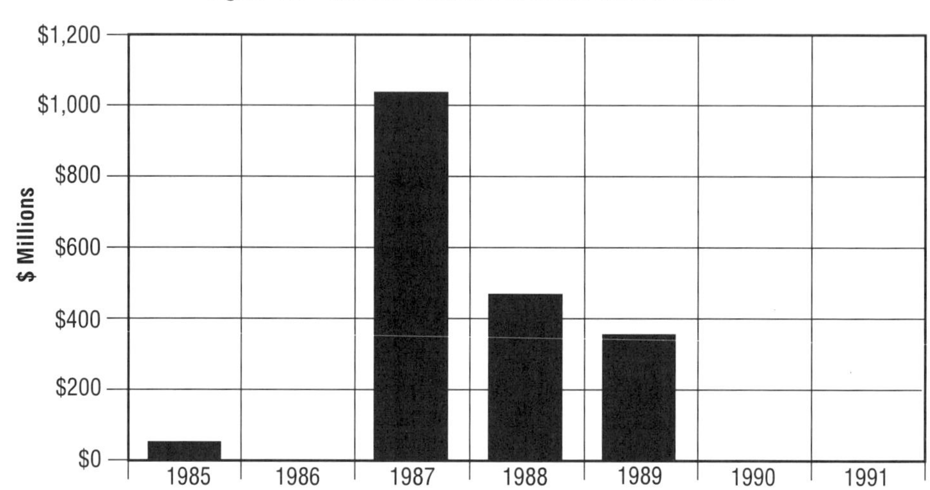

Midland Bank in May 1985 to introduce the initial securitization backed by a pool of retail installment sales contracts for the purchase of automobiles. *Marine Midland 1985-1 CARS Trust* was a public offering of $60.2 million of pass-through securities, rated AAA by Standard & Poor's, with a coupon rate at 9.63 percent and an offering discount that provided investors 9.73 percent—37.5 basis points over the 2-year Treasury rate then in effect.

Marine Midland Bank was a major issuer of securitized auto loans from 1985–89 as it sought to grow into the dominant bank originating and servicing auto loans nationwide, funding the expansion largely off its balance sheet with securitization. This business strategy was a key factor in the decision by the Hong Kong Shanghai Banking Corporation to purchase the Marine Midland Bank. Over $1.9 billion in securities were issued before the bank changed its strategy and reduced its commitment to auto loan financing (Figure 9.6).

"Big Three" finance companies.
Securitization has become a competitive strategy employed by finance companies to enable these firms to secure the franchise for profitable origination and servicing fees. The lessons from the prior decade with the securitization of home mortgages seem to have been well learned by the finance companies. They benefit from a weak regulatory environment that facilitates their use of securitization, particularly the use of senior/subordinated structures in which the subordinated tranches are held (at least initially) by the finance companies. Banks are penalized by their regulators if they employ a similar strategy. The dominant finance companies are the "Big Three," led by Chrysler Finance Corp., yet many others have also securitized auto loans (Figure 9.7).

Commercial banks. Of the $78.3 billion cumulative auto loan securities issued, banks were responsible for only 17 percent. Seven banks dominate bank securitizations, although the seven banks in total constitute only 9.5 percent of total auto loan securitizations (Figure 9.8)

Thrifts. The leading thrift in the auto loan securitization business, Western Financial Savings Bank, has come to the market 18 times for a total of $2.512 billion. The firm was aided in its securitization strategy by Drexel Burnham before its demise, and thereafter by the same team after they switched from Drexel to Donaldson Lufkind Jenrette (Figure 9.9).

Truck manufacturers. Aside from banks and thrifts and the finance subsidiaries of the auto manufacturers, other firms in the securitization market are the finance subsidiaries of major truck manufacturers. A total of $900 million of truck receivables was securitized in 1987–90 by Mack Truck and Navistar.

Since 1960, Mack Financial Corporation has operated as a wholly owned financial subsidiary of Mack Trucks, Inc. The parent company, owned since 1990 by Renault, is a major manufacturer of heavy-duty trucks and engines that it sells and distributes in 65 countries. The finance subsidiary funds retail purchases of new and used, medium-

Figure 9.7—Three Dominant Issuers of Auto Loan Securities

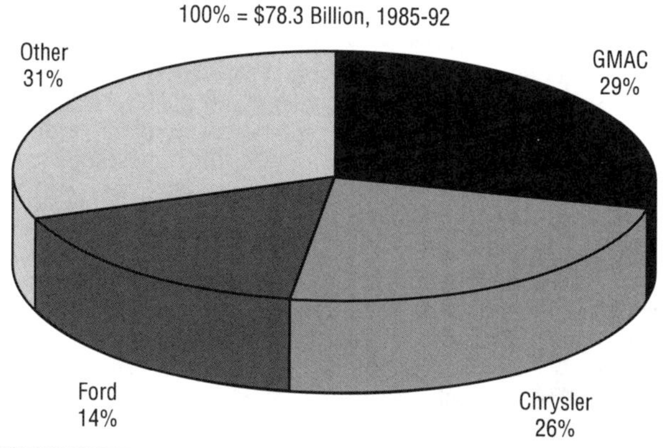

Figure 9.8—Major Banks Securitizing Auto Loans

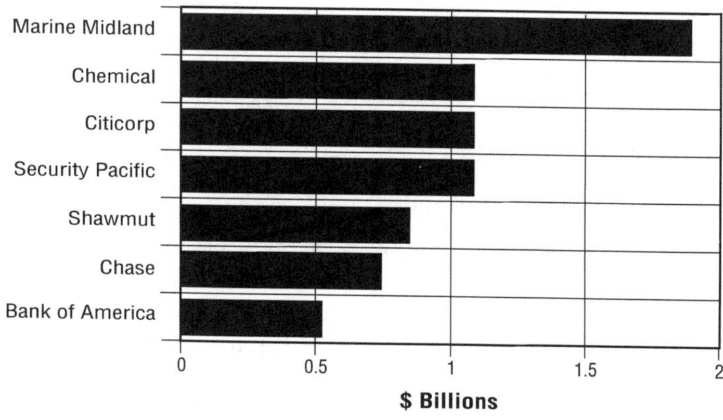

Figure 9.9—Auto Securitizations by Western Financial Savings Bank

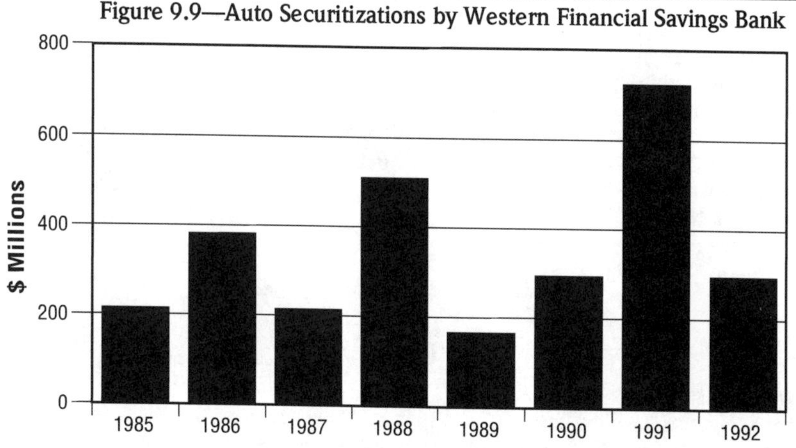

and heavy-duty trucks as well as wholesale distributor floor plans. Mack favors asset-backed securitization because Mack Trucks, Inc., does not have an investment grade rating and because securitization produces a better match of assets and liabilities and a reliable source of competitively priced funds.[6] The firm was concerned about being the first truck company to enter the securitization market. Firm officials found the transactions to be highly complex, and they were concerned about the potential inconvenience to customers as well as their own administrative operations. Their securitization vehicle, known as TRUCS (Truck Receivables Underlying Certificates), has a pay-through rather than a pass-through format for three of the four issues, with two tranches with different maturities to appeal to different investor classes. The securities are debt on the balance sheet. A total of $600 million was securitized in three public offerings in 1987–89 and in one private placement—all AAA-rated and all with Shearson Lehman as lead manager. The 13–14 percent credit enhancement level was somewhat high for the industry and may have reflected the greater concern of the rating agency with truck receivables compared to auto receivables.

Navistar is a prime competitor of Mack Trucks. It has securitized manufacturer wholesale dealer notes, bank floor planning, and manufacturer floor planning assets. In 1990, Navistar securitized $300 million of truck receivables in three public offerings through Prudential Securities with a senior/subordinated structure and retention by Navistar of the subordinated securities. The 15.5 percent credit enhancement reflected the same concerns as experienced earlier by Mack Trucks. Multiple tranches were indexed to the one-month LIBOR because it is preferred in Europe, and over 30 percent of the issue was marketed in Europe. Prudential Securities' analysis as of September 1991 suggests that the cost for 5-year receivables financing was 8.28 percent, compared to 5-year BB senior debt funding of 10.98 percent (including a capital charge assuming 10 percent equity and 15 percent cost of equity).[7]

The Navistar transaction was followed by Chrysler's CARCO series of securitized financings.

AUTO LOAN SECURITIZATION STRUCTURES

In this section, we examine auto loan securitization structures more closely by analyzing (a) underwriters, (b) legal vehicles, (c) debt instruments, (d) levels of credit enhancement, (e) pricing spreads over 2-year Treasuries, (f) transaction size, and (g) geographic concentration.

Underwriters[8]

First Boston has dominated the auto loan securitization market with an estimated 43 percent market share (dollar-weighted transactions with full credit to lead manager). The firm served as lead manager for 72 of the transactions in our data base, including 9 of the 16 $1+ billion transactions by Ford, Chrysler, and GMAC.

Salomon Brothers introduced the initial auto loan securitization on behalf of Marine Midland Bank in May 1985. The firm continued to serve as lead manager for seven additional Marine Midland transactions through 1989. Its market share was 18 percent and it served as lead manager for two of the $1+ billion transactions for "Big Three" auto finance companies. In addition to Marine Midland, the firm served as lead manager for 10 transactions for Chrysler, seven for GMAC, one for Ford—and individual transactions for Bank of America, Bank Boston, and Home Federal.

Merrill Lynch served as lead manager for three $1+ billion transactions—two for Chrysler and the $1 billion wholesale master trust issue by Ford—as well as smaller transactions for Chrysler and others.

Goldman, Sachs also served as lead manager for two $1+ billion transactions by Ford as well as four individual transactions for banks.

Several of these firms served exclusively or primarily for affiliated companies (e.g., Dean Witter for Sears and Chase Securities for Chase Manhattan Bank) or for a single client (e.g., DLJ for Western Financial Savings Bank) (Figure 9.10).

6 Presentation by Mack Truck officials on February 24, 1992, at IIR *Asset Securitization* Conference in New York.
7 Presentation by Prudential Securities on February 24, 1992, at IIR Asset Securitization Conference in New York.
8 This analysis attributes transactions based upon full credit to lead manager. Some of the transactions in the HML data base do not identify lead manager and, therefore, the analysis is somewhat incomplete.

Figure 9.10—Dealers Share (Full Credit to Lead Manager)

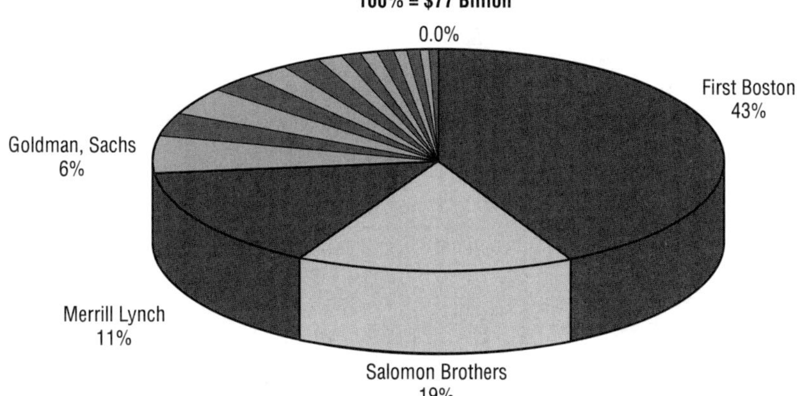

	$Millions	*Share**
First Boston	$33,502	43%
Salomon Brothers	14,581	19%
Merrill Lynch	8,504	11%
Goldman, Sachs	4,536	6%
Bear Stearns	3,408	4%
Chemical Bank	2,794	4%
Drexel Burnham Lambert	1,713	2%
Morgan Stanley	1,648	2%
Donaldson Lufkin Jenrette	1,490	2%
Chase Manhattan Bank	802	1%
Swiss Bank Corp.	650	1%
Citicorp	606	1%
Bankers Trust	575	1%
Shearson Lehman Hutton	573	1%
Prudential	510	1%
Dean Witter	437	1%
Burns Fry	380	0.5%
Kidder Peabody	253	0.3%
Deutsche Bank	150	0.2%
Total	$77,111	100%

*Full Credit to Lead Manager; data not available for $1.2 billion of transactions

Legal Vehicles

The financing of automobile purchases under U.S. law involves "chattel paper," as defined in Article 9 of the U.S. Uniform Commercial Code—namely, "a writing or writings which evidence both a monetary obligation and a security interest in or a lease of specific goods . . . ." Interest in chattel paper may be perfected in one of two ways: (a) by filing a financing statement, or (b) by taking possession of the chattel paper. If a secured party takes possession of chattel paper, its interest in the chattel paper will generally be much more secure than if perfection is obtained solely through filing a financing statement. The UCC treats a sale of chattel paper in the same way as it does a security interest in chattel paper.

Auto loans in the U.S. are typically fixed-rate loans for 2–3 years, although 5-year maturities are increasingly prevalent. Recreational vehicles may be longer than five years. The total principal financed as a percentage of the value is computed using dealer invoice for new cars and the National Automobile Dealers Association Blue Book value for used autos. The original loan/value ratio for a receivables pool is typically below 90 percent.

Auto loans are also differentiated between 24 *direct* and *indirect* financing. With direct financing, the bank or finance company has control of the application process. With indirect financing, the originator (and seller to the securitization structure) is dependent on dealers or other originators for the accuracy and completeness of the credit information submitted by the applicant. In some indirect financing, the lender has recourse back to the dealer or to another third-party in the event of default by the underlying obligor.

In building upon the experience with securitized home mortgages, the auto loan securitization industry adapted several legal and security structures.

Grantor trust. This pass-through vehicle utilizes an old provision under the tax codes to create a single class of investors and allocate principal and interest cash flow to them on a pro rata basis. Variations in the cash flow allocation would threaten the tax-exempt status of the trust itself. The initial auto loan securitization by Marine Midland utilized the grantor trust vehicle because it had been widely employed in home mortgage securitizations.

Master trust. Most recently, major issuers have elected to form master trusts—paralleling a trend in credit card receivables pioneered by Citicorp—in order to link together a series of issues that may have differing terms, conditions, and even ratings while drawing upon a consolidated collateral pool. For example, in February 1992, the Ford Credit Auto Loan Master Trust Series 1992–1 raised $1 billion with this vehicle that also utilized the senior/subordinated structure. Series 2 raised another $700 million. Both transactions involved wholesale financing, unlike the earlier grantor trust vehicles that were for retail financings.

Owners trust. In December 1990, Prudential Securities structured a securitization for Navistar utilizing an owners trust. This approach, like the master trust, was first introduced for credit card securitizations. It permits a revolving purchase of notes, a specific dollar investor portion, and a variable portion to be retained by the seller.

About 18 months later, Chrysler in its Premier Auto Trust 1992–1, 1992–2, 1992–3 and 1992–4 transactions switched from the standard grantor trust to an owners trust. This change affords Chrysler, as it had afforded Navistar, added flexibility to alter cash flows and add new receivables.

Special purpose entity. In 1986–87, the First Boston Corporation used the Auto-Backed Securities Corp. as a "shelf registration" for GMAC ($5.7 billion). This special purpose entity was also used by First Boston in 1987 for several small transactions for GECC ($26 million) and BMW ($106 million). In 1990 Chrysler utilized the shelf in an attempt to widen its access to funds (Figure 9.11).

Another example of a special purpose corporation is the Merrill Lynch Asset-Backed Corporation. This vehicle was created by Merrill Lynch to

Figure 9.11—Asset-Backed Securities Shelf—First Boston

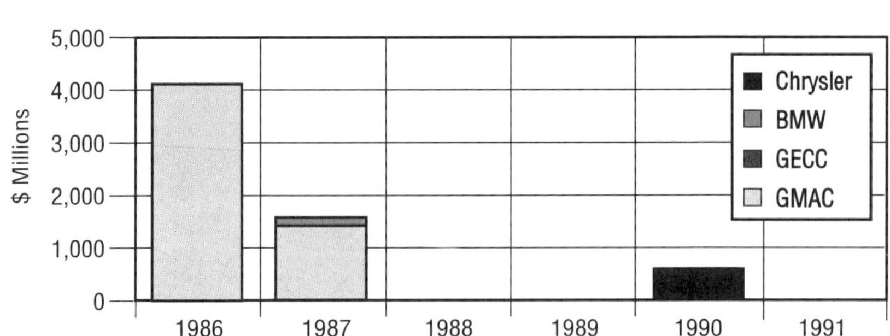

purchase assets from Chrysler and issue senior/subordinated securities for MLABC Automobile Loan Trust 1990-1. The corporation retained ownership of the subordinated securities.

REMIC. Auto loan securitizations cannot utilize the favorable structuring and tax treatment available to mortgages under the statute passed in 1986 for Real Estate Mortgage Investment Conduits ("REMICs").

Debt Instruments

As discussed above, the legal vehicle most widely used is the grantor trust. The securities issued through public offerings by the trusts or special-purpose entities are typically mid-term, fixed rate debt issues. Rarely has commercial paper been used to fund auto loans.

Variable rate debt has been used for a few transactions. Some of these issues were marketed primarily in Europe and utilized variable rate debt pegged to LIBOR—e.g., GMAC 1986-A Euro-Grantor Trust, Chrysler Financial Corporation-Euro Issue, BMWCC 1988 A-1 and A-2 Grantor Trusts. Others were marketed domestically but with variable rate debt—e.g., Shearson (Westamerica Bank)-A1, Mack Truck Receivables Corp-2A, and First American Bank NY 1990-A.

As the market evolved—primarily in response to finance companies whose regulatory environment differed from that faced by banks and thrifts—the structure of securities offering most widely favored became senior/subordinated structures. A grantor trust is used as the legal vehicle; however, the securities offering is divided among two or more tiers of debt with differing priority rights to cash flow. Key features include:

- *Two tiers of debt*—a senior tier for 80–90 percent of the funding and a subordinated "seller certificate" for the balance,
- *AAA rating for senior tier due* to credit enhancement from the subordination of priority return of principal (and sometimes interest) to the holders of the subordinated debt,
- *A rating (or no rating) for the subordinated securities* with credit enhancement from a reserve account, and
- *Retention of the subordinated securities* (at least initially) by the finance companies or by bankruptcy-remote subsidiaries.

The private placement market is another source of funding for a small portion of the auto loans securitized. One-time issuers may also favor this technique for marketing the securities because of the lower fixed costs. Some of the major issuers, like Chrysler, have also utilized private placements from time to time when direct debt placement by the finance company was limited by various conditions. Chrysler Finance Corporation - 16 Grantor Trust, Class A was a $102 million private placement in January 1992. Difficult conditions in the North American automotive market, combined with a historically aggressive financial policy, have hurt Chrysler Corp.'s credit quality, causing Fitch, for example, to downgrade the automaker's senior rating to BB– from BB+ in late January. Because of its affiliation with Chrysler, Chrysler Financial Corporation also is under pressure, and its senior and subordinated debt ratings were lowered to BB+ and BB from BBB and BB–, respectively, in conjunction with the parent's downgrade. Ratings on asset-backed receivables were unaffected.[9]

Banks and thrifts under Federal capital requirements cannot record a "true sale" of the assets associated with the senior securities, with corresponding reduced capital requirements, if the seller retains the subordinated securities that inherit virtually all of the risk.

Type and Level of Credit Enhancement

Most public offerings of auto loan securities are rated AAA. (The small private placement market included AA and A-rated transactions). The public offerings achieve AAA status either by purchasing a financial guaranty from an independent or third party, or through structuring techniques that enhance the *senior* certificates by placing greater risk in *subordinated* certificates. Credit enhancement was purchased for less than one-third of the auto loan securitizations—32 percent by number of transactions (68 out of 212) and 18 percent by dollar value.

The *senior/subordinated* structure was widely used in the past few years, especially by finance companies, in lieu of third-party credit enhancement. This structure provides credit enhancement without payment of a fee to a credit enhancer by leveraging the position of the investors in the subordinated securities.

The *cash collateral account* is a second innovation that avoids third-party credit enhancement. This innovation, developed for credit card securitizations, was adapted for auto loan transactions in

9 Fitch Research Special Report on Chrysler Financial Corp., March 2, 1992.

Figure 9.12—Share of Annual Issues with Fee Enhancement
(Dollar Weighted)

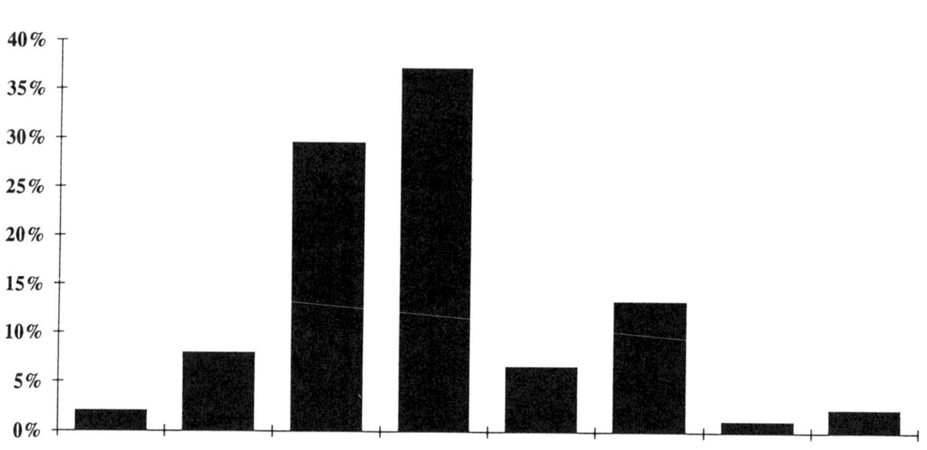

1991 by First Boston on behalf of several clients—Volvo Auto Receivables 1991-A, Security Pacific Auto 1991-A, Rochester Community Savings Bank 1991-B, and Rochester Community Savings Bank 1991-F.

The impact of the growth of senior/subordinated structures and, to a lesser extent, the use of cash collateral accounts, can be seen in the declining portion of the market using third-party credit enhancement after reaching a high of 83 percent in 1988 (Figure 9.12).

Pass-through structures, however, have required credit enhancement from third parties to achieve the AAA ratings. Participants in the credit enhancement industry have provided enhancement for almost $14 billion of securities on 65 transactions. Two types of firms provide credit enhancement: banks that provide letters of credit for 5–15 percent of a total issue, and insurance companies that provide 100 percent surety bonds.

Union Bank of Switzerland (UBS) has dominated the market with 45 percent of the dollar volume and 30 percent of the transactions ($6.1 billion for 20 transactions). Two other Swiss banks (Credit Suisse and Swiss Bank Corporation) and one German Bank (Deutsche Bank), also rated AAA, have been active participants in the letter of credit market. Several other banks have provided letters of credit for only one or two transactions each. The average size transaction for the four major banks is $300 million, but the letter of credit covers losses up to only 5–15 percent of the total dollar amount. However, virtually all risk exposure is contained in that 5–15 percent credit enhancement. Swiss Bank Corporation has provided the largest single letter of credit but has enhanced only the $650 million Euro-placement for Chrysler—CARCO Dealers Wholesale Trust 1990-A.

In addition, two monoline financial guaranty insurance companies—Financial Security Assurance (FSA) and Capital Markets Assurance Company (CapMac)—have been active in the auto loan securitization market. Although the FSA market share on a dollar basis (16 percent) is almost twice that of CapMac (7 percent), FSA has enhanced 18 transactions compared to only eight by CapMac. The average size transaction for the insurance companies is $144 million (Table 9.1).

Pricing

Pricing is typically quoted in two ways:

- *Seller Perspective*—"All-in cost" of funds to the seller, which reflects (a) the coupon on the debt adjusted for the discount/premium at issuance, and (b) transaction costs for dealer commissions, rating agency fees, credit enhancement fees, legal, accounting, printing, etc.
- *Investor Perspective*—Spread over Comparable Treasuries received by the investor with 2-year Treasuries usually deemed the most comparable maturity. The spread is measured on the issuance date for the secu-

Table 9.1—Credit Enhancement from Surety Bonds and Letters of Credit

	$ Million	*Deals*	*Average*	*Share ($)*	*Share (#)*
UBS	6,060	20	303	45%	30%
FSA	2,133	18	119	16%	27%
Credit Suisse	1,909	7	273	14%	10%
Deutsche Bank	1,008	3	336	7%	4%
CapMac	886	8	111	7%	12%
Swiss Bank	650	1	650	5%	1%
Sumitomo	175	1	175	1%	1%
Fuji Bank	143	1	143	1%	1%
Barclays	117	2	58	1%	3%
IBJ	113	1	113	1%	1%
FHLB SF	105	1	105	1%	1%
Bayerische	103	1	103	1%	1%
JP Morgan	89	2	44	1%	3%
Daichi	66	1	66	0%	1%
Nat Union Fire	60	1	60	0%	1%
Total	$13,618	68	$201	100%	100%

rities and is tracked in the secondary market for subsequent trading. This spread is computed differently if the interest rate is variable (e.g., pegged to LIBOR).[10]

The initial auto securitization, Marine Midland 1985-1 Grantor Trust, was a $60.2 million execution by Salomon Brothers at only 38 basis points over Treasuries. However, the spread was never again that tight and has typically ranged between 60 and 100 basis points over comparable Treasuries with a dollar-weighted average spread, 1985–92, of 86 basis points. Spreads were in excess of 115 basis points three times—for one transaction by DBL in March 1987, two transactions after the October 1987 stock market crash, a transaction in December 1989, and for nine transactions in the October 1990 through February 1991 period, peaking on February 22, 1991 with the $150.4 million Union Federal Savings Bank of Indianapolis 1991-A transaction by Morgan Stanley at 145 basis points over Treasuries (Figure 9.13).

A third way to look at pricing is the net cost of the auto loan to the consumer. Although the sources of funding do have an impact on net cost of funds to the consumer, it may be tenuous to attribute differences directly to securitization. The rate on individual auto loans is set in advance of the securitization, although it may be set in *anticipation* of capital market conditions. One way to draw *gross* comparisons between securitization and portfolio pricing is to compare aggregate bank pricing (which is overwhelmingly portfolio-funded) and finance company pricing (which is heavily influenced by securitization).[11] The interest rate advantage typically resided with the banks, except in the 1985–86 period when the major auto manufacturers used their finance companies to implement major discount pricing on loan rates to increase auto sales. In 1991, the falling spreads for finance companies relative to banks appears to reflect the price advantage gained through massive securitization (Figure 9.14).

Transaction Size

The average size transaction for the 212 transactions is $369 million.[12] The average has generally grown from year-to-year as the market matured and the "Big Three" auto finance companies pressed for large-scale efficiency in their transactions. In the initial half of 1992, each of the "Big

10 We analyzed spreads over comparable maturity Treasuries for 167 of the 212 transactions ($68.3 billion or 87% of total issues).

11 Federal Reserve Statistical Release G-19 and G-19A. Consumer Installment Credit.

12 Heritage Management Securitization data base as of June 30, 1992; some private placements may not be included.

Figure 9.13—Spread over Comparable Maturity Treasuries

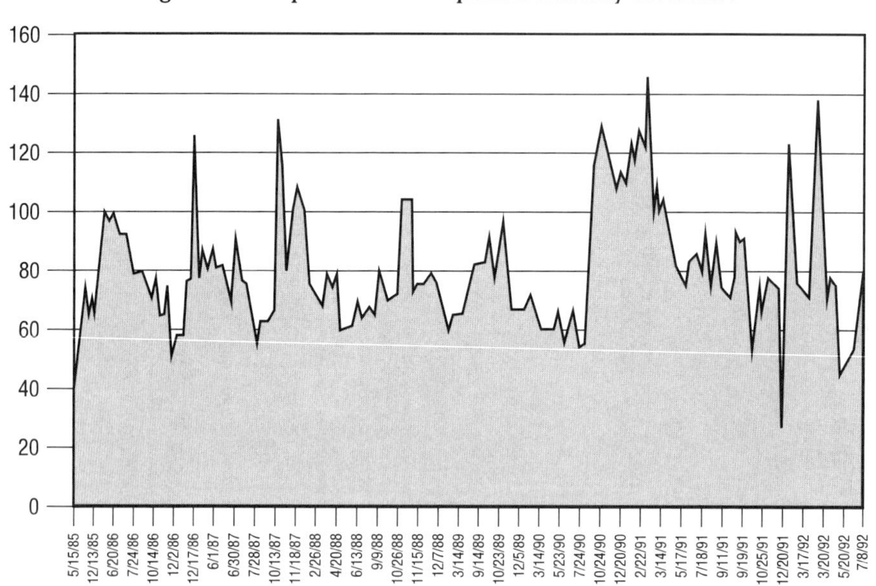

Figure 9.14—Finance Company Rates as Spread over Bank Rates

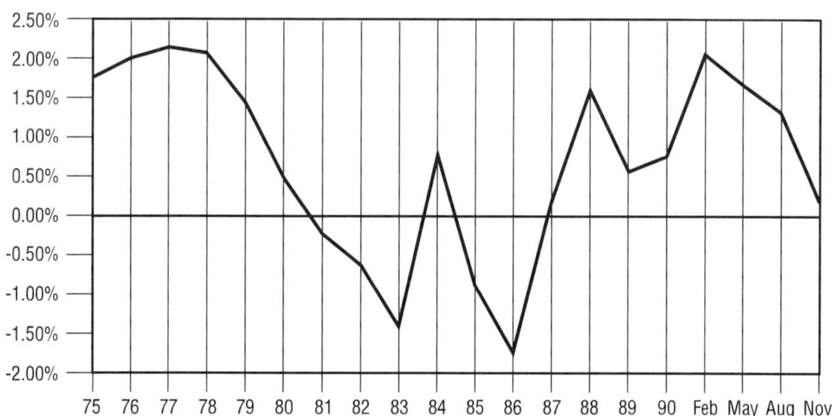

Three" finance companies had transactions well in excess of $750 million:

- ♦ Ford—Two series under the New Master Trust averaging $850 million,
- ♦ GMAC—Four issues averaging $1.1 million, and
- ♦ Chrysler—Four issues under the new Premier series, averaging $761 million (Figure 9.15).

However, certain private placements are not in the data base, and these transactions tend to be substantially smaller than the public placements. Moreover, some transactions are executed at levels below $60 million (Figure 9.16).

Figure 9.15—Average for 212 Transactions = $369 Million

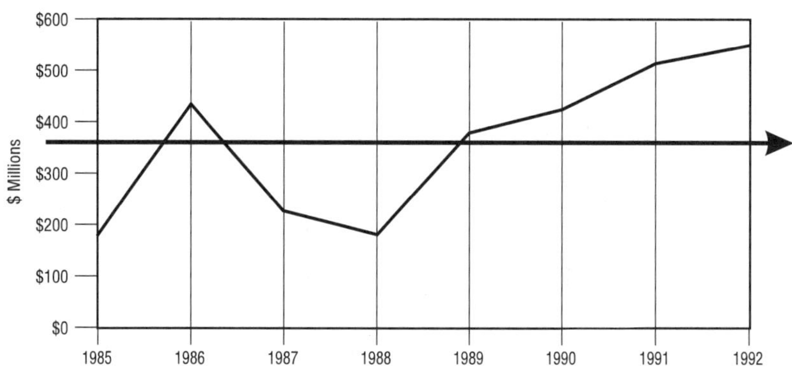

Figure 9.16—Auto Loan Securitizations < $60 Million

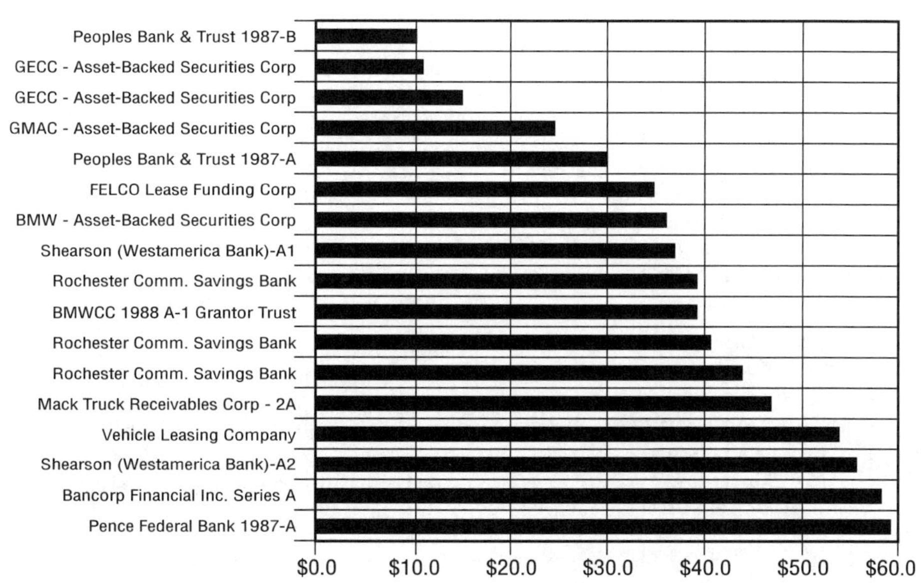

Geographic Concentration

Most securitized transactions are geographically diversified across the United States. In its description of the rating guidelines, Duff & Phelps indicates that:

Pooled receivables should be as geographically dispersed as possible. Ideally, no more than 10 percent of the receivables should be originated in any one State. Geographic diversification reduces the increased default risk associated with regional economic

Figure 9.17—Geographic Concentration

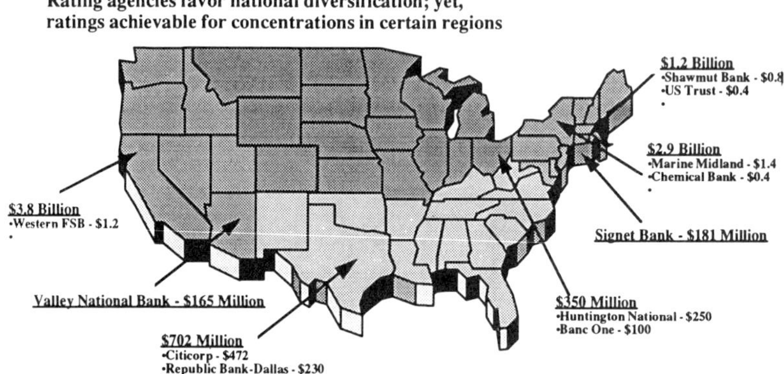

NOTE: Dollar values are for *total* transaction size if 50-100% concentrated with the State

Source: HML Securitization Database

> downturns. The initial pool risk is increased to compensate for significant regional concentrations depending on the economic diversity of that region. The initial risk is adjusted further for concentrations in regions which are currently experiencing economic weakness or that show potential weakness in the near term.[13]

However, the rating agencies have provided AAA ratings for concentrated portfolios in certain states (Figure 9.17).

IMPLICATIONS FOR THE EUROPEAN MARKET

The growth of Euro-auto securitization will undoubtedly differ from the experience in the United States. Few, if any, of the EEC nations have a comparable history of securitizing home mortgages to set the stage for diversification by institutional investors, investment banks, credit enhancers, rating agencies, and government regulators. Moreover, the traditional financing sources are not as highly concentrated as the "Big Three" U.S. auto manufacturers.

On the other hand, the Basle Accord will have a similar impact on commercial banks that fund auto loans from portfolios. Some banks, finance companies, and other financial institutions in Europe—like the "Big Three" auto finance companies, Western Financial Savings Bank, and Marine Midland Bank in the U.S.—will invest the intellectual/analytic capital in securitization and formulate strategies for utilizing this innovative financing technique to gain a compelling advantage over their competitors. And, in all probability, a few of these financial institutions—like Citicorp—will discover that securitization may offer a winning strategy for more than one type of asset.

13 *The Rating of Secured Consumer Receivables*, page 3, undated.

Chapter 10

The Management and Transfer of Credit, Liquidity and Contingency Risks

by Nicholas Millard,
Special Risk Services

Of the many risks which an investor has to assess when deciding whether or not to purchase an asset-backed security—credit, liquidity and contingency risks will rank high in the analysis. In this chapter we will consider how that analysis should be carried out and the relevant considerations that the originator or packager of the security should bear in mind when trying to optimise these aspects of the structure, both from their own and the investors' point of view.

First, we will discuss the *credit risk* associated with the loans in the portfolio. This risk is principally an economic risk; that is, how likely is it that a loan will default and that there will be sufficient collateral to compensate for the default? If there are not sufficient recoveries, then what form of ultimate credit protection (or credit enhancement) would best suit originator and investor?

Second, we will investigate the *liquidity risk*, that is, where there may be a shortfall of payments from a borrower but no final default has been recorded which would enable a specific loss to be crystallised and thereby trigger a claim on the credit enhancement provider. In these circumstances the vehicle company could be left with insufficient funds to maintain current payment of the bonds, although the level of overall credit support may still be adequate.

Third, we will look at *contingency risks*. Contingent risks are those that cause a loss of value in the pool of collateral to the security but may not arise from default or economic circumstances. An example might be a property burning down when there was inadequate fire insurance in force.

Throughout this chapter we will consider to what extent a credit enhancement structure might be subject to *event risk*, or the risk that the rating of the party which has assumed the credit and liquidity risks may have its own credit status lowered, thereby leading to an overall reduction in the rating on the security.

CREDIT RISK

Whether or not event risk arises, or indeed can potentially occur, depends on the choice of the credit enhancement method and demands an evaluation of the potential benefits and risks of that method by the investor. Therefore, selection of the credit enhancement method is one of the fundamental choices that the structuror of the security needs to make. In so doing, the structuror will consider (1) the extent to which an investor is exposed to event risk; (2) the consequence of this on the pricing of the security; (3) any mechanism by which that risk can be ameliorated and (4) whether the event risk is one that the investor might be prepared to incur because the chosen method of credit enhancement offers compensating benefits.

The prospective securitiser now has a broad choice amongst the various credit enhancement methods. These can be listed as follows:

1. An indemnity policy from a multiline insurance company
2. An issue tranched into senior/subordinated bonds
3. A financial guarantee from a U.S. monoline
4. A Letter of Credit from a rated bank
5. Overcollateralisation
6. Cash collateral
7. A hybrid structure involving two or more of the above

A great deal has been written on the merits and defects of these various products, including our contribution to EuroMoney's previous book *Asset Securitisation: Theory and Practice in Europe* where we dealt with the distinctions between the products in the chapter "The Development of Credit Enhancement in Europe." We do not want to repeat much of that ground, which will be familiar to the participants of the asset-backed markets. Instead we would go one stage further and discuss the practical considerations which will determine how a potential issuer comes to a decision about the most suitable form of credit enhancement. From there we will discuss handling the subsidiary risks, namely that of liquidity and event risk.

No decision about risk allocation can take place without regard to the regulatory environment in which the originator funds itself. For example, domestic regulators can and do have very different attitudes regarding the amount of financial support an originator can have in an issue if it is to remain off balance sheet. In France, for example, an originator can invest in its own risk by purchasing the subordinated bonds which enhance the entire issue. In other jurisdictions, including the UK, this would result in the entire issue being placed back on balance sheet. In Spain, until recent changes in legislation, it was impossible to cross-collateralise a mortgage pool so each individual mortgage had to be enhanced separately, rather than the enhancement backing a 'pool.'

In each situation, local regulatory influences will 'suggest' a choice of enhancement. In France it may be, for the reasons expressed above, cheaper for the originator to self enhance via the purchase of subordinated bonds. In the UK this would defeat the purpose of securitisation (since the resulting capital weighting would be calculated on the full face value of the issue) and therefore most issuers have chosen an insurance route, unless they can find a third party to purchase the subordinated bonds.

Regulatory issues are pervasive. Can short-term credits be securitised? Can new credits be sold to the vehicle, after issuance/launch, as the original portfolio amortises? Can transfer of the title to the assets be perfected, or if not, is there a risk that in the event of bankruptcy of the originator, the credit enhancer will be faced with a total loss (because the liquidator will capture the payments from the assets which were thought to belong to the asset-backed securities investors)?

The regulatory background therefore needs careful investigation before analysis of the credit enhancement choices can begin. With a new issuer, or in a country that is just starting to securitise, once the decision to proceed has been made and the structuring bank has been appointed, the study of credit enhancement choices needs to follow rapidly. A long time needs to be spent educating potential credit enhancement parties about the new country or issuer and the sooner that this process can begin, the better.

But, in addition to regulatory issues, what other factors should an issuer consider when trying to make up its mind about the best credit enhancement from its own point of view and that of the investors in its asset-backed securities?

The principle considerations can be categorised into two areas. Clearly, an issuer would like to achieve its credit enhancement needs as inexpensively as possible. There are therefore considerations of pricing. This is a complex area and we will come to this a little later. However, there are also a number of non-pricing considerations which the issuer will have to consider. These are as follows:

1. Most fundamentally, what are the originator's objectives in the securitisation? Is it to diversify their funding? Is it to take assets off balance sheet? Or is it simply to establish the technology in-house and assure themselves that they can securitise as an option when needed? These considerations will determine how important it is to ensure the funding is off balance sheet. This in turn will determine how much financial support the originator can provide to the securitisation.
2. How often is the originator planning to issue? Do they need to establish relationships with a market which is going to provide them with a continuous supply of credit enhancement?
3. What risks is the originator prepared to accept? Is the originator willing to subordinate all the excess cash from the financing vehicle to losses or do they wish to protect the profit stream? (Profit can be protected by limiting the first loss deductible and/or limiting the amount of excess cash[1] from the financing vehicle subordinated to the credit enhancement party.)

1 We will define excess cash as the yield on the securitised assets less the coupon on the securities, administration, trustee fees and various other incidental costs of maintaining the vehicle company.

4. How wide is the realistic choice of enhancement? Can an issuer achieve a sale of subordinated bonds on their first issue if they wish to do so? Alternatively, will insurers have sufficient knowledge about the originator's assets to be able to assess the risks? Do they see sufficient business coming in the future to make it worth their while investigating the portfolio now?
5. Can the originator spend time educating and negotiating with the credit enhancement market to achieve the best possible price or is speed of issue the main objective? Will an issuer trade certainty in the view of the credit enhancer and therefore a lower price for a rapid execution on the enhancement at a higher price?
6. Which potential insurance companies have a licence to issue a contract in the territory where the financing vehicle is located?
7. If the credit risk is transferred to a third party, other than subordinated bond investors, what is the investor perception going to be of this party? Does the investor have too much exposure already to the third party enhancer as a result of other guaranteed asset-backed bonds the investor has purchased?

At the same time as the originator is considering this, it must also draw up another list of issues that need to be determined in calculating the price of the various competing options. These pricing considerations include the following:

1. What is the schedule for premium payments, if an insurance format is used? Will premium be paid up front or on a per annum basis?
2. What level of first loss protection will the credit enhancement party require from the originator and how is this going to be funded?
3. How should the originator calculate the cost of funding this first loss position? Shall they write it off now (but hope to retrieve some of that investment at maturity of the issue) or are they going to be confident that it is never going to be called and only consider its carrying cost?
4. When per annum payments are compared with upfront payments, what discount rate should the originator use to perform the calculation? Are they going to view this as a self-contained financing, and therefore use the funding rate of the asset-backed securitisation as the relevant discount rate, or, because they are employing some of their own capital to pay the premium and to collateralise the first loss position, should they discount at their cost of capital?
5. If a likely pool insurer has a rating lower than the rating required on the funding instrument, or if there are other insurance contracts involved that have a low or nil rating, can some other party be found to upgrade these contracts, and at what cost?
6. Can a financial institution be found to provide liquidity and what will this cost?
7. What is the investor perception of the potential credit enhancement party? Will investors require a premium built into the yield on the securities, either because they already have a large exposure to this enhancer or because they believe there is a risk of down rating in the future?
8. What risks will the credit enhancer really cover? Are there some non-economic risks which they want to exclude and which therefore have to be placed in other markets?
9. Will the rating agencies require that the originator buy additional cover against the risk that, due to insolvency of the originator, it is unable to repurchase loans in the pool which are outside specified criteria and therefore not covered by the credit enhancer? (This is called non-compliance risk.)

At this stage the originator will realise that it has a considerable task on its hands, both in gathering together enough information to ensure that it is properly informed of all these various considerations and also to be able to balance the various costs and non-cost items in such a way that the optimum result is achieved. At this stage we hope an originator will decide that they need professional help and turn to a specialist broker, such as Special Risk Services (SRS). Although the broker should carry out much of the analytical work, the client should understand the reasons behind the broker's recommendations and indeed the originator should keep a watching brief over the credit enhancement process so that they are confident of making the choice that best suits their needs.

Once the originator understands the issues, it can then start asking for bids from suppliers or arrangers of the various forms of credit enhancement. Once an originator has received indications of pricing and conditions from potential credit enhancers it may then proceed to examine the options as follows:

1. Subordinated "mezzanine" bonds—These could be attractive since the risk premium is paid over timeand event risk may be low (but it exists).

   However, for a new issuer it may be difficult to find buyers for the subordinated bonds as the subordinated bond market has traditionally been thin and therefore illiquid. The originator may worry about future capacity of this market if it is going to be a frequent issuer. In addition, if there are elements of unrated credit support, such as, for example, a mortgage indemnity contract in the UK, then the cost of up-rating these must be taken into account. Unless this is done, the rating agencies will regard such contracts as providing negligible support and therefore require the subordinate bond tranche to be increased. This form of credit enhancement does not provide any protection to the issuer for future profits. Rather, all future profits are at risk in this structure. In addition, the amount of cash that has to be built into a "mezzanine" structure may be quite large since it is now necessary to have an investment rating on these notes if they are to be sold.

2. Letters of Credit—This is a limited market given the paucity of remaining 'AAA/Aaa' banks. Some AAA/Aaa banks may only desire to issue LOCs if they have an existing relationship with the originator or if they will be chosen by the originator to lead manage the transaction. Letters of Credit can be issued on a partial guarantee basis which makes them reasonably inexpensive. They can also be paid for annually rather than once up front.

   However, letters of credit are sensitive to the rating of the bank and if the bank is down rated then the whole asset-backed structure may also be down rated. In addition, total subordination of excess cashflow to losses will almost certainly be required, thereby leaving the issuers' profits contingent on the performance of the portfolio.

3. Cash collateral—this is a rare form of credit enhancement but has been employed by issuers of short-term securities—such as Renault's finance arm, DIAC. The problem has been in the availability of sufficient cash and its carrying cost. The cash can either be raised by the vehicle company through the securitisation and retained by the vehicle, invested directly by the originator from his own resources or raised via a borrowing from other sources. This route is limited in event risk, if the amount is sufficient, because there is no dependence on third party support (although the sizing of the cash sum may later prove insufficient to maintain the rating). However, the quantity of cash that it requires and the availability of favourably priced GICs has limited its use.

4. Overcollateralisation is also a rare form of enhancement. It has recently been used by Chemical Bank for a leasing transaction for IFIM Leasing in Italy. In concept, it is similar to factoring, where the assets are sold at a discount—in this case to the issuing vehicle. It may be attractive when, for various reasons, enhancement is difficult to obtain but assets are plentiful. For issuers who wish to *match fund* their assets, overcollateralisation would, however, present a problem and it would not be a route they would choose to pursue.

5. Monoline Insurers—Monoline insurers provide an unconditional guarantee of payments of principal and interest to investors. They are therefore simple for the investors to understand and attractive for that reason. Although not entirely free of event risk it is probably true that, given that the monolines' strongest marketing advantage is their 'AAA' rating, they will take great care to preserve that rating. Any reduction in rating would be disastrous for them commercially. An additional advantage of employing monoline enhancement is that they will have their own liquidity facilities and so this does not have to be separately arranged.

   On the downside monolines will, to protect their own position, require a substantial amount of collateralisation to achieve 'zero loss' exposure. Also, in order to generate a sufficient return on the capital they must allocate to the transaction, they have to charge premiums that make them an expensive source of capacity. Some investors have a substantial exposure already to individual monoline insurers and are beginning to resist taking more paper guaranteed by them, but for large amounts of low-risk capacity the monolines are frequently an excellent source.

6. Multilines—Because multiline insurers are able to absorb credit risk from asset-backed securities within their total book of general business, they do not have to allocate specific capital to any particular transaction of this type. Hence their charges are usually lower than the monolines, although the first loss position which they wish to see collateralised is moving towards a similar size to that of the monolines. Traditionally, the major reason for selecting multiline capacity was price and, to some extent, availability. There are a large number of European companies who participate in these structures, often through the mechanism of reinsurance, and there are also three or four rated leads. Unfortunately not all these leads have 'AAA/Aaa' ratings and the decline in highly rated companies over the past couple of years has done damage to the reputation of this industry. Nevertheless the pricing advantage is such that, even when an upgrade policy is purchased to give the structure its AAA/Aaa rating, the pricing is still attractive compared with many alternatives.

   The guarantee which is offered by insurers is carefully defined. It is an indemnity cover; that is, it will pay only on the net loss created by default on an asset within the portfolio. It will not cover all causes of loss to principal and interest, such as a monoline policy will. Because it only pays a net loss, there may be a time gap between when a borrower defaults on an asset (a mortgage for example), and when the policy finally pays. This gap must be filled by a liquidity facility, something that it is not normally provided by insurance companies.

   In past years a hindrance to selling the multiline approach has been the high level of deductible which these companies have required to be cash collateralised at the inception of the issue. Recently, insurance companies have become more sophisticated about analysing cashflows and many of them will now accept that the subordination of cashflow from the financing vehicle provides them with protection superior to a lump sum cash fund.

7. Hybrid structures—Hybrid structures are, as their name suggests, mixtures of the above approaches. The most common hybrid is a combination of subordinated notes and insurance. It is particularly useful when the subordinated notes may be difficult to place or where there is an arbitrage between the cost of the insurance and the cost of issuing unrated subordinated notes. For example, SRS has created a structure whereby the collateral is guaranteed up to 'AA' standard and then the issue is tranched into senior and subordinated notes. Provided the saving on the lower size and lower yield of rated subordinated notes vs. unrated subordinated notes is greater than the cost of the insurance premium, then this is a route worth following. Event risk is avoided by sizing the subordinated notes so that even if the insurer is down rated, then the subordinated note tranche is still sufficient security to maintain 'AAA/Aaa' rating on the senior notes.

   In another form of hybrid structure, rated financial guarantees are used to upgrade non-rated insurances that may be attached to the portfolio of assets, rather than extending the size of the subordinated tranche which would achieve the same effect. For example, UK mortgage lenders may have purchased unrated Mortgage Indemnity Guarantee (MIG) contracts. The lack of a sufficient rating on these contracts will hinder the structure receiving the AAA/Aaa rating. The pricing of upgrading those contracts via a financial guarantee, is therefore compared to the costs associated with increasing the size of the subordinated note tranche. This increase can be large, in which case it is worth buying upgrades of these unrated insurance contracts.

At this stage of the transaction, an originator would have a range of enhancement bids from its broker and a set of considerations about the relative attractions of each route. The broker and the structuring bank will then run the various submissions on their own pricing models and present the analyses to the originator, demonstrating the various costs associated with each particular route. It will be up to the originator at that stage to decide which of the various routes it prefers.

What should the originator, and its advisers, take into account when considering the cost implications of pursuing different credit enhancement strategies? At SRS we have developed a model which takes into account the points listed below and produces an NPV of the cost of the options. It takes into account the following factors:

Pricing Factors

- Pool size
- Limit of Indemnity (for Insurance and LOCs)
- Mortgage Indemnity exposure (MIG) (if applicable)
- Upgrade cost for pool and Mortgage Indemnity contracts
- Event risk premium
- Guaranteed Investment Contract (GIC) rate
- Subordinated Bond estimated yield
- Liquidity facility costs
- Subordinated Bond placement costs
- Mortgage yield
- AAA Bond yield
- Redemption rate
- Cost of Capital (Discount Rate)

As an example we will assume that the originator has chosen, in common with the first asset-backed issues in the UK, Sweden and Spain, to use the European insurance market for its credit enhancement. In that case it might have a proposal before it as follows:

1. An up front premium.
2. A deductible structure involving a cash deposit, plus a future claim on cash flow should losses to this fund and/or the insurer occur.
3. A rating (of the insurer).
4. A list of qualifications about which loans can be included within the portfolio (e.g., loans in arrears and other loans with unattractive characteristics may be excluded). Substitution of new loans may or may not be allowed, if requested by the issuer, and certain restrictions may be placed on the issuer's ability to make further advances to borrowers within the pool.

LIQUIDITY RISK

The responsibility will then be split for arranging various other parts of the credit enhancement package that remain. One of these will be the liquidity risk. This arises in some, but not all, forms of enhancement. The risk occurs when the form of enhancement only pays for the financial consequences of default of an asset *after* the value in collateral securing the debt has been recovered. For example, in a structure using mortgage pool insurance the policy will only pay a claim once the mortgaged property has been repossessed and sold. Hence there needs to be a liquidity facility which will fund the gap between the time of initial default and the time of making the insurance claim in order to maintain payments to the bondholders.

Liquidity facilities may also be employed in senior/subordinated structures. Many early deals with this form of credit enhancement did not have them and the entire liquidity risk was passed to the subordinated investors. Although the subordinated portion of the financing was sized to meet the liquidity requirements, the rating agencies became worried about the speed at which subordinated note holders would be hit, should the assets be stressed. This in turn, it was feared, would affect the ability to place future issues of subordinated debt. To offset this danger, structures started to include liquidity facilities to protect subordinated note holders and these have now become a common feature.

Letters of Credit are on demand instruments and are therefore a natural source of liquidity. Letters of Credit pay when there is insufficient cash from the portfolio to remunerate the bondholders. Payment under the LOC is therefore not dependent on realising the value of the collateral, although the LOC provider expects to be reimbursed once the vehicle company is in a position to do so. In some structures there may be a certain amount of cash collateral held at the disposal of the trustee which will be called on after losses have exhausted cash flow from the financing vehicle, but before the trustee calls on the LOC. This 'first loss collateral' may be required by the LOC provider in order to protect its own position and ensure the call on the LOC is made only in the case of catastrophe losses on the portfolio.

Monoline guarantees by definition provide liquidity since they guarantee the timely payment of principal and interest so that a liquidity facility additional to the guarantee will not normally need to be arranged. The monoline company, however, will have arranged liquidity facilities for *itself*, so it can honour its obligation of timely payment.

If a liquidity facility is required (for example in a senior/subordinated structure), then we might now see an up-front and ongoing commitment fee plus a 1 percent drawing charge. This pricing reflects recent developments and is significantly more expensive than historical pricing for these facilities.

It is important to understand the mechanism of a liquidity facility. The facility will, if required, make loans to the vehicle company. That loan will be secured on the assets and the cashflow of the vehicle company. In other words, repayment of the loan may come either from the defaulters making up their arrears of payments, from the proceeds of sale of an asset after default or from a claim on the insurance policy.

UPGRADE POLICIES

Once the originator has assessed the offers of enhancements and, let us say, has chosen insurance, then the broker may be asked to arrange the upgrade contract to take the primary credit enhancement to 'AAA/Aaa' if the insurer has a lower rating. There is a reasonably good selection of markets to do this. It is perceived as an attractive risk by the underwriters, although many of them may not wish to take the primary risk themselves. They are therefore underwriting the credit risk of the lower rated underwriter, and only contingently the performance of the underlying portfolio. As with liquidity facilities, the price of upgrade policies has increased over the last few years, although it is also true to say that that cost has not always eroded the advantage of issuing the financing at 'AAA/Aaa' level rather than accepting a higher yield on the bond for launching with a lower rating.

CONTINGENCY RISKS

The broker will also be asked to arrange the contracts for the risks which are not picked up by the primary pool cover. Pool cover is intended to cover a specific economic risk; that of a borrower defaulting and the pledged collateral being worth less than the total value of the debt. However, that is not the only reason for loss of collateral value in the pool and there may be a number of small risks present which need to be covered through what are called *contingency* insurances. For example, there may be problems with title on the collateral so that after default a property cannot be sold and therefore there is no way of crystallising the loss for the purposes of the primary insurance policy. Alternatively, the house may be burnt to the ground and it is then discovered that the fire insurance was not properly in place so that there is then no collateral and no insurance cover to remedy the loss to the portfolio. Another example of this type of risk for the pool is compulsory purchase where the purchase sum offered by the government is less than the outstanding debt. In each of these cases the primary pool policy would not pick up the loss resulting from these risks occurring. Therefore, individual indemnity contracts need to be arranged to secure the portfolio against these exposures. These covers are not particularly expensive and they are reasonably available.

CONCLUSION

To summarise, the major risk associated with asset-backed securities is the credit risk and the major decision which any potential issuer needs to make is which of the various techniques that are available should be chosen in order to accommodate this risk. In this chapter we have tried to summarise some of the considerations which an issuer should bring to bear on this question when making a selection amongst the options. It is of necessity a partial list and those who are interested in taking this subject further can obtain specialist advice from a broker such as SRS or from their merchant bank. Above all, it is important to recognise that the choice of credit enhancement will determine whether associated risks, such as liquidity and down rating, arise and, if so, how they should be handled. There are markets which will handle each of these problems and given each issuer's unique requirements it is likely that a mix of solutions will present the most suitable course. In the early 1990s, it is clear that some structures work better than others, thus insuring subordinated debt issues will, for a 'AAA' rated securitisation, often provide a better execution than one that is dependent just on an issue of subordinated notes alone. Rated subordinated notes are easier to place than unrated subordinated notes and can be placed at a much lower yield. This example is typical of how we expect to see credit enhancement structured in the future. Various markets will be exploited in order to make use of whatever arbitrage is available to produce the most efficient solution for the client.

Chapter 11

Structured Securities: Credit, Cash Flow, and Legal Risks

by Clifford M. Griep,
Executive Managing Director
Financial Institutions/LOC
Standard & Poor's
New York

The analysis of structured securities has several components, but chiefly entails three broad questions. First, what is the relative importance and credit quality of both the assets supporting the transaction and the related parties in the transaction, including the credit and liquidity support providers, the servicer, interest rate or currency swap counterparties, and the investments held in trust. Second, will the cash flow of the assets, supplemented by credit and liquidity supports, meet the terms of the securities and any necessary transaction-related expenses. And third, is the transaction structured in a manner which in all circumstances provides the debtholders with a legally valid right to the assets and the timely receipt of the cash flow they generate. These can be broadly classified into credit, cash flow, and legal risks, each of which is central to the determination of creditworthiness and hence value.

The complexity of these securities, evidenced by the diversity of risks which can affect their creditworthiness, raises unique challenges to portfolio managers who buy and hold them. This chapter outlines the basic methodology S&P utilizes to evaluate these risks and outlines some implications for portfolio managers investing in asset-backed securities, in undertaking their own evaluation and surveillance of them.

The creditworthiness of structured transactions is based primarily on the quality of the assets securitized, the quality and amount of credit and liquidity supports, the credit of the seller, the credit and quality of the servicer of the assets, the credit of several counterparties to the transaction which provide protection from currency and interest rate risks, and finally, the quality of and reinvestment rate on the temporary investments held by the trust for the benefit of debtholders.

The creditworthiness may also be impacted although not directly through the role of the trustee, who performs key operational functions as required by the indenture, or the accountants who provide necessary independent oversight through periodic cash flow audits and other controls.

This fragmentation of influences is a relatively recent phenomenon in the capital markets, having been influenced in the past decade by the enormous growth in structured finance activity and the increasing specialization of roles this has fostered. While this specialization has contributed to the ability of this market to retain its relatively strong credit quality, it also has diminished comprehensive accountability which characterizes simpler corporate or municipal debt issues. The risks of this diminution are mitigated by the extensive documentation, which is increasingly specific in defining roles. To rate any structured financing S&P must be certain that all parties in the transaction can perform their duties and obligations as specified in the documentation.

The central task of credit analysis is the review and evaluation of the assets supporting the transaction. These assets are the investors' principal source of protection in all partially credit-enhanced structures, and an important secondary source of protection in fully enhanced structures. A wide range of assets currently are being securitized and, while there are variations in analytical approach reflecting unique aspects of the assets, the fundamental pattern is largely the same. This includes a review of the seller/servicer of the assets and an analysis of the expected performance of the securitized assets during periods of severe economic stress.

THE CREDIT QUALITY OF THE SELLER MAY BE RELEVANT

This begins with an analysis of both the creditworthiness of the seller/servicer of the assets, as well as a review of the specific business unit originating the assets. The overall creditworthiness of the seller is relevant for several reasons, predominantly relating to the legal risks associated with asset transfers, the potential impact the seller's bankruptcy could have on the quality of its securitized assets, and the sizing of the credit support. Investors in structured transactions should understand the implications of a seller bankruptcy.

Despite efforts to completely eliminate legal transfer risk, there may be risks associated with the legal transfers of assets from the originator to the trust or issuing vehicle. In the U.S. these risks arise from the potential of a bankruptcy court to recharacterize the legal transfer which in most transactions had been intended as a sale of assets, to a pledge of assets, or in some cases, void the transfer altogether. Such a recharacterization could create temporary timing delays in the investors' receipt of cash or, at the extreme, result in a loss of asset protection. This is due to ambiguities in the language of the U.S. Bankruptcy Code and an absence of definitive case law relevant to legal transfers. Outside the U.S., legal systems vary in their capacity to provide definitive guidance on questions of legal transfer. Therefore this risk varies depending upon the type of assets transferred, the type of legal structure used, and the legal framework. Importantly, challenges to a legal structure of a transaction would likely occur only upon the sellers insolvency or bankruptcy. But as a result of this risk the credit ratings of some structured debt could be affected by the credit rating of the seller.

HOW SELLER'S RATING CAN IMPACT CREDIT SUPPORT

In asset-backed structures involving automobile, marine, recreational vehicle, manufactured housing, and other types of secured loan and lease pools, the seller's interest in the receivables contracts is usually transferred to the issuer via a true sale and/or a conveyance of a first perfected security interest in such receivables. However, the seller's security interest in the underlying assets may not be effectively transferred to the issuer. This is due primarily to the expense and administrative burden associated with such a process which includes amending certificates of title and/or filing UCC-1 financing statements. If the seller fails to transfer its security interest in the underlying assets to the issuer, investors may not benefit from any recovery proceeds from the disposition of repossessed assets in the event of a bankruptcy/insolvency of the seller.

As a result of these risks some asset-backed transactions have been done with covenants which require the seller to physically transfer the receivables to the trustee upon the decline in the seller's credit rating. While physical transfer of the receivables at the time of the transaction is a convention in the U.S. mortgage securities market it is sometimes made contingent upon the erosion of the seller's credit quality in the asset-backed market provided the seller is strongly rated. Physical transfer strengthens investor protection by further enhancing the legal transfer by providing the trustee with physical possession of the assets. The surveillance process of the rating agency is intended to assure that such actions are taken promptly when required by the documents.

Also, where such legal uncertainties remain unresolved, then S&P will assume that recoveries may not be available to the transaction when evaluating the credit enhancement level needed to attain a given rating. However, these legal uncertainties will be weighed against the likelihood of a seller bankruptcy during the life of the transaction, and the adequacy of credit enhancement will be judged accordingly.

In credit card structures, the seller's rating can also impact the level of credit enhancement deemed necessary to attain a given rating level. S&P's cash flow analysis of these structures focuses on four major variables, one of which is the portfolio's monthly purchase rate as a percentage of outstanding receivables. The other variables include the portfolio yield, payment rate, and default rate.

Purchase rate is the rate at which the portfolio generates new receivables. But if the seller is bankrupt or insolvent, the trust may not get the benefit of these new receivables. Most credit card structures promise to pay monthly principal amortization equal to a fixed percentage of the pool's principal collections for a given month. Therefore, the higher the purchase rate assumed, the faster the investor is repaid. And the faster the investor is paid, the lower the investor's exposure to credit losses. When S&P determines a worst-case purchase rate assumption for a given transaction, the seller's rating may affect the assumed purchase rate. This is especially true for retail card portfolios. All things being equal, the higher the purchase rate

Table 11.1

An "event risk" checklist for investors

1. *Identify the weak links.*
   Investors should know who the credit enhancer is and be aware of any providers of liquidity support, GICs, interest rate or currency swaps, or tax protection because a downgrade of any one of those parties could cause a downgrade of the transaction.
2. *Identify the trigger events.*
   Investors should be aware of all trigger events in the structure as well as the cash flow implications associated with each one.
3. *Understand the implications of seller bankruptcy/insolvency.*
   The seller may be a weak link in the structure, or a seller bankruptcy/insolvency may be a trigger event. Read the transaction documentation to understand the cash flow implications and consult legal counsel if necessary.
4. *Understand S&P's ratings criteria.*
   Understand how dependent ratings may impact S&P's initial and ongoing rating assessment of an asset-backed transaction. Know what the ratings are intended to address and what the ratings may not address. Refer to the prospectus/private placement memorandum for disclosure of risks not addressed by rating.

assumed, the lower the resulting credit enhancement level that is deemed necessary to attain a given rating.

Retailers pose more of a concern than do bank card issuers with respect to purchase rate. This is because if a bank card issuer fails, the credit card business would most likely be divested, and card usage would continue generating a positive purchase rate. However, if a retailer goes bankrupt and its stores close, the credit card business would also shut down, and no new receivables would be generated. Therefore, S&P assumes a worst-case purchase rate of no less than 2 percent for most bank card issuers but often assumes a purchase rate as low as 0 percent for a lower-rated retailer. However, if a retailer is judged to have significant franchise value such that, in the event of a bankruptcy/insolvency, a reorganization as a going concern is deemed a more likely outcome than a liquidation, then S&P may assume a worst-case purchase rate of greater than zero even if the retailer were unrated or rated speculative grade.

The seller's financial condition may impact the performance of the securitized asset portfolio, either through its effect on receivable collateral value, obligor behavior, or credit quality, or the quality of servicing which is often retained by the seller. While there is evidence of a correlation between seller credit quality and receivable quality, the most meaningful negative impact often occurs upon a seller's bankruptcy. For example, a bankruptcy of a manufacturer can impair product value, which is a source of asset protection in several collateral receivable-backed structures, notably vehicle receivable or vehicle lease-backed transactions. These transactions routinely provide that recoveries on repossessions or residual value of leased vehicles accrue to certificate holders either directly, or indirectly through reimbursement to the credit support provider. Lower recoveries from the erosion of underlying collateral value can diminish investor protection. Similarly, the credit quality of the seller may have some relevance to the obligors on receivables supporting transactions. For example, in auto dealer floor planning loan-backed transactions, the dealer's credit is often directly linked to the credit quality of the supporting manufacturer. More broadly, the bankruptcy of a manufacturer may threaten the credit of its suppliers, distributors, or in some cases customers. These dependencies are the exception for asset-backed financing and are most relevant for single seller trade receivable-backed commercial paper programs. With the corporate sector making more use of securitization such imbedded risk will become more common to structured transactions.

Another risk which becomes more relevant in the seller's bankruptcy is the increasing dilution of trade receivable or retail credit card receivable portfolios. Dilutions are receivable nonpayments which occur for reasons other than credit-related defaults, and the risk of dilutions is factored into sizing the credit support requirements of a particular portfolio. Dilutions are tracked separately from defaults and are most commonly the result of transaction disputes and product returns. Dilutions usually increase following a bankruptcy of the seller, and could have varying impact on transactions depending upon the transaction structure. This risk would routinely be mitigated by the seller's ongoing commitment to replace diluted receivables with new originations. But this capacity may be diminished in bankruptcy, and dilution risk is then covered by the credit support facility.

Another area of risk related to the seller's insolvency is cash flow or prepayment risks associated with seller bankruptcy triggers. Many structured transactions, and all transactions of a revolving nature like credit card or trade receivable issues, contain covenants to amortize the structured debt upon a bankruptcy of the seller. These protective triggers are intended to mitigate credit risk by reducing the duration of the revolving receivable transaction thereby reducing loss exposure. As will be discussed later such triggers are only one of several contractual elements intended to preserve the credit support by structuring debt amortization in response to a negative credit event related to the seller, the servicer, or the performance of the receivables themselves.

In credit card structures, a seller bankruptcy/insolvency causes an early amortization event which will accelerate the payment of principal to investors. This prepayment could adversely impact an investor's overall yield, especially if the structure is intended to provide for the return of principal under a controlled schedule or bullet payment at the scheduled maturity. Furthermore, some structures allow for the liquidation of the trust portfolio upon the seller's insolvency subject to the consent of a majority of the certificate holders. This, in turn, could result in the certificate holders' realizing a loss if the sale proceeds are not enough to cover certificate principal.

It should be noted that the rating S&P assigns to a credit card transaction or to a structured transaction generally does not address the likelihood of any of these early amortization events and their resulting cash flow implications. For example, with respect to "hard bullet" structures, the rating does not address the possibility that investors will, if an amortization event occurs, receive monthly principal rather than a bullet payment. In this case, the rating only addresses the likelihood that investors will receive full return of principal by the "final" (versus the "expected" or "scheduled") maturity date. With respect to "soft bullet" and "controlled amortization" if an amortization event occurs structures, the rating does not address the possibility that investors may not receive the controlled or bullet payments as a result of either (1) an amortization event, or (2) a slower than expected paydown of the receivables pool such that monthly principal receivables collections are insufficient to meet the controlled or bullet schedule. In either case, S&P only rates the likelihood of full principal repayment no later than the final maturity date.

THE SERVICER'S CREDIT QUALITY COULD BE VITAL

The seller often retains servicing of the receivables. Most transactions have a direct financial exposure to the servicer, which through the collection process holds funds arising from payments on sold or securitized receivables. Funds held by the servicer may be at risk in the event of the servicer's bankruptcy. This exposure is normally limited as most structures require that funds collected be remitted to the trustee on a daily basis where they are held in trust for the benefit of certificate holders until disbursement. However, some transactions allow for more periodic remittance, during which the collections on securitized receivables are commingled with the servicer's general operating funds. Some credit card-backed transactions, for example, provide for a commingling period of up to 70 days, during which time a substantial amount of collections may occur. While this heightens a transaction's exposure to the servicer, the risk is mitigated by limiting this to servicers of strong credit quality and by provisions in the documents requiring the servicer to switch from periodic to daily remittance upon a decline in the servicer's credit rating. Part of the surveillance process entails monitoring that such changes occur when required by the documents.

The servicer also may provide a cash advance covering receivable delinquencies that it deems recoverable. This cash advance obligation may protect investors against certain liquidity risks, especially in transactions which have a relatively illiquid form of credit support such as subordination of cash flow or overcollateralization. As a result, the servicer's creditworthiness is directly linked to the credit quality of the structured debt. If this liquidity need is not backstopped by the credit support, a decline in the servicer's rating could jeopardize the rating on related structured debt. Upon issuance, a transaction with an essential cash advance obligation from the servicer will be rated no more than a full category above the unsecured rating of the servicer.

SERVICING RISKS AND PORTFOLIO PERFORMANCE

While the seller's and the servicer's credit quality sometimes remain an important element of a structured financing, the analysis of the assets supporting the transaction and the quality of the servicing of the assets focus on more fundamental risks. The assets supporting the transaction are reviewed within the context of firm specific, competitive, and economic influences, beginning with a review of the business unit which is originating and servicing the assets to be securitized.

The business orientation and operational capabilities of the servicer are a varying but important credit component of structured securities. The increasing consolidation of both residential mortgage and consumer finance coupled with advances in information and communications technology has facilitated more efficient, cost effective, and quality servicing operations. However, this has also tended to create a significant material concentration in the market for servicing the underlying structured debt markets. This concentration has fostered a closer scrutiny of these larger and more influential players. At the same time, the credit pressures in the financial services sector, evidenced by the insolvency and conservatorship or receivership of a substantial number of thrifts and the decline in creditworthiness of the banking system, has highlighted the negative impact a weak servicing operation can have on portfolio performance. This has been especially evident in thrifts and banks under conservatorship or receivership with the RTC, some of which have experienced precipitous increases in residential mortgage delinquency and default, and significant delays in foreclosure and collection actions which are due, in part, to declines in the resources supporting servicing.

In most structured transactions the servicing is retained by the seller of the assets. Therefore, the servicer, and, in the residential mortgage business the master servicer, is evaluated as part of the rating process. These participants are periodically reevaluated as suggested by the performance of the portfolio or the servicer. Given the increasingly important role the servicing of assets has become to securitized debt markets, S&P initiated in-depth servicer evaluations on mortgage servicers. The detailed analysis of servicing capability will become more commonplace in other areas of the structured finance market as well.

MORTGAGE OPERATION REPORT DESCRIPTION AND CRITERIA

The analysis done on mortgage servicers provides a comprehensive evaluation of a mortgage firm's lending and servicing capabilities. It was developed in light of the increased need for a means of evaluating the operating abilities, capacity, and effectiveness of mortgage market players. The analysis is motivated by the significant changes which have taken place in the mortgage and capital markets over the past several years. The mortgage finance industry continues to experience widespread overcapacity and intense competition among market participants. In addition, developments in government, regulatory, and agency requirements, particularly with regard to accounting applications, have given rise to dramatic changes in corporate philosophies and strategies of industry originators and servicers.

Institutions have been forced to reexamine goals and objectives and in many instances to redirect and reposition themselves within the industry framework. Of further significance has been the proliferation of mortgage products, changes in underwriting guidelines, and a heightened pressure on servicing capacity for cost control and operating efficiencies.

A mortgage operation review is based on an assessment of a firm's strengths, weaknesses, opportunities, and limitations through an in-depth analysis of six areas, namely, management and organization, loan production, underwriting and quality control, secondary marketing, loan administration, and financial position. A brief summary of S&P's criteria pertaining to these areas follows below.

Management and Organization

A mortgage company's operating and financial profile is characterized by business cyclicality, thin cash flow coverage, limited equity capital, and aggressive leverage. Within this context, S&P views management as crucial. Ultimately, the best measure of management's capabilities is a proven track record of profitability and economic value added, both in terms of outperforming industry norms and providing an acceptable return on investment.

S&P reviews:

- Historic financial and operating results (comparative review)
- Quality and extent of planning and forecasting
- Philosophy towards credit (recourse) risk, acquisitions, diversification, and leverage
- Controls: management, financial, and internal auditing
- Lines of succession, decision making, and strength of middle management

Loan Production

The commodity-like aspect of mortgage product, combined with industry cyclicality and susceptibility to overcapacity, means that success in this area is driven by cost containment.

S&P reviews:

- Distribution flexibility (retail, wholesale, and bulk)
- Cost to originate and profit center results (comparative review)
- Product-mix adequacy and flexibility
- Contingent liability and counterparty-risk exposure relating to third parties (brokers and correspondents)
- Geographic opportunities and constraints

Underwriting and Quality Control

Taking the perspective of the investor, historical and projected delinquency, foreclosure frequency, and loss severity are assessed.

S&P reviews:

- Credit approval process: review of loan approval system and quality control methodology
- Delinquency and foreclosure results in aggregate on a year of origination basis by product type and location (comparative review)
- Investor and mortgage insurer tenure and experience
- Comparative underwriter tenure and experience
- Loan file sample due diligence

Secondary Marketing

Historic risk tolerance, hedging, and trading performance are reviewed in combination with existing strategies and controls.

S&P reviews:

- Department controls and guidelines
- Pricing philosophies and benchmarks
- Department profit center results (comparative review)
- Historic risk management results
- Current trading positions and strategies
- Sensitivity of current trading and hedging strategies to adverse interest rate movements

Loan Administration

S&P believes that success in this area is driven by operating scale attainment and proactive portfolio mix management.

S&P reviews:

- Loan administration profit center results (comparative review)
- Sensitivity of on- and off-balance sheet servicing value and expected revenue to prepayment
- Servicing value recourse exposure and susceptibility to credit losses, administration, investor accounting and reporting, payment processing, payoffs and assumption, taxes and insurance management, collections, defaults, and customer service
- Quality of on-balance sheet servicing

Financial Position

The focus is on unique mortgage operation issues as they pertain to profitability, capital structure, cash flow protection, and financial flexibility.

S&P reviews:

- Accounting quality-asset sales, hedge transactions, and capitalized and excess servicing
- earnings quality, reliance on nonoperating (sale of servicing) sources
- Reserve policy and adequacy
- Capital adequacy relative to interest rate risk as it pertains to servicing prepayments, warehouse spreads, and secondary marketing strategies
- Capital adequacy relative to credit risk as it pertains to recourse and contingent liability exposure
- Internal and external sources of liquidity
- Evaluation of options under stress: access to various capital markets, affiliations with other entities, ability to sell assets

After completion of our due diligence review, each of the above areas is assigned a ranking of strong, above average, average, below average, or weak. Then an overall ranking is assigned to the mortgage operation. Ranking definitions are as follows:

Strong: A firm in this category demonstrates the highest degree of ability, productivity, and competence through (1) strong and stable management, (2) a highly effective production capacity, (3) the use of conservative underwriting standards and a quality control system that extends well beyond industry standards, (4) a successful secondary market strategy, and (5) a superior loan servicing operation.

Above average: This category signifies a very high degree of ability, productivity, and competence. It differs from higher ranked firms in a small degree, primarily connected with track record, stability, flexibility, or financial condition.

Average: An average firm exhibits a variable track record evidencing recent improving performance. Such a firm may utilize nontraditional underwriting standards and experience delinquencies similar to national averages. Servicing capacity is typically adequate, but systems do not incorporate most recent technological developments.

Below average: Lack of ability, productivity, and competence is evident. This ranking signifies a variable track record evidencing recent declining performance. Typically, underwriting is consistently more liberal than traditional standards and servicing capabilities are marginal.

Weak: A poor track record and recurrent losses are indicative of this category. Underwriting is exclusively nontraditional, quality control is mediocre, and delinquency experience far exceeds national averages. Servicing ability is overextended, and systems capacity is overutilized.

Detailed analyses of this type will become increasingly important to many market participants who require a thorough understanding of the operational capability productivity, and competence of the mortgage lenders and servicers with whom they deal. This includes banks, thrifts, mortgage bankers, investors who trade in whole loans and mortgage-backed securities, state housing agencies, conduits as buyers and issuers, investment banks as underwriters and issuers, and warehouse lenders as credit providers to mortgage firms. Additionally, S&P utilizes this detailed analysis as part of its judgment of credit support levels. Firms securing above average and strong rankings may, as a result, be able to provide slightly lower credit allowance on loss coverage requirements on structured transactions than would weaker servicers.

The Credit Function of the Lender

The originators/servicers competitive strengths and weaknesses in the specific business line generating the assets being securitized may influence the firm's growth strategies and consequently the credit function and the performance of the portfolio.

The influence may be at the front end of the process, during origination, or over the life of the product during servicing. Moreover, the strategic and economic value of the business unit originating or servicing the assets to the overall organization may impact the support or investment they are able to garner should the need arise. Therefore, marketing, financial, and business strategies are evaluated specifically relative to their impact on past and future portfolio quality and servicing capability. Internal shifts in strategy or business needs, and their consequent impact on an originator's credit operation, can materially impact portfolio performance over time. For example, declines in the credit quality of auto receivables evident between 1985 and 1992 for the major captive finance companies, and the consequent increase in delinquency and loss levels reflects a managed relaxation of credit standards including extension of loan terms and reduction of recourse lending, as well as the effects of recession. These changes were captured in successively higher credit support levels on auto receivable transactions done between 1985 and 1992.

The degree of influence of the originator/servicer varies with the type of assets and structure, and the relative degree of decision autonomy provided by the documents. However it may be material. For example, several transactions provide for reinvestment of pool cash flow into new loan originations, or are done through master trusts, which provide for securitization of ongoing originations. In these transactions it is necessary to conduct ongoing due diligence on the originator's changing business strategies and underwriting policies to monitor the quality of new originations relative to outstandings. In some products, like credit cards and home equity loans, servicers retain the authority to make changes in pricing and payment terms, both of which can influence pool cash flow in outstanding structured securities.

As a result of these influences, the rating process entails an ongoing dialogue with the originator/servicer regarding the business and credit conditions in securitized business lines. Overall, this comparative review of underwriting is helpful in explaining past and expected portfolio performance.

Another component of the analysis of the assets is a review of the originator's credit function, including written credit policies and operating practices. The underwriting process, including the sourcing of applications, credit review, appraisals, credit approval guidelines, documentation, and disbursement are discussed and evaluated to gain insight into the relative risk of the portfolio relative to competition and standard industry practices. In pools characterized by higher diversification and broad dispersion, like consumer assets, the rating agencies seldom review actual loan documentation but concentrate instead on the originator's documentation procedures. As such, rating agencies rely on judgments and evaluations of policies and practices as confirmed or evidenced by portfolio performance. Consequently, confirmation of the seller's representations and warranties are monitored through tracking portfolio performance against expectations.

The evaluation of the seller/servicer also includes adequacy of staffing and systems to meet servicing needs specifically in the area of collections. The review of the collection process concentrates on the timing and prioritization of collection actions, policies and practices impacting rewrite, restructuring, extension, and forbearance, all of which could impact portfolio cash flow and loss experience. Past and current charge-off policies are reviewed to determine whether the operating and accounting practices of loss recognition are consistent with both transaction disclosures and the servicing obligations required by the transaction.

The recovery procedures are also reviewed. Recoveries on defaulted and charged-off securitized assets often benefit investors directly or indirectly through the reimbursement and replenishment of the credit support provider.

Structured transactions provide a range of flexibility to the servicers of securitized assets. While most often incorporating standard industry practices, transactions sometimes require practices which are quite specific and which are fully intended to limit the servicer's flexibility. To the extent that S&P's rating methodology reflects certain assumptions about the relevant time frames between defaults and repossessions, foreclosures, and subsequent collections, these are periodically monitored and confirmed or adjusted accordingly. Increasingly, transactions are permitting greater autonomy to the servicer, with the result being that the servicer's judgment regarding values, relative supply and demand trends, the direction of interest rates, and other influential factors are more meaningful to the realization of investor asset value. For example, high yield bond and commercial loan-backed transactions routinely allow an element of value oriented trading. Multifamily and commercial mortgage transactions permit considerable discretion regarding loan restructuring, foreclosures, and other collection actions which could materially affect ultimate recovery value. Where such discretion is significant, periodic review of servicing operations is a meaningful part of the surveillance process.

Servicing costs are normally covered through receivable cash flow, and in rated transactions, the yield of the securitized assets is sufficient to cover both the certificate interest rate and servicing costs. Such costs are estimated based on standard industry costs, and therefore reflect average receivable characteristics and quality, with some cushion to provide for variation in specific portfolio requirements. However, where assets perform particularly poorly, requiring substantial legal collection efforts, the servicing costs may erode investor protection. Consequently, assets for which servicing expenses are widely variable depending upon quality are more vulnerable to such a loss of value.

Control functions, including loan and accounting systems, audit procedures, and results are also often reviewed as part of the initial due diligence. This is done primarily with the purpose of determining if the accounting and loan systems perform consistently with the requirement or needs of the transactions.

PORTFOLIO ANALYSIS AND THE FRAMEWORK FOR JUDGING CREDIT SUPPORT LEVELS

Portfolio performance is the most meaningful component of investor protection in an asset-backed transaction. The analysis concentrates on projecting portfolio delinquency, default frequency, and loss severity in periods of severe economic stress.

The review of the securitized portfolio is oriented toward identifying specific underwriting criteria and other relevant risk concentrations, and includes a comparative analysis of delinquency, loss, prepayment, and in some cases dilution performance relative to industry averages and peers. S&P relies on actuarial analysis if the portfolio is characterized by a high degree of diversification and dispersion, such as consumer loan portfolios. But an obligor-specific approach is used on small, less diversified pools. In small pools each obligor is rated, and S&P utilizes the ratings to determine default probabilities. For secured receivables, S&P reviews underlying asset values. As a result, S&P tracks the business and economic factors affecting securitized asset markets, including residential and multifamily housing, and commercial real estate, both on a national and a geographic basis, particularly with respect to value trends. These factors as well as other relevant value support structures, such as insurance, are reviewed to evaluate expected loss severity. Issuers are often requested to provide breakdowns of portfolio performance by several relevant underwriting or risk-related criteria, geographic concentration, origination method or date, lending officer, or approval process, internal credit score, or other relevant identifying characteristic which could give insight into the quality and performance of the portfolio.

Portfolio performance cannot always be reviewed over economic cycles as a result of limited company or industry history. Therefore, on each receivable type, studies are conducted which capture total or representative industry performance through periods of recession or severe economic stress. These historic examples are helpful in defining expected ranges of performance for each receivable type, and provide the basic framework for determining appropriate credit support levels. For example, residential mortgage foreclosure frequency and severity of loss assumptions, which are the basis for S&P's loss criteria in the residential mortgage sector, are based on both the residential mortgage portfolio experience of the life insurance companies during the 1930s, which were major mortgage lenders during that time, and on the more recent Texas residential mortgage portfolio experience of the 1980s of FNMA, FHLMC, and other major mortgage lenders and mortgage insurers. The more recent experience largely confirms expectations derived from the depression era data. Such illustrative historical examples for other asset types have tended to be relatively more recent, but performance has been tracked through two and sometimes three recent recessions. For auto and credit card receivables, second mortgages and multifamily mortgages, manufactured housing, marine loans, and unsecured personal loans, these more recent recessions have been used to provide a benchmark for asset performance. The benchmark performance is supplemented by a review of current and expected industry and economic conditions which could cause performance to vary from past experience. Generally, stress levels for longer maturity assets, such as mortgages, are based on the worst historical experience, while stress levels on shorter maturity assets would depend, to a greater degree, on current expectations.

Studies formally correlating underwriting criteria to portfolio performance have been relatively rare outside of the residential mortgage market. In that market, substantial performance data are available to distinguish the relative impact of various underwriting or loan factors on performance. Therefore, specific factors such as loan to value, amortization schedule, property type, loan purpose, and several others are factored into the analysis by adjusting either the expected default frequency or loss severity on a particular portfolio. Relative underwriting practices are meaningfully predictive of portfolio performance in all types of lending, but to date, reflecting these factors into the expected performance of the portfolio has been more judgmental than driven by rigorous historical performance comparisons. S&P expects a wide disparity of portfolio performance based on differences in underwriting, servicing, underlying asset protection, and the character and degree of risk concentrations. The process of securitization itself is providing a meaningful data base of portfolio performance statistics describing static pool behavior relative to specific underwriting criteria.

The asset selection criteria used from transaction to transaction may improve or diminish the relative performance of the securitized pool. Asset selection may reflect underwriting, aging, or delinquency or credit scoring criteria which could meaningfully impact pool performance.

THE EVOLUTION OF CREDIT SUPPORT

The credit support or enhancement mechanism used to protect investors has become increasingly efficient but more complex. The efficiency has been driven in part by the bank regulators who, through risk-based capital guidelines and greater attention to the implications of credit and liquidity support arrangements provided by banks to structured financings, have imposed capital charges more consistent with the risks inherent in bank-provided support arrangements.

More important, the broadening market for structured securities coupled with the drive to make the structures more economic and more self-supportive has generated an increasing segmentation along the credit curve, enabling issuers to more efficiently distribute, and price, risk. This segmentation has been achieved predominantly through either tiered credit supports or through the allocation of a receivables cash flow into classes or tranches, with each credit support provider or class of debt having separate sensitivities to credit and cash flow risks.

Use of bank credit enhancement began in the late 1970s in the municipal market when bank letters of credit were used to support municipal and industrial development bond issues.

Both principal and interest of these early structured transactions were fully supported by the letter of credit. That is, if the underlying beneficiary of the financing was unable to repay the offering, the bank was obligated to repay under its letter of credit. Rating approaches for the transaction varied slightly among agencies. S&P's analysis assumed the bankruptcy of the underlying issuer and thus transactions were rated solely on the credit quality of bank and legal structure, with no review and no rating of the underlying project or issuer. The securities were marketed and traded based on the quality and outlook for the bank and the status of the letter of credit, not the strength of the underlying issuer. However, the failure of some large U.S. regional banks which had been active in the credit enhancement business and the current weakness of several others has heightened a disclosure problem. There is often insufficient information and secondary market disclosure on the financial strength of the underlying issuer to value the bonds as the bank deteriorates. Investors and regulators will demand a greater focus on the quality of underlying projects supported by full credit enhancement.

Bond issues fully insured by the financial guarantee industry are similar in many respects, especially with respect to the relative lack of secondary market disclosure on the risks of the underlying issuers. While the financial guarantee industry must conform with conservative credit and financial parameters to preserve their strong AAA repayment capacity, some structured market participants are beginning to demand greater disclosure regarding the quality of the underlying issuer or structure on fully insured issues. As a result of these needs, and in response to modest pricing distinctions relevant to underlying issuer credit quality, S&P has begun to provide ratings on the underlying issuer when the ratings are requested by the issuer. This may become more meaningful in the fully insured taxable structured markets. On fully insured taxable structured transactions S&P reviews the underlying bond structure in much the same way as an uninsured issue is reviewed. The issue is assigned a rating which represents the risk to the insuror, and these ratings are used in the analysis of portfolio risk and capital adequacy of the insuror or guarantor. Consistent with their strong AAA ratings, the financial guarantors generally limit their exposure to only investment grade risk. Consequently, most taxable structured issues with full bond insurance are already of investment grade quality prior to bond insurance.

Most mortgage and asset-backed structures rely on partial as opposed to full credit support. The principal forms of third party support are parent company guarantees, bank letters of credit, and sureties or guarantees, all of which are irrevocable and fully enforceable. The sizing of partial credit supports includes several factors, but predominantly is based on the expected losses on the assets, as previously discussed, and the degree of protection sought. While the credit support is primarily needed to protect against ultimate loss, the form of the credit support, and its use in providing protection against certain liquidity risks, is also important. The highest ratings are intended to provide a level of protection sufficient to cover portfolio losses in an extremely stressful scenario, consistent with a depression or severe recession. Successively lower ratings correspond to successively lower levels of protection.

Credit support for an issue is expressed as a fixed percentage of the notes outstanding or a fixed dollar amount.

In transactions where the receivable pool amortizes, it generally is possible to decrease the credit support either in proportion with the notes outstanding or through reductions based on the performance of the portfolio. In some transactions, such as mortgage securities, the reduction or stepdown of loss protection occurs based on a fixed formula defined in transaction documents. This formula captures the portfolio performance. The stepdown criteria is predominantly based on the expected loss curve of the portfolio as evidenced by static pool performance of similar assets. For example, the credit support for a fixed rate residential mortgage pool would be allowed to stepdown after a period of five years, provided that the pool's delinquency and loss levels were below a certain amount. This gives credit for benefits of seasoning in the portfolio, but limits such reductions to only high quality portfolios. In all cases, third party credit supports have a minimum coverage level. The minimum coverage level reflects the greater cash flow uncertainty existing at and near maturity of the issue. This in turn reflects the uncertainty regarding the statistical validity of the original portfolio analysis for a declining and possibly less diversified pool. It also takes into consideration certain credit policies, which may affect the cash flow availability to redeem notes at maturity.

Adequate credit support reflects the amount and timing of potential charges for losses against assets. Coverage under the credit support decreases when the support is drawn upon.

The credit support will reinstate up to a given percentage of notes outstanding or dollar amount, whichever is applicable, when reimbursed through excess cash flow off the receivables, recoveries on defaulted or delinquent receivables, or otherwise. Where an issue is structured so that excess cash flow either reimburses the entity providing the credit support, or provides direct support in the form of a reserve fund, S&P analyzes the certainty of receiving sufficient excess cash flow.

Once transactions are rated, S&P conducts surveillance which tracks the performance of the securitized portfolio, the amount and quality of the credit support, and the creditworthiness of any related parties to the transaction. Portfolio performance information is derived from monthly servicing reports provided by the servicer which tracks both portfolio credit quality and cash flow performance. Rating changes that have occurred to date have been predominantly based on deterioration in the credit support provider rather than on an erosion of the level of credit support.

S&P tracks credit support levels against expected portfolio losses, and may upgrade or lower ratings over the life of a transaction if the level of credit support is determined to provide significantly greater or lesser protection against expected losses due to varying portfolio performance. However, reflecting the weak link approach, a transaction is normally rated no higher than its credit support provider. Some exceptions exist but these are situations where the exposure to the credit support is limited due to either the availability of sufficient internally generated loss protection, like excess spread or reserve funds to cover expected losses, or the transaction contains a trigger which requires a replacement of the support provider or converts the credit support instrument to cash both upon any decline the credit support providers rating. These triggers have been utilized to permit A-1+ rated credits to provide partial credit enhancement to AAA rated structured transactions. The weak link approach to rating structured transactions with partial credit support providers has been constructive in guaranteeing that only strong credit support providers are utilized, and in alerting investors to an erosion of protection if the credit support provider is downgraded. However, it does limit the extent to which the rating alone can be utilized to convey improvement in the credit support level relative to expected losses. For example, ratings may be lowered on transactions where the credit support provider is downgraded, notwithstanding a relative degree of reliance on the credit support provider.

SELF-SUPPORTING STRUCTURES

The imposition of more conservative bank regulatory treatment and risk-adjusted capital guidelines have increased the capital charges for recourse and made bank letters of credit a more costly form of credit support. The banking and insurance industries were the significant suppliers of credit support to the mortgage and asset-backed markets throughout the 1980s. But over the decade of the 1980s the declining credit quality of the insurance and banking industries has increased the demand for self-supportive issues.

SUBORDINATION STRUCTURES

In response to this deterioration of credit quality, transactions have been increasingly structured to be self supportive, largely through senior/subordination, overcollateralization, spread account, and cash collateral structures. In such transactions, the credit support comes from the subordination of cash flow off the assets, or from excess cash flow off the assets which exceeds the repayment requirements of the securities and the servicing fee accumulated in a reserve fund, or both. Cash collateral accounts, which are normally provided through bank loans, are used as a replacement for a letter of credit. In transactions structured with a cash collateral account, a bank lends funds to the issuing trust for the benefit of debtholders and the cash is held in liquid, high quality investments available to cover portfolio delinquencies and losses.

These structures eliminate the third party dependence, but they may also reduce the third party review of the underlying portfolio. Subordinated and reserve fund structures, for example, increase the reliance on the performance and value of the underlying assets. Therefore the market's pricing of subordinated and reserve fund issues has been correspondingly more sensitive to perceived changes in the quality of the assets.

There has been increasing segmentation along the credit curve. The cash flow to the subordinated tranches is being segmented to create various grades of debt, covering the full rating spectrum. The market for the most junior or equity tranches remains relatively illiquid, and fairly inefficient. The explosive growth of the mortgage pass-through market, and the increasing rise of senior subordinated structures as the preferred form of credit support, is broadening the equity tranch market. Increasingly, these equity tranches have been themselves securitized. The diversity, and consequent risk reduction achieved by pooling such subordinated tranches, has facilitated sellers in securitizing and selling these instruments, removing them from the balance sheet.

Bond structures vary widely as to the release of cash to the subordinated tranches. Several structures, like fast pay/slow pay or shifting interest allocation, provide protection to senior debtholders which has generally increased as the senior tranches amortize. Others, like declining subordination, allow a faster payout to subordinated tranches, often contingent on portfolio performance triggers, similar to the stepdown trigger mechanisms used with third party forms of credit support. Research and analysis of this sector of the market is increasing, aided by the proliferation of modeling capabilities to review cash flow behavior, and therefore tranch performance, under a variety of credit and interest rate environments. Investors will find it increasingly important to distinguish, particularly subordinated securities, by the type of senior/subordinated structure utilized.

The objective in structuring any pass-through is to ensure that, even if the underlying receivable pool experiences substantial losses, interruptions in cash flow caused by delinquencies and defaults do not impair the ability to make distributions of principal and interest to certificate holders. In the case of a senior/subordinated pass-through, that objective translates into making sure that the holders of the senior certificates receive 100 percent of their share of the cash flow by introducing a second, or several, junior classes of certificate holders whose rights to receive their proportional share of the cash flow are subordinated to the rights of the senior certificate holders. In other words, whenever the pool suffers a loss that threatens to result in a shortfall in amounts due to the senior certificate holders, cash flow otherwise due to the subordinated certificate holders may be diverted to cover the shortfall.

In a traditional pass-through, the objective of keeping certificate holders whole is achieved by making available various credit enhancements, chief among which is a pool insurance policy or letter of credit. The credit enhancement provides credit loss protection equal to a specified percentage of the principal balance of the receivables in the pool as of the cutoff date. In a senior/subordinated pass-through, subordination of the rights of the junior certificate holders, becomes the senior certificate holders credit protection. Thus, the initial principal balance of the subordinated certificates should be at least equal to the amount of loss protection provided by the pool policy or letter of credit in a standard pass-through transaction. The analytical process to determine the credit risk posed by a specific loan pool and, therefore, the proportion of certificates that should be subordinated, is basically the same as that used to determine the coverage required for the same pool if loss protection were to be provided in the form of third party supports. However, because loss protection is being provided in the form of subordination, the impact of several factors on the credit analysis requires amplification.

In one critical respect, the protection provided by subordination cannot simulate the protection provided by an insurance policy or a letter of credit. These forms of support are perfectly liquid up to the limit of coverage, whereas the right to receive periodic cash flow is relatively illiquid. If, in a standard pass-through transaction, a portion of the underlying receivable pool defaults, the servicer or the trustee can obtain funds to cover the resulting losses by presenting claims to the credit support provider as soon as the losses are realized. By contrast, in a senior/subordinated structure, because the junior certificate holders can only be asked to give up cash flow that is currently due to them or that previously has been placed in a reserve fund, funds may not be available exactly when needed to cover losses.

Because this lack of liquidity can create two situations in which shortfalls may develop, the legal structure governing the administration of the pass-through trust estate must provide protection to the senior certificate holders against shortfalls to alleviate these risks.

The first shortfall situation is caused by short-term delinquencies. The second results when non-recoverable losses on defaulted loans must be recognized. The legal structure governing the administration of the pass-through trust estate must provide protection against such shortfalls to the senior certificate holders.

Short-term delinquencies are not a factor in determining required loss coverage. Consequently, transactions are not normally structured so as to rely on junior certificate cash flow as the primary source of liquidity. This is often provided by either obtaining a cash performance bond from a rated surety, depositing cash at closing, obtaining a letter of credit from a highly rated financial institution, or relying on a highly rated servicer or master servicer to make advances to cover short-term delinquencies.

If subordination is relied on to provide delinquency-related, short-term liquidity needs, it may be necessary to increase the level of subordination. Whether an increase is required depends on the results of the stressed case cash flow runs.

Short-term liquidity is the one area in which S&P applies a modification of the “weak link” approach in that, if a rated master servicer is relied on to provide advances to cover delinquencies, the master servicer’s rating can be one full rating category below the desired rating of the securities. Thus, a master servicer rated “A” can be relied on to provide short-term liquidity for pass-through certificates rated “AA.”

It should be noted, however, that the modified weak link approach does not apply if some other mechanism is used to provide short-term liquidity. If a letter of credit from a rated institution is used, the institution must be rated as highly as the pass-through certificates. If a cash performance bond is used, the provider of the bond must be rated as highly as the securities.

In the majority of the public transactions rated thus far, the issuer has opted for the cash deposit alternative. This deposit is generally referred to as the initial deposit. In some instances, the issuer retains the right to recover the initial deposit by substituting dollars owed to the junior certificate holders for its own funds, and the issuer's right to recover its funds is prior to the junior certificate holders' rights to receive any cash flow. Hence, the issuer has shifted whatever risk may be associated with ultimate recovery of the initial deposit to the junior certificate holders.

Liquidity to cover nonrecoverable losses: In order to test whether the required level of subordination will provide adequate liquidity when the receivable pool experiences losses, the issuer or underwriter is asked to submit cash flow runs showing how the pool would perform under stress scenarios. Of course, many of the other assumptions needed as inputs to the cash flow model, such as the level of subordination and the prioritization of cash inflows and outflows, are dependent on the specifics of a transaction.

There are four basic types of subordination structures that have appeared in the asset-backed market, each one with many different variations. The four basic subordination structures are: fast pay/slow pay, shifting interest, fixed amount and declining subordination.

In a fast pay/slow pay structure, 100 percent of all principal collections including prepayments is paid to the senior class certificate holders. This accelerates the paydown of the senior certificate holders and shortens the exposure period during which losses can occur. Not only do the senior certificate holders receive all of the subordinated principal, but they get the benefit of the junior class finance charges to cover losses prior to the use of the junior class principal. Simply put, the senior certificate holder receives interest and principal owed to them prior to the junior class receiving anything. Therefore, loan delinquencies and losses will be covered by both excess spread and class B interest prior to the use of class B principal. Since all principal payments are paid to A, there is no release of credit support as there might be in an LOC deal.

Finally, what is common about most fast pay/slow pay senior subordinated structures is that A is only promised interest, scheduled principal, and defaults if the money is available. If funds are not available to make these payments in any given month, the shortfall is carried forward to next month, and the class B amount is usually reduced by such shortfalls. This is not a default, as the investors are only promised payments if available. However, through cash flow analysis, S&P determines that current interest is always paid on a timely basis.

This "if available," structure helps to retain excess spread and class B's interest accumulates for the benefit of A, the senior certificate holders. Both of these sources can be used in future months to cover any prior shortfalls to A holders. Therefore, excess spread and class B interest can have a cumulative effect, since prior losses can be paid from future amounts.

In a fast pay/slow pay structure, all of B's payments including interest can be used for the benefit of A. This accelerates A's payments, reduces A's exposure to losses, causes the credit support on an expected basis to grow as a percentage of remaining collateral, and can provide substantial benefit to A holders from excess spread. For these reasons, S&P views the fast pay/slow pay structure as the strongest of the senior subordination types.

The main difference between shifting interest and fast pay/slow pay structures is that in a shifting interest structure some principal payments can be released to the subordinated classes. In "shifting interest" transactions, all scheduled principal payments and defaults are allocated pro rata between the A and B certificate holders. Note that on a monthly basis all of A's payments must be made before B gets anything, therefore, A receives 100 percent of all principal prepayments. However, since B receives some principal payments there is a release of credit support.

S&P views shifting interest subordination as weaker than the fast pay/slow pay type since some cash is released to B even though credit support as a percentage of current outstanding principal would still be expected to grow with prepayments. Additionally, this structure still provides benefits to the class A holders from class B finance charges as well as excess spread through the "if available" structure.

FIXED AMOUNT

The fixed amount structure was used by Sears, Roebuck & Co. in some of its credit card transactions. Rather than issuing a class B certificate, Sears subordinated up to a fixed dollar amount of seller collections. As an example, Sears issued $250 million of "AAA" rated credit card certificates out of Sears Credit Card Account Trust 1990B. The transaction incorporated a minimum seller price of

15 percent of investor certificates. Sears subordinated up to 9 percent of seller collections. This acts like a flat LOC structure since the dollar amount is fixed, and any use of seller collections for the investors will reduce the subordinated amount. Therefore, there is no additional benefit derived from seller finance charges. Additionally, unlike other senior subordinated structures where the subordinated amount must cover losses of the entire collateral pool, the 9 percent amount in Sears 1990B only covers losses allocated in the investor price. Any losses on the seller price are absorbed by the seller and do not reduce the available subordinated amount.

Another characteristic of the "fixed amount" structure is a monthly liquidity concern. Since the other structures promise investors payments only "if available," monthly cash flow need only be sufficient to cover current investor interest. In the case of the "fixed amount" structure, like a letter of credit-backed deal, the monthly cash flow must cover not only interest and principal received, but also investor defaults on a timely basis. Unlike most senior subordinated structures where the class B is reduced for class A shortfalls, any shortfalls in this case result in a reduction of the class A amount. Whereas in an LOC issue the entire credit support is available on a monthly basis, subordination relies on current monthly payments from the subordinated amount to cover shortfalls. If the monthly payment rate declines materially the monthly cash flow generated from the subordinated amount may not be sufficient to cover the necessary payments to class A investors. Therefore, it is necessary to have a minimum seller price large enough so that the cash flow generated in any month be enough to pay investors as promised. This is the reason for the 15 percent minimum seller price.

To summarize, the Sears structure subordinates a fixed dollar amount of seller collections to cover investor shortfalls, does not allow for any additional benefit from class B finance charges (the seller price in this example), and must provide for a seller price large enough to cover any liquidity needs.

DECLINING SUBORDINATION

S&P has also rated senior subordinated transactions that have incorporated stepdown mechanisms, primarily those with residential mortgages, home equity loans, and manufactured housing loans. With each of these assets, the loss curve is somewhat uncertain. Since S&P does not want any credit enhancement released until after the peak loss period of the respective pool has occurred, the transactions are structured so that the subordination amount is only reduced for losses for a certain period of time. If, at that time, certain performance tests are met, then the subordinated amount can amortize to a reduced level by paying principal to class B. For example, in the Merrill Lynch 1989-1 home equity transaction, the initial subordinated amount was 15 percent. This amount can only be reduced by losses until the class A pool factor is 70 percent. After that, the subordinated amount may step down to satisfactory pool performance. Such declining subordination structures also provide a floor subordination amount.

With assets, such as automobile loans, for which there is considerable evidence that a predictable loss curve exists, an amortizing form of credit support is acceptable. The automobile transactions that have used this form of credit support have not been structured as REMICs and therefore cannot use class A principal collections to pay class A interest. Therefore, the cash flow analysis must demonstrate that the cash generated from class B collections plus class A interest collections is sufficient to pay class A interest. When a declining senior subordinated structure is used, two primary concerns are (1) the cash generated from the subordinated amount on a monthly basis might be insufficient to cover timely interest, and (2) tail-end stress may result due to a less diversified pool and increased delinquencies. S&P's typical floor coverage is 10 percent of the original credit support. If the form of credit support is subordination, a reserve fund in an amount sufficient to cover these two concerns may be used. Sears and Chrysler issued automobile securities with a declining subordination amount and a reserve fund to cover these risks.

Spread account build-up has been another area regarded skeptically by investors, yet has become an increasingly important source of bondholder protection in some structured debt. The value one ascribes to excess spread is dependent on numerous assumptions regarding interest rates, prepayments, delinquency and loss performance, reinvestment rates, and in some cases product pricing decisions. Excess spread is the interest earned on the assets above the pass-through rate and servicing cost. S&P's approach to valuing excess spread is similar to its approach in evaluating portfolio loss potential in that it relies on stressing the factors influencing excess spread including prepayment and losses. Prepayment stress scenarios generally assume that higher coupon or higher-rate mortgages or receivables will prepay sooner and at a faster rate than lower-rate receivables.

Generally stress cases involve a conservative multiple of actual portfolio experience. Investors should carefully review the factors which could affect excess spread and be familiar with the assumptions used to judge whether spread account build-up will be sufficient to provide needed levels of credit support.

COUNTERPARTY RISKS

Structured transactions also have counterparties. These counterparties provide investment agreements, swaps, caps, and various liquidity supports which mitigate interest rate and liquidity risks inherent in structured transactions. Both the credit of these counterparties and a legal review of the relevant contract and its enforceability are also reflected in the ratings of these transactions. Therefore, in addition to knowing and tracking the credit support provider, investors should be aware of any providers of liquidity support, GICs, swaps, tax, interest rate, and currency risk protection. Most issuers use strong counterparties they are usually rated as highly as the transaction. S&P utilizes a weak link approach to rating structured issues in which the rating of an issue will generally be no higher than the rating of its weakest counterparty. Therefore the downgrading of a counterparty may weaken the credit of a structured transaction. The surveillance of these transactions includes monitoring counterparty exposure. If a counterparty is downgraded S&P reviews the significance of the counterparty's exposure within the context of the transaction. The significance of the counterparty exposure is determined by the size and duration of the exposure, whether it provides a primary or contingent level of protection, or the likelihood that protection will be needed, and the willingness and feasibility of the issuer substituting a higher rated counterparty. Several trends, including the development of the derivative markets and the globalization of capital markets, has made the use of counterparties more frequent. As securitization has become a more important funding source, issuers have demonstrated a greater willingness to restructure transactions upon the downgrading of a counterparty as an effort to preserve the credit quality of these instruments. Moreover counterparties are beginning to allow downgrade triggers, converting their obligation to cash.

THE TRUSTEE

The trustee plays a critical role in structured financings. The trustee bank performs the duties necessary to fulfill its indenture obligations and preserve investor rights. S&P relies on the trustee to perform these functions. To ensure this, trustee criteria for structured financing include the following:

- The trustee cannot resign without the appointment of a qualified successor.
- The trustee should hold dedicated assets in funds and accounts designated for a particular transaction.
- The funds and accounts should be held, in trust, for the benefit of investors. Such funds should be held in the trustee bank's trust department.
- The funds should not be commingled with other funds of the trust department.

The presence of trust funds and accounts insulates the structured financing against the insolvency of the trustee. In the event of such adversity, these funds, held in trust for the benefit of the investors, could not possibly be enjoined with the insolvent trustee's estate.

The trustee has primary responsibility for receiving payments from servicers, relevant guarantors, and other third parties, and remitting these receipts to the investors in accordance with the terms of the indenture. The trustee also receives periodic reports with respect to received payments and future projections. Such reports should be audited at least on an annual basis. The complexity of the transaction will determine the frequency and depth of the independent audits. Independent audits should be performed at least annually. Increasingly complex transactions may warrant more frequent independent audits.

Various structures may warrant that the trustee meet specific criteria. Such criteria are stated where applicable, and may include minimum capital and surplus requirements, assets under trust requirements, and recommended familiarity of experience with a given structure. Any warranties and representations that the trustee makes at the closing of a transaction should hold throughout the life of the issue. The trustee also should be willing and able to assume the responsibilities of the master servicer for the eligible asset upon its removal or resignation.

LEGAL RISKS

The intent of securitization is to create securities whose creditworthiness is largely independent from the seller of the assets. This separateness, which allows rating agencies to focus on the assets supporting the transaction more than the seller, is achieved by effectively reducing risks related to a seller's bankruptcy.

For sellers that can file under the Bankruptcy Code, there are potential payment risks that would prevent S&P from rating a transaction supported by a pledge of assets any higher than the rating of the company pledging the assets. There are four reasons for this. First, the automatic stay provision 362(a) of the Bankruptcy Code prevents anyone from taking actions against property of the debtor. Therefore, the automatic stay could prevent secured creditors with a perfected security interest in the debtor's assets from foreclosing on the assets without a court order. S&P's current rating system judges the "timely payment of principal and interest," therefore such a delay would be inconsistent with the high ratings sought on these transactions. Second, Section 363 of the Bankruptcy Code allows a court to require a secured creditor to exchange its collateral for another asset as collateral. For example, a secured creditor with a lien on liquid collateral, such as receivables with a high turnover rate, might be required to give up its lien in exchange for a lien against the debtor's plant and equipment if the court were persuaded the receivables were necessary for the debtor's reorganization. Once again, this could substantially change the cash flow characteristics of the collateral, leading to a default in the transaction. Third, although a secured creditor may have a first lien position with respect to collateral pledged by a debtor, under certain circumstances a court can grant a prior lien to another creditor. And fourth, while both Sections 363(e) and 364(d)(1)(B) of the Bankruptcy Code require secured creditors to be adequately protected in connection with any substitution of collateral or priming of liens, a substitution that conveys "adequate protection," which is the descriptive standard of the law, may materially alter the credit quality and cash flow of the security.

These risks are mitigated by structuring to protect against bankruptcy-related risks. This is frequently done through the creation of special purpose bankruptcy remote issuers, often called special purpose corporations. SPCs are generally created as vehicles to issue debt or pass-through certificates of participation and are structured in such a way as to be unlikely to become subject to Bankruptcy Code proceeding. They may be established as a trust, corporation, or partnership.

The general attributes of a bankruptcy-remote, special-purpose entity are often included in the entity's charter or bylaws. However, these attributes, in the form of restrictive covenants, should also be contained in one or more transaction documents giving the security holders or their representative a right to enforce the restrictions. The entity must limit its activities to the financing transaction, and engage in no other business and must be prohibited from incurring any debt other than the rated debt unless: the debt is rated the same as the original debt; the debt is fully subordinated to the rated debt and does not constitute a claim enforceable against the entity in a bankruptcy proceeding; or the debt is nonrecourse and payable only from excess cash; and, to the extent the excess cash flow is insufficient to pay the additional debt, that debt must not constitute a claim enforceable against the entity in a bankruptcy proceeding. The entity must be prohibited from merging or consolidating with another entity unless the surviving entity is also subject to the bankruptcy-remote restrictions.

In addition to entities which are purposely structured to be SPCs, occasionally S&P may consider an issuer to be bankruptcy-remote even though the entity is not subject to the usual restrictions. This generally occurs with respect to municipal authorities because they cannot become the subject of an involuntary bankruptcy proceeding because the Code only allows them to be filed voluntarily. Also there usually exist strong disincentives which effectively discourage an authority from instituting a voluntary bankruptcy proceeding. Such criteria are monitored closely in an era of increasing financial stress on municipalities and their authorities.

Structuring a transaction so that an SPC issues the securities does not necessarily protect investors from risks associated with the transfer of the assets to the SPC and the intercorporate relationships between the SPC and its affiliates which could, under certain circumstances, result in a default on the rated debt.

S&P wants some assurance that, should a seller become subject to a bankruptcy proceeding, the assets and liabilities of the SPC will not be "consolidated" with those of its parent. This relief under the Bankruptcy Code and its predecessor, the Bankruptcy Act of 1898, is often called "substantive consolidation." Similar relief may be granted under nonbankruptcy state law and is often referred to as "piercing the corporate veil," the "instrumentality rule" or the "alter ego rule."

In other words, a subsidiary could have its assets and liabilities consolidated with its parent in a situation under certain circumstances. The result would essentially be one company comprised of both parent and subsidiary.

Although a creditor of the SPC who has a security interest in the assets of the SPC will continue to have a security interest in those assets after a consolidation, that interest will be subject to the relief found in the Bankruptcy Code noted earlier, such as substitution of collateral.

Elements considered by courts before ordering a consolidation of assets include: the degree of difficulty in segregating and ascertaining individual assets and liabilities, the presence or absence of consolidated financial statements, profitability of consolidation at a single physical location, commingling of assets and business functions, and unity of interests and ownership between the corporate entities.

In order to avoid the risk of consolidation with the parent company S&P requires that the following indicia of corporate separateness are met in rated structured financings. These include assuring that the SPC has and maintains separate officers and directors, separate books and records, regular meetings of the SPC's Board of Directors, separate offices, and separate bank accounts. Also, the SPC should pay its own expenses, have no benefit from intercompany guarantees, and have a representation and warranty from the SPC's parent stating that it will not hold itself out as responsible for debts of SPC. S&P also requests and receives a nonconsolidation opinion from the issuer's or underwriter's counsel citing the transaction's conformity with the standards listed above.

In addition to assuring that the issuer of the structured debt could not be consolidated with the parent company, it is also necessary to assume that the transfer of assets from the seller to the issuer is an effective legal transfer.

It is important that the transfer of assets from the seller to the SPC subsidiary be an absolute assignment or "true sale" of those assets. Even though the transfer is accomplished by means of a "purchase and sale" document, circumstances surrounding the transfer could lead a court to conclude that the transfer of assets was not a sale but a financing transaction whereby the SPC made a collateralized loan to its parent. If such a recharacterization occurred, the transfer of the assets would be viewed as a pledge of collateral by the parent, and the assets will be deemed to be part of the parent's estate under Section 541 of the Bankruptcy Code if the parent became subject to a proceeding. Consequently, the automatic stay (Section 362) and other Bankruptcy Code relief would apply to the assets and their proceeds. Factors examined by courts to determine whether or not the assets have been "sold" or absolutely assigned include:

- whether the assignee has a right of recourse to other assets of the assignor if the assigned assets do not provide sufficient funds;
- whether the assignee's rights in the property would end if the obligation were paid with funds from another source;
- whether the assignee must account to the assignor for any amount received from the assigned assets in excess of the amount of the obligation;
- whether the language used in the transfer document indicates an intention to make an assignment for security; and
- whether the assignment acts to discharge an underlying obligation.

To mitigate this risk S&P requests a legal opinion from underwriter's or issuer's counsel that the transfer of assets from the seller is an effective legal transfer and will not be recharacterized. S&P generally relies on such legal opinions to assure that the legal structure of the transaction conforms with the standards consistent with effective legal transfers. Despite this, some transactions may be structured such that the level of recourse, or some other significant indicia, raises doubts about the validity or effectiveness of the transfer. In those exceptional cases S&P takes what it calls a blended approach in which the rating of the seller, the potential for the transfer to be recharacterized, and the duration of the transaction are each considered and reflected in the rating of the transaction. In such cases, the unsecured rating of the seller may limit the rating assigned to the structured transaction. Therefore, both the probability of a bankruptcy of the seller and the probability of the transfer being recharacterized are reflected in the rating.

Recourse is probably the most meaningful indicia relative to legal transfers. Certain types of recourse may be acceptable. Section 9-502 of the Uniform Commercial Code, which applies to both sales and pledges of accounts and chattel paper, provides that "if the underlying transaction was a sale of accounts or chattel paper, the debtor is entitled to any surplus or is liable for any deficiency only if the security agreement so provides." Also, recourse against a seller for breach of a representation or warranty is unrelated to the performance of the asset. Recourse may be direct or indirect, such as a direct form of recourse, guaranty for losses. S&P believes that any evaluation of the level of recourse should be made within the context of the economic benefit of the transaction for the issuer, as opposed to within the narrow context of historical losses.

Other factors which might influence characterization of the transfer of assets as a sale or pledge include the treatment of the transfer for account and tax purposes, and the seller's ability to exercise control over the assets. The seller/originator often will continue to act as servicer after the sale of assets. As servicer, the seller will be responsible to collect payments on the assets and transfer collections to the purchaser. Commingling of collections by the seller/servicer can jeopardize both the purchaser's perfected ownership interest in the assets (if subject to the UCC) and the sale itself if the seller/servicer has sufficient dominion and control over the collections.

Whether the assets are transferred for cash plus a subordinated note or the purchase price is subject to a holdback which is dependent on asset performance can influence whether the transfer will be viewed as a sale or a pledge. If part of the purchase price is a subordinated note, that note will be paid only if the assets perform satisfactorily. Thus, the seller faces a risk, based on continued asset performance, that it will not receive its full purchase price. Similarly, a partial holdback of the purchase price, which holdback is paid to the seller only if the assets perform satisfactorily, subjects the seller to continued risk dependent upon asset performance. The rating process through the review and reliance of legal opinions and transaction documents largely mitigates these legal risks.

Banks and thrifts are not subject to a variety of conservancy and receivership provisions contained in the Federal Deposit Insurance Act, as amended by the Financial Institutions Reform, Recovery, and Enforcement Act of 1989 (FIRREA). As a result, banks may pledge rather than sell assets and obtain "AAA" ratings from the rating agencies based on the credit quality of the assets themselves independent from the credit quality of the bank.

Chapter 12

Credit Risks and Their Analysis in Asset Securitization

by David L. Gold
and
Julie P. Schlueter,
Duff & Phelps Corp.

I. INTRODUCTION

Asset-backed securities encompass a wide variety of credit risks beyond those present in the securitized asset pool itself. Segments making up the entire transaction package carry unique risks of their own. As investors in asset-backed securities invest only indirectly in the underlying assets, investment focus is directly on the repackaged structure. Here, a transaction structure may unwind (i.e., an early amortization event or event of default) due to even the most obscure credit related problem. Therefore, it is critical for the asset-backed player to be aware of and to cover these risks for the issue to perform at its most optimal risk/return trade-off point. Full consideration and coverage of all credit risks in these deals greatly enhances the security's quality and return.

Of course, not all risks can be fully mollified through structural enhancements. Basic credit risks will remain, but they can be minimized. This is the focal point for the following discussion: an explanation of various credit risks in typical asset-backed transactions and the various methods of mitigating those risks. This chapter will briefly discuss five major credit risk areas Duff & Phelps deems important to analyze and have covered in a high credit quality asset-backed transaction.

Securitization is a process which involves a shift in credit demand away from institutions such as commercial banks and finance companies toward the capital markets—in effect, shifting away from high-cost producers of debt to lower-cost producers. This shift involves the transfer of default risk on the assets sold. For credit protection and low-cost credit production, the credit risk on the assets transferred must be controlled and lowered. Credit enhancement techniques such as overcollateralization, guarantees, subordination, and additional credit facilities on the securitized asset pool lowers the inherent risk to the investor by shifting expected credit risk to a third party. The measurement of this risk and the subsequent "sizing" of the credit enhancement is critical to effect the transfer of the asset pool.

Asset risk analysis is performed through a variety of techniques common to general credit analysis. Asset pools large enough can be analyzed through actuarial techniques. Consumer assets such as credit card receivables, auto loan and lease receivables, residential mortgages, home equity loan receivables, and boat loan receivables, among others, commonly fall into actuarial analytical methods quite easily. Some commercial assets such as trade receivables fall into this category as well. Asset pools too small or with credits heavily concentrated among a few obligors generally cannot be analyzed effectively with the use of actuarial methods. Here, each credit is investigated on its own merit. The resulting small pool risk is a function of the weighted average risk of each individual credit. Corporate assets such as commercial loans and leases and high-yield bond pools fall into this category.

Credit enhancement facilitates the transfer of assets by reallocating a portion of the asset's credit risk to a third party or enhancement vehicle. The enhancement is usually the second layer of loss coverage, with the asset's excess yield or a cash reserve/discount forming the first layer. The risk transferred to the enhancer is then the obligation of the credit enhancer. Thus, the creditworthiness of the enhancer is the analyst's focus here. This risk must be fully understood before any investment decision is made.

Servicers manage and maintain control of the securitized assets and their cash flows. They may also be involved with supporting the transaction through advancement of asset-generated funds, expected but not yet received, to investors. Clearly, the servicer plays one of, if not the most, important functions in an asset-backed security. Duff & Phelps (see Appendices 12A, 12B) pays meticulous attention to a servicer's ability and willingness to perform these and other functions. Paramount to this equation is the servicer's credit quality or, in other words, the ability financially of the servicer to perform over the life of the transaction.

The trustee in a securitized transaction has several critical roles. From making payments to investors to trust account maintenance, the trustee must, like the servicer, be willing and able to perform his/her prescribed functions throughout the transaction. While the credit quality of the trustee is not as immediately important as that of the servicer, it is still a factor in the credit quality of the issue. This subject will be explored further.

Asset-backed securities involve myriad trust funds and accounts. From principal and interest funding accounts to cash collateral accounts, cash proceeds from the issue or from the assets themselves are held for periods of time in trustee/servicer administered accounts. Yield and maturity considerations aside, from a credit risk perspective, these funds and accounts must be invested in high credit quality instruments, for when the cash is ultimately transferred to investors it must be available. Therefore, eligibility requirements are structured into these deals to protect cash proceeds from default risk. This risk variable is critical to the overall credit quality of the transaction.

As the securitized finance field has evolved, more highly complex structures have developed. New ideas involve new risks. These risks should be covered to provide overall protection to the investor. Other variables such as guaranteed investment contracts (GICs) and interest rate swaps carry credit risks all their own which must be explored.

II. ASSET RISK

Not surprisingly, asset risk is the single most important sector of credit risk in a securitized transaction. The majority of the time spent in rating an asset-backed deal is focused on the pool of assets themselves. This section will explore the various elements of asset risk as they pertain to securitization and will be combined with a discussion of Duff & Phelps' analytical approach to these risk elements.

In general, securitized assets can be sorted into three broad categories: (1) consumer assets, (2) commercial assets, and (3) focus (other) assets. Consumer assets, both secured and unsecured, include retail auto loans and leases, credit card receivables, residential mortgages, and home equity loans (second mortgages), among others. These asset pools are typified by a large obligor base, homogeneous origination standards and credit terms, and are usually large enough (at least 250 to 500 individual credits) to be analyzed using actuarial techniques.

Commercial assets include equipment loans and leases, dealer inventor financing (floor plan), collateralized bonds/loans/leases (CBO,CLO), and trade receivables. These asset pools may or may not be able to be analyzed using actuarial methods. For instance, in a CBO or CLO pool with 50 credits, each credit must be analyzed separately to determine overall credit risk. Sampling techniques here cannot be relied on as each credit may have its own origination terms, yield and payment characteristics, and covenants. The same assets with, say, 150 credits, may be subject to an analytical method combining actuarial analysis with single credit risk analysis. Those credits with the highest credit exposure must be evaluated on their own due to the heavy weight each one bares on the entire pool. The remaining credits may be statistically sampled and subjected to actuarial analysis, with those statistical results applied to that portion of the pool. The two results are weighted and combined to determine base risk levels.

Focus assets are those that are both more esoteric and dependent upon special analytical consideration than other asset types. These include franchise agreements, special licensing agreements, student loans, and other less commonly securitized cash flow assets such as oil and gas rights and mortgage servicing rights. This group demands special "focus" on legal and cash flow considerations not found in other assets. Typical analytical techniques have to be augmented and new techniques must be introduced to analyze and control asset risk.

In a top-down analysis, the asset type itself generally determines the broad method of analysis, as briefly outlined above. Secured consumer receivables such as retail auto loans demand an actuarial technique with attention paid to origination and servicing standards and operations. In addition, the collateral itself demands special attention. Recovery rates on the collateral affect net losses, and as such, are important to the overall assessment of the asset risk. Unsecured consumer receivables such as credit card receivables demand similar attention but without focus on collateral. Commercial assets such as trade receivables, depending on the pool composition, may or may not allow actuarial techniques. Additional attention must be paid to seller credit terms, operating procedures, and the seller's own financial health and ability to continue production of its products. All in all, asset type determines the analytical starting point in assessing asset credit risk.

The following list outlines specific pool characteristics critical to a proper actuarial assessment of asset risk. Duff & Phelps' requires this information from issuers for asset risk assessment. Generally, the importance of each variable to the overall analysis is dependent on the asset type.

Pool Characteristics

- aggregate pool balance as of the cut-off date
- number of loans/leases
- average loan/lease balance
- weighted average yield (finance rate)
- range of finance rates
- weighted average remaining term to maturity
- range of remaining terms to maturity
- weighted average original term to maturity
- range of original term to maturity
- weighted average seasoning
- weighted average loan-to-value ratio (secured assets, i.e., mortgages)
- range of loan-to-value ratios
- new/used ratios (autos, boats, equipment, etc.)
- geographic distribution (state, city, etc.)
- pool selection criteria (delinquency status, obligor concentr., etc.)
- prepayment provisions/penalties
- cash flow projections
- fees/expenses
- historical payment and purchase rates (credit cards, student loans)
- average credit limits

This list is by no means exhaustive. Specific asset types demand particular attention to various characteristics. Frequently, such as in consumer assets, data from the selling firm's entire portfolio are requested to ascertain any differential between the pool's performance and the entire company's portfolio performance. Portfolio-wide trends affected by periodic or one-time portfolio purchases, sales, and changes in origination and servicing standards can then be identified and applied to the analysis. Here, the pool's analysis can be adjusted by these factors to properly ascertain the true, normalized base asset risk inherent in the transaction.

Portfolio and pool-specific delinquencies and losses, variables determined through the interplay of aggregate obligor performance and servicer-specific efforts are critical to the assessment of asset credit risk. Perhaps no other indicator has such a high correlation with expected future credit performance than loss and delinquency rates. Generally, Duff & Phelps requires five years of quarterly data at a minimum. A time series which includes performance figures through the latest recession and volatile interest rate period is preferable. Asset performance during expected future economic duress can then be more accurately forecasted if the data are comprehensive and thorough. The following highlights specific loss and delinquency data from the seller and/or servicer requested by Duff & Phelps:

Origination and Servicing Affected Variables (Loss and Delinquency Data)

- origination policies/procedures
- credit policies/procedures
- payment policies/procedures
- collection policies/procedures
- repossession polices/procedures
- 30/60/90-day delinquencies
- repossessions
- gross losses
- recoveries
- net losses
- accounts serviced/personnel ratio
- delinquent accounts/personnel ratio
- operating expenses/accounts

Significant changes in operating policies and procedures having any effect on historical operating performance must be indicated. These also include management strategic focus changes.

Not to be overlooked are basic structural characteristics unique to the asset class itself. Consumer perceptions, attitudes, and behavior are taken into account when determining cause and effect relationships in changes in consumer asset performance. For instance, seasonality inherent in delinquency patterns (i.e., increases in credit card receivable delinquencies are frequently seen in the summer vacation months) are applied to the analysis. Still another example is equipment lease yield changes due to lease prepayments or residual losses affected by equipment obsolescence. These "structural" characteristics are part of the intangible portion of asset credit risk analysis and must be properly weighted in the final analysis.

Unique to some corporate and focus assets are small pools. Single credit risk analysis must be preferred over actuarial techniques for proper risk measurement. A pool of, say, thirty-five corporate obligors under equipment leases to be securitized will require individual corporate credit analysis. In this instance, the company's ability and willingness to perform under the contract is reflected in the firm's senior debt rating. The senior rating is used to give additional credit to the senior, secured nature of the obligation (lease terms and conditions are examined to determine the priority of the specific credit). Weight given to residual values on the underlying equipment is considered to be an intangible factor due to the increasing difficulty in assessing these future values.

III. CREDIT ENHANCEMENT RISK

Once base, underlying asset risk has been quantified, credit enhancement levels are determined through an asset-specific stress test analysis. The stress test places stress on asset performance variables and cash flow determinants. The result is a figure correlating to the expected cumulative future loss on the stressed asset pool. Aggregate enhancement levels are then adjusted for the issue's specific rating level and priority under the transaction structure.

Securitizations involving a rating upgrade from the seller's or asset pool's own rating level typically involves a shift in asset risk away from the investor and toward the enhancer or enhancement vehicle. Where the risk is shifted to the balance sheet of a third party enhancer, risk analysis focuses on that entity. The enhancer's ability and willingness to perform under the various agreements executed in the deal is paramount. Whether in the form of an irrevocable letter of credit, surety bond, or other form of guarantee (full or partial), the provider's own senior rating is the basis for this risk analysis. This risk varies expectedly with the type of support pledged and the role of the supporter in the transaction.

Large commercial banks are typically the providers of letters of credit. The institution's own rating is determined through Duff & Phelps' corporate rating process involving comprehensive financial statement, capital structure, and managerial and strategic analysis, among others. Letters of credit ratings are taken from the provider's own senior debt rating. Standby letters of credit cannot be accepted as a credit enhancement vehicle for the simple reason that the issuing entity's discretion can alter the protection afforded. Discretionary actions are avoided with irrevocable letters of credit for the life of the agreement. Under these facilities, the issuing institution must commit its funds regardless of the circumstance. Downgrade protection is afforded through trigger mechanisms stated in the letter of credit agreement and the issue's indenture provisions. Generally, if the LOC provider's rating falls below a bench mark, the provider must be replaced with a suitable, creditworthy enhancer or some other type of enhancement immune to the added risk due to the downgrade. Duff & Phelps requires this protection on its LOC-enhanced deals.

Surety bonds are guarantees placed on the assets (i.e., student loan guarantees) or on the individual notes or certificates (i.e., financial guarantees) to provide for payment of principal and interest on the defaulted assets or securities. These guarantees may cover 100 percent of the assets, issue principal and interest, or issue interest or principal separately, or may cover that portion of risk just enough to bring up the rating to the targeted level. Financial guarantee firms, property-casualty insurers, and banks are the primary providers of sureties. The selling firm or its parent may also be the enhancer provided its corporate rating is high enough for the desired structured finance rating level. Regardless of the provider, credit risk if focused on the enhancer, much like that on letters of credit.

Although not directly related to asset risk coverage, liquidity facility providers' credit risk weighs heavily in the analysis of the transaction as a whole. Securitizations utilizing the commercial paper markets bear significant liquidity risk related to periodic refunding of the paper. In the event of a market disruption large enough to prevent refunding of the vehicle, a 100 percent liquidity facility must be available to step into the marketplace and reimburse commercial paper holders whose paper has matured. Most commercial paper has a life of 270 days or less and as such, the liquidity facility's own risk is related to this short-term funding need potential. Therefore, the short-term rating of the liquidity facility provider determines the rating of the facility as a whole. Where the facility is syndicated among several institutions, the rating applied is the weighted average short-term rating of the banks' participation. For asset-backed commercial paper programs, backed by corporate trade receivables for example, the liquidity facility's rating dominates the issue's rating.

IV. SERVICER RISK

As mentioned in the introduction, the obligation of the servicer in managing and maintaining control of the assets and the assets' cash flow is one of the most important aspects of a securitized transaction. It is the servicer who maintains the orderly and timely flow of funds from obligors to investors. Without a properly managed servicer, an asset-backed transaction is in serious danger of non-performance. Duff & Phelps evaluation of the servicer's capabilities encompasses several areas of review. They are: servicing history, experience, origination policies and procedures, servicing capabilities, management and human resources, growth/competition/business environment, and financial condition. The credit risk of a servicer is determined through an evaluation of the servicer's financial condition.

The financial condition of servicers varies significantly, and plays an important role in the ability of the servicer to continue to perform its contractual obligations over the life of the transaction. Some servicers have support from a strong parent while others may be start-up operations with limited working capital. Limited capital resources may restrict the servicer's ability to properly staff and equip operations in order to expand or to remain competitive.

The financial statement analysis of the servicer indicates its ability to make servicer advances, if required, and demonstrates its immediate viability. The servicer must exhibit the ability to remain in existence for the life of a transaction. If there is a possibility that the operations may not continue or that the servicer may be unable to fulfill its obligations under securitization documents, provisions must be included to provide for a substitute or master servicer. Servicers not yet profitable must have a source of adequate working capital. In sum, servicer credit risk must be eliminated through strong financial and operating resources or through documented provisions for alternate servicing providers.

V. TRUSTEE RISK

The trustee's role in an asset-backed transaction is, like the servicer's, vital to the execution of the flow of funds from obligors to investors. The trustee must be able to perform its duties over the life of the transaction and, as such, Duff & Phelps evaluates this ability in the overall context of the deal's rating.

Among the requirements of a trustee are: management of the various trust funds and accounts, tracking and reporting monthly (or quarterly, depending on the deal) payment streams, and having the ability to take over the servicing function if the servicer withdraws or otherwise is unable to perform its duties. While trustee credit risk may not directly threaten investor returns, a trustee's sudden inability to perform may temporarily disrupt cash flows. This risk needs to be covered.

To maintain financial confidence in the trustee, the trustee's own long-term rating should be at least investment grade (BBB– or greater), and preferably A or better to protect against downgrade risk. Also, additional protection exists in the securitization documents which provide for the trustee's replacement and the appointment of a successor. This provision intends to protect all parties from risk, yet a suitable replacement must be found. Prior experience as an asset-backed transaction trustee is essential in order to mitigate operational risks going forward. For example, where a servicer is unable to perform the trustee must takeover servicing duties until a replacement is found for the servicer. Inherent in this ability is a trustee's servicing operational ability. Quite often, then, trustees in securitized transactions transcend the traditional role of bookkeeper in "plain vanilla" bond deals, and take on the role as servicer of last resort. Consequently, the trustee must have the financial and operational strength to perform emergency servicing functions. Duff & Phelps measures this ability through a financial and operational review. Trustees with prior experience facilitate this analysis.

VI. FUNDS AND ACCOUNTS RISK (Eligible Investments)

Cash flows from obligors as well as cash reserve funds are held by the servicer/trustee until the stated distribution date when cash is scheduled to be released or when it is needed in case of a distribution shortfall. To ensure timely payments to investors the cash must be held in high-quality, liquid vehicles under the auspices of various trustee accounts. This portion of credit risk attributed to trust investments is insulated through the deal's documented eligibility requirements for such investments. These "eligible investments" ensure risk control of funds and accounts in a securitized transaction.

The following list presents the types of investments permitted in a large, credit card receivables-backed transaction. The list is not exhaustive but provides the reader with a good idea of typical eligibility requirements.

Eligible Investments

- United States government obligations or obligations guaranteed by the U.S. government or its agencies.
- Demand deposits, time deposits or certificates of deposit from a U.S. federal or state chartered institution with certificate of deposit or short-term deposit ratings of at least Duff 1+/P-1/A-1+.
- Bankers acceptances subject to the provisions stated above.
- Commercial paper rated at least Duff 1+/ P-1/A-1+.
- Money market funds rated Duff 1+/ P-1/AAA or with 100 percent of the fund's investments in similarly rated instruments.
- Mutual funds with a net asset value of at least $100 million investing in eligible investments stated above.

Servicers who maintain collection accounts on behalf of the trust must use a depository institution capable of satisfying certain eligibility requirements. An eligible institution is a U.S. federal or state chartered corporation which at all times has either a long-term unsecured rating of A or better, or a certificate of deposit rating of Duff 1+/P-1/ A-1+. Accounts have to be shifted to alternate institutions where the original institution has fallen out of eligibility.

Investment maturity is restricted so that cash outflows are matched with the eligible investment. Liquidity and asset/liability mismatch risk is limited under these requirements. Credit risk is covered by restricting the investment vehicles to top-rated securities.

VII. OTHER RISKS

Transactions encumbered with negative interest rate arbitrage risk (the risk that the net yield on the pooled assets falls below that of the yield on the certificates), certificate yield shortfall potential risk, and servicer performance risk, among others, necessitate additional structural enhancements to maintain the security's creditworthiness. These risks are identified through the normal course of the transaction's asset, legal, and structural analysis. Once these risks are isolated, devices are placed on the transaction to either fully eliminate or drastically reduce the probability of risk occurrence. Yet, the "mechanical enhancements" themselves may carry an element of credit risk. These risks must be identified and covered as well to ensure a strong transaction structure and its subsequent high rating.

Where asset yields may not provide full, adequate certificate yield coverage throughout the deal's life a guaranteed rate agreement, guaranteed investment contract, or yield supplement agreement is used to eliminate this negative interest rate arbitrage shortfall risk. Equipment lease and loan-backed deals, wholesale and retail auto loan and lease-backed deals, and collateralized loan and lease-backed deals are securitized asset types which may employ these mechanisms. For instance, the weighted average asset yield is usually sufficient to make investor interest payments on its own, but several credits in the securitized pool may have an insufficient yield. In similar circumstances, the pool's weighted average yield may decline over time due to prepayments on the higher-yielding assets leaving the lower-yielding assets alone to cover interest payments. Therefore, in both of these situations, a rate guarantee is used to eliminate this risk. The guarantee provider, then, like in other enhancer roles, is the recipient of the risk transfer. The senior unsecured rating of the enhancer for long-term risk is used (i.e., GIC provider and its rating), while the short-term rating is focused on when covering short-term risks (i.e., where a yield supplement is needed during the amortization period for a one-year term transaction).

Transactions involving floating-rate assets coupled with fixed-rate certificates, or vice versa, demand interest rate swap agreements. Here, the servicer delivers the floating yield on the assets while the swap counterparty is contracted to deliver a fixed rate back to the trust and then on to the investors. The potential fixed-floater mismatch risk is transferred to the swap counterparty. Again, the senior unsecured rating of the swap counterparty determines the quality of the swap. Ratings in the AA and AAA category are necessary when employing a swap counterparty. Downgrade risk must be protected through substitution or collateralization provisions in the transaction's documentation.

Servicers who have both relatively low ratings (i.e., BBB servicer on a AAA transaction) and are holding cash flow for the duration of the monthly or quarterly payment period invite commingling risk. The risk that a period's collections of investor funds are held back in the event of a servicer bankruptcy must be eliminated. Immediate transfer of funds to trust accounts and lockboxes are methods used to take out this risk. Another approach is a servicer letter of credit, issued by a financial institution, in the aggregated amount of the maximum amount held by the servicer at any one time during the life of the transaction. Once again, the provider's long-term rating is ascertained as a measurement of the swap counterparty's ability to perform under the swap agreement.

VIII. CASE STUDY NUMBER 1

This case study of a securitization reveals analytical methods and concerns over the various credit risks to the transaction. This transaction was chosen not only because of its landmark nature but because of its complex credit analysis. The discussion will focus on previously mentioned credit issues related to the transaction's structure and assets.

Comdisco Receivables Trust 1991-A 7.70% Lease-Backed Certificates

Transaction Terms:

Issue Size:	$312.22 million
Issue Date:	May 1991
Asset Type:	Computer Leases
Collateralization:	$338.02 million
Original Rating (D&P):	AAA
Payment Frequency:	Quarterly
First Payment Date:	August 1991 (P&I)
First Accrual Date:	April 1991
Seller:	Comdisco Receivables, Inc.
Servicer:	Comdisco, Inc.
Trustee:	First Security Bank of Utah, N.A.
Clean-Up Call:	10%
Lead Underwriter:	Salomon Brothers Inc.
Expected Maturity:	May 1996
Stated Maturity:	May 1996
Expected Average Life:	1.5 years
Original Spread (bp):	+95 over the 2-year Treasury

Structure

Fixed rate, quarterly pay pass-through certificates. The principal amount represents 92 percent of the initial aggregate discounted lease balance (Present value of the remaining scheduled lease payments discounted at the certificate rate plus the servicing fee (8.70 percent)).

See Figure 12.1 for a structural diagram.

Credit Enhancement

Senior/subordinate structure (8 percent subordination) with a 4 percent cash collateral account ($13.57 million) for a total of 12 percent credit enhancement available to cover credit losses on the asset pool. A servicer letter of credit provides protection up to the maximum quarterly accrued payment amount collected by the servicer.

Principal payments received between certificate payment dates are deposited into a guaranteed rate account provided by Morgan Guarantee Trust Company of New York at an interest rate equal to the certificate rate (7.70 percent).

Asset Pool

The trust's assets include computer, electronic, and communications equipment, a pool of leases of such equipment, as well as rights to various trust accounts and early termination lease proceeds.

Pool Size:	$388,016,780	
Number of Leases:	1,900	
Lease Balance:	Between $50,000 and $1,500,000	
Equipment Types:	IBM mid-range CPs, peripherals and misc. equipment	
	PCs and workstations	
	minicomputers	
	related software	
	point of sales devices	
	telecommunications equipment	
	satellite terminals	
Concentration limit:	No lessee has balance exceeding 1 percent of aggregate balance (with exception of four groups of affiliated leases)	
Original Lease Term:	Range from 12 months to 63 months	
Industry Concentration:	manufacturing	32.73%
	service	21.94%
	financial services	17.87%
	retail trade	9.92%
	transportation & util.	8.02%
	wholesale trade	6.34%
	other	3.18%
Gross Charge-offs as % avg. outst.:	3/31/91 – 0.37%	
	9/30/90 – 0.63%	
	9/30/89 – 0.34%	
	9/30/88 – 0.40%	

Figure 12.1

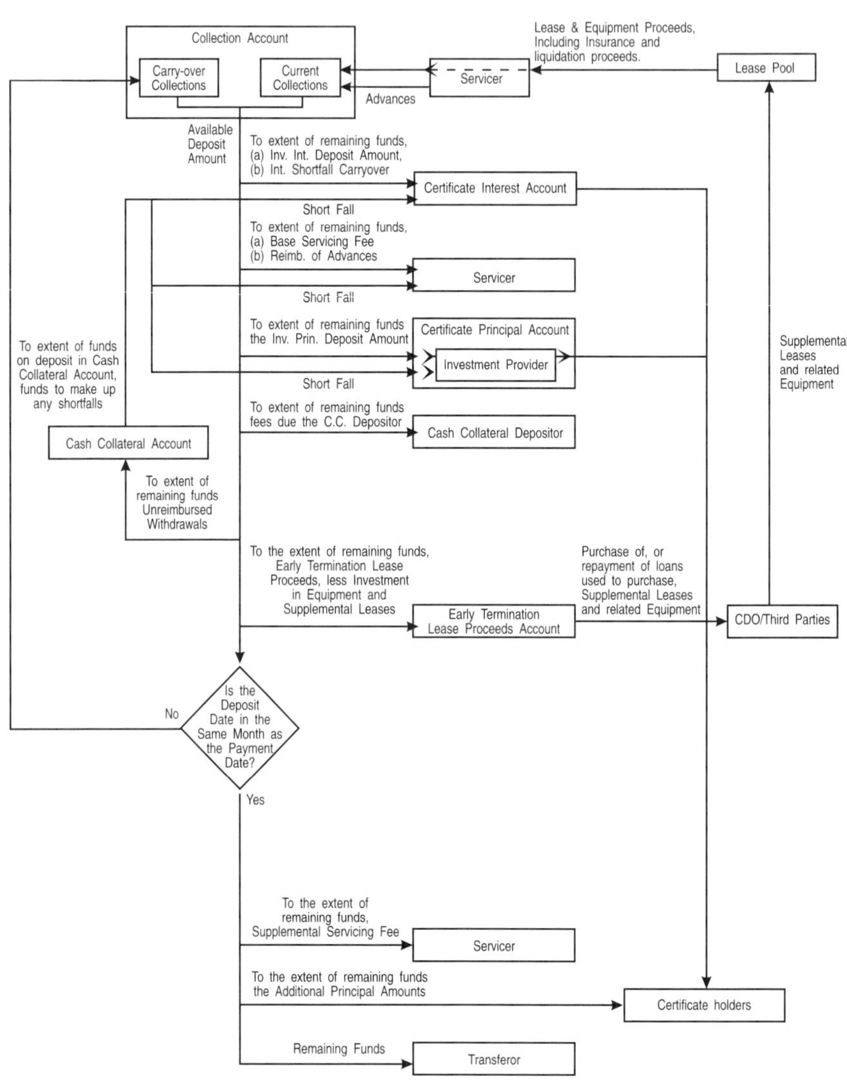

Source: Salomon Brothers, Inc.

Delinquency Rate 31+ days:	3/31/91 – 6.72%	Geographic Concentration:	CA – 17.5%
	9/30/90 – 4.36%		IL – 11.6%
	9/30/89 – 6.18%		NY – 8.4%
	9/30/88 – 6.25%		TX – 7.5%
Operating Leases:	46.8% of pool	Weighted Avg. Maturity:	28.5 months
Direct Finance Type:	53.2% of pool		

Asset Risk Analysis

With an equipment lease portfolio securitization of 1,900 obligor-based leases, the pool is large enough for an actuarial approach in assessing aggregate credit risk. The focus is broadened to include an analysis of Comdisco's origination and servicing standards and procedures, and their effects on asset quality. Because all of the leases are "net leases," where the lessee assumes all responsibility with respect to the equipment, as well as containing "hell or high water" clauses unconditionally obligating the lessee to make payments, obligor payment ability is at the core of the asset risk analysis. Here, the analytical process focuses on obligor credit risk.

Deriving a broad measure of pool credit risk requires an analysis of the 1,900-lease obligor base. The first step is to determine a weighted average senior credit rating of the pool as a fundamental guideline to asset credit risk. Since the leases are both collateralized by the equipment and are critical to the operations of the borrowing companies, Duff & Phelps' approach is to focus its rating level on a senior basis. Public ratings are used in conjunction with Comdisco-based credit scores developed and used in its underwriting process. The analyst must be comfortable with the seller's own assessment of obligor risk before any weight is given to their own scoring system. Comdisco's obligor base contains myriad companies ranging from conglomerates to small service organizations. As such, the pool's credit risk, controlling for underwriting and servicing, generally reflects the broad risk measure in the overall economy, at or below the lowest investment grade rating, BBB–.

Diversification lessens the risk of single industry or regional economic shock-driven defaults. The broader the diversification of obligors, the lower the probability of concentrated charge-offs. Comdisco's portfolio is fairly well diversified. Industry concentrations are spread among several broad categories compared to other lease portfolios which may be highly concentrated (over 50 percent in one single industry) in one business sector. Geographic diversification mitigates effects to the pool of regional economic downturns. Many consumer receivable pools, which because of their large size (i.e., 20,000 obligors) are well dispersed throughout the country, and are granted credit for the risk dispersion. This pool's geographic exposure is fairly well diversified (only 5 states have concentrations above 7 percent of the pool) and as such, is given positive marks for this variable.

Historical delinquency and credit losses are strong indicators of both origination and servicing quality and obligor performance. Delinquent accounts over 31 days are studied as a proxy to portfolio behavior. The historical high of 6.72 percent at March 1991 is used by D&P as a base for its stress test model. The previous years' figures show a consistency in servicing and obligor performance, a positive factor in assessing overall risk.

The gross charge-off table presents the amount of gross losses due to payment failure by lessees for the Comdisco portfolio. Gross losses represent the sum of all unpaid scheduled payments on a lease in default, whether billed or unbilled, which the servicer deemed to be uncollectable. The amounts presented reflect gross losses before recoveries resulting from resale of the related equipment. However, for the purposes of the transaction, Comdisco includes any amount received upon repossession and sale of the equipment under a defaulted lease as liquidation proceeds available for investors. Here, D&P disregarded such proceeds in determining the base asset risk level due to the high volatility of repossession proceeds. This method adds an extra layer of protection due to the conservative nature of the risk assessment. The historical charge-offs reflect a rather stable performance trend, much like in the delinquency statistics. The run-up in charge-offs at year-end September 1990 reflect one-time losses relating to a few lessees rather than the beginning of a broad-based credit problem. This factor is critical in understanding the data. Overall, the relatively low loss history points to consistent, prudent underwriting and servicing performance as well as stable obligor payment behavior.

As Duff & Phelps gave no credit to asset performance from lease residuals, the historical residual performance is not a critical variable in risk analysis. Comdisco's residual realization has been exemplary in the past, yet future residual realization is very difficult to estimate. Future equipment obsolescence, releasing operations and markets, and resale operations and markets are among the determinants of residual values; they are also difficult to forecast. The exclusion of residual values in the overall analysis adds a conservative dimension to the ultimate assessment.

Duff & Phelps' asset risk analysis resulted in the recommendation of credit enhancement in the amount of 12 percent of the original principal balance of the receivables. The credit enhancement number reflects credit protection afforded investors for a AAA-rated security of this type. Lower ratings would mandate a commensurately lower enhancement requirement. The enhancement provides asset credit risk protection and was set to withstand a severely stressed economic environment where both pool delinquency and loss rates increase by a multiple of their historical levels.

The geographic, industry, and obligor diversification worked for the pool. Any heavy over-concentrations would have resulted in a charge against the underlying base risk figure and would significantly increase credit enhancement. This did not occur here. However, the pool's overall credit quality did require added protection. The uncertainty as to which direction the credit quality would head, better or worse, gave credence to a robust enhancement figure.

Servicer Risk Analysis

A top-rated, asset-backed security must have its servicing risk fully covered. As acting servicer for the assets in the transaction, Comdisco's servicing methodology, capabilities, and financial health was investigated. This necessitated a comprehensive due diligence by Duff & Phelps incorporating site tours, systems investigation, management review, and a financial analysis of the servicer, among others items. Since some of the leases pay quarterly rather than monthly, the issue's required periodic payments are quarterly as well. Lessee payments are collected on a daily basis and are held by the servicer until the next deposit date where cash collections are forwarded to the trustee and then on to the investors. The period of time where Comdisco has possession of cash collections creates a risk all its own. Commingling risk, where in the event of a servicer bankruptcy all the assets of the company including the securitized transaction's funds are withheld until further court proceedings can release those funds, is such a risk here. Due to Comdisco's own long-term rating being significantly lower than that of the transaction, its expected bankruptcy risk is relatively high for a AAA-rated securitization. Therefore, any investor cash held by Comdisco must be protected on a one-for-one basis. Comdisco elected to secure a servicer letter of credit in the amount of the maximum dollar amount expected to be held by the servicer at any one time during the life of the transaction. Deutsche Bank, the servicer letter of credit provider, thus provides servicer commingling risk coverage. The bank's own long-term rating marks the degree of risk protection here. The long-term rating is used because the agreement must be in place for the life of the transaction which is longer than one year.

Trustee Risk Analysis

First Security Bank of Utah, N.A., was the acting trustee under the pooling and servicing agreement. The bank must be able to perform the trustee duties as stated in this agreement for the life of the transaction, or otherwise a successor trustee will be named. First Security's financial condition was deemed to be adequate (long-term rating of A or better) for the transaction.

Other Risk Analysis

The incorporation of a guaranteed rate agreement provided by Morgan Guarantee was necessary to boost the underlying asset pool's yield to that of the security. The asset's themselves provide significant yield, however once obligor payments are made that particular asset's yield is terminated. In particular, for those quarterly-pay leases, the cash proceeds cannot be permitted to float for up to three months without a commensurate yield from those funds. Therefore, those funds are deposited with the investment provider at a guaranteed yield equal to the security's coupon, 7.70 percent. Since the funds may be in the account for up to three months at one time, the guarantor's short-term rating is used as a measure of expected performance and reimbursement. Only the highest short-term rating, D-1+, is acceptable to reduce risk. If the short-term rating of the guarantee provider is downgraded or withdrawn the trustee will then invest funds with an alternate investment provided. If an alternate provider is unavailable, the funds are invested in eligible investments (U.S. government securities or short-term securities rated D-1+ or its equivalent).

IX. CASE STUDY NUMBER 2

This case study of a health care receivables securitization reveals analytical methods and concerns over the various credit risks associated with a more novel asset type than those traditionally securitized. This discussion, like the first case study, focuses on previously mentioned credit issues related to the transaction's structure and assets.

National Physicians Funding II-W $50 Million, Health Care Receivables Funding Notes

Transaction Terms:

Issue Size:	$50 Million
Issue Date:	January 1993
Asset Type:	Health care receivables
Collateralization:	Effectively 155% of the issued certificates
Original Rating (D&P):	AA
Payment Frequency	
Interest:	Monthly

Principal:	Monthly upon commencement of amortization period
First Payment Date:	January 1993
Principal Amort. Date:	December 1995
Seller:	Various eligible health care providers
Servicer:	National Premier Financial Services and certain approved providers (sub servicers)
Trustee:	Society National Bank
Placement Agent:	Stephens Inc./Peacock, Hisiop, Staley & Given, Inc.
Stated Maturity:	May 1996

Structure

Fixed rate, monthly-pay notes. Principal payments are withheld until the commencement of the principal amortization period. Principal is then paid monthly to note holders on a pro rata basis beginning in the 36th month, unless a principal amortization event occurs. The rates are not subject to optional redemption prior to their maturity.

See Figure 12.2 for a structural diagram.

Credit Enhancement

Effectively, an overcollateralization structure of at least 155% of the issued notes. Providers are advanced 85%, 80%, or 65% of the net value of the purchased eligible receivables depending upon the terms of an individual provider's sale and subservicing agreement. Three separate minimum seller-specific reserves exist to provide credit and liquidity protection to noteholders. Their levels depend upon the advance rate chosen.

Advance Rate	*Seller Credit Reserve*	*Seller Liquidity Reserve*	*Seller Medicare Offset Reserve*
65%	N.A.	N.A.	5.25%
80%	8.25%	6.50%	5.25%
85%	8.25%	6.50%	5.25%

Figure 12.2—National Physicians Funding II-W

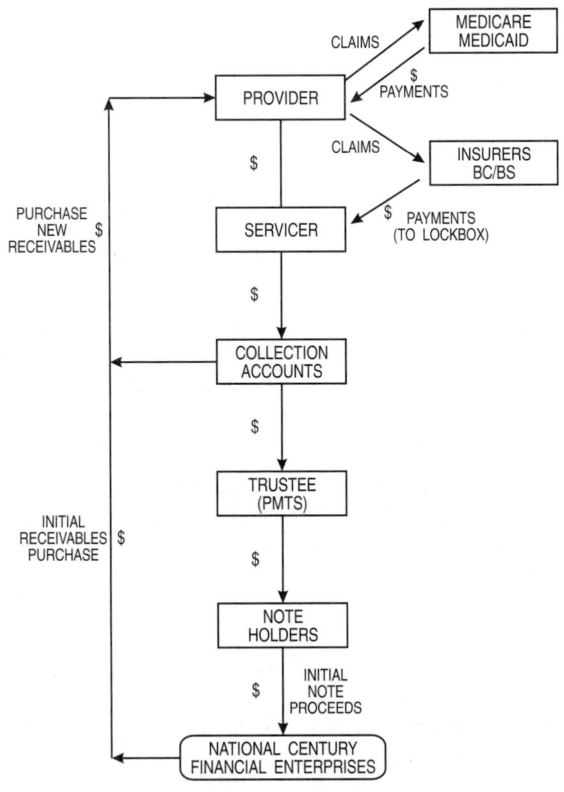

To the extent that there is a draw on any of the reserves, additional amounts equal to the draw are subtracted at the next purchase of receivables from such seller. In the event a seller has an unsatisfied Medicare offset at anytime, such seller is required to maintain a seller Medicare offset reserve equal to the minimum value plus an amount equal to 100 percent of the unsatisfied portion of any Medicare offset irrespective of the applicable advance rate.

Asset Pool

The trust's assets include a pool of eligible health care receivables selected from National Century Financial Enterprises' (NCFE) client base of health care providers. The receivables are purchased by NCFE based upon the following eligibility requirements:

1. Receivables must be payable, in whole or in part, by an eligible third party payor.
2. Services provided must be medically necessary.
3. Health care fees charged must be customary and reasonable.
4. Insurance coverage must have been effective at time of treatment.
5. Health care provider must have pre-verified insurance coverage prior to admittance of patient.
6. Fees may not be excludable due to deductible limitations.
7. Claims must have been submitted to and acknowledged by the payor.
8. All supporting documentation must have been submitted to the payor.

Ineligible accounts include those involving bankruptcies, insolvencies, and disputed claims.

The receivables are obligations of private insurers with implied credit ratings of A or better, HMOs, Blue Cross/Blue Shield, self-funded health plans and government agencies, including Medicare and Medicaid. The receipt of payments from the obligors, less servicing and origination fees paid to NCFE, are the source of quarterly interest payments and final principal repayment. A fee of up to 4 percent of the collected amount of the adjusted billings is retained in an interest funding account to make interest payments. The fee is received each time a receivable is collected during the year. The remaining proceeds are used to reimburse the provider and to purchase additional receivables.

The health care provider is responsible for pre-verifying insurance coverage of a patient before admittance and for submitting a claim to the appropriate payor. National Premier Financial Services (NPFS), the servicer, repeats the pre-verification process and adjusts the patient billings for co-payment provisions. NPFS also performs the collection operations for purchased receivables. NPFS positions affiliates on-site to facilitate the client's billing process. These procedures assist in the prompt receipt of claims payment from payors and reduces the need for resubmission of claims.

When NPFS agrees to purchase a receivable from a health care provider such as a hospital, clinic, or private office, it immediately funds up to 50 percent of the outstanding balance and holds the remainder in reserve. Upon receipt of payment by the intermediary, NPFS retains the portion initially funded, with which it will purchase additional receivables, and funds the reserved balance of the receivables, less a fee, to the health care provider. The fee charged by NPFS is based upon the health care provider's collection history and is up to 5 percent of the collected amount of the receivable. In the event funds received from the intermediary are less than that which is a customary and reasonable charge for the service performed, NPFS offsets this deficiency against the provider's reserves.

Asset Risk Analysis

Health care receivables are unique to the securitization market in form and structure. Risks lie in the origination process and proper valuation of the receivables themselves as well as in the obligors responsible for payment. Extensive due diligence into the receivable generation process, health care provider/administrator billing and claims processing procedures, servicer valuation methods and procedures, and obligor payment mechanisms are necessary to ensure proper asset value maintenance and fluid cash flows from payors to note holders. This evaluation process performed by Duff & Phelps validates the integrity of the transaction structure and verifies that cash will be received by the investors.

Since the receivables themselves exclude any and all self-pay portions of a patient's bill, all asset credit risk falls on the third party payor on that individual receivable. In a program comprised of many health care providers there necessarily exists a multitude of payors. Payor risk is evaluated on the claims-paying ability of the insurer/payor. To limit payor risk, only those private insurers with a claims-paying ability rating of A or better are allowed to participate in the program (including Blue Cross/Blue Shield plans), with limited exception. Government-sponsored programs such as Medicare and Medicaid, an integral part of most providers' third party exposure, are evaluated in a slightly different manner. No government credit risk is assumed except for the possibility of offset risk to an individual health care provider. In the event federal regulators determine a Medicare/Medicaid overpayment to the provider at any time during the previous years, the provider's government funds to cover current billings will be held back until the offset (error) has been repaid. This risk will be further explored in a following section.

Servicer Risk Analysis

As in all securitized transactions, the asset servicer plays a key role in determining the success of the deal. This fact is never more important than in a health care receivables transaction. In this scenario, the servicer must not only properly collect and distribute cash from hundreds of payors but must perform the billing, claims processing and record maintenance on the receivables in a flawless manner. Tens of thousands of individual claims must be verified, re-verified, coded, billed, and followed through to collection on a monthly basis.

As in other asset-backed transactions, the acting servicer's methodologies, capabilities, and financial health was investigated. This necessitated a comprehensive due diligence by Duff & Phelps incorporating site tours, systems investigation, management review, and a financial analysis of NPFS, among other items. Computing and receivables valuation capabilities were stressed during this phase of the analysis.

NPFS' extensive experience and expertise adds significant value to the integrity of the transaction. The complexity of health care receivable valuation and processing must be handled by a skilled professional organization. In respect to the servicer risk present in this transaction, NPFS' presence mitigates this exposure.

Trustee Risk Analysis

The Society National Bank was the acting trustee. The bank must be able to perform the trustee duties as stated under various agreements for the life of the transaction, or otherwise a successor trustee will be named. Society National Bank's financial condition was deemed to be adequate for the purposes of this transaction.

Provider Risk Analysis

The current financial condition of health care providers (mainly hospitals) varies highly across the U.S. While some exhibit strong balance sheets and cash flows, others hover near break-even on an annual basis. The risk here is that if a hospital/provider falls into bankruptcy there exists a risk that those Medicare/Medicaid payments flowing directly to the hospital prior to transfer to the servicer/trustee will become part of the bankrupt estate. The cash flow would become interrupted possibly resulting in losses to note holders. This risk is mitigated through both a diversification of providers in the program and an audit function performed by NPFS to ensure that only those healthy providers remain in the program.

Claim rejection risk exists where improper verification, coding, or billing may occur. The insurer may at times reject a claim for these errors. The claim is then put back to the provider, generating a risk of non-payment. Proper claims management by both the provider and the servicer mitigates this risk. NPFS' extensive experience in health care receivables processing and servicing adds strength to this element of the program. Constant monitoring of the billing process creates a buffer against this risk. Close relationships between NPFS and its program providers is a key element in protecting the value and validity of the receivables.

Payor Risk Analysis

As briefly mentioned above, asset risk falls mainly on the third party payors responsible for payment of the insured portion of the billing. The claims-paying ability of the insurers is a broad measure of the asset risk. Commercial insurers rated A or better are eligible for the program. Those insurers subject to a rating downgrade below that level at any time during the life of the transaction are generally eliminated from the program.

APPENDIX 12A

Long-Term Debt and Preferred Stock Rating Scales

These ratings represent a summary opinion of the issuer's long-term fundamental quality. Rating determination is based on qualitative and quantitative factors which may vary according to the basic economic and financial characteristics of each industry and each issuer. Important considerations are vulnerability to economic cycles as well as risks related to such factors as competition, government action, regulation, technological obsolescence, demand shifts, cost structure, and management depth and expertise. The projected viability of the obligor at the trough of the cycle is a critical determination.

Each rating also takes into account the legal form of the security (e.g., first mortgage bonds,

Rating Scale	Definition
AAA	Highest credit quality. The risk factors are negligible, being only slightly more than for risk-free U.S. Treasury debt.
AA+ AA AA–	High credit quality. Protection factors are strong. Risk is modest but may vary slightly from time to time because of economic conditions.
A+ A A–	Protection factors are average but adequate. However, risk factors are more variable and greater in periods of economic stress.
BBB+ BBB BBB–	Below average protection factors but still considered sufficient for prudent investment. Considerable variability in risk during economic cycles.
BB+ BB BB–	Below investment grade but deemed likely to meet obligations when due. Present or prospective financial protection factors fluctuate according to industry conditions or company fortunes. Overall quality may move up or down frequently within this category.
B+ B B–	Below investment grade and possessing risk that obligations will not be met when due. Financial protection factors will fluctuate widely according to economic cycles.
CCC	Well below investment grade securities. Considerable uncertainty exists as to timely payment of principal, interests or preferred dividends. Protection factors are narrow and risk can be substantial with unfavorable economic/industry conditions.
DD	Defaulted debt obligations. Issuer failed to meet scheduled principal and/or interest payments.
DP	Preferred stock with dividend arrearages.

subordinated debt, preferred stock, etc.). The extent of rating dispersion among the various classes of securities is determined by several factors including relative weightings of the different security classes in the capital structure, the overall credit strength of the issuer, and the nature of covenant protection. Review of indenture restrictions is important to the analysis of a company's operating and financial constraints.

The Credit Committee formally reviews all ratings once per quarter (more frequently, if necessary). Ratings of BBB– and higher fall within the definition if investment grade securities, as defined by bank and insurance supervisory authorities.

Structured finance issues, including real estate and various asset-backed financings, use this same rating scale. Duff & Phelps' claims-paying ability ratings of insurance companies use the same scale with minor modification in the definitions (see following page). Thus, an investor can compare the credit quality of investment alternatives across industries and structural types.

APPENDIX 12B

Short-Term Debt Rating Scale

Duff & Phelps' short-term ratings are consistent with the rating criteria utilized by money market participants. The ratings apply to all obligations with maturities of under one year, including commercial paper, the uninsured portion of certificates of deposit, unsecured bank loans, master notes, bankers acceptances, irrevocable letters of credit, and current maturities of long-term debt. Asset-backed commercial paper is also rated according to this scale.

Emphasis is placed on liquidity which we define as not only cash from operations, but also access to alternative sources of funds including trade credit, bank lines, and the capital markets. An important consideration is the level of an obligor's reliance on short-term funds on an ongoing basis.

The distinguishing feature of Duff & Phelps' short-term ratings is the refinement of the tradi-

Rating Scale	*Definition*
Duff 1+	Highest certainty of timely payment. Short-term liquidity, including internal operating factors and/or access to alternative sources of funds, is outstanding, and safety is just below risk-free U.S. Treasury short-term obligations.
Duff 1	Very high certainty of timely payment. Liquidity factors are excellent and supported by good fundamental protection factors. Risk factors are minor.
Duff 1–	High certainty of timely payment. Liquidity factors are strong and supported by good fundamental protection factors. Risk factors are very small.
	Good grade
Duff 2	Good certainty of timely payment. Liquidity factors and company fundamentals are sound. Although ongoing funding needs may enlarge total financing requirements, access to capital markets is good. Risk factors are small.
	Satisfactory Grade
Duff 3	Satisfactory liquidity and other protection factors qualify issue as to investment grade. Risk factors are larger and subject to more variation. Nevertheless, timely payment is expected.
	Non-Investment Grade
Duff 4	Speculative investment characteristics. Liquidity is not sufficient to insure against disruption in debt service. Operating factors and market access may be subject to a high degree of variation.
	Default
Duff 5	Issuer failed to meet scheduled principal and/or interest payments.

tional '1' category. The majority of short-term debt issuers carry the highest rating, yet quality differences exist within that tier. As a consequence, Duff & Phelps has incorporated gradations of '1+' (one plus) and '1–' (one minus) to assist investors in recognizing those differences.

Duff & Phelps' ratings are recognized by the SEC for broker-dealer requirements, specifically capital computation guidelines. Our ratings meet Department of Labor ERISA guidelines governing pension and profit sharing investments. State regulators also recognize Duff & Phelps' ratings for insurance company investment portfolios.

Chapter 13

Credit Enhancement

by Fredrik Månsson,
Vice President and Head of
Trygg-Hansa SPP Financial Insurance
Stockholm, Sweden

1. INTRODUCTION

In order to describe the most important function that an insurance company performs in a securitisation transaction, I would like to draw a parallel to a more tangible situation. Let us compare a securitisation transaction with a TV set. A TV consists of a great number of different components. Most of us would never want to know how the different parts work and we would expect the manufacturer to sell the TV with a warranty assuring that the TV will work as expected. The buyer of a TV is in a similar position as the investor in an asset-backed security. The investor would, for instance, never consider visiting all homeowners and shaking hands in order to assure himself that the mortgages backing the notes he is about to purchase are of good quality. Here we have an important function that the insurance company performs. The company checks the various components of the security issue and provides a guarantee that the product will work as the buyer expects. By assuming different risks and especially the credit risk in an asset securitisation the insurer can assist the issuer in obtaining the rating aimed at. By doing so the illiquid future cash flow stream will be transformed into a liquid tradable security.

This was just to put the insurance company into the picture. Now, let me examine the most important risks in a securitisation transaction and describe how they can be managed.

2. RISKS

When structuring an off-balance securitisation program you remove financial assets from the originator's balance sheet and place them in a special purpose vehicle (SPV). A SPV is a company established with the sole purpose of buying and owning the assets and funding the purchase through an issue of asset-backed securities. This means that the assets will no longer be supported by the originating company's equity. Since the equity is a buffer for financiers of the originator against the occurrence of, for instance, credit losses, we now will have to find someone else who is willing to pick up the different risks in connection with the issue.

First, I will identify the most important risks in an asset-backed security issue and then present different solutions on how to manage these financial risks. The most important risks are:

- Credit Risk
- Liquidity Risk
- Refinancing Risk
- Reinvestment Risk
- Administration Performance Risk
- Currency and Interest Rate Risk
- Swap Counterparty Risk
- Credit Risk on Mortgage Indemnity Guarantee Provider

Credit Risk

The primary credit risk is on the issuer of the security, i.e., the SPV. However, since the issue is backed by a portfolio of financial assets the actual credit risk is on that asset pool. If the individual borrowers start to go bankrupt during the lifetime of the issue, the SPV will soon go the same route unless the financial structure of the program provides cover against this risk. In case of an issue backed by mortgages the ultimate credit risk depends on the value of the mortgaged home in relation to the loan size. In a securitisation of credit card receivables the creditworthiness of the issue depends on the strength of the individual cardholders. And in a securitisation of car loans you have the value of the car, which is moving around all the time, as last resort.

To summarize I would like to say that each type of asset has its own characteristics when it comes to credit risk. This has the consequence that the credit protection has to be structured individually for each issue. There is very seldom a standard solution available.

Liquidity Risk

Another important risk that potentially can lead to nonreceipt or delayed receipt of interest and principal under the security issue is the risk of liquidity shortfall. The cash flow from the obligors should be structured in such a way that there will be no shortfall of cash when it comes to pay interest or principal under the security. However, if the individual obligors behind the receivables backing the security are late with payments, the cash flow might not be sufficient to pay interest or principal under the notes in time. In order not to pass this risk on to the investors the risk must be covered in some way, which I will come back to later.

Refinancing Risk

In a securitisation there might also be an element of refinancing risk. For instance, in the case of a securitisation of Swedish mortgages you will have this risk. Most mortgages in Sweden amortize over a 40-year period, but they usually have bullet payment obligations that are due after, for instance, five years. At this maturity the homeowner refinances his mortgage. Repayment of principal under the mortgage-backed security relays on the refinancing of the homeowner's mortgage. If the homeowner cannot get refinancing, for instance, due to a substantial fall in property prices, the repayment of principal under the security might suffer. The refinancing risk actually consists of liquidity risk and/or credit risk. If the homeowner eventually obtains refinancing, the investor gets his repayment of principal, *however late*—the risk is a liquidity risk. If the homeowner never obtains refinancing and his house is later sold for a sum less than the principal amount owed, it is a credit loss risk.

The refinancing risk can also be covered as I will show later.

Reinvestment Risk

The cash flow generated by the assets securitized usually remains in the SPV until it is used to either pay interest or principal under the notes. During this time it will be invested and will generate a yield. Here we have a risk that the cash flow invested in this way will generate an interest less than expected and calculated. The SPV can either purchase cover against this reinvestment risk or structure the cash flow in such a way that the need for reinvestment return is limited. However, by a close match of cash flow in and out you will increase the liquidity risk at the same time as you reduce the reinvestment risk, and consequently increase the requirement for cover against the liquidity risk.

Administrator Performance Risk

The SPV has no means to administrate the portfolio of financial assets. Usually, the SPV contracts the originator to continue the administration of the assets. Here, you have the risk that the administrator does not perform according to what has been agreed, or that the administrator goes bankrupt. In either case there is a great risk that the SPV will suffer costs when looking for a replacement to service the portfolio, unless this risk is covered externally.

Currency and Interest Rate Risk

If the portfolio of assets generates cash flow, which does not match, in currency and/or interest rate base, the currency and/or interest under the security, *there will be a need to* swap the cash flow in order to eliminate the SPV's currency and/or interest rate risk.

Swap Counterparty Risk

When introducing a swap into the structure you also create a new risk, the credit risk on the swap provider. If the SPV's counterparty in the swap contract cannot perform according to the agreement, the SPV stands a potential risk of losing money when replacing the swap provider with another entity, unless this risk is managed in some way.

Credit Risk on Mortgage Indemnity Guarantee Provider

In a securitisation of UK mortgages there is also another type of counterparty risk present. The risk of insolvency on the account of the provider of Mortgage Indemnity Guarantees (MIG). A MIG is issued by an insurance company and covers the mortgage lender against the top-slice risk in a mortgage. Normally this insurance covers credit losses in excess of 75 percent in loan to value, i.e., if the original loan advance exceeds 75 percent of the valuation of the property the insurance company issuing the MIG agrees to carry the top-slice risk above 75 percent in loan to value. If the provider of the MIG cover is rated less than the level aimed at for the issue there will be a need to back that insurance company's creditworthiness.

Depending on the individual securitisation structure, the availability of enhancement providers and capacity, the risks I have described can be managed in different ways. I would like to stress that these risks are only the most important present in a securitisation, there are of course other risks as well, e.g., political risks, legal risks and tax risks. I will now describe the most common ways to insure or cover the SPV against the risks I have previously elaborated on.

3. COVER AGAINST THE DIFFERENT TYPES OF RISKS

I will start with the two most important risks, Credit Risk and Liquidity Risk because *how you handle* these risks will have implications for how the other risks will be managed.

There are several ways to manage the Credit and the Liquidity risks. First of all you can decide to use an external third party insurance policy or guarantee, or you can try to structure the issue without involvement of a third party.

Senior Subordinated Structure

Senior subordinated structure is a type of credit enhancement which, for instance, has been used in the UK for mortgage-backed securities. The issuer will issue two or more tranches of notes. Let us assume two tranches and call them A and B notes. The B notes are subordinated to the A notes, which means that the B noteholders will not receive payment of principal until the A notes have been fully paid. The B notes provide in this way a cushion for the A noteholders against the credit risk on the underlying financial assets. I should mention that A notes are often called senior notes, and B notes are called subordinated notes or junior notes. In a mortgage securitisation the senior notes are typically rated AAA and represent something like 90–94 percent of the combined issue size. The junior notes are often unrated.

The liquidity risk can be carried through a line of credit provided by a third party, and if the rating of the third party is not sufficient for the issue there will be a need to upgrade the quality of the provider. For instance, if the bank providing this liquidity facility is rated A or AA and you aim at a AAA-rated senior security, a bank or an insurance company can guarantee the performance of the bank through a performance guarantee.

The refinancing risk, if any, can be covered through the subordination of the B notes. If obligors do not receive refinancing, the B noteholders will represent the investor group who will receive repayment of principal last, i.e., after the A noteholders have received their payment.

The advantage with the senior subordinated structure is that a fee for external credit protection is saved and that you are isolated from the possible downgrade risk of a third-party credit guarantee or insurance. However, the coupon on the B notes will have to be substantially higher than that of the A notes in order to compensate for the higher risk. And then of course you have the question of who will buy the "junk-like" junior notes.

Pool Insurance

An insurance company will enter into an insurance contract with the issuer under which it agrees to indemnify the issuer in respect of credit losses originating from the underlying pool of financial assets. The level of cover needed depends on the rating agencies' requirements and the rating aimed at. In mortgage-backed securitisations in the UK and Sweden the insurance cover required for a AAA has been between 6 percent and 15 percent of the total issue size. The insurance cover includes a deductible or a first-loss position. The deductible has historically been in the region of 0.5 percent to 1.5 percent of the total issue size. However, increasing awareness of the risk of default among homeowners in combination with decreasing property values during the last couple of years has increased the pressure on higher deductible. Today, the first-loss requirement in mortgage securitisations is 1–3 percent of the total issue size. The size of the first-loss is of course highly dependent on the credit quality of the pool of mortgages to be securitised. There are different ways of providing the deductible. It can be provided through either limited recourse not always possible to the originator or through cash in a blocked account set aside by the originator for payment of losses before the pool insurance comes in. For other types of assets, like credit card receivables and automobile loans or leases, the often relatively large spread between funding cost and yield of the portfolio is used to build up a cushion in a blocked account, which will be used to pay losses before the insurance policy comes in. I believe we will see this development in the mortgage securitisation business as well.

You will also need a liquidity facility in this structure to pick up the risk of temporary cash flow shortfall in the SPV.

The big advantage with pool insurance is that you have a well-established market with almost standardised documentation and a reinsurance market familiar with this type of risk. This enables companies underwriting pool insurance business to respond fast and provide the cover needed within a few weeks if necessary.

The disadvantage is the event risk, i.e., the risk of downgrading of the pool insurer. Downgrading will usually lead to the need to bring in another company with the appropriate rating in order not to suffer downgrading of the outstanding notes. This will add to the cost of the transaction.

Partial Principal and Interest Guarantee

One solution to both the credit risk and the liquidity risk is to have a bank or an insurance company with the appropriate rating to issue a guarantee, which covers the SPV against the credit and liquidity risk in the portfolio. In order to receive a AAA rating on the issue it is usually not necessary to obtain a 100 percent guarantee cover. In the case of, for instance, a car loan securitisation there might only be a need for a 20 percent guarantee of the cash flow from the portfolio into the SPV. The guarantee can also be written as a guarantee backing part of the SPV's obligations towards the investors of paying principal and interest under the notes.

The big advantage with this structure is that you protect the SPV against both credit and liquidity risk with one guarantee. If the obligors are late with payments the cash flow might not be sufficient to pay the coupon in time. With a guarantee for principal and interest, the guarantee can be called and the investor will receive payment in time. A pool insurance can only be called when an actual credit loss has occurred. This involves selling the assets. During this process the account overdue must be funded through a line of liquidity. However, this structure is also subject to the event risk as described above under the section "Pool Insurance."

Full Principal and Interest Guarantee

A bank or an insurance company with the appropriate rating provides a 100 percent guarantee, which assures the issuer's timely payment of coupon interest and principal. The guarantee not only covers the direct credit loss risk, but also the liquidity risk and all other risks that the SPV is exposed to. If the issuer experiences temporary liquidity problems the guarantee can be called and the guarantor will be indemnified as soon as the liquidity flows in. The cash flow should be structured in such a way that there will not be any liquidity shortfall in the SPV if the obligors of the underlying asset perform as they should. However, as mentioned above under Partial Principal and Interest Guarantee, if the obligors are late with payments the cash flow might not be sufficient to pay coupon interest in time. In this case the guarantee can be called and the investor will receive payment. The pool insurance structure requires that an actual credit loss has occurred before the insurance will be triggered to pay any loss. During this process the account overdue must be funded through a line of liquidity.

A full guarantee of principal and interest under the notes is of course the most straightforward solution and represents a structure which probably is the easiest for an investor to accept. In this case the investor will not care much about the quality of the underlying financial assets because he will probably take the standing that the risk of the notes are a risk on the issuer of the guarantee, and book the exposure accordingly. Disadvantages with this structure are of course the presence of the event risk, and that the fee or premium for the guarantee will have to be high enough in order to compensate for all risks covered. It is often more cost efficient to manage the individual risks separately than to have the issue "wrapped" with a full principal and interest guarantee.

Cash Collateral

This method of credit and liquidity protection has been used in, for instance, securitisations of credit card receivables in the US. A substantial amount of cash, maybe 6–10 percent of the total issue size, is placed in an escrow account at the beginning of the transaction. The cash is used to pay credit losses in the asset portfolio and to take care of temporary liquidity problems. Cash collateral is often used in combination with other structures (see below).

Combination

The risk-averse trends in today's financial sector have had the effect that it is becoming more and more common to use a combination of enhancement techniques. Insurers and other guarantee providers many times require a cash deposit to be made by the originator of the portfolio to cover the first-loss position. This has in many cases proven to be the most cost-efficient method of providing credit enhancement. The guarantee provider feels confident that there is a buffer before the guarantee or insurance is used and can therefore price the cover accordingly. The originator who has provided the cash deposit will receive all money left in the account after the termination of the issue. Cash has also been used to enhance the junior notes to an acceptable creditworthiness in senior subordinated structures.

If a refinancing risk as previously mentioned is present in the securitisation the credit and liquidity protection will have to be sized in order to provide cover against this risk. All the above-mentioned enhancement techniques can be structures in order to also provide cover against the refinancing risk.

What Type of Credit Protection Structure is Normally Used?

To illustrate how frequent the different types of covers historically have been used, the following figures will give you an idea. Since the first issue of mortgage-backed securities in 1987 in the UK up to and including 1991, over two-thirds of all publicly announced issues have been enhanced through pool insurance. The rest has been issued using a senior subordinated structure. In Sweden so far, since the first issue in 1990, three more issues of mortgage-backed securities have been launched, two have been credit enhanced through the use of pool insurance.

The reasons why pool insurance has been the most cost-efficient credit enhancement method is to a great extent a result of tradition in the UK market. UK insurers had been guaranteeing the top-slice risk for mortgage lending for many years before securitisation was introduced in Europe. They were therefore experienced in the market and felt comfortable with issuing credit insurance protection for pools of mortgages. In turn this has led to the development of a reinsurance market in Europe for pool insurance covers, which can support the primary insurers with risk sharing capacity. However, recent downgrades of several UK and international providers of pool insurance covers will probably lead to an increase in use of other structures and sources for credit enhancement.

Performance Guarantees Manage Third Party Performance Risk

When I described the different risks in an asset securitisation I also mentioned a number of risks related to the performance of the SPV's counterparties in different contracts. If the counterparty does not perform according to what has been agreed, then the SPV stands a risk of losing money which will, in turn, affect the investors in the security. The rating agencies usually want to see a high-rated party to back the different companies who provide services to the SPV. Usually if you aim at obtaining a AAA rating you will need to bring in someone to enhance the chain's links, some of which carry a rating of less than AAA.

The risk of failure on the account of the administrator of the portfolio can be backed by a performance guarantee. The guarantee provider will cover costs incurred if the original administrator is unable to continue servicing the pool of assets and as a consequence has to be replaced by another administrator.

Currency and interest rate risks are swapped away through the exchange of cash flow between the SPV and another entity, usually a bank. If the bank does not carry a sufficient rating the performance risk of the bank can be enhanced in the same manner through a performance guarantee. The guarantee provider will carry all potential costs (basically the cost of replacing the swap provider with another party) incurred in case of non-performance of the swap provider. The guarantee can also be written in such a way that the guarantor itself will step into the place of the original swap provider as a new party in the swap.

I also mentioned the reinvestment risk, i.e., the risk that the SPV cannot generate sufficient yield on cash at its disposal. Some banks have a product they call Guaranteed Investment Contract, which gives you a guarantee of a minimum return. If the provider of this Guaranteed Investment Contract lacks the rating aimed at, there might be a need to upgrade this party through a performance guarantee to the appropriate level.

The credit risk on mortgage indemnity guarantee (MIG) providers present in the UK is also a risk, which has to be covered if the MIG provider is rated below the rating sought for the issue. This can be achieved through a guarantee picking up the risk of insolvency of the MIG provider.

4. PROVIDERS OF CREDIT ENHANCEMENT

There are basically three groups of companies providing cover against risks in connection with asset securitisation transactions. They are:

- Multiline insurance companies
- US Monoline insurance companies
- Banks

Multiline Insurance Companies

In Europe there are a handful of general or multiline insurance companies who provide financial guarantee covers for securitisation. Examples are Trygg-Hansa Insurance Company (Sweden), UNI-Europe (France), UAP (France), Sun Alliance (UK), Commercial Union (UK) and Winterthur (Switzerland). Most of these companies are only involved in carrying the pure credit risk through pool insurance policies. However, there are a limited number of companies who are willing also to cover the liquidity risk present in principal and interest guarantees, e.g., Trygg-Hansa and Winterthur. Several insurers are providers of traditional performance guarantees, for instance, in connection with construction projects. However, in order to be able to issue performance guarantees backing different parties in a securitisation you need a different type of financial knowledge. Most European multiline insurers lack this capacity and are therefore not active in this line of business.

Downgrades of European insurers active in these lines of insurance has decreased the available high-rated risk-carrying capacity provided by European multiline insurers. This has led to an increased interest in the enhancement technique of senior subordinated issues and methods where cash collateral is combined with insurance covers.

US Monoline Financial Guarantee Companies

There are presently seven major monoline companies in the US participating as primary issuers of financial guarantees in the US domestic and international credit enhancement industry. They are AMBAC Indemnity Corp., Capital Guaranty Insurance Co., Capital Markets Assurance Co. (CapMac), Connie Lee Insurance Co., Financial Guaranty Insurance Co. (FGIC), Financial Security Assurance Inc. (FSA), and Municipal Bond Investors Assurance Corp. (MBIA). In addition to these companies there are also four reinsurers who provide the primary US monoline and the international multiline companies with risk sharing-capacity. These four companies are Asset Guaranty Reinsurance Co., Capital Reinsurance Co., Credit Reinsurance Co. and Enhance Reinsurance Co. Credit Re is closely related to Capital Re and Asset Guaranty to Enhance Re.

All US monoline companies are closely monitored by rating agencies and highly regulated. The US monolines engage in providing unconditional and irrevocable guarantees which indemnify the insured against nonpayment by an obligor of principal and interest when due. The lion share of these companies' business originates from guaranteeing US domestic municipal-bonds, however, during the last few years they have expanded their participation in the US, and to some extent also the international asset securitisation market. A few of the companies have representations in Europe with the aim to take part in credit enhancement of European asset-backed financing. The word monoline can be derived from the fact that these companies only participate in one line of insurance business, i.e., the financial guarantee business.

Banks

A number of highly rated international banks have issued letter of credits in connection with asset securitisations, e.g., Union Bank of Switzerland, Credit Suisse and Bayerische Vereinsbank AG. Like the US monoline companies, banks cover the risk of nonpayment or delayed payment of principal and interest under the notes. As in the case of multiline insurance companies banks have suffered a drain on AAA-rated capacity during the last couple of years due to downgrading. The implementation of the Basle Committee's capital adequacy rules has further decreased the capacity available within the banking sector for letters of credit.

CONCLUSION

Securitisations are very complex transactions with a lot of pitfalls, some easy detectable, others more hidden. When contemplating a securitisation it is advisable to, at an early stage, make contact with not only a bank or an investment bank who will structure the deal, but also professional risk carriers as described above. They usually have substantial experience from this type of business and can assist in finding and managing even the more hidden risks. The rating agencies are also highly skilled in finding risks and should therefore be introduced to the proposed transaction at an early stage of the project.

It is essential that the ratings of third party providers like guarantees or pool insurance are at least of the same high rating as the rating aimed at. Therefore, if you want a AAA-rated issue the guarantee provider needs to have a AAA rating. Today, the number of multiline insurers and banks with a AAA rating is limited. There are, however, a larger number of insurers and banks with a rating below AAA active in this business. In addition to this we also have the AAA-rated US monoline insurers. I believe that in the future we will see these companies take a more active role in the international industry for credit enhancement. A likely development might also be the formation of one or more AAA-rated European monoline insurers devoted to providing financial guarantees in connection with European securitisations and other complex financial transactions.

Last but not least I would like to stress that a securitisation transaction exposes the different risks present in the activities of a lender or a credit provider. A securitisation breaks down the elements of risk into pieces and distributes them to parties more suited to carry the specific risk. I believe, even if the start has been somewhat slow, that securitisation in Europe in the long run will prove to be a very efficient method of allocating risk and obtaining optimal funding cost.

CASE—OSPREY MORTGAGE SECURITIES (NO. 1) LTD.

In November 1990, the first mortgage-backed security issued by a continental European mortgage lender was launched by the Swedish mortgage institution, Svensk Fastighetskredit (SFK). SFK and other Scandinavian mortgage lenders have been issuing unsecured mortgage bonds for many years. In contrast to mortgage-backed securities that are secured by a specific pool of assets of an issuer, these bonds are general obligations of the lender. However, as lenders seek to conserve capital and diversify funding sources they have the option to turn to securitisation as SFK did in 1990. The objective to diversify funding sources available to SFK was the most important objective, along with the capital requirement objective, when SFK decided to enter the mortgage-backed security market. Swedish mortgage institutions have traditionally been funded through the domestic medium- and long-term bond market. Prior to deregulation of investment requirements for insurance companies and pension funds in 1986 there were plenty of funds available for the general obligation type of mortgage bonds. The regulation obliged different institutional investors to invest a certain share of their portfolio in mortgage bonds. However, today these investors can be more flexible in their investments, and they are, as a result, in the process of reducing their high share of investments in traditional mortgage bonds. The mortgage institutions also compete with the Swedish government for local investors. The need to finance infrastructure projects and government privatisation programmes along with an increase in the budget deficit has made the competition for funds even tougher. The mortgage lenders have appreciated this reduction of funds available to them in the future, and are therefore expanding funding sources to include securitisation.

Swedish mortgage-backed securities are very attractive to investors in these types of notes mainly due to the fact that Swedish mortgages are not very likely to be prepaid, which means that the expected maturity (usually four to five years) of a Swedish mortgage-backed security is easy to predict. The Osprey (No. 1) transaction was met with great interest from international investors.

THE ISSUE

Issuer	Osprey Mortgage Securities (No. 1) Ltd.
Originator	Svensk Fastighetskredit AB (SFK)
Notes	USD 159,500,000 mortgage-backed floating rate notes due 1995.
Closing Date	November 27, 1990
Interest	Three-month dollar LIBOR + 0.30% per annum, payable quarterly in arrear
Security	The notes are secured by: a a pledge of the portfolio assets b an assignment of the sums standing to the credit of the Collection Account c a pledge of the Dollar Account (an account maintained by the Issuer at Skandinaviska Enskilda Banken for the purpose of receiving dollar payments under the Swap Agreement) d assignment of the Issuer's rights under the Mortgage Pool Indemnity Policy
Rating	AAA (Standard & Poor's Corporation)

The originator SFK sold a portfolio of loans secured on residential property in Sweden to the Issuer Osprey Mortgage Securities (No. 1) Ltd., a private company incorporated in the Island of Jersey with limited liability. The issuer is a wholly owned subsidiary of Osprey Mortgage Securities Holdings Limited. The portfolio compromised around 5,300 loans with an aggregated principal balance at the closing date of approximately SKr 950,000,000. The largest loan in the portfolio was SKr 2,400,000, and the smallest SKr 70,000; the arithmetic mean was close to SKr 179,000. No loan had a Loan to Value greater than 75 percent, i.e., no loan had a relation between principal loan amount and appraised value that was higher than 75 percent. SFK acts as Agent for the Issuer and performs day-to-day management and administration of the portfolio according to the Management Deed. In the event that SFK is for some reason unable to continue the administration Skandinaviska Enskilda Banken or one of its subsidiaries other than SFK will take over the role of the Agent according to the Successor Agent Agreement.

The credit risk of the portfolio is carried by Trygg-Hansa Insurance Company Ltd. through a Mortgage Pool Indemnity Policy. The policy carries losses on defaulted loans up to 10 percent of the aggregated principal balance of all loans in the portfolio at the closing date. This insurance also covers the refinancing risk present in Swedish mortgage-backed securities. Most mortgages in Sweden are scheduled with an amortisation plan of 40 years, but they usually have bullet payment obligations that are due after, for instance, five years. At this maturity the homeowner refinances his mortgage. Since the security is structured with a maturity matching the bullet payment obligation of the mortgage, repayment of principal under the mortgage-backed security relies on the refinancing of the homeowner's mortgage. Should any obligor of the portfolio be unable to find refinancing and the property in question is sold for a sum less than the bullet payment obligation a credit loss will occur. Such loss will be carried by the Pool Policy provided by Trygg-Hansa. Part of the credit protection is a first-loss agreement between the insurer and the originator. The insurer has recourse to the originator for the first 1 percent of credit losses of the aggregated principal balance of all loans. This recourse is also backed by a performance guarantee from Skandinaviska Enskilda Banken.

The Pool Policy does not pay losses until they have been determined through forced sale of the property. This has the consequence that accounts overdue will have to be funded through a Liquidity Facility until settled by the obligor or ultimately through claims payments from the Pool Policy. The Liquidity Facility carrying the liquidity risk is provided by Skandinaviska Enskilda Banken and can be drawn upon up to a maximum of 4 percent of the aggregated principal balance of all loans in the portfolio at the closing date. Skandinaviska Enskilda Banken also provides the Collection Account, which is credited with principal and interest payments from the loans in the portfolio. These amounts are later paid to investors as interest. In order to eliminate the reinvestment risk, i.e., the risk that cash at the Issuer's disposal cannot be invested to generate a sufficient yield, all amortisation of mortgage principal is passed through to noteholders quarterly. The bank has also agreed to pay an interest rate of at least 6 percent per annum on amounts deposited into the Collection Account. Even if principal payments as described above will be passed through to the investors, they will be faced with only limited early redemption. This is mainly due to the fact that in Sweden provisions in the mortgage loan agreements strongly discourage prepayments and that the scheduled amortisation is very small over the lifetime of the security, probably less than 5 percent.

In order to eliminate interest rate and currency risk exposure of the Issuer, a swap agreement converts the cash flow from the mortgages (fixed-rate SKr) into the currency and interest rate of the notes (floating-rate USD). The original swap provider, Barclays Bank PLC, was exchanged for The Swedish Export Credit Corporation due to the downgrading of Barclays in 1991.

SUMMARY OF RISKS AND CONTRACTS MANAGING THESE RISKS

Contractor/Provider	*Risk*
Mortgage Pool Indemnity Policy/Trygg-Hansa Insurance Company Ltd.	Credit risk & Refinancing risk
Liquidity Facility/ Skandinaviska Enskilda Banken	Liquidity risk
Swap Agreement/ Swedish Export Credit Corp. (initially: Barclays Bank PLC)	Currency risk & Interest rate risk
Collection Account Agreement/Skandinaviska Enskilda Banken	Reinvestment risk (most of the reinvestment risk was eliminated through pass-through of all amortisations of principal from homeowners.)
Successor Agent Agreement/Skandinaviska Enskilda Banken	Counterparty risk of the administrator SFK

Since Osprey (No. 1) was the first mortgage-backed issue ever launched by a Swedish originator using Swedish assets, legal fees and structuring costs were substantial. However, SFK has stressed that they will use securitisation as an ongoing source of funding, and subsequent issues will therefore benefit from development costs incurred in connection with the first transaction. The Osprey (No. 1) was followed by Osprey (No. 2 – 6) in July 1991, Osprey (No. 7) in 1992, and Osprey (No. 8) in 1993. (Figure 13.1).

**Figure 13.1—Osprey Mortgage Securities (No. 1) Ltd.
U.S.D. Mortgage-Backed Floating-Rate Notes**

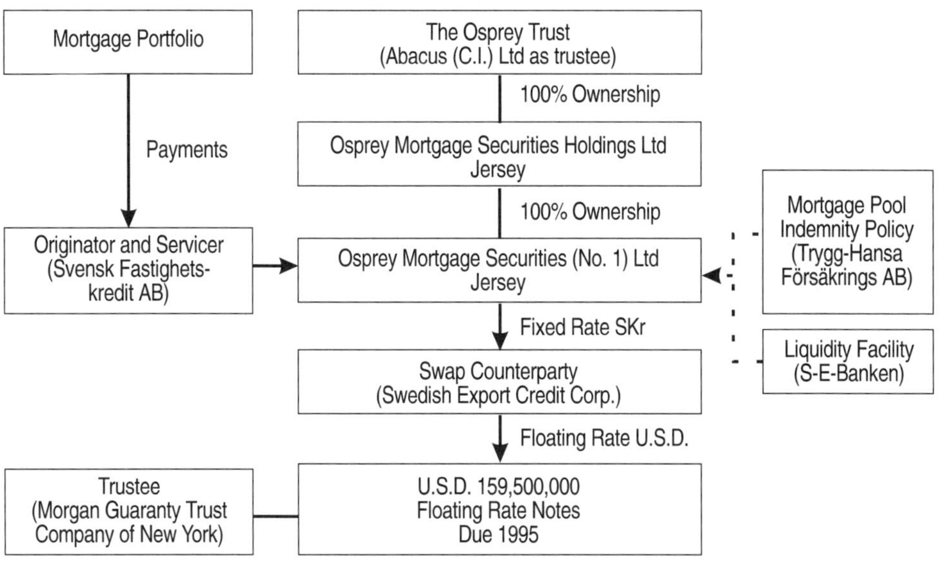

Chapter 14

The Role of the Monoline Financial Guarantor: How Safe Is Safe?

by Henry T. Mortimer, Jr.,
Managing Director,
Financial Security Assurance

INTRODUCTION

Among sectors of the financial community, the monoline financial guaranty industry stands out as one that attracted capital and built strength during the recent recession. Its stable performance—even during an economic downturn—reflects the continued health of the industry over its 20-year history. No monoline financial guaranty insurance company has ever been downgraded. This remarkable record can be explained by the high quality of the industry's insured and investment portfolios.

The nature of the monoline financial guaranty business serves as a basic protection as well. Under the strict regulatory regime governing the financial guaranty industry, monolines are limited to a narrow range of activities. Thus, unlike multiline property and casualty insurers and banks, monoline financial guarantors are not subjected to potential losses from other risk-carrying lines of business.

A BRIEF HISTORY OF THE MONOLINE FINANCIAL GUARANTY INDUSTRY

Financial guaranty insurance originated in the 1970s in the municipal bond market. Because of investor demands and issuer requirements, that business grew explosively during the 1980s. In 1985, financial guaranty insurance was introduced to the asset-backed, taxable market by Financial Security Assurance.

There are currently six AAA-rated monoline financial guaranty insurance companies whose only business under law is providing financial guaranty insurance. Three of these companies, Municipal Bond Investors Assurance Corporation (MBIA), AMBAC Indemnity Corporation (AMBAC), and Capital Guaranty Insurance Company (Capital Guaranty) specialize in municipal bond insurance. Capital Markets Assurance Corporation (CapMac) specializes in structured taxable debt issues, while Financial Guaranty Insurance Company (FGIC) insures mostly municipal issues and some corporate debt. Established as an insurer for corporate asset-backed issues, Financial Security Assurance now also participates in the municipal market.

Each monoline financial guarantor's claims-paying ability carries a AAA rating from one or more of the major rating agencies.

PRODUCTS PROVIDED BY MONOLINE FINANCIAL GUARANTORS

Financial guaranty insurance companies charge a premium to guarantee that the payment obligations of another party in a financial transaction will be fulfilled. The financial guarantor thus provides its high credit rating to the issue it insures, thereby improving an issue's marketability and reducing its cost of funds.

In municipal issues, the creditworthiness of an issue is based on a dedicated revenue stream or the taxing power of a municipality—the financial guarantor enhances an existing credit rating. By contrast, asset securitization creates a financial entity *de novo.* In an asset-backed issue, a special purpose, bankruptcy-remote corporation or trust, which never existed before, has its creditworthiness built from scratch.

The creditworthiness of an asset-backed issue is derived from several sources: the quality of the assets in the portfolio being securitized, the amount of overcollateralization, the amount of liquidity from additional credit lines, and the participation of a multitude of other parties to the

Figure 14.1—Creditworthiness of an Asset-Backed Issue

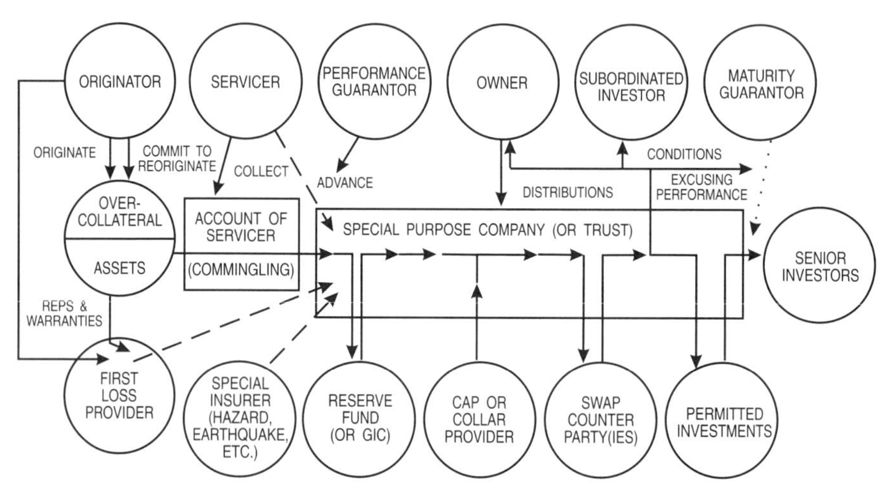

transaction such as trustees, sellers, custodians, primary and backup servicers, performance guarantors, first-loss providers or counterparties for interest and currency swaps. (Figure 14.1.)

By combining these ingredients properly, the special purpose issuer might be able to achieve a credit rating that would be palatable to investors. However, as the dissimilarity of assets and the number of parties and "working parts" increases, the structure becomes more complicated. As complexity increases, there is more potential for asset risk and structural or securitization risks that prudent investors need to identify and assess.

Two kinds of monoline financial guaranty insurance (FGI) are available for asset-backed issues. The first, a partial or typically a "first-loss" guaranty, insures against defaults in the underlying collateral ("asset-risk") up to a specified percentage of the assets, usually in the range of 7 to 15 percent.

Alternatively, the insurance may be applied as an unconditional and irrevocable 100 percent guaranty, covering not just a portion of asset risk but *all* asset risks and *all* securitization risks, including the risks of bankruptcy consolidation, legal or regulatory changes, lawsuits, and fraud and performance failures by servicers, trustees and swap counterparties. In either case, the guaranty is unconditional and irrevocable.

From the investors' perspective, a partial guaranty is comparable to other first-loss protections, like those provided by bank letters of credit and senior/subordinated structures. However, because the rating for a financing will reflect the rating of the first-loss provider, banks' competitiveness in this area has diminished because of the small number of banks that can provide a AAA letter of credit.

Furthermore, the new risk-based capital guidelines adopted for banks make it more expensive for them to offer credit enhancement on low-risk financings—banks have to allocate uniform levels of capital for issues whether or not they are investment-grade or collateralized. Another disadvantage of letters of credit is that they are generally for periods of short duration and thus are not available to support the long-term financing market.

Senior/subordinated structures often provide an effective alternative, although frequently the size of the subordinated piece needed to obtain a AAA rating will make that structure uneconomic to the issuer.

The appropriateness of a partial or 100 percent guaranty will depend on a number of factors, including premium rates charged and the trading value of the insurer's name. In general, the more unfamiliar the assets are to the market or the newer or more complex the structure, the more investors will prefer the comfort of 100 percent coverage.

Conversely, when investors can quickly and cost-effectively make themselves comfortable with the size of a partial guaranty and the body of documents, legal opinions, representations, warranties, and other assurances attesting to the transaction's soundness, they may be satisfied with partial coverage.

However, because 100 percent guarantees fully cover these risks, investors frequently prefer to accept a lower yield in order to have the safety of the 100 percent guaranty. The goal is for the guarantor to add value to transactions that are already very strong so that its premiums can be kept lower than the value added by the policy.

To accomplish this goal, Aaa/AAA-rated monoline guaranty insurers must maintain stringent underwriting standards and structure asset-backed issues to be high quality even before they are insured. Additional protections minimize the guarantor's ultimate losses in the unlikely event of a default.

For example, as part of its underwriting policy, Financial Security Assurance structures all insured issues to an investment-grade level before they are insured. Every issue is backed by collateral equal to at least the par amount. FSA also requires additional protections in every transaction it guarantees such as surplus collateral, spread accounts, and guarantees from investment-grade third parties to minimize losses in the event of default. (For further discussion of credit structuring see the sections on "built-in capital" and "self-correcting mechanisms.")

BENEFITS OF INSURED ASSET-BACKED SECURITIES

In their evaluation of monoline financial guarantors, investors and issuers should first be aware of the numerous benefits of asset-backed securities which are 100 percent guaranteed by monoline insurers.

Investor Benefits

Financial guarantors are in a position to provide thorough analysis more cost-effectively than investors. The guarantor consolidates tasks that would otherwise have to be carried out individually, and hence with duplication of effort, by multiple investors. This review encompasses not only the detailed process of reviewing asset quality, but also the review of securitization risks.

Thorough Analysis: Auto Loan-Backed Example

In the case of an FSA-insured issue backed by auto loans, the asset finance group would evaluate the portfolio's historical performance. Analysts would consider: the interest rate, maturity, and seasoning of the loans; the proportion of new vs. used vehicles; whether there is recourse to dealers on individual loans; and the lender's historical prepayment experience, default, and recovery rates.

To anticipate the future performance of the portfolio, the guarantor would model the portfolio according to expected and stressed loss curves. The guarantor would then structure the transaction to protect itself and investors from losses even under the extreme circumstances implied in the higher curve (Figure 14.2).

Because the difference between the outstanding aggregate par amount of auto loans and the

Figure 14.2—Monthly Losses of Auto Loan Portfolios (As % of Original Number of Contracts)

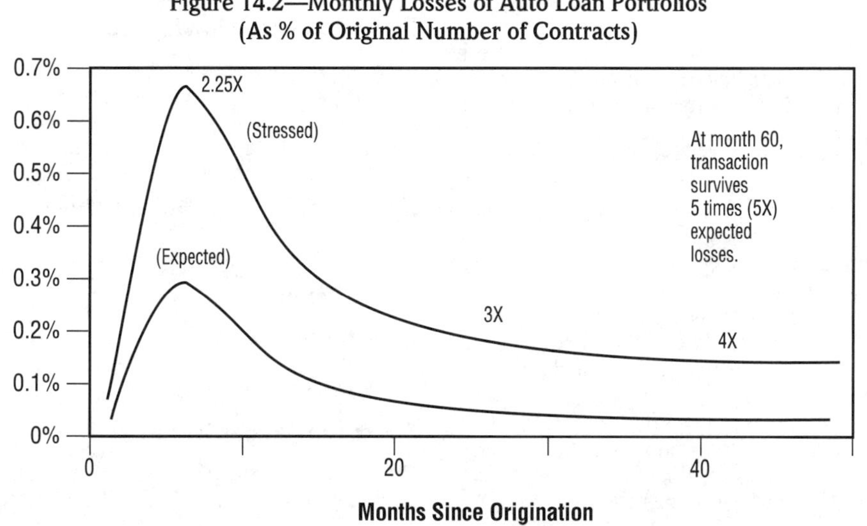

Figure 14.3—Bond Collateralization

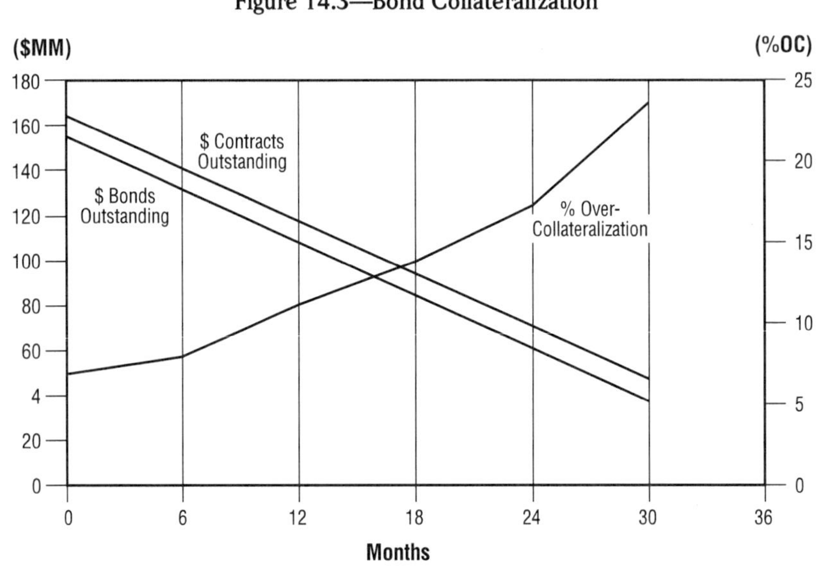

outstanding amount of the bonds remains constant, over time the overcollateralization levels of the transaction would increase. This is because the auto loan contracts are being paid down, as is the bond issue (Figure 14.3).

Monitoring and Surveillance

Asset-backed issues are notorious for the amount of ongoing monitoring and surveillance required to assure not only that assets are performing, but that all the "moving parts" of a transaction are functioning as intended.

When the insurance policy covers 100 percent of principal and interest, the monoline insurer *guarantees* that the investor will not suffer losses as a result of the poor performance of structural elements or other third parties. It therefore assumes the investor's interest in seeing that all facets of a transaction work properly until maturity, and it maintains a staff dedicated to keeping up with the stream of compliance and performance reports attached to these issues. It may also stipulate the proper form for the reports.

If something goes wrong, the guarantor has the standing to do something about it, and can invoke remedies that it required to be built into the transaction at the outset. This could mean replacement of servicers or downgraded first-loss providers, capture of excess cash flows, or in some cases, mandatory infusions of collateral.

Liquidity

Not only can investors in the secondary market buy insured securities without having to duplicate the due diligence of the original investor, but they benefit from the guarantor's ongoing market development efforts. These efforts can broaden investor interest in a guaranteed issue and thus create a liquid secondary market for what might otherwise have been a difficult security to sell or trade because of its complexity.

Protection from Downgrade

Investors benefit from the downgrade protection offered by a 100 percent guaranty because the AAA rating of a financial guarantor supersedes other elements of the transaction. For example, should a letter of credit provider or servicer be downgraded, the issue's rating will remain AAA. In uninsured securities, the downgrade risk is borne by the investor.

Issuer Benefits

In addition to a favorable funding rate, 100 percent financial guaranty insurance offers a number of benefits to issuers.

Structuring Expertise

One benefit of financial guaranty insurance is that the monoline insurer has an abundance of knowledge about all the economic, accounting, structuring, rating agency, and legal elements of an asset securitization. Because it is given an opportunity to see many more transactions than it actually insures, the guarantor is likely to have a broad perspective on the market and the mechanisms that make for successful securitizations. The guarantor can assist at every stage in structuring a transaction that, however complex, will function smoothly until its maturity.

Broadened Market

Securities with 100 percent insurance may appeal to investor classes that would not otherwise show an interest. For example, certain investors might be reluctant to purchase an issue backed by foreign assets because of unfamiliarity with the legal, credit, or other issues related to those assets or their securitization structure. Such investors might purchase the same issue if it is fully guaranteed by a recognized monoline insurance company.

In some cases, the substitution of the guarantor's name for that of the issuer allows the issuer to raise funds without increasing its "name-in-the-market" exposure and to retain capacity within its traditional funding sources. Guaranteed securities that replace rather than augment existing funding programs decrease market saturation in the issuer's name and may thereby improve secondary market pricing of other securities sold by the issuer.

Also, monoline insurers frequently provide marketing support for the issues they guarantee. They will consult with the underwriters at an early stage of the transaction about the most advantageous market, type of debt instrument, call protection, and other factors that can result in the most efficient borrowing. They also maintain ongoing advertising and educational efforts to improve the marketability of the issues they insure.

Timeliness

The use of 100 percent financial guaranty insurance usually reduces the time required for the credit-rating agencies to rate an obligation. This benefit may be particularly important to an issuer seeking to take advantage of a temporary market opportunity, an issuer previously unrated by the rating agencies or an issuer involved in a complex transaction. Some guarantors will manage the entire rating agency process and arrange for delivery of all required rating letters at closing.

Favorable Disclosure, Tax, or Accounting Treatment

Some insured transactions also benefit from reduced disclosure requirements or advantageous tax or accounting treatment. Even though such factors in a transaction are not risk-related, they add value that may be reflected in the insurer's premium, particularly when the issuer seeks to take advantage of a temporary market opportunity.

ASSESSING THE STRENGTH OF MONOLINE GUARANTORS

Recent downgrades in the banking and multiline property/casualty insurance sectors have made investors and issuers realize how important it is to be able to assess the strength of all financial institutions—including monoline guarantors.

There are a number of powerful internal and external factors that sustain the monoline insurer's AAA claims-paying rating. Each monoline guarantor should be assessed according to how well it measures up to those criteria which are described below.

Is the Guarantor's Insured Portfolio of High Credit Quality and Well Diversified?

According to industry statistics, approximately 70 percent of issues insured by the monoline financial guaranty industry are estimated to be in the A or higher range before the monoline applies its guaranty.[1] The credit quality of a monoline guarantor's insured portfolio should be uniformly high, whether its portfolio consists primarily of municipal or taxable financings.

Each insurer maintains an internal rating system that is comparable to those of the rating agencies, which independently confirm portfolio quality for purposes of rating the insurer each year (Figure 14.4).

The monoline's insured portfolio should be well diversified by credit type and by geographic location. Proper diversification prevents problems in one sector or region from severely diminishing overall capital. Moreover, diversification provides the guarantor with several alternative areas of opportunity, so that resources can be shifted away from any line of business whose risk complexion is worsening.

---

1 Association of Financial Guaranty Insurors. *Report of Combined Financial Results and New Business Written: For the Years Ended December 31, 1991, 1990, 1989, 1988.*

Figure 14.4—Financial Guaranty Industry Insured Portfolio Ratings Distribution*

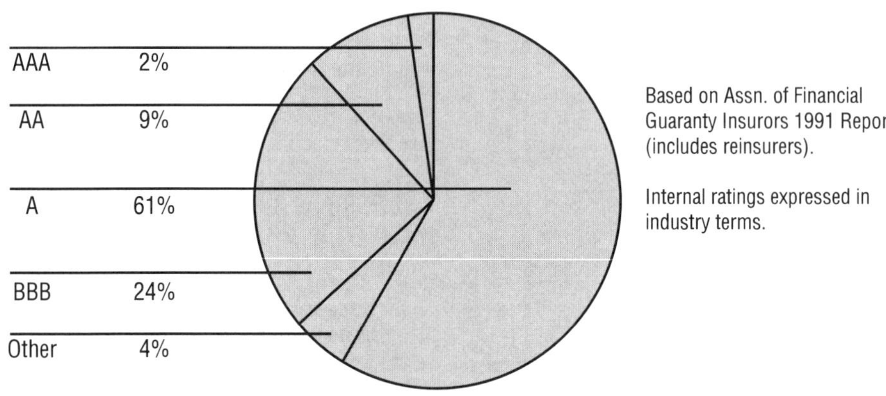

*Internal ratings expressed in industry terms.

Does the Guarantor Adhere to Stringent Underwriting Standards?

In maintaining high credit quality standards for its insured portfolio, a prudent monoline financial guarantor should underwrite to what is called a "zero-loss" standard. Although this is called zero-loss underwriting, the guarantor must recognize that even investment-grade issues can default. Therefore, the guarantor should require collateral or other protections to minimize potential losses.

Protections such as collateral, spread accounts, or guarantees from qualified third parties function as "built-in" capital for the guarantor. All of these would have to be exhausted before the guarantor would suffer a loss to its own capital and reserves (Figure 14.5). When evaluating a transaction insured by a monoline guarantor, investors should look at how well the guarantor's transactions are supported by "built-in capital."

Depending on the nature of the collateral, the guarantor should include different types of "self-

Figure 14.5—Built-in Capital in Asset-Backed Securities

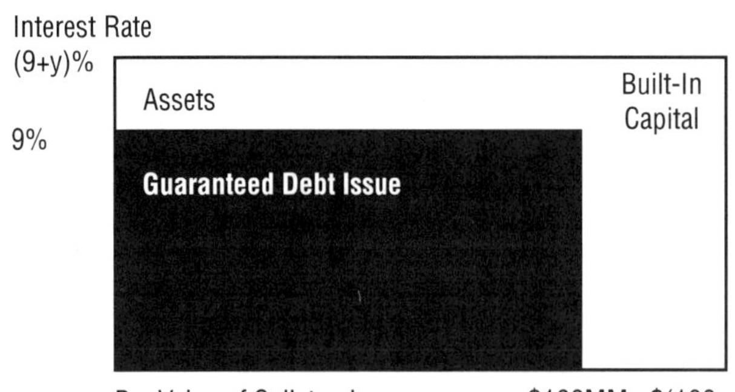

A $100 million asset-backed security with a 9% coupon, represented by inner rectangle, is backed by $(100+x) million of consumer receivables that pay interest at (9+y)% (outer rectangle). There is $x million of excess collateral and a y% interest rate spread. The monoline guarantor requires that these or comparable protections, suited to the specific issue, be in place before it will provide insurance.

Examples of Self-Correcting Mechanisms

Collateralized bond obligations/high-yield bond portfolios. The guarantor should set collateral and portfolio requirements, which include issuer concentration, industry concentration, par overcollateralization, interest coverage, and ratings mix. If ratings fall below prescribed levels, any ineligible collateral should be excluded from pool calculations. If this causes noncompliance, or issuer fails to meet overcollateralization, or interest coverage or diversification tests, issuer must substitute acceptable collateral or defease/redeem senior notes.

Excessive losses from sale or default of underlying bonds should set off triggers requiring the guarantor to approve any subsequent sales/substitutions of collateral. If trading losses plus the amount of ineligible collateral (due to downgrade or default) exceed other specified limits, all cash flow should be diverted (from subordinated tranches) to pay holders of senior, insured bonds until the senior bonds are defeased/redeemed in full.

Senior bank loan portfolios. Portfolios are overcollateralized with a senior/subordinated structure. The guarantor should subject the loan pool to ongoing tests for overcollateralization, industry diversification, credit quality, and interest coverage. If a loan participation becomes ineligible, then cash flow should be allocated to pay down the insured senior tranche.

Consumer receivables/residential second mortgages. Collateral pool is self-liquidating. Excess cash flow is trapped until a reserve is fully funded at a specified level. Should the reserve fund later fall below that level, excess cash flow is automatically diverted again to replenish the reserve. The guarantor should be able to replace the servicer if a predetermined default level is reached on underlying loans. Committed standby servicer receives all data from first day of transaction and can step in immediately.

Commercial mortgages. Mortgage pool contains multiple properties whose mortgages are cross-collateralized. Staggered lease termination dates protect against severe vacancies. If specific financial and performance covenants are not adhered to, excess cash flow from all properties should be trapped in a reserve fund to assure continued debt service coverage.

---

correcting mechanisms" in the securitization structure. If transaction performance falters after the transaction has been closed, these mechanisms will be triggered. These may include replacement of servicers or downgraded first-loss providers, capture of excess cash flows, or mandatory infusions of collateral. Whenever necessary and well before problems become serious, these remedies will be invoked.

In the case of municipal issues, the insured bonds are secured by a dedicated revenue stream or a pledge of taxing power. Some source of tax base or revenues is dedicated to the bonds either by direct pledge or through general obligation status.

Does the Guarantor Meet Rating Agency Capital Adequacy Standards?

Rating agencies provide continual oversight of bond insurers, evaluating capital adequacy by analyzing their claims-paying ability as measured by detailed analyses of financial resources, operations, and exposures in published regular reports on individual guarantors.

In order to receive the agencies' AAA ratings, the guarantor must demonstrate its capital adequacy as stressed under depression-level conditions. The guarantor must meet single-risk limitations and other operating and financial guidelines. By analyzing the reports presented by the agencies, investors can assess how well a financial guarantor has met these guidelines and compare its capital adequacy relative to other financial guarantors.

Examples of Rating Agency Approach

As part of its evaluation of a guarantor, Standard & Poor's Corporation (S&P) employs a capital adequacy model designed specifically for monoline financial insurers. The model analyzes the sufficiency of the guarantor's capital under depression-level economic conditions. The guarantor must demonstrate that it can pay all expected claims forecast by the model and still retain a satisfactory statutory capital base.

Under the S&P model, each municipal and asset-backed transaction is given a capital charge, reflecting an estimate of the loss potential of the transaction in a depression. The model projects three years of aggressive business growth for the guarantor, followed by a four-year depression in which no new business is written.

Expected losses are projected over the four years of the depression by multiplying the weighted average capital charge percentage by the average annual debt service in the case of municipals and by average par in the case of asset-backeds. Therefore, the model assumes that *every* issue the guarantor has guaranteed will default, and the guarantor *will* suffer losses in the amount equal to the capital charge that S&P originally assigned to each issue.

The model takes into account the portfolio composition, as well as projected expenses and investment income under depression conditions. The insurer's third-party capital supports, such as reinsurance and letters of credit, are valued according to the rating of the provider.

At Moody's Investors Service, one tool used to evaluate the guarantor is a bond insurance stress model designed to measure a bond insurer's ability to meet its policyholder obligations. Moody's employs "Monte Carlo" simulation methods, which allow it to test the interrelationships of a great number of variables and the effectiveness of diversification in the insured portfolio, investment portfolio, and group of reinsurance providers, under a variety of economic scenarios.

Drawing on its historical data base on bond default patterns, combined with analysis of how future patterns may differ from those of the past, Moody's assigns probabilities of default frequency and severity to sectors of the insurer's portfolio on the basis of credit quality, type of insured obligations, seasoning, and economic conditions. The model takes into account the tendency of defaults to be concentrated by sector, geographic location, and calendar time period; the variability of premium pricing; and other hazards related to regulation, interest rates, management, and liquidity.

Both S&P and Moody's also consider other factors—ownership, management, quality of underwriting, and financial performance—before assigning a AAA claims-paying rating to a financial guarantor.

The rating agencies revisit the monoline insurer's rating each time it insures a new transaction. In addition, the agencies regularly review the insurer's overall book of business to insure diversification by geography, transaction types, maturities, industry segments, and collateral asset categories.

Does the Guarantor Meet State Regulatory Standards?

In addition to meeting the capital adequacy standards of the rating agencies, monoline guarantors must conform to the requirements of New York State insurance law and the laws of the other state jurisdictions in which they do business. Investors should be aware of what those standards are and how well a guarantor conforms to regulatory requirements.

Under New York State insurance law (Article 69), which applies to all AAA monoline financial guarantors, financial guaranty business must be conducted by separately capitalized corporations. The law sets forth minimum capital requirements for financial guaranty insurers and restricts ancillary lines of business to a narrow range of related activities. It also mandates contingency reserves and sets single risk and aggregate risk limits on the basis of the insurer's policyholders' surplus and contingency reserve.

Like bank regulation, Article 69 uses risk weightings to determine capital adequacy. The insurance law differs from bank regulation in that finer distinctions are made in credit quality in assigning risk weightings. Bank risk weightings differentiate only between certain governmental mortgage or bank credits, with a single capital charge applied to all other liabilities, regardless of ratings. In contrast, Article 69 requires more capital for noninvestment grade and unsecured credits than for investment-grade and well-collateralized credits.

Under law, financial guarantors must invest their capital and reserves conservatively. Over 82 percent of the financial guaranty industry's investment portfolio is rated AA or better, with 98 percent of the investments rated A or higher.[2] Eligible investments include marketable high-quality, fixed-income instruments such as corporate bonds, tax-exempt bonds, and mortgage pass-through securities.

Event risk is virtually absent because New York State insurance law precludes any type of leveraged restructuring of a monoline financial guarantor. Regulation limits indebtedness and payment of dividends, thereby preventing excessive leverage and asset stripping.

2 Association of Financial Guaranty Insurors. *Report of Combined Financial Results and New Business Written: For the Years Ended December 31, 1991, 1990, 1989 and 1988.*

It is also important to recognize that under New York State law, financial guaranty companies can write only financial guaranty insurance, which means their capital cannot be eroded by problems in other lines of business. In addition, once a guaranty is issued, it cannot be revoked by either party, assuring an uninterrupted stream of future revenues.

CONCLUSION

Over the last few years, the structured finance market has grown dramatically and with it the need for financial guaranty insurance. According to the Association of Financial Guaranty Insurors (AFGI), the par amount of new corporate and asset-backed securities insured by monoline financial guarantors in 1990 increased by 51.3 percent from the previous year to $10.165 million. After declining slightly in 1991 to $9,767 million,[3] the insured amount rose again to at least $10,870 million in 1992 according to industry press.[4]

Several factors are expected to make this market expand further:

- The continued entry of new issuers of asset-backed securities as traditional bank borrowers turn to the capital markets in the face of decreased liquidity and higher costs within the banking sector.
- The emergence of structured finance and securitization markets in Europe and Asia and the continued growth of these markets in the United States.
- The increased capital requirements for banks, which will provide pricing advantages to financial guaranty insurers relative to bank letters of credit.
- Heightened credit awareness and trading of credits among international investors, and an increased reliance by borrowers and investors on credit ratings.
- Investor concerns with event risk and voluntary downgrade risk, which are significantly mitigated by the guaranty of a AAA financial guaranty insurer.

The strength of the AAA monoline financial guaranty industry will enable it to continue as a catalyst in the development of the structured finance market.

3 Association of Financial Guaranty Insurors. *Report of Combined Financial Results and New Business Written: For the Years Ended December 31, 1991, 1990, 1989, 1988.*

4 *Asset Sales Report,* January 18, 1993.

Chapter 15

Financial Guaranty Reinsurance: Bridging Global Asset-Backed Securities Markets

by David A. Smith,
Capital Reinsurance Company

INTRODUCTION

During the latter half of the 1980s, increasingly stringent capital requirements and a difficult operating environment for banking institutions encouraged the development of alternatives to the issuance of debt and equity capital. At the same time, restructuring and leveraged buyout activity prompted growing concern among fund managers of potential event risk in holding straightforward corporate debt and equity. The confluence of these factors, together with improving financial technology permitting the rapid analysis of large quantities of financial data, prompted the development of asset-backed and mortgage-backed securities markets on a global scale.

Financial guaranties provided by highly rated insurance and reinsurance companies have increasingly come to be the preferred instruments for the credit enhancement of asset-backed securities issued in North America, Europe, and the Pacific Rim countries. As an example, mortgage pool insurance (covering losses on residential mortgage loans arising from a credit default by the borrower above and beyond any primary mortgage insurance and in excess of a first-loss deductible), and reinsurance upgrades (whereby a reinsurance policy enhances the credit rating of a lesser rated primary insurance company) helped to propel the U.K. mortgage-backed securities market from its infancy in 1987 to over £11 billion in total par amount of securities outstanding by 1991. The lack of large, central government-sponsored financial institutions chartered to support secondary mortgage markets afforded financial guaranty opportunities for the highly rated composite, or multiline, European insurers and reinsurers. Recent developments in Sweden, France, and Australia point to the value of financial guarantors and reinsurers in supporting a global consistency of asset quality and structural protection for investors.

METHODS OF REINSURANCE

Financial guaranty reinsurance plays a pivotal role in the cross-border flow of information, structural techniques, and risk syndication, enabling the bridging of local markets. There are two methods of reinsurance: treaty reinsurance and facultative reinsurance. Treaty reinsurance provides that the company originating the insurance policy, known as the primary or ceding company, or reinsured, and the company accepting or reinsuring the policy, the reinsurer, enter into an agreement for pre-approval of reinsurance within classes of business specified in the treaty. The treaty may define narrow or broad classes of business, and it may place limits on the aggregate volume of business and largest single issue size which may be transferred, or ceded, to the reinsurer under the treaty. Facultative reinsurance is the method of reinsurance used when the primary company and reinsurer individually negotiate each transaction. A reinsurer may limit its activity in new or complex lines of business to facultative acceptances. Facultative transactions often require a substantial amount of documentation, including detailed reinsurance policies or reinsurance slips (a term sheet or summary of the key elements of the reinsurance).

Figure 15.1—Proportional Reinsurance Structure

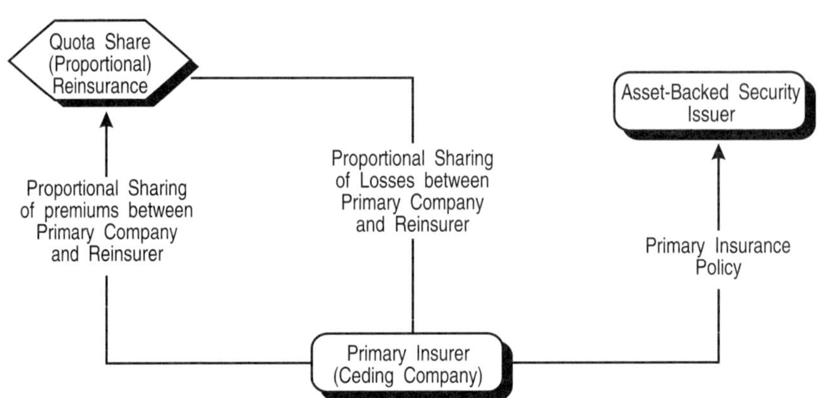

FORMS OF REINSURANCE

Distinct from the methods of reinsurance are two forms of reinsurance: proportional (sometimes referred to as "quota-share"), and non-proportional (sometimes generically described as "excess-of-loss"). Proportional reinsurance, outlined in Figure 15.1, entails a sharing of risk between the reinsured and reinsurer where the only distinction between the risk position of each party is the percentage of the total risk shared by each party. No distinction in temporal exposure (the time periods in which each party has exposure) or in the priority of loss allocation (the order in which losses would be allocated between the reinsured and reinsurer) would be made. In the instance where proportional reinsurance transfers one-half of the risk on a given transaction to the reinsurer, the reinsured and reinsurer have identical risk positions on the transaction. The primary company would customarily keep a percentage of each premium payment, payable monthly, quarterly, annually, or up-front depending on the structure of the insured transaction, as compensation for expenses incurred in originating the insurance coverage. This is termed a ceding commission. A typical amount would be between 20 percent and 30 percent of total premiums ceded to the reinsurer.

Non-proportional reinsurance, outlined in Figure 15.2, generally describes all forms of reinsurance where temporal or priority of loss exposures are not identical between the reinsured and reinsurer. The U.K. mortgage-backed security transaction illustrated below in the case study is an example of non-proportional reinsurance. In general, non-proportional reinsurance strategies permit the synthesis of a wide range of risk positions, including removal from first loss and controlled exposure over time.

DEVELOPMENT OF FINANCIAL GUARANTY REINSURANCE MARKETS

The development of financial guaranty insurance and reinsurance markets is a recent phenomenon, having emerged in the United States in the early 1980s from a confluence of supply and demand factors. On the supply side, a number of highly rated multiline property and casualty insurers were establishing financial guaranty operations as adjuncts to their investment or surety bond operations. The banks, which had previously been the dominant providers of third-party credit support, became increasingly constrained by minimum capital requirements in light of growing non-performing loans in the energy and lesser-developed country sectors. Early projects included the formation of the first monoline financial guaranty insurance company, American Municipal Bond Assurance Corp. ("AMBAC") as a subsidiary of MGIC in 1971, and the Municipal Bond Insurance Association ("MBIA") in 1974, a joint underwriting association of AAA-rated multiline insurers, dedicated to insuring municipal bond obligations. By the early 1980s, corporate surety bonds had emerged as a substitute for traditional bank letters of credit in money market financings. Early transactions included Chatsworth Funding, Inc., a $500 million commercial paper facility established in January 1983 to fund participations in short-term bank loans to major U.S. corporations origi-

Figure 15.2—Non-Proportional Reinsurance Structure

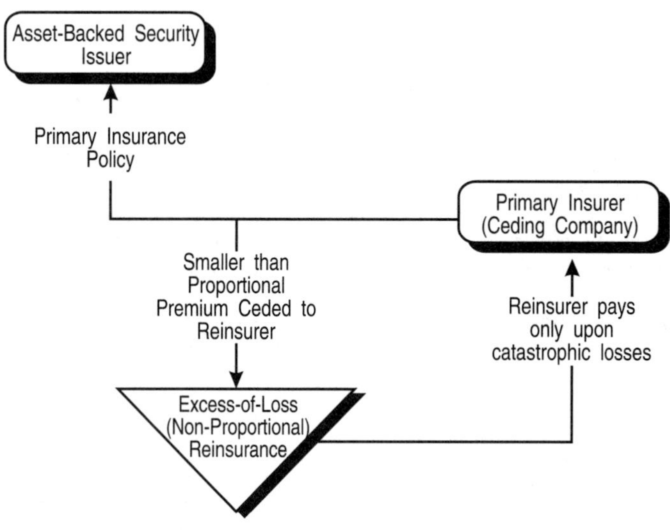

nated by Citibank. The Travelers Indemnity Company provided a surety bond to guaranty the timely payment of maturing commercial paper, enabling the issuer to obtain top commercial paper ratings from the major U.S. rating agencies. As a result, the pricing and availability of standby letters of credit impeded their widespread use, particularly in the last half of the decade.

On the demand side, developing technology in residential mortgage securitization supported by the Government National Mortgage Association ("GNMA") and other U.S. government-sponsored secondary mortgage market makers and the growing power and availability of microcomputers provided the tools for forays into other asset classes, including computer leases, credit card receivables, and automobile loans. Commercial banks, finance companies, and industrial companies sought to securitize assets as a substitute for more direct and costly equity and debt issues.

The use of financial guaranties in the European Community developed initially in the sterling mortgage-backed securities markets, where, in March of 1987, The Mortgage Corporation, a subsidiary of Salomon, Inc., issued a £200 million residential mortgage security, supported by a mortgage pool insurance policy issued by Sun Alliance & London Insurance (then carrying a AAA claims paying ability rating from Standard & Poor's Corp.) The mortgage-backed securities were rated AAA by Standard & Poor's. Over the next three years, more than a dozen mortgage conduits were established, sponsored by commercial banks and investment banks. With total par amounts outstanding of over £11 billion, the sterling mortgage-backed securities market is the largest single asset-backed market outside of the U.S. Of the total par amount of sterling mortgage-backed security issues to date, about two-thirds of the transactions have used financial guaranty insurance.

France adopted securitization legislation in late 1988, providing for special purpose funding vehicles ("Fonds Communs de Créances"). Two constraints on the Fonds Communs de Créances ("FCC") impeded the development of securitization of assets in France: first, loans which had a maturity of less than two years could not be purchased by an FCC and, secondly, an FCC could not substitute new loans for loans which matured or were refinanced. The first residential mortgage securitization, Foncier FCC 1991, received a preliminary AAA rating from Standard & Poor's in November of 1991. Amendments to the securitization regulations passed in 1993 removed the restriction on loan substitution and a forthcoming governmental decree may eliminate the two-year minimum maturity requirement.

Other countries where financial guaranties have been used in securitizations include Sweden, where a mortgage-originating subsidiary of SE Banken has issued over $500 million in mortgage-backed securities (Osprey Mortgage Securities,

Nos. 1-6) covered by pool insurance policies issued by Trygg-Hansa Insurance Co., and Australia, where residential mortgages and private label credit cards have been securitized and co-insured by Financial Security Assurance ("FSA"), a U.S. monoline financial guaranty insurer, and the State Guaranty Insurance Corp. of South Australia ("SGIC"). An asset-backed securities market in Japan may emerge in the next several years with the resolution of various regulatory and legal hurdles.

Financial guaranty reinsurance has been a key factor in the above-mentioned transactions. As new asset-backed securities markets have developed around the world, primary insurance companies have desired to limit their exposure to the relatively uncharted financial guaranty lines, and have thus welcomed cross-border reinsurance. A professional financial guaranty reinsurance company can bring substantial expertise to emerging markets. Asset-backed securities require a large minimum issue size in order to rationalize the up-front costs of structuring; reinsurance provides an effective method of reducing the primary company's single risk exposure. High quality reinsurance can improve the confidence which investors have in the ability of the primary company to perform its obligations in emerging asset-backed markets.

Opportunities available to the U.S. monolines to reinsure financial guaranties in the European markets, and to assume reinsurance from the multilines in certain transactions, have provided a critical link between the markets, allowing for the mutual exploitation of strengths (technical expertise, trading value of guarantor, access to large pools of capital).

The traditional form of reinsurance has been quota share, first introduced by AMBAC to support its municipal bond insurance business. The U.S. monolines have historically used treaties for the covered classes of business agreed upon at the inception of the treaty relationship.

Non-proportional strategies, conducted primarily on a facultative basis, have emerged as an alternative to the traditional quota-share treaty relationships. Non-proportional reinsurance permits a highly rated multiline company desiring to write residential mortgage pool insurance in the U.K. market to issue a relatively large policy, for example, £37.5 million on a total par amount of mortgages of £250 million (15 percent), which would be one of the components required for a high investment grade rating from the major rating agencies. The policy would typically be written with a first-loss deductible sized to be able to withstand the maximum expected cumulative losses on the mortgage pool in a stressful economic scenario. This strategy could allow the multiline company to retain for its own account the first £5 million of exposure above the first-loss deductible together with a premium approaching 50 percent of the total premium for the £37.5 million policy. A disproportionately higher premium would be allocated to the multiline company's first-loss retention to compensate the company for retaining the portion of the policy closer to the level of expected losses in the mortgage portfolio. The remaining £32.5 million in exposure could be ceded to a monoline company where risk/reward preferences would be for exposure much more remote from risk of loss. In return for this exposure, the reinsurance company would receive a share of the premium which is proportionate to the risk of loss, not the nominal value of the principal insured.

Differences in the form of financial guaranties issued in various local markets, and capital positions and single-risk retention policies of the monoline and multiline companies, have enabled professional reinsurers, such as Capital Re, to engineer non-proportional reinsurance strategies that better exploit the strengths of the market participants. The following case study illustrates the use of a non-proportional reinsurance structure in the U.K. mortgage-backed securities market.

CASE STUDY: U.K. MORTGAGE-BACKED SECURITIES

The following presentation illustrates the underwriting and structuring process for a financial guaranty reinsurer in the U.K. mortgage-backed securities market. This case study is drawn from an actual private placement transaction recently insured and reinsured in the U.K. market. The analysis includes a review of the financial and operational capability of the administrator (servicer), deemed to be critical to the ongoing management of asset quality, a discussion of the various insurance coverages employed, and a close description of the reinsurance structure.

ABC Mortgage Company was identified as a strong administrator, benefiting from its relationship with its parent, ABC Bank, in areas such as loan underwriting standards, access to funding, and capital support. ABC Mortgage Company has a 15-year operating history. It commenced business in 1975 as XYZ Finance, Ltd., a consumer finance company, and entered the U.K. residential mortgage loan market in 1980. It was acquired by ABC Bank in 1985. ABC Mortgage's financial performance has been improving, with a 20 percent increase in fiscal year 1991 pre-tax profit reported over FY 1990. Compared to other U.K. centralized residential mortgage lenders, ABC Mortgage has been relatively less active in securitizing its assets. Since 1985, three pools with £750 million in aggregate principal amount of mortgages have been launched. The public deals (ABC Residential Securities Nos. 1 & 2) were rated AAA by virtue of mortgage pool policies issued by DEF Insurance Co., Ltd., which carries a AA claims paying ability rating, and upgraded by GHI Insurance Co. and JKL Insurance Co. (Both of these companies have AAA claims paying ratings.) The upgrade insurance policies provide that if DEF Insurance Co. is unable to pay claims arising under its mortgage pool policy because of insolvency, GHI and JKL will assume the obligations of DEF. Since 1988, ABC Mortgage has funded its mortgage lending entirely through borrowings from its parent company and other banks.

ABC Mortgage turnover (composed of interest income and charges from the mortgage loan portfolio) for FY 1991 was £200 million on total assets of £1.5 billion. ABC Mortgage is moderately capitalized for its status as a centralized lender, with £75 million in capital and reserves equal to 5 percent of total assets. Gross profit (interest income and charges less interest expense paid by ABC Mortgage on its borrowings, or net interest income) totaled £15 million, producing a net interest income to average total assets ratio of 1 percent.

ABC Mortgage's underwriting guidelines, the adherence to which is a precondition of filing a claim for payment under the pool insurance policy issued by DEF Insurance Co., are generally in conformity with the U.K. bench mark pool underwriting guidelines established by Standard & Poor's Corp. Were the underwriting guidelines to deviate materially from the Standard & Poor's guidelines, the administrator would have difficulty in obtaining an investment grade rating for the securitization. The ABC Mortgage credit assessment system has evolved from that used by XYZ Bank for unsecured loans and second mortgages. The maximum loan size is based on a multiple of net take-home pay less a standard cost of living factor (40 percent for single persons and 45 percent for married) less the full mortgage loan payment (not any initial subsidized interest rate). Each loan is individually underwritten after passing the disposable income requirement.

Maximum loan-to-value ratios range between 65 percent and 75 percent without mortgage indemnity guaranties. Mortgage indemnity guaranties are an insurance product provided by composite U.K. insurers for the benefit of mortgage lenders, covering losses a lender might incur from the failure of a borrower to repay a mortgage loan coupled with insufficient proceeds from the sale of the mortgaged property to repay the lender in full. This product is typically required by a lender for mortgage loans with an original or potential maximum loan-to-value ratio of over 70 percent, and is similar to primary mortgage insurance underwritten by monoline mortgage insurers in the U.S. Stabilizer loans (deferred interest features) are limited to 65 percent loan-to-value without mortgage indemnity guaranties. All loans in excess of the 65 percent/75 percent limits require mortgage indemnity guaranties, and are generally limited to 80 percent loan-to-value after the application of the mortgage indemnity guaranties. Only 5 percent of the mortgage loans in the ABC pool have loan-to-value ratios exceeding 80 percent. These loans are termed Ordinary Full Status, have the most conservative debt-to-income multiples, and involve full loan documentation. Recent financial results for U.K. composite insurers writing mortgage indemnity guaranty books dramatically illustrate the potential loss exposure in this line of business. Losses ranging into the hundreds of millions of pounds sterling suggest that either the insurers exit this business or that they tighten underwriting standards and raise premiums.

Mortgage pool insurance, on the other hand, has been a generally profitable line of business for the U.K. composite insurers. Mortgage pool insurance, also similar to the product offered by U.S. mortgage insurers, is a form of catastrophe coverage, responding only after the underlying mortgage indemnity guaranty coverage has been called upon. In addition, the mortgage pool insurance product is typically underwritten with a first-loss deductible substantially in excess of expected mortgage loan defaults.

Following a six-month due diligence process, including a site visit to ABC Mortgage in Northtown, England, DEF Insurance Co. issued a mortgage pool indemnity policy covering 100 percent of the principal balance of the pool mortgages (£200 million in total par amount of mortgages) in excess of an initial 5 percent (£10 million) first-loss deductible. Full 100 percent coverage was motivated by ABC Mortgage's desire to tap the private placement market, rather than issuing mortgage-backed securities through a public issue. The total sum insured was £200 million less the deductible amount of £10 million, or £190 million. The 5 percent deductible is permitted to reduce in sterling the amount, in proportion to the sterling

Figure 15.3—Mortgage Pool Insurance—Risk Run-Off and First-Loss Deductible

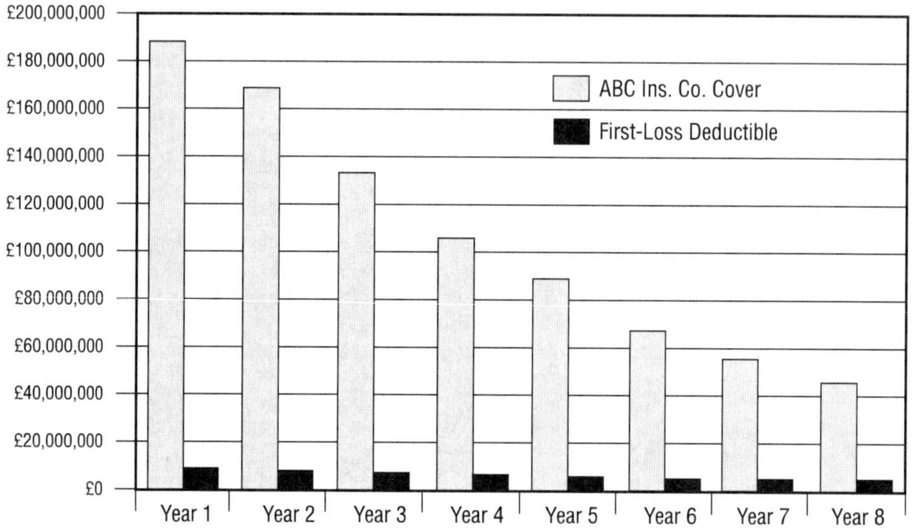

£200,000,000
£180,000,000
£160,000,000
£140,000,000
£120,000,000
£100,000,000
£80,000,000
£60,000,000
£40,000,000
£20,000,000
£0

ABC Ins. Co. Cover
First-Loss Deductible

Year 1 Year 2 Year 3 Year 4 Year 5 Year 6 Year 7 Year 8

amount of pool principal amortized over time, subject to a floor of £4 million (2 percent of the original pool amount) (Figure 15.3).

As illustrated in Figure 15.4, the deductible floor provides an increasing percentage of first-loss protection as the total principal balance of outstanding mortgages declines over time as a result of remortgagings (borrowers moving or refinancing their mortgages resulting in an early principal repayment).

The policy permits ABC Mortgage to substitute new mortgage loans for a three-year period for mortgages refinanced out of the original pool. Substitutions are desirable from the investors' viewpoint, in that principal is recycled for a longer period than would typically be permitted if principal payments were passed directly through to the holders of the securities. Substitutions are subject to criteria imposed by the rating agencies and mortgage pool insurers restricting the aggregate pool from increases in geographic concentration in

Figure 15.4—First-Loss Deductible as Percentage of Pool Insurance In Force

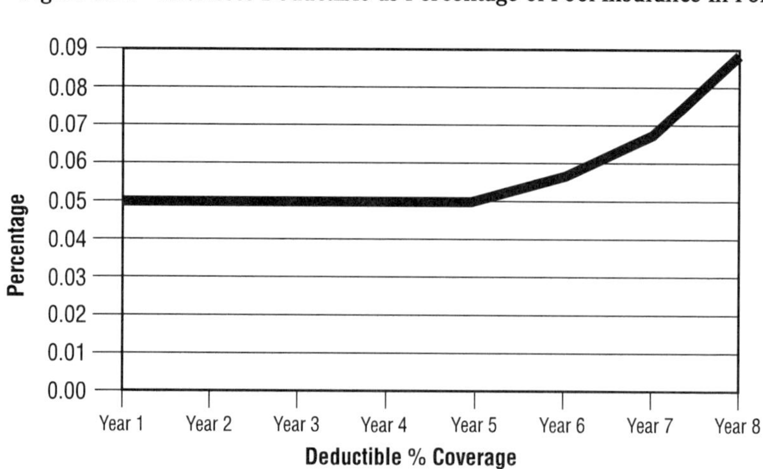

the South East (the region in England with largest house price decline in the past two years), reduced weighted average pool seasoning, increased weighted average pool loan-to-value ratio, increases in self-certified (limited documentation) mortgages, and stabilizer (deferred interest) mortgages. High loan-to-value mortgages and mortgages with substantial deferred interest components have exhibited disproportionately high default rates in the U.K.

It is important to note in this case that the policy was in excess of loss asset insurance coverage where certain rights to deny coverage under the policy have been retained by DEF Insurance Co. Grounds to deny coverage of defaulting loans in excess of the deductible include fraud, untrue statements by ABC Mortgage regarding specific mortgages in the insured pool, non-compliance with the stated loan underwriting criteria and servicing (arrears) procedures, losses pursuant to the lapse of property insurance or the failure of a property insurer to pay any claim, and any policy lapse or failure of any primary mortgage insurer. Any claims that would be absorbed within the first-loss deductible level must be endorsed by DEF Insurance Co. The purpose of this provision is to prevent the depletion of the deductible by invalid or inadequately investigated claims.

As displayed in Figure 15.5, there were six reinsurers participating in this transaction, including two financial risk reinsurers: Diamond Re and Clipper Re. Diamond Re is a U.S. monoline financial guaranty insurer, and Clipper Re is a specialty European multiline reinsurance company writing a financial risk book. DEF Insurance Co. desired to retain 25 percent of the £190 million insurance policy for its own account, reinsuring the remaining 75 percent, or £142.5 million, to the six reinsurers. Four reinsurers agreed to accept a 12.5 percent quota-share (proportional) participation each, totaling 50 percent of DEF's gross policy limit. The remaining 25 percent of the DEF policy being reinsured was offered to Diamond Re. Diamond Re agreed to reinsure the 25 percent share with a gross par amount of £47.5 million. Out of that £47.5 million piece, one "slice" was retroceded (reinsured by a reinsurer) to Clipper Re: the first £1.9 million, equivalent to 4 percent of the gross par amount reinsured by Diamond Re in excess of the 5 percent first-loss deductible. Diamond Re retained the remaining £45.6 million, equivalent to 96 percent of the gross par amount reinsured from DEF Insurance Co. by Diamond Re.

It was envisioned that as the mortgage pool amortizes, with mortgage refinancings taking loans out of the pool after the expiration of the three-year substitution period, the Clipper Re layer will remain at a constant sterling amount (£1.9 million) and will be an increasing percentage of the

Figure 15.5—ABC Mortgage Insurance and Reinsurance Structure

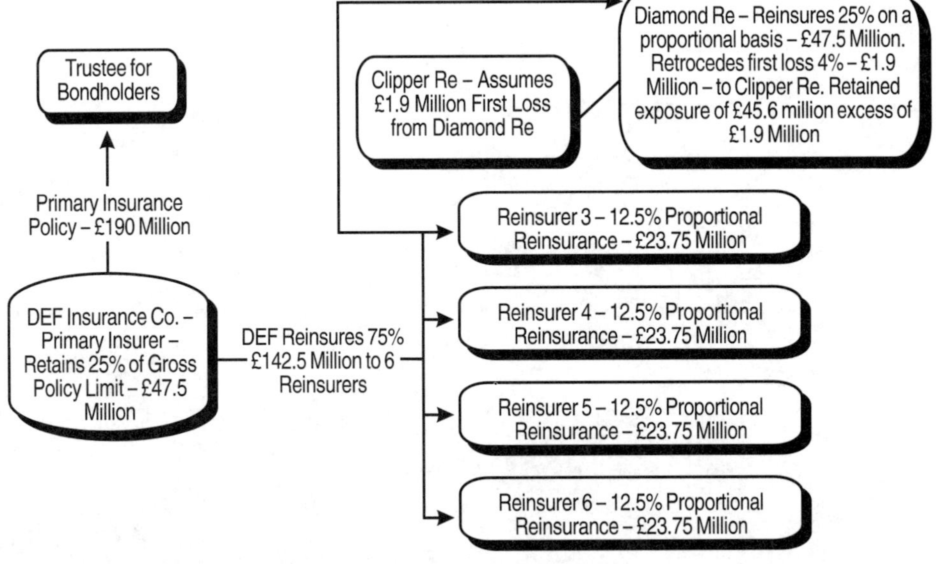

remaining pool. This effectively increases the first-loss protection afforded to Diamond Re over time.

Given the reinsurance structure, gross premium was allocated to produce a higher rate on line (premium as a percentage of the sum reinsured) for the first-loss Clipper Re layer, and a more modest rate on line for the Diamond Re excess layer. The allocation of capacity between Diamond Re and Clipper Re was based on the following factors: (i) the securing of an investment grade level of underlying loss coverage for Diamond Re, (ii) allocation of premium to produce an acceptable return on capital for both reinsurers, and (iii) the objective of a prudent single risk retention for both companies.

The synergistic relationship in the foregoing example arises from the multiline ceding company, DEF Insurance Co., seeking to control exposure on the transaction to a level commensurate with the more traditional lines of property/casualty business. The two reinsurers were able to provide a structure wherein Clipper Re would retain a relatively modest, closer-to-loss exposure layer at a proportionately higher premium. The risk of catastrophic loss was shifted to Diamond Re, which charged a proportionately lower premium than that obtained by DEF Insurance. Nevertheless, the premium provided an acceptable rate of return for the remote risk position of Diamond Re. To the extent that the multiline companies can absorb the first-loss risk layer within their own portfolios of diverse risks, the monoline companies, as illustrated here, can commit substantially larger line sizes and contribute to higher capacity for the entire global market.

CONCLUSION

Reinsurance techniques thus provide a mechanism for the cross-border syndication of financial guaranty transactions which exploit the relative strengths of the global market participants. Reinsurers, to a much greater extent than the policy-issuing companies, have the flexibility to tailor the *method* by which risk is shared (treaty or facultative), and the *manner* in which it is shared (proportional or non-proportional). As asset-backed markets develop in the EC and elsewhere, reinsurance can provide an effective avenue to supporting the growth of financial guaranty insurance.

REFERENCES

Moody's Investors Service. *Structured Finance Research & Commentary*, "Index of Structured Finance Ratings," New York, NY (June 30, 1991).

Standard & Poor's Corp. *Credit Review*. "International Structured Finance," New York, NY (April 15, 1991).

Duff & Phelps, Inc. "Credit Decisions," Chicago, IL (July 29, 1991), Vol. 8, No. 29.

Financial Times, October 4, 1991, p. v.

Standard & Poor's Corp., "CreditWeek International," New York, NY (December 2, 1991) p. 77.

The Economist, November 2, 1991, p. 71.

Part III

Managing Risk

Chapter 16

Evaluating Securitisation—The Perspective of a European Financial Institution

by Jonathan E. Keighley,
Managing Director
Gracebury Securitisation Limited

This chapter addresses some of the reasons why a European financial institution might be interested in securitising some of its assets, and which of those assets might be suitable for securitisation. It discusses some of the reasons why securitisation has been slower to develop in Europe than in the United States. It then examines methods by which a financial institution might analyse the complex economics of securitisation, and looks at some of the practical aspects and difficulties which a European financial institution undertaking a securitisation for the first time might expect to face.

I. REASONS FOR SECURITISING

A financial institution might want to securitise assets for a number of reasons, among which could include a desire to:

- improve capital ratios;
- improve profitability;
- improve its competitive advantage;
- originate assets at a pace which outruns its ability to invest;
- open up new funding sources; or
- alter its risk profile.

Each of these reasons is considered below in further detail:

1) Capital Adequacy

Financial institutions which are regulated by central banks are among the originators of assets which have the strongest motivation for securitsation. Unlike corporations, they can use securitisation as a means of alleviating the capital adequacy pressures brought about by changes in the requirements of their regulators.

Just when financial institutions are facing growing regulatory pressure, the opportunities for raising new capital, particularly equity, are becoming more difficult. Investors have become disenchanted with the under-performance of bank stocks and successive bad debt crisis. In the current climate the possibility of raising new equity on acceptable terms has diminished or even disappeared for all but the most highly rated banks.

The major impetus driving the need for financial institutions to focus on their capital ratios derives from the capital adequacy guidelines laid down in July 1988 by the Basle Committee of the Bank for International Settlements in its report on the International Convergence of Capital Measurement and Capital Standards. The Basle Committee set a minimum capital to risk weighted asset ratio for banks of 8 percent (7.25 percent until the end of 1992) with equity representing 50 percent of this amount, although most bank regulators usually require their financial institutions to exceed these minimum standards.

The BIS recommendations are incorporated in European Community legislation under the provisions of the Own Funds Directive and the Solvency Ratio Directive. The first sets down a strict definition of bank capital. The second sets out a minimum capital ratio and a framework for the risk weighting of assets. The EC requires the full BIS requirements to be met by all banks regulated in Europe from 1993. The EC is introducing a new Capital Adequacy Directive incorporating all the existing directives on the regulation of financial institutions and revising the rules for the risk weighting of assets.

Securitisation has found favour with governments and the regulators who have produced enabling laws and regulations. The French took a pragmatic view and introduced the "titrisation" laws in December 1988 establishing Fonds Communs de Créances and assisted asset assignment with the Loi Dailly. The laws have proved somewhat inflexible in practice, so the securitisation legislation is being amended. In the United Kingdom in February 1989 the Bank of England issued a well drafted but stringent set of rules in a paper called "Loan Transfers and Securitisation," an amendment to which has subsequently appeared covering credit card securitisation. In Italy securitisation was made simpler by the introduction of Law No. 52 in February 1991. In Sweden and Denmark legislation permits mortgage securitisation, and in Germany the Mortgage Banking Act was specifically amended. In June 1991 the Bank of Spain introduced its rules for securitisation, modified in November 1991 in its Circular 4, following the legal changes for mortgage securitisation brought about by the Real Decreto 1289 in August 1991. Enabling legislation has also been tabled in Belgium, but was held up by the elections at the end of 1991.

However, whilst governments and bank regulators have been viewing securitisation in a favourable light, the International Accounting Standards Board in the United Kingdom and the Federal Accounting Standards Board in the United States have all been reviewing and debating the conditions under which securitised assets should be brought back onto the balance sheets of originators. It is a highly complex and controversial subject, but it does not seriously affect the rationale of financial institutions for undertaking securitisations, because such institutions are primarily interested in securitising to obtain zero weighting on the assets for capital adequacy considerations, a matter which is dictated by their regulatory authorities.

Financial institutions across Europe have been progressively waking up to the possibilities of using securitisation as a means of improving their capital ratios. Securitisation is one way for a capital constrained bank to get round the tightening noose being imposed by the regulators on balance sheet size. Securitisation removes risk weighted assets from the balance sheet of the financial institution whilst permitting it to retain much of the earnings stream from the securitised assets. By securitising, a financial institution can effectively reduce the risk weighted assets to be supported by a given capital base, while continuing to enjoy a significant part of the income from the assets securitised. In effect, securitisation can be looked upon as an alternative to raising additional capital for a regulated financial institution which needs to improve its risk asset ratio.

However, when a financial institution decides to use securitisation as a means solely of improving its capital ratios there will inevitably be a consequential reduction in its returns on equity and capital employed resulting from the increased costs associated with securitisation.

2) Profitability

Financial institutions which are not capital constrained can use securitisation as a means of improving profitability. When an increase in profitability is the motive, the securitised assets are moved off the balance sheet, thereby freeing up some of the institution's capital. The capital released by the securitisation can then be redeployed to support further assets.

After a securitisation, an asset originator expects to continue receiving some of the yield spread from the securitised assets. At the same time, the capital required to support securitised assets will be limited to the contribution which the originator may be required to make to the transaction by way of the provision of a cash collateral account, first loss deductible or other support guarantee. (Note: in some jurisdictions the regulatory authorities may not even consider such support to a securitisation transaction as a deduction from the originator's capital base, but the attitudes of bank regulators are rapidly hardening in this regard.) The capital required to support securitised assets will thus be substantially less than when the assets were held on-balance sheet.

If an originator redeploys the capital released by securitisation to put additional interest earning assets onto its balance sheet, there should be a marked improvement in its profitability. There should also be a marked improvement both in its return on equity and in its return on capital employed because, in addition to the income from the new assets, the off-balance sheet assets will also continue to provide the originator with an income stream.

3) Competitive Advantage

The equity markets are now demanding that banks should improve their performance and focus on their return equity. Consequently, banks are scrutinising the returns of their component businesses more carefully so as to generate more acceptable returns.

At the same time as this pressure for bank performance is building up, there is a continuing squeeze on bank margins from increased competition, partly because of the EC's First and Second Banking Directives which are designed to break down protective national barriers and open up the Community to greater competition from cross-border banking services.

The Cecchini report on competition in Europe, published in 1988 by the European Commission, drew comparisons between the spreads on various asset types available to financial institutions operating in specific European countries. The highest average margin over wholesale money market rates found for a specific asset type in one European country was given as a percentage of the lowest average margin found in another country with the following results:

Consumer Credit	383%
Mortgages	276%
Credit Cards	268%
Commercial Loans	157%

Whilst one can be critical of the methodology of these comparisons, the report undoubtedly points out that product pricing across the European banking scene is far from uniform. In a perfectly competitive market there should be no difference at all in product pricing. One may therefore conclude that a European financial institution operating in more profitable market segments in one European country may reasonably expect its profitability to be eroded in the coming period of harmonisation in Europe.

In such circumstances a financial institution can use securitisation to strategic advantage. Assets, when moved off-balance sheet through securitisation, can still yield income but require little (or, in some jurisdictions, no) capital allocation by the originator. Provided an originator can continue to obtain a small contribution margin from the securitised assets, against which he has to allocate little or no capital, it can continue in a business which, as a result of competitive pressures, might not have earned a sufficient margin to meet its return on capital requirements, had it been required to keep the assets on-balance sheet. Hence, the financial institution may still be able to afford to compete in sectors of the market where its margins have been eroded without suffering the detrimental effect on its return on capital, which would otherwise have occurred.

An aggressive institution could consider using its ability to securitise as a means of expanding its market share, or even as a means of fighting a price war. It may be able to afford to accept lower margins on assets which it can securitise because of its reduced capital allocation for such assets, whereas its competitors may not be able to follow suit with similar margin reductions.

A financial institution seeking earnings growth through acquisition could even use securitisation as a means of releasing capital from its target company and, hence, as a form of acquisition finance. For example, a financial institution with an ability to securitise might seek to acquire another institution which did not have that capability. It might be able safely to afford to pay a premium price to make the acquisition in the certain knowledge that it could subsequently reduce its gearing by securitising some of the target company's assets, whilst at the same time gaining economies of scale from combining the servicing and origination operations of the two organisations.

4) Business Expansion

When capital is short the constraint on the business expansion plans of most financial institutions is the permitted size of the balance sheet. If a financial institution services only the assets which it originates and keeps them all on-balance sheet, the size of its servicing operation will be driven by the size of its lending operation. In an age of computerisation there are very significant economies of scale to be achieved in the servicing business. If a financial institution can originate more assets than it can hold on its balance sheet, it is likely to achieve significant economies of scale from its servicing operations.

Securitisation therefore can be used as a strategic tool to permit business expansion and to achieve economies of scale.

5) New Funding Sources

As a direct consequence of the recessionary environment and the extensive bad debt experience of the majority of the world's banks, there are no longer many AAA rated banks. As a result most banks now have to pay a premium for funding over the finest rates. Securitised assets, properly credit enhanced, are usually rated to AAA (long-term) or A1+ (short-term) standards. The top ratings often open up possibilities of funding in markets which might otherwise be closed to an originator or too expensive to tap.

For financial institutions which do not have access to their own retail deposits, obtaining funds from the inter-bank market cannot always be relied upon. The ability readily to securitise assets is becoming increasingly important, as was demonstrated by National Home Loans in the United

Kingdom when it experienced short-term funding difficulties in the autumn of 1991 following the closure of BCCI. As a result of its capabilities and experience in securitising assets, it was rapidly able to shed assets from its balance sheet and reduce its funding requirements.

6) Changing Risk Profiles

By selectively using securitisation, a financial institution can reduce its exposure to the risks inherent in a particular business sector or geographic region. It can utilise the technique of securitisation to off-load risks to which it no longer wishes to be exposed, or as a way of continuing to do business in a sector or country where it feels that the risks are greater than it wishes to accept. The technique has been used, for instance, by banks to reduce exposure to the debts of less developed countries, and also to reduce exposure to the property sector.

By way of example of the way in which the exposure to asset risk can be reduced by securitisation, it is instructive to look at the change in the risk exposure of a British financial institution which occurred when it securitised a portfolio of medium-term consumer credit receivables (Figure 16.1).

Prior to securitisation any reduction in the value of the institution's assets from delinquency or defaults by its debtors was a corporate risk to which it was fully exposed. Following securitisation, the originator retained only a portion of the risk, limited to the value of the cash collateral account (in this case 1.5 percent of asset value); beyond this, the next portion of risk was borne by the credit enhancement provider (in this case 13.5 percent of asset value) and the remainder by the investors in the asset-backed securities issued.

After securitisation, the institution reduced its risk exposure from 100 percent down to 1.5 percent of the value of the assets. While it should be noted that the originator still retained the riskiest portion, the reduction in its total risk exposure to the assets was real and was reflected accordingly in the regulatory treatment of the transaction. (Note: the Bank of England requires the full amount of any monies at risk in a cash collateral account to be a deduction from the institution's capital base, following the rationale that an originator's exposure to the cash collateral account should be treated in the same way for regulatory purposes as would an equity exposure to the transaction).

II. ASSETS SUITABLE FOR SECURITISATION

When a financial institution decides to securitise, it needs to own a portfolio of assets with the following characteristics:

- volume which is sufficiently large and homogeneous to facilitate statistical analysis;
- geographic and socio-economic diversification to minimise credit risk; and
- basic credit quality standards which are capable of being underwritten by a credit enhancer.

The principal assets of financial institutions which meet these criteria are:

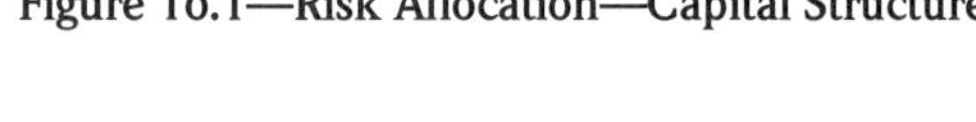

Figure 16.1—Risk Allocation—Capital Structure

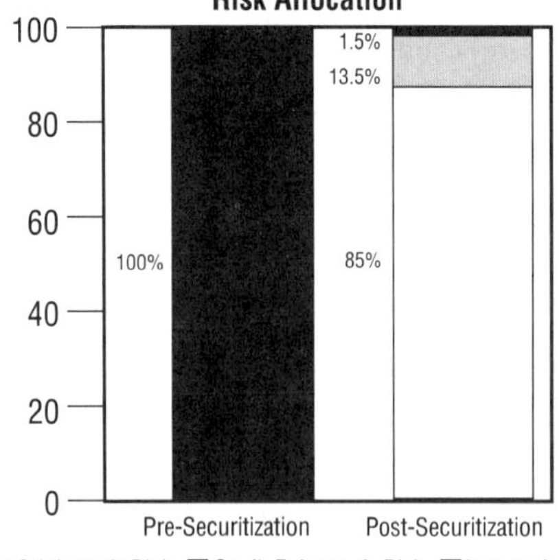

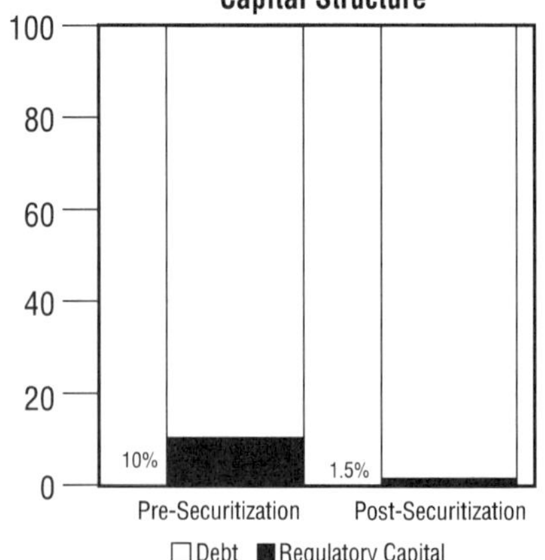

- household mortgages;
- hire purchase receivables;
- lease receivables; and
- credit card debts.

Securitisations have also been engineered for various other assets, including commercial loans, property rentals and, in the commercial sector, trade receivables. Transactions involving the repackaging of a variety of quoted securities have been structured (such as perpetual floating rate notes combined with zero coupon bonds being sold as floating rate notes with definite maturities), but such transactions cannot really be considered as being in the same category as the true asset-backed securities which rely for repayment on the cash flow from a large portfolio of underlying assets displaying statistically normalised characteristics.

In Europe the securitisation of assets started in the United Kingdom with household mortgages. Mortgages have also now been securitised in Sweden, France and Spain. This is still the largest sector of the European asset securitisation market with about £12 billion of securities outstanding. Consumer credit loans are now becoming a popular sector for securitisations in the main European markets. Transactions have been structured successfully in the United Kingdom, France, Italy, Germany and Spain. In the United Kingdom and France several commercial bank loan portfolios have also been securitised, and attention is also now turning to portfolios of leased assets, where to date tax and residual value difficulties have hindered securitisation. The latest asset type on which securitisers are focusing is European credit cards, particularly in the United Kingdom where credit card usage is extensive, following the emergence of the Bank of England's amendments to its 1989 paper on "Loan Transfers and Securitisation."

III. THE SLOW START TO EUROPEAN SECURITISATION

Securitisation has been slow to take off in Europe compared with the United States. To date the principal hindrances to asset securitisation in Europe have been those of cost and the adequacy of the originators' systems. Many of the problems have stemmed from the simple fact that Europe consists of numerous countries, each with its own legal, accounting and regulatory framework. This diversity led to the requirement for different tax and legal structures needing to be devised for each asset type in each country before successful securitisations could proceed. As a result, first-time securitisations of specific asset types in specific countries in Europe have been expensive and required large transactions to carry the costs.

One of the difficulties faced by potential securitisers in Europe has been the legal requirements necessary to achieve effective asset transfer to the special purpose company. Some jurisdictions in Europe require notification to be given to all debtors before any assignment of receivables can be legally effective. The specific requirements in a jurisdiction may even differ for different types of asset. The issue of notification or the consent of the debtor being mandatory has prevented some securitisations proceeding. In other cases securitisations have had to be delayed until changes in the laws of the jurisdiction concerned occurred. Other issues which have proved stumbling blocks for some potential securitisations have been the existence of withholding taxes in some jurisdictions and the differing incidence of corporation tax, value added tax and stamp duties. It is the resolution of difficult legal issues and the devising of elegant tax-neutral structures which has largely caused the structuring costs associated with European securitisations to be so high.

The costs associated with securitisations, over and above the interest cost of the debt and its issuance expenses, are essentially as follows:

- credit enhancement and liquidity support for the assets;
- structuring fees payable to investment bankers;
- legal, accounting and tax advice fees;
- rating agencies' fees;
- systems modifications; and
- management time.

To date, for a transaction involving a single originator, the portfolio size has needed to be of the order of at least the equivalent of $200 million to spread the heavy transaction costs sufficiently and render a securitisation attractive. It is therefore not surprising that in Europe only major institutions have so far exploited the possibilities offered by securitisation.

However, there are smaller financial institutions and finance subsidiaries of major corporations in each European country to whom the technique of securitisation should appeal. For them, a multi-originator programme with a pre-established structure, reasonably standardised documentation, flexible funding sources and sophisticated computer systems is probably the only viable way to securitise their smaller portfolios. Though the option of participating in a multi-originator programme has until recently not been readily available in Europe, several multi-originator programmes sponsored by major banks are now emerging.

Workable structures for the various asset types have slowly been developing throughout Europe, and once satisfactory structures exist, the far lower cost of reproducing them makes securitisation far more attractive. As a result it would seem likely that securitisation will become an increasingly utilised tool in European financial markets.

IV. ECONOMIC ANALYSIS OF SECURITISATION

The economic evaluation of securitisation can appear to be a somewhat complex and daunting exercise for a first-time securitiser. A fully worked example of various approaches described below is provided in the Appendix to this chapter.

One of the simplest ways to measure the impact of securitisation is to compare the weighted average cost of funding of the assets securitised before and after securitisation on an after tax basis.

1) Change in the Weighted Average Cost of Funding Approach

It is first necessary to calculate the all-in cost of funding of the block of assets to be securitised whilst the assets remain on the originator's balance sheet. This funding consists of two elements: capital and borrowings. First, the assumed costs of the required regulatory equity capital and the subordinated term debt capital supporting the assets are weighted by their respective percentages in the overall funding structure. Next, the fixed rate equivalent of any floating rate costs of the on-balance sheet funding of the assets is determined by obtaining the effective swap rate against LIBOR for a similar maturity to that of the funding and adding (or deducting) the margin over (or under) LIBOR at which the originator typically borrows. The percentage of short-term debt funding in the overall on-balance sheet financing structure is weighted by its swapped equivalent cost, and, similarly, the fixed rate (or swapped equivalent floating rate) of any long-term debt funding associated with the assets is similarly appropriately weighted to arrive at the blended cost of the debt funded portion of the assets.

A similar calculation is performed for the cost of funding post-securitisation, but account must also be taken of the cost associated with any notional capital allocated against the cash collateral for capital adequacy purposes by the originator's regulator. In addition to reflecting the costs associated with the financing of the securitised assets, the up-front costs of the securitisation should be spread over the life of the deal and all the annual running expenses factored in.

The change in the weighted average cost of financing the assets being securitised is one way of quantifying the increase in financial efficiency which has been achieved and the resultant benefits which accrue to the originator.

The problem with this approach is that it is necessary to estimate the originator's equity capital cost, which is inevitably subjective. In the Appendix a rough estimate for the cost of equity has been arrived at by taking the current gross dividend yield of the institution and adding the anticipated dividend growth rate. Another method would be to take the inverse of the PE ratio; a third would be to discount future expected dividend flows; and a fourth would be to take the risk free cost of capital rate and add to it an equity premium multiplied by the beta factor associated with the share price. Each method usually yields slightly different results.

Although there is nothing fundamentally wrong with the weighted average cost of funding approach, it is suggested that the analyst in presenting his case for securitisation may find the alternative methods described below give more objective measures of the benefits of securitisation.

2) Alternative Approaches

For any of the calculations which follow, the first step is to arrive at the correct annual pre-tax impact of the costs attributable directly to the securitisation. To do this successfully and to avoid the problems of variations in interest rates, it is suggested that the analyst should always work with the swapped fixed rate equivalent of any floating interest rate figures.

The basic ingredients of the calculation are as follows:

The costs are:

- the interest on the securitised funding;
- the annual costs of credit enhancement/liquidity lines;
- any guarantees to enhance the credit rating of any interest rate or foreign exchange swap counterparty;
- amortised front-end fees (debt issuance, credit enhancement, liquidity lines);
- amortised transaction costs (legal, accounting, structuring, rating, etc.);
- opportunity costs relating to any temporary cash retention in any guaranteed investment contract (GIC); and

- the annual systems/accounting/rating agency costs etc..

From these costs the following benefits must be deducted:

- earnings from any cash collateral deposit; and
- the interest savings on the pre-securitisation borrowings attributable to the assets.

Prior to securitisation, the assets when on the originator's balance sheet were funded partly by money market borrowings and partly by the originator's capital. On securitisation, when the assets are sold and the associated borrowings repaid, the capital previously supporting those assets is released. The amount of capital released by securitsation is calculated by multiplying the volume of assets securitised by the risk weighting attached to those assets (i.e., 100 percent in the case of most non-mortgage assets) and then multiplying the product by the originator's actual risk asset ratio. Any capital support for the securitised assets required by the regulatory authorities to be deducted from the securitising institution's capital base must then be deducted from this figure.

The calculation of the costs and benefits attributable directly to the securitisation described above does not include the benefit that will be derived from the redeployment of this capital released. The value of this benefit is entirely dependent on the manner in which this capital is redeployed.

i) Improvement in the risk asset ratio.

If the financial institution is using securitisation to improve capital ratios, it will merely use the cash from the capital released to repay other borrowings. Alternatively, if the financial institution is using securitisation as a means of improving profitability, it will gear up again on the capital released with further money market or term borrowings to support incremental assets which it will add to its balance sheet.

Aggregating the costs and benefits associated directly with the securitisation with the appropriate benefits derived from the use of the capital released will give the appropriate measure of the effect on pre-tax profits resulting directly from the securitisation. Once the pre-tax impact of securitisation has been calculated, the returns achieved before and after the securitisation on the financial institution's risk assets, on equity capital and on capital employed can be compared.

ii) Improvement in profitability.

The financial institution may be using securitisation as a means of improving its profitability. In this case it will be seeking to maintain its existing risk asset ratio, redeploying the capital released by putting additional assets onto its balance sheet. For the calculations involving incremental assets it is first necessary to calculate the incremental volume of assets which can be added to the balance sheet. This can be done by taking the amount of capital released by the securitisation and multiplying it by the institution's actual risk asset ratio. The cost benefit analysis should now take into account the potential earnings of the incremental assets. When considering the potential incremental earnings of the new assets it is important not to forget the economies of scale which are likely to be achieved as a direct result of the increase in the volume of assets now under the institution's control. There will inevitably then be a marked improvement in the originator's returns on risk assets, on equity capital and on capital employed.

iii) Break-even margin on incremental lending.

If incremental assets are to be added to the balance sheet following the securitisation, a calculation which may be of interest is the determination of the break-even margin on the incremental lending required to make the securitisation worthwhile. Dividing the pre-tax cost of securitisation by the incremental assets which can be added to the originator's balance sheet (maintaining its existing risk asset ratio) will give the required figure.

The resultant break-even margin on incremental lending may sometimes, at first sight, seem a little high. It is, however, important to appreciate that when marginal assets are being added to an existing institution's balance sheet, better use can be made of its infrastructure without a commensurate increase in overhead costs. It is therefore likely to be misleading to directly compare the figure obtained with the institution's estimate of its historical returns on a specific asset type.

iv) Equivalent cost of raising equity.

Finally, it may be useful to consider securitisation as being an alternative to raising new equity. In this calculation, however, any benefits from the earnings on the released capital must be ignored, since they are subsequently derived from the use of that capital. The after-tax cost of the securitisation should then be obtained by applying the relevant tax rate to the pre-tax figure obtained above. Dividing this figure by the amount of capital released will give the after tax cost of the released capital.

It is then assumed that the financial institution would raise additional capital by raising equity and subordinated debt in the most efficient proportion (usually 50/50 for a bank). The current afte- tax cost of raising subordinated debt for the institution should then be determined from the market, and a weighted average calculation is then used to derive the equivalent cost of the equity released by the securitisation from the after tax cost of capital figure calculated above. This equivalent cost of equity figure can then be compared with the estimated real cost of the financial institution raising new equity by means of a rights issue at a suitable discount to its current share price.

Whilst the calculations above will put securitisation into its correct perspective from the point of view of the head office of a group, great care needs to be exercised if the calculations are being performed at the level of a group subsidiary. Very curious results can sometimes be obtained as a result of intra-group financial policy. In European companies it is very rare to find group head offices charging subsidiaries for capital, especially equity, on a realistic cost basis. If the sums are worked on the assumption that equity is being allocated by Head Office to the subsidiary at no cost, or charged for at the same cost to debt, from the subsidiary's standpoint securitisation can appear remarkably uneconomic.

V. PRACTICAL ASPECTS OF SECURITISING

There are two significant hurdles which have to be overcome before any organisation can successfully indulge in a securitisation for the first time: management commitment and computer systems.

Securitisation is a major strategic departure for any institution. Both its strategic and economic implications need to be fully understood by all the members of its board. Even when the board has been convinced of the merits of undertaking a securitisation, senior line management will then have to spend a great deal of time and energy seeing a transaction through to completion, especially if it is the first one.

Management will have to contend with the business reviews conducted by the rating agencies and the credit enhancer. These tend to be very thorough and cover most aspects of the business such as its:

- organisation and management structure;
- financial performance;
- business strategy and planning processes;
- controls and procedures;
- asset origination and credit assessment procedures;
- quality of its loan documentation;
- credit administration and debt recovery procedures;
- treasury management;
- accounting policies; and
- computer systems.

Senior management can expect to have a heavy workload preparing the necessary written submissions for the rating agencies.

The process of securitisation may well cause management to reconsider some of the company's long-standing practices and question them in a new light. Aspects of the business such as funding strategy and interest rate exposures will need to be particularly thoroughly reviewed, because securitisation inevitably will impact directly on the functioning of the treasury area. A thorough audit of a business is usually a beneficial exercise and often draws attention to areas of the business where improvements can be made.

The role of adequate systems cannot be emphasised strongly enough. The systems must be able to:

- produce historical information on the assets to be securitised;
- identify and segregate the securitisable assets and track their cash flows; and
- report on the performance of the securitised assets.

An originator's system will always need to tag the assets to be securitised and divert the cash flows of the securitised assets to the special purpose company. If a stand-alone securitisation is to be undertaken, the system must also be able to sort assets according to specified criteria and be capable of producing separate accounts and regular performance reports for the special purpose company, which may be required to have stricter accounting policies for writing off defaulting receivables than those used by the originator. Some savings on systems modification work are possible if securitisations are to be done through a multi-originator programme. The portfolio selection would then typically be done by the programme sponsor's computer system, as would all the special purpose company's accounting and reporting.

Significant amount of systems work is always required before an organisation can securitise a portfolio of assets for the first time. It is unlikely that it would take a competent team less than two to three months to complete. However, once the systems can handle one securitisation, only very minor work is likely to be required for subsequent transactions.

Inadequate systems have been responsible for several institutions not being able successfully to undertake a securitisation after deciding to proceed. It may come as a severe shock to some senior management, who have managed successful businesses for years, to discover that their systems may not be capable of producing the statistical information on the historical performance of the portfolio of assets to be securitised in the detail required by the rating agencies (and the credit enhancer).

Once a financial institution has undertaken its first securitisation, it is likely that it will discover that it has made a major strategic advance and improved its corporate health. A financial institution should appreciate that securitisations are highly complex financial transactions and a first-time securitisation may even take some six to nine months to undertake. However, once the institution has acquired the technical capability of securitising, subsequent transactions can be put together far faster and assets can then be securitised at a rate in line with the growth of the originator's business.

APPENDIX

PROFILE OF HYPOTHETICAL ORIGINATOR

It is assumed that an Originator wishing to securitise a £250 million portfolio of assets has the following capital structure:

Assumptions	
Tier 1	
Share capital	£50,000,000
Reserves	£80,000,000
	£130,000,000
Tier 2	
Revaluation reserve	£5,000,000
General provisions	£15,000,000
Subordinated perpetual debt	£50,000,000
Subordinated term debt	£50,000,000
	£120,000,000
Capital base	**£250,000,000**

It is also assumed that the Originator has the following asset profile:

Fixed assets	£140,000,000
Money market assets (10% risk weighted)	£100,000,000
Customer debts (100% risk weighted)	£2,600,000,000
Total assets	£2,840,000,000
Total risk assets	**£2,750,000,000**
Risk asset ratio	9.09%
Pre-tax profit	**£30,000,000**

COST OF CAPITAL CALCULATIONS

Assumptions		
3–5 year swap rate against £ LIBOR		10.00%
Current share price (pence)		100
Dividend per share (pence)		4
Corporation tax rate payable		33%
ACT rate		25%
Term debt calculation	**Margin Over LIBOR**	**Swapped Equivalent**
£50 million Sub'd FRN 2000	0.25%	10.25%
£50 million 12% Sub'd Bonds 1998	–	12.00%
Weighted average pre-tax cost of term debt		11.13%
Weighted average after tax cost of term debt		7.45%
Equity calculation		
Current gross dividend yield		5.33%
FTSE 100 Index in April 1982		704
FTSE 100 Index in April 1992		2409
FTSE 100 10-year average growth		13.09%
Approximate rounded after tax cost of equity		**18.50%**

(Current dividend yield + estimated growth rate: this assumes the Originator's dividend will grow in line with the growth rate of the FTSE Index which will itself continue to grow in line with its historic rate.)

	As % of Capital Base	**After Tax Capital Cost**
Equity	60.00%	18.50%
Subordinated debt	40.00%	7.45%
Weighted average after tax cost of capital		**14.08%**

TERMS OF THE SECURITISATION ISSUE

It is assumed that the assets are hire purchase loans of relatively short maturity, previously funded entirely by short-term money market borrowings and associated interest rate swaps.

Transaction size	£250 million
Maturity	5 Years
Asset substitution period	3 Years
Cost of securitised funding	45 basis points over LIBOR
Debt issuance front end fees	65 basis points
Credit Enhancement costs	75 basis points per annum
Credit Enhancement cover required	15.00%
Credit Enhancement front end fees	50 basis points
cash collateral	1.50%
Cost of interest rate swap guarantee	5 basis points per annum
GIC rate	50 basis points below LIBOR
Transaction costs	£400,000
Annual costs	£30,000
Asset amortisation	£0 million Year 1
	£0 million Year 2
	£0 million Year 3
	£135 million Year 4
	£115 million Year 5

COST ANALYSIS OF SECURITISATION

Assumptions

Actual risk asset ratio	9.09%
Cost of Money Market funding (below LIBOR)	0.0625%
3–5 year swap rate against £ LIBOR	10.00%
Swapped fixed rate equivalent cost of Money Market funding	9.9375%
After tax fixed rate equivalent cost of Money Market funding	6.6581%

Annual cost of securitisation	*Note*	*Year 1*	*Year 2*	*Year 3*	*Year 4*	*Year 5*
		£	£	£	£	£
Opening year assets		250,000,000	250,000,000	250,000,000	250,000,000	115,000,000
Average assets outstanding during the year		250,000,000	250,000,000	250,000,000	182,500,000	57,500,000
Average cash collateral balance during the year		3,750,000	3,750,000	3,750,000	2,737,500	862,500
Costs						
Interest on Securitisation debt	1	(26,125,000)	(26,125,000)	(26,125,000)	(19,071,000)	(6,009,000)
Annual fees on Credit Enhancement/Liquidity		(281,000)	(281,000)	(281,000)	(205,000)	(65,000)
Interest Rate Swap Guarantee	2	(125,000)	(125,000)	(125,000)	(91,000)	(29,000)
Amortised front-end fees	3	(458,000)	(458,000)	(458,000)	(334,000)	(105,000)
Amortised transaction costs	4	(101,000)	(101,000)	(101,000)	(74,000)	(23,000)
Opportunity costs of funds held in the GIC	5	(20,000)	(20,000)	(20,000)	(15,000)	(5,000)
Systems/Accounting/Rating Agency fees		(30,000)	(30,000)	(30,000)	(30,000)	(30,000)
		(27,140,000)	(27,140,000)	(27,140,000)	(19,820,000)	(6,266,000)
Benefits						
Earnings on cash collateral (at swapped Libid)	6	370,000	370,000	370,000	270,000	85,000
Interest saved on Money Market funding	1	22,585,000	22,585,000	22,585,000	16,487,000	5,195,000
		22,955,000	22,955,000	22,955,000	16,757,000	5,280,000
Pre-tax cost of securitisation		(4,185,000)	(4,185,000)	(4,185,000)	(3,063,000)	(986,000)

(before benefit of redeployment of capital released)

Notes:

1. Pre-securitisation, 90 percent of value of assets were funded in the money market at the swapped equivalent of its money market cost of funds, whereas post-securitisation 100 percent of the value of the securitised assets is funded in the SPV by the debt securities issued.
2. To neutralise the SPV's potential interest rate exposure the SPV will require to have an interest rate swap with the asset originator. If the originator has a credit rating below that of the securities issued by the SPV, its obligations under this swap will require the guarantee of a AAA rated bank at an assumed cost of 5 bp per annum.
3. Front end fees of the debt issued by the SPV and relating to the credit enhancement amortised over the average life of the transaction.
4. Legal and systems costs amortised over the average life of the transaction.
5. The SPV will pay quarterly interest and settle its accounts with the originator quarterly. The SPV will receive principal and interest from securitised assets daily and invest monies so received in a Guaranteed Investment Contract to the end of the quarter at 50 bp less than money market rates, giving rise to an opportunity cost to the originator, to whom these cash flows would otherwise have accrued directly.
6. Cash deposited in the cash collateral earns interest at swapped LIBOR rate.

Capital released by securitisation	*Year 1*	*Year 2*	*Year 3*	*Year 4*	*Year 5*
	£	£	£	£	£
Opening year assets	250,000,000	250,000,000	250,000,000	250,000,000	115,000,000
Average assets outstanding during the year	250,000,000	250,000,000	250,000,000	182,500,000	57,500,000
Risk weighting of assets securitised	100.00%	100.00%	100.00%	100.00%	100.00%
Originator's pre-securitisation risk asset ratio	9.09%	9.09%	9.09%	9.09%	9.09%
Capital released by sale of assets	22,727,000	22,727,000	22,727,000	16,591,000	5,227,000
Less: average cash collateral balance during the year	(3,750,000)	(3,750,000)	(3,750,000)	(2,738,000)	(863,000)
Capital released by securitisation (average during the year)	18,977,000	18,977,000	18,977,000	13,853,000	4,364,000

Note In some jurisdictions cash collateral balances may not be required to be deducted from the capital base for regulatory capital adequacy reporting purposes.

CHANGE IN WEIGHTED AVERAGE COST OF FUNDING CALCULATION

In the calculation below only the three years of the transaction during which none of the assets has been amortised have been considered. Implicit in this calculation is the assumption that the capital released by the process of securitisation is re-deployed by the Originator to earn the average rate of return on his assets.

Pre-securitisation portfolio funding costs	*As % of Funding*	*After Tax Cost*
Capital	9.09%	14.08%
Debt	90.91%	6.66%
Weighted average after tax cost of funding		7.33%
Post-securitisation portfolio funding costs		
Capital	1.50%	14.08%
Securitised debt (including Credit Enhancement)	100.00%	6.90%
Front-end costs		0.15%
Annual costs plus cash collateral benefit		–0.05%
Weighted average after tax cost of funding		7.10%
Improvement in portfolio weighted average after tax cost of funding		**0.23%**
After tax profit improvement per annum		£571,000
Equivalent pre-tax profit improvement per annum		**£852,000**

USING SECURITISATION TO IMPROVE THE RISK ASSET RATIO

In the calculation which follows it is assumed that the Originator wishes to use securitisation merely as a means of improving its risk asset ratio. Consequently no incremental assets are subsequently added to the Originator's balance sheet. The capital released is used to further reduce money market borrowings.

Pre-securitisation risk asset ratio	
Capital base (Basle Accord definition)	£250,000,000
Risk weighted assets	£2,750,000,000
Risk asset ratio	9.09%
Post-securitisation risk asset ratio	
Capital base (Basle Accord definition)	£250,000,000
Less: cash collateral	£3,750,000
Revised Capital base	£246,250,000
Risk weighted assets	£2,500,000,000
Risk asset ratio	9.85%
Improvement in risk asset ratio	**0.76%**

There will, however, be a detrimental effect on the returns on equity (share capital, retained earnings, revaluation reserves and general provisions) and capital employed. The post-securitisation pre-tax profit is derived as follows:

Pre-securitisation pre-tax profit	£30,000,000
Pre-tax cost of securitisation	(£4,185,000)
Interest saved on redeployment of capital released	£1,886,000
Post securitisation pre-tax profit	£27,701,000
Pre-securitisation return on equity	
Pre-tax profits	£30,000,000
Equity	£150,000,000
Return on equity	20.00%
Post-securitisation return on equity	
Pre-tax profits	£27,701,000
Equity	£150,000,000
Return on equity	18.47%
Change in return on equity	**–1.53%**
Pre-securitisation return on capital employed	
Pre-tax profits	£30,000,000
Capital employed	£235,000,000
Return on capital employed	12.77%
Post-securitisation return on capital employed	
Pre-tax profits	£27,701,000
Capital employed	£235,000,000
Return on capital employed	11.79%
Change in return on capital employed	**–0.98%**

USING SECURITISATION TO IMPROVE PROFITABILITY

In the example which follows it is assumed that the Originator is permitted to operate using its pre-securitisation risk asset ratio. It is assumed that it will seek to restore that ratio, gearing up on the capital released by securitisation.

Assumptions	
The Originator adds hire purchase assets with an APR of	18%
The marginal cost for writing new business is	4%
The average cost of defaults is	1%
Capital released by securitisation	£18,977,000
Former risk asset ratio	9.09%
Incremental 100% weighted assets	£208,747,000
Revenue from incremental assets	£37,574,000
Marginal costs of incremental assets	(£10,437,000)
Cost of new Money Market funding required	(£18,858,000)
Marginal contribution from incremental assets	£8,279,000
Pre-securitisation pre-tax profit	£30,000,000
Securitisation costs	(£4,185,000)
New pre-tax profit	£34,094,000
Pre-securitisation return on risk assets	
Pre-tax profits	£30,000,000
Risk weighted assets	£2,750,000,000
Return on risk assets	1.09%
Post-securitisation return on risk assets	
Pre-tax profits	£34,094,000
Risk weighted assets	£2,708,747,000
Return on risk assets	1.26%
Increase in return on risk assets	**0.17%**
Pre-securitisation return on equity	
Pre-tax profits	£30,000,000
Equity	£135,000,000
Return on equity	22.22%
Post-securitisation return on equity	
Pre-tax profits	£34,094,000
Equity	£135,000,000
Return on equity	25.25%
Increase in return on equity	**3.03%**
Pre-securitisation return on capital employed	
Pre-tax profits	£30,000,000
Capital employed (excluding provisions)	£235,000,000
Return on capital employed	12.77%
Post-securitisation return on capital employed	
Pre-tax profits	£34,094,000
Capital employed (excluding provisions)	£235,000,000
Return on capital employed	14.51%
Increase in return on capital employed	**1.74%**

BREAK EVEN MARGIN ON INCREMENTAL LENDING

In the calculation below it is assumed that the Originator gears up on the capital released by the process of securitisation, at the rate permitted by its target risk asset ratio.

Capital released by securitisation	£18,977,000
Former capital to risk asset ratio	9.09%
Incremental 100% risk weighted assets	£208,747,000
Cost of incremental money market funding required	£18,858,000
Pre-tax cost of Securitisation	£4,185,000
	£23,043,000
Break even pre-tax margin on incremental assets	**1.04%**

EQUIVALENT COST OF RAISING EQUITY

Securitisation can be considered as an alternative to a rights issue. The alternative cost of raising such new equity for the Originator to arrive at similar capital ratios as would be achieved by securitising assets is calculated below.

Capital released by securitisation	£18,977,000
Pre-tax cost of securitisation	£4,185,000
Effective after tax cost of capital released by securitisation	£2,804,000
After tax cost of the capital released by securitisation	**14.78%**
New capital would be raised 50% as subordinated debt and 50% as equity	
Estimated pre-tax cost of raising new 10-year £ subordinated debt	12.50%
After tax cost of new debt	8.38%
Implied equivalent cost of equity	**21.18%**
The above should be compared with:	
Estimated existing cost of equity (see above)	18.50%
Assumed discount for a rights issue	20.00%
Estimated cost of new equity	22.20%

Chapter 17

Asset-Backed Finance—Risk Control for Traders in Asset-Backed Securities

by Paresh Mashru
and
Mark Rhys,
Arthur Andersen, London

Securitisation is a process by which the risks and benefits of income yielding assets are transferred to a third party. In general, any corporation receivable with a contractual cash flow may be suitable for securitisation. Receivables which have been securitised are diverse, and range from credit card debts to home equity loans, as well as other types of receivables such as leases (examples include cars and computers), junk bonds and health care receivables. AT&T is currently considering the securitisation of consumer telephone bills whilst investment bankers are investigating structured financing as a solution to some Third World debt problems. Asset securitisation is limited only by the imagination of the financial engineers at the forefront of this expanding and increasingly complex market.

In this chapter, we consider the risk control issues which should be addressed by corporate issuers of and investors in asset-backed securities. After a brief summary of the characteristics of assets suitable for securitisation, the benefits of securitisation and the risks generated, we describe a framework of control within which investment risks should be managed. This framework encompasses both high level management controls and operational controls.

THE RATIONALE FOR SECURITISATION

The increasing interest in securitisation can be attributed to a variety of economic and commercial reasons. Securitisation provides a corporate originator with a fresh source of funds and can enhance its gearing, return on capital employed and other financial ratios relating to borrowing cost.

Asset-backed securities generally have a relatively low credit risk, are secured by good quality collateral and offer a high yield when compared to other low risk investments such as government bonds. These securities also provide an investor with a mechanism to invest indirectly in a particular class of assets, while limiting the associated asset risk as these issues are usually credit enhanced.

The growth in volume, total value and complexity of the securitisation market can also be attributed to increased competition among financial advisers. They have identified fee earning potential within the market, given the increased volatility in interest rates and changing credit conditions, which result in a greater need to manage, hedge and eliminate risk.

TYPES OF ASSET-BACKED SECURITIES

A corporate issues asset-backed securities to outside investors by repackaging a specific class of its assets. The type of security issued varies, depending on the nature of the cash flow to the investor. The underlying asset generates the cash flow used to finance the return to the investor, both interest and principal. There are, however two distinct types of security.

- Pass-through securities are issued with the assets' contractual cash flows passing directly to the investors in proportion to their participation. The investors would hold participation certificates representing their interests in specific pools of assets. This process is often referred to as "unitisation."

- Asset-backed bonds are debt securities earning a coupon interest, where interest and principal are indirectly funded from the underlying assets' cash flows. In many cases, these assets will have been sold to a special purpose vehicle for securitisation. The special purpose vehicle may or may not be a subsidiary of the original owner.

In all structures, the critical feature is the linkage between the cash return on the security and the cash flows from the asset, rather than the corporation's operations. The key characteristic of such securities is that their credit quality depends directly on the underlying asset and on the issuing entity.

The range of assets suitable for securitisation is diverse. However, they do have the following important risk characteristics.

- The assets should contain sufficiently similar characteristics in order for their cash flows to be pooled.
- The assets should be large enough in number and total value for it to be economical to issue them in securitised form.
- The cash flows generated from the assets should be received periodically and should be relatively predictable.
- The assets should be sufficiently low risk to make them attractive to a potential investor or some form of credit enhancement (such as a guarantee) may be required.

RISK ASSESSMENT

The securitisation process can be complicated and usually involves the creation of highly complex structures. Investment risks arise, which must be identified, assessed, managed and controlled. Risk management and reduction should enhance the attractiveness of an asset-backed issue to the investor. Therefore, risk issues and analysis are of relevance to both the corporate issuer and the corporate investor.

Credit Risk

The main source of risk is the quality of the underlying asset, which determines its value as a source of income and capital repayment. An assessment of such risks may be obtained from the credit rating attached to the issue. Higher risk assets may be subjected to credit enhancement procedures, which can include reserve funds, corporate guarantees, insurance and over-collateralisation.

Other aspects of risk associated with a securitisation transaction are described briefly below:

Market Risk

That there is an adverse movement in the securities' price.

Economic Risk

That prevailing economic conditions do not match the assumptions underlying the pricing of the securities for issue or the purchase of the securities as investments. Political risk will obviously affect economic conditions.

Documentation Risk

That all legal documents associated with a complex securitisation are not properly and accurately prepared.

Regulatory Risk

That changes in the regulatory regime governing accounting procedures or taxation principles will have significant effects on the security's quality or value.

Liquidity Risk

That the securities will not easily be marketable. This risk arises from the currency, size and cash flow profile of the issue. It is borne by both the issuer and the investor.

Gapping Risk

The risk of a mismatch in the timing of the cash inflows arising from the underlying securitised assets, and the outflows required to service the securities.

Event Risk

The risk that an external event or transaction which affects the issuer's financial position, such as a leveraged takeover, will also affect the value of an asset-backed investment.

Reinvestment Risk

This is the risk most commonly ignored by investors unfamiliar with asset-backed securities. A highly rated (AAA rated) bond that has a higher yield than an equivalent government bond seems too good to be true. The extra apparent yield from an asset-backed bond is due to the pricing correction for reinvestment risk (the option adjusted spread).

Most asset-backed securities are backed by third party contracts which may be terminated early at the choice of the third party. To take an example, if a borrower with a fixed rate mortgage sees mortgage rates drop significantly, he will remortgage once the drop in rates is sufficient to cover his transaction costs. If his mortgage is part of an asset pool for a security issue, this prepayment will be passed on to the investor. The investor suddenly has funds to invest (that were previously yielding a rate related to the old mortgage rate) but interest rates have now fallen. The compensation for this reinvestment loss is usually priced into the original extra yield on the AAA-rated securities.

The diversity of the risks involved means that careful risk assessment and monitoring are crucial to the success of a securitisation transaction. The framework of control required is outlined below.

MANAGING RISK

Framework of Control

An overall risk control framework comprises:

- High level management controls such as corporate planning and business strategy, and
- Operational controls over daily trading and support procedures.

These two elements should enable a corporation to control its business, safeguard its assets, prepare financial statements and comply with legislation. Such a framework is obviously a prerequisite of good management in any company, not only in connection with the issue of or investment in asset-backed securities.

The controls over internal procedures can be further classified as primary and secondary controls. Primary controls are concerned with the prevention of errors and irregularities before they occur and with the detection of errors or irregularities which have occurred. Secondary controls include management's regular review and control of budgets, management accounts and other information, transactions and balances and the use of analytical techniques.

A good control framework should include consideration of corporate plans and market strategy, departmental plans and strategies and a well-defined, logical reporting structure.

Corporate Planning and Business Strategy

Senior management should define their corporate goals and develop a corporate plan to achieve them within a medium-term (three to five year) horizon. The formulation of a corporate plan involves the consideration of various factors such as interest and foreign exchange rate forecasts, political, economic and industry trends and the impact of current and proposed regulatory and supervisory requirements. This planning process should also consider other aspects of the business and the risks inherent in them. Examples are exposures to geographical regions and industry concentrations.

A key consideration in the planning process will be the likely level of funding and capital required and how these will be obtained. A source of funds might be the issue of asset-backed securities. An investor will need to plan its desired level of investment in asset-backed securities, both in terms of the quality of the underlying assets and the rates of return.

The corporate plan should also define the overall risk parameters of the business, within the context of its corporate goals. Such a corporate plan is a key component of a framework of control.

Departmental Plans and Strategies

Departmental business plans and implementation strategies should be developed. Departmental plans should be fully integrated with the overall corporate plan, and should encompass and be consistent with all corporate objectives. Clear lines of authority over departmental objectives and responsibilities need to be defined.

Reporting Structure

The organisation and reporting structure within different departments should be clearly defined. Key performance measures should be consistent with the corporate goals.

Limit Structure

The overall control framework established should provide an environment in which risks are managed and controlled within limits which have been approved by senior management. The limit structure should provide sufficient flexibility to enable the business to operate profitably.

It should respond to all the exposures and risks which exist within each product area. A system of delegation or 'stepping' of authorised limits should also be incorporated into the plan and established as a part of the control environment. Management should determine the structure and frequency of reports to identify limit usage and excesses.

For a corporate investor this will involve defining an appropriate limit structure for the treasury department or investment manager.

Transaction Control

This may be defined as the system of internal controls which relates to the execution of transactions. Controls which should be established to ensure proper execution of transactions and detection of errors would typically include the following:

- Transaction authorisation—defining clear lines of authority together with the setting of transaction limits, such that any transaction exceeding that limit would be reported to a higher authority for approval.
- Terms authorisation—establishing procedures for negotiating terms of transactions. These procedures should be formally documented and properly communicated to all parties to whom they are relevant. Adherence to the procedures should be monitored with appropriate authorisation and documentation being required in situations where these procedures are not followed.
- Counterparty approval—establishing counterparty vetting criteria. Formal procedures should be instituted to check counterparty credit quality prior to the completion of any transaction. External credit checks together with internal records of the credit history of each counterparty are normally utilised. The centralisation of this function in a corporation eliminates the possibility that a lack of communication in an organisation results in the failure of its credit control procedures.
- Transaction recording—ensuring accurate and timely recording of transactions. Formalised procedures in this area together with the clear definition of responsibilities and the segregation of personnel duties will meet these objectives. Transaction records should be monitored and reviewed by management on a regular basis.
- Position reporting within a limit framework—establishing reconciliation and reporting procedures. Reports should be prepared on a regular basis by qualified personnel and reviewed by management at an appropriately senior level. Differences and variances should be investigated and resolved on a timely basis.

A key control is the segregation of duties. In particular, different personnel should have responsibility for and access to funds movement, confirmations, settlement functions, and for the information from which management and financial reporting data are assembled.

Operational Control

Operational control aims to ensure accurate and prompt processing, settlement, recording and reporting of transactions. Accurate and timely reporting is critical to enable management to manage risks and monitor profitability.

Management reports should contain information relating to performance and risk management. Such reports should be both accurately and promptly prepared, providing details of all transactions which are in breach of the approved limits. The operational control function should provide not only the statistical and financial data which summarise existing or potential risk and performance but also, where appropriate, sufficient analytical information to assist management in making sound decisions. Such reports should include comparisons against budget, business plan, and authorisation limits, as well as details relating to authorisations for limit excesses.

Risk Management

The risks identified earlier, all of which impact both a corporate issuer and a corporate investor, can be assessed, controlled and managed by the implementation of the control procedures described. These should be present within the accounting and internal control system of any well-run corporation, together with effective procedures designed to address specific risks and achieve the related objectives. Such procedures are outlined below.

Credit Risk

The credit risk to investors in asset-backed securities can be addressed through the formulation of comprehensive procedures to assess the credit quality of the issue and an ongoing assessment of existing counterparties via issuer limits. Detailed upfront procedures may include:

- Review of external credit ratings, for example, Standard & Poor's or Moody's.
- Review of published financial statements and other management information provided by the issuer.
- Performance of external credit history checks.
- Clear definition of position and concentration limits.

Ongoing monitoring should include formal periodic assessments, procedures which identify early warnings of potential default and procedures to deal with problem situations.

A "hands-on" approach by management and regular monitoring should effectively control this risk, particularly where credit control is centralised, allowing effective pooling of information from all parts of a company.

Various securitisation issues are now "graded" by the issuer according to the rights and obligations attached to particular tranches of an issue. It is likely that different tranches securitising the same asset pool will have very different credit characteristics. This should be addressed by the controls discussed above.

Market Risk

Market risk arises whenever variability in exchange and interest rates changes an asset's market price and thus affects the value of that asset or a portfolio of assets. Unlike credit risk, market risk deals only with price variability, which exists regardless of an individual debtor's financial status or the nature of a particular contractual arrangement.

An investor may take a view on market risk with the intention of making profits from favourable price movements. However it is often possible to hedge significant market risks by the judicious use of derivative instruments such as swaps, futures and options. (The use of derivatives for risk control in asset-backed issuance and investment is beyond the scope of this chapter.)

Economic Risk

The external and macroeconomic nature of this risk is such that direct control may not be possible. However, close monitoring by management of the markets in which asset-backed securities are traded, together with the factors influencing the underlying securitised assets, allows a degree of real-time risk management as well as the prompt implementation of contingency strategies wherever necessary. Additional control may be possible where a regular review of financial and management information is performed.

A well run corporation monitors economic risk as an integral part of its business and operational control procedures, with particular emphasis on the market sector in which it operates. An extension of this policy to assess the market sectors in which the issuer operates, together with the overall corporate procedures in place, will allow the company to monitor and assess the effect of economic risk on the investor.

Documentation Risk

Documentation risk can be addressed by the employment of a central legal function, whose task would be to ensure that all necessary legal documentation is properly drawn up or obtained from the corporate counterparty. This would be of particular sensitivity to the corporate issuer. Detailed procedures may include the use of standard contract or certificate formats, as well as written checklists to ensure completeness. The establishment of a close and continuing professional relationship with the firm's corporate lawyers, placing agents and other advisers will add to the controls available to senior management.

Regulatory Risk

A centralised technical department with specialist regulatory expertise is a major risk control mechanism available to the corporate issuer. The hiring and retention of qualified personnel to monitor changes in the accounting environment or tax regime and to recommend mitigating action prior to the introduction of such changes should result in the effective management of regulatory risk.

Gapping Risk

Thorough planning of the issue of asset-backed securities should ensure that the timing of the contractual cash flows from the securitised assets matches the payment terms of the issue, both interest and principal. This should generally avoid the risk that a need for bridging finance will arise during the life of the security, or that surplus cash will be left on hand for which no investment has been planned. In addition, both the corporate issuer and the investor must take into account the potential for unexpected changes in the timing of cash flows and their impact on the risk accepted by the entity.

CONCLUSION

Ultimately, risk control remains a management issue. The way it is exercised within an organisation will depend on the organisation's culture, strategy and objectives. Equally important is the need for a fine balance allowing money to be made but limiting the potential of significant losses. An effective risk control system is an exercise in communication and comprehension. Management must understand the risks being taken, and trading and operational personnel need to be aware of the risk perceptions of senior management and tailor their actions accordingly.

Chapter 18

Asset-Backed Finance—Accounting Issues

by Paresh Mashru
and
Mark Rhys,
Arthur Andersen, London

Securitisations can effectively range from the outright sale of assets to collateralised borrowings. At either end of this range, the accounting is relatively simple and well understood. In the middle ground, however, transactions have characteristics of both sales and borrowings, making accounting issues complex and controversial.

Standard accounting practice has been slow to emerge for securitisation, and it is still evolving. In the absence of definitive rules, it is necessary to develop an approach based on fundamental accounting principles of going concern, matching of revenue and expense, prudence and consistency.

Anglo-Saxon accounting regimes have developed a fifth concept. This requires accounts to reflect the economic substance of transactions rather than their strict legal form. The European Community's fourth company law directive introduced a requirement for all EC-based companies to provide a true and fair view in their accounts; but what is deemed true and fair in one country may not be seen the same way in another. In the U.S. and the UK, the concept of substance over form has generally gained ground. Under the tax regimes of many other countries however, particularly those in continental Europe based on the Napoleonic Code, there is a tendency to require accounting to reflect a transaction's legal form.

THREE KEY ACCOUNTING ISSUES

Sales versus Financing

A common objective in a securitisation is to remove the related assets from the balance sheet. The key issue is therefore whether the economic substance and legal form of the transaction indicate a sale of assets (which can be excluded from the balance sheet), or the form and substance of the transaction is that of a financing with borrowings collateralised by assets.

If it is concluded that the principal risks and rewards of ownership have transferred from the originator to the issuer, the related assets can be excluded from the balance sheet. Conversely, a financing transaction would require both the assets and the related borrowing to be recorded in the balance sheet.

Consolidation

The key accounting question is whether, or in what instances, the SPV or issuer needs to be included in the consolidated financial statements of the originator. The answer will vary depending upon whether or not the issuer is deemed to be a subsidiary of the originator.

Profit and Loss Recognition

Should the originator recognise the profit or loss from the sale of the assets to the SPV immediately, amortise these over the redemption period or defer them until the final redemption of the asset? Similarly, should the originator immediately recognise the costs of the securitisation, amortise them or defer them? The accounting treatment adopted will depend upon the extent to which the risks and rewards relating to the securitised assets reside with the originator. For example, the originator might have provided credit warranties and undertaken to administer the assets and share in any residual profits in the issuer. In this case, the fundamental accounting concept of matching should be applied to ensure that profits are recognised to match the related costs.

U.S. AND UK PRACTICES

Accounting practice in the U.S. is governed by various pronouncements of the Financial Accounting Standards Board (FASB). Statement of Financial Accounting Standard 77 (SFAS 77): *Reporting by Transferers for Transfers of Receivables with Recourse*, and Technical Bulletin (TB) 85-2: *Accounting for Collateralised Mortgage Obligations* stipulate the general rules differentiating sales from financing transactions.

SFAS 94 requires all companies in which a parent has a controlling financial interest to be consolidated, irrespective of the industries in which they operate. The FASB is currently engaged in a project that will address more complex issues, such as the consolidation of "orphan subsidiaries" like securitisation SPVs. Both the FASB and the Emerging Issues Task Force are seeking to address the complexities of the structures that have evolved in the most mature securitisation market. Their efforts cannot be easily summarised in a short chapter.

The UK was the first European country to develop a significant asset-backed securities market, and accounting guidance has only recently appeared. At the end of 1992, the UK Accounting Standards Board (ASB) published a paper detailing its proposals on the appropriate accounting treatment for securitisations. The paper sets out *three* appropriate accounting methods using, throughout, the example of mortgage securitisation. In summary:

- Where the originator has transferred all the benefits and risks relating to the securitised assets, *derecognition* (i.e., off balance sheet treatment) is appropriate.
- Where the originator has retained significant benefits and risks relating to the assets but there is absolutely no doubt that the downside exposure to loss is limited, a *linked presentation* should be adopted.
- In all other cases a *separate presentation* (gross) should be adopted.

The ASB had been grappling with the question of "whether the balance sheet is primarily a statement of an entity's resources and their financing, or whether its primary purpose is to present the entity's exposure to loss and its potential future cash outflows." The solution proposed—linked presentation—accepts that different users have different needs and hence both gross and net information should be shown on the face of the balance sheet.

The proposals are intended to apply to *all* UK companies, not just banking or financial institutions and, once implemented, will apply to *all* outstanding securitisations—potentially bringing previously securitised assets and the related financing back onto the originator's balance sheet, albeit within a linked presentation.

Derecognition (Off Balance Sheet Treatment)

The paper recognises that, where the originator retains no benefits or risks in respect of the securitised assets (true sale), the assets should be removed from the balance sheet and no liability shown in respect of the proceeds of the securitisation. For such derecognition to be appropriate, the ASB sets out the following three requirements (*all* of which must be satisfied):

- The transaction takes place at an arm's length price for an outright sale; *and*
- The transaction is for a fixed amount of consideration and there is *no recourse whatsoever, either implicit or explicit,* to the originator for losses; *and*
- The originator does not benefit or suffer in any way from the future performance of the mortgage.

Linked Presentation

Where any of the conditions for derecognition is not met, it follows that the originator has retained significant benefits and/or risks in respect of the underlying assets. Where "there is *absolutely no doubt* that the originator's downside exposure to loss is limited," a linked presentation should be used. Otherwise, a separate presentation should be adopted.

Thus, a linked presentation should be used where, and only where *all* of the following six conditions are met:

(i) The loan notes finance, and are secured upon, a specific asset portfolio.

(ii) To the extent of any linked presentation on the balance sheet, both the loan noteholders and the issuer have no recourse whatsoever to the originator for losses.

(iii) The directors of the originator explicitly state (in the appropriate published accounts) that they are not obliged to, nor do they intend to, support any losses.

(iv) The noteholders and the issuer agree in writing that they will not seek recourse to the originator for repayment of the loan notes or for losses (usually achieved via the securitisation documentation).

(v) If the funds generated by the assets are insufficient to pay off the noteholders, this does not constitute an event of default for the originator.

(vi) There is no provision whereby the originator has either a right or an obligation to keep the securitised assets on repayment of the loan notes or to reacquire them at any time.

The following example illustrates the application of (vi) to a linked presentation. A portfolio of 100 is financed by 95 of loan notes issued to third parties and 5 of subordinated debt held by the originator. In addition, the originator has an option to reacquire up to 10 of the assets. Assuming conditions (i) to (v) are also met, the balance sheet will present the linked financing within a single asset caption as follows:

Securitised assets:	
Gross assets	100
Less: Non returnable amounts received on securitisation	(85)
	15

The 10 of finance raised by the loan notes corresponding to the maximum that may be repaid upon exercise of the call option would be shown within creditors.

Separate Presentation

In all other cases (i.e., where the originator has retained significant benefits and risk *and* there is some doubt that the downside exposure to loss is limited), a separate presentation should be adopted.

Thus, a gross asset (the assets being securitised) should be shown under assets on the originator's balance sheet, with a corresponding liability recorded in respect of the proceeds of the issuance of the securities shown under liabilities. The relationship between the two items should be disclosed in the notes to the accounts.

Consolidation of SPVs

A previous paper, ED49, required consolidation of quasi-subsidiaries on the basis of control by the parent. The ASB paper argues that indirect but effective control over an issuer is exercised by an originator through securitisation. The ASB therefore expects that, in most cases, the issuer in a securitisation will be a quasi-subsidiary of the originator and must therefore be consolidated.

However, as long as the relevant conditions are present in the group accounts, a linked presentation should be adopted in the consolidated financial statements. The issuing vehicle is viewed by the ASB as merely a means of ring-fencing the securitised assets and their financing; its presence "does not alter the substance of the originating group's assets and liabilities."

EUROPEAN PRACTICES

Although the International Accounting Standards Committee (IASC) has no formal authority, its pronouncements are becoming increasingly influential, since member countries are expected to incorporate IAS principles in local standards. The September 1991 exposure draft IAS ED40 *Financial Instruments* specifically addresses the topic of securitisation, including the general recognition principles discussed above.

The best overview of the various accounting regimes can be provided by a brief survey of the implementation throughout Europe of international accounting standards and, where appropriate, the EC's fourth and seventh directives.

UK practice complies with IAS rulings and the two key EC directives (the fourth and the seventh) have been incorporated in the legal code. The concept of "true and fair" is enshrined in company law. However, the regulatory system has gone beyond this to lay down specific rules on the consolidation of securitisation vehicles.

France has responded to the growing demand for securitisation from French banks with a detailed law. Consolidation accounting may, however, diverge from generally accepted practice in the U.S. or UK. Although French accounting principles do not necessarily require the consolidation of SPVs, vehicles held via an equity shareholding are being consolidated to show the true and fair view required by the fourth directive.

Germany continues to emphasise legal form despite the introduction of the fourth directive. One problem stems from the "imparity principle"—where the accrual principle does not apply, unrealised profits may not be accounted for, although unrealised losses have to be recognised. This has difficult consequences for securitisation where, for example, receivables are sold at a discount but the discount relates to debt quality rather than interest yield.

Spain has historically had tax-driven accounting rules and is to some extent influenced by French practice. The Spanish Ministry of Finance is drafting specific rules for securitisation issues and the associated accounting requirements.

Italy follows international accounting standards and is in the process of fully implementing EC company law directives.

Sweden's accounting rules have in the past followed the legalistic approach of Germany. Recently, however, there have been moves towards substance over form and the UK system of evaluating risks and rewards.

The UK, France, Sweden, Italy and Spain have all seen securitisations. Of necessity, ad hoc solutions have been found for any accounting problems that have arisen. However, as the securitisation market develops and regulators and accounting bodies focus on this area, standard accounting practice will evolve in each country.

Chapter 19

Securitization Trade-Offs—How Deal Structure Can Influence the Future Value of Your Company or Portfolio

by Kathryn A. Cassidy
Vice President Finance (EVP Office)
GE Capital

Securitization has been viewed by many lower rated companies as a means to fund themselves at more attractive interest rates than their underlying rating or lack of rating would normally allow. Many banks and companies have successfully lowered their borrowing costs and accessed the capital markets directly (two very worthy achievements) but by doing so have permanently altered the underlying value of their company and any premium that shareholders could expect to achieve in a buyout or sale of the company or business segment. The structure of the securitization and the unrecorded contingent obligations will have a direct impact on the future value of the company.

Looking at a securitization from the eyes of a potential acquirer of a business or portfolio segment (where a piece of the business or portfolio has been securitized) brings up some issues which a company (and its investment banker) can easily overlook when structuring a securitization transaction. Choices on structures, and which risks to retain, often achieve short-term economic gains but result in long-term lack of flexibility and difficult valuation issues. From an acquirer's point of view, loss of control and flexibility translates to a lesser price and potentially even throws into question the viability of the acquisition of the entire business segment if contractual obligations of the seller/issuer must be assumed. An acquirer will be concerned with what has fundamentally been stripped out of the business (based on economic assumptions and estimates) and the risk he is being asked to take over (valuation).

Securitization can be very complicated (legally, mechanically, and economically) and continuing obligations very broad. What I hope to cover in the following pages is a brief overview of the most important risk elements in a securitization which a potential acquirer of either a business segment or portfolio will or should focus on in determining the value of the business and the price it is willing to pay. Because of the complex nature of securitization contracts, senior management is often unaware of the nature and impact of various decisions made quite often by people in the treasury and accounting functions which can make a future sale of a business segment or portfolio difficult if not impossible.

There are basically six areas of "risk" which can vary tremendously in a securitization transaction which a potential acquirer should be concerned with if they have been asked to look at the acquisition of a portfolio where some of the assets have been securitized. They are: gain on sale/economics; recourse and other risk retention arrangements; representations, warranties, and covenants; control; mechanical arrangements; and servicing arrangements. Each area of risk will be discussed in greater detail. In all cases the analysis assumes that the acquirer has been asked to take over the entire portfolio/business segment including the securitization.

GAIN ON SALE/ECONOMICS

There is probably no one area which brings about greater concern to a future acquirer of a business than how the transaction was recorded and what has been done to recognize future "value" out of the assets which have been sold.

Most securitized transactions are structured to achieve off-balance sheet or sale accounting treatment. The exceptions are generally limited to operating lease transactions where retained residual values generally disqualify assets from being removed from the balance sheet. In addition, there are a handful of sellers/issuers which have structured transactions through bankruptcy-remote subsidiaries where debt characterization in lieu of sale was achieved due to the nature of the securities issued (pay-through in lieu of pass-through securities). For these issuers, access to less expensive funding sources was paramount, and taking the receivables off the books was not.

It is safe to say that in the majority of cases transactions will purports to be sales and will be accounted for under SFAS 77 (which governs accounting and reporting by transferors of receivables with recourse which purports to be "sales" transactions) and EITF Issue No. 88-11 which deals with how to allocate the cost basis of investment in sales transactions which have been creatively packaged (where an economic gain may or may not have occurred).

From an acquirer's point of view, the issue is obviously not whether receivables are on- or off-balance sheet, but rather more substantively, how have the continuing obligations and risks retained by the seller/issuer been recorded? To the extent that a gain on sale has been recorded, a careful review of both loss assumptions and prepayment assumptions will normally lead to varying views on whether an adequately conservative approach has been used and whether or not the yield which remains on any retained risk piece provides to proper compensation for the full spectrum of risks retained: loss risk, prepayment risk, interest rate risk, or any combination of the above. EITF-88-11 provides guidance in dealing with allocating the cost basis between the sold piece of the designated pool of assets, the retained piece of the designated pool (which usually provides the credit enhancement) and the servicing piece of the designated pool (which should cover not only the future cost of servicing the asset, but a profit). However, accounting for a complex transaction is an art at best. While attempts are made to limit the gain taken at sale based on the fair value of the pieces, fair value is quite often an elusive definition, especially when transactions are complicated with fast pay tranches and credit enhancement rolled into one. Careful analysis will be made by any future acquirer to ensure that future income streams from the loans or leases have not been inappropriately stripped by an excessive gain calculation creating an imbedded loss waiting to be recognized in future periods.

When the review is complete a second equally important review will be made in an attempt to size potential adjustments to income which might occur if any of the assumptions (loss, prepayment, servicing) prove to be off target. It is this uncertainty imbedded in future income streams which is extremely difficult to value and which makes most acquirers wary about stepping into the position of the seller/issuer.

RECOURSE AND OTHER RISK RETENTION ARRANGEMENTS

Although the assets may have been removed from the balance sheet and a gain on sale may have been recognized, contingent recourse obligations can impact a seller's income statement down the road.

A financial institution whose income statements and balance sheets are covered by GAAP accounting has more flexibility in establishing recourse arrangements than a bank seeking regulatory accounting sale treatment for the assets. But in either case, a future acquirer will want to understand exactly what future liabilities may be.

Once the acquirer has completed the preliminary economic analysis, a thorough review of the documents is required to determine how much of each of the following four risk elements has been retained:

"Recourse Risk"

How has recourse risk been accounted for? Is the retained risk valued properly? Recourse risk is the limited obligation to pay the securitization investor if the obligors under the securitized assets fail to perform. From the seller/issuer's point of view, recourse is whatever the continuing obligations to the credit enhancer are as defined in the documents. It comes in many forms. It may be a retained class "B" subordinated tranche of the deal; there may be a spread account seeded initially by the seller/issuer and to be built up by the excess spread (customer yield less investor rate less basic servicing) over time. Usually the initial deposit in the spread account is totally at risk as well as the future cash which flows off the assets after the investor and basic servicing is paid. Sometimes this exposure is limited to a defined amount and once that amount has been deposited in the spread account, excess spread is no longer subordinated (except to cover current period losses). An acquirer will focus on how the deposit has been accounted for (write-off vs. receivable).

A detailed review of all contracts is necessary to determine the nature and extent of the recourse obligations of the issuer/seller. Recourse comes in many forms. Today the senior/subordinated structure is most popular. The senior tranche is normally rated AAA and sold to investors based on the overcollateralization of the pool. The subordinated piece is sometimes retained (if the seller is not a bank), or otherwise it is sold off with a surety bond, letter of credit, or cash collateralized.

Additional recourse can be found in any obligations to advance as the servicer, in broad representations and warranties which may lead to loan buy-backs and in interest rate protection (common in commercial paper conduit structures).

"Prepayment Risk"

Another key structural issue which must be investigated is whether the seller or the securitization investor bears prepayment risk on the securitized assets. In many transactions today, fast pay structures actually make the valuation of retained risk much more difficult since principal and interest cash flows may be used to retire the senior certificate as soon as possible. The subordinated tranche retained by the seller becomes much more volatile, and has an extended average life. If loan prepayment risk has been retained, it becomes difficult for a potential acquirer to value the retained risk properly.

"Retention of Interest Rate Risk"

To the extent that there is an intentional mismatch between the asset-backed security and the assets being securitized, it is important to understand the magnitude and the extent to which a changing interest rate environment can be absorbed out of the cash flow of the deal and how it affects the retained risk of the seller/issuer. In many structures for example, fixed-rate assets can be securitized with floating-rate securities. Interest rate swaps can then be used to lock in funding with the seller bearing the differential, if any, when assets pay faster or slower than planned. Sensitivity tests should be run by an acquirer to see what various interest rate scenarios can mean to the deal.

"Adequacy of Servicing Fees"

The last major area to be addressed is whether or not there is sufficient cash to absorb costs plus make a profit on servicing. If an acquirer is to take over, he needs to be comfortable that enough of the yield has been saved to pay adequately for future servicing.

To summarize the impact of recourse risks on acquisition valuations, in evaluating the purchase of the portfolio (including taking over any securitizations) the acquirer most often must look at the "sold assets" just as he would the on-book assets in terms of potential losses and determine if it is feasible to "buy-out" the issuer's position in the subordinated tranche or spread account piece, or if it is better to leave the issuer/seller with the risk. The challenge in estimating the future value of what will be left through the remainder of the transaction, whether in the spread account or from the excess spread from the sold assets, is enormous.

REPRESENTATIONS—WARRANTIES—COVENANTS

After reviewing the economics and the most prominent recourse risks in the transaction, an acquirer will undertake a very detailed review of the contractual obligations documented in the securitization. This adds a complex additional step to the normal acquisition due diligence process. This can be very difficult if the acquirer is not used to the structures and issues involved in a securitization. The review process entails a multi-functional team review of the securitization documentation for economic issues, operational issues, reporting issues, and legal issues. Representations, warranties, and covenants need to be viewed in light of how the business is run to be sure there is no hidden liability or unacceptable operational constraints in the deal over and above the recourse risks retained by the seller/issuer. If the securitization is to stay in place, the acquirer must ensure that the representations, warranties and covenants contained in the securitization will be acceptable on a going forward basis and will not interfere with its strategy for running the business after the acquisition. In some cases it may be necessary to get investor consent if changes in the transaction are necessary to the acquisition deal's viability. In all cases it is necessary to get appropriate indemnifications from the seller/issuer.

As an example of issues which can arise, an acquirer who has stringent negative pledge clauses (as would often be the case for an acquirer who borrows unsecured) needs to review the structure with much care. A seller retained interest and structures which use participations to tie up additional accounts outside the securitized pool are often difficult if not impossible for an acquirer to assume if he is subject to pledge clauses. This contingent use of additional accounts is common in revolving structures for credit cards, floor plan receivables, or other asset classes which are characterized by quick turning receivables where new volume or loans are added monthly or periodically to the securitization pool. Even if the structure doesn't revolve, participation structures can be problematic if the seller/issuer has a pledged, shared collateral interest with the investors in the asset pool. It is, however, generally easier for an acquirer to become comfortable with a non-revolving structure since buying into a transaction when collateral is subject to pre-existing pledges, prior to acquisition, is generally acceptable.

CONTROL

Unlike straight debt transactions which can usually be prepaid, defeased or assumed, a securitization in its most common form—a pass-through structure—generally transfers ownership interest in a pool of assets to investors. This means that the cash flows from the assets support the securities and they are not general obligations of the seller/issuer company. Call provisions are normally not present due to the nature of the transaction, therefore the mechanical arrangements set up to service the transaction will have to be continuing, even if a new servicer comes into the deal.

Quite often, a seller/issuer may continue to "service" the assets, but has effectively turned much of the control over to the trust. Assumption of the role of "servicer" may limit the seller/issuer's ability to work troubled accounts through the use of extensions or adjustments. Similarly they may restrict the ability in remarketing the collateral to wait for the best price. Roles and duties are clearly and restrictively defined in the securitization documents.

Unfortunately from an acquirer's point of view, much flexibility in management of the assets is usually given away.

MECHANICAL ARRANGEMENTS

In order for a low or non-rated company to get a AAA rating in a securitization, it is necessary for the cash coming from the assets to pass through the hands of the seller/servicer quickly to the trust. Commingling of cash needs to be kept to an absolute minimum. This generally means establishing a control account with the trust which will keep the cash until the once-a-month payment to investors. Besides loss of float, this usually entails a change in cash management procedures for the seller/servicer and the set up of bank accounts within the trust and investment procedures to ensure idle cash is invested in highly rated securities until needed. Although usually the trustee can perform the investment function quite easily, the seller/issuer has lost control of its cash.

In addition to new cash management procedures, the far greater challenge for the seller/issuer is the ability to segregate and track cash flows on the designated accounts which have been transferred to the trust. This almost always requires system modifications and new reporting. Because of the kind of audit necessary to ensure conformance to documents, most future acquirers are reluctant to accept servicing/reporting obligations on complex non-standard transactions (especially if the transaction was public).

SERVICING ARRANGEMENTS

There are a number of issues which arise in conjunction with the ongoing servicing of the sold assets. The most important valuation issue, however, is the adequacy of fees in covering the cost of providing the service.

Servicer advancing provisions may require that the Servicer make advances to the investors if the obligors on the securitization assets are delinquent. It is critical to understand the arrangements built into the documents as to when and how the servicer is to be repaid. Cash flows again are of great importance in trying to understand the advancing provisions. How much delinquency is embedded in the pool? Are losses seasonal or relatively constant? What are the payment priorities? When will advances be repaid? What happens during various stages of delinquency? When does advancing stop? What are the mechanics for repossession and what has the servicer contractually agreed to in terms of asset disposal, including advancing and timing? Most documentation will allow the appointment of a sub-servicer but few will allow the responsibility of servicing to be transferred to another party without approval of the rating agencies, the trustees, and the majority of the noteholders. Therefore if the acquirer is willing to assume the servicing, the process for accomplishing that may be time consuming. Normally a release can be easily obtained if the servicer is of higher quality than the original seller/issuer.

As a potential acquirer, taking over as sub-servicer is not necessarily a negative, however the two parties must come to terms on this subject. It is difficult to bear the responsibility of first losses while allowing another party to service and collect the accounts.

One provision which could concern the acquirer is the ability for the trustee to remove the servicer under certain defined conditions. As part of the due diligence, the reasons for removal need to be carefully reviewed to make sure that the servicer can only be removed for a clearly defined cause.

While servicing rights are in some cases assets in their own right (in the case of mortgage and auto loans) it is the most exotic asset classes that pose the challenges: the commercial loan pools, lease transactions, credit cards, boats, recreational vehicles, mobile homes, and computers, to name a few.

CONCLUSION

In transactions which are done publicly or privately in trusts or in conduit structures, stepping into the shoes of the original seller/issuer is not an easy task. It requires a careful review of the documents to be sure the contingent liabilities, recourse, mechanics, and paydown arrangements are well understood. Valuing and paying for what flows back to the seller/issuer is difficult and requires a great deal of historic prepayment data. Servicing arrangements must be carefully reviewed to understand if servicing can be transferred and what is expected of the servicer in terms of advancing for delinquencies, remarketing assets in default or end of term, and what flexibility there is in extending or changing terms. In addition, reporting on sold assets needs to be addressed if the new owner of the business will be servicing securitized assets as well as the assets being acquired. Mechanics will need to be set up to ensure money moves in the fashion documented. This will likely be an issue (or should be anyway), for a highly rated entity who is used to commingling funds and not passing cash received for segregated asset pools daily to a trustee. Not only is it a costly burden administratively, but there is loss of float on the funds which come in on the sold pool.

If a successful acquisition depends upon the entire responsibility for the securitization changing hands, conservative assumptions on prepayments, losses, and cash flows must be made to protect the acquirer who will be unlikely to offer a full value price. If at all possible, an acquirer should leave responsibilities and costs/benefits behind with the original seller/issuer, or defease the debt if economically feasible.

If the securitization transaction has been done through a commercial paper conduit, the easiest execution is usually for the seller to buy-out the securitization transaction (which can usually be done fairly easily) so that the acquirer does not have to value the securitization's impact. More often than not, a better price will be paid for the deal as a whole without the complications of a securitization.

It is very important that up front, as a seller/issuer evaluates the benefits of various securitization structures, that the far-reaching consequences limiting future strategic flexibility not be forgotten. Although exotic structures may create short-term economic pick-ups, sometimes sound, straightforward transactions with conservative documentation and accounting preserve options for the company which may be of far greater value down the road.

Part IV

Structured Finance Within the Law

Chapter 20

Asset Securitisation in the United Kingdom and Other Jurisdictions—Main Considerations

by David Bonsall,
Freshfields

INTRODUCTION

As a response to the growing pressures on the balance sheets of companies, banks and other financial institutions, securitisation techniques are increasingly being developed in a number of European jurisdictions and in the Far East. For a company, securitisation can be attractive as it can lower the cost of funds it raises in the money or capital markets by substituting the creditworthiness of the transaction for its own corporate credit and it helps to diversify its sources of financing. For a bank or other financial institution, securitisation can be even more attractive as it is one method of making more efficient use of its capital resources which are increasingly important as capital and prudential requirements are imposed by international regulators. Securitisation in Europe first began in the United Kingdom in 1987. The market in the UK has seen public issues to date of some £14 billion of securities backed by assets originated in the UK. However, due to the different sets of regulatory, legal, tax and accounting standards, securitisation in Europe has not developed in one common way but more on a country-by-country basis. Similar constraints apply in the Far East where, despite its attractions, securitisation is still relatively untried in Japan and is only just beginning to emerge as a separate market in Hong Kong.

There are many different types of asset that are suitable for securitisation. While historically in the UK residential mortgage loans have been the biggest source of assets for securitisation, there has also been securitisation of vehicle hire purchase and conditional sale receivables, commercial property leases, corporate and consumer loans, trade receivables, lease receivables, as well as dealer finance receivables. In Continental Europe, receivables that have been securitised include residential mortgage loans, corporate loans, lease and trade receivables, whilst in Hong Kong there has been a number of issues of mortgage-backed securities and one securitisation of auto-loan receivables. All of these types of receivable provide a right for the beneficial owner of the underlying asset to receive stable and reasonably predictable payments from third party debtors.

This chapter will consider in some detail the legal, regulatory and accounting issues which arise in connection with the securitisation of assets in the United Kingdom. It will then examine how these same issues are dealt with in France, Belgium, Germany, Italy, Spain, Hong Kong and Japan.

THE UNITED KINGDOM

Introduction

The growth of securitisation in the UK has enabled the range of businesses and institutions entering the market to expand together with the variety of assets securitised. Indeed, the challenges presented have encouraged the development of many different structures, some of them particularly complex, in order to meet individual objectives. As a result of the continued use of securitisation, the regulatory and accounting bodies have published their own guidelines for the treatment of these transactions. This attempt to produce a clear framework is to be welcomed, although it is important that a flexible approach is maintained to permit the securitisation market to develop further.

1. The Assets

The assets that are most securitisable are those that are of a homogenous character. They should generate stable and statistically predictable cash flows which can be used to service debt obligations carrying scheduled interest payment obligations and expectations as to the rate of repayment, or amortisation, of principal.

Most of the assets that have been securitised in the UK to date have been residential mortgages. The UK has a mature and sophisticated home loans market, which grew very significantly during the 1980s. As a result, residential mortgages represented a huge pool of readily securitisable assets. Other assets that have so far been securitised in the UK include commercial mortgages, vehicle hire purchase and conditional sale receivables, corporate and consumer loans, trade receivables, lease receivables and dealer finance receivables.

The basic structure of transactions in the UK has involved the sale of the relevant assets to a special purpose vehicle ("SPV") which has raised the funds for the purchase by an issue of bonds (often bearing interest at a floating rate) to investors in the Euromarkets or by a private placement. The originator of the assets continues to administer the assets. This section will first look at how, under English law, assets may be transferred to the SPV. It will then look at some issues associated with ownership of assets and finally will consider tax issues that arise on transfer.

(a) Transfer of assets/receivables. In the UK, the normal method used for the sale or transfer of an asset/receivable is for a transfer by way of an assignment. An assignment can be effected either at law or in equity. The distinction under English law between the ownership of an asset in law and its ownership in equity and the recognition that these interests can be separated and vested in different persons provides a very flexible tool for the transferring of assets/receivables in the UK and enables payment flows resulting from assets to be effectively split between different parties who have separate interests in the assets. However, in the context of residential mortgages, there can be some restrictions on this splitting of payment flows because of the system known as MIRAS whereby the Inland Revenue gives tax relief at source to borrowers for their mortgage interest payments. This can lead to difficulties in structuring the best means of profit extraction for an originator (see further 6(d) below).

Under English law to effect a legal assignment of an asset/receivable (which would transfer both the legal and the beneficial interest in the asset), the assignment must comply with the provisions of Section 136 Law of Property Act 1925. This provides that the assignment must be in writing and be in respect of the whole debt and notice of the assignment must be given to the debtor.

In practice, because the provision of notice to debtors is often administratively expensive and rating agencies regard it as acceptable for the SPV to have only an equitable interest in the assets/receivables, notice is often not given to debtors so that assignments only take effect in equity with just the beneficial ownership in the assets passing to the SPV.

The lack of notice has several theoretical legal consequences. The most significant is that the debtor could obtain a fully effective discharge of his obligations by paying the underlying debt to the originator. However, protection is built into the structure so that the SPV is only at risk in the event of fraud or mistake on the part of the originator. Equally, until notice is given to the original debtor, equitable rights (such as to obtain damages for misrepresentation or breach of contract) may accrue in favour of the original debtor and allow him to set-off amounts due to him against his obligation to make payments under the relevant receivables contract. Where notice of assignment is given to the original debtor, certain rights of set-off will crystallise and may not accrue after the date of that notice.

In relation to particular types of assets securitised to date in the UK, the following additional issues arise on transfer:

(i) *Mortgage backed transactions:* There is a system of registration of title to land in the UK but it does not yet have full effect throughout the country. As a result, two distinct systems of administering title to land still exist. Land is, therefore, commonly referred to as registered or unregistered and different procedures apply when purchasing the underlying property; however, there is no distinction in value between the two types of land and security can be taken equally well over both types. The transfer from the originator to the SPV of a portfolio of mortgages over unregistered land will often have the benefit of Section 114 Law of Property Act 1925. This provides that, unless a contrary intention is expressed, a transfer of a mortgage by deed will operate at law (without notice to the borrower) to transfer the right to receive and give receipts for the mortgage moneys, the benefit of all the securities for the mortgage moneys and the right to exercise all powers of the mortgagee. However, mortgages over registered land can only be transferred at law (rather than in equity only) by changing the details at H.M. Land Registry at a cost, which is currently £25 per title to be registered. Given this cost (which would be substantial when applied to a large portfolio), the administrative expense of giving notice to original debtors and the acceptance by the rating agencies and the Bank of England of transfers by way of equitable assignment, most mortgage-backed issues in the UK now use the equitable assignment route.

(ii) *Other types of receivable:* Without having to contend with the restrictions on splitting payment flows from residential mortgages which result from the application of the MIRAS system, the structure used for the car hire purchase receivables and lease receivables securitisations involves a transfer by way of an equitable assignment of the receivables to a "receivables trustee" rather than directly to the SPV. The reason for this is to make profit extraction easier. As the average fixed yield from the purchased receivables is typically much greater than floating interest rates payable by the SPV to investors, significant amounts of profit could be locked up in the SPV if the traditional method of transfer is adopted. Instead, the receivables trustee holds the receivables on trust for various beneficiaries, including the SPV, which is entitled to receive only what is needed to fund its payment obligations to investors and other related expenses. The originator is the other main beneficiary under the trust and extracts any residual profit in the transaction. Again, no notice is given to the underlying debtors. It is likely that transfers of other types of receivables such as credit card receivables will follow the same format.

Generally, no approvals or filings are required by the SPV in order for it to obtain valid title to the receivables.

(b) Ownership issues. The ownership of an asset often brings with it a number of continuing obligations under the underlying contract such as, for example, maintenance and insurance of the asset. There are two concerns here. First, if the SPV has purchased just the receivable and not the underlying physical asset, then to the extent that the owner fails to perform these obligations there is a risk for the SPV that the ultimate user of the asset (the underlying debtor) will no longer pay rentals or finance payments under the contract. The risk of such non-performance and consequent non-payment is something that could impact upon the commercial viability of the transaction and is a matter that an SPV will have to deal with by taking an indemnity from the originator and/or being able to obtain performance by a third party and/or through insurance.

The second concern arises either if the SPV is the owner of the physical asset or if a third party is the owner and the viability of the transaction depends upon the continued existence of that third party owner. In either case, owner liabilities and obligations imposed by operation of law must be considered. Obligations and potential liabilities can arise for the owner under the Supply of Goods and Services Act 1982 and the Supply of Goods (Implied Terms) Act 1973 as to the quality and fitness of the goods and the right to enjoy or to sell the assets, as the case may be. Other legislation where liability can arise includes the Consumer Protection Act 1987 (strict liability for defective products causing damage), the Health and Safety at Work Act 1974 (duty of care imposed on suppliers of articles as to their safety) and the Consumer Credit Act 1974 (liability for misrepresentation by a creditor or his agent). Finally, there are also residual liabilities which arise by operation of the English common law.

There may or may not be defences available to owners/suppliers of the assets from some of these liabilities. However, the suitability of such defences will depend upon the particular circumstances prevailing. Given the nature of some types of assets, it is clear that the SPV in a securitisation will not want to be burdened with the liabilities and obligations that ownership brings. Indeed, in the vehicle receivables transactions to date, ownership of the underlying assets, the vehicles, has remained with the originating finance company.

(c) Tax issues on transfer.

(i) *Stamp duty:* A transfer of mortgages will normally not be chargeable to stamp duty as a result of Section 64 Finance Act 1971. The assignment of charges over life policies or other collateral security should also be exempt from stamp duty. In respect of a transfer of other types of receivable, stamp duty will be payable on their transfer. However, payment can be deferred by the sale being concluded by means of a written offer accepted through conduct (such as the payment of the purchase price) and with any related documents and payment arrangements taking place outside the UK. Stamp duty on transfesr of assets other than land is due to be abolished when a new paperless share transfer system (TAURUS) is introduced, probably in the spring of 1994.

(ii) *Value added tax:* The VAT treatment will depend entirely on the type of asset/receivable that is being disposed of. For a securitisation of mortgages, no VAT cost should arise on the disposal of the mortgages by the originator to the SPV since the sale of mortgages is an exempt supply for VAT purposes. In many other cases (such as hire purchase, lease or credit card receivables) the assignment of the relevant receivables will also be an exempt supply by the originator so that VAT will not be payable on the sale. However, the effect of an exempt supply by the originator on the originator group's own ability to recover input VAT needs to be carefully considered. It is also important to remember that certain receivables, for example lease rentals, themselves attract VAT and that, following the assignment, VAT will remain payable by lessees on the lease payments. The structure needs to accommodate this feature.

2. Basic Structural Considerations—On-Or Off-Balance Sheet

It will often be a key objective for originators to structure the securitisation in such a way that the securitised assets do not appear on their consolidated balance sheets for regulatory purposes and also, if at all possible, for statutory accounting purposes. This section discusses the regulatory, accounting and legal requirements in the United Kingdom with which any such originator must comply in order to obtain the correct treatment.

(a) Regulatory Aspects.

(i) *Bank of England:* Originators which are, or are members of a group of companies which are, supervised by the Bank of England are required to allocate capital to their assets/receivables while they remain on-balance sheet. Other originators who may be actually or potentially involved in securitisation are also regulated by being required to maintain certain prudential ratios e.g., building societies and insurance companies. One major advantage of securitisation to such institutions will be to remove the assets/receivables off-balance sheet in order to reduce the capital required to be allocated. In a Notice entitled "Loan Transfers and Securitisation" (BSD/1989/1) (the "1989 Notice") the Bank of England specified the circumstances in which it will be prepared to treat securitised assets/receivables as having ceased to be on-balance sheet thereby freeing up capital for redeployment. The 1989 Notice laid down a number of criteria which must be observed to achieve this treatment.

The main impact of the 1989 Notice on the structure of any transaction is to restrict the type of support which the originator can provide to the SPV. The originator may provide a one-off financial contribution to the SPV on its establishment and it may make a long-term subordinated loan to the SPV. However, any such loan must be entered into and be fully drawn at the outset of the transaction and can only be repayable when the transaction is wound up. Further, in order to ensure that the originator is completely distanced from the SPV, the originator is forbidden to hold shares in the SPV or exercise any control over its board of directors. The originator is permitted to service the asset portfolio and, where applicable, to exercise discretion on behalf of the SPV in fixing the interest rate chargeable to the underlying debtors. As a result, the originator will have no legal powers to exert control over the SPV although, in practice, the SPV will be constrained in what it is permitted to do by the documentation governing the transaction.

The Bank of England has amended the 1989 Notice to expand its scope and bring it into line with current market practice and to deal with specific new areas, namely the treatment of the risks arising from equipment finance transactions (e.g., lease and hire purchase receivables) and the securitisation of revolving credits such as credit card receivables. These guidelines are set out in the Bank of England's Notice BSD/1992/3 (the "1992 Notice").

The amendments to the 1989 Notice are relatively minor in nature. However, with regard to equipment finance receivables, the Bank of England has made it clear that the ownership risks noted earlier have to be addressed appropriately before a nil capital weighting for the leased assets/receivables sold will be ascribed. Some sensible guidelines to address these risks are suggested (e.g., through insurance).

The 1992 Notice lays down new criteria for achieving off balance sheet treatment for the securitisation of revolving credits such as credit card receivables. The Bank believes that, if carefully structured, such assets can be successfully securitised by transferring the risk on a pool of such assets to noteholders. The Bank's prime concern, however, is that repayment and amortisation arrangements do not leave selling banks exposed to deteriorations in the performance of the pool. Some account balances will be of cardholders who pay off their card balances every month, whereas others will relate to those who make only the minimum payment. The latter are perceived to be worse credits. If the proceeds of repayment from cardholders that repay each month in full are available to the issuer, the noteholders may be repaid very quickly from the proceeds of the better credits, leaving the originator with the worse credits who make only the minimum payment each month. In view of this, the 1992 Notice recommends that the issuer receives payments only as and when the account balances outstanding at the beginning of any amortisation period are collected so that the issuer, like the originator, remains exposed to the worse credits. The Bank, however, recognises that this might not be feasible in practice. Therefore, to satisfy concerns that the Bank has in this regard, any originator must demonstrate (e.g., on the basis of historical data or because of specific mechanisms built into the transaction) that at the point when the noteholders are fully repaid there will not remain outstanding more than 10 percent of the aggregate balance on cardholder accounts which was outstanding at the beginning of the amortisation period. The Bank has also imposed a limit, initially of 10 percent of a bank's solo capital base, on the amount of revolving credits which can be securitised.

(ii) *Building Societies:* No building society has, as yet, undertaken a securitisation of its mortgage assets, although they have what would seem to be a large and ready resource of securitisable assets. However, increasing pressure is being placed on the capital of building societies and with opportunities for societies to raise new capital externally becoming increasingly difficult, the removal of assets from the balance sheet through securitisation is looking a more likely alternative.

Building societies are regulated under the Building Societies Act 1986 and supervised in prudential matters by the Building Societies Commission (the "BSC"). It was not until the enactment of the Building Societies Act that many of the fundamental powers were granted. The building societies would be required to structure the securitisation. However, even with these wider powers there are still a number of technical difficulties with the Act that any society would have to overcome.

Supplementary to, and superimposed upon, the statutory requirements are the BSC's prudential requirements. The BSC, like the Bank of England, has a very wide discretion to require capital backing for any kind of asset.

The BSC is very much a "hands-on" regulator and its statements, in the context of securitisation, are of considerable importance. Its Prudential Note 1988/2 entitled "Capital Requirements For Off-Balance Sheet Mortgage Lending" lays down criteria which a securitisation structure would need to satisfy for the Commission to accept that a building society would no longer need to hold capital to back the securitised mortgages. In addition, in August 1991 the BSC published a Consultative Paper proposing certain changes to Prudential Note 1988/2 which were an attempt to bring that Note more up to date with current market practice and the Bank of England's 1989 Notice. A revised draft of Prudential Note 1988/2 is still awaited. However, it is reasonably safe to assume that the requirements for a building society to securitise mortgages are likely to be similar, in many respects, to those applicable to a bank regulated by the Bank of England.

(b) Accounting aspects. The accounting treatment of securitisations has been a matter for individual originators to agree with their auditors without (until recently) clear guidelines from the various accountancy governing bodies. For over two years, the position has been under review as the accountants have included securitisation in their consideration of various off-balance sheet financing techniques, some of which have been designed as little more than "window-dressing" rather than intended to produce genuine commercial benefits. In May 1990 Exposure Draft 49 entitled "Reflecting the Substance of Transactions in Assets and Liabilities" was issued by the Accounting Standards Committee on behalf of the Institute of Chartered Accountants in England and Wales. It required that the accounting treatment of a transaction should reflect the commercial reality of what had occurred and provided guidance on determining the substance of a transaction by setting out examples of "general recognition tests" and "specific recognition tests" for assets and liabilities. If the originator retains a significant share of the risks and rewards in respect of the assets sold, those assets should continue to be recorded on the originator's balance sheet. Annex D to the Exposure Draft set out common characteristics of a securitised mortgage transaction and the conditions which must be satisfied in order to achieve off-balance sheet status. These conditions closely resemble the requirements set out in the Bank of England's 1989 Notice referred to earlier.

In October 1991 the Accounting Standards Board (the "ASB") (the successor to the Accounting Standards Committee) stated that, while it was broadly happy with the approach adopted in ED49 and would be producing a Financial Reporting Standard based on ED49, it wanted to see a different accounting treatment implemented with respect to securitisations. These proposals would have significantly reduced the instances in which securitisation could be treated as off-balance sheet financing. After much debate and discussion the ASB published revised proposals in November 1992 which reflect a new and more flexible approach.

The ASB's fundamental concern in the debate on the proper accounting treatment of securitisations is that, where an originator continues to enjoy rights to certain benefits from an asset sold to an SPV (e.g., through the right to surplus income from the transaction after financing costs and other expenses have been paid) and continues to be exposed to limited risk from the asset (e.g., through bearing the first losses suffered on the asset transferred), the accounts of the originator should reflect the true position of the originator. The November 1992 paper attempts to do this by what is known as a "linked presentation."

The linked presentation operates by showing on the originator's balance sheet the external finance raised from the sale of the securitised assets (to the extent that recourse is limited to only those assets) deducted from the related gross assets. An example of this is as follows:

Securitised mortgages:	£
Gross mortgages	X
Less: non-returnable amounts received on securitisation	(Y)
	Z

For a linked presentation to be used there must be absolutely no doubt that the noteholders cannot claim repayment from the originator but must look only to the proceeds generated by the securitised assets, and there is no provision for the originator to re-acquire the assets in the future. The ASB has laid down a set of six criteria that have to be met in order for these objectives to be satisfied. If the originator retains significant benefits from the assets but there is no doubt that the originator's exposure to losses is limited to a specific amount, a linked presentation may be appropriate.

If the criteria for linked presentation are not met, the accounts must use "separate presentation" showing the gross assets and related liabilities without any deduction or offset. On the other hand, there may be cases where the originator has no significant benefit or risk in respect of the underlying assets that are securitised. Here the ASB will allow complete "derecognition" with the originator's balance sheet showing merely a net asset on the assets side of the balance sheet (e.g., the cash proceeds of sale) and no related liability.

On the whole the ASB paper is to be welcomed. Discussion with market practitioners continues with regard to some of the criteria required for a "linked presentation" but if the proposals are implemented in the Financial Reporting Standard (a draft of which was published in February 1993) it should enable most corporates and bank originators to continue to securitise their assets in the UK and obtain off-balance sheet treatment for most of the financing.

(c) Legal aspects. The Companies Act 1989 introduced into English law a new definition of "subsidiary undertaking" for accounting purposes.

This had the effect of requiring consolidation, as a matter of law, of most of the off-balance sheet vehicles which had been previously set up in reliance on a mismatch between statutory definitions under English tax law and company law. As a result of these changes, off-balance sheet corporate structures are now created by way of the "orphan structure" whereby the entire issued share capital of the SPV is held by an unconnected third party on discretionary trust for a group of charitable institutions. In order to issue its securities to the public (which is very broadly defined) the SPV must be a public company with a minimum authorised share capital of £50,000 which must be, at least, one-quarter paid up. For tax reasons, the SPV will normally be expected to make a profit, which need only be fairly modest.

3. Credit and Securities Regulation

The acquisition by the SPV of a portfolio of assets/receivables and the issue of securities in the Euromarkets raise a number of issues regarding authorisations, licenses and consents. These issues arise as a result of the Consumer Credit Act 1974, the Data Protection Act 1984, the Financial Services Act 1986 and rules on the issue of debt securities that are listed on the London Stock Exchange or the Luxembourg Stock Exchange and, for authorised institutions, Bank of England requirements. Each area is briefly discussed below.

(a) Consumer Credit Act 1974. This Act primarily regulates the making of loans and other credit provisions to individuals. It is unlawful for a person to make a regulated loan unless the lender is licensed to do so under the Act. Regulations under the Act lay down detailed requirements regarding the conduct of businesses making regulated loans, the form and content of documentation and the nature of any publicity material.

Failure to comply with these requirements can result in the loan being unenforceable, although in most circumstances the loan can be enforced after obtaining an order of a court. Credit card arrangements, consumer loans and lease and hire purchase agreements are often subject to the Act. However, loans of £15,000 or more are exempt and so are certain loans of less than £15,000, if made for various prescribed purposes including the purchase of land or the improvement or extension of property. Certain new consumer protection rules are expected to come into force this year; these relate to "tying-in," a sales technique whereby a borrower wishing to take out a residential property loan is forced to receive certain related services (e.g., insurance or property valuation) from the lender or an affiliated company. Unless specified conditions are met, directors and other officers of the lender will be guilty of a criminal offence. However, the enforceability or validity of the loan itself will not be affected. It is normal that, on a sale of the assets/receivables to the SPV, the originator will be expected to warrant compliance with the various legal requirements and to repurchase any assets/receivables which do not comply.

(b) Data Protection Act 1984. The administration of debts is normally a highly computerised affair with records of debtors and correspondence being computer stored and generated. As such, the originator will need to have been registered as a "data user." Similar registration is appropriate for the SPV on the sale of the portfolio and as a precaution for any security trustee.

(c) Financial Services Act 1986. This Act prohibits the unauthorised carrying on of investment business in the United Kingdom. Each aspect of the transaction must be analysed to see whether the relevant activity constitutes "investment business," whether it involves "investments" and whether, as a result, authorisation is required under the Act. A criminal offence is committed by the carrying on of unauthorised investment business and civil sanctions can also apply. There are a number of areas in a securitisation where the Act can raise difficulties. Although it is beyond the scope of this chapter to discuss these, one example relates to the use of spare cash in a transaction. To the extent that cash is received in respect of any of the assets/receivables between note interest payment dates, it will usually be the responsibility of the administrator to reinvest that cash on behalf of the SPV. Commercially, it may be desirable to buy short-term government securities or commercial paper.

However, the administrator is unable to invest cash in "investments" (as defined in the Act) unless it is either authorised or exempted under the Act since to do so would involve "managing investments" on behalf of the SPV which is an investment business activity under the Act. Other examples of where the Act may apply abound (e.g., swaps between various parties) and careful consideration of the terms of the transaction and the various exemptions and exclusions in the Act need to be examined when looking at a particular transaction. To date, authorisation has not been required for most issuers and administrators although it is by no means certain that this will always be the case.

(d) Listing and selling restrictions. All of the public UK asset-backed note issues have to date been listed on either the London Stock Exchange or the Luxembourg Stock Exchange. If the issue is to be listed on the London Stock Exchange, Part IV of the Financial Services Act 1986 requires that listing particulars be prepared. The London Stock Exchange has issued specific listing requirements for asset-backed securities. These are less extensive than for a domestic share offering. London Stock Exchange issuers are also subject to continuing obligation rules requiring them, broadly, to keep the market informed of important developments which might affect the securities. Issues listed on the Luxembourg Stock Exchange are, in theory, subject to a slightly more relaxed regime and do not have to comply with the provisions of the Financial Services Act but are subject to the requirements of Part III of the Companies Act 1985 relating to the form and content of the prospectus, which must be delivered to the Registrar of Companies. Part III of the Companies Act will be repealed and replaced in due course by Part V of the Financial Services Act, although it is to be hoped that the generally relaxed approach will be maintained.

Notes listed in either London or Luxembourg which are genuine debt obligations rather than, say, undivided interests in a pool of assets can be widely distributed. In practice, this is not a problem given the mature nature of the markets in which such securities are sold. In any event the managers for the issue are likely to have to be authorised under the Financial Services Act in order to sell and distribute the securities.

(e) Bank of England requirements. When the Bank of England first published its approach on implementation in the UK of the EC Solvency Ratio Directive (see Notice BSD/1990/3), authorised institutions holding mortgage-backed securities were to be required from 1 January 1993 to give a 100 percent risk weighting to such securities for the purpose of calculating the solvency ratio of the holding institution. However, following much lobbying from market participants, the Bank of England indicated in November 1992 (Notice BSD/1992/6) its acceptance of the argument that the EC Solvency Ratio Directive does in fact permit a 50 percent risk weighting to be applied to mortgage-backed securities provided that the transaction terms satisfy certain conditions—these are consistent with market practice and should cause no difficulty.

4. Insolvency Considerations

(a) Of the SPV. The SPV's finances must be carefully balanced so as to match its assets (assets/receivables and cash) with its liabilities (repayment of notes and other costs and expenses). The SPV must not be rendered insolvent as a result of any particular feature in the structure of the transaction other than non-payment on the securities. This is sometimes known as making the SPV "insolvency remote" and great care is taken to ensure that the SPV is not exposed to liabilities to third parties not involved in the transaction.

(b) Of the originator and administrator. Unless these parties are themselves rated (thus making the rating of the transaction dependent on their corporate rating), the rating agencies will assume that the insolvency of the originator or administrator will occur at some (usually inconvenient) stage of the transaction. In these circumstances, the liquidator of the originator or administrator must not be able to take any action which would adversely affect the SPV. There are a number of grounds upon which some of the arrangements between the originator and the SPV could potentially be attacked under the Insolvency Act 1986 (e.g., preferences and transactions at an undervalue). One example may illustrate the difficulty. If a mortgage is warranted by the originator to have certain characteristics (e.g., its loan to value ratio) but the warranty is untrue, the SPV will want to sell the mortgage back to the originator at the price it paid (usually the face amount) and use the proceeds to buy another mortgage or to pay down the notes issued. If the originator is solvent when the breach of warranty is discovered and it performs its repurchase obligation but soon thereafter becomes insolvent, the liquidator may try to recover the money paid to the SPV. If that claim is successful, the SPV may not have any funds available (e.g., because it has paid the noteholders) and it could be rendered insolvent. The legal analysis of the transaction must address this situation and, either by meeting certain legal tests or by requiring certain factual circumstances to exist, prevent this risk jeopardising the transaction. For example, it is common practice to require the originator's directors to give certificates confirming the originator's solvency when the portfolio is sold to the SPV and on certain occasions thereafter and it is becoming standard practice to ensure that a competent administrator "of last resort" is committed to take over servicing of the portfolio if the originator cannot continue with this role.

As can be seen, the circumstances of each transaction will need to be carefully scrutinised and protections built in to the satisfaction of the rating agencies in this regard. Similar concerns can obviously arise in non-rated transactions.

5. Security Considerations

In the standard structure the SPV will create security interests over the assets/receivables and any related security acquired by it from the originator in favour of a trustee for the secured creditors to secure its obligation to repay the finance raised. The SPV will also grant security over its interest under any insurance contracts and its rights under other contracts entered into in the transaction and give a floating charge over all its remaining assets. If the SPV only has an equitable interest in the assets/receivables, the security interest granted to the trustee must necessarily also be equitable and will not usually be notified to borrowers. English law recognises the concept of subordination of creditors under which the rights of certain secured creditors of the SPV (e.g., certain facility providers and the originator itself) are postponed or subordinated behind others—most notably the trustee and administrator and the holders of the securities.

All security created by a UK company in these circumstances must be registered at Companies House. Prescribed particulars of the security together with the security document must be lodged at the Companies Registry within 21 days of the creation of the charge. Failure to register on time will mean that the charge becomes void against the liquidator or administrator or any creditor of the company.

Should it be necessary for the trustee to enforce the security and only an equitable assignment has been taken, the trustee would arrange for a transfer of the legal title to the assets/receivables to the SPV and for the creation of a legal security interest in favour of itself. The trustee would then, as chargee, be able to exercise its rights and powers of sale over the assets/receivables. However, in respect of a securitisation of mortgages created over registered land, the trustee would be unable to exercise the rights under the mortgage until it had become registered as proprietor of the charge at H.M. Land Registry. Since registration at H.M. Land Registry takes time, the trustee will normally take security powers of attorney from the originator and the SPV authorising it to take such action as it may wish during the intervening period. It is, of course, worth noting that the trustee may only take action against the underlying debtors if they are themselves in breach of the obligations owed to the SPV. If only the SPV is in default, the trustee may have to seek other remedies, e.g., selling the performing portfolio to a third party at the best price reasonably obtainable.

6. Tax Implications

(a) Disposal. The UK tax treatment of the disposal proceeds arising from the sale of the assets/receivables to the SPV will vary depending on the nature of the asset/receivable:

(i) *Mortgages:* Mortgages will commonly be sold by the originator to the SPV for a price equal to the outstanding principal amount of the mortgages, often without any accrued but unpaid interest. The technical analysis of such a disposal can be quite complex depending on the status of the mortgages as capital or revenue assets in the hands of the originator and the SPV and whether the SPV is in the originator's tax group.

However, in principle the disposal of the mortgages at cost should be neutral from a corporation tax point of view. The same analysis will generally apply to the ancillary security sold with the mortgages such as charges over life policies and insurance policies.

(ii) *Credit card receivables:* Where an originator carrying on a credit card business disposes of the credit card debts to the SPV, the price will be brought into account in computing its trading profit.

(iii) *Hire purchase receivables:* Whether a tax charge will arise on disposal depends on whether the hire purchase receivables are sold at a profit or loss by reference to the net carrying value of the receivables in the originator's accounts.

(iv) *Lease receivables:* The sale by a leasing company of its lease receivables gives rise to some difficult questions. A basic issue is the effect that any disposal will have on the capital allowance position of the originator/lessor. On a sale of leased assets by a leasing company, to the extent the originator/lessor obtains a capital receipt, there will be a clawback of capital allowances relating to the leased assets. Difficulties can arise in determining whether such a clawback occurs where receivables only, rather than the leased assets, are sold. There is also a concern that a sale of receivables only may result in accelerated receipt by the originator of taxable income which could be commercially disadvantageous.

(b) The SPV. The tax position of a UK controlled and organised SPV depends on whether it is treated as a trading company or an investment company. Broadly a company is more likely to be regarded as a trading rather than an investment company if it has a substantial degree of turnover of its assets (including "substitution" by using redemption proceeds to buy new assets), as opposed to simply holding a closed fund of assets to their maturity.

(i) *Trading company status:* The profits or losses of a company carrying on a trade will be subject to corporation tax on income. The tax treatment of a trader is generally more favourable than that of an investment company, particularly as the category of those expenses which can be deducted in computing taxable trading profit is wider, and it should be possible to avoid the tax difficulties which can arise when funding in a foreign currency or holding assets denominated in currencies other than sterling. Trading profits are ascertained by deducting revenue expenses from trading income adjusted to exclude disallowable items such as depreciation charges. A trading deduction will be available for items such as specific bad debts (though not a general provision) and fees and other expenses of a revenue nature related to the trade. Income and revenue expenses of a trading company are usually brought into account on an accruals basis. Interest paid on the bonds issued by the SPV is relieved when paid.

(ii) *Investment company status:* Investment companies hold their assets on capital account, not trading account. Any gain or disposal may give rise to corporation tax on chargeable gains or an allowable loss. The gain or loss is ascertained by deducting from the proceeds of disposal the acquisition cost (indexed to allow for inflation) and incidental expenses in acquiring, enhancing and disposing of the asset. Income and revenue expenses are brought into the charge to corporation tax on income on a cash basis rather than an accruals basis. The categories of expenditure for which the company will be able to claim a deduction are narrower than for a trading company, though interest on the bonds will be deductible.

(c) The Investors. Normally an issue of debt securities by an SPV is structured so that the bonds fall within the definition of "quoted Eurobonds" in Section 124 Taxes Act 1988, i.e., they are interest bearing securities quoted on a recognised stock exchange and are in bearer form. Consequently, interest is generally payable without the deduction of UK income tax by the SPV. Furthermore, investors in asset-backed issues in the Euromarkets are prepared to invest in an issue where there is no obligation upon the issuer to "gross-up" if a withholding tax is imposed.

(d) Profit Extraction. Profit extraction presents a number of problems and will inevitably depend on a number of factors, in particular the tax treatment required by the originator and the SPV. The Inland Revenue have given some general indications of their views of the tax treatment relevant to the more commonly encountered methods of profit extraction:

(i) Traditionally, the simplest way of extracting profit is by way of dividends on shares in the SPV held by the originator. This method is only available where the originator does not seek off-balance sheet financing and so can hold shares in the SPV. Dividend payments are not deductible expenses for the SPV which must also account to the Inland Revenue for advance corporation tax (ACT) of (currently) 25/75ths of the dividends paid. However, the dividend is not taxable in the hands of the originator and may relieve it of ACT on its own dividend payments.

(ii) The use of an interest rate swap, where the SPV pays out (say) the mortgage rate less an amount to cover its expenses and the originator pays the bond rate, is another possibility. It is, of course, necessary to ensure that such a swap will benefit from the Inland Revenue's current concessionary treatment for swaps, particularly taking into account whether the interest rate could be regarded as "excessive."

(iii) The mortgages may be sold for a price in excess of par, i.e., the originator would sell the mortgages to the SPV for a price comprising their face value and an element of deferred consideration (calculated by reference to the transaction profit). The main concern here is that, since any payment will be taxed in the hands of the originator, it is essential that the payment is a deductible expense for the SPV. Where the SPV can be regarded as a trading company this treatment may be available.

(iv) The payment of administration fees to the originator, acting as administrator, might prove to be an effective extraction method. The fees payable would include the costs of the administration and an element to take out further "profit." The fee must be a deductible expense of the SPV to avoid double taxation. The provision of administration services would amount to a taxable supply for VAT purposes. As the SPV will not usually be able to recover any VAT which it pays (and the administrator must account for VAT which it should have charged on its taxable supplies), this method will result in a tax leakage of (currently) 17.5 percent of the fees payable.

(v) An alternative regularly used is to extract profit by the payment of interest on a subordinated loan from the originator. The loan may be made by the originator either to the SPV to fund its initial expenses or to provide a layer of credit enhancement to the SPV. The interest charged would be in excess of the market rate so as to accommodate the extraction of profit. If the interest exceeds a commercial return on the principal borrowed it will, for tax purposes, usually be treated as a distribution, the tax treatment being broadly the same as in (i) above. To the extent that the interest does not exceed a reasonable commercial return, it will be treated as true interest for tax purposes and, provided it is annual interest (which will normally be the case), the SPV should obtain relief in computing its liability to tax.

(vi) Finally, the originator might opt to transfer the assets to a trustee, the terms of the relevant trust providing that the originator shall be entitled to any remaining profit after all the expenses of the SPV have been taken into account and met out of the trust's income and capital receipts. The purpose of this method is to ensure that the SPV has sufficient moneys to meet its funding costs and expenses but that the major part of the profit never belongs to the SPV. The trust should be tax efficient, as the profit on the assets which the originator would have obtained had it retained the entire interest in them should generally be received in the same tax accounting period as it would have been received had no securitisation occurred. As noted earlier, this method has not been used for mortgage securitisations, as the Inland Revenue have indicated that a mortgage, the interest from which is held in trust for two or more persons concurrently, cannot fall within the MIRAS scheme and such a structure would therefore disadvantage the individual borrowers.

SCOTLAND

Introduction

Securitisation in Scotland has developed rather more slowly than in England. The principal cause for this lies in fundamental differences between the English and Scottish legal systems. However, as methods of overcoming the legal obstacles to securitising Scottish assets have been devised there is good reason to believe that there is considerable scope for expansion in this jurisdiction.

Many of the considerations involved in a Scottish securitisation are the same as those in England and this section concentrates on the principal areas of difference—transfer and insolvency.

1. The Assets

(a) Types and transferability of assets/receivables. Scotland has seen the securitisation of both residential mortgages and hire purchase receivables. However, since Scottish law does not recognise equity, the usual method of transferring the assets/receivables in England by way of equitable assignment is not available.

(i) *Mortgages:* The early securitisations of Scottish mortgage portfolios relied upon full legal transfers and charges. The title to the individual mortgages was transferred from the originator to the SPV by two block assignations—one for each of the two Scottish land registers (Sasine or Land Registry depending on the area) and thereafter sub-charges created in favour of the security trustee over the portfolio on a fully registered basis.

Although this structure has the advantage of offering full security to the trustee it presents a number of difficulties and by its nature is rather inflexible. The Land Registry may, for example, reject registration in the event of an error in the details of the mortgage. Particular problems arise where block transfers are effected since one error in one mortgage could cause the whole block to be rejected resulting in protracted delays. If this "legal transfer" approach is adopted one of two alternatives should be considered—either to securitise only "seasoned" mortgages whose details are known to be accurate, or to obtain the trustee's consent to there being a period of delay before the Scottish fixed charges are put in place. The fees for registering a block of mortgages are currently only a few hundred pounds. However, it is possible that the Scottish Land Registry will in the future take the view that this should be increased so as to fall into line with the English system.

Due to the inflexibility, potential administrative delays and costs of legal transfers an alternative structure has been devised employing the concept of a "trust," which Scottish law does recognise. Using this method, following the sale of the mortgage portfolio, the originator undertakes to hold the Standard Security (the Scottish equivalent of a mortgage) on trust for the SPV. Under Scottish law this gives the SPV enforceable rights similar to those afforded by equity in English law which survive the receivership or liquidation of the originator.

The SPV will in turn undertake that it holds its beneficial interest in the Standard Security on trust for the lenders/investors, thus creating a "sub-trust." The SPV will agree to enforce its rights under the main trust as directed by the lenders/investors/security trustee and, ultimately, to make a full assignation of the Standard Security. These rights will be enforceable against a receiver or liquidator of the SPV (and, through the SPV or its receiver or liquidator, against the originator or its receiver or liquidator). In addition, the SPV will create a floating charge over its interest in the Standard Security.

The sale of the Standard Securities to the SPV and the charging of those Standard Securities by the SPV to the lenders/investors are not made by way of full registered assignations. This avoids increased administrative expenses, delays in registration of up to one year and the need to give notice to the borrowers.

(ii) *Hire purchase receivables:* Although the structure of a securitisation of hire purchase receivables is similar to that used in England, there will be differences arising from the need to use the "trust" method of transferring title to the assets/receivables. In this structure also two trusts are created. The first is effected by the originator declaring that it holds the receivables on trust for the receivables trustee absolutely, with effect from the closing date. The second is created by the receivables trustee declaring that it holds the receivables as a bare trustee for the SPV and for any other beneficiary (usually the originator) according to their respective entitlements. In this case the property subject to the trust will be the rights of the receivables trustee under the first trust.

A trust will be properly constituted only when all of the necessary elements have been put in place. First, the declaration must be in writing and must be drafted in terms which describe the exact property which is to be made subject to the trusts. This declaration will not of itself create a trust over that property, i.e., the underlying debts, since it is axiomatic in Scots law that a trust cannot be created without delivery of the property or the equivalent of delivery. When a person declares himself trustee of his own property, the equivalent of delivery is "intimation" to the beneficiary. For this to be effective it is essential that all of the items of property to which the intimation relates are already in existence and must be referred to in the intimation. Once constituted, the trust will prevail over the rights of any liquidator, administrator or receiver and should not be vulnerable to attack as an unfair preference or gratuitous alienation if full value is given.

The only third party who may become entitled to a receivable in priority to the receivables trustee as beneficiary under the first trust is what is known under Scottish law as a "bona fide onerous transferee without notice" of the trust. This equates to the position in English law whereby the rights of an equitable assignee can only be defeated by a bona fide purchaser for value without notice or "equity's darling." In the absence of fraud or mistake by the originator, this risk should not become a problem.

Notice need not be given to the hirer; if, however, it were given it would prevent the hirer from prevailing against the trust in respect of any rights acquired after its creation. Rights of set-off would arise if notice were not given and three such rights exist in Scots law—compensation, balancing of accounts and insolvency, and retention. As in England, nothing can be done to avoid rights of set-off which arose before the trust was created. One important distinction between the trust and an equitable assignment is that in Scotland notice to a hirer does not oblige him to pay the receivables trustee directly.

2. Insolvency Considerations

Under Scottish common law a gratuitous alienation (roughly equivalent to a transaction at an undervalue under English law) is open to challenge on the insolvency of the person making it, regardless of when it was made. Such a challenge can be made by any creditor, or any person representing creditors such as a liquidator. The person making the challenge must show that the debtor is insolvent at the time of the challenge and either was insolvent at the time of the alienation or was made insolvent by it, that the alienation was made without adequate consideration and that the alienation was to the prejudice of the challenging creditor.

This common law right has been embodied in statute by Section 242 of the Insolvency Act 1986. Under Section 242(3), a two- or five-year limit applies to any challenge (five years in the case of associates) and it is unnecessary for the challenging creditors to show insolvency at the date of alienation. There are two main defences stated in Section 242(4)(a) and (b): that immediately, or at any other time, after the alienation the company's assets were greater than its liabilities or that the alienation was made for adequate consideration.

Under Scottish common law an unfair or fraudulent preference can be challenged on the insolvency of the grantor. Any creditor of the insolvent or his representative may challenge voluntary transactions by which, after insolvency of the debtor, another creditor receives a preference. The strongest common law defence to a challenge is showing that the transaction involved *nova debita*, that is the parties undertook reciprocal transactions for full consideration.

The statutory power under Scottish law to challenge unfair or fraudulent preferences is now contained in Section 243 of the Insolvency Act 1986. There is a time limit of six months before the date of winding up, and it must be shown that the effect of the transaction is to create a preference in favour of a particular creditor, but there is no need to establish the debtor's insolvency. The important defence is provided by Section 243(2)(c) where the parties to the transaction are under reciprocal obligations for full consideration (unless the transaction was aimed at prejudicing the general body of creditors). The adequacy of consideration must be measured by the price paid for the Scottish receivables. A discount to allow for credit, bad debts and the like is not inconsistent with full consideration being paid.

FRANCE

Introduction

Asset securitisation in France has been the subject of specific legislation: law No. 88-1201 of 23 December 1988 (the "Law of 1988") and decree No. 89-158 of 9 March 1989 (the "Decree of 1989") which have created a strict regulatory environment for securitisation.

Up to July 1992, 37 issues had been launched. In total, approximately Fr 22.4 billion of debts have been securitised, representing Fr 9.3 billion of consumer loans, Fr 9.5 billion of interbank loans, Fr 1.5 billion of loans to provincial authorities, Fr 1.1 billion of industrial loans (two issues) and Fr 1 billion of residential mortgages (one issue only).

The slow development of asset securitisation in France compared to the UK is generally attributed to a number of factors, notably the lack of suitable high yielding assets. For instance, residential mortgage portfolios in France, unlike the UK, are not necessarily suitable for securitisation due to the system of state interest rate subsidies in the sector, the effect of which would make securities backed by such mortgages *prima facie* uncompetitive with other investments available in the market.

The Law of 1988 has now been amended by law No. 93-6 of 4 January 1993 (the "Law of 1993") which makes the legal framework of securitisation less rigid. Since governmental decrees will have to be passed to implement some of the rules set out in the Law of 1993 and, at the time of writing, these have yet to be published, it is not possible for the moment to have a clear picture of all the applicable rules, as will be seen below. However, the overall scheme is already in existence.

As a result of the rigidity of the regulatory framework of the Law of 1988 some transactions have been launched outside the territorial effect of the Law of 1988 using offshore SPVs and private international placings. It is difficult to ascertain precise details of such transactions because of their confidential nature, but one significant transaction for Renault used this means. Overall the importance of offshore transactions appears to be marginal (a few billion Fr at the most) but this could change if securitisation develops further in France, partly as a result of the amendments to the Law of 1988 made by the Law of 1993. This section of the chapter will deal only with securitisation schemes falling under the Law of 1988 as amended.

1. The Assets

(a) Nature and type of assets. The Law of 1988 provides that the assets/receivables which can be securitised are those held by financial institutions or, since the Law of 1993, insurance companies representing debts owed to them by their clients (either individuals or corporate clients).

These debts, under the Decree of 1989, must have a minimum initial life of two years and must not be considered as fixed assets or be in litigation or be likely to default. Each "package" of debts sold must also be of the same type (i.e., car loans, mortgages, etc.) so that they represent an homogenous portfolio. The two-year restriction has meant that many securitisable receivables cannot be financed through "Fonds Communs de Créances" ("FCCs") and resulted in a narrower usage of this technique than might have been expected. However, the Law of 1993 provides that the requirements as to the characteristics of the debts will be defined in a future decree. It is expected by the financial community that the two-year requirement will be repealed.

The servicing of the debts is normally continued by agreement by the originator or seller of the debts. It is possible to transfer this task to another person but only if, at the time of the assignment, the underlying debtor accepts in writing the change in servicing. This requirement has not been changed by the Law of 1993 and could theoretically be a drawback if the originator/servicer becomes insolvent. The servicer can be remunerated by way of a fee.

(b) Transfer of debts. There is only one method recognised by the Law of 1988 for the transfer of the debts, which derives from the 1981 law on the assignment of trade receivables to financial institutions, known as "Loi Dailly." The mechanism is very simple: the assignor fills in a form, the format of which is set out in the Decree of 1989, which must identify the debts assigned. The form is delivered by the assignor to the assignee and mere delivery transfers the debts between the parties. The assignment is enforceable as against third parties as of the date of delivery of this form.

The Law of 1988 provides that the debtors must be notified of the assignment by means of a simple letter, but does not provide for any time limit for issuing the notice nor for any sanction if this obligation is not complied with. After the notice has been issued, the assignor will normally still continue to collect the debts.

However, even though notice is given to the debtor, the assignment of the debt does not prevent the debtor raising (as against the assignee) any legal or contractual set-off rights which it may have against the assignor. To cover the risk on a securitisation of the debtor successfully raising a set-off claim, a guarantee is often provided to the assignee.

On the transfer of a mortgage over land, the transfer of the benefit of a "registered" security such as a residential mortgage could theoretically give rise to difficulties in terms of enforceability vis-a-vis third parties because of the imprecise drafting of the Law of 1988. However, these difficulties have been remedied by the Law of 1993, which provides that the transfer form will transfer title to the security and that this transfer will be enforceable against third parties without any formalities being necessary.

(c) Tax issues on transfer.

(i) *Stamp duty:* An assignment of debts made by simple contract between the assignor and the assignee does not have to be registered. If the assignment contract is voluntarily registered or is made by notarised deed, registry tax will be due at the fixed amount of Fr 500.

(ii) *Value added tax ("VAT"):* The sale of debts is exempt from VAT.

2. Basic Structural Considerations

(a) Legal aspects. The Law of 1988 provides that financial institutions (and now insurance companies) can assign certain debts to FCCs. These entities do not have a separate legal personality and are managed by a company (the "Manager") whose sole purpose is the management of FCCs. Under the Law of 1993, the Manager must be approved by the French stock exchange authority, the Commission des Opérations de Bourse ("COB"). The assignor of the debts cannot hold, directly or indirectly, more than one-third of the issued share capital of the FCC and must not be in control of it by any other means. The Manager is not the custodian of the FCC's assets. These are deposited generally with a third party credit institution in France (the "Depositary"). The Depositary has two roles to play in a transaction: first, to look after the assets of the FCC (the debts and the cash they generate) and, second, to supervise the Manager and ensure its decisions are "regular."

The creation of an FCC was, under the Law of 1988, subject to the prior approval of the COB. In this context, the COB would act upon the advice of the Banque de France which would check that the transaction met all legal and regulatory requirements and would examine the transaction documentation and the financial arrangements of the FCC. This procedure has been simplified by the Law of 1993, which has removed the need to involve the Banque de France and provides that the Manager and Depositary have to issue a "note d'information" (prospectus) for the subscribers of the units issued by the FCC. Such "note d'information" must receive the "visa" (prior approval) of the COB before the issue is launched: this means that FCC public issues are now subject to the same administrative supervision as any ordinary security issues. However, the Law of 1993 has maintained the requirement set out in the Law of 1988 that the units issued by the FCC should be rated by an approved rating agency.

An FCC does not have a minimum capital requirement because it is not a legal being. The amount of units issued should match (except for expenses) the amount of the debts acquired. The FCC is not required to make a minimum taxable profit since it is not subject to tax. Profits of the FCC are distributed to its investors under the terms provided in the articles of association of the FCC.

After the issue of securities to fund the acquisition of the debts, the FCC cannot borrow or sell the debts it has acquired. Under the Law of 1988, it was necessarily a "one-off" structure which had to be wound up and liquidated at the latest within six months of the last debt being extinguished because it could not buy any debts after the issue of the units. The Law of 1993 has introduced, in principle, the right for an FCC to acquire new debts but rules governing the way in which such acquisitions will take place have yet to be published. When debts are repaid, the FCC can also invest the moneys until the FCC's liquidation or the next payment on the units, but there are limitations as to the type of securities in which the FCC can invest. These limitations might be changed by the new decree.

It should be noted that an FCC is not necessarily a "pass-through" structure: a surplus of cash can arise during the life of the transaction (e.g., in the form of interest earned on investments made with debts repaid during the life of the FCC). It is possible that a 1 percent tax ("droit de partage") may be due on the division of any surplus among unit holders on the liquidation of an FCC.

Finally, an FCC must have accounts which are audited. The auditors' task and duties in this regard are comparable to the ones which they have vis-a-vis the shareholders of a company.

(b) Accounting aspects. The assignment of receivables under the regime of the Law of 1988 is given a favourable accounting treatment: article 6 of regulation No. 89-07 of 26 July 1989 of the "Comité de la Règlementation Bancaire" (the financial institutions' administrative regulatory authority) provides expressly that the debts assigned to an FCC are taken off the assignor bank's balance sheet even where the assignor has acquired subordinated securities issued by the FCC as credit enhancement or has given a guarantee to the FCC or has a right over the liquidation surplus (if any) of the FCC. However, where a guarantee is given, it must be recorded in the assignor's profit and loss account and appear as an off-balance sheet commitment in the notes to its accounts. If the assignor has a right over the liquidation surplus of the FCC, it must be recorded as an asset in its balance sheet. However, this preferential treatment could be open to question for several reasons. For instance, it could be argued that, when the assignor has a right over the liquidation surplus, it has de facto control over the FCC and should be obliged to consolidate the FCC in its accounts, which could defeat one objective of the transaction. The banking authorities ("Commission Bancaire") have not questioned the existing FCC issues on this ground and do not seem likely to do so in the near future. Nevertheless, there is uncertainty on this matter which might be remedied by the new decree.

(c) Regulatory constraints. In view of the nature of the securitisation market in France and the desire of the French authorities to provide protection to subscribers of units in FCCs, it was compulsory under the Law of 1988 for the FCC to provide credit enhancement to protect subscribers against default risk. There were several methods of doing so: a bank guarantee or letter of credit or pool insurance from an appropriate insurance company; overcollateralisation with the assignor selling to the FCC an amount of receivables which exceeds the amount of debt securities it issues; or the issue by the FCC of subordinated units which bear the first loss on any principal shortfall on the underlying debts. Of these three methods, the first and third have been widely used. The subordinated securities are usually subscribed for by the assignor itself, which of course contradicts the principle that the assignor is fully transferring the debts and the risks they bear. Surprisingly this has not so far prevented off-balance sheet treatment being granted under regulation No. 89-07.

Pursuant to the Law of 1993, the permitted credit enhancement techniques will probably be changed in the future decree and it is not yet certain whether such credit enhancement will be compulsory.

The Law of 1988 prohibits the taking of security over the debts acquired by an FCC. Thus, investors in the securities issued by an FCC will not have the benefit of a security interest in the underlying debts. However, this is not a real concern given the nature of the FCC and the constraints on its activities.

Finally, the previous requirement that the FCC units be of a minimum amount of Fr 10,000 has been lifted by the Law of 1993.

3. Credit and Securities Regulation

(a) Data protection and consumer law. There are provisions under French law which protect consumers who are unable to pay their debts and give wide powers to the courts to impose reductions of the debts, grace periods and payment moratoria; these provisions continue to apply after the assignment of any debts. Similarly, the FCC (in reality, the Manager and the Depositary) will also be bound by the rules restricting the use of electronic data banks for commercial purposes known as "loi informatique et libertés."

(b) Securities regulation. FCC units are treated as ordinary "valeurs mobilières" (securities) and can therefore be placed domestically or internationally, publicly or privately, in accordance with standard practice. Public placing of the units is not compulsory but, at the moment, units with a nominal value in excess of Fr 1 million must be listed. The entity in charge of the operation of the stock exchange, known as "Conseil des Bourses de Valeurs," has issued detailed rules on the admission to the stock exchange list of FCC securities. One main difference on the listing of securities by an FCC compared with other securities is that the COB's regulations of 1989 provide that there can be a public placing of an issue of FCC units where there are more than 25 original subscribers (whereas the figure is 300 for other securities).

A prospectus giving the details of any FCC must be provided to the subscribers of both publicly listed and privately placed securities. In September 1989 the COB issued an "instruction" setting out detailed requirements on the information to be disclosed. The requirements are naturally more stringent in the case of a public placing, but the subscriber must be provided with full information on the transaction.

It is unlikely that these rules will be fundamentally changed once the decree implementing the Law of 1993 is passed but there may be some modifications.

4. Insolvency Considerations

(a) The FCC. As it is not a legal body, it cannot be subject to any insolvency proceedings.

(b) The assignor. As a matter of law in France, if the sale of the receivables took place where there had been a preference or fraud, the sale could be annulled by a court, either acting on its own or upon the request of any interested party, provided that the sale took place within 18 months of the commencement of the insolvency proceedings.

(c) The Manager and the Depositary. When considering whether to approve an FCC, the COB takes into account the financial and technical capacities of the Manager and the Depositary. In practice, given the nature of the entities that take on such roles, their insolvency during the life of the FCC is a relatively unlikely event. However, if insolvency does occur, it would probably not cause a major problem to the transaction since neither the Manager nor the Depositary has any direct financial commitment to the FCC. This aspect is obviously considered carefully by the rating agencies in transactions which involve them.

5. Tax

(a) The FCC. The FCC is an unincorporated entity established specifically to acquire debts owned by financial institutions or insurance companies. It issues units to investors who receive a payment stream backed by the flow of receivables paid to the FCC. After the issue of units, the FCC can invest only to manage its cash. The FCC is not subject to corporation tax.

(b) The assignor. For the assignor, the transfer of debts to the FCC is treated as an outright sale. The difference between the sale price and the net book value of the debts will give rise to a taxable gain (at the rate of 33.33 percent) or deductible loss for the seller.

(c) Investors. Investors will be taxed in accordance with their nature and residence. Different rules and rates apply to French corporate and individual investors as well as certain non profit-making entities and special investment vehicles such as SICAVs or FCPs. Genuine non French-resident investors will usually be exempt from withholding tax on income or tax on capital gains. Distributions of surplus on the winding up of an FCC may be subject to withholding tax unless an applicable double tax treaty provides effective relief.

BELGIUM

Introduction

Securitisation of receivables has not to date occurred in Belgium due to a number of legal obstacles that impede its efficient structuring. However, the Belgian business and financial community as a whole sees securitisation as being a useful tool to tidy up balance sheets and to obtain relatively low cost funding. As a result of pressures from various entities, new laws have been enacted and other draft statutes are still under consideration by Parliament to facilitate securitisation by way of assignment. An alternative technique involves the SPV acquiring rights in respect of the underlying debts by way of subrogation (Code Civil, Articles 1249-1252). The application of this technique to securitisation, while innovative in Belgium, is receiving more interest as it may avoid some of the difficulties currently associated with assignments of assets/receivables.

1. The Assets/Receivables

(a) Transfer of assets/receivables. The main legal constraints at present which hinder securitisation under Belgian law are:

(i) For an assignment of assets/receivables to be effective and enforceable against third parties (including the underlying debtor), the assignment must be notified to the debtor by a bailiff delivering a notice of assignment or it must be accepted by the debtor in a notarised deed (Code Civil, Article 1690) ("Article 1690"). These formalities are cumbersome and relatively expensive and from a practical point of view complying with such requirements where there are hundreds or thousands of loans has effectively prevented securitisation of Belgian receivables taking place.

(ii) For mortgage-backed securities, Article 5 of the 1851 Act on Mortgages ("Article 5") requires a transfer to be noted explicitly in the margin of the registration deed of the mortgage at the public register of mortgages ("conservation des hypothèques"). Again, for a transaction involving many mortgages this is a cumbersome and expensive procedure.

In order to get around the difficulties caused by Article 1690, a draft statute (dated 15 February 1991) proposes to make an assignment of assets/receivables effective and enforceable against third parties (excluding the debtor himself) simply by the execution of an assignment agreement. The assignment would be enforceable by the assignee against the debtor only after the existence of the agreement has come to the debtor's knowledge. If a debtor, in good faith, were to pay the assignor before the assignment had been brought to his knowledge, he would be validly released from his debt and would be entitled to defeat any claims the assignee might make against him.

Article 51 of the Law of 4 August 1992 in respect of mortgage-backed loans provides that the formalities imposed by Article 5 are not applicable to the securitisation of a portfolio of such loans. However, only the assignor of the loan is entitled to exercise the mortgage rights on behalf of the assignee. The mortgage rights are exercisable by the assignee (or their exercise may be further transferred) only after the marginal notation required by Article 5 has been effected.

In addition, the Law of 12 June 1991 in respect of consumer credits which has been modified by the Law of 6 July 1992 provides that in order for an assignment of a consumer loan to be valid as against third parties, the underlying debtor must be notified of the assignment by a registered letter. This approach is not the same as that proposed in the draft statute to amend Article 1690 discussed above, which simply requires that an assignment of receivables is valid against the underlying debtor the moment the assignment is brought to the knowledge of the debtor and is valid against third parties the moment the actual assignment is entered into. However, notifying the debtor by registered letter is one way of ensuring that the assignment is brought to the debtor's knowledge.

(b) Tax issues on transfer of assets

(i) *Registration tax:* An assignment of mortgage-backed receivables will attract a registration tax of 1 percent of the nominal amount of the assets transferred.

(ii) *VAT:* A transfer of assets to the SPV will not be regarded as a taxable supply. It is worth noting that an SPV established in Belgium will normally not be a VAT taxpayer since it will have no activities which are subject to VAT. Any VAT charged to it (normally at 19.5 percent) for certain supplies of goods or services will, therefore, not be recoverable.

2. Basic Structural Considerations

(a) Legal aspects. The Law of 4 December 1990 in respect of financial transactions and financial markets creates a legal framework for collective investment undertakings and it has been proposed that this law be amended to permit special purpose companies to be established for use in securitisation. The Law of 5 August 1992 provides that two types of SPV can be established and organised as a "receivables unit trust" either on a contractual basis or in the form of a statute based corporation. The first is a contractual entity known as an "investment fund of receivables" (the "Contractual SPV") while the other is a statutory entity known as a "company for investment in receivables" (the "Statutory SPV"). A Statutory SPV can take the form of a corporation with limited liability or a partnership limited by shares.

Both Contractual SPVs and Statutory SPVs fall under the Law of 4 December 1990 and are subject to the general regulatory provisions of that law and applicable decrees. They would, as a result, be subject to the detailed regulations and supervision of the Banking and Finance Commission which has the power to review, and must approve, the management structure, charter and bylaws of all such vehicles.

A management company is required for both Contractual SPVs and Statutory SPVs. A single management company can manage several SPVs and its role would simply be to advise the relevant SPV on all questions of a commercial and financial nature and to collect payments on the receivables. In addition, the SPV will be required to use the services of a depositary which will hold the assets as a custodian on its behalf. The depositary would serve as an additional safeguard to investors and watch over the activities of the management company. In this respect, the proposed Belgian legislation follows that in France for FCCs.

(b) Regulatory and accounting aspects. Although the Banking and Finance Commission has not, as yet, issued guidelines in respect of the regulation of the securitisation market, it is generally expected that it will issue guidelines along similar lines to those of the Bank of England. However, under regulations currently in force, the Banking and Finance Commission has ruled that zero weighting of a securitised loan portfolio (through an assignment to a foreign SPV) for capital adequacy purposes requires that the risks of the assets be transferred "in a complete and final manner." Similarly no special accounting rules for securitisation have, as yet, been laid down. In respect of off-balance sheet financing generally, the transaction must be structured in such a way that any asset purported to be transferred off the balance sheet of a selling company, will only be regarded as being off-balance sheet if, upon a liquidation of the selling company, a liquidator could not claim ownership rights in respect of that asset.

3. Credit and Security Regulation

(a) Consumer credit and data protection legislation. Depending upon the type of asset/receivables to be securitised, a Contractual SPV and a Statutory SPV would require authorisations under consumer credit and mortgage-backed loans legislation. A Royal Decree of 20 November 1992 regulates the use of data in respect of consumer credits. A general law in respect of data protection of 10 December 1992 is expected to enter into force in March 1993. While the consumer is entitled to ensure that accurate information is held on him, he cannot generally prevent that information being lawfully transferred.

(b) Securities laws. Debt instruments issued by an SPV can be issued to the "public" (as defined by Royal Decree of 9 January 1991) or be privately placed. Pursuant to the Law of 5 August 1992 in respect of Contractual SPVs and Statutory SPVs, securities which have been publicly issued have to be listed on the Belgian Stock Exchange and the general rules in respect of public issues and Belgian Stock Exchange listings will apply. Essentially these provide for extensive disclosure in any prospectus and for prior approval by the Banking and Finance Commission. The law requires the quarterly publication by any SPV of its assets, liabilities and operating results.

4. Insolvency

Under Articles 445–448 of the Belgian Bankruptcy Act wide powers are granted to a court to intervene in any transaction depending upon the particular circumstances. Thus, if the transaction was made fraudulently to the detriment of creditors, a court can hold that the transaction is void *ab initio.* If the transactions were made by a debtor within a period of six months before the debtor was declared insolvent by the court, the transactions are voidable by the court if the party with whom the transaction was made had knowledge of the impending insolvency. Equally, a court under the Belgian Bankruptcy Act has power to recharacterise the sale of the assets/receivables from the assignor to the SPV as one of loan and security rather than true sale and could rescind the assignor's obligations under the sale agreement with the SPV.

5. Security Considerations

Under Belgian law it is difficult for investors in securities issued by an SPV to hold any security interest in the underlying assets purchased by the SPV for two reasons. First, the concept of a security trust is not recognised under Belgian law. Second, any security interest in receivables is subject to the same requirements as an assignment of the receivables and, according to court decisions, a pledge of receivables can only be perfected if the pledgee holds "possession" of the assets pledged to him. In the context of a pledge of a large portfolio of hundreds or possibly thousands of receivables, possession by the pledgee is not practicable. Accordingly, under the draft statute of 15 February 1991, possession by the pledgee would be deemed to result from the mere execution of the pledge instrument and the pledge would be enforceable against the underlying debtor only after he had been given notice of its existence. However, once the pledge is made and validly perfected, the pledgee will have preference over other creditors in respect of the pledged receivables.

6. Tax Issues

(a) For the SPV. If the SPV is a Statutory SPV it will be subject to corporation tax on any profits it may make at the standard tax rates applicable under Belgian law for corporations. If the SPV is a Contractual SPV its profits will be taxed on the same basis as its management company.

(b) For the investor. The Law of 5 August 1992 on the establishment of SPVs provides that all payments of interest to investors in issued securities must be subject to a 10 percent withholding tax. Belgian tax resident investors will obtain a tax credit from these withholdings against their Belgian tax liabilities, but securities issued by such SPVs may be unattractive to foreign investors as a result of the withholding tax.

(c) For the assignor. Receipt of the purchase money by the assignor in respect of the receivables will not give rise to any taxable profit or deductible loss if the sale was made at a price equal to the book value of the receivables in the assignor's balance sheet at the date of transfer.

GERMANY

Introduction

Unlike France, there is no special legal framework for the securitisation of assets in Germany. However, asset securitisation is, as a matter of German law, possible. It appears that so far only one transaction involving the securitisation of German assets has been completed. It is fair to say that as yet asset-backed securitisation in Germany has not been of great interest to German banks. This is partly due to the fact that while banks in most European jurisdictions sometimes have difficulties meeting capital ratio requirements this is not yet a concern for most of the German banks. In addition, the asset-backed market has yet to prove that it can provide German financial institutions with cheaper funding costs than the markets that already exist and with which they are familiar. However, the fact that German assets have actually been securitised coupled with stronger international competition and new market demands could see a renewal of interest in such structures for assets originated in Germany.

1. The Assets

Types and transferability of assets/receivables. There are no legal considerations in Germany that would necessarily eliminate any of the types of assets that have customarily been securitised in other countries. Loans are generally freely assignable in Germany without the consent of the debtor, unless the loan documentation requires such consent or prohibits the assignment. An assignment does not require notice to the debtor, but notice is necessary in order to exclude the debtor's right to discharge his obligations by payment to the assignor.

Despite the giving of notice of the assignment to the underlying debtor, under German law the underlying debtor will still be able to raise against the assignee any defences or rights of set-off that he has against the assignor. However, the underlying debtor may only set off such claims that he had already acquired before he was notified of the assignment or, broadly speaking, which are due before the debt assigned falls due.

The assignment of unsecured receivables does not usually require any filings or approvals with any regulatory authority. In addition, no fees or stamp duties are payable in relation to the assignment and the sale of receivables will be VAT exempt.

2. Basic Structural Considerations

(a) Legal aspects. In both the UK and France asset-backed securities issuers are established by the forming of special purpose vehicle companies or trust funds. German law does not recognise the concept of trusts. The most appropriate legal structure for a German SPV would probably be a limited partnership (Kommanditgesellschaft) of which the general partner is a limited company (Gesellschaft mit beschränkter Haftung). While an entity (called GmbH & Co. KG) provides advantages from a tax point of view, there can also be a number of difficulties. First, the GmbH & Co. KG set up for the purpose of loan securitisation may qualify as a bank under para.1 sec.1/7 of the Kreditwesengesetz (Banking Act) which provides that entering into an obligation to buy receivables generated by loan contracts before they fall due is considered to be banking business. The second problem in using a GmbH & Co. KG as an SPV is that the company will be subject to trade tax (see later under "Tax").

(b) Accounting and regulatory aspects. There are no specific accounting regulations for asset-backed securitisation in Germany. However, the general rules for off-balance sheet financing are that a seller of an asset will be regarded as having removed that asset from its balance sheet if it does not retain any rights in the asset, e.g., there is no right to have the assets retransferred nor is there an option to ask for a retransfer. If the seller of the assets is a German bank it will be important to obtain correct treatment of the transaction for bank regulatory purposes. The German Banking Supervisory Authority has not to date issued specific regulations for the transfer of loans off-balance sheet. In any case, the desired off-balance sheet regulatory treatment for the seller of the assets could only be achieved if the transaction qualified as a "true sale" by the selling bank for accounting purposes and if the SPV was not owned or controlled by the bank to an extent requiring consolidation under accounting rules. Further conditions will also have to be met.

There appears, however, to be some concern on the Federal Banking Supervisory Authority's part that even if the transaction qualified as a "true sale" by the selling bank, some residual obligations could remain with the selling bank and that, therefore, assets sold could nevertheless not be totally ignored for capital ratio requirements.

3. Other Regulatory Issues

(a) Data protection/banker's duty of confidentiality. A practical problem with assigning financial assets may arise under German data protection legislation. These laws contain restrictions on the disclosure of personal data (data on individuals) to the assignee and other parties, such as rating agencies. The basic principle of the German data protection legislation is that data may be disclosed to a third party which has a legitimate interest in knowing the information. This rule should allow the disclosure of such information to the assignee as is necessary to enable an assignee to assert and enforce the assigned claims. It will probably not, however, permit giving details of individual debtors to rating agencies other than by code to enable them to evaluate the pool of the assigned assets. Further, any banker's duty of confidentiality would have to be complied with. German bank general business conditions require the customer's explicit consent before any information about the customer can be passed on to third parties.

(b) Securities laws. Under the German Prospectus Act, the public offer of debt securities in Germany generally requires the publication of a prospectus at the time the offering commences. Certain exemptions are provided, notably for Euroissues.

Where the securities issued are denominated in Deutsche Marks, they would need to comply with the Bundesbank requirements for the issue of DM-denominated securities. The requirements, among other things, include a minimum term of two years for DM-denominated debt securities issued by foreign credit institutions. There is not, however, a requirement for German law to be the governing law of the issue nor are the securities required to be listed on one of the German stock exchanges.

4. Insolvency

In the event of the bankruptcy of the originator or the SPV the receiver appointed has no right to re-characterise the sale between the originator and the SPV provided that, on the basis of the tests referred to in 2(b) above, it cannot be regarded as a secured loan. Under German law the overriding concern is to protect the interests of creditors and consequently the receiver may set aside any contract which was entered into to defraud creditors or which was made at an undervalue.

5. Security

The creation of a security interest in the assets themselves should not pose any problems under German law. The customary way of granting a security interest in a receivable is to assign the obligation to the secured party. In an asset securitisation transaction, this would generally be the trustee, acting for the benefit of the investors.

6. Tax

Under recent legislation, it is unlikely that payments in respect of underlying financial assets would be subject to withholding tax. Payments made by a German SPV to the holders of asset-backed securities could, however, be subject to withholding tax. For a German SPV, the transaction will need to be structured so as to avoid both corporate income and trade taxes payable by the issuer. The trade tax (Gewerbesteuer) is a local tax based on income and net assets. Its rate varies depending on the municipality. Only 50 percent of interest payments on long-term debts (such as bonds) are deductible for the purposes of calculating the SPV's income subject to trade tax.

SPAIN

Introduction

Asset-backed financing is not a new concept for Spanish financial institutions. Mortgages have been used to secure credit in the past, but normally with recourse to the original lender. The most widespread forms of asset-refinancing used in the last few years in Spain have been various assignments of credits (mainly commercial credits) by financial institutions to their clients. The Royal Decree 1,289 of 2 August 1991 (the "August Decree") has further developed Spain's Mortgage Market Law of 1981 (the "1981 Law"). Its aim was to promote and liberalise the secondary mortgage market by broadening the range of potential issuers and clearing the way for the removal of mortgage loans from the balance sheet of originating institutions through the use of "Participaciones Hipotecarias" (mortgage stakes) created by the 1981 Law.

Prior to the August Decree, mortgage loan transfers had been confined to a limited group of banking institutions whose mortgages represented more than 30 percent of their loan portfolio; and the mortgage bond market was restricted to the issue of the so-called "cédulas" by such banking institutions. The August Decree widened the category of potential originators and confirmed the creation of Participaciones Hipotecarias ("PHs") as an effective way to remove mortgages from the balance sheet of the originator issuing them. The August Decree helped in the development of a mortgage-backed securities market, with issues by Banco Bilbao Vizcaya (BBV), Citibank Espana, Banco Santander and Citifin. These changes, however, were insufficient as they did not address two major issues which are important if the market is to develop further: the insolvency rule relating to the so-called "black period" and withholding tax problems.

These issues have now been addressed by Law 19/1992 of 7 July, (the "1992 Law") together with the creation of a domestic mortgage securitisation structure involving an insolvency remote "Fondo de Titulizacion Hipotecaria" ("Fondo") (a form of mutual fund) and a "Gestora" (management company).

1. The Assets

Types and transferability of assets/receivables. Generally, there are no constraints on the removal of debts from a balance sheet. The principle under Spanish law is that debts can be assigned absolutely, although this must be done on an arm's length basis. It is, therefore, acceptable to remove any debt/mortgage loan from the balance sheet of the originator and replace it with the cash consideration received from the SPV for the assignment. There appear to be no particular rules which must be observed to obtain off-balance sheet treatment provided that there is a genuine sale.

Under Spanish law, the benefit of a contract can be assigned without the assignor obtaining the consent of the other contracting party. Furthermore, there is not even any requirement in the case of such an assignment to notify the other party that the transfer has taken place. However, failure to notify means that payment by the debtor to the assignor will discharge his obligations.

However, even though it is possible to assign the benefit of the contract without consent, if the assets to which it refers are subject to some security which needs registration, notification to the borrower will be necessary. For such a right to be transferred the relevant register would have to be changed to show the new assignee. In this sense, the August Decree has effectively encouraged the securitisation of mortgages over land through the creation of PHs without the need to alter the underlying registration details, especially where the purchaser is a Fondo.

2. Basic Structural Considerations

(a) Legal aspects. Spanish law does not recognise the concept of a trust. Therefore, before the 1992 Law came into force, the use of an off-balance sheet Spanish resident charitable trust-owned SPV as transferee and issuer was difficult to achieve in practical terms. Four different structures were used in Spain prior to the 1992 Law: (i) The direct placing of PHs with no intermediate vehicle (BBV); (ii) the issue of PHs to an intermediate vehicle (Banco Santander); (iii) sub-participation (Citifin); (iv) the placing of percentage interests in a non-corporate "comunidad de bienes" (community of assets) (Citibank Espana).

Law 19/1992 provides for the following Spanish resident structure:

(i) A Fondo (which is not a separate legal entity) purchases the PHs from the originator with funds received from a bond issue ("Bonos de Titulizacion Hipotecaria").

A new Fondo must be created for each issue. Consequently, the Fondo's assets must have the same maturity as the bonds it issues. Substitution is permitted if expressly contemplated by the documentation but is limited in that funds so used must derive from PHs which have been prepaid.

(ii) The Fondo is administered by the Gestora. The creation of a Gestora requires authorisation from the Ministry of Economy and Finance and must be registered at the Comision Nacional del Mercado de Valores (the National Securities Market Commission). To date four Gestoras have been authorised. The Commission has stipulated in each case a minimum capital requirement of 100 million pesetas with no one shareholder holding more than 25 percent of the capital (although there has been some flexibility in applying this requirement). The four existing Gestoras are headed by Banesto, Argentaria, Banco Santander and AB Asesores. Other institutions are expected to follow suit soon.

(b) Regulatory aspects. Where the originator is not a financial institution, there are no particular rules which must be observed to obtain off-balance sheet treatment provided that there is a genuine sale or true assignment. Where the originator is a financial institution (which will usually be the case) special rules apply (Section 15 of Circular 4/1991 of the Bank of Spain). The 1981 Law provides that, for a PH to be created over an underlying mortgage and then securitised off-balance sheet, the underlying loan must have been granted for one of the following reasons:

(i) for the purchase of land which has been built on;

(ii) for the construction of buildings on the relevant land; or

(iii) for the improvement of buildings on the relevant land.

In addition, the securitised mortgage must be a first mortgage, relate to the whole of the property and must not be subject to a charge or any other encumbrance.

The significance of PHs is that the underlying costs (notarial fees, stamp duty and registration expenses) otherwise incurred by the assignment of mortgages do not apply. Each PH represents the entitlement, depending on the terms of the issue, to the benefit (or a percentage stake in the benefit) of one particular mortgage loan.

3. Insolvency

In the event of the insolvency of the originator, it is very important to be aware of the Spanish mechanisms regulating bankruptcy proceedings, as the outcome can depend on the discretion of the judge. A Spanish judge may determine that the originator became bankrupt at an earlier date than the official commencement of bankruptcy proceedings (the "black period"). If this occurs, any transaction (whether or not for value) after the date of actual bankruptcy (as determined by the judge) will be void. Unless the assignment has been notarised, the issuer (which now finds itself a creditor of the originator) will rank relatively low among the unsecured creditors.

However, the 1981 Law made an important exception to the discretionary retroactive powers of the judge in bankruptcy proceedings. The exception relates to mortgage loans and mortgages created in favour of financial entities which operate in the mortgage market. The 1981 Law provides that mortgages will not be regarded automatically as null and void, even if they fall within the retroactive bankruptcy period, and will only be invalidated if fraudulent preference is proved. The intention of the 1981 Law was to introduce a degree of certainty into the secondary mortgage market so that the potential bankruptcy of the original lender would no longer be an issue.

Unfortunately, the transfer of interests in an underlying mortgage by means of a "PH" was outside the terms of this exception. A change in the law was, therefore, imperative if mortgage securitisations were to develop in Spain, and such a change was implemented by the 1992 Law by extending the exception to the creation and transfer of the PHs.

4. Security

Under Spanish law, assets can be charged and security interests created without any special considerations. A limited number of security interests and charges are regulated by Spanish law, which draws a distinction between moveable and real property. In the case of moveable property, the possible charges are the "prenda" (a pledge which requires possession of the relevant asset or document representing it, for example a document of title); an "hipoteca mobiliaria" (where transfer of possession is not required but entry on a registry is) and a limited number of "prendas sin desplazamiento" (pledges which do not require transfer of the relevant asset or document representing it).

In the case of real property the basic form of express security interest is the "hipoteca" (mortgage) which is perceived as a guarantee (secured on immoveable property) of the performance of an obligation, which must be monetary in nature or capable of quantification in monetary terms.

5. Securities Law

In June 1988, the Spanish Parliament passed a new Act ("Ley del Mercado de Valores") regulating the securities markets. In addition, a series of regulations have implemented this Act, making up a legal framework substantially similar to that of other western countries. Article 25 of the Spanish Securities Market Act, whilst recognising the general principle of freedom of issue, authorises the Ministry of Economy and Finance to make the issue of certain types of securities in Spain subject to prior approval. The Ministry's prior approval is not required for Spanish listed peseta denominated issues by non-resident companies or institutions but the Ministry is not currently in favour of the development of a Euro-peseta market.

Companies making peseta denominated issues are subject to the requirements of the National Securities Market Commission which are based on the EC Directives applicable to listings.

6. Tax

(a) Withholding tax. The general rule under Spanish law is that any interest payment or capital gain, where the payment is made by one Spanish resident to another, gives rise to an obligation on the part of the payer to withhold a percentage (normally 25 percent). A major exception to this arises where the payments are made to a financial entity registered as such with the Bank of Spain. The exception therefore applies to institutional mortgage lenders. Consequently, payments made by mortgage borrowers in respect of their loans will be free from withholding taxes. However, payments from the originator/mortgage lender (even where it is registered as a financial entity with the Bank of Spain) to the issuing vehicle are subject to withholding tax where the issuing vehicle is Spanish resident and is not itself a registered financial entity. The 1992 Law has created an exception from withholding taxes for payments to a Fondo by the originator.

Withholding tax will apply also where the issuing vehicle is based outside Spain subject to the terms of the relevant double tax treaty between Spain and the country in question, although the level will normally be below 25 percent. This is subject to an exception in relation to non-resident legal persons or entities who have their residence in EC states other than Spain and do not operate through a permanent establishment in Spain. The exception does not, however, extend to territories listed as tax havens.

(b) Stamp duty and transfer tax. Both stamp duty and transfer taxes are payable in Spain and their applicability will depend on the particular facts. Stamp duty at a rate of 0.5 percent of the value of the asset transferred is generally applicable if details of the transfer have to be entered on a public register but stamp duty is not chargeable if the transfer is also subject to transfer tax.

Transfer tax at the rate of 1 percent is payable on the creation of mortgages over real property and, if more than 18 months remains to maturity, on transfers of such mortgages. However, an exception from transfer tax and stamp duty is available on the creation of PHs and their sale to a Fondo. The transfer of other assets (whatever their maturity) may be subject to transfer tax at higher rates (on average 4 percent) but the tax will generally not apply where an originator of business assets, e.g., car loans, sells those assets to an SPV.

ITALY

Introduction

The comparatively slow development of a securitisation market in Italy can be attributed largely to the complexities of assigning title to the assets/receivables. However, Law No. 52 of 21 February 1991 ("Law No. 52/1991") was enacted in order to simplify the procedure relating to the assignment of business receivables. Following this liberalisation there have been transactions involving Citibank receivables through Banco Commerciale Italiana, IFIM car lease receivables and Gruppo Sipi lease receivables.

1. The Assets

(a) Types and transferability of assets/receivables. To date securitisations in Italy have been restricted to trade receivables, car hire purchase and lease receivables and certain other lease receivables. No mortgage loan securitisations have been effected primarily because of the cost of registering each mortgage.

The most appropriate method of transferring the receivables from the originator to the SPV is by way of assignment. A written assignment is not necessary but the assignment will be effective against third parties and the assigned debtor only if certain formalities are complied with. Where the receivables assigned represent debts owed by the Public Administration the assignment agreement must be notarised.

Whilst no formalities are required in order for the assignment to be valid and effective between the parties, Article 1406 of the Italian Civil Code states that the assignment of contractual rights and obligations can be effected only with the consent of the debtor. Furthermore, Article 1264 provides that an assignment of receivables is effective as against the underlying debtor when he has been notified of the assignment or has accepted it. Failure to comply with these formalities entitles the debtor to be discharged from his obligations by paying the assignor directly, except where the assignee can show that the debtor is aware of the assignment having taken place.

Assignment will be ineffective as against third parties pursuant to Article 1265 unless the debtor has been "officially" notified by way of a deed having a date certain at law. A notice is considered "official" when served by a court bailiff or, possibly, by way of a public announcement expressly authorised by the court. In the event of a failure to notify, the assignment will be ineffective against any creditor or trustee in bankruptcy of the assignor.

However, the notification requirements in Article 1265 are not necessary where the transfer of receivables is made under Law No. 52/1991. This states that the assignment of receivables to a "factoring company" should be deemed effective as against third parties provided that the assignor carries on a business activity and the assigned receivables are related to this activity, the assignee is a "factoring company" and the payment of the purchase price has been effected on a date certain at law. A "factoring company" is defined as a company registered as such with the Bank of Italy and with a capital of at least 2 billion lire and whose corporate objects permit the purchase of the receivables.

Under Italian law rights of set-off occur only between two debts consisting of a sum of money or quantity of fungible assets of the same type, both of which are liquid and collectable. Article 1248 defines when a right of set-off can arise between the originator and the debtor in the case of an assignment. If the debtor has accepted the assignment unconditionally he is prevented from setting-off against the assignee the claims which he could have set-off against the assignor. Where the debtor has been notified of the assignment he is prevented from setting-off claims which arise after the notice. Finally, if the debtor has neither accepted the assignment nor been notified of it, he could continue to set-off claims against the assignor against obligations arising from the receivables both before and after the assignment.

There are no approvals or filings to be made in order for the SPV to obtain valid title to the receivables.

(b) Tax issues on the transfer of assets. The agreements effecting the assignments are subject to a 0.5 percent registration tax and to stamp duty of 10,000 lire for every four pages of documentation, unless the agreements are executed outside Italy or by an exchange of letters. However, in the case of assignments of sums owed by the State these taxes may arise whether or not the assignment is executed offshore or by exchange of letters. If the agreements are subsequently filed in an Italian court, so as to be enforced against third parties, they become subject to registration tax and stamp duty at that time.

No VAT is payable on the assignment as the transfer of receivables is not regarded as a supply.

2. Basic Structural Considerations

(a) Legal aspects. Until recently trusts were not recognised by Italian law and it was not possible to give effect to a receivables trust corresponding to that used in the structure for non-mortgage securitisations in the UK. This position has changed following the ratification of the Hague Convention on the Recognition of Trusts dated 1 July 1985. However, as no practical application of the Convention has yet occurred, the response of the Italian courts in relation to trusts is difficult to predict. Therefore, to date, the SPV has always been constituted through the incorporation of a company rather than by the creation of a trust.

In general, there is no minimum capital requirement for the SPV nor a minimum level of taxable profits. However, in order to gain the benefits provided by Law No. 52/1991 the SPV must be incorporated under Italian law and have a minimum subscribed capital of 2 billion lire (which would require a minimum paid-in capital, at the time of incorporation, of 600 million lire).

The SPV will not be treated as a subsidiary of the originator provided that it is not subject to the control of the originator in any of the ways specified by Article 2359. This provides that an SPV is a subsidiary of another company if that other company holds the majority of the voting rights, or holds voting rights sufficient to exercise a predominant influence at a shareholders' meeting, or has a predominant influence over it by virtue of particular agreements. Law Decree No. 356/1990, which regulates banking groups, states that an SPV within the group will be regarded as a subsidiary if a bank within the same group is able to exercise a predominant influence by way of shareholding, to coordinate the respective managements for the achievement of common purposes, to determine the composition of the board of directors, or where there is common management due to the composition of directorships.

(b) Regulatory and accounting aspects. General Italian accounting principles apply to off-balance sheet financing. An assignment of receivables without recourse is the only means by which the originator will be able to obtain off-balance sheet treatment for the receivables sold. The SPV would not be treated as a credit or financial institution or subject to the supervision of the Bank of Italy or any other authority except where there has been a transfer of "business receivables" pursuant to Law No. 52/1991.

3. Other Regulatory Issues

(a) Data protection and consumer credit law. There are no authorisations, licences or consents required for data protection or consumer credit law purposes. However, a new consumer credit law is to be enacted in the near future.

(b) Securities regulations. Strict controls are imposed on the issue of debt securities by an SPV incorporated in Italy. Debt securities may only be issued by a company limited by shares ("Società per Azioni") and for an amount which does not exceed the paid-up share capital of that company.

The official listing of securities on the Italian Stock Exchange is primarily regulated by Article 6 of the Presidential Decree No. 138 of 31 March 1975 and by the Regulation of the National Commission for Companies and the Stock Exchange ("CONSOB").

Pursuant to Law No. 216 of 7 June 1974 any public offer of securities is subject to prior notice to CONSOB and to the publication of a prospectus outlining the organisation, financial position and future prospects of the offeror's activity. Furthermore, Article 11 of Law No. 77 dated 23 March 1983 provides that, in order to control capital raising activities, the issue of securities on the Italian market is also subject to the approval of the Bank of Italy. The listing requirements for the admission of debt securities to the Italian Stock Exchange are contained in legislative provisions and a CONSOB Resolution which relates to both the issuing company and the securities intended to be listed.

4. Insolvency Considerations

Pursuant to Article 1362 the courts may recharacterise an assignment as a secured loan, although this is unlikely if the sale is construed as a non-recourse sale.

An assignment is effective as against a liquidator of the originator only if it has been notified to, or accepted by, the debtor or the assignment was effected in accordance with Law No. 52/1991. Article 66 of the Italian Bankruptcy Law states that once a debtor has been declared bankrupt the trustee in bankruptcy is entitled to ask the court to revoke the assignment if it prejudices his creditors, but only if the originator was aware of, or intended to cause, such prejudice and the SPV was aware of that prejudice.

Italian courts may set aside transactions for no value under Article 64 and the payment of unmatured debts within two years of the declaration of bankruptcy pursuant to Article 65. Transactions entered into for inadequate consideration within two years of bankruptcy may be set aside under Article 67 unless the SPV can prove that it was unaware of the originator's insolvency. Payment of matured debts, transactions for value and transactions creating preferential rights for the creditor in relation to contemporaneously created debt within one year of bankruptcy may be set aside if the liquidator shows that the SPV knew of the originator's insolvency.

5. Security

Under Italian law, a security interest may be granted by the SPV over the receivables either through a pledge or through an assignment by way of security. The formalities to be complied with for the creation of a pledge are similar to those for the assignment of receivables (i.e., notification to, or approval by, the relevant debtor) but, in addition to such formalities, delivery to the pledgee of the documents evidencing the pledged receivables is required by Italian law. Pledge deeds, which need to be executed in writing, are subject to registration tax at a rate of 0.5 percent, although this tax may be avoided if the deeds are executed abroad or through an exchange of letters.

6. Tax

Under Italian law any interest payment, if made by an Italian resident to a non-Italian resident, is subject to withholding tax (at the usual rate of 15 percent). Therefore, interest payments made by Italian resident debtors to an SPV will be liable to withholding tax only if the SPV is not Italian resident. The same rule applies to interest payments made by an Italian resident SPV to its creditors. Such payments are subject to withholding tax if the creditors are non-Italian residents, but are exempt if the SPV's creditors are residents of Italy.

If the SPV is domestically controlled and operated, it is subject to Italian taxation. In calculating its profits for tax purposes, the SPV can deduct all payments it makes to its creditors from all the receipts it collects from the debtors.

The originator is subject to tax in respect of the amounts paid by the SPV for the purchase of the receivables to the extent this exceeds the face value of the receivables sold. However, if the purchase price under the assignment is lower than the face value of the receivables, this difference is considered as a loss which is tax deductible for the originator.

JAPAN

Introduction

The idiosyncrasies of Japanese law as it applies to securitisation, and in particular to assignments of the receivables, have caused a number of problems in the development of capital market products in Japan. However, increased interest in the issue of asset-backed securities has resulted in proposals for new legislation in this field being passed in June 1992, although detailed regulations implementing the new regime have yet to be introduced. As it currently stands, the new legislation is relatively limited in scope and does not envisage the creation of a public market in asset-backed securities. Certain banks have raised finance backed by Japanese assets from the US capital markets by means of offshore transactions and this technique may continue to develop.

1. Assets

(a) Types and transferability of assets/receivables. Trade receivables have been the only type of Japanese assets so far securitised. However, there are discussions between the Japanese Ministry of Finance (the "MOF") and Ministry of International Trade and Industry (the "MITI") for the securitisation of automobile lease receivables. In addition, studies are being made into the feasibility of securitising other lease receivables and credit card receivables. As it currently stands, the new legislation referred to above extends only to lease receivables, and certain consumer finance and credit card receivables.

The originator may continue to service the assets (and is required to continue as servicer under the new legislation) for an arm's-length fee after the sale of the assets.

The sale of receivables is by way of assignment, preferably in writing. Generally, the underlying assets can be assigned with the receivables by agreement between the parties. Subject to the perfection requirements mentioned below, it is not necessary to obtain other approvals or to make filings to obtain valid title to the receivables.

Perfecting the assignment has been perceived as one of the greatest obstacles to securitisation in Japan. Notice to, or consent from, the debtor of receivables is not a condition precedent for the acquisition by the SPV of receivables. However, a transfer will only be perfected as against the debtor and other third parties (such as creditors or a liquidator or receiver of the originator) if such notice or consent has a confirmed date ("kakutei hizuke") attached to it.

Unless notice is given to, or consent is obtained from, the debtor of receivables assigned, an assignment cannot be effective as against the debtor and, therefore, is subject to the debtor's right of set-off. Even if notice is given to the debtor, the debtor can still exercise his right of set-off if, and to the extent that, such right of set-off is exercisable at the time that such notice is given.

The effect of the new legislation is to do away with the existing perfection requirements in the case of those assignments to which it applies. It will be possible to perfect such assignments by issuing a public notice in an official gazette. However, the new legislation will only apply to assignments:

(i) of particular types of assets, as mentioned above;

(ii) made to special purpose companies licensed jointly by the MOF and MITI (subject to exemptions in the case of banks and certain other regulated institutions); and

(iii) made pursuant to certain specified types of transaction structure, none of which would permit the special purpose company to issue freely marketable securities backed by the assets.

Under existing legislation, a receivables trust may be created to hold the underlying assets although asset-backed instruments issued by the trustee would have to be in the form of certificates representing a beneficial interest in the trust. However, these are not easily assignable and do not fall within the definition of "securities" under the Securities and Exchange Law 1948. Securities Investment Trusts overcome this problem but cannot be used as vehicles for buying the loan assets.

(b) Tax issues on transfer. A master assignment agreement whereby a series of assignments is contemplated will attract stamp duty of ¥4,000. An individual transfer agreement covering a one-time assignment will attract stamp duty of ¥200. As a result of the Consumption Tax Law Enforcement Order Article 9(1)(4), no Japanese consumption tax is imposed on an assignment of receivables.

2. Basic Structural Considerations

(a) Legal aspects. As mentioned above, the new legislation prescribes certain transaction structures which must be adopted if advantage is to be taken of the relaxed perfection requirements. The inflexibility of the legislation in this respect may cause problems in structuring a transaction efficiently.

Under Article 8 of Financial Statement Rules an SPV will not be treated as a subsidiary so long as the originator does not own a majority of the SPV's voting rights.

The minimum capital requirement for a corporation to be used as the SPV is ¥10,000,000. However, this minimum capitalisation requirement will be irrelevant if a foreign entity and a Japanese branch of such foreign entity are used for the proposed transaction (see 6 below).

(b) Regulatory aspects. The MOF has issued a number of circulars relating to the liquidation of assets by banks but it has issued no special rules for obtaining off-balance sheet treatment.

Under Article 3 of the Money Lenders Law 1983 a person engaged in the business of money lending or acting as an intermediary in money lending must register the required information with the Minister of Finance and the Governor of the relevant prefectures in which such money lender or intermediary has offices. A Japanese branch of a foreign-based SPV may be regarded as a money lender if:

(i) the purchase price of the receivables is paid by promissory notes;

(ii) the transfer of receivables is structured as a secured loan rather than a sale of receivables;

(iii) proceeds of receivables collected by the originator acting as collecting agent are not immediately paid over to the Japanese branch of the foreign-based SPV but will be paid over at a later date with interest; or

(iv) receivables with installments which contain an amount equivalent to interest are assigned.

A money lender whose outstanding loan balance exceeds ¥50 billion must submit copies of its annual reports and financial statements to the Minister of Finance and the Governor of the relevant prefectures in which it has offices.

(c) Accounting aspects. Neither the Business Accounting Council nor the Association of Certified Public Accountants has published rules dealing with the procedure for obtaining off-balance sheet treatment. However, it is likely that the following tests might be regarded as important:

(i) if a monetary claim is sold to another outright and without recourse such a claim will be written off from the balance sheet;

(ii) if the monetary claim is sold to another with recourse but such a sale is notified to the debtor in respect of such a claim, then such a claim will be written off from the balance sheet with a remark in the accompanying notes;

(iii) if a monetary claim is sold to another with recourse and without notice to the debtor in respect of such a claim, then such a claim will remain on-balance sheet.

3. Credit and Securities Regulation

A special purpose company formed to take advantage of the new legislation will need to be licensed (renewable every three years) by the MOF and MITI. The business and investments of the special purpose company will be restricted, and there will be limitations on its transfer or sale. In addition to the licensing function, MITI is required to conduct a credit review of the portfolio of assets to be sold in each individual transaction.

With the exception of obtaining a licence under the new legislation and registration as a money lender under the Money Lenders Law 1983 no authorisations, licences, notices or consents in respect of the originator, the administrator or the SPV are required for data protection or consumer credit purposes. However, the MOF and MITI have issued a number of circulars relating to information held by financial or credit institutions regarding, *inter alia*, the scope of persons whose credit information is made available and the scope of persons who can utilise such credit information.

The listing requirements for an issue of debt securities by the SPV on the Tokyo Stock Exchange and the contents of the prospectus are extremely detailed. However, these will not be of concern if an offshore structure is used for the issue (as set out in 6 below).

4. Insolvency Considerations

A trustee in bankruptcy or reorganisation administrator has no general powers under insolvency statutes to re-characterise a sale of receivables as being one of loan and security.

Pursuant to Article 72 Bankruptcy Law a trustee in bankruptcy has the right to nullify a transaction which is a preference or has been effected for no value. Factors considered include the knowledge and intention of the company making the payment and whether the interests of creditors have been prejudiced. Under Article 7 of the Bankruptcy Law an immediate stay on proceedings is effected on the commencement of a "corporate reorganisation."

Apparently there is no means of ensuring that the SPV is "insolvency remote." However, care should be taken to minimise the activities of the Japanese branch of a foreign-based SPV.

5. Security Considerations

A security interest may be created by way of a trust, for example "Shasai" Bonds secured by a trust holding on behalf of the holders of such bonds. To perfect the security interests as against a debtor and other third parties the procedure referred to in paragraph 1(a) should be used.

6. Structure

Pending implementation of the new legislation (which seems likely, in any event, to prove relatively restrictive) the following structure appears to present the most tax efficient and administratively convenient means of effecting a securitisation in Japan.

A Japanese corporation (the "Originator") will establish a special purpose vehicle ("SPV") to be incorporated in a foreign jurisdiction. The receivables will be sold to a Japanese branch of the SPV ("SPVJ"). The branch will raise funds to purchase the receivables by way of yen-denominated financing from the SPV's head office. This in turn will be financed by way of an issue of securities outside Japan.

This method has a number of advantages and circumvents some of the obstacles presented by Japanese law. A foreign-based SPV is used because the amount of bonds which a Japanese company is permitted to issue is limited according to the extent of its net assets. Although this difficulty may be overcome if the securities are issued in the form of commercial paper, this itself is affected by other restrictions such as the fact that financial institutions are not permitted to issue domestic commercial paper in Japan.

Regulations under the Foreign Exchange and Foreign Trade Control Law ("FEFTCL") require that the Minister of Finance approves the assignment of receivables by a Japanese resident assignor to a non-resident assignee. This is frequently difficult to obtain. However, as the SPV has a Japanese branch to which the receivables are sold the need for MOF approval will be avoided because the SPVJ would be regarded as a resident of Japan for the purposes of FEFTCL.

There are also a number of tax advantages in using a foreign-based SPV and a Japanese based SPVJ. As the bonds issued by the SPV and the loan financing from the SPV to the SPVJ are directly related to each other on a "back-to-back" basis, the structure will be able to avail itself of the following tax law provisions:

(i) the SPVJ may deduct from its income the interest to be paid to the bondholders through the SPV;

(ii) the interest on the yen loan financing paid by the SPVJ to the SPV does not constitute Japanese source income to the SPV or bondholders under Japanese Income Tax Law and is not subject to withholding tax;

(iii) interest on the bonds realised by the holders does not constitute Japanese source income under the Income Tax Law and the Corporate Tax Law and is not subject to Japanese net basis taxation unless the bondholder has a permanent establishment in Japan;

(iv) payments by the underlying debtors will also be exempt from withholding tax.

HONG KONG

Introduction

There have been a number of privately placed securitisation issues in Hong Kong but, as yet, no public issue. This is not due to any apparent legal constraints on the development of a securitisation market in Hong Kong but rather to a lack of variety of institutional investors. The impetus for development of particular investor markets in Hong Kong mainly comes from US banks. To date potential investors in a securitised mortgage market have not felt that the rewards which investment in asset-backed securities would bring are any greater than other, more liquid and better established, forms of investment.

1. The Assets

(a) Types and transferability of assets/receivables. Although Citicorp International packaged an issue of securitised auto-loan receivables in Hong Kong in mid-1992 the principal assets to have been securitised in Hong Kong to date are residential mortgages.

As in the UK the normal method used for the sale of an asset or receivable is for a transfer by way of an assignment. Section 9 Law Amendment and Reform (Consolidation) Ordinance deals with the assignment of debts and is substantially the same as Section 136 of the Law of Property Act 1925 ("LPA") in England. An equitable assignment of receivables may be made without notice to the original debtor but, as in England, this will not operate to transfer legal title to the receivable. In respect of residential mortgages, because they constitute an interest in land, an assignment in writing, by deed, under Section 3 Conveyancing and Property Ordinance is required.

The transfer of the mortgages will be registrable at the Land Office.

The principles of set-off between the original debtor and the assignor in Hong Kong are much the same as in the UK.

(b) Tax issues on transfer. An assignment of receivables (which do not constitute bearer instruments) does not attract stamp duty. Stamp duty may be payable on an assignment of mortgages if a strict interpretation of the Stamp Duty Ordinance is taken. However, the Inland Revenue of Hong Kong have indicated that they would not seek to recover stamp duty on such assignment. There is no VAT payable in Hong Kong.

2. Basic Structural Considerations

(a) Legal aspects. In order for an SPV to avoid treatment as a subsidiary of the seller, Hong Kong company law requires that the seller must not control or have the ability to control the composition of a majority of the board of directors or more than 50 percent of either the voting power of the company in a general meeting or of the issued share capital of the company. There is no minimum capital requirement for an SPV nor any minimum level of taxable profits.

(b) Regulatory aspects. No guidelines have been issued by the Banking Commissioner of Hong Kong for banks seeking to obtain off-balance sheet treatment for SPVs. Each transaction is reviewed on a case-by-case basis. However, a former Banking Commissioner has explained that for "guidance" he adopted the Bank of England's guidelines for banking regulation. It seems likely, therefore, that when guidelines for off-balance sheet treatment are issued, they will be similar to the Bank of England's 1989 Notice as amended and supplemented from time to time.

In addition, the Money Lenders' Ordinance states that no person may carry on a business as a money lender without a licence. This results in the SPV not being allowed to assume any obligation to make further advances to the underlying borrowers.

The Protection of Investors Ordinance contains a basic prohibition on advertisements inviting the public to acquire or subscribe for securities, which may for these purposes include notes issued by an

SPV. However, provided, *inter alia*, that the prospectus complies with the requirements of the Companies Ordinance the SPV will not be affected by the prohibition.

(c) Accounting aspects. The Hong Kong Society of Accountants issues Accounting Guidelines and Statements of Standard Accounting Practice but these do not address off-balance sheet financing.

3. Credit and Securities Regulation

(a) Data protection and consumer protection law. There are no data protection regulations in Hong Kong and the only consumer credit regulations which may be relevant are contained in the Money Lenders Ordinance referred to above.

(b) Securities regulations. The principal requirement is that if the issue is not made or guaranteed by a listed company, the issuer must have shareholder funds of HK $100 million and the nominal amount of debt securities must exceed HK $50 million. Provided that the prospectus is registered the securities may be offered to the Hong Kong public.

The Companies Ordinance requires that a prospectus contains a Chinese translation. Although a Certificate of Exemption from these provisions may be sought from the Securities and Futures Commission, these are not often granted. If the securities are listed on the Hong Kong Stock Exchange the contents of the prospectus should also comply with the listing rules.

4. Insolvency Considerations

A liquidator has no power to change the character of the transaction. Under Section 268 Companies Ordinance a liquidator may disclaim certain property but this power is exercisable only if the property binds the relevant company to the performance of an onerous act or payment of any money. A transaction may be declared invalid as a fraudulent preference if it is entered into within six months before the commencement of winding up proceedings and if the dominant intention is to prefer one creditor over another. On the making of a winding up order an automatic stay is placed on all actions involving the relevant company. The methods of ensuring that the SPV is "insolvency remote" are broadly analogous to those employed in the UK.

5. Security Considerations

A security interest is usually granted over the receivables by the SPV by way of a charge. A charge created in these circumstances by an SPV incorporated in, or having a place of business in, Hong Kong must be registered at the Companies Registry within 5 weeks of its creation. Failure to register on time will mean that the charge becomes void against the liquidator and any creditor of the SPV. A charge over the mortgage pool may also be registrable at the Land Office.

6. Taxation

Under Section 14 Inland Revenue Ordinance Hong Kong profits tax is imposed on any person carrying on a business in Hong Kong to the extent that such person derives Hong Kong-sourced revenue profits from that business. If the SPV derives its income from Hong Kong mortgages and carries on its business in Hong Kong it will be liable to profits tax (currently at the rate of 16.5 percent). However, it will be taxed only on net interest receipts; principal payments are not taxable as they represent repayment of capital.

There is no withholding tax in Hong Kong. Moreover, pursuant to Section 16(2)(f)(ii)(A) Inland Revenue Ordinance the SPV will be allowed to make a deduction for interest paid to noteholders to the extent that the SPV is under a legal obligation to make such payments and as long as the notes are marketable in Hong Kong or another approved financial centre. Fees paid to the administrator and security trustee will be a deductible expense under Section 16 Inland Revenue Ordinance.

If the securitisation operations are moved offshore, i.e., if the SPV does not carry on any business in Hong Kong, it should be possible to eliminate the SPV's Hong Kong profits tax liability on the net interest receipts from the mortgage pool. In this case the security trustee should also be a non-Hong Kong resident.

Chapter 21

Multi-Country Securitization and Currency Hedging Programs

by Stephen Oxenbridge,
Morgan Grenfell & Co. Ltd.
and
C. Mark Nicolaides,
Mayer, Brown & Platt

One of the most intriguing applications in Europe of U.S. style securitization structures is to support the hedging of anticipated foreign currency earnings against foreign exchange fluctuations. The first portion of this article outlines a structure for the securitization of multi-country trade receivables, and briefly discusses some of the financial, legal, and accounting issues which might arise as such a structure is implemented in a specific transaction. The second portion of this article suggests a method by which a multi-national company can, by using such a securitization structure, implement a currency hedging program against the anticipated future earnings of its group subsidiaries.

Securitization is complex by its nature, but this article suggests that such complexities can be managed and residual legal risks and uncertainties can be reduced to acceptable levels by experienced professional advisors acting for parties' whose purposes for seeking to securitize financial assets are soundly based.

MODEL TRANSACTION STRUCTURE

The proposed securitization structure is diagrammed in Figure 21.1. In addition, Figure 21.2 provides a brief description of the some of the parties that would be involved in a transaction based upon such a structure.

The essential purpose of the proposed structure, from a securitization standpoint, is the same as with most others—to provide a legal framework that insulates the financial assets being acquired from the claims of parties other than the Purchaser (and, as a result, any Investors and, after payment of the Investors, the credit and liquidity providers), thereby permitting the timely transfer of payments from the account debtors to the investors. However, the proposed structure also incorporates financial and legal mechanisms currently in use in U.S. structures which eliminate or reduce excess costs found in older securitization programs—especially costs arising from the mismatch of collections and payments and capital costs arising from liquidity and credit facilities and daylight advances to fund commercial paper rollovers.

The structure outlined in Figure 21.1 would involve two types of sales of receivables or interests in receivables. The first type of sales would be intercompany sales from the Operating Companies to the Seller. The structure and terms of the intercompany sales would be evaluated to ensure that they would qualify as "true" sales. Figure 21.4 provides a more detailed discussion of the characteristics of "true" sales. The second type of sales would be sales from the Seller to the Purchaser. The Seller's sales would constitute sales of "undivided interests" in the pool of receivables owned by the Seller. A more detailed discussion of the characteristics of "undivided interests" is provided later in this chapter.

The purpose of the two-sale structure is to accommodate the various interests of the participants. First, the Purchaser will desire to have adequate (albeit limited) credit protection for uncollected receivables. This aim is protected by "overcapitalizing" the Seller with extra receivables or other financial assets and rendering it "bankruptcy remote" (See Figure 21.3). By overcapitalizing the Seller and rendering it "bankruptcy remote," the Seller is thus less likely to become insolvent or bankrupt. As a result, the Seller sales

Figure 21.1—Model Transaction Structure

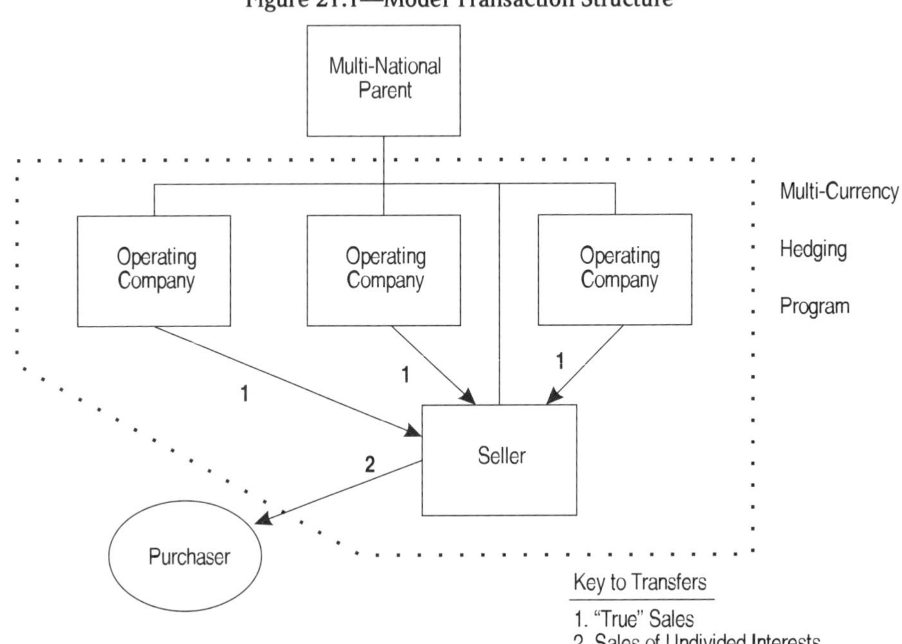

do not need to be "true" sales from a bankruptcy standpoint and the Purchaser may therefore obtain more credit protection from the Seller for defaulted receivables without compromising the Purchaser's access to the entire pool in the event of the insolvency or bankruptcy of any of the Operating Companies. Second, the Purchaser will desire to be insulated from the risks associated with the bankruptcies of the Seller and the Operating Companies. Overcapitalizing the Seller provides one aspect of this protection (with respect to the Seller) and structuring the intercompany sales as "true" sales provides another aspect (with respect to the Operating Companies).

INTERCOMPANY SALES MADE AS "TRUE" SALES

The intercompany sales could be made for cash and on a frequent (even daily) basis, so that this financing structure could be used to finance the Operating Companies' trade receivables portfolios as they are generated in the ongoing course of business.

As mentioned above, each of the intercompany sales would be structured as "true" sales (as opposed to loans) for commercial and bankruptcy law purposes. A "true" sale is one which validly removes the receivable from the assets of a seller, thereby making the receivable unavailable to satisfy claims of third party creditors of the seller (including such seller's bankruptcy receiver).

Whether a sale of receivables is a "true" sale will depend upon the law applicable to such sale. Where the seller's creditors are seeking access to the seller's receivables by claiming that sales were not "true" sales (whether before or after the seller's bankruptcy case has commenced), the relevant court will as a general rule apply its own "local" law to evaluate such sales. The relevant court might also accept the seller's and the buyer's choice of a different law, but such a choice will be contested by the seller's creditors (and perhaps successfully so) if it would deny them access to receivables they could otherwise seize if "local" law applies. Given that the Operating Companies will be located in a number of jurisdictions, it would be prudent to anticipate that the terms of the intercompany sales will differ from country to country. Figure 21.4 provides a more detailed discussion of the various "true" sale requirements of several European countries.

SELLER'S PURCHASE PRICE

Ordinarily, the Seller will prefer to pay the Operating Companies a purchase price for receivables equal to some discount from the face amount of

Figure 21.2—Parties to a Securitization Transation

Parent: A multi-national company.

Operating Companies: Subsidiaries of the Parent operating in various countries.

Seller: A special purpose company formed as a wholly owned subsidiary of one or more of the Parent and the Operating Companies. The Seller can be formed in a tax-efficient manner, such as a Belgian coordination center. The Seller will be overcapitalized in an amount sufficient to provide adequate credit protection against uncollectible receivables, and will be rendered "bankruptcy-remote." See Figure 21.3 for "bankruptcy-remote" elements.

Purchaser: The company purchasing an interest in the Seller's pool of receivables. The Purchaser may be a bank or a special purpose company. If the Purchaser is a special purpose company which issues rated securities, it will be rendered "bankruptcy-remote." See Figure 21.3 for "bankruptcy-remote" elements.

Servicers: The parties (normally, the Operating Companies or affiliates) who collect the receivables and account for and report on their collections.

If the Purchaser issues rated securities, the following additional parties will be involved:

Investors: The purchasers of the Purchaser's securities from time to time.

Credit Enhancer: One or more banks or insurance companies which provide liquidity and credit enhancement to the Purchaser.

Managing Agent: A bank acting on behalf of the Purchaser (and at its direction (to supervise and manage all operations of the Purchaser in connection with (i) the Purchaser's investment in receivables and other financial assets and related rights, (ii) the issuance and sale of securities to fund the Purchaser's investments, and the payment of such securities, (iii) the implementation and administration of the liquidity and credit facilities, and (iv) related operation and activities of the Purchaser.

Dealers: Such dealers as the Managing Agent may engage to place the Purchaser's securities.

Depositary: The bank acting as depositary and paying agent in respect of the Purchaser's securities.

the receivables purchased. The amount of the discount would be determined by reference to a large number of factors, including the Seller's cost of funds and its losses on the receivables.

However, the Seller's determination of the price it will pay for receivables must also be evaluated against the "true" sale requirement referred to above and described in Figure 21.4. In some countries, the Seller might need to pay the entire face amount of each receivable to the relevant Operating Company as the purchase price therefor (if, for example, the purchase is by way of subrogation). In such a case, the Seller would want to charge the Operating Companies a management fee for providing its financing service, the fee representing the sum of the factors which ordinarily would have made up the discount portion of the purchase price.

The Seller's purchase price should be determined in a manner which supports its financial viability. Therefore, the discount (or fee) should be calculated so as to reimburse the Seller for the various costs otherwise borne by it of operating the securitization program—including amounts in respect of the Seller's own cost of funds (as received from the Purchaser), a financing charge for the discounting services it provides, an amount in respect of Servicers' fees and fees of the Depositary and the Managing Agent, a discount in respect of historical losses on the receivables Pool, an amount in respect of "dilution" of the pool caused by discounts and credits provided by the Operating Companies and adjustments for incorrect billings, and other miscellaneous matters.

SELLER'S SALES

From time to time, the Purchaser would buy an undivided percentage ownership interest in the pool of receivables owned by the Seller. As with the intercompany sales, the Seller's sales would be completed without notice to the various account debtors.

The Seller's sales would also be structured to constitute "true" sales, if possible. However, because the Seller might retain a subordinated undivided interest in the receivables (see below), it might thus provide a great amount of "credit protection" to the Purchaser. For this reason, and because the Seller's sales are completed for a price that effectively fluctuates, there may be a risk that the Purchaser's purchases of undivided interests in receivables could be treated by a bankruptcy court as loans instead of "true" sales. Although the structure will seek to minimize this risk, it has been compensated for by "overcapitalizing" the Seller.

Figure 21.3—Bankruptcy Remote Elements

The purpose of making a company "bankruptcy-remote" is to reduce the possibility of its being declared bankrupt, and thereby to avoid the potential delays and other difficulties such bankruptcy proceedings might cause in transferring collections from account debtors to the Investors. When rendering a company bankruptcy-remote, one or more of the following steps (among others) can be taken:

- The company would not be allowed to incur any debt other than in connection with the securitization transaction.
- Certain of the company's creditors would agree not to file an involuntary bankruptcy petition against the company.
- In some cases, the outstanding shares of the company would be owned by a neutral entity which has no incentive to cause the company to file a voluntary bankruptcy petition and which is distinct for bankruptcy consolidation purposes from the parties to the transaction.
- The company's corporate purposes would be limited to drawing funds under the credit and liquidity facilities, issuing securities, and using proceeds from the securities or the facilities to invest in receivables or interests in receivables.
- The providers of the credit and liquidity facilities would be obligated to fund in all events other than, in the case of the liquidity facility only, the company's bankruptcy.

The amount invested (or reinvested, as the case may be) by the Purchaser from time to time as payment for its undivided interest in the receivables is the Purchaser's "investment" in the receivables. As a result of the Seller's sales, the Seller would receive cash in the amount of the Purchaser's investment in exchange for its sale of an undivided interest in the pool of receivables.

At the time of each sale by the Seller, the Seller would inform the Managing Agent of the amount the Seller wishes to raise through such sale and the desired duration of the initial settlement period (which would need to be acceptable to the Managing Agent). The duration of the initial settlement period could be different than the anticipated average maturity date of the receivables in which an undivided interest is purchased. The Purchaser would fund its investment in the manner described below.

UNDIVIDED INTEREST

An undivided interest is a form of shared ownership, pursuant to which the purchaser acquires ownership of a portion of the cash flow and related rights arising from the entire pool of receivables rather than ownership of specified receivables in the pool.

One very important advantage of having the Purchaser purchase undivided interests in a pool of receivables rather than discrete batches of receivables is that it avoids the need for the Purchaser to match the maturities of its own funding to the anticipated repayment dates of the receivables. Throughout the term of the transaction, the Purchaser would maintain the principal amount of its investment in the receivables pool at a level constantly equal to the outstanding principal amount of its own funding by reinvesting its share of collections (those collections not allocable to its yield) back into the pool of receivables. After the term of the facility has expired and the reinvestment process has stopped, the Purchaser's investment in receivables naturally liquidates itself.

A second important feature of the Seller's retained undivided interest in the receivables is that it may be functionally subordinated to the undivided interest purchased by the Purchaser. Basically, the Seller's retained undivided interest can constitute a "residual" interest in the receivables following the Purchaser's collection in full of its investment, its yield and other amounts owing to it.

UNDIVIDED INTEREST CALCULATION

The amount of the Purchaser's undivided interest in the receivables pool is *deemed* to be calculated daily. Under most circumstances, however, the Seller would actually be required to calculate the undivided interest only as of the end of each month and (if a liquidation occurs) on the day before the first day of the liquidation. In most circumstances it is unnecessary to calculate the undivided interest more frequently because (i) it can generally be assumed that the Purchaser's share of collections, if calculated, would be adequate to cover the Purchaser's yield and the Servicers' fees, and (ii) prior to a liquidation the amount of the Purchaser's

Figure 21.4—Elements of "True" Sales

Three factors can generally be relevant when evaluating whether a sale of a receivable is a "true" sale, although the importance of these or other factors will depend upon the applicable law. First, how much credit protection is provided by the seller? Second, are the account debtors notified of the sale? Third, is the purchase price paid by the buyer adjusted from time to time after the sale? Other factors may be relevant in a particular country, such as whether the seller retains the right to collect the receivables and use the proceeds in its business, but are not discussed in detail here.

What follows is a non-exhaustive summary of methods for transferring trade receivables which would qualify as "true" sales under the laws of several European countries. We have assumed that the sales will be pursuant to a written contract, and that neither any applicable law (as in the case of governmental receivables) nor the documents evidencing the receivables prohibit such transfer.

It should also be noted that, in most countries, a bankruptcy trustee can void sales of receivables occurring during the "suspect" period prior to bankruptcy if not for fair value.

Belgium: Belgium is at the time of press amending Article 1690 of the Belgian Civil Code to permit the assignment of a receivable without notice to the account debtor. Until then, transfers could occur by subrogation (see note below), which does not require notice to the account debtor. There are other methods of transferring receivables under Belgian law (such as endorsement of invoices), but none are available to a special purpose vehicle such as in the proposed transaction.

England: Under English law, an equitable assignment would qualify as a "true" sale and would not require notice to the account debtor. Recourse would generally not undermine this "true" sale treatment if not in excess of some low multiple of historic losses. Similarly, modest adjustments to the purchase price would also be tolerated.

France: Without giving notice to the account debtors pursuant to Article 1690 of the French Civil Code, subrogation is the only method at present to transfer short-term trade receivables to a special purpose company under French law as a "true" sale. Neither the French securitization law (relating to *Fonds Communs de Créances*) nor the Loi Dailly permits transfers of short-term receivables to special purpose vehicles. Even with a modest amount of recourse and/or price adjustments, French courts would likely recognize the formalities of the transfer as a "true" sale.

Germany: Under German law, the assignment of receivables does not require notice to the account debtors to be a "true" sale. Neither recourse nor price adjustments should affect the buyer's legal title in such receivables.

Italy: Under the new Italian law (effective February 1991) relating to receivables sales, it is possible to have a "true" sale of a receivable without notice to the account debtor provided certain requirements are met. If the minimum capital requirement for the Purchaser (Lit. 2 billion) under the new law cannot be met, however, a transfer by subrogation is also possible. Both recourse and price adjustments should be permitted if structured properly. In Italy, sales during the seller's suspect period can be voided under certain circumstances, even if for fair value, unless sold pursuant to the new law.

Netherlands: Under current Dutch law, the assignment of receivables does not require notice to the account debtors to be a "true" sale. Both recourse and price adjustments should be permitted if structured properly. However, the new Dutch civil code (which went into effect January 1, 1992) requires transfers of receivables to be structured differently if they are to qualify as "true" sales.

Spain: The sale of receivables can be a "true" sale under Spanish law without notice to account debtors. Neither recourse nor price adjustments should affect the buyer's title in such receivables. It is at present unclear whether the formalities of creating an *escritura publica* for the sale of commercial receivables are required by law.

Switzerland: Pursuant to Articles 164 and 165 of the Swiss Code of Obligations, a receivable can be transferred without notice to or consent of the account debtor, provided that certain relatively simple documentary formalities are met. Neither recourse nor price adjustments should affect the buyer's title in such receivables.

Note on Subrogation: A party that pays the amount of a debt to the existing creditors stands in the shoes of (or is "subrogated" to) the prior creditor *vis a vis* the debtor. With subrogation, recourse is generally not allowed, although a separate repurchase agreement should be acceptable. Later purchase price adjustments should also be acceptable.

share of collections in excess of its yield and the Servicers' fees is simply reinvested in the pool, resulting in no net change in the amount of the Purchaser's investment.

This analysis would change during a period when the Purchaser's investment was being liquidated, when reinvestments would halt and the excess of the Purchaser's share of collections over amounts held for its yield and the Servicers' fees would be applied to pay back the Purchaser's investment. The potential complexity involved here is avoided to a large extent by providing that during a liquidation period the amount of the undivided interest is deemed to remain at the level it was at on the day before the first day of such liquidation period, unless the Managing Agent requests that it be recalculated. In addition, in practice few transactions actually liquidate when the Seller wishes to terminate the financing. Instead, the Purchaser would normally agree to sell the undivided interest back to the Seller for a price equal to the Purchaser's investment plus accrued, unpaid yield. Of course, if off-balance sheet treatment is required, there can be no prior binding agreement to do this.

The formula used for determining the amount of the Purchaser's undivided interest at any point in time is designed to assure that the Purchaser's share of collections from the pool of receivables is sufficient to pay the sum of (i) the Purchaser's investment, (ii) the Purchaser's yield, (iii) fees due to the Servicers, and (iv) a loss reserve. At any point in time, the undivided interest can be expressed as a percentage interest in the pool and related collections. This percentage is determined by dividing (x) the aggregate claims which the Purchaser has on the pool in respect of the undivided interest (see Figure 21.6) by (y) the aggregate unpaid balance of receivables in the pool, after adjustments which remove amounts in excess of concentration limits applicable to any individual account debtor. The amount of the undivided interest will vary over time with changes in the various components of the Purchaser's aggregate claims and the aggregate unpaid balance of receivables in the pool.

Figure 21.5—Miscellaneous Legal and Accounting Issues

The legal and accounting issues in a multi-country securitization transaction tend to be complex and numerous, but also manageable. Some of those issues are highlighted below:

True Sales: In most countries there is an existing method for the transfer of receivables in a manner which is enforceable against the creditors of the Seller and without notice to the account debtor. See Figure 21.4.

Withholding Taxes: Payments of collections on trade receivables from the Operating Companies to the Seller and from the Seller to the Purchaser should not attract withholding taxes because such receivables do not bear interest. In addition, the transaction can be structured in most countries so that fees, discounts and other amounts paid from one party to another also do not attract withholding taxes.

Capital Commitments: Based on present risk-based capital guidelines, the liquidity and credit facilities, if structured correctly, would carry the following capital requirements if provided by a bank: (1) the liquidity facility, being a "commitment" having a term of one year or less, would have a conversion factor of zero percent, and (2) the default facility, as a "direct credit substitute," would probably be brought onto the balance sheet at a conversion factor of 100 percent. The Depositary's "daylight" loans to fund commercial paper rollovers should carry a credit weighting of zero percent.

Deductibility of Interest on the Securities: There are many jurisdictions where the Purchaser could be formed with a minimum amount of equity capital without risking recharacterization of its securities and/or borrowings under the liquidity and credit facilities as equity. This is important because interest on the Purchaser's securities and borrowings under the facilities must be fully deductible against its income.

Licenses, etc. to Conduct Activities: There are a number of jurisdictions where both the Seller and the Purchaser can be formed where they would not be required to obtain banking or similar licenses from applicable authorities as the result of their activities.

Off-Balance Sheet: Under applicable generally accepted accounting principles, the Seller's sale of undivided interests in the receivables would permit it to remove such interests from its balance sheet. In addition, the Purchaser would be structured to avoid the potential problem of the Purchaser's accounts needing to be consolidated with the accounts of the Purchaser's sponsor on the grounds that the sponsor has the right to "exercise a dominant influence" over the Purchaser.

Figure 21.6—Aggregate Claims Against the Pool

The aggregate claims of the Purchaser against the pool of receivables will generally consist of the following four components:

Purchaser's Investment. This component equals the amount paid by the Purchaser for the Undivided Interest. This component remains constant until a liquidation occurs.

Yield Component. This component equals the sum of (a) accrued, unpaid yield through the date of computation, (b) yield over an estimated liquidation period, and (c) any additional amount necessary to reimburse the Purchaser for breakage-type losses.

Servicers' Fees Component. This component includes the same elements as the yield component, but relating to the Servicers' fees.

Loss Reserve. This component includes the loss reserve, if any, to be funded from collections of receivables in the pool.

PURCHASER'S FUNDING

The Purchaser will need to fund its investment in the Seller's receivables pool. Typically, the Purchaser will be either a bank or a special purpose company, and there are several trade-offs involved. A bank Purchaser's investment in the Seller's receivables pool would be funded in its ordinary course of business, but would attract capital adequacy costs which would need to be reflected in the Purchaser's required yield. However, where a bank Purchaser also provides the currency hedging program described below, its required yield could reflect the benefit of this hedging business and could thus be quite competitive with the yield required by special purpose Purchasers. In addition, bank Purchasers can frequently be very flexible in negotiations with a Seller compared to the detailed purchasing and operating standards of special purpose Purchasers funded by rated securities.

If the Purchaser is a special purpose company formed to purchase investments in the Seller's receivables pool, it would be rendered "bankruptcy-remote" and would raise funds by issuing securities to investors directly in the capital markets. Because of the Purchaser's special purpose status, those securities would typically be rated by an independent rating agency in order to be acceptable to the widest possible group of investors. Figure 21.7 provides an outline of the issues a rating agency would typically investigate if asked to provide a rating.

Where the Purchaser funds itself by issuing rated securities, on the date of a Seller sale the Managing Agent would inform the Seller of the all-in interest rate on securities issued by the Purchaser (including the various costs described below), which rate is used to calculate the Purchaser's required yield on its investment in receivables.

COSTS

The Purchaser's required yield would be determined by its costs of doing business.

These costs would include the following:

- **Base Funding Cost.** Paid by the Purchaser for the funds it needs to purchase its interest in the receivables pool, reflected as either interest or as original issue discount.
- **Dealer's Fees.** Paid to the parties which place the Purchaser's securities, if any.
- **Arrangement Fees.** Paid to the party which arranges the securitization structure.
- **Management Fees.** Paid to the Managing Agent for the ongoing monitoring and administration of the securitization structure on behalf of the Purchaser.
- **Liquidity and Credit Enhancement Fees.** Paid to the providers of liquidity and credit enhancement, if any. Liquidity enhancement should be less expensive than credit enhancement, because the former carries less risk and less credit weighting than the latter.
- **Servicing Fees.** Paid to the originators for their collection and monitoring of the receivables.
- **Rating Agency Costs.** If the Purchaser raises funds by issuing rated securities, there will be an initial fee payable to the rating agencies for the rating and an annual monitoring fee.
- **Legal Fees.** These would usually include counsel for the Purchaser, the Seller and the arranger. There would be the costs of local counsel as well.

Figure 21.7—Rating Process

In the event that the Purchaser's securities are to be rated by one or more internationally recognized rating agencies, the rating agencies would conduct a detailed investigation of the transaction structure. The investigation would evaluate three major issues:

Credit Quality of Receivables. The rating agencies would want to evaluate the nature of the financial assets involved as well as their historical performance. Their evaluation would consider (among other factors) the Operating Companies' underwriting guidelines, historic and current credit criteria, collection and administration procedures, exposure to customer and industry concentrations, historic and prospective values of the collateral, origination and repayment statistics, auditing and accounting procedures and systems, computer systems backing the operations and criteria for the selection of the receivables in the pool. Variations in any of these factors might justify different rating levels; hence it is difficult to predict rating agency requirements with any precision, even for the same type of asset.

Financial Mechanisms. The rating agencies would also want to ensure that collections and other procedures of the receivables would be transferred without interruption from the Servicers to the Investors, both in terms of amount as well as timing. The rating agencies would look at, among other factors, where and how cash is received, systems to record and identify the receipt of cash, mechanisms which pass the cash through the structure to the Investors and the effect of mismatched collections (including negative spreads on reinvestments).

Legal Structure. Finally, the rating agencies would evaluate the laws which govern the ownership of the collection of proceeds thereof, and the laws which govern the insolvency of the parties to the transaction. The rating agencies would seek to assure themselves that the legal structure would operate in a manner which provides for repayment of the Securities on a timely basis, despite the insolvency of the Parent, the Seller or the Operating Companies.

MULTIPLE SELLER VEHICLES

Given that there is a cost to creating each securitization structure, a highly economic approach is for the Purchaser to be a "general purpose" vehicle which can make multiple purchases of a wide variety of types of receivables from a variety of sellers, thus amortizing the costs over a larger variety and volume of transactions. A cost-effective vehicle would, by reducing its per-transaction operating costs, be able to appeal to more potential customers. In addition, a multiple-seller vehicle would reduce the time and cost necessary to complete each additional transaction, and could simplify the documentation to be reviewed by the Operating Companies. Finally, a multiple-seller vehicle could benefit from the diversity of its assets, and might obtain name recognition which could help in its marketing efforts.

The structure of a transaction involving such a multiple-seller vehicle would look somewhat different than that illustrated in Figure 21.1, but many of the legal, accounting and business principles discussed herein would otherwise remain unchanged.

NOTICE TO ACCOUNT DEBTORS

As a matter of commercial necessity, both the Intercompany sales and the Seller's sales will be made without notice to account debtors. Although structuring receivables sales without notice to account debtors will impose certain requirements in certain countries (see Figure 21.4), in most countries such sales can be nevertheless structured as "true" sales even without such notice.

However, in most countries it is also true that, prior to an account debtor's receiving notice of a sale of receivables, the buyer is subject to all defenses which such account debtor may have against the seller, even if such defenses arise after the time of sale. In addition, prior to its receiving notice of the sale of a receivable owing by it, an account debtor can generally discharge such receivable by paying the seller.

A standard element of any securitization transaction is the Purchaser's retained right to notify account debtors of the Purchaser's purchase of receivables upon the occurrence of pre-agreed events. Many of the pre-agreed events relate to the financial condition of either the Operating Companies or the Seller. Such notices when given would cut off later-arising defenses the account debtors may have against the Operating Companies. The notices could also be accompanied with a request to make future payments of receivables into a new account of the Purchaser, although it is generally provided that the Purchaser will simply take title to the existing collections accounts where possible.

COLLECTIONS

Ordinarily, the Operating Companies would be responsible, at least as long as the Purchaser was satisfied with their financial condition, for collection of the receivables from the various account debtors. In the event that the Purchaser was not satisfied with the financial condition of the Operating Companies, the Purchaser could appoint other entities to act as its Servicers. Given the short-term nature of the receivables, it would be necessary for all collections to be identified promptly (i.e., preferably overnight and in any event within several days) and it may be advisable for such collections to be held in segregated bank accounts until identified and either paid over to the Purchaser or reinvested in further receivables.

From a legal standpoint, the transaction would need to be structured carefully so that the collections which are held temporarily by an Operating Company as Servicer are not deemed to have been advanced by the Purchaser to the Operating Company as an unsecured loan. Thus, collected amounts representing the Purchaser's investment or yield are either reinvested in further receivables generated by the Operating Companies or deposited in an account of the Purchaser maintained at the Managing Agent.

REPORTING AND SETTLEMENT PRODECURES

In addition to their collections responsibilities, the Operating Companies would periodically monitor and report on several aspects of the receivables collections process, including aggregate amounts collected and aggregate defaults in the receivables pool, listings by account debtor of outstanding receivables (with aging and default information), and listings of receivables subject to warranty claims, rebates and other adjustments.

Following the Purchaser's purchase of an undivided interest in a receivables pool, but prior to a liquidation, the Servicers would be required on each day to set aside out of the Purchaser's share of collections (i) for payment to the Purchaser, amounts equal to the Purchaser's yield accrued on such day, and (ii) for payment to each Servicer, such Servicer's fee accrued on such day. The remainder of the Purchaser's share of collections is deemed to be reinvested in an additional undivided interest in the pool (which is then deemed to be aggregated with the existing undivided interest). On the last day of each settlement period, the Servicers pay to the Managing Agent the amounts set aside throughout the settlement period for the Purchaser's yield and the Servicer's fees, and the Managing Agent pays such amounts on to the Purchaser and the Servicers, respectively.

If the Purchaser issues commercial paper to fund its operations, a special arrangement must be made on rollover dates. Given that commercial paper typically must be paid early in the day, the Depositary would fund the repayment of the commercial paper by making an advance to the Purchaser (unless it has notified the Purchaser on or prior to the Business Day preceding the repayment date that it will not do so). When the new commercial paper is issued later on the same day, the proceeds thereof, combined with the yield received from the Servicers, are used to reimburse the Depositary. The agreement of the Depositary to provide this liquidity would be structured so that it is not a "commitment" for capital adequacy purposes. Depending upon the parties' preferences, other payment arrangements can be made.

LIQUIDITY AND CREDIT ENHANCEMENT

If the Purchaser funds itself by issuing rated securities to Investors, it would typically be supported by two facilities, a liquidity facility and, if necessary, a default facility.

The liquidity facility would be designed primarily to cover mismatches in timing between receipt of cash by the Purchaser from its investments and obligations of the Purchaser to repay maturing securities. The liquidity facility would normally take the form of a loan facility, but it could include other types of facilities (such as a letter of credit facility or a secondary receivables purchase facility) should the need exist. The amount of the liquidity facility would be limited to the Purchaser's share of the non-defaulted receivables in which it has an interest (or a percentage thereof).

The default facility is designed to protect the Purchaser's securities from the effect of excessive defaults within the receivables portfolio in which the Purchaser has purchased an interest. Depending upon the level of credit protection provided by the Seller, a default facility may not be required. The default facility could be structured in a number of ways, including for example a letter of credit, an insurance policy or a commitment of a bank to make revolving loans. The default facility would be also available to pay maturing securities of the Purchaser when the liquidity facility is unavailable or exhausted.

If the facilities were provided by commercial banks, they would be structured so as to minimize capital costs associated with them. Thus, each would have a term of 365 days, but would be extendable from time to time.

CURRENCY CONVERSIONS

Given the multi-currency nature of the Operating Companies' various businesses, it will always be necessary for at least part of the receivables collections (which will be in a number of currencies) to be converted into the currency of the Purchaser's investment (which will typically be in one currency). Of course, the creditworthiness of the entity making these currency conversions will affect the creditworthiness of the Purchaser's investment in the receivables pool and the creditworthiness (and rating) of the Purchaser's securities, if any. In addition, it is the need to make such conversions which also provides the Parent with the basis on which to support a hedging program of the anticipated foreign currency income of the Operating Companies.

There are two basic methods to accomplish these currency conversions. First, one or more of the Operating Companies or the Seller can themselves commit to make the necessary conversions. For example, the various Operating Companies could commit to convert all collections of the sold receivables into one uniform currency. In order for this arrangement to be viable from the standpoint of the Purchaser, the Operating Companies would need to demonstrate an ability to absorb the potential losses of converting such collections. However, the Seller could also provide this currency conversion by, for example, purchasing forward currency exchange contracts. In any case, a creditworthy party could guarantee the obligations of the Operating Companies and/or the Seller if that would be necessary to obtain the desired rating on the Purchaser's securities, if any.

The second method of dealing with the currency exchange problem is for the Purchaser to enter into currency swap contracts with acceptable counterparties. This second method would have the advantage of putting within the control of the Purchaser the currency exchange arrangements.

HEDGING PROGRAMS

A multi-national Parent can use a securitization structure of the nature described above to support a program to hedge the anticipated foreign currency earnings of its Operating Companies. Such a hedging program can provide desired period-to-period consistency to the Parent's consolidated balance sheets and income statements, especially when significant shifts in currency exchange rates are expected.

In the case of any hedging program, however, the requirements of generally accepted accounting principles ("GAAP") must be taken into account. For example, U.S. GAAP makes it difficult for a multi-national Parent to defer recognition of the gain or loss on foreign currency hedges written solely against anticipated foreign currency earnings, because such hedges do not normally satisfy the requirement that the hedge relate to a firm foreign currency "commitment." Figure 21.8 contains the text of the relevant U.S. GAAP provisions. More obviously, if such hedges must be marked-to-market on a current basis, the intended beneficial balance sheet effect is not achieved and the economic rationale for purchasing such hedges in the first place will be substantially undermined.

Given the objective of deferring recognition of foreign currency hedging gains and losses, there are several methods by which a multi-country securitization structure can help achieve this objective. In the case of a U.S. Parent, for example, where the Operating Companies are located in Europe and could sell receivables to a Seller based in the U.S., such a securitization structure could support hedges converting the anticipated foreign currency income of those Operating Companies into dollars (the reporting currency of the Parent).

First, the Parent would arrange hedges against the dollar for a number of years (three, for example) of anticipated income of the Operating Companies. The hedges would be arranged to have such exercise dates (at monthly intervals, for example), strike prices and other terms as are agreed between the Parent and its hedge counterparty, based upon the Parent's financial goals and means.

Second, the Operating Companies would enter into a multi-country securitization transaction pursuant to which they are, as Servicers under the securitization transaction, committed to convert their foreign currency collections into dollars and to remit those dollars to the Purchaser. If such a commitment is drafted properly, it would satisfy the requirements of U.S. GAAP and would thus, effectively, permit the Parent to defer gains and losses relating to hedges of anticipated foreign currency earnings until the exercise dates of such hedges.

The volume of receivables sold by the Operating Companies to the Seller during any settlement period could be adjusted carefully so that the amount of collections to be converted on any hedge exercise date would equal as closely as possible the amount of foreign currency hedged by such Operating Company on such exercise date.

Figure 21.8—Statement of Financial Accounting Standards No. 52

Paragraph 17 of FAS 52 provides, in relevant part, as follows:

"A gain or loss on a forward contract that does not meet the conditions described in paragraph . . . 21 shall be included in determining net income in accordance with the requirements for other foreign currency transactions . . . ."

Paragraph 21 of FAS 52 provides, in relevant part, as follows:

"A gain or loss on a forward contract or other foreign currency transaction that is intended to hedge an identifiable foreign currency commitment . . . shall be deferred and included in the measurement of the related foreign currency transaction . . . . A foreign currency transaction shall be considered a hedge of an identifiable foreign currency commitment provided both of the following conditions are met:

a. The foreign currency transaction is designated as, and is effective as, a hedge of a foreign currency commitment.

b. The foreign currency commitment is firm."

This structure thus implies a multiplier effect between the size of the securitization program and the amount of the hedging program. For example, a securitization program where the Seller is constantly (by regularly reinvesting collections) investing in an aggregate of $10 million face amount of receivables having an average life to maturity of 30 days, would provide an ongoing monthly foreign exchange commitment sufficient to support $120 million of hedging on an annual basis.

However, such a structure may not be optimal. In part, such a structure may lack sufficient flexibility for a multi-national Parent as it arranges its global hedging strategy. With the Operating Companies committed, by GAAP as well as the securitization program, to convert a fixed amount of foreign currency into another currency on each settlement date, it becomes difficult for the Parent to adjust its global hedging program without also changing its currency exposure in a converse manner with respect to the underlying securitization transaction.

Fortunately, a solution to this problem exists, at least under U.S. GAAP. By making certain adjustments to the structure described above, a U.S. multi-national Parent will be able to maintain full flexibility to adjust the parameters of the hedging program without increasing the currency exchange exposure of the group under the related securitization program. In fact, several such "second-generation" combined securitization/hedging programs have already been put into place.

CONCLUSION

Current innovations in the securitization market are providing multi-nationals with an effective and competitively priced method of supporting hedging programs against anticipated foreign currency earnings. The complexities of such combined securitization/hedging programs can be managed and the residual legal risks and uncertainties can be reduced to levels which make such programs a new—and viable—tool for financial management.

Chapter 22

Asset-Backed Commercial Paper Programs

by Barbara Kavanagh,
Federal Reserve Bank of Chicago
and
Thomas R. Boemio
and
Gerald A. Edwards, Jr.,
Division of Banking Supervision and Regulation
Federal Reserve Board

In existence since 1983, asset-backed commercial paper programs have grown substantially over the past two years. These programs involve the securitization of assets and are attractive to companies because they provide a stable source of funding. At the same time, they appeal to banking organizations because they provide a means of earning fee income and meeting customers' needs for credit and, at the same time, eliminate the need to maintain the amount of capital that would be required if loans were extended directly to the companies.

Further incentive for participation in these programs has been provided by recent revisions to the Securities and Exchange Commission's rules limiting the amount that money market mutual funds may invest in commercial paper issues rated less than the highest quality. Through these programs, companies whose own commercial paper is rated below A-1/P-1 can continue to have access to the commercial paper market, despite the lower demand for commercial paper with such ratings.

This article examines the benefits and the risks of asset-backed commercial paper programs. First, it provides an overview of the commercial paper market and asset-backed commercial paper programs. Next, it discusses the mechanics of the securitization process, the role of banking organizations in the process, and the incentives for banks and customers to participate in such programs. Then it outlines the risks to which asset-backed commercial paper programs may expose banking organizations. It also addresses the risk-based capital treatment of the liquidity facilities and other supporting arrangements provided by banking organizations. Last, the article discusses how existing guidance on securitization activities that the Federal Reserve has provided its examiners pertains to asset-backed commercial paper.

OVERVIEW OF THE COMMERCIAL PAPER MARKET

Commercial paper, one of the oldest money market instruments, is used to raise short-term funds. Typically, commercial paper is an unsecured, short-term promissory note issued in bearer form by a financial or nonfinancial company to satisfy its funding needs. Its popularity as a funding mechanism stems from (1) its availability as an alternative to short-term bank loans and (2) its lower relative costs when compared with bank loans or debt issuance.[1] To be exempt from securities registration requirements of the Securities

1 By issuing commercial paper, companies are able to secure funding directly from investors in the market instead of using banks as intermediaries and paying for their services.

and Exchange Commission (SEC), commercial paper must have a maturity of 270 or fewer days.[2] In practice, most commercial paper issues mature in 30 days or less, and the maturities of longer-term issues rarely exceed 90 days. While it is sometimes sold in denominations as small as $10,000, commercial paper is generally issued in denominations of millions of dollars to meet the requirements of money market funds and other institutional investors, which are the major purchasers.

The origins of commercial paper can be traced back to the 1800s. Because banking organizations were restricted to operating in one state, and often in only one location, companies in one area of the country might not be able to borrow needed funds from banking organizations in other regions. Thus, regions of the country with problems regarding the availability of credit often had interest rates higher than those in other regions. During times of high seasonal demand, companies in areas with relatively higher rates found the issuance of commercial paper to be a more cost-effective means of obtaining financing than borrowing under bank lines of credit.[3]

The growth of the market, however, essentially ceased from the Great Depression through World War II because of prevailing economic conditions. In the postwar economic boom, commercial paper again became a source of funding. During the 1960s and 1970s, growth in the commercial paper markets accelerated. One cause of the acceleration was the inability of banks to raise funds sufficient to meet corporate loan demand, which forced borrowers to look to the commercial paper market for credit.[4]

Many commercial and financial companies also discovered the commercial paper market to be a viable, cost-effective alternative to bank credit. Rates on commercial paper, Treasury bills, and certificates of deposit tend to move closely together, and all three generally change more quickly than the prime rate. During periods of falling interest rates, obtaining funds through the issuance of commercial paper may be cheaper because rates on such paper tend to move downward more quickly than the prime rate. Conversely, many commercial paper issuers have relied on bank loans during periods of rising interest rates because rates on these loans tend to change more slowly than rates on commercial paper.[5]

The growth of the commercial paper market continued to accelerate during the early 1980s as investors, because of their uncertainty regarding future rates, favored shorter maturities and as corporations waited for lower interest rates before issuing bonds. During this period, money market mutual funds grew exponentially and became the largest purchasers of commercial paper. The net effect of these vents was a continued increase, not only in the dollar volume of the commercial paper market, but also in the number and type of issuers.

The amount of commercial paper outstanding in today's market is well above $500 billion (Table 22.1). This amount represents obligations of domestic financial and nonfinancial companies as well as of multinational corporations and foreign firms and shows a growth in volume of more than 90 percent from 1985 to 1990. Although commercial paper issues are generally unsecured, the liquidity of most issues is fully supported by bank lines of credit. Most borrowers in the market reissue or "roll over" commercial paper as the primary method of financing maturing paper. Although some secondary market activity is associated with commercial paper issues, original purchasers generally hold the paper to maturity.

Table 22.1—Outstanding Amount of Commercial Paper, Selected Years, 1960–91

Billions of dollars

Year	*Outstanding amount*
1960	4.5
1965	9.3
1970	33.4
1975	48.4
1980	124.4
1985	298.8
1990	566.9
1991 (to October)	528.3

Source: Federal Reserve Bulletin.

2 Other conditions that commercial paper must meet to be exempt from registration requirements include the following: The proceeds of the notes are to be used for current transactions, and the notes are not ordinarily to be advertised for sale to the general public.

3 Marcia Stigum, *The Money Market*, rev. ed. (Dow Jones-Irwin, 1983), p. 626.

4 Timothy D. Rowe, "Commercial Paper," in Timothy Q. Cook and Timothy D. Rowe, eds., *Instruments of the Money Market* (Federal Reserve Bank of Richmond, 1986), pp. 111–35.

5 Evelyn Hurley, "The Commercial Paper Market," *Federal Reserve Bulletin*, vol. 63 (June 1977), p. 530.

OVERVIEW OF ASSET-BACKED COMMERCIAL PAPER PROGRAMS

Like other securitization programs, asset-backed commercial paper programs segregate assets into pools and transform these pools into market instruments. The payment of principal and interest on these instruments stems from the cash flows collected on the underlying assets in the pool. In such programs, the underlying assets are the receivables of corporations, and the market instrument that is issued is commercial paper.

Asset securitization began in 1970 when the federal government through the Government National Mortgage Association (GNMA) stimulated the securitization of residential mortgages by guaranteeing investors the timely receipt of principal and interest on the securities issued under the GNMA program. Soon after, the Federal Home Loan Mortgage Corporation (FHLMC) and the Federal National Mortgage Association (FNMA) also began issuing mortgage-backed securities. In 1985, securities backed by computer leases, credit card receivables, automobile loans, and other types of loans began to be issued.[6]

Asset-backed commercial paper programs use a vehicle called a special purpose entity (SPE) to issue commercial paper. The programs provide a service basically similar to that offered by a factoring company in that the SPE finances the receivables of corporate clients. In other respects, however, the SPE differs from a factoring company. Typically, a factor assumes the role of a credit department for its clients to evaluate the creditworthiness of the clients' customers. While it finances a client's receivables by purchasing them, the SPE does not perform a credit evaluation of each obligor associated with the receivables in the pool as a factor would, but relies instead on an actuarial review of the past performance of the client's portfolio of receivables. Also, with an SPE, the corporate client usually performs the servicing function whereas in a factoring arrangement the factor generally services the receivables.

Unlike more familiar mortgage or credit card securitizations, asset-backed commercial paper programs are ongoing activities that do not wind down by themselves after a few years. Generally, in the more traditional securitizations, the SPE holds a definitive pool of assets that back a specific issue of securities. Once the securities have been paid off, the transaction unwinds. In asset-backed commercial paper programs, the SPE continually purchases new receivables and usually rolls over the outstanding commercial paper.

Asset-backed commercial paper programs may differ from the more traditional securitization programs in several other ways. First, these programs issue short-term commercial paper as the instrument to fund the purchase of the underlying assets. Most other asset-backed instruments have maturities of more than two years. Second, the banking organization advising the program may provide credit enhancements or guarantees because the commercial paper is backed by assets sold to the SPE by unrelated third parties. Generally, in the more traditional securitizations, in which the acquired assets are sold by the advising banking organizations, credit enhancements are obtained from nonrelated third parties to ensure that, for accounting purposes, the selling institution can treat the transaction as a sale. Third, the commercial paper issued by these programs is less liquid than mortgage-backed securities and other types of asset-backed securities because no active secondary market exists.

At present, more than seventy asset-backed commercial paper programs are in operation, and estimates of the size of the market for this paper currently range from $50 billion to $70 billion. In the 1980s, programs advised by domestic banking organizations dominated the asset-backed commercial paper market. Currently, participants in this market also include foreign banking organizations, retail companies, and finance companies, which are estimated to account for one-half of the outstanding commercial paper issued by asset-backed commercial paper programs.

Standard & Poor's Corporation rated the first commercial paper program backed by pooled receivables in April 1983 and the second in January 1985 (Figure 22.1). By year-end 1988, Standard & Poor's had rated eleven programs with the total capacity of issuing more than $16 billion of commercial paper. By November 1991, Standard & Poor's had rated sixty such programs, which have the capacity of issuing more than $48 billion of commercial paper.[7] (See Table 22.2 for the various credit ratings and their definitions.)

6 Thomas R. Boemio and Gerald A. Edwards, Jr., "Asset Securitization: A Supervisory Perspective," *Federal Reserve Bulletin*, vol. 75 (October 1989), pp. 659–69.

7 Avi Oster and Barry Wood, "Commercial Paper: Pooled Receivables' Robust Growth," *Standard & Poor's Creditweek* (March 27, 1989), p. 90.

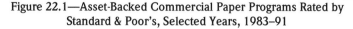

Figure 22.1—Asset-Backed Commercial Paper Programs Rated by Standard & Poor's, Selected Years, 1983–91

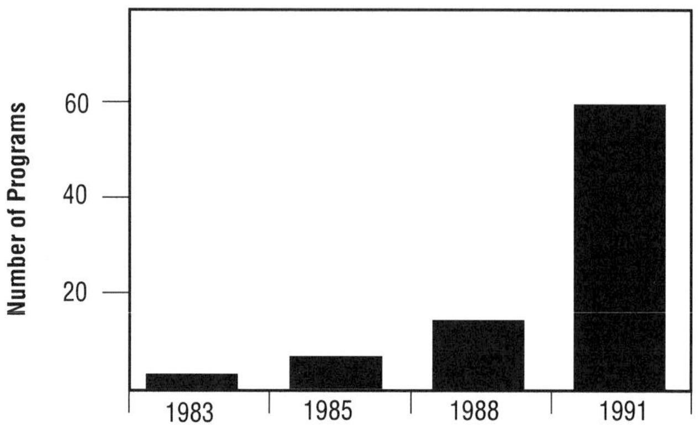

Table 22.2—Definitions of Commercial Paper Credit Ratings

Standard & Poor's Corporation		*Moody's Investors Service*	
Definition	*Rating*	*Definition*	*Rating*
Capacity for timely payment		*Ability for repayment*	
Extremely strong	A-1+	Superior	Prime 1 (P-1)
Strong	A-1		
Satisfactory	A-2	Strong	Prime 2 (P-2)
Adequate	A-3	Acceptable	Prime 3 (P-3)
Speculative	B	. . .	. . .
Doubtful capacity for payment	C	. . .	. . .
Debt in payment default	D	. . .	. . .
. . .	. . .	Not of prime quality	NP

THE SECURITIZATION PROCESS

Asset-backed commercial paper programs use an SPE to acquire legal title to receivables directly from corporations. To date, the type of receivables that have been included in such programs are trade receivables, installment sales contracts, financing leases, noncancelable portions of operating leases, and credit card receivables. By using these programs, a bank can help arrange the financing of receivables for its corporate customers without having to make loans or purchase assets, which could inflate its balance sheet and increase its capital requirements. In some instances, these programs are designed to remove assets (typically credit card receivables originated by the bank) from the advising bank's books.

To avoid having to consolidate an SPE on its balance sheet, the advising bank does not own any of the capital stock.[8] Employees of an investment banking firm or some other third party generally own the equity of the SPE. As previously noted, to obtain funding the SPE issues commercial paper, which is ultimately repaid from the cash flow of the underlying pools of receivables. The rating agencies require that the entire amount of out-

8 Under generally accepted accounting standards and SEC reporting requirements, consolidation of the SPE is usually expected if the banking organization has a controlling financial interest in the SPE. A controlling financial interest would generally be presumed if the banking organization had a majority ownership interest in the outstanding voting shares of the SPE, although control might also be deemed to exist in certain situations involving minority ownership.

Figure 22.2—An Asset-Backed Commercial Paper Program: Structure and Cash Flows

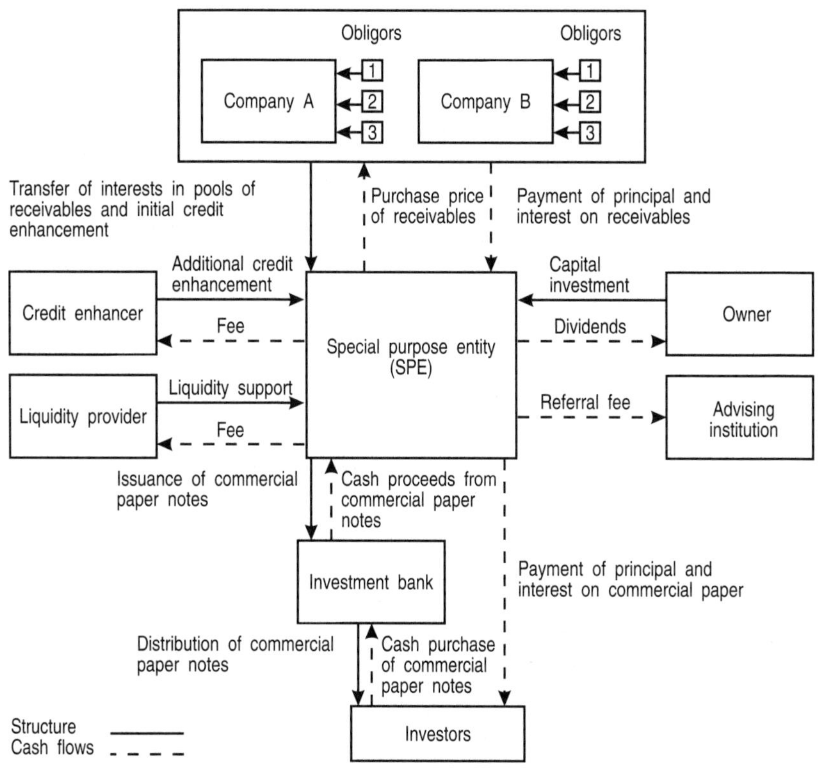

standing commercial paper be covered by liquidity and credit enhancements before the program can receive the highest investment rating (see Figure 22.2).

Bank involvement in an asset-backed commercial paper program can range from advising the program to advising and providing all of the required credit or liquidity enhancements needed to support the SPE's commercial paper. In most cases, the advising bank or an affiliate performs a review to determine whether the receivables of potential participants in the program—that is, the corporate sellers—are eligible for purchase by the SPE. The review is somewhat similar in scope to the review used in structuring securitizations backed by credit card receivables or automobile loans. It covers the credit origination standards of the corporation and the current and historical quality and performance of its portfolio. Ideally, the bank traces the performance of the corporation's portfolio through a complete business cycle and evaluates the current portfolio's expected performance. The bank reviews the receivables in the portfolio to make sure that they are widely distributed across regions of the country and among obligors and industries. Once a bank or its affiliate determines that a corporation's portfolio has an acceptable credit-risk profile, the bank or an affiliate approves the purchase of the company's receivables portfolio by the SPE.

The bank or an affiliate may also act as the operating agent for the SPE. Acting as operating agent entails structuring the sales of pools of the corporate client's receivables to the SPE and continuously monitoring the performance of the pools. The SPE then issues commercial paper in an amount equal to the discounted purchase price of the receivables and uses the proceeds of the sale to buy the receivables from the seller. A company that sells its receivables to an SPE traditionally acts as the servicer for the receivables and, as such, is responsible for collecting interest and principal payments on the amounts from the obligors and for periodically passing these funds to the SPE.

Credit Enhancements and Liquidity Facilities

Asset-backed commercial paper programs typically have several levels of credit enhancement to protect investors from loss. The first level of protection in these programs is generally the difference between the face value of the receivables purchased and the discounted price paid, known as a hold-back or overcollateralization. In some cases, the terms of the sale also give the SPE recourse back to the seller if there are defaults on the receivables. The amount of overcollateralization varies from pool to pool and depends mainly on the asset quality of the receivables originated by the corporate client and the desired credit rating for the commercial paper issued by the SPE. Usually, the level of credit protection provided by overcollateralization is specified as a multiple of historical losses.

The second level of credit safeguards is designed to absorb any losses that exceed the sum of the overcollateralization and recourse. Secondary credit enhancements include letters of credit, surety bonds, or other backup facilities, such as agreements that obligate a third party to purchase pools of receivables from the SPE at a specific price. The loss protection provided by the overcollateralization and secondary credit enhancements may range from 15 percent to 35 percent of the amount of commercial paper outstanding.

Besides the support provided by these credit enhancements, asset-backed commercial paper programs usually have support from a liquidity facility. The general purpose of the liquidity facility (sometimes referred to as a liquidity backup line) is to provide funds to the SPE to retire maturing commercial paper when a mismatch occurs in the maturities of the underlying receivables and the commercial paper obligations or when a disruption occurs in the commercial paper market. Thus, in its purest sense, the liquidity facility's purpose is to cover temporary shortfalls in the cash flows of the SPE that do not result from credit losses on the underlying receivables.

The credit enhancements and liquidity facility of an asset-backed commercial paper program may be provided separately or they may be provided together under a single arrangement with a bank. In a combined arrangement, a bank may be required to purchase pools of receivables to provide funds to the SPE to pay off maturing commercial paper, regardless of whether the funding shortfall resulted from credit deterioration in the particular pool or a liquidity problem in the overall commercial paper market.

When one bank provides both the credit and the liquidity support enhancements, whether in separate facilities or in a combined arrangement, the commercial paper's rating is integrally tied to the bank's own short-term rating. Recently, Standard & Poor's placed several asset-backed commercial paper programs on "Creditwatch," with negative implications, after the short-term deposit rating of the bank that provided the credit and liquidity enhancement was downgraded from A-1+ to A-1. The reason for the close scrutiny of these programs was their reliance on just one bank for both liquidity and credit support. In other asset-backed commercial paper programs, the A-1+ ratings for the commercial paper were maintained, despite the deterioration of one bank's short-term rating because the bank was part of a diversified group of banks providing credit and liquidity support.

In rating the commercial paper issued through these programs, the rating agencies consider the protection provided investors by credit enhancements and backup liquidity facilities. Two criteria used by rating agencies are of particular importance. First, to obtain the highest credit rating, commercial paper issued by the SPE must generally have 100 percent liquidity support, which may be provided by a combination of the liquidity and credit enhancements. For example, if the program is protected by a 15 percent credit enhancement, a liquidity backup line of 85 percent will be necessary. Second, the rating on the commercial paper is integrally tied to the rating on direct obligations of the bank providing the enhancements. Thus, if the short-term deposit rating of the bank providing the enhancements is A-2/P-2, the commercial paper of the SPE will be given a similar rating at best and never a higher one.

Incentives for Banking Organizations

Through asset-backed commercial paper programs, banking organizations can help arrange short-term financing support for their customers without having to extend them credit directly. Thus, by keeping these potential loans off their books, banking organizations effectively reduce their capital requirements. Banking organizations also earn fee income for the service of packaging and monitoring pools of receivables as well as for providing liquidity facilities and credit enhancements. The programs therefore improve the performance measures of banks involved, not only because the fees earned add to revenue but also because revenue is increased without a corresponding increase in the banks' asset levels. Banks also contend that these vehicles allow them to help meet the financing needs of investment-grade customers that have relied on commercial paper in lieu of bank borrowing, and thus enable the banks to regain market share.

Incentives for Participating Companies

Companies wishing to obtain financing choose asset-backed commercial paper programs for several reasons. First, these programs provide participating companies with an additional, reliable source of funding at a relatively stable cost. This stability of funding costs results from the diversified pool of assets that back the commercial paper issued by the SPE and the extensive credit and liquidity support involved. Also, unlike traditional commercial paper programs, the cost of funding associated with these asset-backed programs is considered relatively stable because adverse conditions experienced by an individual participant generally do not affect the overall program's cost. Second, companies may want to clean up their balance sheets by reducing their total assets to improve performance ratios or by limiting the amount of their own paper outstanding in the market and, instead, issuing new paper through the SPE. Third, the funding costs associated with these asset-backed programs may be less than the direct funding costs for customers with a commercial paper rating below A-1/P-1. Finally, these arrangements may provide indirect access to the commercial paper market for companies that are unable to gain direct access.

Risks Associated with These Programs

Three fundamental models, with variants of each type, seem to underlie the structuring of the credit and liquidity support of these programs. First, a program can combine the credit and liquidity support into one arrangement; such a combination generally results in an effective guarantee of the entire amount of outstanding commercial paper. Second, a bank can provide separate credit and liquidity enhancements. Third, some programs have separate credit and liquidity support mechanisms provided by one or more third-party institutions. This last model is generally used when a bank is selling its own assets, typically credit card receivables, to the SPE. The bank uses this model to ensure that the transfer will be treated as a true sale of assets, that is, without any recourse to the bank. The resulting sales treatment allows the bank to remove the assets from its books and thus reduce its capital requirements.

The banking organization providing credit or liquidity support to one of these programs may have to raise funds itself in connection with these obligations to provide funds to the SPE. For example, the downgrading of the short-term deposit rating of a bank providing the credit or liquidity support could result in a simultaneous downgrading of the commercial paper issued by the SPE. In such an event, the SPE may be unable to roll over, or pay off, some or all of its outstanding commercial paper at maturity. In this circumstance, the credit deterioration in the bank providing credit or liquidity support could create a liquidity problem for the SPE. Furthermore, if cash inflows from the underlying receivables are insufficient to pay off the maturing commercial paper issued by the SPE, then the liquidity facility could be drawn down. These potential liquidity problems are exacerbated because the SEC now restricts money market mutual funds, which are major purchasers of asset-backed commercial paper, to investing no more than 5 percent of their assets in paper rated A-2/P-2 or worse at the time of purchase.[9]

Finally, a significant deterioration in asset quality—one exhausting the overcollateralization or recourse credit enhancements—could result in losses being absorbed by the secondary credit enhancements, usually letters of credit or cash collateral.

The liquidity or credit problems previously mentioned, in effect, could bring some portion of the SPE's assets onto the balance sheets of the banking organizations providing the credit and liquidity support enhancements. In such a case, the banking organizations providing the enhancements would have to acquire some portion of the assets of the SPE or extend credit to the SPE, both of which actions would increase the total assets of the banking organizations. This increase would adversely affect their capital ratios and certain performance ratios. Because the structures of asset-backed commercial paper programs usually differ, a case-by-case analysis of these programs is necessary to ascertain the exact nature and the extent of the risks in any credit or liquidity enhancements supporting an SPE's commercial paper.

---

9 In June 1991, the SEC adopted amendments to its rule 2a-7 that essentially require a money market fund to limit its total investment in securities rated A-2/P-2 or below to 5 percent of its assets and to limit investment in such securities of any one issuer to 1 percent of its assets.

RISK-BASED CAPITAL IMPLICATIONS FOR ASSET-BACKED COMMERCIAL PAPER

A question arises as to whether the liquidity and credit enhancements supporting asset-backed commercial paper constitutes a commitment or a direct credit substitute, that is, a guarantee of the banks providing these enhancements. The Board's risk-based capital guidelines require banks to hold less capital to support a commitment than to support a guarantee. Therefore, determining whether liquidity and credit enhancements are commitments or guarantees may affect the pricing of these off-balance-sheet obligations and, in turn, the profitability of these programs.

Under the risk-based capital guidelines, direct credit substitutes include any irrevocable arrangements that guarantee repayment of financial obligations, including commercial paper. These guidelines contain the following definition of a financial guarantee:

> the combination of irrevocability with the fact that funding is triggered by some failure to repay or perform an obligation. Thus, any commitment (by whatever name) that involves an irrevocable obligation to make a payment to the customer or to a third party in the event the customer fails to repay an outstanding debt obligation . . . is treated, for risk-based capital purposes, as . . . a financial guarantee.[10]

Such off-balance-sheet guarantees are converted at 100 percent to a credit equivalent amount on the balance sheet and then weighted according to the risk of the counterparty, after taking into account any eligible collateral or guarantees.

These direct credit substitutes or guarantees must be supported by the same amount of capital as if the obligation were held directly—as a loan—on the bank's balance sheet. The reason for this treatment is that the bank providing the guarantee faces the same credit risk as if it had a direct on-balance-sheet loan to the beneficiary of the guarantee. Thus, assuming that a loan to a borrower would be assigned a risk weight of 100 percent, a guarantee of the borrower's financial obligations would generally be assigned the same risk weight of 100 percent.

A guarantee, or direct credit substitute, is normally drawn down when the primary obligor has experienced some difficulties and therefore is unable to pay its financial obligations. A distinguishing feature of an irrevocable guarantee arrangement is that it does not customarily contain a "material adverse change" (MAC) clause or similar provision that would enable the bank providing the guarantee to escape its obligation.

In contrast to a financial guarantee, a commitment is defined for risk-based capital purposes as an arrangement that obligates a bank to extend credit in the form of loans or leases, or to purchase loans or other assets. The important difference between a financial guarantee and a commitment is that the latter is usually drawn down in the normal course of business rather than when a party cannot meet its obligations. A commitment generally will contain provisions abrogating the lender's obligation and thus helping to limit its risk if the borrower's condition worsens. However, the presence or absence of a MAC clause or other escape mechanism has no bearing on the appropriate capital treatment.

Under the risk-based capital guidelines, if the original maturity of a commitment exceeds one year, then it is considered "long term" and is converted at 50 percent to a credit equivalent amount on the balance sheet. Alternatively, if the original maturity of the commitment is one year or less, it is considered to be "short term" and the conversion factor becomes 0 percent. Thus, a bank is not required to hold capital in support of a short-term commitment.

Backup facilities under asset-backed commercial paper programs that meet the definition of guarantees for risk-based capital purposes are to be treated as guarantees. For example, there are "commitments" that obligate a banking organization to loan against or to acquire the underlying receivables at the price paid by the SPE, regardless of the quality of the receivables or any losses on them. In this structure, the SPE would use the proceeds to retire the commercial paper. Under these arrangements, banks cannot revoke their obligation to purchase the underlying receivables, regardless of any deterioration in quality; likewise, there is generally no limit on the amount of credit loss the bank may be subject to, that is, 100 percent of the enhancement is available to absorb credit losses. Consequently, the banks providing these

---

10 Board of Governors of the Federal Reserve System, *Capital Adequacy Guidelines* (Board of Governors, 1989), p. 13 and p. 41 (12 C.F.R. pt. 208, app. A, sec. III.D.1 and 12 C.F.R. pt. 225, app. A, sec. III.D.1).

enhancements ultimately protect the commercial paper investors against loss by guaranteeing that the SPEs will have funds to redeem their commercial paper. Arrangements that have characteristics of a financial guarantee are regarded as direct credit substitutes for purposes of the risk-based capital guidelines. Such an agreement, even when called a commitment, should be converted at 100 percent to a credit equivalent amount on the balance sheet and generally is risk weighted at 100 percent.

In contrast, other facilities differentiate between what is potentially available to absorb credit losses and what is available to facilitate liquidity. These liquidity facilities are most commonly characterized by, at the very least, a test for some minimum asset quality that must be met before funds will be extended to the SPE. For example, funds may not be drawn against receivables of lesser quality, in other words, those in default. Therefore, these facilities could be considered commitments and may be treated as such for purposes of risk-based capital.

EXAMINER GUIDANCE

In 1990, to ensure consistency during examinations, the Federal Reserve provided guidance to its examiners to use when reviewing an institution's involvement with asset securitization transactions. Although not specifically directed toward asset-backed commercial paper programs, many aspects of these existing examination guidelines are applicable to these vehicles. For example, the guidance instructs examiners to check that a banking organization participating in a securitization transaction—whether an asset-backed commercial paper program or some other type—has clearly and logically integrated these activities into its overall strategic objectives. In addition, it states that examiners should determine that the management of the organization understands the risks associated with the various roles that the institution can assume in such programs.

Examiners are also instructed to determine that appropriate policies, procedures, and controls, including well-developed management information systems, are in place before the banking organization participates in these programs. They should ascertain that the banking organization's board of directors periodically reviews significant policies and procedures relating to these programs before approving them.

Based on this guidance, a banking organization involved in asset-backed commercial paper programs should establish overall limits on the actual amounts of credit and liquidity commitments. Institutions involved in these programs should also analyze the underlying pools of receivables and the structure of the commercial paper program. This analysis should include a review of the following:

- The characteristics, credit quality, and expected performance of the underlying receivables
- The banking organization's ability to meet its obligations under the securitization arrangement
- The ability of the other participants in the arrangement to meet their obligations.

A banking organization involved in an asset-backed commercial paper program needs to have established policies and procedures to ensure that it follows prudent standards of credit assessment and approval. Such policies and procedures would be applicable to all pools of receivables to be purchased by the SPE as well as the extension of any credit enhancements and liquidity facilities. Procedures should include an initial, thorough credit assessment of each pool for which the bank has assumed credit risk, followed by periodic credit reviews to monitor performance throughout the duration of the exposure. Furthermore, the policies and procedures should outline the credit approval process and establish "in-house" exposure limits, on a consolidated basis, with respect to particular industries or organizations, that is, the companies from which the SPE purchased the receivables as well as the receivable obligors.

For those banking organizations providing credit enhancements and liquidity facilities, an analysis of the institution's funding capabilities should be performed to ensure that these institutions are capable of meeting their obligations under all foreseeable circumstances. In addition, an analysis should be completed to determine the effects of the fulfillment of these obligations on the banking organization's interest rate exposure, asset quality, liquidity position, and capital adequacy.

Examiners, in reviewing backup lines supporting this type of commercial paper, will distinguish between guarantees and commitments. A backup arrangement is considered a direct credit substitute and, thus, is risk weighted at 100 percent if it provides credit enhancement to the asset-backed commercial paper program. In contrast, if the facility is determined to be solely for liquidity support and meets the definition of a short-term commitment with a maturity of one year or less, as outlined in the Federal Reserve Board's risk-based capital guidelines, a zero conversion factor applies.

CONCLUSION

In recent years, commercial and investment bankers have become involved with new asset securitization programs at an increasing rate, and this trend is likely to continue. A relatively new form of securitization, asset-backed commercial paper appears to be growing in popularity, from the perspective both of the investor and of the companies using these programs for financing. To date, there are no indications that investors are reaching a point of saturation with these commercial paper issues. Rather, these issues appear to be a favored means of providing investors with a method of achieving even greater diversification of credit risk.

The market appears to be evolving in the direction of programs that involve an SPE that accommodates referrals of corporate customers from multiple banks rather than from just one institution. Also, the market seems to be moving toward having several parties provide credit and liquidity enhancements. Mechanisms such as cash collateral, which minimize the effects of a downgrade of the ratings of the associated instruments of one party, seem to be growing in popularity. These developments may limit the risks associated with asset-backed commercial paper programs.

Asset securitization activities should remain beneficial to banking organizations when conducted in a prudent manner. Banking organizations, however, must carefully evaluate the risks inherent in any new form of asset securitization and maintain appropriate controls, systems, and other measures to minimize these risks. Banking regulators will continue to review new asset-backed security structures as they develop in order to assess the associated risks to banking organizations and to the financial system.

REFERENCES

Board of Governors of the Federal Reserve System, *Capital Adequacy Guidelines.* Washington: Board of Governors, 1989.

Boemio, Thomas R., and Gerald A. Edwards, Jr. "Asset Securitization: A Supervisory Perspective." *Federal Reserve Bulletin*, vol. 75 (October 1989), pp. 659–69.

Cook, Timothy Q., and Timothy D. Rowe, eds. *Instruments of the Money Market*, 6th ed. Richmond: Federal Reserve Bank of Richmond, 1986.

Duff & Phelps Credit Rating Agency, *Performance Trend Report.* Chicago: D&PCRA, Second Quarter 1991.

Duff & Phelps, Inc. *Rating Approach for Asset-Backed Commercial Paper.* Chicago: D&PI, March 1990.

Hurley, Evelyn M. "The Commercial Paper Market since the Mid-Seventies," *Federal Reserve Bulletin*, vol. 68 (June 1982), pp. 327–34.

________________. "The Commercial Paper Market," *Federal Reserve Bulletin*, vol. 63 (June 1977), pp. 523–36.

Kravitt, Jason H.P., ed. *Securitization of Financial Assets.* Englewood Cliffs, N.J.: Prentice Hall Law & Business, 1991.

Kuhn, Robert Lawrence, ed. *Mortgage and Asset Securitization.* Homewood, Ill.: Dow Jones-Irwin, 1990.

Oster, Avi, and Barry Wood. "Commercial Paper: Pooled Receivables' Robust Growth," *Standard & Poor's Creditweek* (March 27, 1989), pp. 89–91.

Stigum, Marcia. *The Money Market*, rev. ed. Homewood, Ill: Dow Jones-Irwin, 1983.

Part V

Mortgage-Backed Securities

Chapter 23

MAES ECP No. 1 PLC: An Example of the Risks and Rewards of Asset-Backed Euro Commercial Paper

by Candy Helman,
Vice President
J.P. Morgan Securities Ltd.

Although asset-backed commercial paper (CP) is a common concept in the United States where outstanding short-term asset-backed paper tops $50 billion, the European markets have seen no more than three or four such programmes. Precedents such as the MAES ECP No. 1 programme backed by a portfolio of UK residential mortgages and the Hifin programme for Union Carbide backed by trade receivables have existed for several years, but they have yet to be copied. Although the lack of asset-backed Euro commercial paper (ECP) programmes results in part from limited demand from European borrowers for off-balance sheet finance, unfamiliarity also plays a part in restricting the development of the market. However, there are many reasons for borrowers throughout Europe to find asset-backed finance more attractive than in the past including growing leverage concerns, decreasing availability of bank finance and higher short-term borrowing costs. Equally, as European investors gain sophistication and come to have greater confidence in public ratings, asset-backed ECP, provided it offers a slight yield premium, should become recognised as an attractive investment.

Despite the high credit ratings of most asset-backed debt, this type of structured debt does expose investors to a wide range of different risks. However, it is the responsibility of all parties to a transaction—the arranger, the originator, the rating agencies, the trustee and the lawyers—to review these risks and to address them through the transaction structure and the legal documents. This article will aim to explain the various risks that arise and to describe the structures designed to protect investors against them. Throughout this article, I will use an existing European programme, the residential mortgage-backed MAES ECP deal, as an example. Although I expect the growth in the asset-backed ECP market in the next several years to come from securitisation of short-term trade receivables rather than mortgage or other long-term assets, the risks that arise and the ways of addressing them are similar regardless of the actual assets securitised. However, before describing the MAES structure in detail, I will briefly discuss the advantages of asset-backed ECP compared with other types of securitised debt.

THE BENEFITS OF ASSET-BACKED ECP

Lower Cost

Compared with other longer-term forms of securitised debt, asset-backed CP or ECP offers a number of economic and non-economic benefits to a borrower. First, because the debt issued is short term, it tends to carry a lower margin than long-term asset-backed bonds. Even after taking into account the costs of various other elements of an ECP programme, primarily the backstop facility, the financing cost of an asset-backed ECP programme may be significantly less than that of a bond. The incremental cost of financing assets through securitisation is a major objection raised by borrowers, so that the lower rate can be an important attraction to them. In addition, many of the upfront structuring expenses of a short-term deal such as rating fees and legal fees (reflecting more streamlined documentation) will be lower. Depending on the period over which they are amortised, upfront fees can add significantly to the all-in cost of a financing, so again savings on fees can improve the economics of a transaction for a borrower.

Flexibility

In addition to its cost advantages, asset-backed ECP tends to be more flexible than other longer-term forms of securitisation. In particular, ECP is well suited to assets such as trade receivables or credit card balances which experience fluctuating principal balances due to repayments by borrowers and new purchases of goods during a period. Specifically, the amount of ECP issued on any day can be adjusted to match the current principal balance of the receivables. By issuing ECP in a number of tranches, which can be as small as $10 or $20 million, it is easy to stagger interest periods and roll-over dates. This reduces an issuer's exposure to volatile market conditions and to sudden temporary spikes in interest rates.

Simplicity

Lastly, asset-backed ECP programmes can be easier to structure than longer-term securities because of less onerous rating requirements. Whereas long-term investors have a strong preference for AAA ratings, CP or ECP investors are generally satisfied with A-1/P-1 ratings. These short-term ratings categories encompass a range of long-term ratings down to A– and A3 for Standard & Poor's (S&P) and Moody's respectively. This means that a borrower can involve credit enhancement and other facility providers of a lower rating in an ECP programme than he could for a longer issue. Therefore, the universe of potential facility providers is larger, leading to greater competition and finer pricing.

THE DISADVANTAGES OF ASSET-BACKED ECP

Although asset-backed ECP offers significant benefits to borrowers, it is not without its disadvantages. Among the major disadvantages is the need for a committed backstop facility from a group of banks to support the programme (see "Backstop Facility" below). As banks cut back on both lending and commitments to lend in order to meet BIS target capital ratios, these facilities have become more difficult to arrange. The shortage of potential facility providers is further aggravated by the rating agencies' strict credit requirements for the participants in rated securitisations. For any asset-backed programme seeking an A-1/P-1 rating, all backstop banks must themselves be A-1/P-1 rated. Following the well publicised problems of the banking industry and the widespread deterioration of individual bank's credit ratings, the universe of eligible backstop providers has contracted. However, provided the facilities are properly structured, they can be both attractive business for bank providers and economically priced for borrowers.

Despite the low volume of asset-backed commercial paper issued to date in Europe, JP Morgan Securities Ltd. has had an excellent experience as dealer for an existing asset-backed programme, MAES ECP No. 1 PLC. The MAES programme finances a pool of UK residential mortgages and carries an A-1 rating from Standard & Poor's and a P-1 rating from Moody's. It was voted ECP Programme of the Year in 1989 by International Financing Review, a major Euromarket publication, and has consistently provided competitive off-balance sheet funding for CIBC Mortgages ("CIBCM"), a subsidiary of Canadian Imperial Bank of Commerce and the originator of the securitised mortgages. Although I expect the growth in the asset-backed ECP market to come from securitisation of short-term assets such as trade receivables, the experience of establishing the MAES programme and its structure can provide a useful example of the risks that a borrower and his advisor must address in bringing an asset-backed ECP programme to market.

DESCRIPTION OF THE MAES STRUCTURE

MAES ECP No. 1, the issuer, is structured as a so-called "orphan" company with no direct links to CIBCM as originator and administrator of the securitised loan portfolio. Rather, an independent trustee holds the shares of the company on behalf of a charitable organisation as owner. Although CIBCM has no control over MAES ECP, its interests are protected by a representative on the company's board and, more importantly, by the legal contracts that strictly limit MAES ECP's rights and obligations. In fact, the company has very little discretion to take decisions which might conflict with CIBCM's interest.

The sale of the original mortgage portfolio by CIBCM to MAES was entirely without any recourse to CIBCM or any other CIBC company. Only in the event that warranties given by CIBCM at the time of sale on the characteristics and quality of the mortgages later prove to be untrue will CIBCM be obliged to repurchase any assets. In addition to the original sale, CIBCM has agreed to generate mortgages in the future on behalf of MAES which will act as direct lender. New mortgages can be used to replace original mortgages that have repaid or to increase the programme size subject to arranging additional backstop facilities.

Although practices vary from country to country, generally accountants and regulators will require both an independent issuing company and a non-recourse sale as preconditions to achieving off-balance sheet treatment of the securitised debt. The rating agencies will also be concerned to insure that the issuing company is unconnected to the originator and would not be adversely affected by the originator's bankruptcy. In the MAES case, CIBC achieved off-balance sheet treatment of the securitised debt both for accounting and regulatory purposes.

In the MAES transaction, where the securitised assets are residential mortgages, the rating agencies stipulate that each borrower must have made at least one payment before a loan can be included in the pool. MAES addressed this requirement by holding new loans in a separate so-called "seasoning" pool for several months before transferring them to the securitised pool and financing them with ECP. For other asset types where the risk of non-performance can be better judged, this may not be necessary. For instance, in the case of trade receivables, where the rating agencies can assess the credit quality of specific obligors or rely on their past payment history, seasoning will not be a major credit issue.

In securitisations such as MAES where a changing body of investors have an equal claim on a changing pool of assets, it is normal for a trustee to hold security over the assets on behalf of all lenders. In addition to investors and backstop banks, the issuer may have various other creditors such as swap or foreign exchange counterparties. The security arrangements are set out in a charge document which includes the rankings of the various creditors. In general, the lenders, be they banks or noteholders, will have a priority position second only to the fees of the trustee and any administrator, if appointed.

CREDIT RISK AND CREDIT ENHANCEMENT

Outside of the assets themselves, credit enhancement is probably the most important element of any securitisation. Because the special purpose issuer has only nominal capital and no resources other than the asset pool, it is important to insure that investors are protected against losses due to defaults on the assets. This protection is generally called credit enhancement and can be provided in different forms including insurance policies, guarantees, bank letters of credit, overcollateralisation, cash cushions and subordinated debt. Regardless of its form, the purpose of credit enhancement is to insure timely payment of interest and principal to investors even when non-payment by the underlying borrowers causes a cash shortfall in the special purpose issuer.

In the MAES ECP programme, credit enhancement takes the form of a pool insurance policy from UK insurer Eagle Star. Under the terms of the policy, Eagle Star agree to cover losses arising on individual loans following repossession and sale of the defaulting borrower's property and after claims on any other existing insurance policies up to a maximum amount equal to 10 percent of the mortgage pool. In addition to principal losses, the Eagle Star insurance covers accrued but unpaid interest and enforcement expenses.

Because MAES can only claim on the Eagle Star policy after sale of a property, it also requires interim finance for overdue interest payments pending crystallisation of a loss. MAES relies on a committed liquidity facility from Morgan Guaranty Trust Company of New York to finance this temporary cash shortfall. The combination of the committed liquidity facility and the pool insurance assures investors that they will receive timely payments of interest and principal even if the issuer suffers credit losses, subject only to the performance of the credit enhancement providers and to the sufficiency of the enhancement.

In order to achieve an acceptable rating for a CP or ECP programme, credit enhancement and liquidity facilities must be in place only for the life of the outstanding paper. However, if the life of the assets will exceed that of the notes, the party assuming the implicit refinancing risk, usually the backstop banks, may require the term of the credit enhancement to match that of the assets. This was the case in the MAES transaction where the Eagle Star pool policy insured the loans for their full lives.

Because the credit enhancement is a key element of a transaction's credit structure, the rating agencies will carefully scrutinise the enhancement arrangements. In particular, the agencies will want to confirm that the enhancement will be available in all circumstances and that the enhancer will be able to meet its obligations at all times. On the latter point, Standard & Poor's so-called "weak link" theory states that none of the component parts of a structured financing may be rated lower than the overall rating of the transaction. Therefore, the credit enhancement provider for an asset-backed ECP programme must be at least as highly rated as the programme itself. Although there is greater flexibility to use lower-rated providers in short-term financings where a single rating category encompasses a range of long-term ratings, choosing a weak enhancement provider increases the risk of downgrade of the programme.

Another important credit consideration arose in the MAES transaction because CIBCM wanted the ability to substitute new loans for those that had repaid and to increase the size of the ECP programme by adding new mortgages to the pool. Clearly, such substitution and expansion options could lead to a substantial change in the composition of the pool over time. Therefore, it was necessary to incorporate controls in the programme documentation to insure that the credit quality of the total pool was not reduced. A similar concern will arise in securitisations of most short-term assets, such as trade receivables, where a portfolio can turn over as many as four or five times during a year.

The MAES transaction addresses this credit risk initially by setting certain minimum eligibility criteria for individual mortgages which roughly correspond to CIBCM's lending criteria. Further, to insure that the overall risk profile of the pool remains unchanged, the agencies require that CIBCM as administrator carry out periodic checks on the pool composition. CIBCM accomplishes this by feeding certain key criteria on the assets in the new pool (product breakdown, geographic distribution, loan to value ratios, etc.) into a computer model to derive the implied credit enhancement requirement of the current portfolio. Provided that the result of the analysis is no higher than the original requirement of 10 percent, the agencies will be satisfied that credit quality is maintained. In addition, certain other triggers related to the performance of assets in the pool, such as arrears rates, are set as a precondition to MAES' ability to include new assets in the pool.

In a trade receivables securitisation, the risk of deteriorating asset quality is more likely to be addressed by setting concentration limits on the percentage of the total pool that a particular obligor or certain groups of obligors' receivables may constitute. In addition, the agencies will monitor the actual performance of the receivables compared with expectations by reviewing aging data and loss statistics. Given the very short-term nature of trade receivables, it is fairly easy to wind-down a programme if asset performance falls below acceptable levels.

If a borrower believes his asset quality may decline or that it will be too difficult or inconvenient to monitor credit quality throughout the life of a transaction, he may opt for a full guarantee of his debt. Such a guarantee effectively provides investors with 100 percent loss coverage and, provided that the guarantor is satisfactory to the rating agencies, they will simply extend his rating to the programme. Though a full guarantee simplifies rating agency and investor credit analysis, potential guarantors will no doubt have the same concerns about maintaining credit quality of the pool as the rating agencies and will probably impose similar concentration limits and performance tests.

An originator can provide credit enhancement himself in the form of overcollateralisation or a holdback of a portion of the purchase price of the assets. Alternatively, enhancement can be purchased from third parties as in the MAES transaction. Whilst it will be most economic for the originator to provide the enhancement, this will only make sense if the seller's accountants allow off-balance sheet treatment despite retention of risk. In the U.S., corporate sellers of receivables or other assets can achieve off-balance sheet treatment for transactions involving overcollateralisation, but European accountants tend to be considerably more conservative than their American counterparts. Therefore, it is doubtful that European sellers of assets could take securitised debt off-balance sheet if they retain exposure to all of the expected losses. It is more likely that European sellers will take a small "top slice" risk with the remaining credit enhancement provided by a third party bank or insurance company.

REFINANCING RISK AND THE BACKSTOP FACILITY

Although in most asset-backed CP or ECP programmes including MAES, the borrower plans to repay outstanding notes by issuing new paper, the rating agencies will not rely on an issuer's continued access to the market. Rather, they will require some guaranteed source of refinancing if the maturity of the assets stretches beyond that of the outstanding notes. This refinancing risk is normally covered by a committed bank facility and in the MAES transaction an original group of 15 banks provided such a backstop. In the event that ECP becomes unavailable generally or unavailable to MAES because of specific investor concerns, MAES will use the proceeds of a drawing on the backstop facility to repay its noteholders.

If a borrower succeeds in tapping the ECP market and does not draw on the backstop facility he will pay only a commitment fee to the banks rather than a drawn margin. This lowers a borrower's all-in financing cost. Borrowers may be able to reduce fees further by limiting the term of the backstop facility to no more than 364 days.

Because BIS capital guidelines do not require a bank to allocate capital to undrawn commitments of less than one year, the fees on these short facilities tend to be substantially lower than for longer-term commitments.

In structuring a backstop facility, it is important to balance the facility banks' credit concerns and the rating agencies' desire to insure that noteholders are adequately protected against refinancing risk. Noteholders are best protected by a facility that is unconditionally available for drawing by the issuer. However, if the facility is so structured, the backstop banks effectively provide a guarantee to the noteholders and will price their commitments to reflect the credit risk that they are assuming. This is likely to prove uneconomic if the borrower has also purchased third party credit enhancement as he will be paying twice for credit protection.

In the MAES transaction, these conflicting interests are addressed by incorporating two "stages" of defaults into the facility agreement—a limited set of conditions that apply whilst paper is outstanding in the market and a fuller set of terms in force when, and if, all of the assets are financed by the backstop facility. In addition, the facility agreement contains a number of credit-related events which, if they occur, require suspension of the issuer's substitution rights and lead to the gradual wind-down of the programme. These triggers are designed to protect banks against the risk of further asset deterioration when the existing pool has performed significantly below expectations. With this type of risk sharing agreement, the backstop banks and noteholders can rank *pari passu* in proportion to their actual outstandings.

Both rating agencies consider the financial condition of the backstop banks to be very important and will not allow any participant in a facility to have a rating below that of the intended rating of the programme. This requirement imposes limits on the universe of eligible candidates and leads, inevitably, to higher pricing for the facility. Further, because the backstop banks constitute dependent ratings for an ECP programme, there is a risk that the downgrading of a single facility participant will jeopardise the programme rating. In order to avoid the cost and inconvenience resulting from a downgrade, it is important that the facility documentation provide for the resignation or replacement of any participant that is downgraded. Alternatively, the issuer may have the right to draw and redeposit the downgraded bank's share of the facility. Whilst this mechanism will address the rating agencies' credit concerns, it will increase a borrower's costs. If a programme finances short-term assets, such as trade receivables, a borrower can choose to reduce the programme size rather than suffer downgrade, although this will reduce the efficiency of the financing for the borrower.

In the case of the MAES programme, the intended maturity of the programme was five years and, hence, the borrower arranged a five-year committed facility which included an option to extend the facility annually for a further year with the lenders' approval. In addition to taking the credit risk of the loans during the life of the transaction, because MAES' mortgages are as long as 25 to 35 years, the backstop banks also face a refinancing risk at maturity of the facility. At the time that the facility was arranged, finance was freely available to UK mortgage lenders and most banks were willing to rely on MAES' ability to refinance.[1] However, in today's very different environment for mortgage finance, it would be very difficult, if not impossible, to arrange such a facility at an economic cost and this is a major reason why other mortgage lenders have not copied the MAES structure.

As mentioned earlier, the availability of 364-day facilities is greater and consequently the cost lower. However, a short facility is suitable only

1 The MAES programme is still active. The backstop facility supporting the programme was renewed in part once, extending its final maturity from 1993 to 1994. It was not renewed subsequently. Therefore, the refinancing risk that I refer to will arise in 1994. It is as yet unclear what will happen then. There are several options: MAES may attempt to sell the mortgages to a third party, which might include a CIBC company although obviously CIBC has no obligation to buy the mortgages; MAES may arrange a new backstop facility for the principal value of mortgages outstanding with a group of banks that may include many of the existing facility providers and continue the ECP programme; or MAES might arrange a different type of securitised financing, such as, say, a mortgage-backed floating rate note. In the unlikely event that none of these forms of refinancing can be accomplished, there is a risk that the facility must be renegotiated.

In any event, the portfolio will naturally shrink over time if assets that prepay are not replaced through substitution. UK mortgages tend to turn over quickly and many lenders such as CIBC experience repayment rates as high as 20–30 percent per annum. A lender can cause even faster prepayment by raising his mortgage rate well above the average in the market, although most lenders are unwilling to do this for commercial reasons.

when the assets themselves are very short as in the case, for example, of trade receivables. Otherwise, potential lenders may be concerned that they will be forced to roll over their commitments and may view their participations as effectively longer term. A borrower whose assets are of short duration may be able to reduce his costs by providing a backstop for less than 100 percent of the value of the financing. Depending on the characteristics of the securitised assets, the rating agencies may agree to rely on scheduled liquidations of the assets to provide part of the repayments due on outstanding notes. However, they are unlikely to rely solely on liquidation of receivables to repay debt.

HEDGING FOREIGN EXCHANGE RISK

If a borrower plans to securitise assets that are denominated in a currency other than that of the financing, the rating agencies will require all foreign exchange risks to be fully hedged. This type of exposure can be covered in one of two ways: either through a rolling series of short-term foreign exchange spot and forward transactions or through a single long-term cross currency swap. In the MAES ECP programme, where notes were issued in U.S. dollars against a pounds sterling denominated mortgage portfolio, MAES chose the former alternative. Whilst both forms of hedging cover foreign exchange risk equally well, they each have their advantages and disadvantages. The considerable flexibility afforded by the short-term method of hedging attracted MAES. However, this technique does not fix a borrower's all-in financing cost. An element of uncertainty arises because a borrower's all-in cost is dependent not only on the ECP yield but also on the forward foreign exchange rates which can be quite volatile. Simply put, dollar paper issued at a LIBOR flat yield may not equate to a LIBOR flat borrowing cost in the foreign currency after taking account of forward foreign exchange rates.

Hedging Foreign Exchange Risk

When the issuer first acquires the assets from the originator, it enters into a spot foreign exchange transaction to convert the dollar proceeds of the notes into foreign currency which it pays over to the originator as consideration for the purchase of the assets. At the same time, the issuer enters into a short-term foreign exchange forward contract, agreeing to buy dollars forward in return for delivering an agreed foreign currency amount. The term of the forward contract must match that of the notes issued in order to eliminate any residual currency or interest rate exposures.

At the maturity of the notes and the forward contract, the borrowing company issues a new tranche of dollar notes and again converts the proceeds into foreign currency in the spot foreign exchange market. The borrower delivers the foreign currency to the forward foreign exchange counterparty in satisfaction of the forward contract. Unless the assets have matured, the borrower must look to the proceeds of this new tranche of dollar notes to generate the foreign currency amount he must deliver under the forward contract. Therefore, the principal value of the new tranche of notes he issues is equal to the amount of foreign currency he must deliver translated at the then current spot rate. This form of hedging requires a large number of foreign exchange trades and creates an administrative burden. The hedges must be renewed constantly in order to insure that the issuer's assets and liabilities are always fully matched.

Hedging with Cross Currency Swaps

Hedging through longer-term cross currency swaps is considerably easier than the above mechanism. The issuer enters into the swap for the life of the assets (or for the expected life of the financing) at the transaction's start. The terms of the swap may include an initial exchange of principal at the current spot foreign exchange rate. Alternatively, the borrower may choose to exchange the dollar proceeds of the notes in the spot foreign exchange market himself. Thereafter, the issuer will make periodic payments of interest in the foreign currency to the counterparty in return for receiving dollar interest payments. The interest rates in the respective currencies are agreed at the start of the swap as are the nominal principal values on which the swap payments are calculated. The issuer uses the dollar payments from the counterparty to meet its dollar interest obligation on the notes and receives the foreign currency amounts that it owes from its assets. At maturity of the swap, the issuer and the counterparty will exchange the nominal principal amounts of dollars and foreign currency.

A currency swap has the advantage of locking in the exchange rate between dollars and the foreign currency for the full life of the financing thus providing greater cost certainty than a short-term hedging programme. However, this alternative has several disadvantages. A currency swap allows the borrower very little flexibility which may negatively affect both the availability and the pricing of the ECP. Because swap payments will occur on a regular, set cycle a borrower will find it difficult to issue ECP of odd maturities or differing periods without causing interest rate and/or currency mismatches unacceptable to the rating agencies. A borrower having to issue a high volume of paper on a single day will probably pay a premium yield in order to insure that the full amount is placed. In addition, he will also face exposure to sudden, temporary upward moves in interest rates.

An issuer that wishes to lock in a long-term hedge can increase his flexibility somewhat by entering into a series of swaps with differing interest rate reset dates and differing payment cycles. This way, he can issue smaller tranches of paper on a number of different dates throughout the month and reduce exposure to poor market conditions or interest rate spikes. Entering into short-term basis swaps can also help by changing the payment cycle of a swap from, say, three monthly to six monthly. However, multiple swaps add complication and increase an issuer's administrative burden.

Regardless of which of the two forms of hedging an issuer chooses, it is again important that any foreign exchange or swap counterparties be adequately rated. In the case of an A-1/P-1 rated ECP programme, for instance, each counterparty must itself be A-1/P-1 rated.

HEDGING INTEREST RATE MISMATCHES

In addition to currency exposure, an asset-backed issuer may face some interest rate exposures if the rate basis of his assets differs from that of his liabilities. ECP tends to be pegged to LIBOR and, therefore, using ECP to finance assets which are not tied to LIBOR may give rise to a so-called basis risk.

The mortgages owned by MAES carry a mortgage rate which is set from time to time at the company's discretion, in practice this right being delegated to CIBCM as administrator of the portfolio. However, because this mortgage rate is not explicitly linked to LIBOR or the actual rates achieved on the ECP, it was necessary to incorporate in the structure a mechanism to insure that the rate earned on the mortgages always exceeds the rate payable on the outstanding notes. Given that MAES has a legal right to set its mortgage rate without regard to external factors, basis risk can be addressed by a covenant obliging MAES always to charge the minimum rate necessary to allow it to generate sufficient income to service its liabilities. This rate is called the threshold rate and is calculated using a mathematical formula which includes as variables all of MAES' known and predicted expenses for the period.

The MAES case is slightly unusual in that an issuer rarely has complete control over the rate that it earns on its assets. Interest rates or payment amounts are more usually fixed or linked to some external index. There are several ways to provide basis risk protection for these types of assets. The most common alternative is a basis swap in which the issuer exchanges its income in return for payments from a counterparty with a rate basis matching that of its liabilities. However, it will be difficult to arrange such a swap in the market if the basis used to calculate the issuer's income is not a market index. In this case, sellers themselves are often willing to assume this risk provided that their accountants and regulators will allow off-balance sheet treatment of the debt despite the link between seller and issuer created by the swap. If the originator himself is not adequately rated to provide the swap directly, he will need a more highly rated intermediary to front the swap for him.

Although swaps are by far the most straightforward means of hedging basis risk, they may present difficulties in financings that prepay at unpredictable rates. In such a transaction if the swap itself does not amortise in line with prepayments of the debt, the issuer can, in fact, face an open interest rate exposure. Again, the rating agencies would find such an exposure unacceptable. In many types of swaps, genuine third parties will not agree to allow the swap to prepay freely. Therefore, swaps often only work in amortising transactions if the seller himself is standing behind the swap and is willing to assume the mismatches arising from unpredictable prepayments.

Interest rate caps can also serve to hedge an issuer's basis risk in some transactions and may, in fact, be more suitable than swaps in certain circumstances. A cap will fix the maximum interest rate payable on an issuer's liabilities and, provided this will always be below (by a margin to cover expenses) the rate earned on the assets, the issuer will have sufficient cash to pay its debts. Caps can be better suited to transactions that experience unpredictable amortisation than swaps. This is because, unlike swaps, caps need not be cancelled in line with prepayments. However, many issuers prefer to use swaps, if possible, in order to avoid paying upfront premiums.

Although swaps or caps will usually be the neatest tool for eliminating basis risk, it is also possible to rely on a cash fund or overcollateralisation to provide the necessary cushion to cover potential interest rate mismatches. The drawback of this method, however, is that unless the magnitude of the mismatch is known, the rating agencies will make very conservative assumptions about its size in order to insure that no shortfall will ever occur. This leads to a fund that will almost certainly be well above the actual amount required and will increase the cost of the transaction.

REPAYMENT MISMATCHES AND REINVESTMENT RISK

Whenever the timing of repayment of the assets in a securitisation does not coincide with a repayment date on the debt, a potential reinvestment risk arises if the issuer cannot reinvest the funds it has received at a rate at least as high as that charged on his liability. The nature of an ECP programme—the ability to stagger repayment dates by issuing multiple tranches of paper maturing on different dates—reduces this risk. However, in many asset-backed CP or ECP programmes, including the MAES transaction, it is necessary to anticipate the need to reinvest amounts of principal for short periods.

There are several layers of protection against reinvestment risk for the investor in the MAES ECP programme. MAES' substitution rights allow it to replace loans that repay with new loans paying the same return. However, it is impractical and uneconomic to substitute new loans too frequently so, in practice, funds will require reinvestment for short periods pending maturity of an outstanding tranche of paper. This will also be the case if MAES' substitution rights are suspended for any reason.

In the MAES programme, as in many transactions, a guaranteed investment contract (GIC) covers the reinvestment risk arising from early repayments. Under the terms of the MAES GIC, the GIC provider agrees to pay a guaranteed interest rate on all amounts invested with him during the specified period. The return guaranteed to MAES is set at an absolute rate based on the actual LIBOR rate quoted on the first day of the period. By setting the rate at the start of the investment period, MAES is assured that the rates on its assets and liabilities will be matched even if interest rates have moved since the start of the period. In other types of transactions, the GIC may only need to guarantee a minimum margin under a specific index, with the absolute rate set at the time of investment. In Europe, such GICs are generally provided by banks.

In the MAES transaction, there is a final protection against rate mismatches in the form of the threshold rate calculation which effectively requires that the mortgage rate on loans remaining in the pool be raised in order to generate sufficient income to cover any shortfall arising from a negative carry on reinvestment of redemption proceeds. This mechanism alone is inadequate to cover reinvestment risk because MAES may be unable to raise its mortgage rate quickly enough or to collect increased payments in time to make up the shortfall.

Exposure to reinvestment rates does not arise to the same degree in trade receivables transactions for several reasons. Because receivables are usually sold at a discount equal to the implied financing cost, the issuing company is assured of sufficient cash flow at maturity of the receivables to meet its interest expenses regardless of when assets mature. Instead, early prepayments may reduce the efficiency of the financing for the borrower unless funds are reinvested in new receivables. In fact, many originators are able to designate new receivables on a very frequent basis thus reducing almost to nil the risk that funds will be reinvested in low yielding assets.

As with the other components parts of a rated securitisation, any investments held by the issuer must be with obligors whose credit quality is acceptable to the rating agencies. For an A-1/P-1 rated transaction, therefore, cash can be invested only with parties themselves rated A-1/P-1.

DOWNGRADE RISK

Although investors often favour asset-backed debt because it is not vulnerable to the same "event risk" as corporate obligations, highly structured securitised transactions do suffer from substantial risk of downgrading due to the deteriorating financial condition of even a single participant in the transaction. As we have seen, many of the other risks of an asset-backed financing are addressed by facilities or other support from third parties including such pieces as the credit enhancement, backstop facility, GIC and swaps. Clearly, the greater the number of parties to a transaction, the greater the risk of a "knock-on" downgrade.

Again, downgrade risk is less serious in a short-term financing such as a CP or ECP programme. Because the agencies' top short-term rating categories cover a range of different credit standings, an institution's financial condition or performance may deteriorate somewhat before its short-term rating is affected. In addition, it is often easier to replace facility providers in short-term transactions not only because the term of their involvement is less, but also because a wider universe of potential replacements exists. Because ECP does not trade actively, if at all, investors need not be concerned by the risk of price falls resulting from a programme downgrading. Lastly, investors are protected somewhat by the presence of the backstop facility which continues to be available to refinance maturing notes regardless of the programme rating. Conversely, backstop banks will be concerned by the risk that a drawing will occur due to a downgrading that restricts the issuer's access to the ECP market and will wish to be satisfied that sufficient precautions have been taken to avoid the occurrence of a downgrading.

EXPOSURE TO THE ADMINISTRATOR

Administration of the securitised assets, including the collection of payments and chasing of arrears, normally remains with the originator. An administration agreement sets out the administrator's duties and any failure to carry out these obligations properly will constitute a default under the agreement and may lead to involuntary resignation of the administrator. The administrator plays a key role in insuring that the issuer receives the cash that it needs and the investors in any asset-backed debt should review the administrator's competence and creditworthiness. Often when the originator himself is not of sufficient size and creditworthiness to meet investors' standards, it will be necessary to provide for a stronger institution to act as backup servicer. This institution would have a legal commitment to service the assets in the event of default or bankruptcy of the original administrator.

In the MAES transaction, CIBCM's parent, CIBC, was a party to the management agreement governing the programme. Given the financial strength of CIBC and its clear competence in carrying out its duties, no backup servicer was required.

In a short-term financing such as an asset-backed ECP programme, a noteholder's exposure to the risk of incompetence or default of the administrator is substantially lower than, for instance, in a 20- or 30-year mortgage securitisation. This means that the investor can take a shorter-term view of administrator risk. In any event, the rating agencies include a review of the administrator in their credit analysis and will require a backup servicer or other support arrangements where they consider it necessary in order to protect investors' interests.

ASSESSING RISK DURING THE LIFE OF A TRANSACTION

The rating agencies continue to monitor the credit quality of a securitised transaction throughout its life in order to judge whether or not the assets are performing as expected. In order to carry out this performance review, the agencies require issuers of asset-backed ECP to submit various reports on a quarterly or semi-annual basis. MAES prepares such a report quarterly detailing mortgage repayments and additions to the pool under the substitution option as well as arrears rates, loss statistics and claims on the pool insurance policy. The report also includes simple financial statements. As European investors are growing more familiar with asset-backed debt, they are increasingly asking to receive this type of information directly and there is a growing trend for issuers to make pool performance information available. This information allows investors themselves to make judgments about the relative credit risk of different asset-backed deals in the market.

THE COSTS OF ASSET-BACKED ECP

The all-in cost of asset-backed ECP for an issuer consists of a number of different components. Most important, of course, is the yield which is achieved on the paper and JP Morgan Securities Ltd.'s experience with the MAES ECP programme suggests that European investors will accept returns of around LIMEAN to LIMEAN plus several basis points on A-1/P-1 rated asset-backed paper.[2] After taking into account placement fees payable to dealers, the financing cost of a programme will be about LIBOR flat. In addition, a non-dollar borrower must include the cost of foreign currency hedges. This cost will differ from currency to currency, but is likely to add five to 10 basis points to the total cost. A borrower must also pay commitment fees on the backstop facility whilst paper is outstanding. Again, the level of these fees will differ depending on factors such as the perceived credit quality of the assets, the facility term and the identity of the seller. However, a borrower can

2 LIMEAN is the mid-rate between LIBOR and LIBID. The historic spread between LIBOR and LIMEAN is 12.5 basis points so that LIMEAN is 6.25 basis points below LIBOR. Thus, when I say that MAES paper is placed around LIMEAN to LIMEAN plus several basis points, this equates to LIBOR – 6 to 3 basis points. Dealer fees in the ECP market tend to be 3–5 basis points, bringing the all-in financing cost for MAES to around LIBOR flat.

expect to pay between 15 and 20 basis points per annum in commitment fees. Finally, credit enhancement fees will add another six to 12 basis points to the all-in cost depending on the amount of enhancement required and the form chosen. Based on these figures, it is reasonable to assume an all-in financing cost for asset-backed ECP of between LIBOR + 26 – 42 basis points per annum. This is, however, before upfront expenses which again vary greatly but can be as much as $500,000 to $1,000,000.

CONCLUSION

Each of the component parts of an asset-backed ECP programme described above addresses one of the various risks that arise for investors in holding this paper. Although asset-backed ECP is a more complex investment than corporate ECP or bank deposits, its credit quality can be high and investors are handsomely rewarded for the greater complexity of the instrument with a yield premium.

The primary risks associated with asset-backed ECP are credit risk, refinancing risk, currency risk, basis risk and reinvestment risk. In addition, the existence of numerous third parties in an asset-backed financing creates substantial downgrade risk. Credit enhancement, including liquidity facilities, protects investors against credit losses. A backstop facility provides investors with a known source of refinancing. Currency and basis swaps cover foreign currency and interest rate mismatches. A GIC will eliminate reinvestment risk. Although the nature of asset-backed finance makes it difficult to do away with downgrade risk, arrangers and issuers will increasingly strive to create less vulnerable structures and to incorporate contingency plans into the documentation to deal with threatened downgradings. In addition to these structural risks, there are various legal risks which arise in asset-backed transactions stemming from events such as the formation of the issuing company, the transfer of the assets and the creation of a security interest over the asset pool. The various legal documents governing the transaction must address these risks and the law firms acting for the issuer and arranger must satisfy the rating agencies in their legal opinions that the risks are adequately covered. For a transaction involving multiple jurisdictions, the legal issuers will be considerably more complicated and lawyers must review carefully any potential conflicts of law.

Provided a programme is properly structured, documented and managed, asset-backed ECP can be a very attractive and secure investment for noteholders. Although the concept of asset-backed debt is still relatively new in Europe, I am optimistic that many ECP investors will welcome high-quality asset-backed paper in the future. Equally, I expect that a growing need for off-balance sheet finance, coupled with greater familiarity, will lead more European borrowers to turn to the asset-backed ECP market for funds.

Chapter 24

Managing Risk in a LIBOR-Plus Fund

by Paul Derosa,
Eastbridge Capital Inc.
and
Laurie Goodman,
Merrill Lynch

In the past several years, there has been a proliferation of offshore US Government security funds which pay 3 month LIBOR plus a spread of 60–75 basis points. The LIBOR rate is reset every 3 months, but the spread remains constant over the life of the fund. In addition to the spread paid to investors, the funds generally have expenses on the order of 50–65 basis points. Thus, to pay LIBOR + 70 for example, the funds must accrue at the rate of LIBOR plus 120–135 basis points. If the fund makes more than the accrual rate, the additional profit is added to the net asset value of the fund. If there is a shortfall, the amount of the shortfall is subtracted from the net asset value of the fund. Thus the spread on these funds or the total return is in no way guaranteed. Most of these funds have a maturity of 5–10 years and rely primarily on U.S. Government and agency mortgage securities in order to meet the return target.

This chapter is intended to provide a glimpse of how Eastbridge Capital Inc. manages its LIBOR plus fund. This fund, known as the ECI Adjustable Income Portfolio, N.V., pays 3 month LIBOR plus 75 basis points. To cover expenses, the fund accrues at the rate of 3 month LIBOR plus 125 basis points. Table 24.1 shows the performance of the Eastbridge fund since its inception on April 18, 1990. The net asset value of the Eastbridge Fund currently stands at 102.49. Thus, the investor has enjoyed a return of LIBOR + 75, and experienced additional appreciation of 2.49 percent. This represents an annualized net total return of 10.83 percent. This portfolio performance reflects primarily our decision that the best relative value was to be found in fixed rate pass-throughs rather than adjustable rate mortgages used by many other funds.

The Eastbridge Philosophy

Eastbridge believes that the best way to maximize the yield on the portfolio over time is to trade actively. This is done by purchasing securities when they represent good relative value. When securities are sold, they are replaced with other securities that represent more attractive relative value. These securities will not always offer the highest current yield, but their total return should be bolstered by price appreciation. Eastbridge management is willing to give up yield in order to maintain liquidity.

Eastbridge Capital's procedure for managing mortgage portfolios emphasizes risk control. Since no funds manager meets success on every investment, the ability to avoid excessive concentration and work within well-defined risk limits is essential to long-term profitability.

In order to ensure we are adequately controlling our risk, we have a four-step procedure for mortgage portfolio management:

- Use quantitative analysis to construct a portfolio with low convexity risk
- Control duration risk
- Manage the LIBOR-Treasury spread risk
- Monitor the mortgage-Treasury spread risk

USE QUANTITATIVE ANALYSIS TO CONSTRUCT A PORTFOLIO WITH LOW CONVEXITY RISK

The primary problem in managing mortgages is maintaining a predictable duration, and substantial effort is required to avoid securities whose dura-

At the time this chapter was written, Laurie Goodman was with Eastbridge Capital, Inc.

Table 24.1—Performance of Eastbridge ECI Fund

Month	*3 Month LIBOR Paid*	*3 Month LIBOR +75*	*Days per Period*	*Net Interest Paid per Period*	*Net BEY per Period*	*1 yr CMT per Period*	*Net BEY versus 1 yr CMT*	*NAV*	*Change in NAV per Period*	*Annlzd. Net Total Return per Period*	*Net Income per Period*
Apr '90 – Jun '90	8.41%	9.16%	74	1.88%	9.40%	8.26%	1.14%	$100.17	0.17%	10.64%	2.05%
Jul '90 – Sep '90	8.28%	9.03%	92	2.30%	9.25%	7.82%	1.42%	$100.74	0.57%	11.97%	2.87%
Oct '90 – Dec '90	8.06%	8.81%	92	2.23%	8.96%	7.30%	1.66%	$100.55	–0.18%	8.47%	2.05%
Jan '91 – Mar '91	7.51%	8.26%	90	2.05%	8.42%	6.43%	1.99%	$101.52	0.96%	12.92%	3.02%
Apr '91 – Jun '91	6.37%	7.12%	91	1.77%	7.17%	6.21%	0.96%	$101.83	0.30%	8.62%	2.07%
July '91	6.31%	7.06%	31	0.60%	7.10%	6.27%	0.82%	$102.49	0.65%	15.71%	1.25%
4/18/90 – 7/31/91	7.61%	8.36%	470	10.91%	8.57%	7.11%	1.46%	$102.49	2.49%	10.83%	13.40%

tions fall when interest rates decline and rise when interest rates rise. Stated differently, prepayments increase and hence many mortgage securities shorten as rates decline, thereby reducing their potential for price appreciation. As rates rise, prepayments slow, lengthening the security and thereby increasing their potential for price depreciation. This property, in which you lose no matter which way interest rates move, is called negative convexity and is the greatest source of unsatisfactory results in mortgage investing. Those mortgage portfolios that consistently outperform Treasury issues do so because of their managers' ability to maintain a stable duration under a variety of market conditions.

Eastbridge employs quantitative techniques for security selection and portfolio construction, ensuring we limit the amount of negative convexity in the portfolio. Mathematically, an investment in a mortgage-backed instrument can be viewed as a short position in a complex call option, with the value of the security depending crucially on the value of this option. It would be nice to say that Eastbridge has a precise, non-judgmental method for evaluating the options embedded in mortgage-backed securities, but this is not the case. To the best of our knowledge, a completely satisfactory technique for this purpose does not exist. In the absence of something better, Eastbridge employs a somewhat eclectic three-stage method that employs the best quantitative tools currently available. Binomial option pricing allows for a comparison of relative value across securities. Interest rate scenario simulation allows for a cross-check of performance. The third and final stage is complimentary securities selection via a linear program which allows construction of a portfolio with stable returns.

The binomial option pricing model allows an investor to evaluate the cost of the call features of mortgage-backed securities by computing the equivalent value of the security if it had no options. This is done by valuing the option under hundreds of different interest rate scenarios. Thus, the results of option-adjusted pricing provide a consistent framework within which the relative value of different mortgage-backed securities can be compared. One limitation of this procedure is that is compresses the results of many equally likely interest rate paths into one number.

This is too concise for practical applications. Two securities with the same option-adjusted yield may be equivalent from a probabilistic point of view. However, their actual returns over finite horizons will differ greatly, depending upon how interest rates change and upon such factors as their coupon and degree of seasoning in the mortgages. To avoid this difficulty, it is necessary to supplement option-adjusted pricing with simulation analysis to see how different securities perform under different scenarios.

The last consideration emphasizes the need for optimal portfolio selection. It is important to select securities that complement each other and produce a portfolio with stable returns under different market conditions. Eastbridge performs this function using a linear programming technique. Having obtained consistent measures of yield, duration, and convexity using option-adjusted methods, we then select a portfolio that generates maximum total return over a six-month horizon under five equally weighted interest rate paths, between down 1 percent and up 1 percent. The portfolio also must conform to a predetermined limit on duration and not be subject to negative convexity. Individual securities may have very long durations, and some may be negatively convex, but the overall portfolio must conform to preset requirements.

Through the first half of 1991 the bulk of our portfolio holdings consisted of 30 year fixed rate pass-throughs. The core holdings of the fund consist of $100 million in mortgages in the following coupons:

- $40 million slightly seasoned FHLMC and FNMA 8.5
- $10 million FNMA 9.0
- $30 million GNMA 9.5
- $20 million GNMA 10.0

We also hold some options on bond futures in order to add positive convexity to the portfolio. In addition, we hold a small amount of mortgage derivative products to enhance yield ($7.5 million in a $100 million fund). The bulk of these are interest only (IO) securities. In an interest only security, a lump sum is paid up front for the right to all or a portion of the interest payments. When prepayments occur, the interest also ceases on the prepaid amount.

Once an optimal portfolio has been selected, we subject it to a final test for reasonableness. This involves applying our accumulated market experience to judge whether any pending event is likely to threaten some part of the portfolio.

Portfolio holdings must be adjusted as market conditions change. We rerun our quantitative analysis whenever there is a major change in our prepayment modeling, when interest rates move more than 25 basis points, or whenever we believe there might have been a change in relative value in the marketplace. Moreover, we also try to anticipate prepayment trends and review the prepayment model embedded in our quantitative analysis. Any mortgage model is only as good as the prepayment model that lies behind it. There are instances in which one can anticipate prepayment trends, and use these prepayment estimates to do our quantitative analysis rather than rely solely on historic prepayments.

CONTROL DURATION RISK

The next step is to hedge the portfolio down to our target duration. Hedging is relatively straightforward and standard techniques can be used because we have constructed a portfolio with no negative convexity. The portfolio will hence maintain its duration across a wide variety of interest rate movements.

The Eastbridge offshore fund has a target duration of .75 years. We do not vary the target duration much from month to month. This practice reflects a view that while the proper objective of investing is total return over a finite horizon, mortgages are not a vehicle for interest rate speculation. In the case of our offshore fund, the reset period is 3 months. Thus, to be immunized against rate risk, the duration of the fund should be the time to reset the liabilities. However, we feel 3 months is too short a duration, because when the Treasury market rallies, mortgages tend to lag. Similarly, when the Treasury market falls, mortgages outperform. This effect requires that we run the portfolio slightly long.

As a practical matter, we vary the target duration of the portfolio between .5 years and 1.0 years, depending on our view of interest rates. If we are neutral on rates, our portfolio duration is .75 years. If we expect rates to fall, we will run the portfolio slightly long. If we expect rates to rise, we will run the portfolio at a .5 year duration.

To illustrate how we hedge a thirty-year pass-through position, assume we purchase a portfolio consisting half of FNMA 8.5 percent thirty-year pass-throughs and half of GNMA 9.5 percent mortgage pass-throughs. Portfolio yields and durations are as follows (as of July 2, 1991):

Security	*Price*	*Market Value Weight*	*Yield*	*Duration*
FNMA 8.5	96-15	50%	9.21	5.04
GNMA 9.5	101-30	50%	9.21	4.75
Portfolio		100%	9.21	4.90

These durations are based on estimates as to how much the market price would change for a small change in interest rates. This, in turn, is dependent on a model as to how prepayments change as interest rates change.

The average duration for the portfolio is 4.9 years. With no hedging, this portfolio would entail far too much interest rate risk for investors funded on a 3-month LIBOR base.

In order to shorten the duration of this 4.9 year portfolio to .75 years we must shorten duration by 4.15 years (4.90 – .75). If we were to shorten duration by shorting the 8.5 of 11/2000, we would need to short $.65 market value of notes for each $1.00 market value of the portfolio. This number is obtained by dividing the amount of duration to be shortened (4.15 years) by the duration of the security to be used as a hedge (6.35 years).

In order to sell short a security we do not own, we must borrow it. This is done via a repurchase agreement (repo). We take the cash we obtain from shorting the security and simultaneously loan the cash at the repo rate, with the security we are short being used as collateral on the loan. Since we are short the security, we must pay the coupon. We receive the repo rate. The yield on the security is 8.31. The repo rate is expected to be 5.85 over the next six months, producing negative carry of 246 basis points. The cost of shorting the security is 160 basis points, which is the negative carry of 246 basis points times the size of the short (.65). Thus the yield on the hedged portfolio is the yield on the mortgage securities (9.21 percent) less the hedging costs (1.60); 7.61 percent. At the present time, this is equal to 3-month LIBOR plus 148 basis points.

In addition to shorting cash Treasury securities there are two other commonly used methods to shorten the duration of a fixed rate mortgage portfolio: selling futures or using swaps. We have used both short sales of Treasury securities and sales of bond and note futures contracts. A short position in a futures contract is roughly comparable to a short position in the underlying instrument. Consider a position in the 10-year note contract rather than a position in the cheapest to deliver 10-year note (8.5 of 11/2000). Prior to the expiration of trading on the June note futures contract, the June and September futures contracts were trading 20/32 apart. If rates remain constant over the next three months, and there are no changes in the relative value of the futures contract, the September contract will converge to the current price on the June contract. This is a pick up of 20/32 over 3 months or 2.48 percent per year. This can be compared to the carry of 246 basis points on the 8.5 of 11/2000.

We have not used swaps to hedge the duration of the base position because our long mortgage positions will change as we actively manage our portfolio. This will change our duration and the amount of the hedge that is necessary. Swaps are less liquid than Treasury securities or note futures—10-year swaps trade in 5 basis point markets. This is equivalent to 10/32, or 10 times the average transactions costs of the alternatives. Thus, swap positions are much more expensive to adjust as warranted by changes in the underlying portfolio. Moreover, swaps lock a manager into a short on a particular point on the yield curve. By using futures and short positions in cash instruments, we can be short whatever sector of the Treasury yield curve we regard as the most expensive.

This represents another opportunity to enhance total returns through active management. Since the inception of the fund, we have hedged with three-year notes, five-year notes, current and off-the-run seven-year notes, current and off-the-run 10-year notes, the long bond, and note futures. Our turnover on our short position has far exceeded the turnover on our long mortgage position.

Many managers of LIBOR plus funds use adjustable rate mortgages rather than a hedged position in fixed rate mortgages. These adjustable rate mortgages generally reset at a margin above the one-year constant maturity treasury (CMT) index. One-year CMT ARMs have, on average, six months to the next reset. The duration of these instruments is the time to the next reset plus the duration created by the annual and lifetime caps. Thus, a typical Treasury ARM would have a duration of approximately .9 years. The yield on the one-year ARM is approximately 120 basis points above the one-year CMT (6.20). Thus the yield is 7.40, rather than the 7.60 from our hedged fixed rate position. In addition these securities have substantially more negative convexity then our hedged fixed rate portfolio. We firmly believe that at current levels these securities, after hedging out the negative convexity from the caps, are substantially more expensive than fixed rate mortgages. If there were to be a substantial realignment in the mortgage market, with these securities cheapening substantially relative to fixed rate products, we would look to sell our fixed rate securities and buy adjustable rate product.

MANAGE THE LIBOR-TREASURY SPREAD RISK

Our fund pays out a spread over LIBOR, but our assets are mortgage and Treasury based. If we did not hedge the LIBOR-Treasury spread, and the spread between the one-year Treasury rate and LIBOR were to increase from 46 basis points to 135 basis points as it did in September through November of 1990 the fund would not show very good performance. That is, with the asset side of the portfolio unchanged, the LIBOR reset by the portfolio would be substantially higher. This would reduce the net asset value of the fund. The average spread has been 61 basis points, but it is very volatile, ranging from –8bp to 163bp over the past 5 years. We manage this risk by using leverage. An alternative method to hedge this risk, as well as shorten duration, is to use swaps. By paying fixed and receiving LIBOR, fixed rate mortgage income is transformed into LIBOR based income. However, we do not find long-term swaps very flexible, as explained earlier.

Our prospectus allows us to use up to 50 percent leverage. Stated differently, borrowed money may not exceed more than 50 percent of total assets. Thus, for a $100 million fund, we may hold up to $200 million in assets. Leverage is employed by financing our entire position in 30-year pass throughs. We use a small amount of the proceeds to enhance yield by purchasing mortgage derivative products, and most of the balance to purchase LIBOR based assets.

We use two different financing techniques for the mortgage securities. We have taken delivery of the slightly seasoned (1987 production) 8.5s and one large ($18 million) pool of GNMA 10s. These pools are financed using repurchase agreements. The other $42 million of mortgage positions are purchased forward, in TBA form, and rolled from month to month. Each month, we sell the current month and buy the same coupon for the next month. The one-month difference between the prices is called the drop. It reflects the carry on the mortgage security over the course of the month. On occasion, the drop can be larger than is indicated by the carry, reflecting demand from dealers who are short in the front month. This also represents an opportunity to enhance the fund's returns.

Some managers of LIBOR plus funds use AA and AAA mortgages rather than agency mortgages. These private label mortgages yield 35–45 basis points more than their agency counterparts. They are, however, much less liquid, and trade in markets of approximately 5–10 basis points. In addition, they finance at much higher rates than agency mortgages, and opportunities to roll these securities are unavailable. After considering these effects, we feel the true yield advantage from these securities is a more modest 10–15 basis points. Thus, we use agency securities although our prospectus would allow us to use AA product.

Approximately half of our LIBOR assets are placed in 3-month LIBOR time deposits. These deposits are rolled over on the same dates the liabilities reset. The other half of the financed funds were used to purchase asset-backed securities. We hold the asset-backed securities in eight different pieces to provide diversification. Two pieces are LIBOR based. The other six pieces are swapped into LIBOR based funding. We are achieving a yield of approximately LIBOR + 60 basis points on the position. This adds roughly 24 basis points to the incremental yield on the portfolio (60 basis points times 40 percent of the net position).

MONITOR THE MORTGAGE-TREASURY SPREAD RISK

The major risk in our portfolio and in most other LIBOR-plus funds is the widening of the mortgage-Treasury spread. If we anticipated the widening, we would reduce the mortgage holdings in the portfolio, or would hedge our mortgages with other mortgages. However, switching our long positions into Treasury securities or moving our short position into mortgages involves forfeiting the mortgage-Treasury spread. Spreads can widen 17–18 basis points over the course of a year before a mortgage position actually underperforms a Treasury position. It can widen only about 8–9 basis points over a six-month period.

The superior performance of the Eastbridge Fund is in large measure due to the narrowing of the mortgage-sTreasury spread. At the inception of the fund, the spread between the current coupon GNMA (the GNMA 9.5) and the 10-year Treasury was 130 basis points. At the end of July 1991 the spread between the GNMA 9.5 and the 10-year stood at 92 basis points. This 38 basis point move translates into an increase of 1.71 percent in net asset value (38 basis points times the average duration of the mortgages of 4.5 years).

In future years, we do not anticipate achieving the rate of price appreciation that has been achieved over the past year and a quarter. A good deal of our excellent performance to date is due to a tightening of the mortgage-Treasury spread. We do not expect spreads to tighten considerably from these levels, and some widening is likely. We have already adjusted our holdings accordingly. Going forward, Eastbridge expects to continue to deliver superior returns by careful security selection, portfolio construction, and active management.

Chapter 25

Developments in the UK Mortgage Securities Market

by N.S. Terrington,
National Home Loans Holdings PLC

The UK mortgage-backed securities market sprang into life in early 1987. It was born into a period of deregulation and substantial opportunity, and was presented against the background of a housing sector that had only seen sustained asset value appreciation and where losses were "de minimus."

Today the market is perceived to have faltered. An economy in recession, a housing market without confidence, limited new supply and a contracted investor base have all served to depress activity and question the future viability of this funding technique.

The UK market considered Standard & Poor's misguided in trying to transport US depression scenarios to the UK. Loss severity of 37 percent at AAA level was considered quite outrageous. However, house price depreciation has been heading toward this level and, at the time of writing, the signs of an improvement have yet to translate into stemming of price falls.

This all looks rather gloomy; and yet, the UK mortgage-backed securities market is alive and performing. No rated security has experienced a principal loss nor a missed interest payment. Only one subordinated tranche has experienced a deferral of interest on a part of its issue for one quarter which was subsequently met from future cash flow. The experience has served to demonstrate the extraordinary resilience of the mortgage-backed securities market.

The following pages have sought to explore some of the implications of both a general and a specific nature of the changing market in the UK over the last five years or so. In order to do so it is necessary to appreciate the backgrounds to the UK housing market and the UK mortgage-backed securities market.

RECENT DEVELOPMENTS IN UK HOUSING MARKET

The UK has a mature private sector housing market. Home ownership is among the highest in the world at 67.5 percent of the population (and expected to rise) and is certainly the highest in Europe. Cultural attitudes together with a weak private rented sector had already established the housing market as the largest form of private wealth holding in the country when the Conservative Government swept to power in 1979.

The Thatcherite dream of returning to the private sector state assets previously acquired under Labour governments and deregulation was to have a profound effect on the housing market.

Although the private rented sector was virtually non-existent, the Government through its municipal authorities held a substantial portfolio of properties for social housing. A programme was established over a number of years to offer tenants the opportunities to purchase these houses at heavily discounted prices. This created an increased demand for mortgages and reduced the alternatives to home ownership.

The mid-1980s saw two significant pieces of deregulation:

1. The Building Societies, which had dominated the UK housing market for 200 years and, by the mid-1980s, were funding 80–90 percent of all mortgages in the UK. In addition, through their heavy branch representation and image of security, they had a strong position in the retail deposit-taking market.

For many years mortgage rates were set by reference to a cartel agreement. However, by 1982 it was decided that this cartel arrangement would cease. For the first time competition would exist within the industry.

2. Through the Building Societies Act (1986), societies were permitted to diversify their source of funding to the wholesale markets and to make loans into certain non-housing sectors, e.g., unsecured and commercial property. Again the seeds of competition were being sewn.

The resultant market rate for mortgages and genuine availability of funds led to the creation of a new breed of mortgage company, the centralised lenders. These institutions, such as The National Home Loans Corporation PLC, The Mortgage Corporation (subsidiary of Salomon) and Household Mortgage Corporation, were established with varying strategies in mind but with certain common principles. They operated without a branch network, with a low cost base, funded themselves solely from the wholesale markets and sourced assets via the new and developing intermediary or broker market. They were also the founder members of the UK mortgage securities market.

Their style was brave, aggressive and swift. New technology and a philosophy of intermediary support enabled mortgage products to be delivered to the market ahead of the slumbering societies. New participants in the housing market quickly increased with the clearing banks probably providing the biggest impetus in volume terms. It was not long before Building Society levels fell to a nadir of 43 percent of total new lending.

The new centralised lenders were the pioneers of product innovation. Historically, the UK mortgage market had been restricted to simple unimaginative forms of lending. New products such as those incorporating negative amortisation, i.e., the payment rate being only 10 percent where the charging rate was 13 percent. (The three percent difference being capitalised to the account.) Additionally, a plethora of products with varying forms of interest rate setting, i.e., LIBOR-linked, three-year fixed rate, capped, collared and the first real attempt to mimic the US market 25-year fixed rate mortgage.

The development of the housing market was greatly assisted by the economy. An already strong economy in the UK was enhanced by a seemingly continuous round of deregulation in the financial services sector. Relaxation of monetary conditions to assist the expanding economy prior to the 1987 General Election laid firm foundations for a housing market where the level of demand for home ownership was increasing for demographic reasons and through the release of municipal housing. House prices were already increasing at 30 percent when in the Budget of 1988 the Chancellor laid fuel to the flame. Three factors converged in a "triple witching hour."

1. The 1988 Budget announced that the top marginal tax rate was reduced from 60 percent to 40 percent.
2. The Budget also announced the abolition of joint MIRAS (tax deductions) on a single property. The error however was that it did not take effect for four months thereby opening a window to meet the tax break.
3. Sterling interest rates were falling rapidly to stem the currency appreciation against the Deutschemark. Base rates fell as low as 7.5 percent.

The result was unprecedented levels of turnover in the housing market. House price inflation fueled confidence, which in turn increased activity. Rising house prices led to equity withdrawal taking place at unprecedented levels with an estimated increase in annual personal disposable income equivalent of 8 percent in 1988.

As quickly as the bubble was blown up during 1988, it burst in the months following the closure of the double MIRAS tax relief. The reality was that the feeder to the market, the first-time buyer, had disappeared because house purchase decisions had been accelerated to meet the MIRAS tax window. This, together with rising debt costs, served to turn off market demand virtually overnight.

The surge in the economy, especially in the consumer market, led to a rapid deterioration in the country's balance of payments as imports were sucked in to meet demand. Inflation threats soon followed and the government which had fostered the economic boom had to take corrective action.

During the course of the next year interest rates rose further peaking at 15 percent. Rates stayed at this level for a further 14 months, the longest period in recent times without a movement in base rates.

Western economies were generally slowing down towards the end of the 1980s but the severity of the UK government's monetary policy dropped the UK into the longest and deepest recession the economy had experienced post 1945. The housing market has been particularly badly affected. The excesses of the housing boom ensured the landing was severe.

Figure 25.1

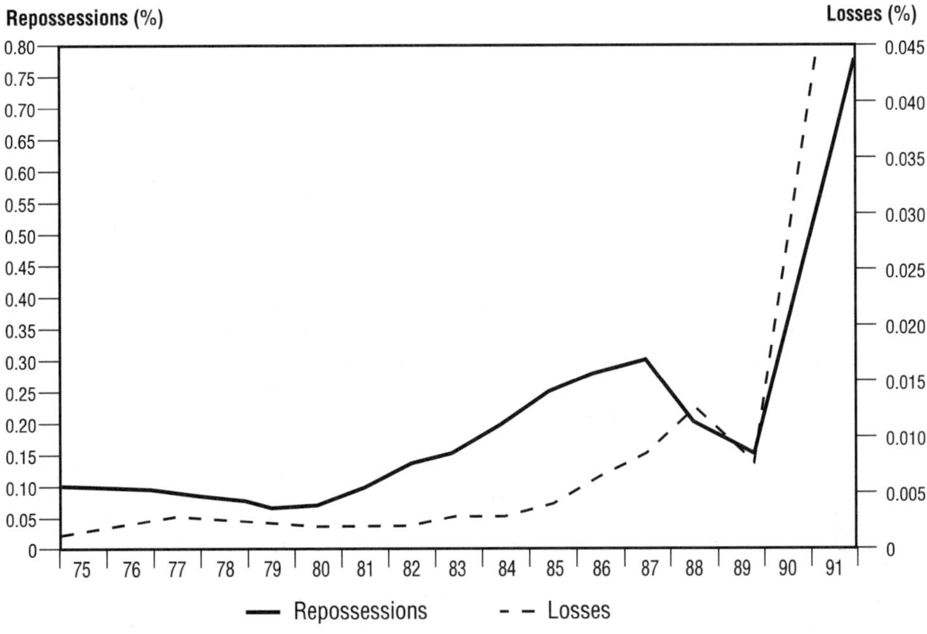

Figure 25.2

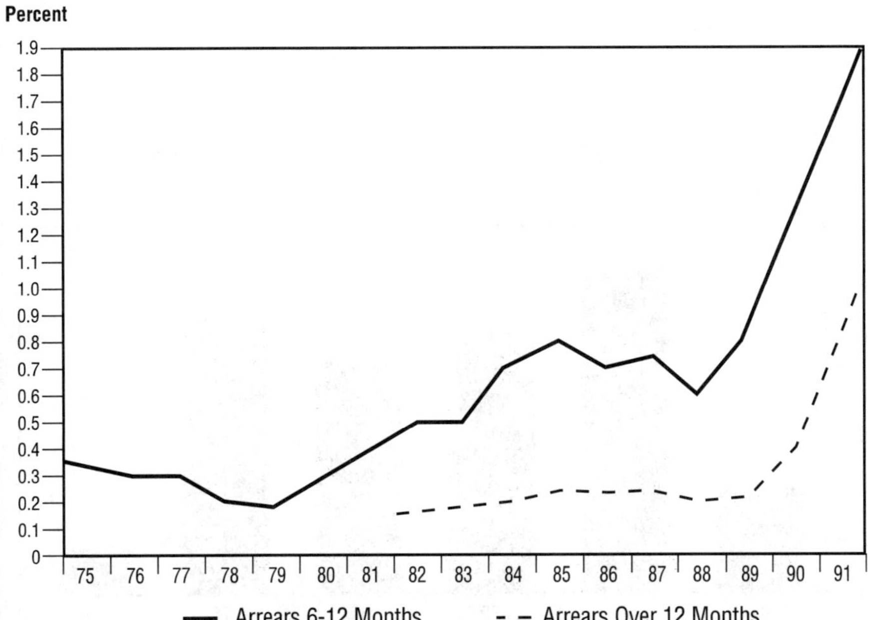

Figures 25.1 and 25.2 show the trend in arrears and properties possessed by the mortgage industry.

Turnover in the housing market is now at historically low levels and prices do not appear, yet, to have found a firm floor. This house price/income multiple is back to a more normal ratio of approximately 3× whereas 1988/89 saw the multiplier hitting 5.2×—clearly an unsustainable level of gearing.

House prices, particularly in the once prosperous South of England, have fallen sharply since 1988/89. Clearly houses became overvalued and the market has undergone a sharp correction. The house price index has seen price falls of around 25 percent, although in security value terms, losses will almost certainly be higher. The result is that consumer confidence has been shattered.

So, as can be seen in Figure 25.3, the mortgage-backed securities market has certainly had a baptism of fire. It was formed as the market expanded and peaked during 1989 as the UK housing market was about to turn.

The major issuers have virtually all stepped aside from the new lending market either by choice or due to availability of warehouse lines. Most centralised lenders did not have the benefit of a mature lending base going into the boom/bust period and consequently have been more exposed to the highly geared borrowers and inflated asset values of 1988 and 1989.

The mortgage-backed security market itself has reflected this position in a number of ways, many of which will be discussed further on. However, Figure 25.4 reflects the new issue yields, and the dramatic reversal of fortunes is clearly seen in the spike of yields.

Figure 25.4 also shows the comparability with new issue yields on Building Society FRNs. Although the top-rated society is only AA, their pricing has consistently outperformed the mortgage securities market, principally due to complexity perception and uncertain amortisation schedules.

As mentioned at the beginning of this section, the securities have proven highly robust despite the environment and it is my firmly held belief that these securities are heavily undervalued compared to alternative instruments, despite the underlying housing market. It is perhaps the destiny of the market to have to prove the depression scenario can be survived before investors begin to believe in the strength of the underlying structures.

INVESTOR BASE DEVELOPMENT

The early transactions in the mortgage-backed securities market were highly illiquid. An investor base had not been cultivated and given the nature of the security, FRNs, the most logical route was to the banking market. The new issues were relatively small and frequently sold to the commercial banking divisions with the benefit of a put at 5 and 7 years, thereby converting it to a banking asset.

Things began to improve as the sterling shook off its poor investment image and overseas interest was seen particularly from the Far East. The UK corporate sector, which was experiencing record levels of liquidity and a retracting gilt market,

Figure 25.3—Mortgage Security Issuance Volume as of July 1992

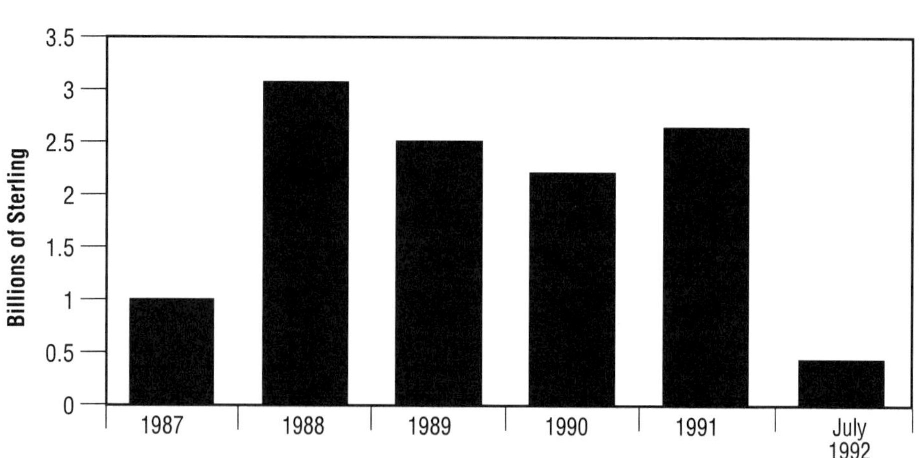

Figure 25.4—Sterling Mortgage-Backed Floating Rate Note Issues—Discount Margin

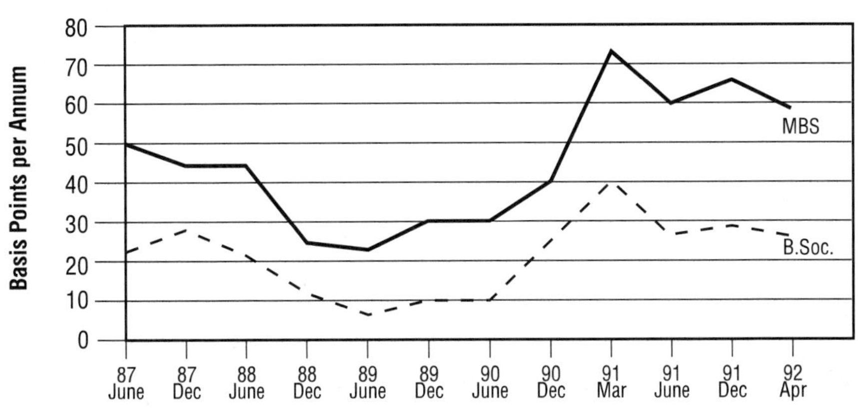

became active participants. A number of new investors seeking to establish particularly large holdings were regularly taking 25–40 percent of every issue. Banks remained buyers but the emphasis was switching to the treasury division who were using their surplus funding position to achieve something better than interbank rates. In all, the market appeared to be developing but it was still exposed to risks.

The immaturity and weak foundations became apparent as the housing market started to deteriorate. Discount margins increased as arrears rose and gloom on the housing market spread. The concentration of paper in relatively few hands, once perceived as an advantage in boosting demand, actually proved negative. The individual investors began to realise the strength of their position and began dictating terms. In effect, the market pricing level was being set by a few investors and a number of new issues were probably not far from private placements.

Another factor which affected the investor base was regulatory intervention. The banking sector had been attracted, amongst other reasons, by the risk asset weighting. There are discrepancies between the Basle Agreement which allocated a 0.5 weighting (so long as the transaction met certain conditions) and the implementation of EC Directives which allocated a 1.0 weighting with effect from 1 January 1993. It is quite inconceivable how you can take a mortgage, locate it in a special purpose company, add credit enhancement to protect the value of the mortgage and then consider it twice as risky. Eventually, the decision was taken to retain the 0.5 weighting, however, it took virtually two years and the uncertainty erroded investor confidence.

So what have the market participants done to either broaden the investor base or to diversify away from the core securitisation funding source?

MULTI-TRANCHE STRUCTURES

A number of transactions have included recasting the cash flows to make certain structures more appealing to different classes of investors.

Until 1989 the Bank of England prohibited capital market issuance with maturities of less than 5 years. In the case of mortgage-backed securities where principal repayments are passed through quarterly this was interpreted as the average life. Whilst a standard FRN had tended to create average lives of 5 years, or longer with substitution, it posed a significant problem for multi-tranche structures as the concept appeared diametrically opposed to the regulations.

Following the lifting of the restrictions, two transactions were launched into the market. The first by CIBC, MAES Funding No. 2 PLC. This was a £300 million FRN with a call and price step-up at 4 years. Assumptions of 25 percent straight line repayment created an average life of 2 years and consequently the relatively short-term nature of the security enabled pricing to be pared to LIBOR +15 bp, the finest seen in the market and certainly a far cry from today's margins.

Shortly afterwards National Home Loans, through SPV Collateralised Mortgage Securities (No.1) PLC launched the UK's first multi-tranche structure. The US has a deep market for tranched

Figure 25.5

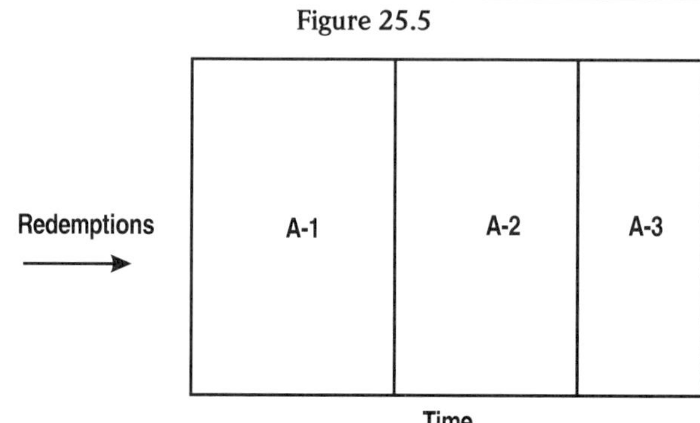

securitisations although principally by way of repackaging securities rather than whole loans. The US market played heavily on yield curve arbitrage opportunities whereas the principle of the UK multi-tranching was to widen the investor base to encourage its continued development. Although there were savings by the NHL CMO structure they were in the scheme of things marginal.

Before moving on, it is appropriate to set out briefly the nature of multi-tranche structures. In an FRN every £1 of redemptions proceeds is used to prepay the noteholders, either pro rata or selected by lot. Consequently, each noteholder experiences the same prepayment experience. In the CMO that £1 of redemption proceeds may be directed to certain of the noteholders depending on their particular class.

Figure 25.5 explains the most straightforward of the structures.

As redemptions occur they are initially applied to tranche A-1 until A-1 noteholders are prepaid in full. When complete paydown of this tranche has taken place, the subsequent proceeds are all directed to tranche A-2 noteholders, again until full paydown. Proceeds are then directed to tranche A-3.

The result is that the investor in tranche A-1 experiences a very fast payback period. Assuming tranche A-1 represented 50 percent of the total pool and prepayments occurred at the rate of 20 percent per annum, investors would experience an average life of 18 months and a final maturity of 3.2 years. This is as compared to an investor in a standard FRN who would experience an average life of five to eight years (depending on whether substitution was included or not) and a final maturity of 13–16 years.

Tranche A-2, assuming it constituted 30 percent of the total portfolio, would experience an average life of five years. The final tranche, A-3, would experience an average life of 9.6 years.

It is immediately clear that by recasting the cash flow into a fast, medium and slow payment tranches, it is possible to appeal to different maturity preferences of investors. The fast-paying piece should appeal in particular to the money market investor, the slow-paying piece to the investor who prefers a constant principal balance, with the option of writing asset swaps to convert the note into a five-year gilt/US treasury linked instrument.

It is quite apparent that the CMO structure assists with one of the problems identified by investors with the FRN. Investors now have a substantial degree of certainty with which to establish their credit and return horizon.

A derivative of the CMO has extended this certainty even further. This is by means of the Planned Amortisation Class—or PAC tranche.

Diagrammatically this is presented in Figure 25.6.

As redemptions occur, in common with the previous example, they pay down tranche A-1. However, in year three (for example) any redemptions that take place are passed through to the PAC tranche up to the (say) £10 million limit for that year. Any prepayment flow proceeds over and above this amount are passed through to tranche A-1 (until it is paid down in full). The same takes place in years four and five. If there are insufficient funds to pay down the PAC tranche within any particular year then the tranche is effectively carried over to the following period. The shortage of funds does not create an event of default but just defers prepayment of the notes.

The PAC tranche gives substantial prepayment certainty to investors and it is structured to ensure the annual limit is achievable under most circumstances.

This derivative of the multi-tranche structure has not been used in the UK although Mortgages Securities (No. 2) PLC, a vehicle of First Mortgage Securities, was able to construct a controlled am-

Figure 25.6

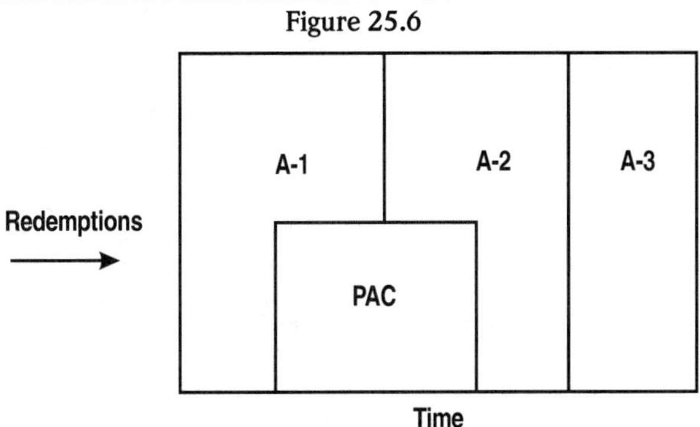

ortisation option whereby any surplus principal receipts over and above 2.5 percent per annum could be applied in acquiring further collateral.

The value of multi-tranche structures is heavily dependent on the likely (and the sellable) cash flows from the underlying securities. UK mortgages are generally written for periods of 25–35 years with the majority of recent origination based on bullet repayments, although fully amortising loans appear to be making a degree of a comeback. In reality, however, mortgages rarely last this long.

The concept of average lives is defined as the expected weighted time from launch to final repayment of the securities, usually assuming a call at either 7 or 10 years, clearly allowing for the quarterly partial mandatory redemptions. At the commencement of the mortgage-backed securities market, the only form of analysis was based on a survey conducted by the Building Societies Association which indicated the average life of a mortgage was approximately 6.6 years.

It is quite extraordinary to think that the foundations of a £12 billion market were based on the responses of 1,102 people. The UK market has always suffered from lack of data and analysis (of which more later), a situation certainly not evident in the USA.

The actual experience has proven quite different. The dramatic changes in the mortgage market already referred to had the effect of increasing turnover and hence reducing the average life. During 1987 through 1990, a refinance market developed to meet the growing levels of competition, as did a plethora of new mortgage products and the means for individuals to extract equity, or in a number of cases, consolidate debt. Again the effect was to accelerate redemptions and reduce average lives. Table 25.1 is a list of the average lives for all the NHL public securitisations.

Table 25.1

	CPR	*Average Life from Launch*
NHL 1	25%	Redeemed
NHL 2	33%	Redeemed
NHL 3	29%	Redeemed
NHL 4	28%	2.4 years
CMS 1	26%	2.2 years
CMS 2	25%	2.2 years
CMS 3	25%	3.2 years
CMS 4	10%	5.7 years
CMS 5	10%	5.8 years
CMS 6	9%	5.8 years
CMS 7	8%	5.7 years
CMS 8	8%	6.2 years
CMS 9/10	10%	2.5 years
CMS 11	11%	6.2 years
CMS 12	13%	5.7 years
Homer 1	14%	5.0 years

The constant prepayment rate or CPR is the effective redemption rate. In the above list the experience to date is extrapolated forward using constant assumptions. When projecting it is important to understand that a CPR of, say, 20 percent per annum is the estimate that redemptions of the notes will, on an annualised basis, reduce at the rate of 20 percent of the previous quarter's balance. The market has generally accepted between 15–20 percent CPR as the basis for determining the discount margins although, as can be seen above, the true experience has been faster resulting in improved yields for investors and higher real financing costs for issuers.

Somewhat perversely, NHL's experience was that redemption levels were faster during 1989/90 when interest rates were higher compared to today when base rates stand at 40 percent of their peak levels. The reasoning would appear to be that the availability of remortgage finance today is heavily restricted by the need for acceptable levels of equity which, as a result of house price falls, have been eroded and in a number of cases are non-existent to negative.

In current market conditions it is likely that a significant premium would have to be offered for the tail pieces of multi-tranche structures because of their extended average life. In recessionary times the marginal cost arbitrage opportunities would turn negative and consequently standard non-substituting, non-tranched FRNs have become the norm.

During the growth phase of the mortgage securities market, many issues included an option for issuers to substitute a new origination when mortgages in the original pool redeemed. Typically this was available for periods of up to three years. The resultant extension in the average life did not however get adequately priced by the market and, in effect, became a zero cost or low premium option. In today's market, substitution is a difficult "sell" and a significant premium would probably be necessary.

COMMERCIAL PAPER

Mortgage- and asset-backed structures have been created to enable funding to be met from these deep and highly liquid markets. To date, they have appeared in three forms:

1. Euro-CP Programme

This is being covered separately in another chapter but, in essence, provides for the sale of mortgages to an SPV with funding created through the issuance of CP. In order to protect against the loss of liquidity in the CP market, a standby bank syndicate is in place.

The advantage to this sort of programme would be the flexibility in issuing at various interest periods compared to the rigidity of the FRN which market convention dictates at 3 months. Additionally, it could prove price competitive. To the CP issuing prices needs to be added the cost of the back-up lines in order to compare against straightforward discount margins. Although the cost of FRN mortgage securities has risen sharply, the cost and availability of bank credit lines have had similar experiences.

The only issue of this type launched and used was a CIBC programme, MAES ECP. Whilst certainly attracting a range of new investors to purchase the CP, these investors were backing into the rating of A1/P1 created by virtue of the bank back-up lines. Therefore, it could be argued that whilst the primary funding had moved to a new market, the commercial banking sector had long been funders of mortgages and, therefore, the secondary level of funding had not created much in the way of diversification.

2. Domestic US Commercial Paper

There are, it is believed, only two transactions where this market has been tapped, both quite different.

1. Mortgage Funding Corporation utilised the Citibank Columbus Capital programme where the US bank's CP-issuing vehicle purchased rated securities and issued CP into the market to fund the consideration. Effectively MFC creates a relatively standard FRN and instead of it being sold to the market it is packaged directly into the Columbus structure. A major advantage is that, similar to the ECP issuance above, interest rate settings can be quite flexible and minimise gapping risks.
2. NHL created a hybrid securitisation in conjunction with the US monoline insurer FSA. The programme, available for 4 years renewable annually, permitted the sale into and out of the SPVs. CP was issued to finance the acquisitions and was repaid from time to time when assets were re-acquired or transferred into another securitisation. The programme attracted a back-up syndicated facility similar to all asset-backed CP programmes but had one significant distinction. Both the CP and the bank syndicate were guaranteed by FSA. The advantage was "two-fold"—first the CP rates were aligned to AAA corporations because the securities were sold on the back of FSA's credit (typically they trade 5 basis points through the AA federal composite index). Secondly, the bank back-up group did not know what assets they were supporting. This structure acted as a bank warehousing line, offered interest rate arbitrage opportunities and genuinely opened a new investor base.

3. Commercial Paper Conduit Financing

This particular section of the market has seen rapid growth in recent years with major banking institutions leading the field in setting up what is effectively their own programmes.

The forerunner to these schemes was the Citibank Columbus Capital transaction which MFC employed in 1989, as mentioned above. However, since that time, it seemed virtually every major commercial bank either directly or in conjunction with an investment bank was tapping the market. The most recent announcement has been by National Westminster Bank and is known as Thames Funding.

The programme involves the sale of receivables to an SPV or a trust structure providing bankruptcy-remote protection. The commercial paper issued into the US debt markets can have a maximum maturity of 270 days. Typically the sponsoring bank (or if it is an investment bank then the commercial bank as a partner) will write a 364-day back-up credit line to ensure liquidity to the CP and protect its rating. This will be done either solely or jointly with a few other players. It is essential therefore that, given the credit quality requirement of the CP market for minimum A1/P1 paper, the back-up facility must be provided by a bank of equal rating. Credit risk is protected through structures although because the paper is issued at A1/P1 (min) levels, their underlying credit support can afford a degree of relaxation from AAA. Interestingly, the NatWest programme is planning to utilise corporate credits the bank had previously made. The criteria of A1+/P1 corporates has resulted in no additional credit support being necessary.

Banks have written substantial programmes of this type. The trick is that a 364-day credit facility carries a 0 percent risk asset weighting under banking capital adequacy requirements. Therefore despite, say, a US$1 billion committed credit line, the bank requires no capital to support it so long as these facilities remain undrawn. The return on regulatory capital for the bank is infinite. The Fed has certainly looked at these arrangements and it may be that regulatory change will kill off this developing market. Alternatively, it should be remembered that regulators have flexibility to set the minimum level of capital to any level above the 8 percent determined by Basle rules. A commercial bank may well find its minimum ratios being increased if the level of "zero weighted" commitments appeares out of line with the existing balance sheet capacity. It may therefore not be the "free lunch" it is perceived to be.

FIXED RATE ISSUES

There have, to date, been five fixed rate mortgage issues in the UK. These can be divided into two types:

- ♦ 5-year non-amortising bullet
- ♦ 25-year fully amortising

They will be dealt with in turn.

1. 5-Year Bullet Maturities

Given that the UK market is dominated by variable rate collateral and that maturities of the underlying loans are for 25 years and longer, the ability to create a 5-year bullet maturity involves some quite complicated structuring.

Four issues have fallen within this category—HMC 101, 102, 103 and CMS 10. They are opportunistic issues. The securities are sold into the fixed sterling markets where investor demand and yields are more volatile on a day-to-day basis. In addition, a swap from fixed to floating is required to match the SPV cash flows and therefore the timing is dependent on the window of opportunity between the swap and bond market.

Certainly CMS 10 produced significant cost savings compared to the alternative FRN at the time. Additionally, these fixed rate issues have performed well in price terms since issued despite the poor trading levels in the FRN market.

So why is the UK mortgage-backed securities market not built around the fixed rate issues rather than FRNs? Well, first is the opportunistic nature of the fixed rate. It is generally perceived that the FRN market is always open at a price whereas this is certainly not the case in the Eurosterling market. Secondly, the complexity of the structure requires a variety of additional credit supports to ensure the AAA rating.

The structure employed in the CMS 10 issue can be diagrammatically represented in Figure 25.7.

NHL sold £200 million worth of mortgages to an SPV (CMS 9). This vehicle created three tranches of security of equal amounts similar to the multi-tranche issues. The fast and medium paying tranches of £100 million in total were sold to the market. The slow paying tranche was sold to another SPV, CMS 10.

CMS 10 is the fixed rate issuer and sold 5-year fixed rate bonds in the amount of £100 million. The SPV's primary income was generated from the £100 million FRN. How then can it ensure its AAA rating? This is achieved through three mechanisms.

Figure 25.7

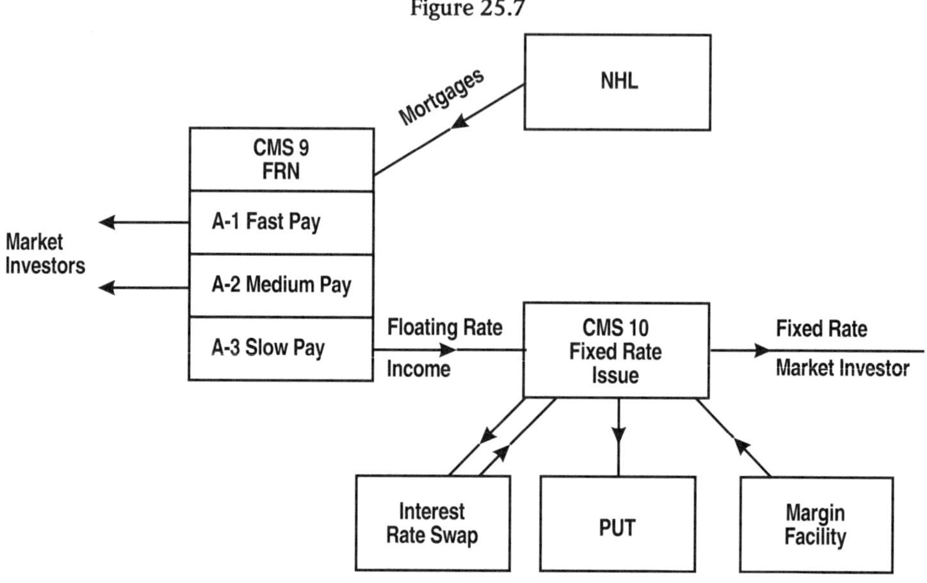

1. Interest rate swap—the SPV enters into a fixed/floating interest rate swap with a bank converting its fixed rate interest obligation to floating rate in order to match the income stream on the FRN. Of course the swap must be with a AAA-rated institution.
2. The FRN purchased by the fixed rate issuing SPV will have a final maturity of 37 years (35-year mortgage plus 2-year assumption to foreclose). How then can repayment be "guaranteed" to AAA standard at the end of year 5? The fixed rate issuer enters into a put agreement with a third party (who must be AAA-rated) who agrees to purchase the FRN at the end of year 5 at a pre-agreed price assuming it has not been sold by the SPV to the market earlier. Typically the pre-agreed price will be set at a premium to discourage the put from being exercised.
3. It is important to understand why it is the slow paying tranche of the FRN issue that is sold to the fixed rate issuer. All early mortgage redemptions will be applied in paying down the fast paying tranche which has been sold into the market. Only then will proceeds be applied in paying down the slow paying tranche. This therefore makes it remote that there is any paydown under the slow pay FRN tranche. The reinvestment risk of this happening however needs further support to meet rating requirements.

The sizing of the tranching has, for the issuer, protected what it believes is the economic risk. Further protection is afforded by the ability to substitute mortgages after redemption into the fast paying tranches. However, the rating test required protection should mortgage redemptions far exceed expectations and substitution not be possible. This risk was covered by a margin facility which would fund the difference between an agreed deposit rate and the rate on the slow pay FRN tranche. This operates in a similar fashion to a guaranteed investment contract. In reality it is highly unlikely the margin facility will be necessary but is a product of achieving the rating.

2. 25-Year Amortising Fixed Rate

The US mortgage market is dominated by long-term fixed rate mortgages with an ability of the home owner to exercise their option at any time and prepay, irrespective of interest rates.

This provides a substantial reinvestment risk to the mortgage provider in a falling interest rate environment and was a major contributor to the problems of the US savings and loan sector in the early 1980s.

This risk of adverse performance is known as negative convexity and is clearly not within the bounds of a mortgage lender to manage to any great degree. Hence the US passed the management of this risk on to the financial markets who were able to analyse the various embedded options and, using prepayment projections, could attempt to value the risk. Option adjusted spread (OAS) has become the main method of valuing a mortgage security in the USA.

The UK market is not subjected to the same levels of consumer protection laws and therefore has no depth in a long-dated fixed rate mortgage sector. Separately, the UK is particularly weak on statistical analysis of its mortgage industry, and the ability to analyse and value these securities would be inherently problematical.

Bear Stearns Home Loans, the mortgage subsidiary of the US investment bank, did make a brave attempt however. In April 1990 it issued Bear Stearns Mortgage Securities No. 1 PLC, a £106 million fully amortising long-dated issue.

Bear Stearns had previously originated fixed rate mortgages at quite attractive pricing. It charged a 3 percent upfront fee to deter early prepayment (negative convexity risk) and protected its trading position—the time between originating the mortgage and sale through to the securitisation—by way of gilt options. This would have protected the majority of interest rate risk although an element would have to be absorbed in respect of basis risk, i.e., the spread over gilts that the securities would have to be issued at.

Bear Stearns developed an econometric model of UK prepayment spreads for use in the transaction. It was adapted from their US models and attempts had to be made to convince the UK investor base, typically gilt players, that this additional level of risk had been adequately compensated. Now that UK interest rates have fallen sharply, it will be interesting to see how these securities will perform.

The market did not take kindly to the transaction. Criticism was leveled at the price at which securities were being sold—180 bp over the 10-year gilt; whereas with the inverse yield curve the securities were thought to be nearer 140 bp over the 7-year gilt. The reality was that the investor base, who had largely been participants in a fixed rate non-callable market were not yet prepared for innovation.

Although Bear Stearns was criticised for pricing the securities too tightly, the reality of the problem was two-fold. First, the UK investor base has a somewhat limited vision and is not forced by the volume in the market to come to terms with the complexity of valuing interest rate risk and option adjusted spreads (unlike the US where the size of the mortgage securities market means this form of investment cannot be disregarded).

Secondly, the ability to create the right quantity of mortgage product is going to be dependent on either a very steeply inverted yield curve (making long-term fixed rate competitive with variable rates adjusting for the need to factor interest rate risk into the price) or a structural change in the mortgage market which will widen mortgage spreads to more appropriate levels. Despite the structural changes in the market during the mid-1980s, mortgage products are sold too cheaply by the building societies compared to alternative investments, especially now that the gloss of their low non-risk nature has evaporated. The over competitive market does not provide for a sufficient spread to be earned and increased risk to be compensated. A more economically based margin would be to all participants' benefits, except perhaps the UK home owner.

CREDIT ENHANCEMENT STRUCTURES

The market's development has centered around two main forms of enhancement—pool insurance and senior/subordinated structures.

Pool insurance will in addition require the availability of a liquidity facility to cover the cash flow shortfall between borrower default and foreclosure/sale of the property. Senior/subordinated structures cover this cash flow risk through the surplus cash funds generated by the higher level of assets compared to senior debt.

Each form of enhancement has its advantages and disadvantages and has experienced mixed performances during the last few years. These will be dealt with separately.

Pool insurance originally required the need for a deductible fund of typically 0.5 percent of the issue to be held in the form of cash. The first level of losses would be taken from this reserve. The insurance company would meet losses between 0.5–10 percent. This ensured the rating level. For issuers such as NHL and HMC where capital preservation was important, this structure did not compare well against senior/subordinated where the level of risk capital exposure was considerably smaller. Alternative structures were developed in due course to cope with these requirements by reducing the level of upfront deductible funds to say, 0.25 percent in compensation for the ability to redirect the issuer's surplus cash flows to "topping up" this deductible if exhausted, subject to an ultimate cap of, say, 1 percent. The insurers were therefore likely to have greater levels of loss protection ahead of their exposure if necessary whilst the issuer could preserve capital.

The pool insurance market has suffered in recent years from contracting capacity. The main participants, Sun Alliance and Eagle Star, have suffered severe losses on their separate MIG (Mortgage Indemnity Guarantee) policies. Some losses can be expected in certain pool insured transactions for the insurer but not remotely like the problem in the MIG divisions. But the general corporate view to mortgage risk has clearly been clouded. Separately, the pool insurers would reinsure themselves within the industry typically in the European markets. The reinsurers' view of the UK economy and the UK housing sector has resulted in a withdrawal from this market. Therefore, pool insurance capacity is today heavily constrained. Premiums are higher and deductibles and top-up structures enhanced in the insurer's favour.

At heart I am a contrarian and believe the insurance industry which is forcing today's market to pay for yesterday's problem is missing out on an opportunity. If the UK housing market is set to lose as much money on new lending today as it has done in recent years' originations, then there is no hope for any of us. Clearly, today is when they should be actively courting new business not frightening it away.

Senior/subordinated structures commenced life as cheaper alternatives to pool insurance. Pricing at about 100 bp over LIBOR was almost certainly too cheap with the benefit of hindsight. However, one of the major attractions to the B piece investor is the availability of the issuer's profit (or servicing strip) to support its performance. Essentially this means that the SPV cannot extract profit from the transaction unless the B piece is current. However, the B note is there to provide liquidity and credit support to the senior debt and with high arrears levels, interest deferrals could occur in similar fashion to drawings being made on liquidity policies ahead of foreclosure. Three further aspects need to be drawn out. First, these securities are proving their robust nature, with only transactions having experienced one B note interest deferral for one quarter which was subsequently paid. Secondly, the securities were sold to an investor base that did not expect interest deferrals and hence their original mis-pricing. Thirdly, the market has now moved to a tranching of the security to provide increased credit support to the subordinated piece. This has come in the form of creating a third tier of security making the B note a mezzanine piece. The B note will typically carry its own rating of single A and have the benefit of the liquidity and credit support of the C note sized at approximately 2–3 percent of the issue.

EVENT RISK

One of the main issues surrounding credit enhancement has worked against the market as a whole. Event risk in this situation can be defined as downgrading of a mortgage-backed security as a result of the downgrading of one of the constituent external credit supports to the transaction. By way of example, if the pool insurer were to fall from AAA to AA+, the rating on the dependent mortgage-backed security could fall simultaneously unless the issuer purchased a new upgraded level of insurance. As the main providers of pool insurance have suffered in the current recession, their own corporate downgrades have dragged the rating of the mortgage securities down with them.

Separately, the plethora of new mortgage products required credit support either by way of committed facilities, swaps or interest rate caps. These would typically have to be provided by AAA-rated banks. As bank after bank lost this status again, the mortgage-backed securities ratings fell in tandem. Many of these support facilities were of a contingent nature and, on analysis, the market's belief in the underlying strength and integrity of transactions was largely preserved. However, it does cause confusion and disruption. Investors are now aware of the risks and will analyse transactions in more detail to determine the degree of an individual deal's exposure to third party downgrade. With more complicated mortgage products in the portfolio, the risk is obviously higher.

Some issuers were keen to maintain their SPVs' ratings to protect future issuance and purchased additional credit support. Some others were fortunate in being able to alter their structures to accommodate the additional enhancement with little or no cost, whilst others, for regulatory or principle reasons, could not support the transactions. In reality it has not caused a major widening of spreads between issues but has served to maintain the overall high spread to LIBOR that mortgage securities command.

COLLATERAL QUALITY ISSUES

The depression in the housing market has and remains the single biggest factor affecting the mortgage securities market. The availability of new mortgage supply, capacity for credit enhancement and the pricing of securities have all been adversely affected as a consequence.

Delinquencies have been at historical highs in the industry although it is likely each separate transaction will have different experience depending on its demographics and other characteristics, especially period of mortgage origination. It is also important to understand that a transaction is likely to experience a relatively predictable pattern. On day one with zero arrears it is likely that in the first few months to two years a relatively sharp acceleration of delinquency will occur. This will eventually flatten out and indeed cash flow shortfalls will start to improve. However, the improvement is likely to be gradual as the period to foreclosure has proven to be somewhat longer than expected. Beyond a certain period the propensity for borrowers not to perform will reduce thereby justifying the value in a seasoned portfolio.

NHL's experience in its four oldest securitisations (originated 1988-1989) is exactly as described above. It has seen a flattening of the arrears curve and, recently, improvements.

One consequence of the current recession has been the need to invest in adequate delinquency control systems. With arrears and losses being miniscule in the UK for as long as anyone could remember, the industry was caught under-invested in this part of its business. Managers with inadequate experience of coping with the rising arrears trend and manual systems which failed at the beginning of the tidal wave all contributed to the greater level of losses experienced in the industry. Frighteningly, there are still members of the industry who have not responded to this problem.

We at NHL have invested substantially in arrears management systems developed initially in the USA. For an investor in mortgage-backed securities this should be just as important a consideration as knowing the characteristics of the portfolio.

Portfolio performance disclosure has become a topical debate in the recent past. Transactions have been launched with relatively limited information, and unlike the USA, there is very little in the way of ongoing statistically based research. Consequently, investors in a housing-based securities market are naturally concerned when the underlying collateral in the industry experiences such problems. The securities have been robust but the investor is naturally keen to be aware and price the risk of the different performances accordingly. It will almost certainly be a requirement of future transactions that ongoing statistical research will be published, and it is likely to be to the benefit of future issuers to publish experiences of their past transactions.

ARREARS SECURITISATIONS

The difficulties in the housing market have led to the need for originators to develop structures to securitise non-performing loans. Unusually, new structures had to be developed for the UK as no "blue print" could be lifted from the USA.

There are two principle factors to consider (which although they appear to be statements of the obvious have to be handled in different ways to standard securitisations). These factors are:

1. Credit quality—whilst the rating agency assumptions do not vary, the level of house price declines built into the model do assume all, or virtually all, of the mortgages will go into foreclosure and therefore the overall losses within the portfolio will be consequently higher. This 100 percent foreclosure frequency has a particularly important consequence in that the modeling will assume the interest losses that occur will affect the whole of the portfolio.

2. Liquidity—with all the mortgages non-performing, the portfolio clearly would ordinarily not be able to meet its interest and other expenses as they fell due.

The above two issues have been handled separately in the three securitisations of arrears mortgages launched to date. Undoubtedly there will be more and undoubtedly they will be refined and improved upon.

1. CIBC had originated mortgages with the benefit of a 100 percent pool insurance policy. Any losses on the portfolio would be for the account of the insurer thereby making the collateral issue redundant.

   Liquidity risk however was covered by a substantial credit facility to ensure timely payment of interest. The sizing of this facility is stressed under rating conditions and would exceed 20 percent of the size of the issue.

   In CIBC's case, the whole transaction was wrapped under an FSA guarantee thereby providing AAA securities.

2. NHL did not have the benefit of 100 percent pool insured mortgages and it is impossible to purchase insurance on a portfolio already in arrears. Therefore an alternative method of credit enhancement had to be used. This was achieved by two elements of the structure.

   - Credit quality was provided by over-collateralisation through a subordinated tranche of debt. This was large because of the 100 percent foreclosure frequency assumption and consequent interest loss projection.

- Repayment was assumed by the agencies in the long term although liquidity aspects were covered by structuring the bonds with the risk of deferral. However, this risk was protected by the ability to use principal receipts (i.e., repayments of loans by natural redemption or through foreclosure) to pay interest. The experience of this transaction is that it has been highly cash generative with all interest being met as it fell due and, in addition, principal paydowns occurring. It could be expected that arrears transactions would perform in this way, as with effective arrears management non-performing accounts should be foreclosed quickly. Their average life will therefore be relatively short at 18 months–two years.

3. HMC launched the most recent public arrears securitisation and was an adaptation of the NHL structure set out above.

The refinements were in two areas:

i) The over-collateralisation to the senior bonds was provided by two tranches, mezzanine and subordinated pieces. This enabled the level of originator capital held in the transaction to be minimised as the mezzanine tranche was given an A rating and thereby saleable.

ii) Liquidity was provided by a cash reserve fund which was sized to meet rating stress levels.

As mentioned above, there is still a lot of non-performing collateral looking for finance and it is likely more transactions will occur in the future.

CONCLUSION

Securitisation in the UK has certainly not had an easy or indeed happy childhood. The depth and longevity of the recession has put the assets through real life stress tests and it is a testimony to the robust nature of their structures that all issues are performing.

The generally accepted view is that the market will not progress until a more developed investor base is created. What is needed is supply from the largest sector in the UK housing market, the Building Societies. The absence from this form of fund raising is a product of their closeted and oligopolistic position. They compete with each other but have no means of accountability for their performance except to the extent that any weak society is forced into an arranged marriage of unequal partners by the Building Societies Commission. In the USA, investors cannot ignore the mortgage-backed securities market because of its size. In the UK, increasing new issuance, particularly from society originators, will develop a similar mentality. Investor awareness will be greater, investment banks will make more resources available and liquidity will develop in the secondary market.

The market has survived the toughest baptism any fledgling industry could have experienced. It has adapted and developed to accommodate the issues of the day. It will certainly survive but it needs additional support to enable it to achieve its potential.

Chapter 26

The Risks and Opportunities of the Canadian NHA MBS Market

by Lori Terry,
Burns Fry Limited

OVERVIEW

The relative unsophistication of the Canadian Mortgage-Backed Securities market provides a unique investment opportunity for those interested in investigating and evaluating the risks pertaining to a highly profitable instrument.

Prepayable MBSs resemble Government of Canada bonds in terms of credit but, unlike Canada bonds, are callable by virtue of the prepayment option afforded mortgagors on the underlying loans. Prepayment features create investment risk by creating cash flow timing uncertainty. Monthly cash flows to investors consist of scheduled principal due on the pooled mortgages, coupon interest due on the MBS, and any additional (or unscheduled) principal and penalty interest occurring as a result of partial and/or full loan principal repayments. The potential for unscheduled principal payments gives rise to investment risk.

Succinctly stated, the risk is twofold.

1. *Pricing Risk:* In the absence of a consistent valuation methodology which incorporates both the benefits and drawbacks of cash flow timing and duration uncertainty, investors bear the risk that the likelihood of prepayment, and therefore the price of the security, will not be valued accurately at the time of purchase or sale.
2. *Reinvestment Risk:* Given that some level of prepayment will occur, investors assume the risk of future reinvestment rate uncertainty. In the face of unfavourable reinvestment opportunities, the investor may not be able to achieve the same yield as would have been realized had the security not prepaid.

Increasing prepayment activity and the impact of such payments on the realized value of an investment provide a compelling argument to include prepayment assumptions when valuing prepayable MBSs. In an effort to reduce investment risk, the marketplace has moved to incorporate a rudimentary level of prepayment analysis. Referred to as *Option Adjusted Spread Pricing,* prepayment assumptions are being incorporated into the pricing of prepayable issues trading at a premium. As the market matures, we should expect similar treatment with respect to prepayable MBSs trading at a discount.

Understanding unscheduled principal payments and the impact they have on both duration and realized yield, knowledgable investors can manage the risks associated with prepayable MBSs to their advantage. Three fundamental opportunities exist.

1. *Prepayable MBSs Priced at a Premium:* Given the rudimentary level of prepayment analysis in Canada, traders will typically overestimate prepayment activity when valuing MBSs trading at a premium. This works to an investor's advantage since, generally speaking, if prepayment activity falls below the assumed rate, the investor's realized yield will be greater than that anticipated at the time of purchase.
2. *Pricing off Stated Maturity:* Canadian MBSs are priced based on the security's stated maturity. In a positive yield curve environment investors benefit from a yield pick-up at the time of purchase since the purchase yield is based on the stated term and the theoretical value is based on a term short-

ened by prepayment. The yield pick-up is the difference between the purchase yield and the theoretical value assuming a greater than 0% prepayment rate.

3. Short Term Reinvestment Rates: The yield impact of short term reinvestment rates, subsequent to purchase, is solely a function of short term rates relative to the purchase yield. Reinvestment opportunities at rates higher than the purchase yield offer investors the potential for an enhanced realized yield.

The following chapter explores the risks and returns associated with prepayable MBSs in Canada.

THE CANADIAN NHA MBS MARKET

Enthusiasm swept the Canadian fixed income markets in January 1987 with the introduction of the Canadian National Housing Act Mortgage-Backed Securities Program (the "Program") and the issuance of the first Canadian mortgage-backed security ("MBS"). Sponsored by the federal government under the National Housing Act ("NHA"), the Program provides for a direct federal government guarantee of full and timely payment on all issues. The Program is administered by Canada Mortgage and Housing Corporation ("CMHC"), a federal Crown Corporation created pursuant to the National Housing Act. The Program was modeled after the highly successful U.S. Government National Mortgage Association (Ginnie Mae) MBS Program.

NHA MBSs result from the packaging, or pooling, of homogeneous NHA-insured, first residential mortgages. The resulting certificates, when sold, represent an undivided ownership interest in the mortgage loans underlying the issue. Monthly payments of principal and interest are made to investors according to a modified pass-through structure which means that while all principal is fully passed through every month, only that portion of the interest payment required to meet the negotiated MBS coupon rate is paid. The remaining interest portion is retained by the originating institution as a servicing fee. Only CMHC approved institutions can issue NHA MBS.

Since its inception in 1987, the Canadian MBS market has experienced exponential growth (Figure 26.1). In December 1992 the market surpassed $14 billion (Cdn) in cumulative new issue volume and appears to have secured a permanent position within the Canadian capital markets.

Canadian MBSs are grouped according to the characteristics of the mortgage loans underlying each issue. Four distinct categories currently exist: Prepayable, Non-Prepayable, MMUF, and Hybrid. A brief synopsis of each is provided below.

Prepayable. Prepayable MBSs result from the pooling of NHA-insured, single-family, prepayable, first residential mortgage loans. Typically these loans have an amortization period of 25 years, an initial financing term of 5 years, and permit early principal repayment. In most cases, penalty inter-

Figure 26.1—Canadian NHA Mortgage-Backed Securities Market

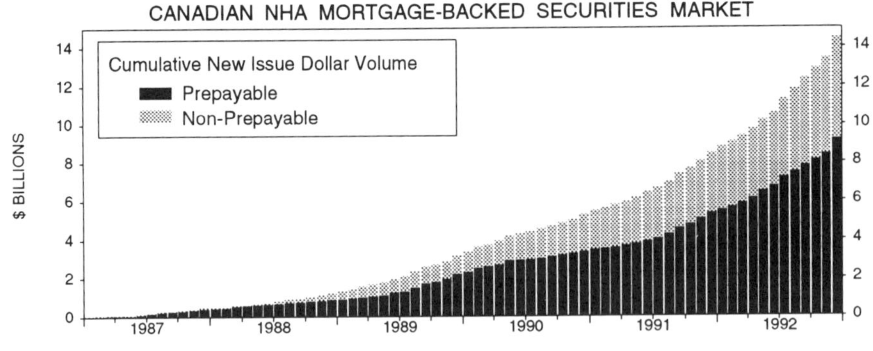

est charges will be levied against mortgagors for making early or unscheduled principal payments. Penalty interest is usually, but not always, passed through to the MBS holder.

Non-Prepayable. Non-prepayable MBSs result from the pooling of multi-unit, social housing, non-profit mortgage loans. Typically these loans have an amortization period of 35 years, an initial financing term of 5 years, and do not permit early principal repayments. These mortgages result from initiatives at the federal and/or provincial level to provide subsidized housing for low-income Canadians. Government subsidies match the operating deficits of the non-profit corporations running the projects, thereby rendering default virtually impossible. In the absence of prepayment privileges, non-prepayable MBSs provide investors with predictable cash flows.

MMUF. MMUF MBSs contain **m**arket **mu**lti-**f**amily mortgages (also known as rental loans) and most closely resemble the characteristics of non-prepayable MBSs. Typically these mortgages involve large multiple-unit properties which are not government subsidized and prohibit prepayments. Foreclosures, if any, will result in lump sum repayments of principal. MMUF issues may therefore experience some prepayment risk as the underlying mortgages are market loans susceptible to early prepayment due to default under severe economic conditions. MMUF issues may contain social housing loans.

Hybrid. Hybrid MBSs contain a combination of prepayable and non-prepayable mortgages.

Current market share in terms of new issue volume for each of the four categories is presented below:

Canadian NHA MBS Market as at December 31, 1992

NHA MBS Type	*# of Issues*	*New Issue $ Volume (Market Share)*
Prepayable	680	$ 8,865.89 MM (61.5%)
Non-Prepayable	443	$ 4,749.91 MM (32.9%)
MMUF	17	$412.37 MM (2.9%)
Hybrid	25	$390.51 MM (2.7%)
Total Market	1165	$14,418.68 MM (100.0%)

Since 1987 prepayable MBSs have dominated the Canadian MBS Market in dollar volume and number of issues. Secondary in both respects, non-prepayable MBSs trail largely due to limitations imposed at the onset of the Program. It was not until August 1988 that multi-unit, social housing, non-profit mortgage loans were permitted for securitization under the Program and the first Canadian non-prepayable MBS was issued. Program expansion continued in September 1990 when minimum term loan restrictions were reduced from 4.5 years to 6 months. Since that time, MBSs with initial terms of as low as 6 months have been issued.

During the first year of the Program roughly 90% of the market supply was absorbed through participation by the retail investor. By 1988, the increasing monthly production volumes, due in part to the introduction of non-prepayable MBSs, exceeded the industry's aggregate retail distribution capacity and necessitated the widening of spreads to attract institutional investors. While close to 90% of the demand now comes from institutional investors, retail demand continues to be strong.

Conventionally MBSs have been valued on a spread basis over similar term Government of Canada bonds. As both of these instruments represent the unconditional obligation of the federal government and are AAA rated, the yield differential is not credit related, but speaks more to cash flow timing. Prepayable spreads in the 5-year area have remained relatively stable at 65-85 basis points over similar term Government of Canada bonds with non-prepayable MBSs trading 10-20 basis points narrower than prepayable issues (Figure 26.2). The 10-20 basis points differential is directly attributable to the call feature of prepayable pools.

Since the majority of Canadian MBSs are 5-year prepayable and non-prepayable issues the analysis presented herein will be confined to this group.

INVESTING IN PREPAYABLE CANADIAN MBS

The greatest risk to investors of prepayable Canadian MBSs is the absence of a consistent valuation methodology which incorporates both the benefits and drawbacks of cash flow timing and duration uncertainty. It is one thing to be cognisant of the factors affecting cash flow timing uncertainty, but quite another to devise a uniform means of forecasting the collective influence these factors will have on the value of the security. The lack of any such standardized forecasting model creates a unique arbitrage opportunity for investors, whereby institutions valuing MBSs will, based on

Figure 26.2—Canadian NHA Mortgage-Backed Securities

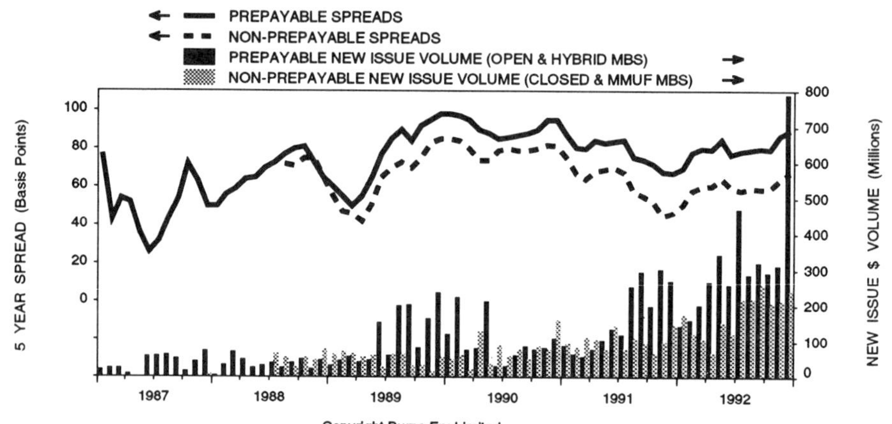

differing assumptions, attach different value to the same security.

Valuation of the yield differential between prepayable MBSs and similar term Government of Canada bonds necessitates a thorough understanding of the attributes affecting cash flow timing and hence the implicit value of the investment. Fundamentally, the bond characteristics which impact on the value of the respective securities are as follows:

- Cash Flow Frequency
- Timing of Capital Gain/Loss Realization
- Duration Uncertainty
- Subsequent Reinvestment Opportunities

Each of these attributes is discussed below.

Cash Flow Frequency

Cash flow frequency marks the primary difference between NHA MBSs and traditional Government of Canada bonds. Unlike semi-annual-pay instruments, MBSs employ a monthly-pay modified pass-through structure. Payments of principal and interest are made to MBS holders on or about the 15th day of every month. The principal payment includes scheduled principal due pursuant to the amortization schedule of the underlying loans, plus any additional principal occurring as a result of prepayment privileges. The interest payment includes coupon interest (as calculated at the monthly equivalent coupon rate based on the remaining principal balance of the security) and may include penalty interest. Subject to policies of the lending institution, penalty interest may be levied against a mortgagor for early principal repayments, and when charged, may be passed through to the investor. If received, penalty interest is viewed purely as additional income. The absence of any "rule of thumb" regarding penalty interest has resulted in discrimination between issuers in the Canadian market.

Mortgage prepayment privileges vary among lending institutions. CMHC requires that NHA-insured, single-family, first residential mortgage loans allow a minimum of 10% prepayment each year for the first three years without penalty. Thereafter, any amount of principal can be prepaid with a maximum penalty equal to three months interest. Most NHA MBS issuers extend more liberal prepayment privileges. Typically, prepayment privileges are as follows:

1. The mortgagor has the right to prepay up to 15% of the original principal balance once each year for each of the first three years without penalty.
2. The entire loan or any portion thereof may be repaid following the third anniversary date upon a penalty payment equal to three months interest at the mortgage rate.
3. Scheduled payments can be increased by 15% annually without penalty.

4. The entire mortgage may be paid-off after one year, upon bona fide sale of the home, and subject to three months penalty interest.

Prepayment privileges are disclosed on the information circular of each issue.

Timing of Capital Gain/Loss Realization

NHA MBSs provide a monthly cash flow of interest *plus principal.* The monthly payment of principal accelerates the realization of a capital gain or loss relative to a bare interest paying investment. Partial prepayments and full loan repayments further precipitate a capital gain or loss realization. Investors focusing on the present value of a gain or loss will prefer to accelerate the realization of a capital gain and defer the realization of a capital loss.

Duration Uncertainty

Duration is the weighted average time to receipt of the present value of both principal and interest cash flows. An accelerated rate of principal redemption has the effect of shortening duration. To the extent that prepayment activity cannot be accurately predicted, prepayable MBSs are susceptible to high duration uncertainty.

Duration uncertainty has a direct impact on the purchase price of an MBS and is considered to be one of the key factors contributing to the yield differential between prepayable and non-prepayable MBSs. Historical spread data indicates that investors will typically give up the yield equivalent of 10-20 basis points to obtain duration certainty.

Since Canadian MBSs are bought and sold off their stated maturity, prepayments and hence duration uncertainty also impact on the theoretical value of the investment. In a positive yield curve environment, investors benefit from the price advantage created from spreading MBSs off the point on the Canada bond yield curve matching the MBS stated maturity. Assuming a prepayment rate of greater than 0%, and hence a shorter duration, the theoretical relative value of the MBS at the time of purchase (i.e., its value against an equal duration Government of Canada bond) is higher than initially assumed. Conversely, if the curve is inverted, the shorter duration impacts negatively since the theoretical value of the security is measured off a less expensive bond.

Subsequent Reinvestment Opportunities

Unscheduled principal payments increase an MBS investor's exposure to future reinvestment rate uncertainty. The risk therefore, is not that prepayments will occur, but rather that subsequent reinvestment opportunities will not be sufficient to achieve the same or better results as would have been realized had the security not prepaid. Reinvestment at rates higher than the MBS purchase yield will serve to enhance the investor's realized yield while reinvestment at rates lower than the purchase yield will have an adverse effect. Penalty interest, reinvested at any rate, will enhance the realized return.

THE PREPAYMENT OPTION

As previously outlined, single-family, first residential mortgage loans afford borrowers the option to make early principal repayments in accordance with the terms or privileges extended by the lending institution. In assuming a slightly higher mortgage rate than would be negotiated on a non-prepayable mortgage, the borrower purchases the option to exercise prepayment privileges at one or more future points in time. For the investment community it is this issue of the potential for prepayments and associated cash flow timing uncertainty which creates ambiguity in the valuation of prepayable MBSs in Canada.

Projecting prepayment activity necessitates consideration of both economic and non-economic related factors. Economic events, such as a drop in refinancing rates may increase a borrower's propensity to prepay. Theoretically, borrowers will prefer to pay down existing loans and seek refinancing when rates fall to a level such that they can more than recoup the penalty charges and transaction costs incurred as a result of refinancing. Non-economic events such as death can also impact on prepayment activity and occur regardless of the interest rate environment. Mortgage loans may be fully repaid as a result of foreclosure, sale of property, or natural disaster, or partially prepaid due to the availability of excess cash. Lump sum payments frequently coincide with the availability of excess cash due to the tax treatment of mortgage interest expenses in Canada. In contrast to the United States, mortgage interest is not deductible under the Canadian tax system thereby doubling the borrower's effective mortgage rate. Excess cash is, therefore, better put toward paying down a mortgage loan than toward investment elsewhere. With respect to home sales, tax implications are again different. In contrast to the United States, capital gains realized on the sale of a principal residence under Canadian tax laws are tax free.

Since the accurate prediction of any one of these factors is difficult, predicting their collective impact on a mortgagor's propensity to prepay is equally, if not more, difficult. Furthermore, not all borrowers will exercise their prepayment option simply because it is advantageous to do so. They may be either transaction adverse or simply unaware of what is occurring in the market. The complexity surrounding the propensity to prepay reinforces the need to devise a meaningful, measurable method for predicting prepayment activity. The greater the accuracy in forecasting the factors affecting prepayment, the more accurate the MBS valuation. As a starting point, we can look to historical performance in an attempt to identify general trends which may be applicable to a forecasting model. While forecasting based on historical performance is by no means definitive of future activity, it represents greater accuracy than would be attained from assuming a 0% prepayment rate.

UNSCHEDULED PRINCIPAL PAYMENTS

Unscheduled principal is that amount of principal received from partial prepayments or full loan repayments which, together, create cash flow uncertainty and increase reinvestment risk. The term used to describe the frequency of unscheduled payments of principal is known as the unscheduled principal payment ("UPP") rate. UPP can include both CPR and SMM (described below) and is expressed as an annualized rate. The constant prepayment rate ("CPR") is the constant annual percentage of outstanding principal being partially prepaid on a monthly basis throughout the life of the MBS. SMM (single month mortality) measures whole loan liquidations from a pool. SMM is measured on a monthly basis similar to CPR and is expressed as an annual percentage of those mortgages which have been liquidated from a pool relative to the amount then outstanding.

At the end of 1992, the weighted average UPP rate for the universe of prepayable NHA MBSs was 10.07%. Table 26.1 illustrates the upward trend which has occurred over the past 12 months. While the rise in UPP rates is coincident with a dramatic fall in Canadian interest rates, high UPP can also be explained by the natural propensity for prepayment to occur as pools age. The 6-month weighted average UPP rates represent a trailing average based on the latest 6 months. Six-month rates allow investors to identify any significant changes to the underlying UPP trends. The variance in UPP rates suggests that prepayment assumptions should reflect the prepayment privileges extended by a specific issuer.

Historical UPP Experience

The UPP analysis which follows has been confined to prepayable NHA MBSs with an initial 5-year term to maturity, issued prior to 1991. The 5-year initial term represents the majority of NHA MBSs issued to date.

Figure 26.3 illustrates the weighted average UPP rates from January 1987 through December 1992.

In each of the four origination years UPP rates exhibit an upward trend over time. At the end of 1992, the weighted average UPP rate for 1987 issues was 7.53%. Curves for pools issued in 1988, 1989, and 1990 appear slightly steeper with UPP rates of 12.45%, 15.73%, and 13.25% respectively. The constant UPP rate shown in 1992 for 1987 issues results from issues reaching maturity and, in part, from the current unavailability of UPP data in the final 6 months of a pool's term. (Note: UPP volatility in the year of issuance results from the weighting in of new issues and should not be confused with sporadic prepayment activity).

Of interesting note is that the increase in UPP for all four origination years seems to have occurred before the dramatic drop in 5-year mortgage rates in the third quarter of 1991. This suggests that short-term rates may have enticed mortgagors to prepay and refinance for terms less than 5 years.

Figure 26.4 illustrates 6-month and 1-year lending rates from January 1991 through December 1992. Anticipating a continued rate decline, mortgagors may have seized the opportunity to refinance for 6 months or 1 year to avoid getting locked in for 5 years at a higher rate. The upturn in UPP appears to occur in March 1991, at which time 5-year residential mortgage rates were roughly 11.50%. The weighted average initial mortgage rates for the pools in this study by year of origination are as follows: 1987 issues = 10.63%, 1988 issues = 11.33%, 1989 issues = 11.83% and 1990 issues = 12.21%. The 6-month and 1-year mortgage rates in March 1991 were roughly 11.75% and 11.0% respectively. As the above initial mortgage rates by year of origination are averages, the 11.75% rate may have been low enough to attract borrowers at the higher end of the range to refinance based on their expectation that 5-year rates would continue to fall. Through a period of falling rates it is conceivable that mortgagors opted for interim 6-month and 1-year refi-

Table 26.1—Prepayable NHA MBS UPP Rates

	As at December 31, 1991				As at December 31, 1992			
Issuer	*# of Pools*	*Volume Issued ($MM)*	*UPP (%)*	*6-MTH UPP (%)*	*# of Pools*	*Volume Issued ($MM)*	*UPP (%)*	*6-MTH UPP (%)*
Bank of Nova Scotia	3	150.11	8.27	13.36	3	$150.11	11.66	23.34
Bayshore Trust	7	75.08	3.71	7.47	7	75.08	12.90	15.34
Canada Trust	2	105.20	1.19	1.28	3	205.18	4.94	8.03
CIBC	7	150.00	10.95	13.23	7	150.00	13.10	16.96
Central Guaranty Trust	22	690.41	9.29	15.11	22	690.41	15.51	33.89
Family Trust	4	15.51	6.83	7.08	9	40.57	3.65	5.90
Fiducie Desjardins	5	21.32	7.41	13.10	7	36.85	7.65	15.50
Financial Trust	11	88.48	6.23	10.26	11	88.48	7.71	14.57
FirstLine Trust I*	86	799.31	5.99	12.61	86	799.31	15.44	43.54
FirstLine Trust II**	102	819.78	5.88	8.87	195	1,558.65	12.12	19.60
Fortis Trust	2	4.81	1.96	1.58	4	10.93	2.24	1.98
Guaranty Trust	5	35.06	10.47	14.00	5	35.06	11.88	17.96
Household Trust	4	16.57	9.34	14.42	5	21.33	17.29	43.54
London Life	1	4.99	0.07	0.07	56	487.72	3.88	4.03
Montreal Trust	1	15.00	6.88	22.16	1	15.00	6.88	22.16
National Bank of Canada	13	391.41	6.21	6.70	46	1,858.25	4.80	5.27
National Trust	1	20.71	3.39	3.39	1	20.71	6.86	7.13
Pacific Coast	–	–	–	–	1	3.96	3.41	3.41
Peoples Trust	12	40.18	7.87	18.57	16	55.27	11.73	21.91
Royal Trust	20	664.95	6.84	10.20	30	1,147.98	7.87	13.22
Security Home Mortgage	–	–	–	–	1	2.03	0.00	0.00
Shoppers Trust	64	469.56	3.28	5.90	75	583.53	10.58	21.90
Standard Trust	46	292.95	5.32	12.84	46	292.95	11.43	29.87
Surrey Metro	–	–	–	–	1	16.44	11.44	11.44
Toronto Dominion Bank	12	100.26	7.41	10.59	29	155.17	8.52	16.91
Trust General	1	5.90	6.17	14.90	1	5.90	9.67	14.99
Vancouver City Savings	6	144.04	8.59	8.41	12	359.03	21.86	28.68
Universe	437	5,121.59	6.49	10.53	680	8,865.89	10.07	18.57

* FirstLine Trust I (pools issued prior to March 1, 1990)
** FirstLine Trust II (pools issued since to March 1, 1990)

Source: Burns Fry Limited, February 1993

nancing rates while waiting for the decline to level off. An observable lag exists between the decline in 5-year mortgage rates and the upturn in UPP activity. The onset of declining mortgage rates occurred in August 1990, whereas the upswing in the weighted average UPP rates did not occur until March/April 1991. In addition to any correlation between UPP activity and mortgage rates, rising UPP rates can also be attributed to the natural aging of the mortgages.

UPP Versus Initial RAM and WAM

In an effort to extrapolate general trends, a preliminary analysis has been conducted on UPP rates relative to the Initial RAM and WAM attributes for a group of prepayable MBS issues. RAM is the

Figure 26.3—Historical UPP Experience

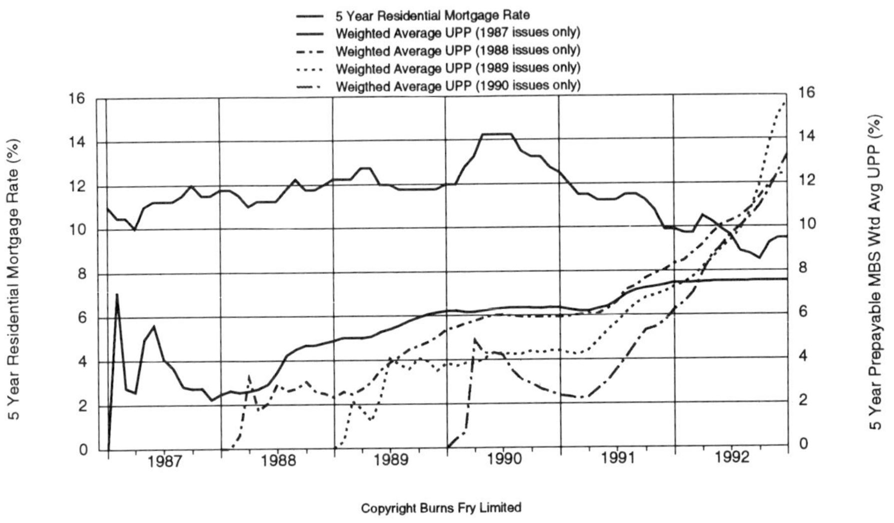

Figure 26.4—Mortgage Rates

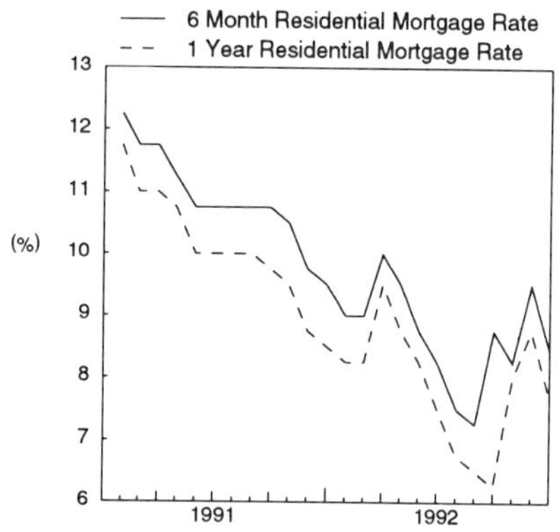

weighted average remaining amortization period of the loans underlying an MBS. The Initial RAM is the RAM at the time of issue. The Program stipulates that the difference between the longest and shortest amortization period of mortgages within a pool cannot exceed 30% of the latter. WAM is the weighted average mortgage rate of the mortgages within a pool. Program regulations command that each mortgage within a pool must bear a rate of interest at least 50 basis points higher than the coupon on the MBS. The difference between the highest and lowest mortgage interest rate within a prepayable pool cannot exceed 100 basis points. An MBS Initial WAM is the pool's WAM at the time of issue.

For the purposes of this analysis, a sample indicative of the majority of Canadian prepayable MBSs was studied. As pools should be at least one year old to provide meaningful statistical data, the sample includes prepayable pools issued prior to January 1, 1992 bearing an initial term of 5 years. Initial RAMs for this group range between 150 and 300 months. Initial WAMs span 9.64% to 13.61%.

Table 26.2 presents the weighted average UPP rates for specific Initial RAM ranges. Seasonality would suggest that pools exhibiting longer amortization periods (i.e., 300 months) should prepay slower relative to those with a shorter remaining amortization (ie: 240 months). One would therefore expect UPP rates to be higher on issues with shorter Initial RAMs; the assumption being that older mortgage loans will be repaid at an accelerated rate over new mortgages. Table 26.2 neither confirms nor refutes this hypothesis (possibly due to the relatively small sample size) and shows UPP to be highest in pools exhibiting Initial RAMs of 280 to 290 months. Tables 26.3 and 26.4 illustrate

Table 26.2—Weighted Average UPP Rates as at December 31, 1992

Initial Term 5 years; MBS grouped by Initial WAM, Initial RAM

Initial WAM (%)	*Size ($MM)*	*# of Pools*	*Initial RAM (mths)* < 270 mths	270–280	280–290	> 290 mths	*Wtd Avg UPP (%)*
> 13.00	152.78	16	–	–	15.26	14.37	14.67
12.50 – 13.00	204.34	23	15.65	23.76	20.78	11.86	16.62
12.00 – 12.50	474.40	31	30.49	16.13	17.36	16.03	16.68
11.50 – 12.00	1,524.68	102	9.28	11.97	14.65	14.70	14.45
11.00 – 11.50	1,548.68	98	9.20	8.28	14.61	10.73	10.69
< 11.00	471.87	48	8.41	8.98	10.59	7.73	8.16
Total:	$4,376.75	318	9.70%	9.90%	15.44%	12.98%	12.79%

Source: Burns Fry Limited, February 1993

that a finer segregation of the data may not yield the same observation.

Table 26.2 also includes weighted average UPP rates for pools grouped by Initial WAM. Since refinancing rates are considered by the marketplace to be one of the key factors influencing prepayments, one would expect pools with a high Initial WAM to prepay at a rate notably faster than pools with lower Initial WAMs, particularly in a declining mortgage rate environment. Table 26.2 reveals that UPP activity on a weighted basis is relatively consistent throughout the sample. Tables 26.3 and 26.4 provide a further breakdown of the data showing where high and low prepayment exists. As high UPP rates do not consistently correspond with high Initial WAMs, forecasting UPP on the basis of Initial WAM alone would be highly suspect. For the most part, Table 26.2 serves to emphasize that regardless of the Initial RAM and WAM, the variance in UPP activity on these pools is quite small.

Table 26.5 provides the weighted average UPP rates for pools with initial terms of greater than 5 years (mostly 10 years). Observe in Table 26.5 that the lowest weighted average UPP rate occurs in the group with the longest weighted average Initial RAM. Pools with shorter Initial RAMs appear, for the most part, to be exhibiting a higher weighted average UPP rate. This supports the theory that prepayment increases as mortgages age. Table 26.5 offers no correlation between UPP and Initial WAM.

The impact of transaction costs (including penalty interest) on a mortgagor's propensity to prepay has thus far been ignored. Some lending institutions offer mortgages that have few, if any, such costs. Securities created from these loans have become known as fully open prepayable MBS. Table 26.6 presents statistical data for 14 fully open issues meeting the criteria of our sample group. (Fully open pools have previously been excluded from the sample.) The salient difference between this group and the last group is the opportunity to refinance, at any time, without incurring penalty charges. As Table 26.6 illustrates, significantly higher UPP activity is occurring on these pools relative to the group analyzed in Table 26.2. The data in Table 26.6 further supports the hypothesis that high UPP rates will generally correspond with high Initial WAMs.

The above comparison strongly suggests that penalty interest charges represent a barrier to refinancing. UPP rates presented in Table 26.2 (for pools subject to penalty interest) are drastically lower than those presented in Table 26.6 (where penalty interest is not charged). While factors other than penalty interest should be considered when forecasting UPP, Table 26.6 illustrates how pronounced the impact of any one factor can be.

It should be noted that high UPP on fully open issues may not be due solely to the characteristics of the mortgages but instead may be affected, in part, by the characteristics of the borrower. Presumably mortgagors opting for specific prepayment privileges on their loans are more sophisticated. Borrowers opting for fully open loans are likely more interest rate conscious, and perhaps have a naturally higher propensity to prepay due to higher disposable incomes and the availability of excess cash.

Table 26.3—Weighted Average UPP Rates as at December 31, 1992

Initial Term 5 years; MBS grouped by Initial WAM, Initial RAM

Initial WAM (%)	*Initial RAM (mths)*	*Wtd Avg Init WAM (%)*	*Wtd Avg UPP (%)*	*Wtd Avg 6-mth UPP (%)*	*Total Size ($MM)*	*# of Pools*
> 13.00	> 290 mths	13.29	14.37	21.58	101.32	12
12.50 – 13.00	> 290 mths	12.84	11.86	19.68	95.27	12
12.00 – 12.50	> 290 mths	12.20	16.03	34.90	315.35	25
11.50 – 12.00	> 290 mths	11.71	14.70	39.18	1,152.25	79
11.00 – 11.50	> 290 mths	11.21	10.73	22.64	479.39	52
< 11.00	> 290 mths	10.66	7.73	12.49	361.24	37
> 13.00	280 – 290	13.15	15.26	27.65	51.47	4
12.50 – 13.00	280 – 290	12.85	20.78	38.03	85.04	8
12.00 – 12.50	280 – 290	12.18	17.36	34.06	135.05	3
11.50 – 12.00	280 – 290	11.75	14.65	38.38	248.69	15
11.00 – 11.50	280 – 290	11.29	14.61	21.37	342.15	19
< 11.00	280 – 290	10.35	10.59	15.71	47.21	5
>13.00	270 – 280	–	–	–	–	0
12.50 – 13.00	270 – 280	12.87	23.76	45.06	15.00	1
12.00 – 12.50	270 – 280	12.16	16.13	35.72	15.00	1
11.50 – 12.00	270 – 280	11.77	11.97	27.60	114.99	6
11.00 – 11.50	270 – 280	11.24	8.28	10.44	308.32	8
< 11.00	270 – 280	10.24	8.98	16.43	41.05	4
>13.00	< 270 mths	–	–	–	–	0
12.50 – 13.00	< 270 mths	12.60	15.65	23.50	9.03	2
12.00 – 12.50	< 270 mths	12.25	30.49	57.52	9.00	2
11.50 – 12.00	< 270 mths	11.69	9.28	5.96	8.75	2
11.00 – 11.50	< 270 mths	11.25	9.20	14.62	418.81	19
< 11.00	< 270 mths	10.71	8.41	14.66	22.37	2
	Total:	11.59%	12.79%	26.95%	$4,376.75	318

Source: Burns Fry Limited, February 1993

THE IMPACT OF UPP ON PRICING

Unscheduled principal payments have a direct impact on the realized yield of a prepayable MBS. The magnitude of this impact will increase the further the purchase price is from the issue's parity price. Parity price is the price at which any UPP rate projection will have no effect on the yield-to-maturity. The parity price for a 5-year MBS will typically be around $99.625. Investors purchasing MBSs at a discount assuming 0% UPP will benefit from the ensuing yield enhancement occasioned by an accelerating realization of the capital gains component of their effective yield. Conversely, for MBSs purchased at a premium assuming 0% prepayment the occurrence of UPP will have a diminishing effect on the yield. Adjustments made to reflect anticipated UPP activity have a mitigating effect on the yield impact.

Table 26.4—Weighted Average UPP Rates as at December 31, 1992

Initial Term 5 years; MBS grouped by Initial WAM,, Initial RAM

Initial WAM (%)	*Initial RAM (mths)*	*Wtd Avg Init WAM (%)*	*Wtd Avg UPP (%)*	*Wtd Avg 6-mth UPP (%)*	*Total Size ($MMM)*	*# of Pools*
> 13.00	> 290 mths	13.29	14.37	21.58	101.32	12
> 13.00	280 – 290	13.15	15.26	27.65	51.47	4
> 13.00	270 – 280	–	–	–	–	0
> 13.00	< 270 mths	–	–	–	–	0
12.50 – 13.00	> 290 mths	12.84	11.86	19.68	95.27	12
12.50 – 13.00	280 – 290	12.85	20.78	38.03	85.04	8
12.50 – 13.00	270 – 280	12.87	23.76	45.06	15.00	1
12.50 – 13.00	< 270 mths	12.60	15.65	23.50	9.03	2
12.00 – 12.50	> 290 mths	12.20	16.03	34.90	315.35	25
12.00 – 12.50	280 – 290	12.18	17.36	34.06	135.05	3
12.00 – 12.50	270 – 280	12.16	16.13	35.72	15.00	1
12.00 – 12.50	< 270 mths	12.25	30.49	57.52	9.00	2
11.50 – 12.00	> 290 mths	11.71	14.70	39.18	1152.25	79
11.50 – 12.00	280 – 290	11.75	14.65	38.38	248.69	15
11.50 – 12.00	270 – 280	11.77	11.97	27.60	114.99	6
11.50 – 12.00	< 270 mths	11.69	9.28	5.96	8.75	2
11.00 – 11.50	> 290 mths	11.21	10.73	22.64	479.39	52
11.00 – 11.50	280 – 290	11.29	14.61	21.37	342.15	19
11.00 – 11.50	270 – 280	11.24	8.28	10.44	308.32	8
11.00 – 11.50	< 270 mths	11.25	9.20	14.62	418.81	19
< 11.00	> 290 mths	10.66	7.73	12.49	361.24	37
< 11.00	280 – 290	10.35	10.59	15.71	47.21	5
< 11.00	270 – 280	10.24	8.98	16.43	41.05	4
< 11.00	< 270 mths	10.71	8.41	14.66	22.37	2
	Total:	11.59%	12.79%	26.95%	$4,376.75	318

Source: Burns Fry Limited, February 1993

Market Control of Risk

From both a practical and theoretical viewpoint, the impact of prepayments on price, yield and duration necessitates that UPP rate assumptions be incorporated into the investor's purchase price. A breakdown of historical payment data indicates that approximately 87% of UPP has resulted from whole loan liquidations (SMM) while the remaining 13% represents partial prepayments (CPR). While MBS valuations should reflect a similar breakdown, the marketplace typically incorporates only CPR assumptions, and has thus far, done so only on premium priced issues. The use of CPR was adopted following an initial misconception crediting partial prepayments as the main contribu-

Table 26.5—Weighted Average UPP Rates as at December 31, 1992

Initial Term 10+ years; MBS grouped by Initial WAM

Initial WAM (%)	*Total Size ($MM)*	*# of Pools*	*Wtd Avg Init WAM (%)*	*Wtd Avg UPP (%)*	*Wtd Avg 6-mth UPP (%)*	*Wtd Avg Init RAM (mths)*
12.00 – 12.50	10.00	2	12.18	8.76	13.48	289.56
12.50 – 13.00	43.89	8	12.73	11.76	23.70	287.79
> 13.00	25.00	2	13.06	10.32	16.85	286.58
11.00 – 11.50	136.99	17	11.32	13.80	38.40	285.23
11.50–12.00	123.13	24	11.69	16.20	41.40	261.50
< 11.00	25.93	3	10.74	10.88	27.30	252.87
Total:	$364.94	56	11.72%	13.78%	34.70%	275.44

Source: Burns Fry Limited, February 1993

tor of UPP. As the market matures, we can expect to see the inclusion of UPP rate assumptions (as a function of CPR + SMM) in the valuation of prepayable MBSs trading both above and below par.

Option Adjusted Spread Pricing

Option adjusted spread pricing was introduced to the Canadian MBS Market early in 1992. The term "option adjusted" was adopted given that the impact being incorporated into the price of the security results from the option extended to borrowers to make partial prepayments or full loan repayments. The adjustment represents the basis points spread over similar term Government of Canada bonds assumed to be required to protect investors from the impact of prepayments.

Table 26.6—NHA MBS Prepayable Fully Open as at December 31, 1992

Pool Number	*Size ($MM)*	*Issue Date*	*Maturity Date*	*Init RAM (mths)*	*Initial WAM (%)*	*UPP (%)*
96-402-714	$3.02	Jul-90	Jul-95	283.92	12.80	56.09
96-402-698	$5.00	Sep-90	Oct-95	288.60	12.66	77.00
96-402-763	$5.00	Aug-90	Jul-95	293.88	12.62	51.68
96-402-722	$4.01	Jul-90	Jul-95	293.16	12.08	79.12
96-402-912	$5.00	Oct-90	Oct-95	280.80	11.83	85.59
96-403-092	$5.00	Dec-90	Jan-96	287.64	11.47	53.21
96-403-324	$5.50	Feb-91	Jan-96	265.20	11.40	53.68
96-401-583	$2.14	Jun-89	May-94	297.60	11.17	41.66
96-402-656	$8.00	Jun-90	Apr-95	290.28	10.91	48.34
96-401-732	$4.51	Aug-89	Jul-94	293.16	10.68	34.77
96-402-441	$5.00	Apr-90	Apr-95	291.36	10.59	52.13
96-402-185	$9.00	Jan-90	Jan-95	292.32	10.54	41.79
96-401-989	$5.00	Oct-89	Oct-94	288.36	10.53	41.53
96-404-561	$2.01	Dec-91	Nov-96	281.88	9.99	39.27
Total:	$68.19			287.78	11.33%	53.90%

Source: Burns Fry Limited, February 1993

Two numerical examples are presented in Tables 26.7 and 26.8 to illustrate the impact of CPR on the price and yield of a prepayable MBS. (CPR is used to reflect current market practice.)

Prepayment assumptions incorporated into the valuation of MBSs priced at a premium serve to compensate buyers for the negative yield impact resulting from a constant rate of unscheduled principal payments. The immediate effect is a decrease in purchase price. The realized yield is contingent upon the actual UPP. A pool which performs at the expected UPP rate yields the base spread over the Government of Canada bond. In the event that UPP performs at a rate different from that anticipated at purchase, the degree of the positive or negative realized yield impact is a function of both the premium paid and the magnitude of the variance between the assumed and actual UPP rates. Generally speaking, if actual UPP activity falls below the anticipated rate, the realized yield will be greater than anticipated at the time of purchase. Conversely, if UPP activity is higher than expected, the realized yield will be lower than anticipated at the time of purchase. Keep in mind that while a higher than expected UPP rate has an adverse yield impact, the duration of the security will be shorter than expected. A positive yield curve at the time of purchase coupled with a shorter than expected duration creates an additional yield curve pick-up on the theoretical value of the security. While this is true, the point at which the yield advantage afforded by the shortened duration offsets the realized yield impact resulting from an underestimation of UPP has yet to be analyzed in detail.

Table 26.8 illustrates how prepayment assumptions effect the anticipated yield on pools priced below par. In contrast to issues priced at a premium, UPP on pools bought at a discount signifies the early recognition of capital gains and ensuing yield enhancement.

Prepayment assumptions incorporated into the valuation of MBSs priced at a discount have the effect of reducing the gap below par that a seller can expect to receive on a sale.

The preceding examples illustrate the price/yield relationship as it occurs under various CPR assumptions. Valuations which incorporate prepayment assumptions produce an effective yield equivalent to the market level assuming 0% prepayment. These examples emphasize that prepayment consideration and hence increased accuracy in MBS valuations work to the market's advantage in reducing the risks associated with market mispricing.

CURRENT/FUTURE OPPORTUNITIES

Inconsistent pricing assumptions with respect to the implicit value of expected future unscheduled principal payments presents an extraordinary investment opportunity. While in the U.S. all MBSs trade on formulated prepayment information, the infancy of the Canadian market affords the opportunity for investors to capitalize on the excessive spreads associated with a steep learning curve. The greater the understanding of the cause and effect of prepayments, the greater the opportunity to benefit from a developing market.

Two potentially profitable opportunities exist:

1. Yield Curve Advantage
2. Total Return Enhancement

Yield Curve Advantage

Canadian MBSs are priced based on the stated maturity of an issue, not its weighted average life (the weighted average principal repayment term) as done in the U.S.. The potential to benefit from this practice lies in the impact prepayment assumptions have on the expected average life of the MBS. To the extent that some level of prepayment will occur, the average term to principal repayment of a prepayable MBS will be shorter than expected at the time of purchase. In a positive yield curve environment investors benefit from a yield pick-up at the time of purchase since the purchase yield is based on the stated term and the theoretical value is based on a term shortened by prepayment. The yield pick-up is the difference between the point on the Canada yield curve at which an issue is priced and the yield which corresponds with the average life assuming prepayment greater than 0%.

The impact of prepayments on average life (and duration) is shown below. The data in the table assumes a 5-year prepayable MBS with the following characteristics: Coupon 10%, RAM 270 months, WAM 11.75% and an MBS Yield of 8.75%. The impact is as follows:

CPR (%)	*0%*	*5%*	*10%*	*15%*	*20%*
Average Life (yrs)	4.90	4.24	3.71	3.27	2.92
Modified Duration	3.91	3.44	3.06	2.74	2.47

Until such time as Canadian MBSs are priced based on their expected average life or duration, investors can benefit in a positive yield curve environment, at the time of purchase, from the price advantage resulting from valuations based on stated term.

Table 26.7—Prepayable MBS Priced at a Premium

Assume the following:

MBS Issue date: January 1, 1993
Maturity date: January 1, 1998
Coupon: 10.00 %
Initial RAM: 280 months
Initial WAM: 11.50 %

Government of Canada bond yield 8.00%
MBS base spread 80 basis points
Desired Yield (8.00+0.80) 8.80%
MBS Price assuming 0% prepayment $104.22

Incorporating prepayment assumptions of 0 to 15%:

CPR Assumption	*0%*	*5%*	*10%*	*15%*
at a price of $104.22:				
Effective BEY (%) assuming CPR	8.80	8.64	8.47	8.29
Negative yield impact of CPR (%)	0.00	–0.16	–0.33	–0.51
Option Adjusted (O/A) to provide a uniform effective yield of 8.80%				
At an effective yield of 8.80%:				
O/A Price ($) assuming CPR	104.22	103.66	103.20	102.82
O/A Yield (%) at O/A Price, 0% CPR	8.80	8.94	9.06	9.16
Adjustment Over Base Spread (%)	0.00	0.14	0.26	0.36
O/A MBS Spread (%)	0.80	0.94	1.06	1.16

Note: The above example illustrates that by accounting for the effects of CPR the option adjusted MBS price will produce a consistent effective yield of 8.80%.

Total Return Enhancement

Unscheduled principal payments present the opportunity for an enhanced realized yield over a 0% UPP experience. Monthly cash flows reinvested at rates comparable-to or better-than the purchase yield will result in a higher-than expected total return. Figure 26.5 illustrates the actual performance of a matured 5-year prepayable MBS against alternate fixed income investments. Note the variability in monthly cash flow resulting from unscheduled principal payments.

The analysis presented in Figure 26.5 assumes cash flow reinvestment in money market instruments. In this example, actual total return exceeded the expected total return because short term rates were relatively high over the life of the MBS. To the extent that monthly cash flows may be greater during periods offering low reinvestment rates, investors risk that the return on the reinvested cash flow will not be sufficient to equal or exceed the yield that would have been realized had prepayments not occurred.

Penalty interest passed through to MBS investors provides additional income. Regardless of the reinvestment rate environment, this additional income impacts positively on the realized return.

For a simplified explanation of the potential for heightened total returns, given a favourable reinvestment rate environment, consider cash flows received on a prepayable MBS versus those received on a non-prepayable MBS over the same period. Recall that in the absence of prepayment privileges, monthly payments on the non-prepayable security are confined to scheduled principal and coupon interest only. In general, monthly cash flows will be smaller in comparison to those received on a prepayable pool since the potential for

Table 26.8—Prepayable MBS Priced at a Discount

Assume the following:

MBS	Issue date:	January 1, 1993
	Maturity date:	January 1, 1998
	Coupon:	7.60 %
	Initial RAM:	280 months
	Initial WAM:	9.25 %

Government of Canada bond yield 8.00%
MBS base spread 80 basis points
Desired Yield (8.00+0.80) 8.80%
MBS Price assuming 0% prepayment $95.15

Incorporating prepayment assumptions of 0% to 15%:

CPR Assumption	*0%*	*5%*	*10%*	*15%*
at a price of $95.15:				
Effective BEY (%) assuming CPR	8.80	8.97	9.14	9.32
Yield impact of CPR (%)	0.00	+0.17	+0.34	+0.52
Option Adjusted (O/A) to provide a uniform effective yield of 8.80%				
At an Effective Yield of 8.80 %:				
O/A Price ($) Assuming CPR	95.15	95.69	96.14	96.50
O/A Yield (%) at O/A Price, 0% CPR	8.80	8.65	8.53	8.44
Adjustment Over Base Spread (%)	0.00	–0.15	–0.27	–0.36
O/A MBS Spread (%)	0.80	0.65	0.53	0.44

Note: The above example illustrates that by accounting for the effects of CPR the option adjusted MBS price will produce a consistent effective yield of 8.80%.

additional cash flow due to prepayment and penalty interest does not exist. While cash flow reinvestment occurs at the same rates, the yield impact from reinvestment will not be as pronounced. Under favourable reinvestment conditions, the actual return on investment in the case of the nonprepayable MBS will be better than expected, but will not be as good as in the case of the prepayable security.

Figure 26.5 illustrates the actual monthly principal and interest payments (per $1 MM) received on prepayable MBS pool # 96400015 over its 5-year term. Since reinvestment rates during this period were high relative to the coupon on the security, the short term market provided for the realization of a higher than expected total return. The opposite would have been true had reinvestment rates been consistently low relative to the coupon rate. Cash flow reinvestment at rates lower than the monthly coupon rate has a diminishing yield impact. While the potential for a higher than expected total return in an inverted yield curve environment is evidenced in Figure 26.5, the marketplace has yet to explore the return potential resulting from prepayment activity in a positive yield curve environment.

CONCLUSION

With increasing monthly new issue volumes and a market size in excess of $14 billion, NHA Mortgage-Backed Securities have established a permanent position within the Canadian fixed income capital markets. Increased trading and investor participation provide a compelling argument for both traders and investors to give careful consid-

Figure 26.5—Pool # 96-400-015 Performance Evaluation at Maturity

POOL # 96-400-015 PERFORMANCE EVALUATION AT MATURITY

POOL CHARACTERISTICS

Issuer	CIBC
Issue Date	Jan. 1/87
Maturity Date	Aug. 1/91
Pool Size	$ 20.33 MM
Coupon	9.250 %
WAM Initial	10.755 %
WAM Final	10.760 %
RAM Initial	293.20 mths
RAM Final	230.76 mths

FINAL PRINCIPAL PAYMENTS

		Actual Per $1MM	
Months to Maturity	Projected	Scheduled[1]	Unscheduled
5	-	$ 705	$ 1,779
4	-	709	1,711
3	-	702	9,760
2	-	705	2,077
1	10 %	52,459	9,984
at Maturity	90 %	439,969	

[1] Includes amortizing and maturing principal

Actual Monthly Cash Flow Per $1MM

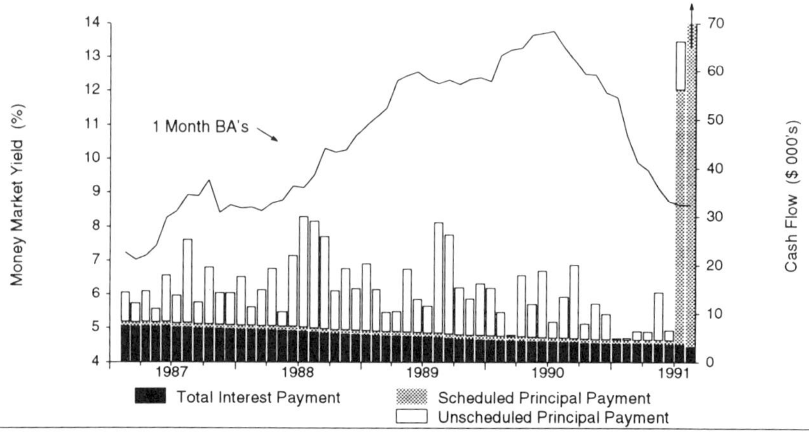

UNSCHEDULED PRINCIPAL PAYMENT & PENALTY INTEREST PAYMENT RATES

UPP at Maturity	13.51 %	
PIP at Maturity	0.01 bp	
Issuer Weighted Average UPP	12.42 %	(6 pools)
All 1987 Issues Weighted Average UPP	6.98 %	(45 pools)

TOTAL RETURN ANALYSIS

	Price [1]	Yield [1]	Compound Yield at Maturity[2]	Compound Yield versus Initial Yield
Assumed Cash Flow[1]	$ 100.00	9.15 %	9.62 %	+ 0.47 %
Actual Cash Flow	$ 100.00	9.15 %	10.08 %	+ 0.93 %
			Yield Impact	+ 0.46 %

[1] At Issue Date, calculated using the C3I Mortgage-Backed Analyzer assuming 0% UPP
[2] Cash Flow reinvested and compounded using 1 month BA's

eration to the risks and rewards associated with this unique investment. The uncertainty surrounding prepayment expectations communicates the potential for inaccurate MBS valuations. Prepayment assumptions are incorporated into the value of an MBS as a function of the dealer's expectations based on past and expected future market performance. Assumptions are rarely related to individual pool performance but speak to the aggregate MBS UPP experience. Prepayment assumptions are critical as they affect pricing and therefore impact directly on an investor's realized return. Clearly there is a need for a uniform means of forecasting prepayment activity and the impact the resulting cash flow uncertainty will have on the realized yield. Towards this end the marketplace has begun to incorporate a rudimentary level of prepayment analysis into the price of prepayable MBSs trading at a premium. Deficient by way of standardized forecasting mechanisms, the Canadian MBS market offers investors a unique arbitrage opportunity whereby those who perform some basic analysis will be able to profit from the market's current valuation imperfections.

Chapter 27

The Australian Mortgage-Backed Securities Market: The Role of Mortgage Insurance in Reducing Credit Risk

by Brian W. Richardson,
Manager of the Securitization and Banking Division
MGICA Ltd.

BACKGROUND

The securitization market in Australia has operated to a limited degree and on varied bases for a number of years but it first began gathering momentum around the middle of 1986.

The establishment in the mid-80s of corporations such as National Mortgage Market Corporation Limited (NMMC), sponsored by the Government of Victoria and First Australian Mortgage Acceptance Corporation Ltd. (FANMAC), sponsored by the Government of New South Wales, provided the impetus for its strong growth.

From a development perspective, the timing of the entry of these and other privately sponsored companies such as MGICA Securities Ltd. ("MSL," a wholly owned subsidiary of the mortgage insurer MGICA Ltd., itself a wholly owned subsidiary of AMP Society, Australia's largest life insurer) and Security Pacific Securities Australia Limited ("SECPAC," a wholly owned subsidiary of Security Pacific Australia Limited), which were formed closely upon the birth of their government sponsored counterparts, could not have been much better.

The Australian property market had been stable for some time following major downward corrections in 1981 and 1984 and confidence was running high. This positive environment, fuelled by the availability of significant levels of funding at competitive interest rates, provided a nucleus for establishment of the market.

The major financial institutions were initially reluctant to involve themselves in securitization other than as issuers or potential issuers of mortgage-backed securities. Finance brokers, backed by issuers who were anxious to establish outlets for their funds, found the ideal vehicle for development of their own mortgage (origination) banking businesses. Broking backgrounds gave many originators the opportunity to enter the business with an existing client base and the issuers with a market hungry for funds.

Following the stock market crash of October 1987, property prices in Australia soared and by the end of 1988 they were virtually double what they were in 1985/86. As the economy heated, interest rates rose significantly to the extent that bank bill rates exceeded 20 percent. This gave further momentum to mortgage securitization as bank borrowers sought relief—albeit to rates around 18 percent—from these crippling costs.

In October 1990 the bubble burst.

There were a number of reasons for the collapse but, significantly there was,

1. a drying up of funds as a result of the "flight to quality" of the major investors, and
2. the influences of an emerging recession which has subsequently gripped Australia and much of the world.

Overnight the fledgling industry was left to ponder its future and for around twelve months the market remained virtually stagnant. However, during that period there were a number of significant happenings. On the positive side,

- the ratings agencies reviewed their ratings criteria,
- existing issuers,
  - reviewed their systems and procedures, and
  - developed new and improved existing products
- new issuers such as Prudential Bache, Macquarie Bank Limited and the Queensland-based Graham and Company Mortgages Limited, developed their programs.

On the other hand,

- the recession took a firm hold with devastating effect on business. As failures occurred, rental arrears increased and premises were vacated. This had the snowballing effect of causing loan defaults as landlords' cash reserves were eroded.
- the property market, particularly in the commercial and industrial sectors, failed. In the worst affected areas value drops of 50–60 percent were evidenced.
- a number of high profile entrepreneurs and development companies failed adding to the erosion of confidence in the property market.

Side effects of the change included:

1. entry into the Australian market of the American monoline insurers, bringing with them the strength of their balance sheets for ratings purposes as well as access to standby facilities,
2. a revision of the use of mortgage insurance by those issuers not attaching to a monoline to lessen the burdening cost of standby facilities, and
3. a move to expand the market from a predominantly 3/5 year, fixed interest, commercial based program to one which also includes a 25 year principal and interest, variable rate residential based program.

MORTGAGE INSURANCE AND SECURITIZATION

Because senior/junior issues have been rare in Australia, issuers have been very much dependent upon the mortgage insurers to enhance their pools. Except for a limited number of issues by FANMAC on behalf of the New South Wales Government in the area of special housing, the lack of availability of sufficient junior stock and the capital to fund it has cast pool mortgage insurance into its present significant role.

Two mortgage insurers, MGICA Ltd. ("MGICA") and the Australian Government owned and guaranteed Housing Loans Insurance Company ("HLIC") have been deeply involved with the securitization industry—virtually from the outset—and they have remained in the forefront in providing credit enhancements for mortgage securitization.

In the early 1980s, MGICA, through its previous Managing Director Peter Bradford, had expressed a desire to see a secondary mortgage market develop in Australia. To this end the company sponsored visiting speakers from overseas to tour the country and speak to interested groups. Although these visits were generally well received, HLIC, because of its sovereign, triple-A rating was chosen as the pool insurer for both the NMMC and FANMAC programs and was seen by many as the only mortgage insurer capable of supporting the industry. To overcome this perception, MSL was formed and its first issue, rated double-A by Australian Ratings (which has since been acquired by Standard and Poors) and covered by an MGICA pool policy, was issued in March 1987. MGICA has gone to become one of the major participants in the market.

To reinforce its stated position of not being tied to one issuer, on 31 December 1990, MGICA sold its entire shareholding in MSL to AMP Society. Subsequent to the sale MSL changed its name to Australian Mortgage Securities Ltd ("AMS").

The mortgage insurers have provided the industry with a springboard towards success, albeit at some cost to themselves and their reinsurers. Their enhancements have included both pool and primary mortgage insurance, cash flow insurance—which guarantees, in the event of default by the borrower, timely payment of interest of the trust—and early repayment damages insurance.

Cash flows to some trusts are also supported by way of Mortgage Manager Obligation Guarantee ("MMOG"). Traditionally, mortgage insurers have refrained from providing cover against fraud by the trustee, the trust manager, the mortgage originator/manager or any of their agents or employees. When required, protection against these forms of risk has been provided by the general insurance industry in the form of professional indemnity cover. The purpose of the MMOG is not to support the fraud/dishonesty cover but to provide protection to the trust against the inability of a mortgage manager to meet its interest obligations to the trust as a result of the failure of a borrower to pay loan interest on the due date.

Traditionally, pool mortgage insurance policies in Australia do not have provisions for a deductible; i.e., the pool insurer has no recourse to either the issuer or the mortgage originator and is therefore responsible, in terms of the policy, for all losses which are not covered by primary mortgage insurance. As a consequence of the insurers' loss experiences, which have been exacerbated by the lack of a deductible, they also have undertaken a reassessment of their position in the period since October 1990 and a number of changes have occurred.

It was mentioned earlier that a majority of issues to date in Australia have been in respect of three- to five-year fixed interest loans. With some exceptions (notably some FANMAC and Prudential Bache program loans) they have been bullet mortgages with no provision for early repayment of principal—except at a premium. The break funding cost ("early repayment damages") has been set by the issuers at an amount sufficient to cover any shortfall between the reinvestment interest on prepaid loan funds and the coupon rate on the bond to the end of its life.

The mortgage insurers originally provided an early repayment damages cover, but with no mechanism available in the insurance system to manage the risk, and as a consequence of:

1. a record number of distress sales brought about by the recession,
2. low property prices, and
3. a large fall in interest rates,

losses mounted to a level where it was no longer prudent for them to continue to provide that cover. Issuers have therefore been forced to look to other forms of enhancement, notably guaranteed investment contracts ("GICs"), for their protection.

Other changes made by the mortgage insurers include:

1. a reduction in the minimum loan size from $5M to $1.5/2M.
2. a requirement that primary mortgage insurance be obtained on all commercial loans sufficient to reduce exposure to 50 percent. (Some insurers require this only if the loan to value ratio exceeds 65 percent.) Residential investment properties geared in excess of 65 percent and owner occupied residential properties geared in excess of 70 percent require 100 percent primary cover.
3. a tightening up as to of the types of properties which are acceptable as security. A non-exclusive list of properties not acceptable would include:
   - abattoirs, amusement parks/centers, brothels, caravan parks, car yards, hostels, funeral parlors, health clubs/gyms, holiday villages, dog kennels, kindergartens, licensed clubs, hotels, inns, liquor stores, taverns or wine bars, marine parks/marinas, motels, night clubs, nurseries, picture theaters, properties modified to meet the specific needs of the occupier and which would have limited appeal in the event of a forced sale, rural properties, schools, service stations, ski lodges, sporting facilities, and veterinarian hospitals/surgeries.

   Significant restrictions have also been made in relation to owner occupied business properties.
4. a tightening up of the loan purposes; e.g., some insurers will now no longer insure loans required for,
   - carry on funds for a business, or
   - future property investment where no purchase contract has been entered into.
5. a tightening up of requirements in relation to borrowers; e.g.,
   - all borrowers and guarantors are to be personally interviewed by the mortgage manager who is not to rely solely on submissions from finance brokers, and
   - loans to mortgage managers, their associated companies, family, and staff will not be insured.
6. development of policies precluding from pool mortgage insurance, loans secured by properties contaminated or exposed to the possibility of environmental contamination.
7. the assumption of a high profile in the area of risk assessment by undertaking, in certain circumstances, internal inspections of properties offered as security in the company of the borrower. Mortgage insurers have traditionally maintained a low profile in underwriting risks, preferring to restrict contact to the insured (lender). However, because of the levels of risk associated with securitization covers, a higher exposure in the market is considered appropriate.

The mortgage insurers have provided new initiatives which have reduced the reliance of issuers on standby funds which, very often, are not available, or are not available at levels sufficient to ensure a continuity of business. Cash flow insurance is one obvious example of support which relieves dependence upon standby facilities to meet bond coupon payments. A new offering has been cover for five years, including cash flow insurance, in relation to a five-year bond supported by three-year loans. This cover reduces the repayment of principal on maturity risk as, in the normal course, a majority of loans will repay or be rolled over at the end of three years and the remainder, being in default of the terms of the mortgage, will be cleared by way of recovery action against the borrower in the remaining two years of the life of the bond.

THE NEW GENERATION

A new generation of mortgage securitization will be launched in Australia early in 1992. The industry is vastly different to what it was in October 1990. Some issuers have gone and others have taken their place. One thing is for sure though, those who have remained and those who are now starting have a much greater understanding of the market and its problems than those who pioneered the industry a few years ago.

The first open market, pure residential, triple-A, program will issue and for the first time a large financial institution, the Credit Union movement, will throw its considerable weight behind the industry as a mortgage originator/manager.

The Macquarie Bank, long respected as a commercial lender (amongst other things), will assume the role of issuer in its own right of a commercial mortgage program after gaining experience in securitization as a mortgage originator.

A significant amount of time and energy has been expended by all those involved in the industry and those supporting it to ensure strong growth in the future through the issue of quality paper which meets the high ratings requirements of the investment market.

Chapter 28

Mortgage Securitisation in Developed Housing Finance Systems

by Douglas B. Diamond, Jr.
and
Michael J. Lea,
Cardiff Consulting Services, Cardiff California

INTRODUCTION

Securitisation is a financing technique that potentially expands the funds available for housing through tapping new investors and reallocating the risks of mortgage lending. By repackaging the cash flows from a pool of loans in such a manner that an investor has recourse only to the cash flows or accompanying credit enhancement, a lender can finance a portfolio without expanding the balance sheet. Thus, securitisation differs from more traditional forms of wholesale funding in the form of on-balance sheet obligations of the lender (either collateralized as in the case of mortgage bonds or uncollateralized in the form of unsecured debt). Securitisation can provide an alternative funding source to traditional methods of financing housing (e.g., deposits, mortgage bonds), and enable lending institutions to better manage their balance sheets and risk.

Securitisation was introduced by the Government National Mortgage Association (Ginnie Mae) in the U.S. in 1970. A major feature of securitisation in the U.S. is credit enhancement. Ginnie Mae, an agency of the U.S. government, essentially provides pool insurance for FHA (Federal Housing Administration) insured mortgages allowing originators to pool loans into securities for sale in the capital markets. The other major institutions in the U.S. secondary mortgage market, Fannie Mae (Federal National Mortgage Association) and Freddie Mac (Federal Home Loan Mortgage Corporation) add pooling and security issuance to the credit enhancement function. These institutions are private shareholder-owned entities with explicit borrowing privileges from the U.S. Treasury. They purchase loans from lenders and (often simultaneously) issue securities collateralized by these loans.

The activities of these entities have greatly improved access to the financial markets for lenders in the U.S. Their guarantees obviate the need for investors to look at the collateral or credit worthiness of the originator to assess credit risk. Credit enhancement permits small, locally based and thinly capitalized institutions to provide a substantial portion of housing credit in the country. The need for credit enhancement arose in large part from the prohibition on nationwide banking in a geographically large and economically diverse country.

Outside the United States, mortgage securitisation has been successfully incorporated into the housing finance systems of Australia and the United Kingdom. More recently, it has been introduced in France, Spain and Sweden. However, questions have been raised over its viability in the U.K. and it has yet to be adopted in other European countries.[1] It can be argued that securitisation has not been needed in the past in many developed countries. Well developed mortgage bond markets have existed in continental Europe for over 100 years, providing lenders with access to wholesale (i.e., financial market) funds. Mortgage banks have overcome the credit risk concerns of investors by issuing bonds which are credit enhanced by the capital of the bank and extensive cross-collateralization. In addition, their activities are regulated closely by governmental authorities which generally restrict access to mortgage bond financing.

1 For a recent review of U.K. mortgage securitisation, see Pryke and Whitehead (1991).

Larger depositories have direct access to the financial markets through unsecured debt issues and smaller depositories often have access through wholesale banks (e.g., the Landesbanken in Germany). Thus, unlike the U.S., lenders have generally not seen the need for off-balance sheet financing or financial markets access.

Interest in securitisation in Europe derives from adoption of the BIS (Bank of International Settlements) capital adequacy standards. These standards will increase capital requirements for some depositories and mortgage banks, reducing their funding advantage and possibly motivating them to securitize their loans. Perhaps more importantly, securitisation allows small competitors to enter new markets at relatively low cost, because it does not necessitate the high fixed costs of a retail branch system or large capital investment to credit enhance security issuance. Thus, in an environment in which subsidies to particular lenders are being reduced and barriers to entry to mortgage markets are being removed as part of the creation of the single market in financial services, there is a growing realization of the advantages of securitisation.

Although interest in securitisation is increasing, there are still numerous obstacles to its successful introduction. In particular, the legal, tax and regulatory systems of individual countries often have to be modified to accommodate new contractual and institutional forms.[2] Equally important are the economic aspects of each country's housing finance system. To be successful, securitisation must be competitive with other forms of financing mortgage assets. In turn, its competitiveness is affected by the existence of subsidies to other means of fund raising and ways in which risks are allocated under existing forms of mortgage finance.

The purpose of this chapter is to review how funds are raised and risks are allocated in financing owner-occupied housing in four European Community countries (Denmark, France, Germany and the United Kingdom). This review will allow us to highlight the economic conditions that are conducive or adverse to the introduction of securitisation. Based on this analysis, we will comment on the prospects for introduction and/or expansion of securitisation in these countries.

The analysis in this chapter is based on a study of the efficiency of housing finance arrangements commissioned by the Federal National Mortgage Association in 1991.[3] In this chapter, we focus on securitisation and expand our analysis of this aspect of housing finance.

FUNDING HOUSING

There are a number of financing circuits that have been used for providing housing finance in developed countries.[4] Retail funding can be available through universal banks or specialized depositories (e.g., savings banks or building societies).[5] These institutions mobilize funds from savers in the form of deposits. More recently, depository institutions have accessed the capital markets directly through issuance of unsecured debt. Non-depository intermediaries typically rely almost completely on the financial markets to mobilize funds. Mortgage banks have existed in Europe for over 200 years, funding home loans almost exclusively through issuance of mortgage bonds. Securitisation is a relatively new phenomenon in European mortgage finance. It involves the creation of new special purpose entities which finance pools of loans through collateralized security issuance.

Table 28.1 summarizes the housing finance arrangements in the subject countries as of 1991. These countries offer a broad array of institutional arrangements and government policies. Mortgage loan funding ranges from heavy dependence on retail depository institutions (France, U.K.) to extensive capital markets funding. Government support ranges from subsidies for contract savings plans to government backing or ownership of lending institutions. Dominant contracts range from 30-year prepayable fixed-rate mortgages (Denmark) to reviewable-rate mortgages (RRM) with rates administered by the lender (Germany, U.K.). Various forms of adjustable-rate mortgages (ARM) are also available (France, Germany).

Table 28.2 contains a more detailed summary of funding arrangements by country. The focus of this summary is on the market structure, regulation and subsidization of intermediaries as well as the degree of integration of the funding markets into the overall capital markets. We focus on these aspects of the market in order to assess the eco-

2 For a recent review of these issues see articles in Stone, Zissu and Lederman (1991).

3 The study has been published in its entirety in the *Journal of Housing Research* (1992).

4 For a survey see Boleat (1985).

5 Contractual savings schemes also provide funds for housing. In Germany, such funds are mobilized by specialized depositories known as Bausparkassen. In France, such schemes are offered by commercial and savings banks.

Table 28.1—Mortgage Market Comparisons

Country	Mortgage Originations	Funding Instruments (in order of importance)	Market Structure	Role of Government	Dominant Contract	Average Mortgage Yield (1990)	Average Gross Spread[1]
Denmark	Mort. Credit Instit. (80%) Depositories (12%) Other (8%)	Mortgage Bonds Deposits	Oligopoly (Mort. Credit Institutions) Depositories mainly do "top-up" and short-term loans	Control over MCI entry, mortgage contract terms, insurer/pension investments	20–30-year fixed rate	11.33%	120 basis points (10 yr. govt.)
France	Depositories (85%) Specialized Lenders (10%) Other (5%)	Contract Savings Deposits Collateralized Debt	Competitive; dominated by depositories with advantaged access to funds	Subsidized contract savings; deposit rate regulation; state ownership of banks	15-year fixed rate[2]	11.09%	175 bp (10 yr. govt.)
Germany	Depositories (55%) Mortgage Banks (22%) Bausparkassen (13%) Other (10%)	Deposits Mortgage Bonds Contract Savings Uncollateralized Debt	Segmented funding by regulation; significant affiliation across segments	Control over terms and institutional use of mortgage bonds and contract savings; limits on insurer investments; subsidized contract savings; state-owned savings banks	25–30-year first[3] a. fixed rate from mortgage bank b. reviewable rate from depository	a. 9.66% b. 9.58%	a. 125 bp (10 yr. govt.) b. 128 bp (1 yr. govt.)
United Kingdom	Depositories (94%) Centralized Lenders (6%)	Deposits Uncollateralized Debt Mortgage-Backed Securities	Competitive with free entry	Prudential regulation	25-year reviewable rate	15.12%	117 bp (3 mo. govt.)

1 Spread to comparable duration government bond yield, bond equivalent basis including annualized fees
2 Typically combined with contract savings loan through depository
3 Typically combined with contract savings loan through affiliated Bausparkassen

Table 28.2—Funding Market by Country

Country	*Depositories*	*Specialized Lenders*	*Market Shares*
Denmark	Lack of long-term mortgage lending	Investment limits on insurers and pensions as well as capital requirements favor mortgage bonds	Government directed; growing role for depositories through acquisitions/affiliations
	No money market mutual funds; deposit rates below market rates	Well developed mortgage bond markets	
	Banks cannot issue mortgage bonds	MCIs exceed BIS requirements but may have capital needs in 1995 when 100% risk wt. on commercial mortgages becomes effective	
	Depositories exceed BIS requirements		
France	Rate regulation (current accounts/ST deposits)	Tight limits on holdings of one issuer	Depositories have used funding advantage to dominate the market
	State ownership of banks	Favorable capital requirements for senior-subordinated securities	
	Only banks offer contract savings		
	Banks can refinance through CRH		
	Unknown capital adequacy of banks		
Germany	No money market mutual funds; deposit rates below market rates	Only specialized mortgage banks can issue Pfandbriefe	Market determined; banks have purchased specialized instit. and operate on an integrated basis
	State ownership of savings banks	Only Bausparkassen can issue contract savings	
	Banks can issue unsecured debt, but not mortgage bonds	Investment limits on insurers favor mortgage bonds	
	Depositories exceed BIS requirements	MCIs exceed BIS requirements but may have capital needs in 1995 when 100% risk wt. on commercial mortgages becomes effective	
United Kingdom	Open and intense competition for funds	Centralized lenders primary issuers of MBS	Market determined
	Depositories issue unsecured debt	EC capital requirements potentially adverse to MBS	
	Building societies face limits on unsecured debt		
	Building Societies are mutual organizations with limited capital raising capabilities		

nomic feasibility of and thus market prospects for mortgage securitisation.

Denmark

The Danish system relies on a very well-developed market in mortgage bonds for the vast majority of mortgage funding. Mortgage bonds are obligations of the mortgage credit institutions. They are cross-collateralized with large mixed pools of residential and commercial mortgages and, until recently, the joint and several liability of all borrowers in the issue. This market is well-integrated with the overall capital markets. Historically the bond market has been segmented by maturity with government predominant in the short portion of the market, and mortgage bonds predominant in longer maturities. In fact, mortgage bonds are about 60 percent of the total bond market and an even greater share of longer maturities.

Historically, there has been some channeling of funds from pension plans and insurance companies towards domestic government and mortgage bonds. These entities hold 45 percent of mortgage bonds. Such restrictions could imply a segmentation of the mortgage bond market. However, the relative price of government and mortgage bonds has recently become less sensitive to fluctuations in their supply, which suggests greater integration of markets. The fact that 40 percent of mortgage bonds are now held by foreigners and individuals suggests that any remaining degree of segmentation is small.

Although the mortgage bond market is well developed, it has not seen the introduction of mortgage-backed securities. This is partially because of the lack of regulatory approval. However, there has not been a perceived market demand because the mortgage credit institutions (MCI) which dominate the market have been well capitalized and implicitly backed by the government. In addition, under Danish regulation, all interest rate risk is passed through to investors.

The number of mortgage credit institutions themselves had been limited to three until recently, implying a significant potential for distortions in pricing and other forms of competition due to market power. Mortgage rates were determined by adding a fixed spread over the mortgage bond yield—a spread that was constant throughout the 1980s. During this time, the MCIs appear to have competed almost exclusively on a non-price basis. One form of this competition, the loosening of underwriting guidelines, contributed to extraordinary losses at the turn of the decade.

Depository institutions appear to have been discouraged by the government from actively competing in longer-term mortgage lending, and have confined themselves to provision of top-up loans.[6] This restriction has denied consumers a potentially attractive contract form (the ARM or RRM). Depository institutions have also been somewhat shielded from competition. Although there is no rate regulation, savings rates are considerably less than prevailing market rates and there are no money market mutual funds to provide competition. Thus, in an open market it is likely that savings deposit rates, and thus top-up loan rates, would become more market sensitive over time. However, the existence of below-market funding sources may retard the development of securitisation if the banks become more involved in long-term mortgage lending.

Also, securitisation has not been attractive because intermediary default risks are carefully regulated and are generally minimal. In addition, the government pursues tight regulatory oversight and an active mergers policy, as well as probably a too-big-to-fail policy, implicitly backing the major intermediaries.[7] Danish capital adequacy rules are generally more strict than those of the E.C. or BIS. In particular, capital standards are based on liabilities rather than assets. Currently, the major Danish mortgage credit institutions and banks exceed 8 percent of risk-weighted assets requirements set to go into force at the end of 1992.

The demand for securitisation may arise with increased competition. In 1990, the Danish government deregulated the mortgage bond market, allowing the possibility of new entry. In addition, the existing MCIs may face some capital adequacy issues in the future. Denmark was given until 1995 to implement a full 100 percent risk weighting on commercial mortgages. As the mortgage credit institutions fund both residential and commercial loans with on-balance sheet mortgage bonds, implementation of this standard may motivate adoption of off-balance funding techniques for commercial mortgages.

6 Top-up loans are typically unsecured personal loans for the amount over 80 percent LTV. One form of discouragement is the fact that capital requirements favor mortgage bonds over mortgage whole loans with a capital risk weight of 20 percent versus 50 percent for whole loans.

7 For example, the loss experience of KD, the largest mortgage credit institution, induced the Parliament to pass legislation authorizing the issuance of a special form of preferred stock enabling KD to remain within capital adequacy guidelines.

France

In France, the great majority of housing finance to individuals is provided by depository institutions. These institutions draw on regular time and sight deposits and wholesale funding (unsecured debt), as well as the funds generated by the contract savings schemes.

France has been experiencing the money market fund revolution since 1985, and this has eroded the base of low-cost sight deposits enjoyed by the banks, and also the special liquid tax-favored Livret accounts. There has also been a sharp growth in reliance on market-rate CDs rather than ordinary term deposits. However, the bedrock of bank lending for housing has remained the contract-savings schemes {the Epargne-Logement (or E-L) plans}, which pooled funds sufficient to back 55 percent of the housing loans outstanding from banks in 1990.

The E-L schemes are not a closed loop, like the Bauspar system, simply converting savings at below-market interest rates into below-market rate loans. They were designed to raise below-market funds for other types of housing loans as well as for the loans under the schemes. To do so, they benefit from two subsidies, both a bonus payment from the government and tax-exemption of interest paid. Only depository institutions offer E-L plans.

The presence of the E-L programs, together with restrictions on interest on current accounts and short-term deposits, gives a significant advantage to depositories in funding mortgages. As a consequence, banks funded mortgages at rates less than or equal to government bond rates during periods between 1987 and 1991, as part of a strategy to increase market share after removal of credit controls in 1987. Thus, the vast majority of French mortgage loans were originated at rates lower than true market rates and could not be securitized without a loss. However, current trends indicate a decline in the E-L treasuries of banks (funds available for loans other than E-L loans), pushing the banks toward greater wholesale funding and reliance on CDs and other more market-related accounts.

French banks benefit from another form of subsidy. The French government also provides an implicit guarantee of bank deposits, in addition to a formal, but modest, deposit insurance fund.[8] This is important not only because of the dominance of the banks in mortgage lending, but also because the banks in France take on more interest rate risk than do those in any of the other countries. If this were not the case, there would be more potential for a market in mortgage-backed securities, given the popularity of FRMs.

France has taken a step towards efficiency in funding markets by creating the legal framework for a mortgage-backed securities market, but the market is not yet a competitive source of funds, primarily because of the indirect subsidies to the depository institutions.[9] Although the MBS market has yet to develop, there does exist a collateralized mortgage bond option, something like the German Pfandbriefe, through the CRH (Caisse de Refinancement Hypothecaire). However, activity in this market has been depressed by aggressive pricing by depository institutions. In addition, there are active (but not very liquid) long-term funding markets for fixed-rate unsecured debt, but not for adjustable-rate debt.

Another important facet of the French market is a regulation restricting institutional investors from holding more than 5 percent of their portfolio in any one issuer of debt, other than the state itself. At the time of its imposition, this restriction seems to have added 30 basis points to the spread of issuers of mortgage bonds over state debt, thus making this form of funding (but not MBSs, since they have special purpose issuers) less competitive with deposits.

Germany

Germany has an institutionally segmented system on the funding side. However, strong competition exists in mortgage lending as the commercial and savings banks appear to have overcome the funding segmentation through ownership of the specialized institutional funding sources (e.g., mortgage banks and Bausparkassen which originate contract savings loans). Although no one funding source, type of loan, or lender dominates the market the major competition is between institutional families headed by a commercial or savings bank.

Funding markets are probably not fully integrated. Banks and savings banks have been becoming more market sensitive in competing for term

8 In France, not only does the "too-big-to-fail" principle apply, but also the government itself currently owns a majority of the banking sector. Although they purport to be profit maximizers, the fact that the top managers come from government agencies suggests a high degree of influence of the government on the decision making of the banks.

9 The first French MBS was marketed in December 1991.

deposits, but money market mutual funds have not been permitted to compete for sight deposits. Thus average deposit rates are still well below government bond yields. The bond market is segmented with only mortgage banks issuing collateralized bonds. Commercial and savings banks issue unsecured debt, primarily to fund corporate lending (until recently corporations could not issue uncollateralized debt). As in Denmark, a high proportion of these bonds are purchased by domestic institutions with restricted choice sets, and spreads over government debt may be reduced because of this.

Germany is like Denmark in its reliance on regulatory processes to minimize intermediary default risk in funding markets. The mortgage banks are permitted to take on only minimal credit risk, and no interest rate risk. All financial institutions are subject to close scrutiny by government regulators. There is some explicit involvement by state and local governments through ownership of savings banks as well as affiliated Bausparkassen and mortgage banks. There is also clear confidence that the central government would act to prevent failure of major banks, and there is a system of private deposit insurance protecting smaller depositors.[10] The situation with respect to intermediary risk in Germany is exemplified by the fact that mortgage-backed bonds trade at only five to ten basis points above government bonds, and even unsecured bank debt trades at only ten to fifteen points above government debt.

About an eighth of German mortgage lending originates through the contract-savings system. The German system is completely self-contained and relatively isolated from the rest of the financial market; the flow of new contracts, though, does respond somewhat to changes in market rates, as well as the level of tax or other subsidies to the scheme.[11] The Bauspar system may survive despite a sharply reduced subsidy because it serves an important signaling function by establishing a track record of steady payments before the home purchase, and provides cross-selling opportunities for other banking services.

German regulators have yet to endorse the concept of mortgage-backed securities. In part this may reflect a lack of demand for this funding option on the part of well capitalized German banks. However, as in Denmark, German lenders have until 1995 to implement higher (100 percent risk weight) capital requirements against commercial mortgages. These loans are primarily funded by mortgage banks using on-balance sheet mortgage bonds. Implementation of these requirements could spur interest in off-balance sheet funding techniques.

United Kingdom

The U.K. has perhaps the most fully integrated and developed funding markets of the countries in this study. Funding for housing finance comes from a variety of sources, including mortgage-backed securities which were introduced in 1987. Despite the highly competitive nature of the U.K. market and the lack of explicit subsidies for particular lenders, the building societies dominate the mortgage market. Their market share has fluctuated significantly during the last decade. With the elimination of credit controls from the commercial banks in 1981, their share of the mortgage market rose from 8 percent to 32 percent in less than a two-year time period. Relatively high margins in the mid-1980s encouraged the entry of the centralized lenders which funded the vast majority of their originations through MBS issuance. The centralized lenders' market share rose to almost 15 percent of the market in 1987 and 1988 before falling to 5 percent in 1991.

In large part, the recent domination of the building societies can be traced to the dynamics of the deposit market and the nature of the mortgage instrument used. After the stock market crash of 1987, the building societies were able to attract new savings at relatively low rates of interest. In addition, because building society deposits display some interest-rate insensitivity the building societies' funding advantage further increased when[12] market interest rates began moving sharply up in mid-1988 as a result of tightened monetary policy. Reviewable-rate mortgages are priced off the societies' average retail cost of funds, mortgage rates lagged market rates during the rising rate period, decreasing the mortgage-to-LIBOR yield spread. Thus, the building societies were able to recapture their market share, particularly from the centralized lenders which rely on LIBOR-indexed MBS as

10 The European Community has moved to require public notification of depositor insurance coverage, something previously prohibited in Germany. This has hastened the spread of such coverage.

11 Segmentation of the contract savings system can have beneficial effects in terms of the stability of the system. The fact that below market rate funds are not generally fungible within depository institutions reduces the potential for distortionary lending rates (as exists in France). Segmentation, along with limits on alternative funding sources, reduces the chance that loan commitments are granted in excess of available savings.

12 For a recent examination of building society mortgage pricing, see Diamond and Lea (1992).

their main funding source. The continued consumer preference for dealing with the societies has preserved a degree of segmentation in the retail deposit market, but a steady erosion in this segmentation is evident in many ways.[13]

The wholesale funding markets in the U.K. are well developed. There is an active market in long-term, unsecured, floating-rate notes, usually indexed to LIBOR, as well as the usual commercial paper market for the larger societies. Mortgage-backed securities have been almost exclusively used by the centralized lenders. Recent regulatory uncertainty has affected the competitiveness of the centralized lenders. In particular, the possibility of a risk-weight of 100 percent on MBS when the underlying collateral has a weight of 50 percent increased MBS spreads (approximately 50 percent of MBS had been purchased by financial institutions) in 1991. Also, concern about financial health of the insurers in the U.K. has led to increases in spreads on both FRNs and MBS.

In the United Kingdom all financial institutions are scrutinized by the Bank of England and other regulatory bodies. Building societies that show any possibility of failure are merged rapidly into another stronger society. As a result, building societies have traditionally enjoyed a very favorable perception in the minds of consumers, particularly relative to the commercial banks which have fallen in consumer esteem recently due to publicity about loan losses. The weakest link in the U.K. system of risk allocation appears to be the private insurance companies, who provide coverage not only for the top portion of most loans, but also have been active in the pool insurance market. The significant losses borne by these entities recently has brought on an increase in spreads of unsecured depository debt and MBS over the government rates (reflecting a concern that insurers could fail). The impact of losses on market pricing is a notable difference between the entirely private system of the U.K. and a government-guaranteed system, as in the U.S.

CREDIT RISK ALLOCATION

Mortgage credit risk allocation is summarized in Table 28.3. Credit risk in the mortgage market can be allocated and priced in a number of ways. It can be priced through the mortgage rate, covered by third party insurers (and also the government) or minimized through relatively low maximum LTV ratios. There is some specialization wherein certain institutions lend based only on property characteristics and others take on higher risk by underwriting the borrower. Understanding the sources and allocation of credit risk is key in assessing the viability of securitized finance.

Denmark

In Denmark, borrower credit risk was traditionally handled by regulatory segmentation. Specifically, before 1983, the LTV ratios on loans on existing homes made by mortgage credit institutions were restricted to levels at which borrower credit risk did not arise.[14] However, in the last decade, LTV ratios were liberalized (although not deregulated), and significant additional credit risk was borne by the MCIs. Removal of rationing was accompanied by an increase in lending through formal channels and a rise in house prices. These trends came to a halt in 1986 with a shift towards a restrictive monetary policy and a cut-back on tax incentives for owner-occupied housing. As a result, house prices fell and record default losses have been recorded by the MCIs and banks.

A specific fee is incorporated in all mortgage rates by the MCI to account for credit risk. Unfortunately this fee was not raised at the time of liberalization of LTVs, but has now been adjusted to reflect the recent serious loss experience, and to vary some with the LTV ratio.

Danish mortgage bonds trade at option adjusted spreads of 70 to 80 basis points over comparable maturity government bond yields. Although a portion of this spread may represent a liquidity premium, it is likely that there is some credit risk premium in these spreads. The actual credit risk in these bonds does appear to be low as the mortgage credit institutions are well capitalized. In addition, risks are limited by several factors: (1) strict matching requirements, (2) the allocation of prepayment risk to investors, (3) the cross-collateralization of mortgage bonds, and (4) the joint and several liability of borrowers.

The bulk of the credit risk on housing loans in Denmark (i.e., for loans with LTVs over 80 percent) has been borne by the commercial banks through their top-up lending. The rates and terms on such loans have been freely negotiated and usually reflect the financial characteristics of the borrower. The average spread for a bank top-up loan relative to the 2 year Treasury yield between

13 The societies funded over half of their net new originations on the wholesale markets in recent years. Also, building society deposit rates have become more responsive to capital market rates.

14 As in other cases where regulation seriously restricts market transactions, the market adapted by developing an active resale market in owner-financed second mortgages.

Table 28.3—Credit Risk Allocation by Country

Country	*Allocation*	*Underwriting*	*Pricing*	*Other Aspects*
Denmark	Government determined: ≤ 80% – MCI	MCI – property underwriting only – quarterly pay mortgages	Some risk-based pricing by LTV (started in 1991)	Mortgage bonds cross-collateralized Mortgage bonds secured by joint & several liability of borrowers
	> 80% – bank "top-up" unsecured	Banks – borrower underwriting	Borrower specific pricing (avg. spread of top-up to 2-yr. govt. bond – 305 bp)	
	No mortgage insurance			
France	Lenders	Weak collateral access by borrowers Reliance on borrower underwriting	Some risk-based pricing by LTV	High costs to foreclose (strong borrower protection)
	Extensive mort. payment ins. – no mort. collateral ins.		Borrower specific pricing (700 bp spread to 10-yr. govt. bond for 80% to 90% portion)	Poor appraisal system
Germany	Packaged: ≤ 80% – lenders (secured) > 80% – banks (unsecured) top-up loans	LTV > 80% only available for repeat buyers	Some risk-based pricing by LTV	Extensive housing allowance program covers defaults
	Lack of mortgage insurance	Regulatory constraints on Pfandbriefe LTV (55%) and mortgage bank & Bausparkassen LTV (80%)	Borrower specific pricing (avg. spread of top-up to 5 yr. govt. bond 276 bp)	Mortgage bonds cross-collateralized
United Kingdom	< 75% – lenders	Loans up to 75% LTV available without insurance	Market pricing (one price up to 80%)	Unemployment ins. covers mort. payments for 1 yr.
	≥ 75% – insurers	Loans up to 100% LTV available with insurance	Ins. premium 4.5% of amount over 75% (565 bp over 3 mo. govt. for 80% to 90% portion) Higher prices for 95%+ in 1991	Extensive use of pool ins. for MBS (recent increase in cost)

1982 and 1991 was approximately 300 basis points. This spread widened to over 400 basis points in 1988 and has remained in excess of 300 basis points since that time, reflecting increased default risk in the Danish market.

Two other considerations affecting the treatment of credit risk in Denmark are (1) the tradition of quarterly payments on fixed-rate first mortgages, and (2) the provision of unemployment compensation at levels of 80 to 90 percent of full-time wages. The quarterly payment system reflects the fact that bondholders prefer quarterly or semi-annual payments, but introduces a significantly higher exposure in cases of default. The liberal unemployment system provides an element of insurance somewhat comparable to the mortgage insurance utilized in the U.S., in light of the inability of lenders to diversify across geographic markets.

In a small country like Denmark, the inability to diversify credit risk suggests that domestically provided mortgage and pool insurance may not be viable forms of credit enhancement. Credit enhancement may come through the emergence of European-wide mortgage insurance and/or reinsurance of domestic pool insurers. An alternative being discussed in Denmark is to limit LTVs on collateral for mortgage securities to 60 percent with the banks becoming more active in 60 percent to 80 percent LTV lending.

France

There are two distinctive aspects of the market in credit risk in France. First, there are very high costs to foreclosure under French legal procedures. Strong borrower protection translates into a 2 to 4 year process to foreclose on a borrower. Because of this length of time, even a 25 to 30 percent equity cushion may be insufficient to protect lenders against loss. Second, mortgage insurance against a shortfall upon foreclosure is not available commercially.

The response of French lenders has been to price loans according to LTV ratio and borrower characteristics. Although time series data on French mortgage rates by LTV are unavailable, results of lender surveys suggest a substantial premium for high ratio loans, as high as 700 basis point spreads to the 10-year government bond yield for the 80 percent to 90 percent increment in financing a 90 percent LTV loan. This high spread also reflects the trend towards higher default rates in recent years—which in turn reflects increasing indebtedness of French consumers. Concern over indebtedness led to the passage of the Neiretz Law in 1990 under which French borrowers can seek debt relief.

Most underwriting is based on borrower characteristics as the French appraisal system is regarded as weak and unreliable. As a consequence, loans over 80 percent LTVs are more difficult to obtain than in other countries. Lenders in France also commonly require insurance against disruptions in repayment ability, i.e., unemployment or disability. Although the French system has adapted to an inability to secure easy access to the collateral, it is clearly a second best situation and has reduced credit availability. Also, these imperfections suggest that third party credit enhancement will be difficult to obtain in France.[15] As a result, French asset-backed securities have been senior-subordinated in structure, with the lender retaining default risk. French regulatory authorities have required financial institutions to hold capital against only the subordinated security and not the entire issue. As this appears not to be in the spirit of the BIS standards, it is unclear how long it will continue.

Germany

In Germany, the situation is very similar to that of Denmark in that there are regulatory constraints on LTV ratios for certain types of loans and lenders, and a significant portion of the credit risk is borne by commercial and savings banks through top-up loans underwritten based on borrower characteristics. The average spread on unsecured loans relative to the 5-year government bond yield was 276 basis points between 1982 and 1991, but rates vary considerably across borrowers. This relatively low spread may reflect the low default rate in Germany, which in turn is a function of relative stability in prices and employment as well as conservative underwriting. Also, the system of housing allowances covers mortgage payments for low- and moderate-income homeowners (as well as renters) in cases of temporary financial difficulty, which reduces the incidence of default.

First-time buyers find it difficult to obtain top-up loans and tend to be excluded from the market until they accumulate a 25 percent downpayment. High downpayment requirements for first-time

15 An alternative to the traditional mortgage, the "caution" has enjoyed some success in recent years. The caution is basically a guaranteed personal loan which avoids the high costs of registering a mortgage. To date, it has been offered primarily to high-quality borrowers and cannot be considered a true form of mortgage insurance. For more details, see Lancereau and Robert in Stone et. al. (1991).

buyers may be responsible for the relatively low homeownership rate and late age of first purchase (36). The gradation of rates and loans by LTV is an efficient pricing mechanism, but the lack of credit for higher LTV loans suggests market imperfection. In part, the conservative underwriting may reflect the lack of a market for private mortgage insurance against shortfalls at foreclosure, despite the relatively diverse housing market.

Both mortgage bonds and unsecured bank bonds trade at very tight spreads to comparable duration government debt. Mortgage bonds are obligations of the mortgage banks but investors enjoy preferential access to collateral pools backed by residential and commercial mortgages. In addition, mortgage bond collateral is regarded as very safe because of the maximum 55 percent LTV.

United Kingdom

In the U.K., third party insurance companies bear most of the credit risk and high LTV loans are available, even to first-time buyers. A few building societies bear the credit risk themselves and charge for it through a sliding scale of interest rates.

There are no government-sponsored insurance programs. As on the Continent, though, there is strong desire to avoid foreclosure, and thus a greater use of insurance against disability or other loss of repayment ability. In fact, the unemployment compensation program of the government provides significant assistance specifically for mortgage repayment, and probably subsidizes the cost of private mortgage insurance. All building societies bear some residual credit risk below the portion shifted to the private mortgage insurers.

The pricing of mortgage insurance during the late 1980s and early 1990s did not appear to be risk-based. A flat fee of 4.5 percent of the amount above 75 percent was charged at loan origination. This fee translates to a spread of 565 basis points over the 3-month government bond yield for the 80 percent to 90 percent loan increment. This spread is somewhat higher than the other countries (except France), perhaps reflecting greater use of high LTV loans and higher house price volatility. Mortgage insurance fees were raised in 1991 and higher fees have been instituted for loans over 90 percent LTV.

All MBSs are credit enhanced, either through pool insurance or senior-subordination. Pool insurance rates increased sharply in 1991, reflecting the downgrading of the major insurance companies. Although a portion of the insurance company problems are due to their exposure in the U.K. housing market, their loss experience also reflects commercial property and other lines of business. Thus, the competitiveness of lenders using pool insured funding sources is dependent on events outside the housing market.

INTEREST RATE RISK ALLOCATION

Since market interest rates are uncertain in the future, some party in a long-term investment or lending transaction may be bearing interest rate risk. The risk may be the classic sort for a financial intermediary not matching the interest sensitivities of liabilities and assets. Or, it can be the risk borne by a borrower as to future cash flows. Finally, it may be the risk borne by an investor or depositor with respect to future cash flows.[16] The risk can be managed by purchasing options or it can be simply borne. The different ways interest rate risk is allocated is summarized in Table 28.4.

One of the key advantages of securitisation is the ability of lenders to manage interest rate risk by passing it on to investors in the financial market (mortgage banks can be required to do this also). The viability of securitisation in turn depends on a demand to reduce this risk. Such demand may be lacking if significant interest rate risk taking by financial institutions does not impose appropriate capital requirements, or is subsidized or contractually precluded.

Denmark

The Danish system of housing finance limits consumer choice with respect to interest rate risk. For the most part, it is allocated to the investors in mortgage bonds. There is no market provision of first-mortgage ARMs. We cannot determine whether this is due to regulatory constraints or lack of demand. In the future, there does not appear to be any reason why additional options cannot be developed if desired.

16 The literature does not commonly treat the choice of portfolio maturities as involving risk, but clearly it does involve uncertainty of nominal outcomes. This uncertainty is the risk determined here, and it arises in any portfolio with a horizon longer than the maturities of its assets. This perspective permits us to treat classic interest rate risk and prepayment risk within the same context, since they reflect the same uncertainty as to the course of interest rates, and thus cash flows. Our focus is on the allocation of interest rate risk, not its magnitude (e.g., as determined by the underlying interest rate volatility in the country).

Table 28.4—Interest Rate Risk Allocation by Country

Country	*Borrower*	*Investor*	*Role of Government*
Denmark	Lack of long-term ARMs; no prepayment penalties on FRMs	MCI must match fund by loan; bonds are callable Mortgage bonds cross-collateralized with commercial and residential loans	Regulators have not yet allowed derivative mortgage securities
France	Wide range of contacts Limited prepayment penalty	Significant interest rate risk for depositories Significant prepayment risk for specialized lenders Use of MBSs deterred by depositories funding advantage	State encourages contract savings despite instability
Germany	Lack of prepayment option on ARMs Lack of FRMs	Mortgage banks must match fund portfolio Some maturity mismatch by banks Mortgage bonds cross-collateralized with commercial and residential loans	Regulators have not yet allowed derivative mortgage securities or MBSs
United Kingdom	Full range of contracts; little FRM borrowing	Full range of alternatives to manage risk	

Mortgage bonds are prepayable at the option of the borrower without penalty. However, the prepayment premium is not very large, especially considering that there is no due-on-sale or significant costs of prepayment. This may be due to the segmented nature of the investor market for mortgage bonds, or the presence of an original issue discount in most mortgage bonds.[17]

France

In France, a degree of interest rate risk is borne by borrowers. FRMs can be prepaid but are subject to prepayment penalties of the lesser of 3 percent or 6 months interest (although enforcement varies and the penalty is frequently negotiable). There is also a wide range of choices of ARMs. Most ARMs have some form of interest rate cap, thus sharing risk between borrower and lender.

The majority of French mortgages are still FRMs, funded by depositories. These institutions bear considerable interest rate risk because of their reliance on contract savings plans and short-term deposits. Because of this distortion, as well other distortions in mortgage pricing in France, prepayment risk is currently not priced through any active market such as one in MBSs.[18]

Germany

In Germany, the borrower must bear some interest rate risk. There is a wide array of consumer choice on the period of fixity on what are essentially all adjustable-rate mortgages (with up to ten year adjustment periods), but there are no caps, and the borrower rarely has a prepayment option. Until recently, lenders also bore little or no interest rate risk, as depositories primarily originated reviewable rate loans and mortgage banks originated 5 to 10 year ARMs backed by 5 to 10 year mortgage bonds. Recently, though there has been a trend towards savings banks offering loans with rates fixed for 5 to 10 years backed primarily by the usual shorter term deposit mix.

There appears to be a regulatory bias against callable debt, but this could change due to pressure from the European Community or competition from outside lenders. The market demand for shifting this risk to investors is uncertain, given the relative stability of interest rates.

United Kingdom

In the United Kingdom, long dominated by reviewable-rate lending providing little interest rate risk, there is a small amount of fixed-rate lending returning (rates are typically fixed for up to 5 years).[19] As the advantages to depositories of obtaining retail funding fade, there will be increasing reliance on wholesale funding, which can be used to manage the risks of fixed-rate lending, with or without prepayment options. A sophisticated MBS market has developed incorporating derivative securities allowing investors to more effectively manage interest rate risk. However, investor appetite for long-term fixed-rate mortgages with prepayment has yet to develop, as the relatively poor market reception for the first MBS backed by FRMs indicated.

LIQUIDITY RISK

The ability to supply funds to the housing market depends on the ability of intermediaries to attract sufficient funds to meet the demand. To do so efficiently means there must be no barriers to market pricing of funds and ease in refinancing existing mortgage portfolios and reselling wholesale funding instruments. The refinancing risks for depositories and wholesale-funded lenders are summarized in Table 28.5.

Denmark

In Denmark, investors in mortgage bonds enjoy a very liquid market with low bid-ask spreads. The high degree of liquidity reflects the standardized design as well as the financial characteristics and implicit government support of the MCI. There does not appear to be a well-developed unsecured debt market for depositories, limiting their refinancing abilities if they become more involved in mortgage lending. Also, there is no whole loan sales or trading evident in Denmark.

---

17 Bonds must be issued at yields at least 7/8 of the average redemption yield of all open series quoted on the Copenhagen Stock Exchange during the 20 business days prior to June 15 and December 15 each year. Higher coupon bonds have experienced significantly higher prepayment rates and have a larger call option yield component.

18 There are markets in options involving future movements in interest rates. Apparently, the cost of such options is more than the price for prepayment risk implicit in market mortgage rates.

19 For example, in the last several years, a centralized lender, UCB, has originated a significant volume of loans with rates fixed for five years, with a yield maintenance penalty. Recently, building societies have been offering loans with an initial fixed-rate period.

Table 28.5—Liquidity Risk Allocation by Country

Country	*Depositories*	*Wholesale-Funded Institutions*	*Role of Government*
Denmark	Banks can't issue mortgage bonds	Very active mortgage bond market	Implicit support of MCIs
	No whole loan trading	Bid-ask spreads < 10 bp	
France	Banks can issue collateralized debt through CRH; little trading volume	Use of CRH has declined significantly	Implicit guarantee on bank and CFF bond issuance
	No whole loan trading	Bid-ask spread CRH, CFF – 25 to 30 bp	Limits on holdings on non-govt. debt
	Lack of mortgage performance info		State owned/backing of banks
Germany	No whole loan trading	Very active mortgage bond market	State-owned wholesale banks issue debt for savings bank families
	Banks can issue uncollateralized debt	Bid-Ask spreads on mortgage bonds < 10 bp	
United Kingdom	Growing trading of whole loans	Active FRN & MBS markets	Adverse capital requirements for MBSs
	All lenders access wholesale market	Bid-Ask spreads on MBSs 20 to 30 bp	
		Lack of standardization of MBSs	

France

In France, neither the whole loan market, nor the mortgage-related debt markets are very liquid. The major exception is for a range of mortgages that enjoy special access to a refinancing market, through bond issuance by the CRH or for issuance by Credit Foncier. Average bid-ask spreads on this debt appear higher than mortgage-related debt in other countries and this market does not experience large volume of resale and trading.

Transfer of mortgage portfolios is subject to some degree of uncertainty. Lenders must notify borrowers, which is costly, and the ability of new owners to perfect security interests has yet to be tested in the courts.[20] Lack of portfolio performance information also retards liquidity.

Germany

In Germany, investors in mortgage bonds enjoy a very liquid market. Again, there is a long history of the mortgage banks issuing standardized securities which, when combined with low risk and tight supervision, enhances liquidity. Larger commercial and savings banks actively issue unsecured debt. Smaller savings banks and credit cooperatives have access to the capital markets through wholesale funding banks (Landesbanken for the savings banks and the DG Bank for the credit cooperatives). However, no market exists in whole loans. Borrowers must be notified of such transfers, suggesting a relatively high cost to transferring servicing.

United Kingdom

In the U.K., major lenders have ready access to wholesale funding markets on an unsecured and, to a growing degree, secured basis. Mortgage loan portfolios are relatively easily transferable. There are no legal impediments to transfer assets or servicing and an increasingly active market is developing.

The MBS market is still in somewhat of a developmental stage. A very liquid resale market has yet to develop, partially because of the lack of standardization and uncertainty regarding the regulatory treatment of MBSs (with respect to financial institution capital requirements and the use of MBSs as liquid assets for building society portfolios, which is a potentially strong source of demand). Recent developments in the U.K. demonstrate the difficulty of establishing MBSs as a consistent funding sources for housing. MBSs have been increasingly customized for investors, both in terms of credit enhancement (given the costs and downgrades of the insurers) and cash flow management (e.g., CMOs). While customization clearly enhances the pricing of the initial issue, it does tend to reduce the ease of future sale, ultimately increasing the liquidity premium for all issues.

PROSPECTS FOR SECURITISATION

Numerous documents have extolled the benefits of securitisation over the years. In most countries in Europe, lawyers, accountants, regulators and bankers are hard at work establishing the guidelines and framework for securitisation. However, the near-term prospects for the introduction of securitisation are anything but certain and, as the centralized lenders in the U.K. have found, the success of lenders using this funding source after introduction is not guaranteed.

The conditions favorable to the successful introduction of securitisation are numerous. In this chapter we have focused on the economics of mortgage funding and risk allocation as major factors related to the demand for and eventual introduction of mortgage securitisation. There are several observations that can be drawn from this review:

1. Funding markets must be open and competitive. Utilization of a capital markets-based funding source will be impeded by the existence of low cost and/or subsidized deposits. This has clearly been the case in France. Although banks in Denmark and Germany do not have access to subsidized or rate-regulated deposits, the lack of competitive alternatives (e.g., money market mutual funds) has allowed them to retain a low cost deposit base. However, there are signs that this advantage is eroding throughout all of Europe as consumers become more rate sensitive and governments cut back on subsidies.
2. Risk taking cannot be subsidized. Intermediaries that are allowed to take on extensive interest rate or credit risk without appropriate capital will undermine the need for and thus competitiveness of securitisation, as may be the case in France.

20 For more information, see Moodys (1990).

3. Contract sets must be complete. If certain types of contracts are not allowed, the demand for securitisation may be reduced. This is the case in Germany wherein prepayment is precluded on mortgage loans with rates fixed for more than 6 months. Allowing this feature might spur introduction of securitisation.
4. Performance information is essential in gaining investor acceptance. The costs of credit enhancement and investor yield requirements are both clearly influenced by the quantity and quality of information. In turn, good quality performance information along with standardized design will reduce liquidity premiums.
5. If MBSs in Europe are ever to achieve the degree of acceptance they enjoy in the U.S., there must be a greater standardization of design and credit enhancement. Creation of separately capitalized institutions with government support has been suggested as a vehicle to speed adoption of MBSs, but is unlikely given the highly developed nature of Western European mortgage markets. However, a consortium of insurance companies offering standardized loan and pool insurance, diversified across Europe, could serve a similar function and reduce the likelihood of a repeat of the U.K. MBS experience.

A level playing field will encourage the use of securitisation in countries where it is not in use currently, both in Europe and elsewhere. This is especially true in the short term as financial institutions seek to modify their balance sheets to conform to stricter capital standards. However, it should be recognized that the dominance of mortgage securitisation in housing finance as in the U.S. cannot be expected to necessarily occur elsewhere. In the absence of government-related credit enhancement, other means of wholesale and retail fund raising may remain superior to securitisation. In any case, securitisation will probably gain momentum slowly and only with some clear encouragement from statutory and regulatory actions by government.

REFERENCES

Boleat, M., *National Housing Finance Systems: A Comparative Study*, Building Societies Association, London, 1985.

Diamond, D. and Lea, M., "Housing Finance in Developed Countries: An International Comparison of Efficiency," *Journal of Housing Research,* 3,1, 1992.

Moodys Structured Finance, "French Real Estate Loans: Creation, Enforcement and Assignment of Security Interests," June, 1990.

Pryke, M. and Whitehead, C., *Mortgage-Backed Securitisation in the U.K.: A Wholesale Change in Housing Finance?* University of Cambridge, Department of Land Economy Monograph 22, 1991.

Stone, C., Zissu, A., and Lederman, J., *Asset Securitisation: Theory and Practice in Europe,* Euromoney Books, London, 1991.

Chapter 29

The Hazards of Default

by Robert Van Order,
Chief Economist
Freddie Mac

Were it possible to foretell at origination whether a particular loan would default, then there would be no such originations and no defaults. The most we can hope to understand is the probability that a loan will default (or the fraction of a pool of loans that is expected to default) over time and some of the factors that affect this probability.

The probability that a loan will default this year (or the fraction of loans that start the year and default sometime during the year) is often referred to as the conditional default rate because the rate is conditional on the loan being "alive" at the beginning of the year. When applied to other fields, this concept is known as the hazard rate.

HAZARD MODELS

Hazard rates and the models that explain them are used in research in such diverse areas as life insurance, quality control, and unemployment. For instance, a hazard might be a piece of equipment breaking down or a worker becoming unemployed, and the hazard rate would be the probability of these events occurring in a particular period given that the equipment or employee was working at the beginning of the period.

A hazard model might simply estimate the hazard rate, that is, the probability of job loss in the first year, the second year, and so on. It might go further and analyze factors that affect the hazard rate in each year, such as the age or experience of the worker.

By estimating hazard functions statistically, rather than "eyeballing" the data, measures of the separate effects of various factors on the hazard being analyzed can be obtained. In addition, once hazard functions are estimated, they can be used for "what-if" analysis and ultimately for pricing and cost control.

APPLICATION TO MORTGAGE DEFAULT

For purposes of managing and pricing credit risk, it is not enough to know the general characteristics of mortgage risk, for example, that high loan-to-value ratio (LTV) loans default more than low LTV loans. (See "Those Were the Days," *SMM*, Spring 1990.) It is also important to quantify the elements of mortgage risk, so that you can answer questions like, "How much greater is the chance of default for a 95 percent LTV loan than it is for a 75 percent LTV loan?" Other dimensions of mortgage credit risk can also stand closer scrutiny to answer such questions as, "Holding LTV constant, how much more likely is someone to default if the payment burden is high?"

Answering these questions requires statistical modeling. We estimated a hazard model using data for about 725,000 single-family, fixed-rate, conventional loans originated from 1976 through 1983 and purchased by Freddie Mac under its cash program. The data base includes default experience on these loans through the middle of 1990. (See "Estimating the Hazard Function" on p.)

Figure 29.1 depicts hazard rates estimated for loans with different original LTVs. The curve at the bottom of the figure shows average default rates (averaged across all origination years) by loan age for loans with original LTVs of 80 percent or less. The second curve from the bottom shows the effect of increasing LTVs to the 81 to 90 percent category; the third curve is for LTVs from 91 to 94 percent; the top curve is for 95 percent LTVs. Each curve resembles the typical time profile of conditional default rates, which start out low, increase in the early years after origination, hit a peak, and then fall. Higher LTVs shift the entire profile up.

Figure 29.1—Estimated Default Rates by Loan-to-Value Ratio

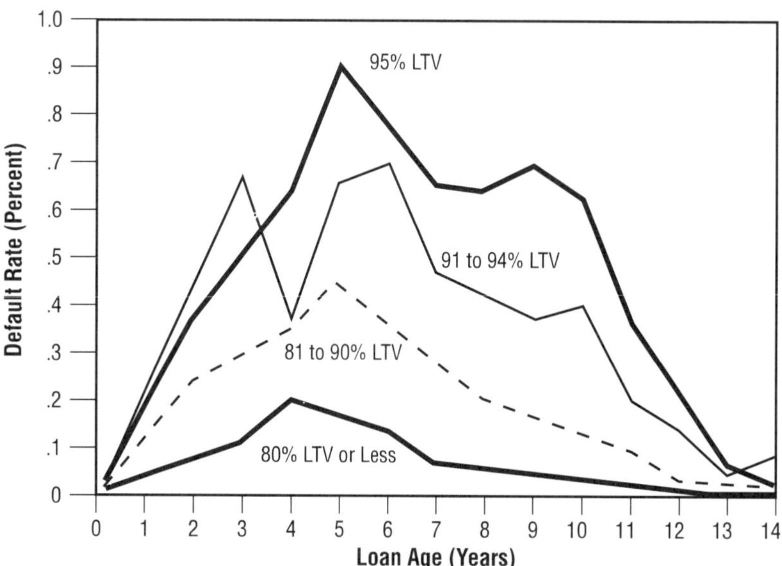

Note: Estimated using a proportional hazard model and Freddie Mac data on single-family, fixed-rate loans.

Figure 29.2—Estimated Default Rates by Origination Year

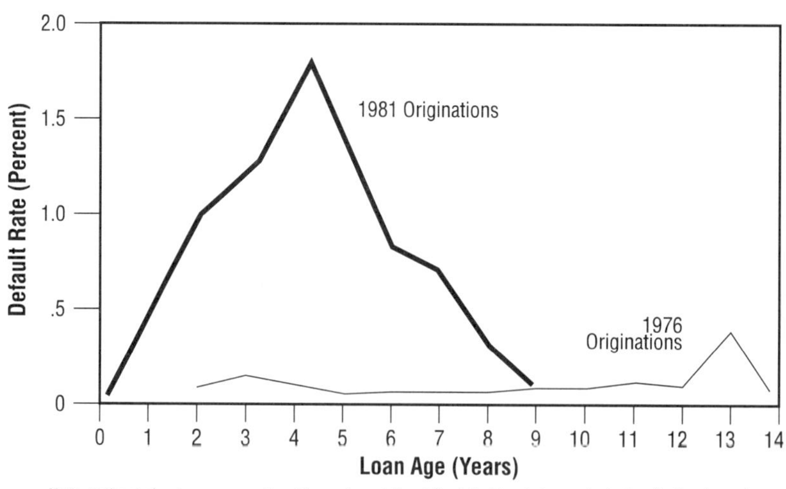

Note: Estimated using a proportional hazard model and Freddie Mac data on single-family, fixed-rate loans.

Table 29.1—Simulations of Cumulative Default Probability within 10 Years of Origination (Percent)

	Loan-to-Value Ratio			
Origination Year	*80% or Less*	*81 to 90%*	*91 to 94%*	*95%*
1976	.08	.31	.45	.63
1977	.15	.59	.86	1.23
1978	.39	1.53	2.23	3.16
1979	.73	2.87	4.16	5.89
1980	1.36	5.31	7.70	10.89
1981	1.86	7.26	10.51	14.85
1982	1.57	6.15	8.92	12.60
1983	1.03	4.02	5.84	8.26

Note: Estimated assuming a prepayment rate of 6 percent per year using a proportional hazard model and Freddie Mac data on single-family, fixed-rate loans.

Figure 29.2 shows hazard rates estimated using mortgages originated only in 1976 or 1981, the best and worst years for mortgage defaults in the sample. The figure shows that different origination years can have quite different time profiles of default.

Overall, original LTV and origination year matter most in explaining default patterns. The level of default varies considerably by origination year, while the separate effect of LTV on default is about the same for different origination years. For example, we divided our sample into two groups, 1976 to 1979 originations, which were followed by years with high inflation rates, and 1980 to 1983 originations, which experienced much less inflation. Loans originated during the first period had much lower default rates, as expected, but the effect of LTV was about the same. In both time periods, a loan with an initial LTV of 95 percent was about 8 to 10 times more likely to default than a loan with an LTV of 80 percent or less.

Table 29.1 summarizes projections of cumulative default rates over a 10-year period. For simplicity, we assume that 6 percent of the loans remaining each year prepay. This assumption will cause over or under predictions of default depending on whether prepayment rates are more or less than 6 percent. If prepayments are greater, fewer loans will be available to default.

According to our model, an 80 percent or below LTV loan originated in 1976 had about an .08 percent chance of defaulting in the first 10 years, while a 95 percent LTV loan originated in 1981 has about a 15 percent chance. All other origination years and LTVs have estimated cumulative default rates in between these extremes.

To this point the discussion has been limited to a few dimensions. Using complex models, the effect of additional variables on default can be quantified and isolated from the effects of other factors, such as LTV.

Our analysis included the separate effects of several borrower characteristics on default. For example, we examined the effect of the borrower's payment burden, measured by the ratio of the mortgage payment to the borrower's income as of the origination date. A higher payment burden only slightly increases the chance of default in our sample. This conclusion is tentative, however, because we have little experience with loans with high payment burdens. The borrower's age also seems not to affect the likelihood of default. The borrower's income has a small effect; high-income borrowers tend to be a little more likely to default. While all of these variables need further study, that they appear to be relatively unimportant in determining default is illuminating.

IMPLICATIONS FOR PRICING

Once estimated, a hazard function can be used to analyze default costs and, in turn, mortgage pricing. Suppose that the estimates for 1980 originations are expected to hold true for future defaults. Using Table 29.1, an 80 percent or below LTV loan originated in 1980 had about a 1.4 percent chance of defaulting in the first 10 years (after that, the changes are quite small). The loss per default, in present value terms, is typically about 25 cents on the dollar for an 80 percent LTV loan. Hence, an upfront charge of $.25 \times 1.4$ percent of .35 percent would cover the losses. This is roughly equivalent

ESTIMATING THE HAZARD FUNCTION

In statistical terms, hazard models can be thought of as an extension of multiple regression or logic models. The most common type of hazard model is the proportional hazard model. It is broken down into two proportional parts. The first is the baseline function, which gives the baseline time path of the hazard. The second function moves the baseline function up or down proportionately, incorporating the effects of other variables on the hazard's time profile.

When applying hazard models to mortgage default, the baseline function is the "normal" time profile of conditional default rates; that is, the probability of default in the first year, the second year, and so on, for some baseline, such as loans in a particular LTV class that were originated in a particular year. The proportional part shows how explanatory variables such as other loan-to-value ratios or origination years shift the time profile.

To estimate the hazard function, a specific mathematical form must be specified. Freddie Mac's analysis uses the standard form:

$$h(t) = \lambda(t)e^{bx}$$

where t is time; h(t) is the hazard rate after t years; $\lambda(t)$ is a series of "dummy" coefficients giving the baseline hazard rate for each year after origination; e is the exponential function; x is the explanatory variable(s); and b is the coefficient(s) to be estimated that measures the effect of x on the hazard function. Standard statistical packages can be used to estimate h and b, and using those results, the baseline rate λ can be calculated. Because of the exponential form of the function, e^b measures the percentage change in h brought about by a unit change in x.

The estimated coefficients (b's) were:

LTV Class	*Effect*
81 to 90%	1.37
91 to 94%	1.74
95%	2.09

Origination Year	*Effect*
1976	–2.58
1977	–1.91
1978	–0.97
1979	–0.34
1980	0.28
1981	0.59
1982	0.42

While this looks complicated, the interpretation is straightforward. The coefficients show how LTV and origination year shift the entire baseline hazard curve. Positive coefficients mean upward shifts and negative ones mean downward shifts, relative to the reference point of 1983 originations with LTVs of 80 percent or less. Looking at the LTV, a mortgage in the 81 to 90 percent LTV class has a higher hazard rate than does an 80 percent or below LTV, by a factor of $e^{1.37}$ or almost 4. That is, an 81 to 90 percent LTV is about 4 times more likely to default (holding origination year constant) than is a below 80 percent LTV. For LTVs from 91 to 94 percent, the effect is greater; the effect is greater still for 95 percent LTV loans, $e^{2.09}$ or more than 8.

Origination year has a similar interpretation. Holding LTV constant, a 1976 origination is less likely to default than is a 1983 origination, by a factor of $e^{-2.58}$ or about .08. That is, 1976 was such a good year that a loan originated then had less than one-tenth the probability of defaulting than a 1983 origination has. The pattern of the coefficients, rising and reaching a peak in 1981, reflects the general worsening of economic conditions, which peaked with the 1981 recession.

---

to an annual charge of 8 basis points. Using the same approach, loans with 95 percent LTVs originated the same year would require an annual charge of about 60 basis points. However, 95 percent LTV loans typically carry mortgage insurance. As a result, losses to the investor after insurance are smaller per default, perhaps more like 15 percent. This reduces the appropriate charge to about 35 basis points annually.

Going beyond this single-scenario analysis, one might assign to each origination year the probability that its economic environment would be repeated. For instance, we could use an average of the costs for the seven origination years in the sample if each year is thought to be equally likely to recur. For loans with 80 percent and below LTVs the average 10-year default rate is about .9 percent, which implies an annual cost of about 5 basis points. For 95 percent LTV loans the average cost (after insurance) is about 25 basis points annually.

The trick is to estimate probabilities for the future. Perhaps monetary policy is tightening and a repeat of the early 1980s is more than equally probable. More detailed modeling of the economy, however, is better deferred to another occasion.

Like the Moliere character who discovered he had been speaking prose all his life, mortgage market analysts have long been analyzing hazard rates in the guise of conditional default rates. What is important is not the new jargon; it is the statistical technique along with computer capacity and programs that allow analysis of large data sets like Freddie Mac's purchased mortgages. Applying hazard models to default takes us one step further in understanding its determinants and estimating its costs.

Chapter 30

Credit Intensive Mortgage Securities: B Pieces

by William F. Wallace,
Morgan Stanley & Co.

INTRODUCTION

Insurers are constantly looking for higher-yielding assets. One asset class that offers these higher yields is the subordinated class of AAA/AA-rated mortgage pass-through securities. These securities, often referred to as "B" pieces, currently have spreads of approximately 300 to 500 basis points over the Treasury curve and are prepayment buffered. In addition, their credit risks are measurable and, with proper diversification, may be small in comparison to other high-yielding securities. The credit risk profiles of B pieces can be improved further through the use of Letters of Credit (LOCs), the creation of "C" pieces, first loss insurance or other credit enhancement techniques. These enhancements, however, will reduce the yields offered.

These securities are generally well-suited to interest-sensitive life insurance liabilities. With the choices of Cost of Funds Index (COFI), one-year Constant Maturity Treasury (CMT) or fixed-rate issues, portfolios with high correlations to Single Premium Deferred Annuity (SPDA), Flexible Premium Deferred Annuity (FPDA), and Universal Life (UL) reset rates can be created.

ORIGINATION AND SECURITIZATION PROCESS

AAA/AA mortgage pass-throughs are created when a mortgage originator pools its nonconforming mortgage loans for sale into the secondary market. Since these mortgage loans are primarily nonconforming due to size or documentation, they cannot be sold to the traditional agency issuers (i.e., GNMA, FNMA, FHLMC). They must instead be pooled and sold under the originator's name. With no agency backing, Moody's and S&P require that some form of credit enhancement exist for these pools to receive a AAA or AA rating.

In the past, four methods of achieving credit enhancement for these mortgage loans have been used. In order of 1990 size of insurance, these methods are:

- Senior/subordinated structure
- Pool insurance
- Letter of credit
- Parent guarantee.

In 1990, just over 50 percent of the private pass-through productions were senior/subordinated structures (see Figure 30.1). We expect that in the future this percentage will increase to the levels of 1988–1989, which was roughly two-thirds of the market.

In a senior/subordinated pass-through structure, monthly payments of principal and interest are passed through to the investors in a predetermined order of priority. At time of issue, the subordinated, or class B, holders generally represent 6 percent to 10 percent of the outstanding balance but bear the full risk of losses from the entire pool. In this fashion, the B piece is providing the credit protection for the senior piece. In turn, the B piece is buffered from prepayments by the senior piece. To achieve this, most AAA/AA mortgages allocate all prepayments from the underlying collateral to the senior piece until it is paid off or for the first 10 years, whichever occurs first. Beginning in Year 11, prepayments are allocated in increasing percentages to the B piece until it is receiving its full prorated share of prepayment in

Figure 30.1—Private Pass-Through Production By Type of Credit Enhancement

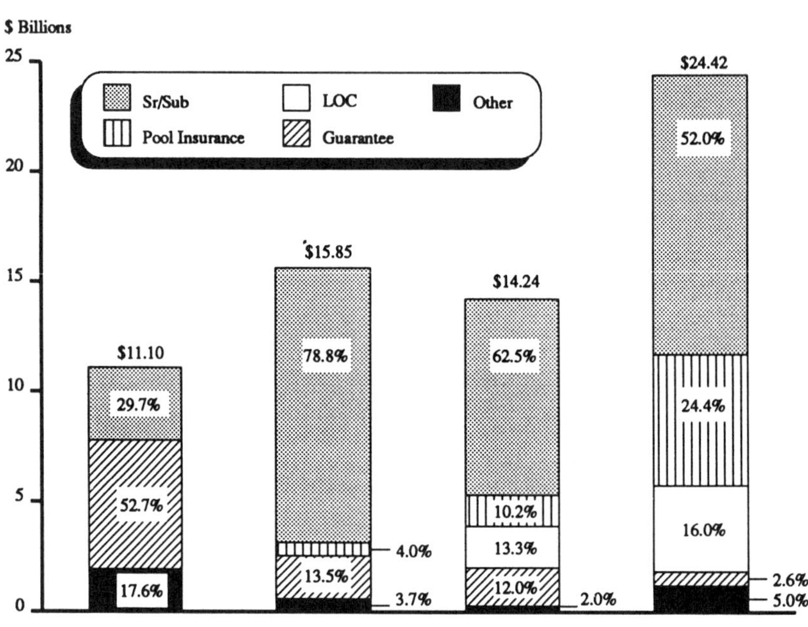

Source: Inside Mortgage Capital Markets

Year 15.[1] This structure, along with the discount price, keeps the prepayment costs small.

B pieces have been issued with ratings from AAA to BBB, however the majority are not rated but carry shadow noninvestment grade ratings.

CREDIT RISK

The risk in B pieces derives from the negative leverage of owning 6 percent to 10 percent of the mortgage collateral while bearing 100 percent of the risk of loss. Therefore, it is important to find ways of both subjectively evaluating the quality of the underlying mortgages and quantitatively estimating their default costs. The following are some of the most important factors in assessing the underlying quality.

Loan-to-Value Ratio (LTV)

The LTV is the original dollar amount of the mortgage loan divided by the original market value of the property. This ratio has been a very good indicator of default risk. In Figure 30.2 we see that there are nonlinear increases in the default risk as the LTVs rise. For this reason it is as important to know the distribution of the LTVs in the issue as it is to know the weighted-average LTVs.

Seasoning

The age of a pool of mortgages has been found to have an impact on the pool's default rate. We see in Figure 30.3 that defaults, on average, begin at very low levels, peak in Year 5, and are by S&P's estimates 95 percent complete by Year 7.

1 This structure is generally true of adjustable-rate B pieces. Fixed-rate B piece structures are similar, but the allocation of prepayments will generally begin in Year 6.

Figure 30.2—FNMA Default Experience 30-Year Fixed-Rate Texas Loans

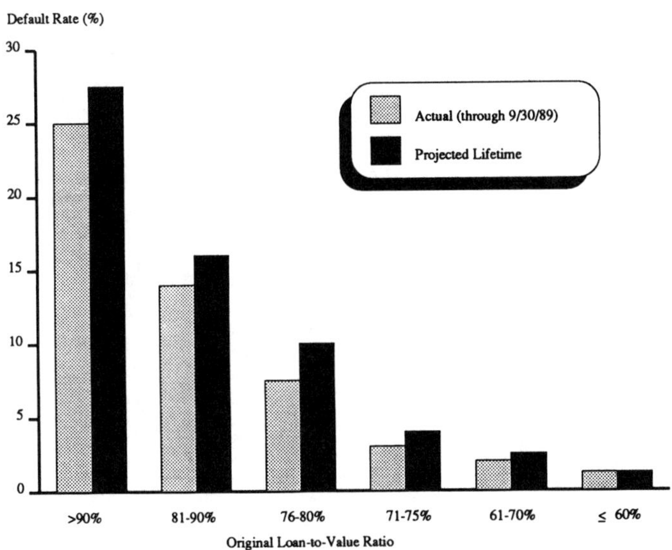

Source: FNMA

Figure 30.3—Annual Default Rates 1973–1989 Mortgages Nationwide (Covered by PMI)

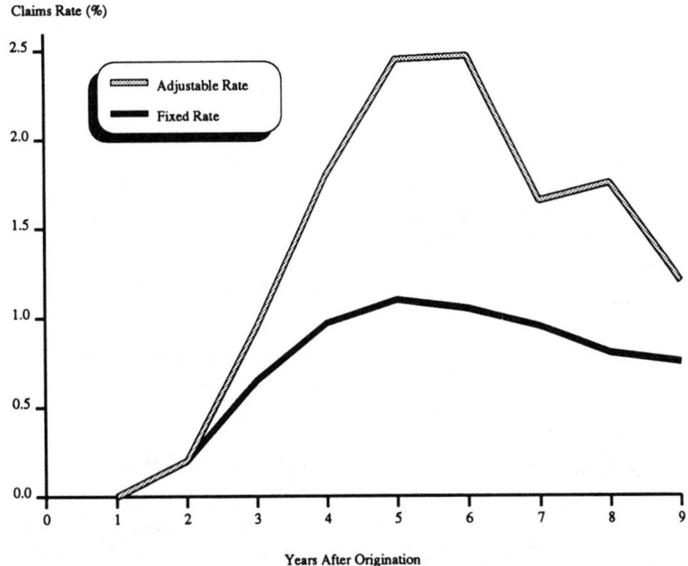

Source: Moody's Annual Report of the Private Mortgage Insurance Industry

Figure 30.4—Annual Default Rates
1973–1989 Mortgages Nationwide (Covered by PMI)

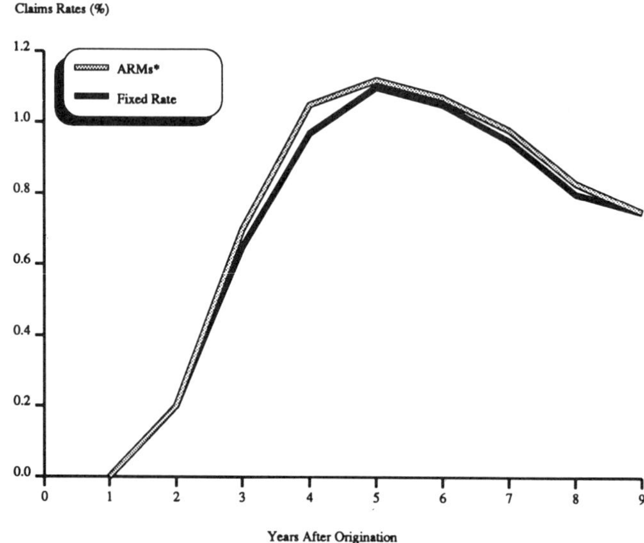

* Excluding 1980–1983 negative amortization ARMs
Source: Moody's Annual Report of the Private Mortgage Insurance Industry

Mortgage Type

Is the mortgage a fixed rate, ARM, negative amortization ARM or graduated payment mortgage (GPM)? Most investors believe that ARMs have had a higher default rate than fixed-rate mortgages. However, if we disaggregate the ARM category into fully amortizable ARMs and negative amortization ARMs (including GPMs and GEMs) we find that most of the additional risk is coming from the negative amortization ARMs written between 1980 and 1983 (see Figure 30.4). Since 1983, ARMs, including negative amortization ARMs, have shown default rates nearly equivalent to those of fixed-rate loans.

Underwriting Standards

These standards are the amount of documentation and verification required for the borrower to receive its mortgage. Full documentation requires:

- Application by borrower
- Verification of employment
- Verification of income
- Verification of down payment
- Source of down payment
- Credit checks
- Settlement statement on sale of previous home
- Appraisal.

Any loan origination in which less documentation is required is considered a *low-documentation* loan. Most AAA/AA mortgage pass-through issues contain these low-documentation loans. These loans are not inherently bad, however they do carry higher risks then full-documentation loans. Therefore, it is important to understand which underwriting procedures were omitted. As an example, loans with low LTVs may be good quality low-documentation loans.

Property Type and Purpose

Is the loan secured by an owner-occupied single-family dwelling or a rental condominium? Single-family and owner-occupied dwellings traditionally have the lowest default rates.

Property Location

Geographic diversification is important. A location with high economic diversity will be less susceptible to single industry recessions than a town or state with one major industry. In addition, the state and local laws will affect the ability of the servicer

Table 30.1—Delinquencies, Foreclosures and Loss Experiences for Select Mortgage Issuers

	The Travelers Mortgage Services			
	1987	*1988*	*1989*	*1990*
Loan Portfolio ($MM)	3,898	5,620	9,067	12,220
Delinquency (%)	1.11	1.00	1.38	2.82
Foreclosure (%)	0.20	0.23	0.14	0.19
Loss (%)*	0.01	0.06	0.04	0.05
	Western Federal Savings & Loan Association			
	1987	*1988*	*1989*	*1990*
Loan Portfolio ($MM)	3,443	4,815	8,051	9,128
Delinquency (%)	1.10	0.41	1.57	1.97
Foreclosure (%)	0.01	0.005	0.005	0.267
Loss (%)*	0.0002	0.089	0.0079	NA
	Marine Midland Mortgage, Inc.			
	1987	*1988*	*1989*	*1990*
Loan Portfolio ($MM)	2,678	4,916	11,998	14,678
Delinquency (%)	1.68	2.78	3.63	2.89
Foreclosure (%)	0.08	0.06	0.06	0.36
Loss (%)*	0.00	0.00	0.00	0.00

* Cumulative losses for total originations

Source: Morgan Stanley

to foreclose as well as the foreclosure costs involved.

Underwriter/Servicer

Know your issuer! Not all issuers/servicers have had the same loss experiences on residential mortgage loans. The experiences of three prime pool issuers/servicers are presented in Table 30.1.

We will now lay out a framework for quantitatively estimating the cost of defaults. To do this we examine the sources of loss in these securities and review the historical data for these components in both Texas (as a presumed worst case) and the nation as a whole.

Foreclosure Rate

The foreclosure rate is the percentage of the outstanding balance of mortgage loans for which the subject property is under foreclosure (see Figure 30.5). National foreclosure rates for the period 1980–1990 averaged 0.16 percent per quarter, apparently peaking in early 1990 at approximately 0.21 percent. The experience in Texas during this same period saw lower foreclosure rates than the national averages through 1984 but experienced a dramatic rise thereafter. Rates peaked on a quarterly basis at 0.65 percent in the third quarter of 1986. The worst one-year period encompassed the second half of 1986 and the first half of 1987 at 2.16 percent.

Property Value Declines

These are the percentage declines in the market values of the properties versus the values at times of origination (see Figure 30.6). On a nationwide basis, during the last 10 years housing prices have grown at an average annual rate of 4.5 percent.

The experience in Texas has clearly been worse. Using 1983 as a base (the start of the Houston decline), a diversified portfolio of Texas mortgage loans showed a total market value decline of 5 percent as of the first quarter of 1988, with Houston showing a 25 percent market value decline. As of the third quarter of 1990, the same diversified Texas portfolio was off 3 percent, with Houston again the only loss of the group at 15 percent. It is important to note that this period includes the full peak and trough in the Houston market, and that for both periods, Houston was the only city among the Texas cities shown whose property values were below their 1983 values. The

Figure 30.5—Texas Foreclosures Rates versus National Foreclosure Rates for 1–4 Family Residential Mortgages 1980–1990

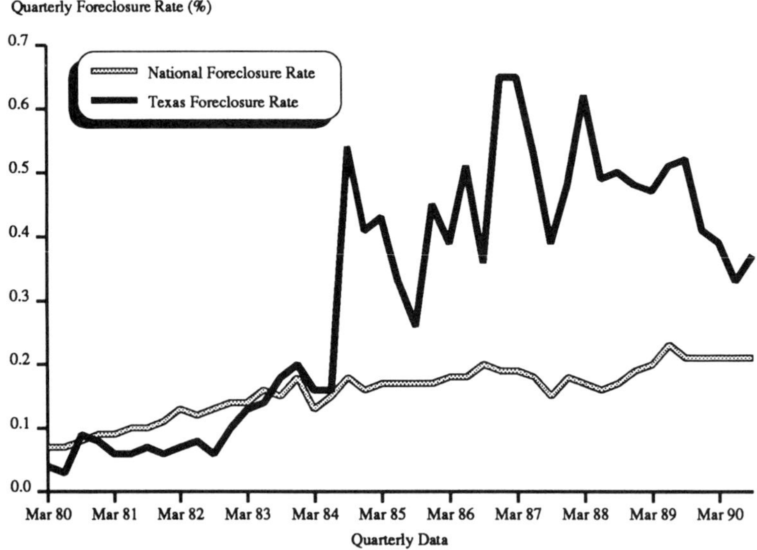

Source: Mortgage Bankers Association of America Delinquency Survey—Historical Series

Figure 30.6—National versus Texas Home Sales Price Indices 1980 Base

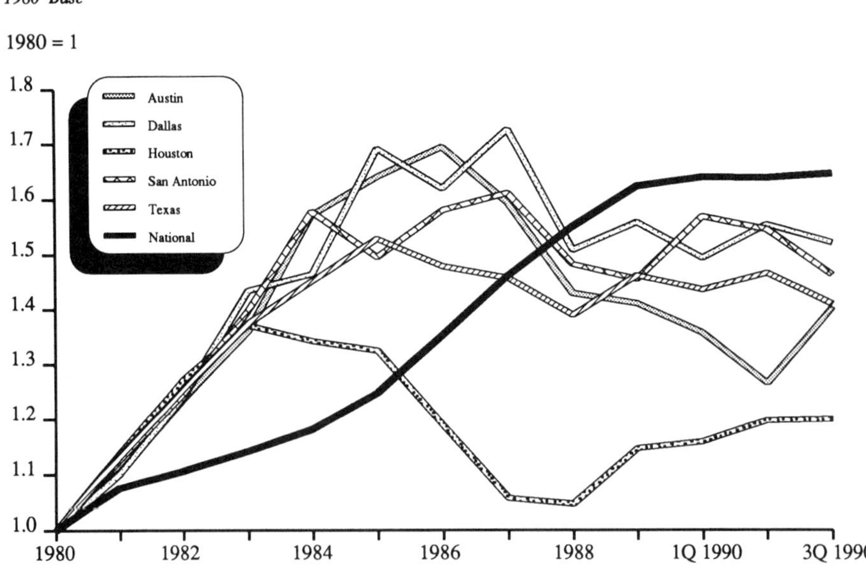

Source: Real Estate Center at Texas A&M University (based on Multiple Listing Serviced), National Association of Realtors

Table 30.2—Implied Loss Severity Calculation

	Property Value Decline	
	30%	*15%*
Initial Home Value ($)	100	100
Property Value Decline ($)	(30)	(15)
Foregone Interest (One Year) ($)	(8)	(8)
Foreclosure Costs ($)	(6)	(6)
Net Realized Property Value ($)	56	71
Original Mortgage Amount (80% LTV) ($)	(80)	(80)
Loss ($)	(24)	(9)
Implied Loss Severity (%)*	30	11

* Loss + Original Mortgage Amount = Implied Loss Severity

Source: Morgan Stanley

Houston experience again points out the importance of diversification.

Implied Loss Severity

Implied loss severity is the percentage of the original mortgage loan that may be lost in a default situation. It is calculated from the LTVs, property value declines, foregone interest, and foreclosure costs, as shown in Table 30.2. This analysis assumes an 80 percent LTV and 7.5 percent of the loan balance for foreclosure costs. Lower LTVs decrease the loss severity, higher ones increase it.

Utilizing the Formula

Credit Risk = Foreclosure Rate × Implied Loss Severity

We can create a matrix for estimating the yearly cost in basis points of default/credit risk for an entire pool of collateral. The matrix presented in Table 30.3 assumes 80 percent of LTVs with a variety of property value declines and foreclosure rates.

Since the subordinated class bears the full risk of loss on the mortgage loans, the numbers shown in Table 30.3 must now be used to calculate the cost of defaults to the subordinated class. The model that we have developed allocates the principal, interest, and prepayments generated by the mortgage loan collateral to the senior and subordinated tranches according to their predetermined schedules. The model then utilizes the credit risk from Table 30.3 to determine the net cash flows and post-default yield received by the subordinated class. In this fashion the effects of leverage and the reduction of principal and future interest flows are modeled correctly.[2]

To estimate the default risk of B pieces we have utilized a generic AAA/AA ARM structure with the B piece equal to 8 percent of the initial collateral. No credit enhancement is assumed on the B piece. Additionally, no prepayments go to the subordinated class until after Year 10 and then they go to the subordinated price in an increasing, predetermined share. At inception, the mortgage loans are required to be current and can have had only one 30-day delinquency in the preceding 12 months. Because the loans are current at issue and we have assumed the loss of one year's interest in the implied loss severity numbers, we further assume that no defaults take place in the first year.

Table 30.4 presents the default costs to the subordinated piece of different default experiences for the entire collateral. As an example of how the table works, most real estate market estimates point to potential foreclosure rates of 0.75 percent and market values bottoming 15 percent below initial home values. We can take these estimates into Table 30.3 (across the 5-year nationwide average foreclosure rate row, and down the 15 percent property value decline column) to arrive at a default experience rate of 0.08 percent. We then input this 0.08 percent experience into the model for Years 2 through 30 and arrive at our best estimate default cost of 40 basis points per year.

If we use more severe estimates for foreclosure rates and/or property value declines to arrive at

2 The model will *overstate* the credit risk because we have assumed that defaults continue for the entire 30 years and we have not reduced the loss severity of principal repayments (both scheduled and prepaid) that reduce the LTVs with time.

Table 30.3—Effect of Foreclosures on Entire Structure's Yield (Percent per Year)

		Texas			
Property Value Declines (%)		30.00	15.00	10.00	6.00
Implied Loss Severity (%)		30.00	11.25	5.00	0.00
Foreclosure Rate (%)					
Worst Experience	2.16	0.65	0.24	0.11	0.00
10-Year Average	1.28	0.38	0.14	0.06	0.00
5-Year Average	1.86	0.56	0.21	0.09	0.00
1-Year Average	1.83	0.55	0.21	0.09	0.00
Best Experience	0.24	0.07	0.03	0.01	0.00
		Nationwide			
Property Value Declines (%)		30.00	15.00	10.00	6.00
Implied Loss Severity (%)		30.00	11.25	5.00	0.00
Foreclosure Rate (%)					
Worst Experience	0.88	0.26	0.10	0.04	0.00
10-Year Average	0.61	0.18	0.07	0.03	0.00
5-Year Average	0.73	0.22	0.08	0.04	0.00
1-Year Average	0.84	0.25	0.09	0.04	0.00
Best Experience	0.16	0.05	0.02	0.01	0.00

Source: Morgan Stanley

default experiences for the entire pool of 0.10 and 0.25, we would see expected yield reductions due to a default of between 50 and 129 basis points for the B piece. A Texas-type scenario would cost approximately 307 basis points. It is important to note once again that these numbers are based upon 80 percent LTVs and 18 percent ownership of collateral initially. Reduction of the initial LTVs would improve these numbers; a decrease in the initial senior/subordinated leverage would decrease default costs.

CORRELATION TO SPDA, FPDA AND UL RATES

It has been shown in earlier studies that a high correlation exists between the 11th District COFI

Table 30.4—Effect of Default Experience on Subordinated Tranche's Yield

Default Experience (%)			*Cost of Default (bp)*
Year 1	*Year 2*	*Years 3–30*	*Effect on B Piece per Year*
0	0	0	0
0	0.08	0.08	40 (Best estimate)
0	0.10	0.10	50
0	0.10	0.25	84
0	0.25	0.06	84
0	0.25	0.10	93
0	0.25	0.25	129
0	0.55	0.55	307 (Houston experience)

Source: Morgan Stanley

Figure 30.7—Universal Life versus COFI ARMs

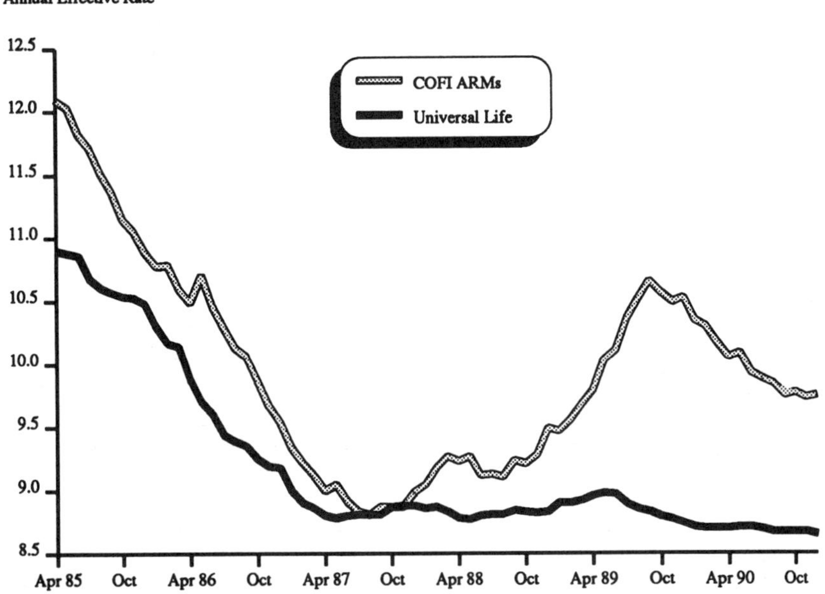

Source: Morgan Stanley

and UL crediting rates.[3] Figure 30.7 shows that this high correlation remains in effect.[4] These high correlations also exist between SPDA/FPDA reset rates and one-year CMT rates, and these correlations provide an opportunity to construct portfolios that are sensitive to crediting rate needs.

AN SPDA EXAMPLE

For most interest-sensitive portfolios, portfolio managers are forced to go too long in duration in order to achieve their yield targets. This duration mismatch translates into both parallel and nonparallel risk. The parallel risk arises when rates rise, but the portfolio rate does not rise quickly enough to keep policyholders from lapsing. The nonparallel risk comes in the form of a change in the rates used for resetting the crediting rate without a corresponding change in the portfolio rate. One-year CMT-based B pieces, with their high yields and short durations, help reduce this disintermediation risk.

As an example, we will use a generic new issue SPDA. The insurer guarantees the current three-year Treasury rate to the policyholder for a period of three years. After the initial period, the rate resets annually to the one-year Treasury rate. There is a surrender penalty of 7 percent, which declines by 1 percent per year.

Expenses and other product features lead to an "all-in cost" for the SPDA of 74 basis points above Treasuries. This 74 basis point spread is known as the "required spread"[5] and includes the cost of the

3 For more information see the Morgan Stanley publication *Investing for Interest-Sensitive Insurance Products: Adjustable Rate Mortgages*, April 1989.

4 It has been hypothesized that the divergence seen between September 1988 and September 1990 is due to the weaker savings and loan institutions bidding up the Cost of Funds Index; then the Index declined as these pressures subsided.

5 A more detailed discussion of the required spread concept can be found in the Morgan Stanley publication *The Excess Spread Approach to Pricing and Designing the SPDA*, December 1989. The required spread is the spread that equates the present value of the liability and expense cash flows to the market value of assets. Liability cash flows are generated along a carefully constructed set of interest rate paths so that all the interest-sensitive characteristics of the product are recognized.

Table 30.5—Portfolio 1

	Yield (%)	OAS (bp)	OAD (Yrs.)	Credit Risk (bp)
95% 3–4 Year Noncallable Bonds*	8.45	110	3.1	35
5% Top-Tier High Yield	12.00	450	3.4	200
Weighted Average	*8.63*	*127*	*3.1*	*43*
Credit Risk		43		
Credit-Adjusted OAS		48		

	Change in Interest Rates					
	–200 bp	*–100 bp*	*0*	*+100 bp*	*+200 bp*	*+300 bp*
Market Value ($ Thousands)	994	964	935	907	881	855
Earned Spread on Assets (bp/year)	84	84	84	84	84	84
Required Spread on Assets (bp/year)	82	76	74	75	76	79
Expected Profit (bp/year)	2	8	10	9	8	5

* This portion of the portfolio is composed of A/BBB noncallable corporates, clean CMO tranches, and asset-backed securities.

Source: Morgan Stanley

interest-sensitive withdrawal feature that is part of any SPDA liability.

The price-sensitivity duration (otherwise known in investment literature as "option-adjusted" or "effective duration") of the generic product is 3.1 years. We now construct and test two portfolios. Both portfolios will be duration-matched, without regard to a profit target. Table 30.5 shows a traditional asset mix for this type of product, emphasizing noncallable corporates. Table 30.6 includes a small position in one-year CMT B pieces to examine what benefits can accrue from the inclusion of this asset.

Table 30.6—Portfolio 2

	Yield (%)	OAS (bp)	OAD (Yrs.)	Credit Risk (bp)
46% One-Year CMT Agency ARMs	7.70	90	0.4	5
5% One-Year CMT B Piece	10.35	375	0.5	125
46% 7–10 Year Noncallable Bonds*	9.15	115	5.9	35
3% Top-Tier High Yield	12.00	450	3.4	200
Weighted Average	*8.63*	*127*	*3.1*	*30*
Credit Risk		30		
Credit-Adjusted OAS		97		

	Change in Interest Rates					
	–200 bp	*–100 bp*	*0*	*+100 bp*	*+200 bp*	*+300 bp*
Market Value ($ Thousands)	995	964	935	908	882	851
Earned Spread on Assets (bp/year)	97	97	97	97	97	97
Required Spread on Assets (bp/year)	81	76	74	74	75	84
Expected Profit (bp/year)	16	21	23	23	22	13

* This portion of the portfolio is composed of A/BBB noncallable corporates, clean CMO tranches, and asset-backed securities.

Source: Morgan Stanley

The portfolio shown in Table 30.6 has several advantages:

- Higher expected profitability
- Lower credit risk with no giveup in yield or OAS
- Average rating of AA3 versus A3 for the portfolio in Table 30.5
- Diversification of risk away from the junk market
- 50 percent of the portfolio resets at the same frequency and against the same index as the renewal crediting rate.

These advantages are available because the high yields on the B piece allow the use of agency securities and a larger floating-rate component. This short component in turn allows us to extend the duration of the balance of the portfolio and thus pick up the 70 basis point yield curve advantage between three and seven years.

SUMMARY

Opportunities exist to use B pieces effectively in insurance company portfolios. The credit risk in the subordinated pieces of AAA/AA mortgage securities is measurable and, depending upon one's outlook for real estate values, likely small or very small. The nominal yield spreads on these securities are high, and credit enhancement is available for investors desiring an investment grade rating or a further reduction of default risk.

Chapter 31

AAA Senior Mortgage-Backed Securities versus AAA Insured Mortgage-Backed Securities

by Charles Austin Stone,
Université Paris Dauphine
Anne Zissu,
Temple University
and
Jess Lederman,
Author and Private Investor

I. INTRODUCTION

The securities which a special purpose vehicle issues in order to fund the purchase of a pool of mortgages are mortgage-backed securities. Investors in these mortgage-backed securities have claims on a share of an undivided interest of the cash flows net of a servicing fee, credit enhancement fees, and trustee fees which are generated by the pool of mortgages. The magnitude, timing, and value of the cash which flows from the mortgages to the owners of the mortgage-backed securities via the special purpose vehicle are uncertain. The sources of the uncertainty are the ability of the mortgagor to refinance his mortgage (prepayment risk), the ability of the mortgagor to default on his mortgage (credit risk), and the volatility of interest rates (interest rate risk).

Consider a bank which originates mortgages and funds these mortgages by issuing a combination of government insured deposits, senior debt of various maturities, subordinated debt of various maturities, preferred stock, and common stock. Each class of liabilities has a claim on the value of the mortgage portfolio which is senior relative to another class of liabilities except for common stock which is a claim on the residual value of the mortgage portfolio. Losses to the bank's mortgage portfolio arising from default, prepayment, and interest rate volatility will be allocated across the various classes of investors according to the priority of each investor's claim with respect to the other claims. Common stock absorbs the first level of losses while insured deposits only absorb catastrophic losses (the insurance fund becomes insolvent and cannot be refinanced). Preferred stock would absorb losses before the payments to the subordinated bonds would be disrupted. Subordinated bonds would be devalued before the value of the senior debt was affected. Debt with relatively long duration funds a larger proportion of interest rate risk than relatively short-term or floating-rate debt.

When the bank's mortgages are securitized, the special purpose vehicle may issue a single class of securities to fund the purchase of the mortgages or it may issue multiple classes of securities. The objective of the SPV is to structure the classes of mortgage-backed securities (MBS) to minimize its cost of capital.

The original GNMA pass-through security was an undivided interest in a pool of FHA/VA mortgages. A single class of securities was issued to fund the purchase of the mortgage collateral. The Government National Mortgage Association (GNMA) guaranteed the timely interest and principal payments of the GNMA pass-through security. The guarantee of GNMA is equivalent to a guaranty of the U.S. government. The interest rate risk and prepayment risk remained tied together in the GNMA pass-through security while the credit risk was isolated and funded by the Government National Mortgage Association. The trend in the market since the first CMO was issued by Freddie

Mac in 1983 has been for SPVs to issue multiple classes of securities which have claims on different parts of the cash flows which are generated by the securitized assets. For example an SPV might issue one class of securities which has a claim on all interest payments (interest only strips) and one class of securities which has a claim on all principal payments (principal only strips).

In this chapter we consider two structures which are used to allocate the credit risk associated with a securitized pool of mortgages. The two structures are the senior/subordinated structure and the pool insurance structure. In the senior/subordinated structure the SPV issues two classes of securities, the senior class and the subordinated class. The subordinated tranche is obligated to absorb all credit losses on the underlying collateral. Defaults will not disrupt the cash paid to the senior security unless credit losses exceed the size of the subordinated tranche. The subordinated securities are equity from the perspective of the investors who own the senior class of securities. The senior MBS funds only a catastrophic level of credit risk. If the level of defaults in a period are greater than the amount of cash which is due to the subordinated securities, there will be a liquidity problem. Funds in excess of the payments due to the subordinated securities have not materialized and therefore cannot be diverted to the senior securities. A common technique of solving this liquidity problem is for the SPV to utilize funds from the mortgage collateral to finance a third-party liquidity facility. The liquidity facility guarantees that the owners of the senior MBS receive timely payment of interest and principal.

An alternative to allocating the credit risk of the mortgage collateral to a subordinated security is a pool insurance policy issued by a third party. The insurance policy insures a specified percentage of the value of the mortgage principal which has been purchased by the SPV. Pool insurance is an indemnity policy. If mortgages in the pool default, the insurance company will indemnify the SPV for the value of the defaulted mortgage principal after the foreclosure proceedings have been completed and the mortgaged property has been liquidated. Foreclosure is a process which often takes a significant amount of time to complete. In France the process can take up to three years. The time delay between default and foreclosure poses a liquidity problem. The SPV can solve this liquidity problem by diverting cash from the underlying mortgage collateral to fund a third-party liquidity facility. The liquidity facility insures that owners of the MBS receive timely payment of principal and interest.

The purpose of this chapter is to compare the values of the senior tranche of securities issued in the senior/subordinated structure (from now on referred to as "senior MBS") with the single class of securities issued in the pool insurance structure (from now on referred to as "insured MBS"). Both the senior securities and the insured securities are assumed to be structured so as to receive a AAA rating from Standard and Poor's, Duff & Phelps, Fitch, and Moody's. In order to receive the top credit ratings the subordinate security and the insurance policy must be able to absorb credit losses of the securitized assets which are a multiple of historical loss experience.

The insured MBSs are exposed to the risk that the supplier of the liquidity facility and/or the provider of pool insurance may suffer losses to the extent that they cannot fulfill their commitments. This type of risk is referred to as event risk. The "senior MBS," although not subject to the event risk associated with the insurance company becoming insolvent, is still subject to the risk that the liquidity facility cannot perform as expected (NB: it is possible to completely eliminate event risk by structuring a senior MBS to accrue {negatively amortize} shortfalls of cash flow}). Although both the "senior MBS" and the "insured MBS" are both rated AAA with respect to credit risk, the prepayment risk of the subordinated security has been partially allocated to the "senior MBS." The allocation of the subordinated tranche share of prepayment risk to the "senior MBS" causes the price dynamics of the "insured MBS" and the "senior MBS" to differ substantially. Section II of this chapter summarizes the information which is critical to understanding our model and the results of the model. In section III we build the model. Section IV of this chapter is the interpretation of our results. Section V is the conclusion.

II. THE SENIOR/SUBORDINATED AND INSURED STRUCTURES

The senior/subordinated pass-through structure that we analyze has the following characteristics:

- The subordinated tranche is a 10 percent undivided interest in the pool of mortgages.
- For the first five years, all prepayments of mortgage collateral are allocated to the senior MBS.
- From year 6 to year 10, the percentages of the prepayments which are allocated to the subordinated security increase.

Table 31.1

From year 1 to year 5
100% of prepayment on the entire pool is shifted to the senior MBS.

Year 6
The subordinated MBS receives only 30% of its share of prepayments. The remaining share (70%) is allocated to the senior MBS.

Year 7
The subordinated tranche receives 40% of its share of prepayments. The remaining share (60%) is allocated to the senior tranche.

Year 8
The subordinated tranche receives 60% of its share of prepayments. The remaining share (40%) is allocated to the senior tranche.

Year 9
The subordinated tranche receives 80% of its share of repayments. The remaining share (20%) is allocated to the senior tranche.

Year 10 to year 30
The subordinated tranche is allocated 100% of its share of the prepayments.

- From year 11 to year 30, the subordinated security is allocated its full share of the prepayments.[1]

The size of the subordinated security is in effect set by rating agency criteria. In order for the senior MBS to receive the top credit rating, the subordinated tranche will have to be able to absorb a loss rate on the securitized assets which is a multiple of historical loss severity.

The senior/subordinated structure we have described implies that the credit risk of the pool of mortgages is allocated to the subordinated tranche and the prepayment risk is allocated to the senior MBS. For the first 5 years the senior class of securities receives all principal which is paid into the SPV. Table 31.1 illustrates the share of prepayments the senior MBS receives relative to the share of collateral allocated to the senior MBS.

In order to isolate the effect which prepayments have on the value of the senior MBS relative to the insured MBS we make the following assumptions:

- The pool coverage provided by the pool insurance policy is equivalent to the original size of the subordinated tranche. The subordinated tranche covers 10 percent of the original mortgage pool.
- The mortgages which have been securitized are exactly the same for both the senior/subordinated structure and the insured structure.
- The securitized assets correspond to 100 30-year fixed-rate mortgages, with same coupon rate.
- The insured MBS has the same servicing fee as the senior MBS.
- The cost of the equity cushion which protects the senior MBS (the subordinated security) and the insured MBS (the pool insurance policy) is equivalent. The cost of insurance is the present value of an annual premium and an up-front deductible. The cost of the subordinated tranche is the present value of the difference between the pass-through rate on the subordinated tranche and the pass through rate on the senior tranche.
- The cost of third-party liquidity support is equivalent for both the insured MBS and the senior MBS.
- The insured MBS has the same pass-through rate as the senior note.
- The pool of mortgages purchased by the SPV prepays at a constant rate (CPR).
- The rate at which mortgages prepay is a function of the future difference between the interest rate on the mortgages which

1 There are alternative forms of the senior/subordinated structure. See Finnerty (Chapter 3) and Griep (Chapter 11) in this volume.

Table 31.2

(assuming cpr = 4%)

t (1)	%Sen. (2)	%Sub. (3)	%cprSen. (4)	%cprSub. (5)	G (6)
0	90%	10%	0%	0%	0%
1	89.5833	10.4167	111.1111	0	0
2	89.1493	10.8507	111.6279	0	0
3	88.6972	11.3028	112.1714	0	0
4	88.2262	11.7738	112.7431	0	0
5	87.7357	12.2643	113.345	0	0
6	87.378	12.622	109.7851	30	30
7	87.0624	12.9376	108.6672	40	40
8	86.8468	13.1532	105.9441	60	60
9	86.7372	13.2628	103.0291	80	80
10–30	86.7372	13.2628	100	100	100

have been securitized and the current market rate at which these mortgages can be refinanced.

- It is possible to summarize the expected periodic prepayment of principal with a constant prepayment rate.
- When the pass-through rate is equal to the market rate, there is a "natural" prepayment rate. The "natural" prepayment rate corresponds to prepayments which are not motivated by refinancing opportunities. The "natural" level of prepayment is due to reasons such as moving to a different area, divorce, death, unemployment, financial distress, depreciating property value, etc.[2]

Higher interest rates increase the opportunity cost of refinancing a mortgage. Prepayment rates will fall below the natural rate when the prepayment option is out of the money.

- There is a minimum prepayment rate (CPR_{min}) which can be interpreted as systematic credit risk. CPR_{min} is the level of prepayment associated with relatively high rates of interest. The prepayment which takes place at these high levels of interest is primarily a result of mortgagors exercising their default option.

III. METHODOLOGY

Equation (1) is the prepayment function which is the foundation of the analysis.

$$cpr = \text{Max}\{[cpr_n \pm b(ptr - r_m)^2], cpr_{min}\} \quad (1)$$

where

cpr = constant prepayment rate

$(ptr - r_m)$ = pass-through rate minus market rate

(cpr_n) = natural prepayment rate

b = constant

cpr_{min} = minimum constant prepayment rate

for $(ptr - r_m) > 0$

$cpr = \text{Max}\{[cpr_n + b(ptr - r_m)^2], cpr_{min}\}$

for $(ptr - r_m) < 0$

$cpr = \text{Max}\{[cpr_n - b(ptr - r_m)^2], cpr_{min}\}$

Once we have determined (cpr), the constant prepayment rate, we allocate the prepayments to the senior and subordinated tranche according to the structure described in Table 31.1.

The pool of mortgages underlying the senior/subordinated structure consists of 100 30-year fixed-rate mortgages with coupons of 10% per year, and original balances of $100,000. The senior note corresponds to 90% of the original mortgage principal which has been securitized, and the subordinated tranche is a claim on 10% of the mortgage principal. The cost of servicing the senior MBS is 25 basis points per year, and the cost of credit enhancement is 25 basis points per year. The 25 basis point per annum cost of credit enhancement is the additional yield earned by the subordinated tranche as well as the cost of the liquidity facility. The senior note has a pass-through rate of 9.5% per year.

2 The "natural prepayment rate" includes the expected rate of defaults. We have assumed that the level of defaults never exceeds the size of the subordinated tranche or the percentage of principal insured by a third party.

The pool of mortgages which is securitized and insured is composed of 100 30-year fixed-rate mortgages each with a coupon of 10% per year, an original balance of $100,000. The servicing fee is 25 basis points per year, and the insurance premium is 25 basis point per year (cost of insurance + liquidity). Therefore the pass-through rate is 9.5% per year (Table 31.2).

Column (1) corresponds to time.

Column (2) represents the senior note as a percentage of the total outstanding mortgage pool at each point in time.

Column (3) represents the subordinated tranche as a percentage of the total outstanding pool of principal at each point in time. The size of the subordinated tranche relative to the senior tranche increases over time. This implies that the equity cushion protecting the senior note increases as the mortgages amortize and prepay.

Column (6) is the share of the prepayments which are allocated to the subordinated tranche. Therefore, (1–column 6) is the share of prepayments which are diverted from the subordinated tranche to the senior MBS. Column (4) is the ratio of total prepaid principal allocated to the "senior MBS" (inclusive of prepaid principal shifted from subordinated tranche) over the prepaid principal payments which correspond to the size of the "senior MBS."

Column (4) at time (t) is computed as follows:

$$(col4)_t = [(col2)_{t-1}+(1-(col6)_t)*(col3)_{t-1}]/(col2)_{t-1}$$

For example at t=3: %cprSen=112.1714%

$$112.1714\%=[89.1493\%+(1-0)*10.8507\%]/89.1493\%$$

where 89.1493% is the percentage of the senior note with respect to the entire pool at time 2; 10.8507% is the percentage of the subordinated note with respect to the entire pool at time 2; (1–col6) is the percentage (100%–0%), at time 3, of the subordinated tranche's prepaid principal which is allocated to the "senior MBS."

The %cprSen equal to 112 means that the "senior MBS" received 12% more prepaid principal than is represented by an undivided interest in 89.1493% of the pool of mortgages.

The additional wealth which can be accumulated by investing in the insured MBS rather than the senior MBS can now be calculated. We calculate the difference in the present values of the cash flows generated by the insured MBS and the senior MBS across a range of CPR/market rate combinations.

Figure 31.1—Constant Prepayment Rate as a Function of Market Rate

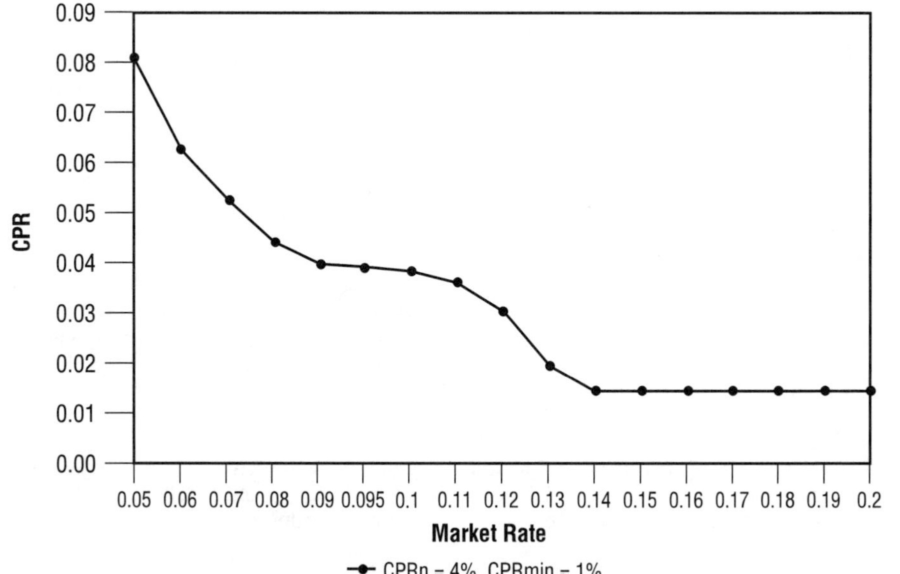

Figure 31.2—Benefit of Insured MBS over Senior Note

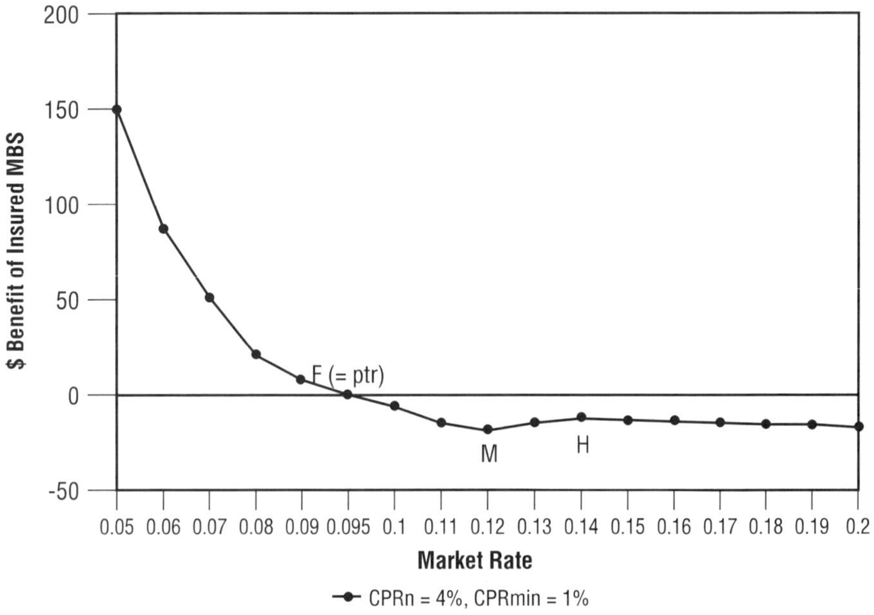

IV. RESULTS AND INTERPRETATION

Figure 31.1 shows the constant prepayment rate as a function of the market rate.

Figure 31.2 shows the benefits of investing $10,000 in the insured MBS relative to a $10,000 investment in the senior MBS given that prepayments are explained by equation (1).

We observe the following:

0 < Ben < F

When ($0 < r_m < ptr$), the benefit of the insured MBS is positive and decreases as the market rate (r_m) approaches the pass-through rate (ptr) (the CPR decreases as r_m increases)

Ben = F

When $r_m = ptr$ an investor would be indifferent between investing in the insured MBS and the senior MBS. When the market rate (r_m) equals the pass through rate (ptr) the benefit curve intersects the horizontal axis at a market rate which corresponds to the natural level of prepayment (CPR_n).

F < Ben < M

When ($r_m > ptr$) the benefit of investing in the insured MBS rather than the senior MBS is negative and this disadvantage increases as the market rate increases until it reaches a *local* minimum, (point M).

Ben = M

When ($r_m > ptr$) the value of the senior MBS increases relative to the "insured MBS" as r_m increases, until the relative benefit of the "senior MBS" reaches a local maximum (or local minimum for insured MBS), at point M.

M < Ben < H

The senior MBS's benefit decreases as interest rates increase and the constant prepayment rate continues to decrease until the prepayment rate equals the minimum constant prepayment rate (cpr_{min}).

Ben > H

As interest rates increase beyond the rate associated with CPR_{min} the benefit of the senior note once again begins to increase.

Figure 31.2 is based on the data from Table 31.3.

Table 31.3—Benefits of Insured MBS over Senior Note

r_m (1)	cpr_n (2)	Benefit (3)
.00	.2205	655.9002
.01	.1845	529.0277
.02	.1525	412.2040
.03	.1245	307.8470
.04	.1005	218.4870
.05	.0805	145.9953
.06	.0645	90.81056
.07	.0525	51.51375
.08	.0445	24.98000
.09	.0405	7.06767
.095	.0400	0.00000
.10	.0395	−6.33373
.11	.0355	−15.98630
.12	.0275	−19.76190
.13	.0155	−15.26010
.14	.0100	−11.9771
.15	.0100	−13.4865
.16	.0100	−14.7236
.17	.0100	−15.7335
.18	.0100	−16.5534
.19	.0100	−17.2140
.20	.0100	−17.7407

Where column (1) is the market rate, column (2) was computed using equation (1):

$$cpr = Max\{[cpr_n \pm b(ptr - r_m)^2], cpr_{min}\} \quad (1)$$

We used as the natural prepayment rate (cpr_n) 4% per year, a minimum prepayment rate (cpr_{min}) of 1% per year, and a coefficient b=20.

Column (3) was computed with the use of column (1) and Column (2):

Column (2) was used to determine the pass-through for the "insured MBS" and the "senior MBS." We then discounted the difference in the cash flows received by the "insured MBS" and the "senior MBS" at the rates which appear in column (1). The benefit is the difference between the present value of the insured MBS and the senior MBS (value of insured MBS–value of senior MBS).

For example, if an investor expects the market rate r_m to be equal to 5% per year, he will use that rate in equation (1) to find the corresponding constant prepayment rate. The investor will have an a priori estimate of the natural prepayment rate, i.e., 4% per year, and an a priori estimate of the minimum prepayment rate CPR_{min}, i.e., 1% per year. The investor decides that the appropriate b is 20. The investor would use this information to calculate column (2):

$$cpr = Max\{[.04 + 20(.095 - .05)^2], .01\}$$

$$cpr = 8.05\% \text{ per year}$$

The prepayment function is illustrated in Figure 31.1.

The investor then, uses the constant prepayment rate of 8.05% to compute the cash flows for each note, takes the difference at each point in time between such cash flows and discounts them to the present using the market rate of 5%. He finds that the benefit of investing $10,000 in the 100% AAA-rated note over that of investing $10,000 in the AAA-rated senior note is equal to $145.9953 (see column (3)). Under these conditions, the investor would choose to invest in the "insured MBS." It is not necessary to predict interest rates to conclude that the insured MBS is the preferred investment. For example, an investor who assumes a neutral probability distribution with respect to market rates will reach the same conclusion.

Figure 31.3 plots two benefit functions which only differ with respect to the natural prepayment rate. The higher natural level of prepayment increases the benefit of the "insured MBS" for interest rates less than the rate which corresponds to the natural level of prepayment and increases the benefits of the "senior MBS" for interest rates greater than the rate which corresponds to the natural level of prepayment.

The senior/subordinated structure we have examined creates a senior security which is secure with respect to credit risk. The true cost of insulating the "senior MBS" from credit risk is the premium which must be paid to the subordinated security for funding the credit risk, and the premium which will have to be paid to the "senior MBS" for the additional prepayment risk it has assumed from the subordinated tranche. Since the prepayment risk was shifted to the "senior MBS" from the subordinated security, the subordinated security must be exposed to less prepayment risk than the "senior MBS" and the "insured MBS." The "senior MBS" is leveraged with respect to prepayment risk and the subordinated security is leveraged with respect to credit risk. Will an SPV be indifferent between the "insured structure" and the senior/subordinated structure? If the "senior MBS" trades at a discount from the "insured MBS" the market is discounting for prepayment risk. This

Figure 31.3—Benefit of Insured MBS for Two CPR Functions

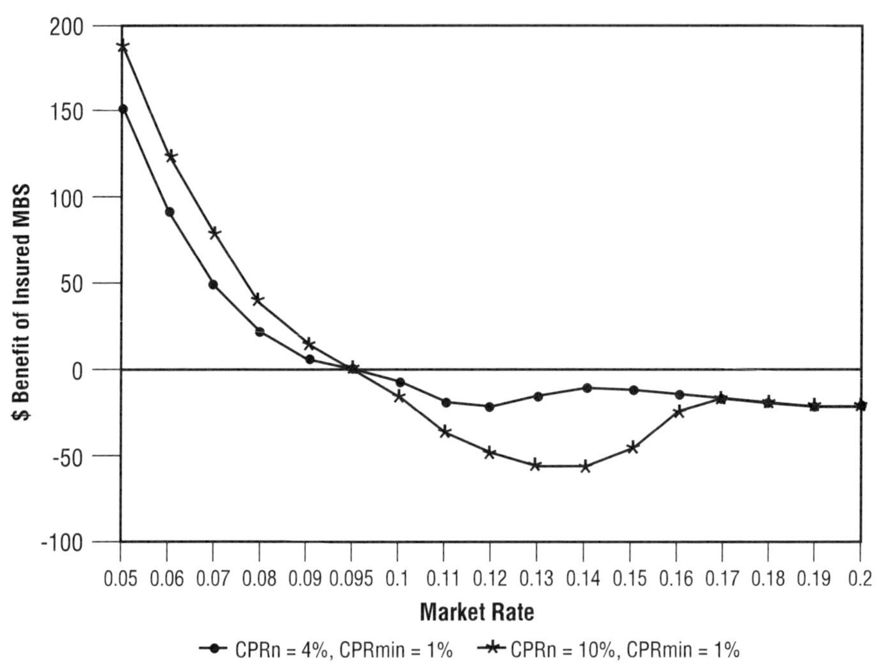

should enhance the value of the subordinated tranche which has been stripped of its prepayment risk. If the "senior MBS" trades at a premium to the "insured MBS" the market is anticipating relatively low levels of prepayment. This implies that the market would discount the fact that the subordinated tranche has very little prepayment risk and would instead focus on the subordinated tranche's high leverage.

It is important to note that the comments above apply only to the simple pass-through structure that has thus far dominated the European MBS market. The introduction of a greater number of classes, with differing cash flow characteristics (floaters, inverse floaters, PAC and TAC bonds, etc.) and thus differing sensitivities to prepayment risk, greatly complicates the analysis. For example, suppose that two identical pools of mortgages are stripped into IO and PO classes, and one PO class is then credit enhanced through subordination while the other is credit enhanced through insurance. If we then subject the two resulting AAA securities to the analysis presented above, the results would be approximately the opposite: the PO strip enhanced by way of subordination would generally be the preferred investment. This, of course, is because PO securities are issued at deep discounts from par and will always benefit from earlier prepayment.

It is common for mortgage-backed and asset-backed securities in the U.S. market to consist of multiple classes. Each class is designed to fund a designated portion of a specific type/types of risk. It is possible to fund a pool of mortgages by issuing N classes of securities. (i=1 . . . N) Class N-1 could be subordinated to class N, class N-2 could be subordinated to class N-1, . . . etc. Although class (N-N-1) would be a highly leveraged security with respect to credit risk it would be quite secure with respect to prepayment risk. Securitization is a technique which makes specific forms of risk more transparent and liquid. It is also possible for the company which insures the pool of mortgages to cede a portion of the insurance policy to a reinsurance company and for the reinsurance company to retrocede part of its reinsurance policy to another reinsurance company, etc. The primary insurer may fund the first level of losses, the first reinsurance company may fund losses up to a specified level, and the last reinsurance company in the line may fund losses above and beyond losses associated with a very unlikely scenario. Mobilizing equity and deploying it efficiently is the basis of designing an efficient securitization architecture.

Chapter 32

CMO Volatility Ratings

by Stephen W. Joynt,
Executive Vice President
Financial Institutions/Structured Finance,
James D. Nadler,
Managing Director, Volatility Ratings
and
Robert E. Phelan, CFA,
Managing Director, Market Risk Products
Fitch Investors Service, Inc.

SUMMARY

Fitch announces ratings of collateralized mortgage obligation (CMO) volatility. V-Ratings offer a balanced view of the relative volatility of total return, price, and maturity for each CMO tranche.

CMOs are fixed income investments supported by U.S. government agency or whole loan collateral and structured into specific classes of securities known as tranches. All CMOs have high credit quality reflecting their support by federal agency certificates of Fannie Mae, Freddie Mac, or Ginnie Mae, or backing from whole loan collateral rated AAA.

Individual tranches, however, have varying degrees of market risk. CMOs differ from pass-through certificates because cash flows from the collateral are structured to prioritize payment among tranches. Pass-through certificates are sold and priced with an expected yield and maturity based on an assumed mortgage prepayment rate. All pass-through certificate holders share symmetrically in this prepayment risk. CMO tranches are individually priced for expected return, maturity, and assumed prepayment rates based on their unique characteristics. Because cash flows are specifically allocated as part of structuring a new issue CMO, there is an assymetrical distribution of prepayment risk among the tranches.

FIVE LEVELS OF VOLATILITY

Until now, there was no standard measurement of potential CMO performance. Fitch CMO Volatility Ratings, scaled V1 through V5, provide a relative measure of the volatility of individual tranches given changing interest rates. The volatility of current coupon agency certificates refer to current rates on new Fannie Mae, Freddie Mac, or Ginnie Mae mortgage participation certificates. Tranches assigned ratings of V1, V2, and V3 demonstrate volatility less than or equal to current coupon agency certificates over a range of interest rate scenarios. Tranches rated V4 or V5 demonstrate greater volatility over a range of interest rate scenarios than do current coupon agency certificates. Fitch has created an analytical model to assess changes in total return, price, and expected maturity by testing performance in 10 divergent interest rate scenarios given correlated prepayment expectations and considering specific collateral characteristics. In rating tranches, the combined results are contrasted with current coupon agency certificates and all other CMO tranches. V-Ratings analyze the potential impact of interest rate movements on individual tranches but do not rate the probability of specific interest rate scenarios.

TRANCHE ASSESSMENT

Volatility ratings on CMOs provide a valuable reference point for investors to understand relative tranche risk when buying new issue CMOs. V-Ratings are an easy-to-use scale that simplifies a complex analysis of prepayment expectations, interest rate scenarios, and individual CMO issue structures. V-Ratings also provide a common framework and an independent assessment of all new-issue CMOs offered in the market. While V-Ratings offer relative volatility measures across all individual CMO tranches, retail and institutional investors must separately analyze each CMO considering their risk/reward preferences and investment needs.

MARKET RISK

All fixed income investments have degrees of market risk affecting total return and price. V-Ratings are defined as relative measures of CMO market risk volatility that can be contrasted with other fixed income instruments. Volatility ratings should be differentiated from credit ratings in that the scale is not absolute. Credit ratings assume U.S. government bonds to be the highest rated securities, i.e., the bench mark, among fixed income investments. Volatility ratings do not. When subjected to the same interest rate scenario testing, Treasury securities are not all rated V1.

For example, 30-year Treasuries subjected to the same interest rate scenario testing for CMOs appear in the V3 category, indicating they too experience a decline in total return and price in rising interest rate environments.

Because volatility ratings are derived by testing wide movements in interest rates and since the ratings are relative performance indicators, the majority of individual tranche volatility ratings are expected to remain constant. However, given extreme interest rate movements, certain CMO tranche ratings may change because of cash flow prioritization or due to the individual characteristics of the tranche structure. Separately, since maturity is an important variable in market risk analysis, as individual CMO tranches shorten in life, volatility potential will decrease and volatility ratings will naturally improve. Fitch will monitor all tranche volatility ratings and will make quarterly rating adjustments to reflect these factors.

Figure 32.1 indicates the approximate distribution of the V-Ratings.

V-RATING DEVELOPMENTS

CMO tranches are purchased by a variety of investors. Retail buyers typically purchase individual tranches, and therefore are most interested in specific tranche performance indicators. Insurance companies tend to be strongly influenced by cash flow and duration measurements as they balance their insurance product offerings. CMO bond funds often compete on, and are most interested in, total return measurements. Fitch V-Ratings represent a standard framework in which to provide the diversity of analytical information required by different investor segments. At the end

Figure 32.1—Volatility Ratings

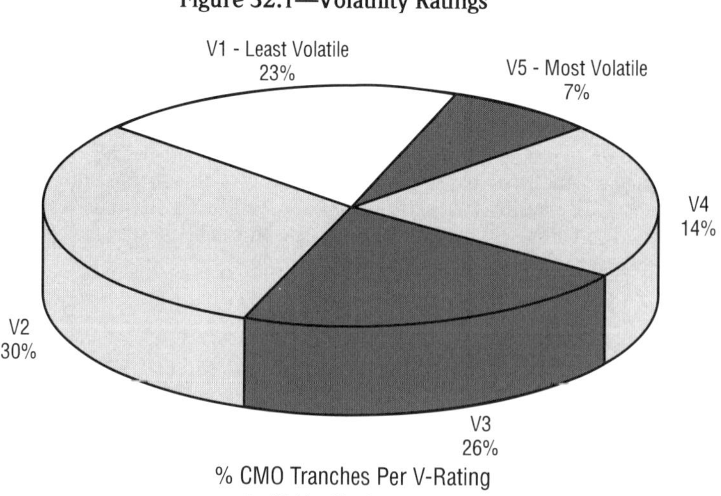

V-RATING DEFINITIONS

Fitch Indicated Volatility: Low to Moderate

Securities rated V1, V2, or V3 perform predictably over a range of various interest rate scenarios. On balance, total return, price, and cash flow indicators are less volatile than current coupon agency certificates.

V1 The security exhibits relatively small changes in total return, price, and cash flow in all modeled interest rate scenarios.

V2 The security exhibits relatively small changes in total return, price, and cash flow in most modeled interest rate scenarios. Under certain adverse interest rate scenarios, one or more of the indicators are more volatile than securities rated V1.

V3 The security exhibits relatively larger changes in total return, price, and cash flow in all modeled interest rate scenarios. However, on balance, total return, price, and cash flow indicators are less volatile than current coupon agency certificates.

Fitch Indicated Volatility: High

Securities rated V4 or V5 perform less predictably over a range of various interest rate scenarios. On balance, total return, price, and cash flow indicators are more volatile than current coupon agency certificates.

V4 The security exhibits greater changes in total return, price, and cash flow than current coupon agency certificates in all modeled interest rate scenarios. However, most indicators show less volatility than securities rated V5.

V5 The security exhibits substantial changes in total return, price, and cash flow in all modeled interest rate scenarios compared to current coupon agency certificates. Under the most stressful interest rate scenario tests, negative total returns may result.

---

of 1992, Fitch separated the components of its analysis to provide the following information within the framework of its V-Ratings standard. This includes:

- Indications of volatility by individual measures of total return, price, and duration.
- Identification of key contributing factors to individual tranche volatility, such as high coupon/low coupon, individual tranche prepayment collars, etc.
- An indication of the interest rate environments in which individual tranches show the greatest positive and negative performance potential.
- An indication of price volatility using option-adjusted spreads (OAS).
- A volatility rating on a CMO portfolio that analyzes the combined cash flows of individual tranches.

This portfolio analysis capability has been specifically requested by investors in mortgage bond funds and clearly is important to institutional investors given the limitations of individual tranche V-Ratings for portfolio analysis.

Please Note:

Volatility ratings are assigned to individual tranches only. CMOs of all tranche types across the V-Rating spectrum are purchased by institutional investors and are constructively used as part of institutional asset and liability management programs, hedging and/or duration matching programs. For institutional investors, quantifying a CMO portfolio by the percentage of individual tranches in any V-Rating category would not be a representative indicator of portfolio risk. Fitch is developing an analytical model to combine cash flows to provide a portfolio volatility rating for CMO funds, institutional investors, and their regulators.

THE MODEL

The Fitch CMO model (Figure 32.2) provides an independent assessment of the potential volatility of a CMO tranche. V-Ratings are derived by analyzing the relative performance of CMO tranches compared to the current coupon agency. Current coupon agency certificates are the median benchmark for all new issue ratings and consequently would carry a V3 rating. A series of analytical computer programs, including Global Advanced Technology Corp.'s Precision™ system, produce statistics on each CMO, which are reviewed by analysts to determine the final V-Rating. Investors can use the V-Rating as a summary of the major components of market risk on a scale that ranks a CMO relative to a known bench mark and to other CMOs. A V-Rating describes the potential rate of

Figure 33.2—Fitch CMO Model

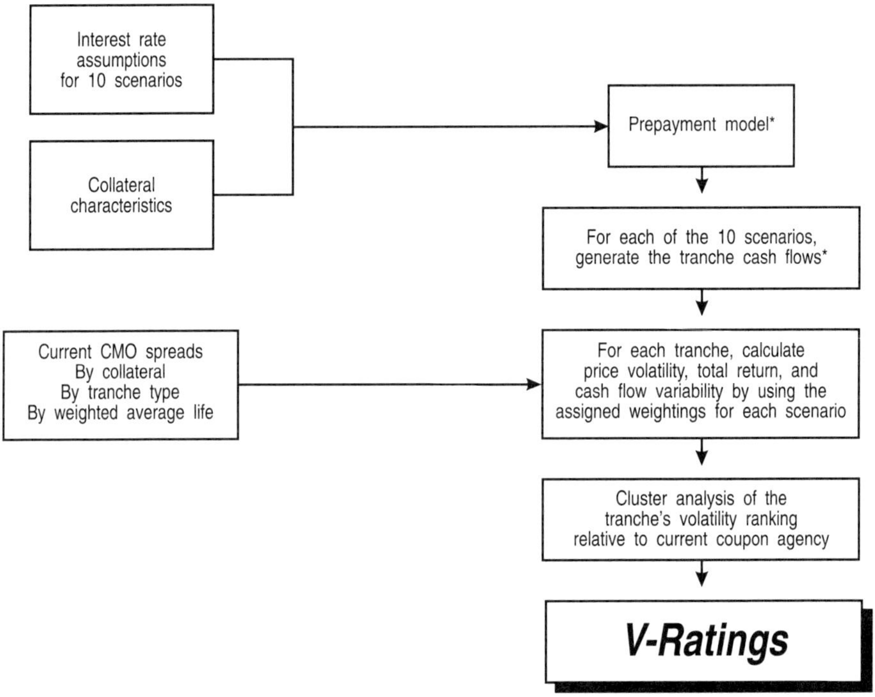

Interest rate assumptions for 10 scenarios

Collateral characteristics

Prepayment model*

For each of the 10 scenarios, generate the tranche cash flows*

Current CMO spreads
By collateral
By tranche type
By weighted average life

For each tranche, calculate price volatility, total return, and cash flow variability by using the assigned weightings for each scenario

Cluster analysis of the tranche's volatility ranking relative to current coupon agency

V-Ratings

* CMO cash flow and prepayment forecasts by Precision™ from Global Advanced Technology Corp.

change in price, total return, or cash flows if the investor were to encounter periods of increased interest rate volatility or prepayments.

Fitch prepayment rates used for analyzing outstanding deals have been compared to those of investment banking firms and are in an acceptable range of Wall Street estimates. In addition, CMO spread and price data used in the Fitch CMO model have been provided from three separate sources. More importantly, Fitch's model ranks relative performance in wide rating categories, mitigating the impact of small differences.

Fitch investigated over 20 different analytical indicators before deciding on the final volatility measures. The Fitch CMO model employs six independent views of volatility, which are calculated for each interest rate scenario. For each tranche, a change in total return and cash flows is calculated for each scenario and compared to results calculated if interest rates remain constant. Price changes are measured based on an instantaneous change in interest rates. The six volatility measures together were chosen because they provide an indicator of market risk if the investor must sell before maturity, reinvest for a longer horizon, or match cash flow liabilities.

The Fitch CMO model calculates the six volatility measures based on the weighted average of results from 10 different interest rate scenarios. Stress scenarios incorporate larger interest rate movements and are useful in discriminating among tranches that have different prepayment protection over widely varying prepayment speeds.

Cluster analysis is performed separating the changes in the six measures into rating groups. Cash flow variability is weighted approximately equal with changes in total return and price to arrive at the V-Rating.

FITCH SCENARIOS

The scenarios are best described in two broad categories: (1) Moderate and Historical Scenarios and (2) Stress Scenarios.

Moderate and Historical Scenarios

Scenarios 1 and 2 project interest rates moving up and down 100 basis points (bp), respectively, over the first two years and remaining at that level through maturity. Scenario 3 is based on relative interest rate changes that replicate the 1980-1981 period. Scenario 4 is based on the same period except the interest rate movements are the inverse of scenario 3. After the initial movements, which last two years, interest rates in scenarios 3 and 4 are constant through maturity.

Stress Scenarios

Scenarios 5–10 represent large movements in interest rates. In scenarios 5 and 6, interest rates move up and down 300 bp, respectively, over an 18-month period and remain at that level until maturity. Additionally, scenarios 5 and 6 were tested with initial interest rates 150 bp lower and 20 bp higher. Scenarios 7 and 8 have an instantaneous 300-bp change in rates, then constant through maturity. Scenarios 9 and 10 are whipsaw scenarios where rates fluctuate 200 bp up and down over two years, then remain constant until maturity.

VOLATILITY MEASUREMENTS

Unless specifically noted in the descriptions below, volatility measures were calculated from the weighted average result across 10 scenarios.

1. Change in Total Return

The change in total return of the CMO tranche is determined from its current expected return. The total return measure uses the largest decrease in weighted average expected total return from either the rising or falling interest rate scenarios. A single horizon of three years was used, enabling a uniform test across CMOs of all maturities. Using this measure, a significant decline in expected total return indicates a volatile CMO tranche.

2. Duration Change Relative to Current Collateral

The relative change in the modified duration of the tranche with respect to the modified duration change in a current coupon agency certificate is an indicator of cash flow variability. Using this measure, a CMO tranche is volatile if, relative to a current coupon agency certificate, its duration extends during rising interest rate scenarios, or shortens during falling interest rate scenarios. A current coupon agency certificate is a median-ranked security under this volatility measure.

3. Change in Effective Duration

Effective duration provides an indication of price sensitivity to changes in yield. The change in effective duration provides an indication of the price variability given potential changes in interest rates. A tranche with large negative convexity is considered more volatile than a tranche exhibiting positive convexity.

4. WAL Variability

The absolute change in the weighted average life (WAL) of the CMO tranche is a cash flow variability measure. This measure does not distinguish between extending and shortening the WAL. A large absolute change in WAL indicates a volatile CMO tranche.

5. Change in Hedge Ratio

The change in the ratio of the tranche's modified duration to the modified duration of a duration-matched Treasury is another indicator of cash flow variability. The hedge ratio measure designates as volatile those CMO tranches experiencing large cash flow variability compared to holding Treasuries of similar duration.

6. Percent Change in Price

The difference in the current price compared to the price determined by an instantaneous 300 bp increase or decrease in interest rates. Large declines in price of the CMO tranche indicate high volatility under this measure.

STABILITY TESTING

The stability of the ratings is important, therefore Fitch ran independent tests to assure the V-Ratings were consistent even under interest rate or prepayment conditions not modeled. The following additional tests (Tables 33.1, 33.2) were used to check the stability of the Fitch V-Rating under alternative interest rate scenarios.

The Fitch CMO model produces stable V-Ratings under all but extreme interest rate movements.

Table 32.1—Stability Tests

Event	*Result*
Nonparallel shift in the yield curve	Stable
Varying the investment horizon from one year to five years	Stable
Assumes only mild interest rate changes	Stable
Assumes only stress scenarios	Stable
Simulates two immediate, back-to-back stress tests	Approximately 15% of the ratings changed
Rating over passage of time	The ratings improve to higher rating classes due to duration drift

Table 32.2—FNMA Series 91-132

Volatility Rating	*Tranche ID*	*Type**	*Original WAL*	*Coupon*	*Original Amount ($000)*
V1	A	PAC	2.4	6.00	40,658
V1	B	PAC	2.4	12.00	40,658
V1	C	PAC	4.4	7.00	57,844
V2	D	PAC	5.9	8.00	42,457
V2	E	PAC	7.9	8.00	82,460
V4	W	PACZ	10.7	7.50	34,837
V4	X	PACZ	13.6	7.50	12,959
V3	G	PAC	15.9	7.50	20,422
V4	Z	PACZ	21.1	8.00	7,784
V4	H	PACIO	5.9	1,015.72	239
V4	J	PIOZ	11.7	1,018.77	71
V3	K	PIOZ	18.7	994.05	39
V5	L	TCIO	5.5	1,088.82	42
V1	M	TAC	1.5	7.00	27,981
V1	N	TAC	1.5	12.00	18,654
V3	F	FTAC	5.5	5.62	73,427
V5	S	IFTAC	5.5	20.72	17,278
V3	FA	FTAC	20.4	8.60	44,000
V4	SA	IFTAC	20.4	9.81	22,000

* PAC: Planned Amortization Class; PACZ: Planned Amortization Class Accrual Bond; PACIO: Planned Amortization Class Interest Only; PIOZ: Planned Amortization Class Interest Only Accrual Bond; TCIO: Targeted Class Interest Only; TAC: Targeted Amortization Class; FTAC: Floating Rate Targeted Amortization Class; IFTAC: Inverse Floating Rate Targeted Amortization Class.

Chapter 33

CMO Tranche Risk Revealed*

by James D. Nadler,
Managing Director, Volatility Ratings
and
Brandon H. Einhorn,
Senior Analyst
Fitch Investors Service, Inc.

SUMMARY

Each year, the growing collateralized mortgage obligation (CMO) market attracts new investors with its relatively high yield and AAA credit quality. At the same time, the payment structures of these securities are becoming increasingly complex. Unexpected changes in interest rates and mortgage prepayment rates can surprise investors by drastically affecting the amount and timing of cash flows. These changes impact total return and price, and complicate investment decision making. Fitch V-Ratings is the first analytical system that describes each tranche's relative volatility under various interest rate scenarios.

CMOs are sliced into tranches that receive principal and interest based on the priorities defined by the payment structure. Each tranche has unique characteristics appealing to different types of investors. Insurance companies and pension funds are concerned with changes in duration. Mutual funds and retail investors are generally most interested in total return. Banks want short-term, more liquid bonds. The various tranche labels are not sufficient for investors to determine which tranches meet their investment needs. V-Ratings provide an evaluation of cash flow, price, and total return variability, without regard to the tranche label.

Among the hundreds of CMOs issued last year are dozens of tranche types with names, symbols, and features unfamiliar to most investors. The following sections describe the most frequently issued tranche types and highlight their generic characteristics. The corresponding graphs provide an overview of volatility tendencies by tranche type, while pointing out the disparity in market risk between individual tranches of the same type. All buyers of individual tranches should use V-Ratings to measure tranche-specific volatility and not rely solely on the tranche label.

PAC: PLANNED AMORTIZATION CLASS

PACs are the most frequently issued tranches, accounting for 40 percent of outstanding tranches. PACs tend to have predictable returns and low volatility, factors that appeal to risk-averse investors. Yields tend to be lower than those of more risky tranches. PACs receive principal payments according to a planned schedule and perform predictably across a wide range of interest rates. As such, their total return, price, and cash flows are among the most stable. Average lives on most PACs range from two to 10 years. PAC stability is often supported by a companion bond, described later in this chapter, which provides call and extension protection. Highly rated PACs (V1 and V2) typically have shorter average lives, dampening price and duration volatility. PACs rated V3 and V4 typically have longer average lives, smaller companions, or narrow prepayment collars (Figure 33.1).

---

* The authors wish to acknowledge Byron D. Klapper; Robert E. Phelan, CFA; Glen Costello; and Henry Wilson who contributed to this Chapter.

Figure 33.1—PAC V-Rating Distribution

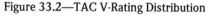

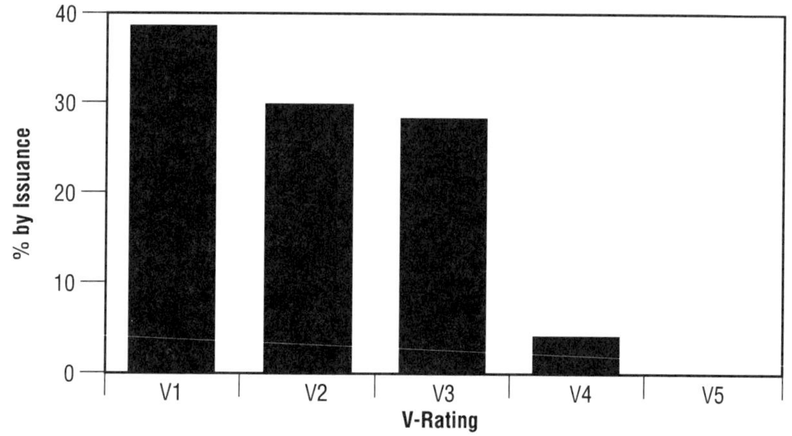

Advantages

- Cash flow stability.
- Stable total return.
- Price stability.

Disadvantages

- Lower yield.
- Protection depends on number and size of companion bond.

TAC: TARGETED AMORTIZATION CLASS

Like PACs, TACs are protected from falling interest rates and are popular with safety-oriented investors. Unlike PACs, they lack protection against delayed return of principal should rising interest rates slow mortgage prepayments. Volatility is low to moderate, with about 55 percent rated V1 and V2, and 30 percent V3. TACs account for 10 percent of newly issued tranches. TACs can provide a slightly better total return than PAC bonds, while still providing a high degree of safety. Highly rated TACs (V1 and V2) typically have shorter average lives, dampening price and duration volatility. TACs rated V3 and V4 typically have longer average lives, smaller companions, or narrow prepayment collars (Figure 33.2).

Advantages

- Cash flow stability.
- Stable total return.
- Higher yield than PACs.

Figure 33.2—TAC V-Rating Distribution

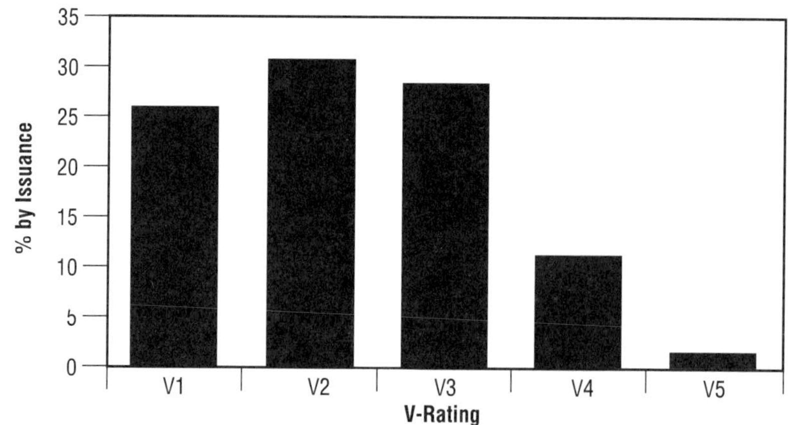

Figure 33.3—VADM V-Rating Distribution

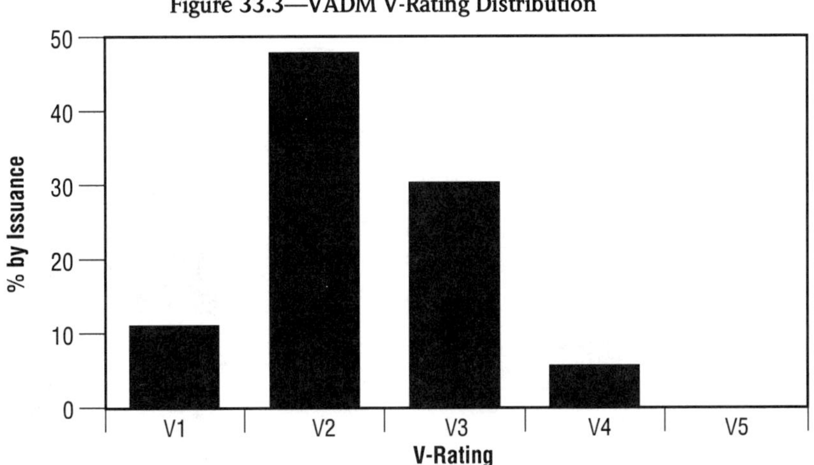

Disadvantages

- Susceptible to extension risk as prepayments slow.

VADM: VERY ACCURATELY DEFINED MATURITY

The precise maturity targets of this tranche appeal to investors seeking predictable returns on their investments. VADMs are protected from extreme interest rate movements. Volatility is moderate, with 90 percent of VADMs in the V1 to V3 range, 50 percent being rated V2. Buyers tend to be banks, pension funds, insurance companies, and individual retirement accounts seeking specific maturities. Highly rated VADMs (V1 and V2) typically have shorter average lives, dampening price and duration volatility. VADMs rated V3 and V4 typically have longer average lives, smaller companions, or narrow prepayment collars (Figure 33.3).

Advantages

- Cash flow stability.
- Stable total return.
- Predictable amortization schedule.

Disadvantages

- Lower yields.

COMPANION BONDS

Companion bonds are securities that support PACs, TACs, or other tranches with defined amortization schedules. When rates fall, companions provide stability to the other classes by absorbing excess principal payments. When interest rates rise, a companion bond's claims to principal payments are subordinated to the tranches it supports. Companions generally demonstrate moderate-to-high volatility, with a very small percentage having low volatility. Companion bonds rated V4 or V5 support a larger dollar amount of scheduled classes or support scheduled classes with wider prepayment collars (Figure 33.4).

Advantage

- Provide higher yields than bonds they support.

Disadvantages

- Cash flows and price are not predictable when interest rates fluctuate.
- Total return is more volatile due to prepayment option premiums inherent in yield.

PAY: SEQUENTIAL PAYMENT BONDS

Bonds in this group receive principal payments in sequence after an earlier tranche is retired. Unlike PACs, sequential payment bonds lack a predetermined schedule for amortization of principal. When rates fall, principal payments accelerate. When rates rise, principal payments to the tranche slow. Volatility is moderate, ranging from V2 to V4. Without an amortization schedule, PAY bonds have no internal resetting mechanism to stabilize prepayment rates during interest rate swings. Susceptibility to principal prepayments increases with

Figure 33.4—Companion V-Rating Distribution

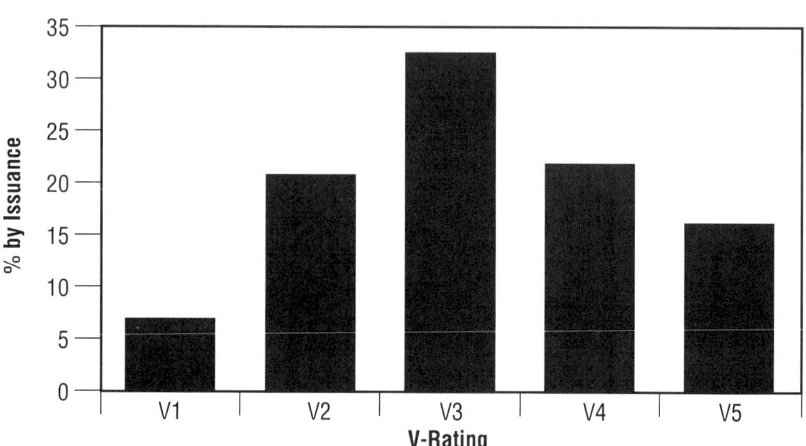

longer average life. For example, as interest rates rise dramatically, a PAY with a three-year weighted average life (WAL) can extend 1½ years, while a PAY with a 10-year WAL can extend 4½ years (Figure 33.5).

Advantages

- Because cash flow from the collateral is tranched, PAYs are available in a wide range of maturities.
- Perform well in stable interest rate environments.

Disadvantage

- Maturity and cash flow variability are susceptible to prepayment variations in fluctuating interest rate environments.

FLOATERS

Floaters are bonds with interest payments tied to an index, typically the London Interbank Offered Rate (LIBOR). Payments may be reset monthly or quarterly, depending on the tranche's structure. These are bound by a rate cap and floor. Price and total return on floater bonds tend to be more stable across interest rate scenarios. As a result, floaters have low-to-moderate volatility. About 80 percent of floaters are rated V1 or V2. Floating tranches are susceptible to variations in cash flow as prepayment rates change. Floaters rated V3 and V4 are more susceptible to the impact of prepayments on maturity (Figure 33.6).

Figure 33.5—PAY V-Rating Distribution

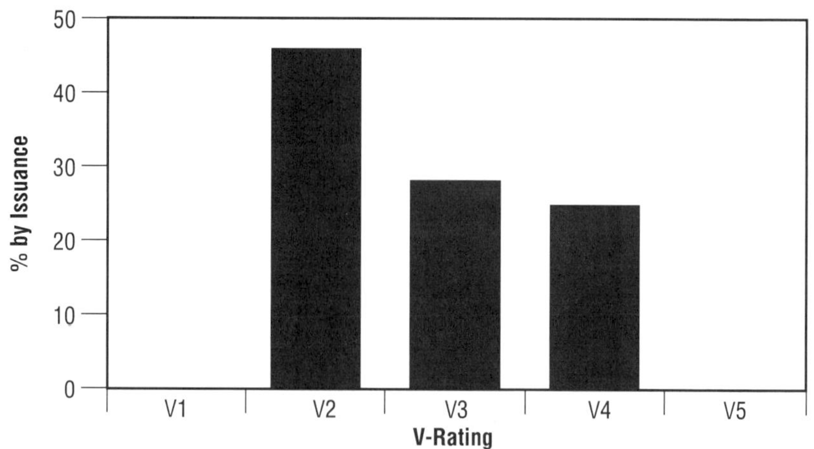

Figure 33.6—Floater V-Rating Distribution

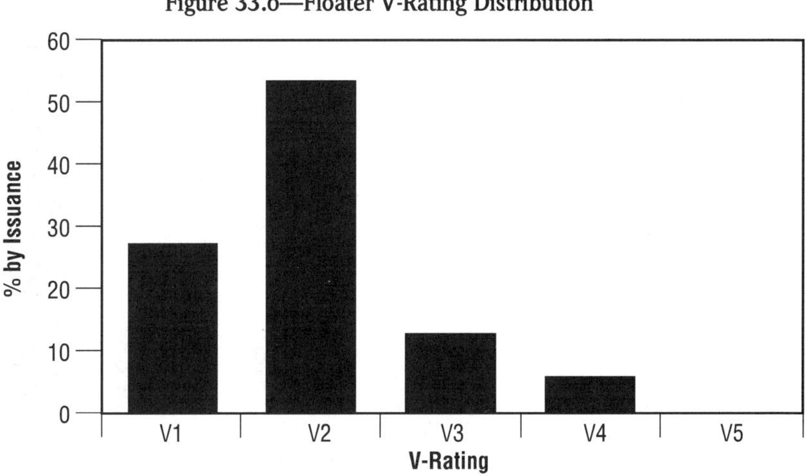

Advantages

- Stable total return.
- Price stability.

Disadvantage

- Lack cash flow stability as interest rates fluctuate.

IF: INVERSE FLOATERS

Inverse floaters are structured to offset floating-rate tranches described above. Interest payments on IFs vary inversely with an index, typically LIBOR. Because inverse floaters are more leveraged than other tranches, they have high price volatility as interest rates move. As the rate of the index drops, the interest rate on the IF rises at an accelerated pace. Conversely, rising rates cause an IF's interest payments to drop dramatically. Price and total return can be very unstable. In the worst case, rising rates will lower interest payments and extend return of principal beyond the expected time frame. Inverse floaters rated V5 have been structured to incorporate greater coupon leverage than those in higher V-Rating categories. IFs are suitable for the investor with a higher risk profile or a comprehensive hedging strategy (Figure 33.7).

Advantage

- Interest rate play for sophisticated investor.

Disadvantage

- Moderate interest rate changes can cause large changes in price and total return.

IO: INTEREST ONLY

These tranches only receive the interest portion of the cash flow. The principal cash flow is directed to other tranches in the structure. Since interest-only tranches have little or no principal, prepayments wipe out future cash flow. As prepayments accelerate in declining interest rate environments, investors could lose a portion of their initial investment. Conversely, investors benefit when rising rates extend interest payments beyond the targeted maturity. IOs exhibit "negative convexity" and are considered a bearish investment. IOs are predominantly rated in the V4 category, with about 20 percent rated V5 (Figure 33.8).

Advantage

- Typically a good hedge in rising interest rate environments.

Disadvantages

- Potential loss of original investment.
- Volatile total returns.

PO: PRINCIPAL ONLY

These tranches receive only the principal component of the cash flow; they receive no interest. POs have more cash flow volatility than IOs. POs are sold at a large discount from face value. Price volatility increases when rates rise, because the bulk of cash flows, normally received near maturity, are pushed further out as prepayments slow. POs perform best as interest rates fall. PO tranches are heavily influenced by maturity, with V1-rated

Figure 33.7—IF V-Rating Distribution

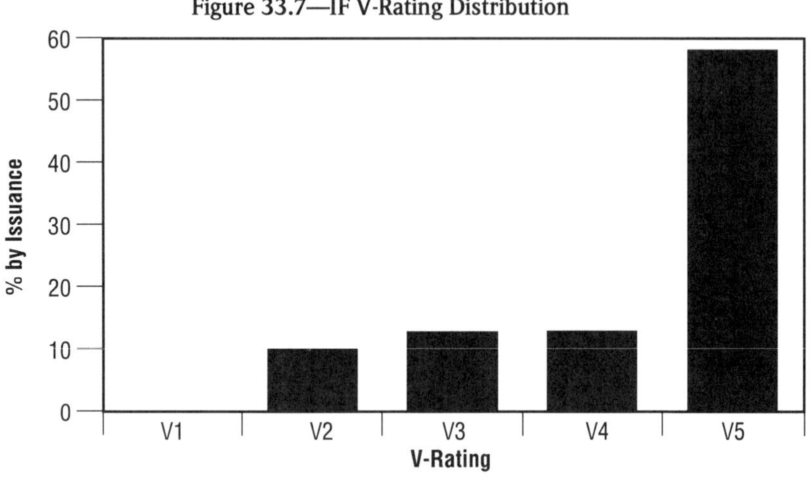

POs having short maturities and V4- and V5-rated POs having longer maturities, making them susceptible to greater price volatility (Figure 33.9).

Advantage

- Typically a good hedge in declining interest rate environments.

Disadvantages

- Total return fluctuates in rising interest rate environments.
- Longer maturities create greater price volatility in rising interest rate environments.

Z BONDS: ACCRETION BONDS

In general, Z bonds do not pay interest. Interest accretes, being added to principal, and is compounded through the accretion period, which can extend beyond 20 years. Thereafter, interest payments begin and continue through maturity. Z bonds have characteristics similar to zero coupon bonds. They stabilize other bond classes by absorbing excess principal payments. Thus, their accretion period may be shortened substantially, due to unpredictable cash flows. Average life, total return, and cash flows are subject to wide swings as interest rates rise or fall. Among variations of this

Figure 33.8—IO V-Rating Distribution

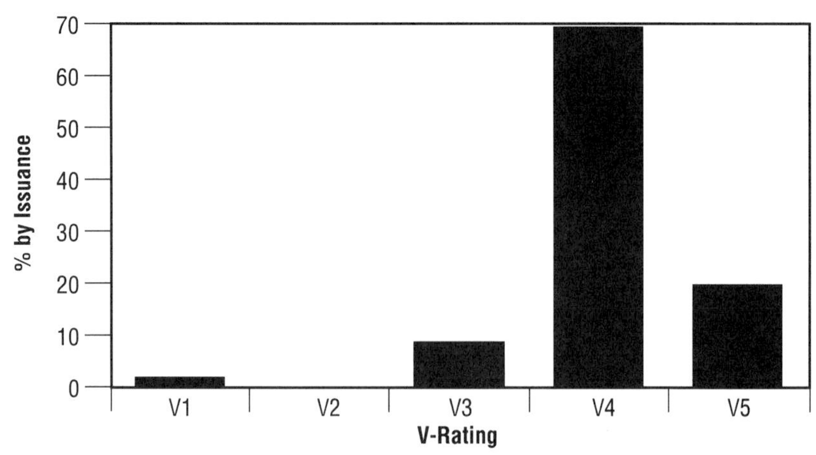

Figure 33.9—PO V-Rating Distribution

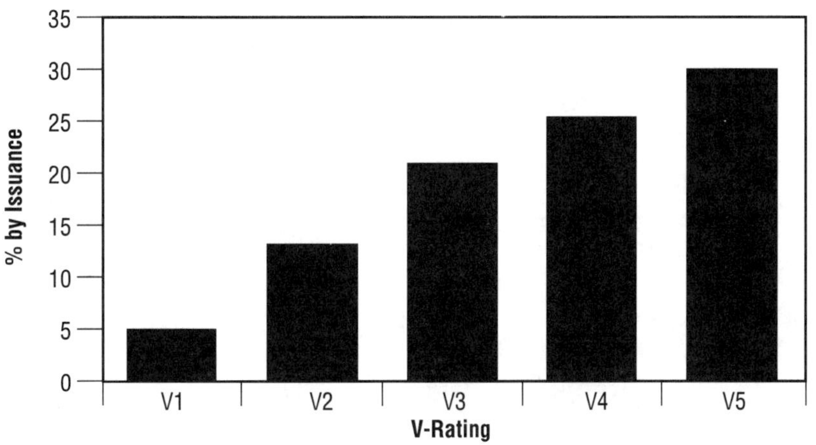

tranche type are Jump Zs, where payments can accelerate or recede based on prepayments, and Sticky Jump Zs, which become sequential pay bonds once triggered by accelerated prepayments. Scheduled or PAC Z bonds typically are rated V1 through V3, and support Z bonds typically are rated V4 and V5 (Figure 33.10).

Advantages

- If held to stated maturity, total return is higher.
- Interest compounds.

Disadvantages

- High cash flow volatility.
- Total return and price become volatile as interest rates fluctuate.

V-RATING DEFINITIONS

Fitch Indicated Volatility: Low to Moderate

Securities rated V1, V2, or V3 perform predictably over a range of various interest rate scenarios. On balance, total return, price, and cash flow indicators are less volatile than current coupon agency certificates.

V1 The security exhibits relatively small changes in total return, price, and cash flow in all modeled interest rate scenarios.

Figure 33.10—Z Bond V-Rating Distribution

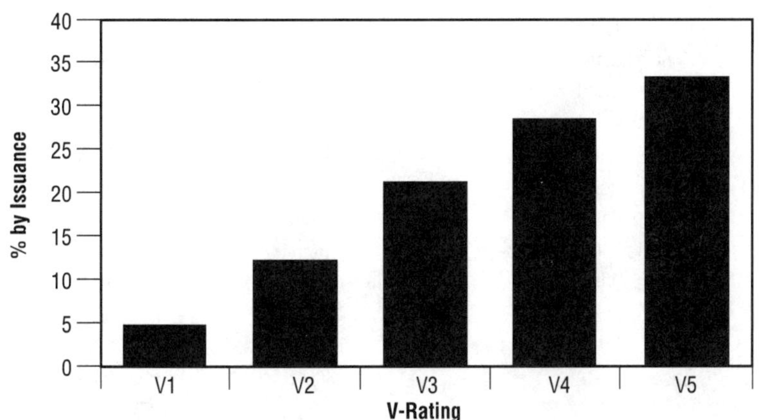

V2 The security exhibits relatively small changes in total return, price, and cash flow in most modeled interest rate scenarios. Under certain adverse interest rate scenarios, one or more of the indicators are more volatile than securities rated V1.

V3 The security exhibits relatively larger changes in total return, price, and cash flow in all modeled interest rate scenarios. However, on balance, total return, price, and cash flow indicators are less volatile than current coupon agency certificates.

Fitch Indicated Volatility: High

Securities rated V4 or V5 perform less predictably over a range of various interest rate scenarios. On balance, total return, price, and cash flow indicators are more volatile than current coupon agency certificates.

V4 The security exhibits greater changes in total return, price, and cash flow than current coupon agency certificates in all modeled interest rate scenarios. However, most indicators show less volatility than securities rated V5.

V5 The security exhibits substantial changes in total return, price, and cash flow in all modeled interest rate scenarios compared to current coupon agency certificates. Under the most stressful interest rate scenario tests, negative total returns may result.

Table 33.1—Common Tranche Types

Fitch analyzed more than 2,000 tranches issued in the last year. Among that group, some of the more common tranche types, ordered by relative par issuance, are:

Tranche Type	*Description*	*Agency Symbol*	*Number of Tranches*	*Relative Issuance ($000)*
PAC	PAC Bond	PAC	618	22,639,296
PAY	Sequential Pay Bonds	SEQ	141	8,312,723
COMP	Companion Bond	SUP	173	4,101,497
TAC	TAC Bond	TAC	81	3,843,376
SPAC	Secondary PAC	PAC	158	3,060,505
F	Floating-Rate Bond	FLT	33	2,567,600
CF	Companion Floater	FLT	51	1,908,458
VADM	Very Accurately Defined Maturity	VADM	105	1,402,357
PACZ	PAC Accrual Bond	PACZ	48	931,514
CIF	Companion Inverse Floater	INV	68	828,323
SF	Super Floater	FLT	18	791,324
STAC	Secondary TAC	TAC	25	735,419
PO	Principal-Only Bond	PO	30	569,557
LIQ	Liquidity Bond	LIQ	50	552,036
RTL	Retail Bond	L	15	517,256
Z	Accrual Bond	Z	24	496,768
COMBO	Combination Bond	SUP	10	310,034
IF	Inverse Floater	INV	31	301,441
PACPO	Principal-Only PAC	PO	12	221,552
PACIO	Interest-Only PAC	IO	118	69,862
IO	Interest-Only Bond	IO	65	17,250
TCIO	TAC IO Bond	IO	12	1,468
SPCIO	Secondary PAC IO	IO	20	979

Chapter 34

Optional Plays

by Donald R. Rindler,
Securities Sales and Trading Group, Freddie Mac

The roller coaster interest rate environment of the past few years has turned hedging the mortgage pipeline into a major challenge. Closings on loan commitments are increasingly sensitive to rate fluctuations. This sensitivity undermines a technique that would otherwise be the perfect hedging tool, forward sales of mortgage product, and exposes the lender to interest rate risk. Fortunately, a new hedge alternative has emerged to help lenders reduce this risk exposure: options on mortgage-related securities (MRSs). Mortgage lenders are tuning into the advantages this new instrument can provide. The popularity of MRS options has soared since their introduction in the early 1980s, boosting trading volume to over a billion dollars a day.

THE NEED FOR OPTIONS

If lenders could predict with certainty the percentage of loan applicants who would go to closing (the closing rate), hedging would be simple. Lenders could lock in a profit by selling forward—that is, by agreeing to deliver their mortgages or MRSs backed by those mortgages on a future date at a given price. In such a world, they need not worry about interest rate fluctuations between loan commitment and delivery—their interest rate risk would be fully hedged.

In the real world, interest rate volatility and borrower sensitivity to rates thwart lenders' hedging plans. When interest rates rise, borrowers tend to close more loans at a given commitment rate than lenders had expected. Consequently, forward sales tend to fall short of loan closings. The excess loans, now at below-market rates, can be sold only at lower prices. In periods of falling interest rates, the reverse happens. Borrowers abandon commitments and search for better rates elsewhere.

This pipeline fallout may force lenders to meet their forward sales commitments by purchasing loans (or more typically MRSs) bearing the required coupon at a premium over the forward sale price. In today's volatile rate environment, even lenders who take great care to hedge their pipelines with forward sales can experience considerable losses.

Over-the-counter (OTC) options on MRSs can help lenders hedge their interest rate risk. Options give the holder (the buyer) the right, but not the obligation, to buy or sell a security at a specified price on a specified date. In return, the holder pays the writer (the seller) a fee to compensate for assuming the risk of a price movement in the underlying security. Typically, mortgage lenders are the holders or buyers of options; investors are the writers or sellers. MRS options are over-the-counter because they represent two-party contracts between buyer and seller rather than standardized options traded on an exchange.

MRS options have two key advantages for mortgage lenders. First, options provide protection against interest rate volatility. In effect, lenders holding options to sell securities have bought insurance against rising interest rates. They are guaranteed the right to sell MRSs at a set price even if interest rates rise.

Second, MRS options can be tailored to each lender's unique needs. The OTC feature means that lenders can buy options that provide them with the greatest hedge effectiveness at the least cost. These features make options the optimal hedge for the portion of the mortgage pipeline that is sensitive to interest rates.

OPTIONS TRADING STRATEGIES

Although dealers offer many complex options strategies, mortgage lenders can stick to a few basic techniques that reduce risk at minimum cost.

The Long Put

The most straightforward strategy is for the lender to purchase the right, but not the obligation, to sell a security at a specific price (the strike price). This contract is known as a put. If security prices fall, the lender acts on the put, thereby selling the security at a higher price than is currently available in the secondary market. If security prices rise, the lender lets the option expire, forfeits the fee, and sells the product in the forward market. In general, lower security prices make the put profitable by enabling the lender to sell at an above-market price.

Figure 34.1 illustrates the relationship between the option's value and the forward security price on the expiration date. In this example, the option fee is 1 $^{16}/_{32}$ or 1.5 percent of the par amount. The strike price for the put is 99. If the market price is 99 on the expiration date, the lender is indifferent between exercising the put and letting the option expire. He loses the option premium whether he exercises the put or not, and the security price is the same either way.

At prices above 99, the lender will let the option expire. At any price below 99 on the expiration date, exercising the option will be beneficial because the lender sells above the current forward market price. That allows recovery of at least some of the fee. As the figure shows, at a price of $97^{16}/_{32}$ on the expiration date, the lender recoups all of the option premium. For prices below this level, the put becomes more profitable than an unhedged position.

There are several factors to consider in buying puts. The first is the settlement date. As they do for forward trading, lenders should analyze their loan pipelines to determine the expected date that the security can be delivered.

The second factor is the relationship between the expiration date and the settlement date. As a general rule, options are set to expire one or two weeks before the regular settlement date (as determined by the Public Securities Association each month) on the underlying security. Options markets are most liquid on those dates, which is to say that the difference between the bid and offer prices is narrowest. Lenders who purchase puts should set the expiration date as near to the option trade date, and as far from the settlement date, as their loan pipeline permits to minimize premiums paid on the options.

The third factor is the coupon on the underlying security. The best strategy is to trade options on securities in the coupon the lender is most likely to form. Lenders who issue less marketable securities, such as quarter-coupon or discount securities, may prefer to hedge their pipeline by buying puts on more liquid securities because option prices on these securities are cheaper. This is known as a "cross-hedge." Cross-hedging, however, is not without risk. A cross-hedger gambles that the price of the hedge instrument will move in tandem with the price of the hedged security.

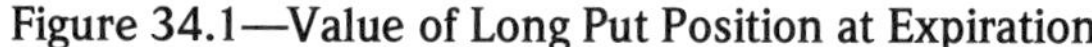

Figure 34.1—Value of Long Put Position at Expiration

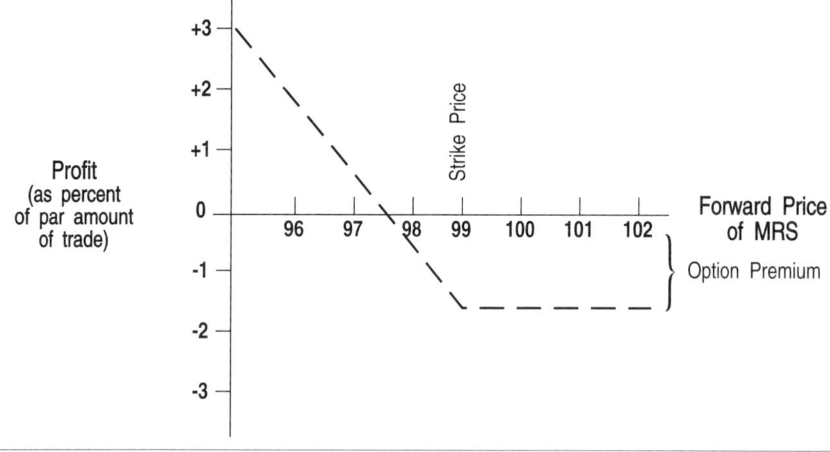

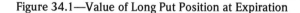

The final consideration is the relationship between the strike price and the forward market price of the underlying security. Those who buy puts granting the right to sell at the current forward market price (at-the-money puts) essentially have decided to buy insurance with no deductible. They pay a higher fee and assume little risk. Such a strategy is appropriate for lenders who expect interest rates to rise or whose pipeline is highly sensitive to interest rate movements. Those who buy puts that allow them to sell MRSs at a price lower than the current forward market price (out-of-the-money puts) want insurance with a deductible. They are willing to assume some risk on a decline in security prices in order to save on cash outlays.

The Split-Fee Option

Split-fee options are a variation on puts. They let a buyer pay a reservation fee upfront to receive a limited period for deciding whether to pay the remaining or "back" fee and turn the position into a put. In effect, the lender buys time, protecting himself against interest rate risk for less cash upfront than with a put option. In a bull market, split-fee options can often save money compared to puts. If forward market prices are higher on the window date (when the buyer must decide whether to pay the back fee), obtaining a put option at the same strike price may cost less than paying the back fee. In this case, the buyer can let the option expire on the window date and obtain a new OTC put option at lower cost.

Split-fee options have certain downside risks. When bond prices are generally declining, the front and back fees will cost the buyer more than an OTC put. Buyers of split-fee options may also fare worse than put buyers in a very volatile market. Buyers may exercise the front option on the window date only to find that the put expires worthless.

If bond prices decline continuously following the trade, the option holder will earn the difference between the exercise price on the option and the current market price, less the outlay on the front and back fees. If bond prices rise continuously after the trade, the option holder could limit losses to the front fee only.

Figure 34.2 illustrates the lender's choices where the current forward price is 99, the front fee is 24/32, and the back fee, 1 8/32 on a split-fee option. If the cost of a put at 99 on the window date is less than 1 8/32, the lender should let the option expire. He will forfeit the upfront fee, but should be able to obtain more favorable terms on another put option. If security prices decline after the trade date and the lender pays the back fee, his total outlay is 2 percent of the par amount. The lender will let the put expire if the forward market price on the expiration date is above 99; he will exercise the put at any price below 99. At any price below 97, exercising the option produces a profit relative to an unhedged position: the difference between the strike price and the current forward market price exceeds the 2 percent option premium.

Figure 34.2—Value of Long Split-Fee Option Position at Expiration

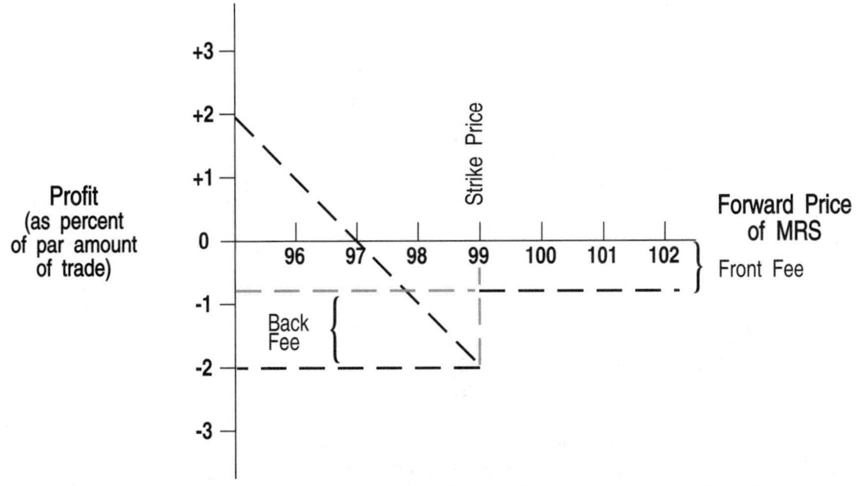

Figure 34.3—Value of Long Call and Short Forward Position at Expiration

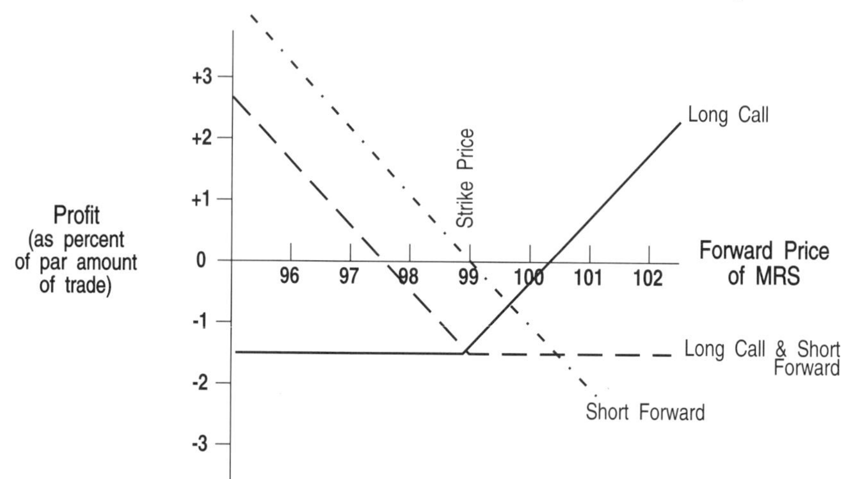

The buyer of split-fee options considers the same elements that the purchaser of puts does: the appropriate settlement date, final expiration date, the coupon on the underlying security, and the relationship between the strike price and the forward market price on the underlying security. The size of the front fee and the placement of the window date are also important. The lender should tailor these two variables as closely as possible to the characteristics of the underlying pipeline.

The Long Call

Occasionally, lenders will buy the right to purchase a security—a call option. This transaction generally occurs in conjunction with a previous forward sale of the underlying security. The purpose is to protect the lenders from pipeline fallout caused by a drop in interest rates.

A combination of a forward sell and a call buy is often termed a "synthetic put" because the profit/loss tradeoff is identical to that of buying a put (compare Figures 34.3 and 34.1). If market prices decline, the value of the forward sale increases; if market prices rise, the call allows the security to be repurchased just as borrowers fail to take down loans.

Pairoffs

If circumstances change, the mortgage lender may no longer need the interest rate protection obtained through options purchases. For instance, pipeline fallout may rise despite higher interest rates, eliminating the need for put options. In such cases, lenders may pair off their outstanding options trades. A lender that previously purchased puts may sell the identical option and obtain a fee from the buyer. A lender that bought a call on a put (split-fee option) may sell it. In this manner, lenders can close out the hedge and sometimes even realize profits on their outstanding options positions.

Valuing Options

Buying an option requires a cash outlay. Lenders want to make sure they get adequate return for their investment. Economists have identified three main factors that determine options value:

The Difference Between the Price of the Underlying Security and the Strike Price of the Option

Options derive value from the probability of their being exercised. An option that grants the right to buy or sell securities at a better price than the current market price is more likely to be exercised than one that is "struck" at a price that is worse than the current market price. Options are priced accordingly. Those that give the holder the right to buy or sell at better than market (in-the-money) cost more than options struck at the market price (at-the-money) or worse than market (out-of-the-money).

Volatility

An option's price varies with expected fluctuations in the price of the underlying security. High volatility increases the likelihood that the price of the

Table 34.1—Translating Options Talk

At-the-Money	An option that has a strike price equal to the forward price on the underlying security. If an option is at-the-money on the expiration date, the holder is indifferent between exercising and not exercising the option.
Back Fee	Fee paid by the split-fee buyer on the extension date if he exercises the front option.
Call Option	The right, but not the obligation, to buy the underlying security at a specified price on a specified future date.
Exercise	Action by option holder to require option writer to buy or sell securities.
Expiration Date	For "European" options, the only day that an option may be exercised; for "American" options, the last day that an option may be exercised. Also called notification date.
Extension Date	The date that the holder of a split-fee option must notify the writer of his intention to exercise his right to buy the underlying option. Also called window date or first expiration date.
Front Fee	Initial fee paid by the buyer of a split-fee option when the trade is executed.
Holder	Buyer of an option.
In-the-Money	An option with intrinsic value (see intrinsic value). If an option is in-the-money on the expiration date, the holder will want to exercise the option.
Intrinsic Value	The extent to which the option conveys the right to buy or sell the underlying security for a better price than the current market price. For a call: the security price is less than the strike price. For a put: the strike price is less than the security price.
Out-of-the-Money	An option with no intrinsic value (see intrinsic value). If an option is out-of-the-money on the expiration date, the holder will not want to exercise the option.
Premium	Fee paid by the buyer.
Put Option	The right, but not the obligation, to sell the underlying security at a specified price on a specified future date.
Settlement Date	Settlement date on the forward trade underlying the option.
Split-Fee Option	The right, but not the obligation, to buy an option (generally a put) for a specified premium on a specified future date. Also called a compound option, an extendable option, or a call on a put or call.
Strike Price	The price at which the option seller has agreed to buy or sell securities. Also called the exercise price.
Time Value	The difference between the market price of the option and its intrinsic value. At expiration, time value equals zero.
Underlying Security	The security that is bought or sold upon exercise of the option.
Writer	Seller of an option.

underlying security will move enough to precipitate exercise of the option. The seller of the option, therefore, demands a large premium to compensate for the risk.

Price volatility differs among securities. For example, MRSs trading above par tend to have more stable prices than those trading below par, making options on premium securities less costly than those on discount securities. Expected volatility also varies with market trends. When interest rates are stable, investors may not expect future prices to fluctuate much. A forecast of future volatility is crucial to determining the value of an option.

Time to Expiration

The price of an option is related to the number of days to expiration. Typical maturities for MRS options are 60 to 90 days, but terms as short as one week or as long as one year can be negotiated. The longer the term to expiration, the more likely it is that a major price fluctuation could increase an option's value. To compensate themselves for this risk, options writers demand higher premiums for longer terms.

The option premium increases with the time to expiration but at a decreasing rate. This means that doubling the term of the option less than doubles the cost. For example, a two-month option will generally cost less than 50 percent more than a one-month option. A three-month option is just over 20 percent more expensive than a two-month option.

PREPARING TO TRADE

Once lenders decide to integrate options into their hedging plans, they should prepare for the task.

Understand Trading Mortgage Pass-Throughs

An OTC option, if exercised, results in a forward trade of a mortgage pass-through security. A lender should thoroughly understand pass-through trading before trading options on these securities (see "Freddie's Travelogue to Trading," *Secondary Mortgage Market*, Winter 1986/87).

Obtain Authorization to Trade

Lenders often need the approval of their board of directors before trading in OTC options. Lenders should also investigate accounting, statutory, and regulatory requirements that must be met for certain types of institutions.

Set Up Dealer Relations

Many securities dealers that trade MRSs, including Freddie Mac's Securities Sales and Trading Group (SS&TG), also trade options on these instruments. But choosing a securities dealer for options trades requires particular care. The option buyer is entrusting an options premium with the dealer in exchange for a distant future commitment. Before automatically establishing an options account with its existing dealer, therefore, a lender should carefully review the dealer's integrity and capital.

Analyze the Pipeline

To maximize the effectiveness of the hedge for the smallest cash outlay, lenders should determine what their options needs are. For instance, loan commitments that have little chance of closing or whose probability of closing is unrelated to interest rate movements need not be hedged. At the other extreme, loans with a high probability of closing can be hedged effectively with forward sales. Options can be used to cover the residual portion of the pipeline for which loan closings are sensitive to interest rate fluctuations. For each group of loan commitments, the lender can best determine the likelihood of closing the loans by reviewing past experience and using professional judgment.

EXECUTING THE TRADE

As with forward trades, an option transaction begins with a phone call to a dealer (see "Trading Steps"). The customer provides the dealer with specifics of the trade: Is it a buy or sell? Is a put, a call, or a split-fee option involved? What is the type of security: PC, MBS, or Ginnie Mae? Is it a 15- or 30-year security? The trade amount? The security coupon? The settlement date? Thus far, the information is nearly identical to the information provided in a forward trade.

Options require several additional parameters. For puts and calls, the customer must also specify the expiration date and the strike price. The customer either states the desired strike price (for example, "98") or the desired relationship between the strike price and the forward market price on the underlying security (for example, "at-the-money").

For split-fee options, the customer must identify several other features: the first expiration date; either the front or the back fee; and whether the split-fee option is intended to resemble a put or a call (that is, a "call on a put" or a "call on a call").

EXERCISING THE OPTION

Most options on mortgage-related securities are written European style, which means that the buyer can exercise them only on the expiration date. On that morning, the buyer should carefully monitor the market to see whether exercising the option is desirable. The exact procedure varies from dealer to dealer, but generally the buyer must notify the seller by phone by a particular time of day, followed by written notification within 24 hours.

More mortgage lenders are entering the options market every day. Recent bouts with interest rate volatility have heightened their awareness of the need for more effective hedging tools, and lenders are finding that options serve that need. MRS options are a unique and valuable hedge for that portion of the mortgage pipeline which is sensitive to interest rate movements. They serve as insurance, protecting lenders against big losses in a volatile market at a comparatively low cost. Moreover, options are widely available. Many investment bankers act as dealers, as does Freddie Mac's SS&TG. In today's volatile markets, no mortgage lender can afford to exclude the options weapon from its hedge arsenal.

Table 34.2—Trading Steps

Following are the typical steps that precede and compose an options transaction. The parties involved in this example are a dealer from Freddie Mac's Securities Sales & Trading Group (SS&TG) and a mortgage lender.

Loan Side		*Hedge Side*
Lender gives borrowers commitments to provide mortgages at a rate that is fixed for 60 days.	Jan 1	
	Jan 15	Trade Date. Lender buys a split-fee option from SS&TG and pays the front fee.
	Feb 1	
	Feb 15	First Expiration Date. Lender decides whether to buy a put or to extend the split-fee option. Lender pays premium.
Lender closes on a portion of January loan commitments.	Mar 1	
Lender processes loan documents for delivery to Freddie Mac.	Mar 16	Final Expiration Date. Lender decides whether to exercise the put or to sell the security at the current forward market price.
Lender delivers loan documents to Freddie Mac.	Apr 1	
Freddie Mac processes loan documentation.		
Lender receives PC in exchange for loans.	Apr 20	Settlement Date. Lender delivers PC to fulfill its obligation on the forward sale.

Chapter 35

Strategic Options

by Donald R. Rindler
Securities Sales and Trading Group, Freddie Mac

Today's markets offer the investment manager a wide array of financial instruments, but finding the right combination of tools can be difficult. That is why a growing number of managers have turned to options. With options, investors can construct portfolios to meet a variety of investment objectives. Success requires a clear understanding of how to put an options strategy together.

For those portfolio managers with substantial investments in mortgage securities, over-the-counter (OTC) options on mortgage securities can be especially appropriate. An OTC option is a flexibly structured agreement between the portfolio manager and a securities dealer. Managers can employ these options for various objectives: to enhance current income, to hedge against interest rate volatility or a shift in rates, or to benefit from such rate movements.

WHY OPTIONS?

The first step on the road to trading OTC options is to acknowledge a simple truth: most investments already contain some form of embedded option. An option is simply the right, but not the obligation, to buy or sell a security at a specified price on a specified date. Securities that allow the issuer to buy back the bonds at a specified price on a specified date contain "call" options. Such call provisions are common on corporate debt, municipal securities, and even agency and Treasury issues. Another set of securities allows the investor to "put" the securities back to the issuer on a specified date, delivering the bonds to the issuer and receiving a specified price (often par) in return.

Mortgage securities also have embedded options. The mortgage borrower usually has the right, but not the obligation, to prepay the loan at any time; that is, the borrower has the right to call the loan from the lender. Thus, investors in securities that contain embedded options bear similar risks to those who sell options outright.

As the saying goes, we have been talking prose our entire lives without knowing it. In contrast, portfolio managers for thrifts, commercial banks, and mutual funds have knowingly been using options for years, without talking about it. As old prejudices fade, portfolio managers are beginning to make options an explicit component of their risk/return strategy.

Investment managers may use options for several purposes: to enhance income; to reduce risk; to benefit from market volatility or stability (volatility strategies); or to benefit from changes in the level of interest rates (directional strategies). Carefully structured options positions can produce risk/return profiles that are unavailable in the underlying securities, and can offset exposure in the rest of the portfolio.

STRATEGIES FOR CURRENT INCOME

For managers who expect interest rates to remain relatively stable, selling (writing) options—calls or puts—is a strategy for improving current income. However, these strategies do contain considerable risk if the market moves against the option writer.

Short Calls

The most common options trade by portfolio managers is selling calls. Call sellers agree to sell securities at a specified price on a specified future date, at the discretion of the option holder. In exchange for granting this right and assuming the risk that the security price will rise, the call seller receives a premium or fee.

If security prices remain stable or fall, the call expires unexercised and the call seller earns a profit equal to the fee received. If security prices

Figure 35.1—Value of Short Call Position at Expiration

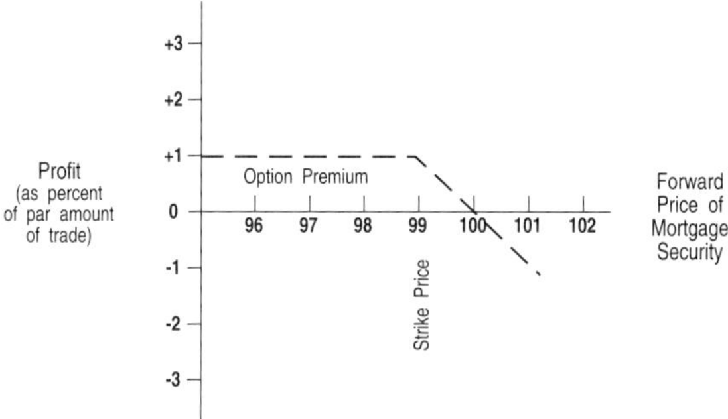

rise, the option holder will act, forcing the call writer to sell the security at a price which is now below market. The call seller's potential loss equals the amount by which the market price exceeds the strike price (the agreed-upon price), less the fee received.

Figure 35.1 illustrates the profit/loss characteristics of a short call option at expiration (the last date that the option can be exercised). In this example, the call seller receives a fee of 1 point, or 1 percent of the par amount, for a call option at a strike price of 99.

If the market price of the security is 99 at expiration, the call holder may or may not exercise the option, and the seller would be indifferent to that decision. If the option is exercised, the call seller must sell the security at 99, but can buy it back at the same price. At any price below 99, the call holder will not exercise the call. Thus, if the market price is at or below the strike price on the expiration date, the call seller earns profits equal to the option premium.

If the security price is above 99 but below 100, the call seller earns a profit on the trade even though the security is sold at 99, a below-market price. The premium received still exceeds the loss on the security. At market prices above 100, the call seller generates a loss.

Because the OTC market is flexible, call sellers can alter their risk/return profile in various ways. They can have their choice of underlying mortgage security, term-to-expiration, and strike price.

The call-selling strategy produces a fixed income in a stable or declining price environment but potentially unlimited losses in a rising price environment. Call selling is thus appropriate only for investors who can afford to absorb substantial risk.

Covered Calls

Generally, investment managers selling calls either have the security in portfolio or purchase it when the option agreement is made. Calls written on securities in portfolio are known as "covered" calls because gains on the underlying security will cover losses on the short call in a market rally. Calls written on securities not held in portfolio (for example, short calls) are known as "naked" calls.

Covered calls have a very different risk/return profile than naked calls, as Figure 35.2 illustrates.

Figure 35.2—Value of Covered Call Position at Expiration

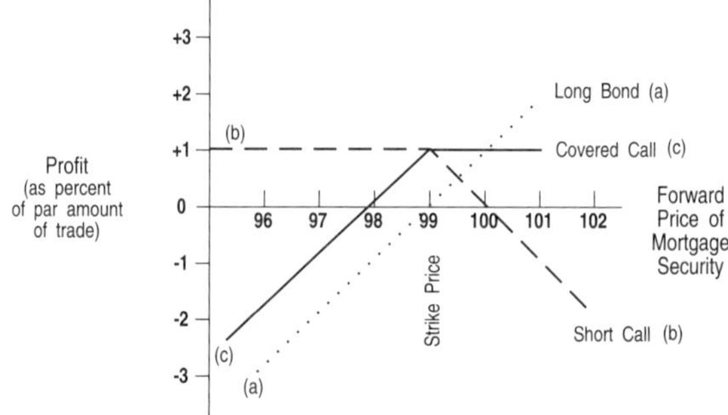

In this example, the investor buys a security at a price of 99 and simultaneously sells a call on that security at 99.

On the expiration date, the investor has profits and losses on the two positions. At a market price of 97, the loss on the long position in the underlying security is 2 points (see line (a)). The gain on the call is 1 point (see line (b), which duplicates Figure 35.1). The net loss is 1 point (see line (c)). At a market price of 101, the gain on the long position is 2 points and the loss on the short call is 1 point, giving a net profit of 1 point.

Covered call sellers can structure these options to suit their specific needs and expectations. For example, they might set the strike price above the current market price in order to reap some gains from a rising market. Also, by writing calls on just a portion of their portfolio, managers can reduce their exposure to a market rally.

The covered call strategy produces a fixed amount of income in a stable or rising price environment (bull market) but potentially large losses in a falling price environment (bear market). It is profitable in markets where naked call writing is unprofitable and vice versa. Covered call writing is considered a current income strategy because in stable markets the option fee enhances the coupon yield. It is appropriate for investors who want to sell long-term assets in a bull market.

Short Puts

Some portfolio managers use a strategy of selling puts. Put sellers agree to buy the security at a given price on a specified date, at the option of the put buyer. The option holder has the right to "put" the securities to them. For assuming the risk of price fluctuations, the put seller is paid a fee.

When security prices remain at or above the strike price of the security, the option remains unexercised, and put sellers earn a profit equal to the option fee. On the other hand, when the market price on the expiration date is below the strike price, the put buyer will exercise the option. The put seller's loss equals the difference between the strike price and the market price of the security at expiration, less the fee received.

The profit/loss profile of a short put position at expiration appears in Figure 35.3. In this example, the investor sells a put at 99 for a fee of 1 point. At a market price above 99, the put expires unexercised and the put seller pockets the premium. At a market price of 99, put sellers earn the same profit whether the put is exercised or not. They can sell any securities put to them at the same price. At prices between 98 and 99, put sellers earn a net profit equal to the fee received less the loss on disposing of the security. At any price below 98, the put seller incurs a loss.

The profit/loss profile for short put positions is identical to the profit/loss profile for covered call positions (compare Figures 35.2 and 35.3). For this reason, covered call positions are sometimes called "synthetic puts." Short put positions are appropriate for investors who can afford to add securities to their portfolios in a bear market. The fee income helps to reduce the cost of the purchase.

HEDGE STRATEGIES

Investment managers sometimes use the OTC options market for mortgage securities as a hedge vehicle. For example, they may buy put options. (See Chapter 34 for a more complete discussion of hedging strategies.) These long puts can protect them from losses if interest rates rise.

Buying puts may also provide valuable protection for portfolios that are hedged against small interest rate changes, but that would incur losses if rates move substantially. To protect against extreme market moves, some fund managers buy puts with strike prices below the current market

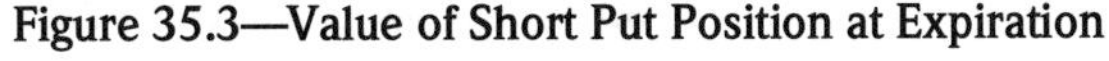

Figure 35.3—Value of Short Put Position at Expiration

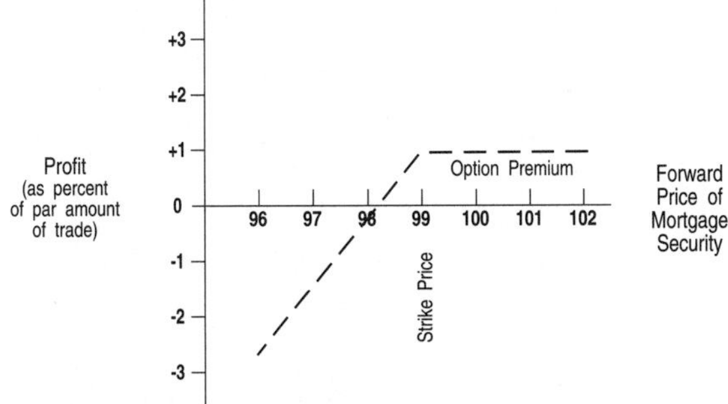

price (out-of-the-money) on a small portion of their portfolios.

Similarly, portfolio managers sometimes buy calls as a portfolio hedge. For example, long calls can hedge current-coupon mortgage portfolios financed with long-term debt. If interest rates fall, prepayments may accelerate, leaving the investor with too few long-term assets. The securities obtained by exercising the call can restore the balance between long-term assets and liabilities.

VOLATILITY STRATEGIES

In some recent periods, interest rates have been extremely volatile, swinging widely within a short time span. At other times, rates have remained quite stable for extended periods.

Volatility strategies try to take advantage of expected volatility or stability in interest rates. A volatility strategy implies a point of view about *how much* interest rates will change, but not about whether the move will be up or down. In fact, holders of mortgage securities use volatility strategies all the time—financing an investment in mortgage securities with long-term borrowings implicitly reflects a market view that rates will remain stable. A volatility strategy, like other options strategies, should be viewed within the context of the overall portfolio: profits or losses from the strategy can offset losses and gains in the rest of the portfolio, reducing the firm's exposure to market fluctuations.

Straddles

A straddle is the simultaneous purchase or sale of both a put and a call on a security, at the same strike price for the same expiration date. The term "straddle" refers to the fact that the strike prices sit astride the market price.

A long straddle protects the investor against increased volatility in market prices. The portfolio manager buys both a put and a call at the same strike price and earns a profit if the market price at expiration differs from the strike price by more than the sum of the put and call premiums paid. Assume, for example, that an investor buys a put and a call at a strike price of 99 for fees of 1 point each, or 2 points in total (see Figure 35.4). If the market price at expiration is either below 97 or above 101, the profit from exercising the put or the call exceeds the option fee paid. Between prices of 97 and 101, the long straddle position incurs only a limited loss. For extreme market moves, by contrast, straddle buyers can rack up extraordinary gains. Because mortgage securities often suffer dramatic losses when volatility increases, hedging a mortgage security portfolio with a long straddle may be a sensible strategy when more volatility is expected.

The short straddle position is the inverse of the long straddle (see Figure 35.4). With a short straddle, the investor sells both a put and a call on a security at the same strike price, and receives fees on each. The straddle seller earns a profit when the difference between the market price at expiration and the strike price is less than the sum of the options fees received. Straddle sellers exchange limited profits in stable markets for potentially large losses in volatile markets. A short straddle may be a suitable current income strategy if low volatility is expected.

Strangles

A strangle, like a straddle, represents the simultaneous purchase or sale of puts and calls for the same expiration date. However, with a strangle, both options are struck out-of-the-money: that is, the put has a strike price below the current market price and the call has a strike price above the

Figure 35.4—Value of Straddle Positions at Expiration

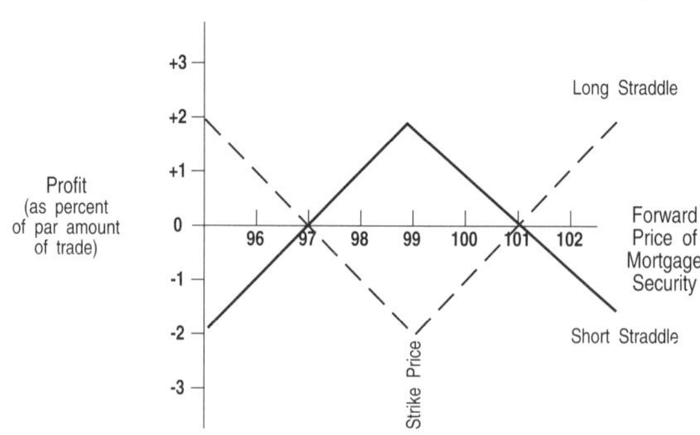

Figure 35.5—Value of Strangle Positions at Expiration

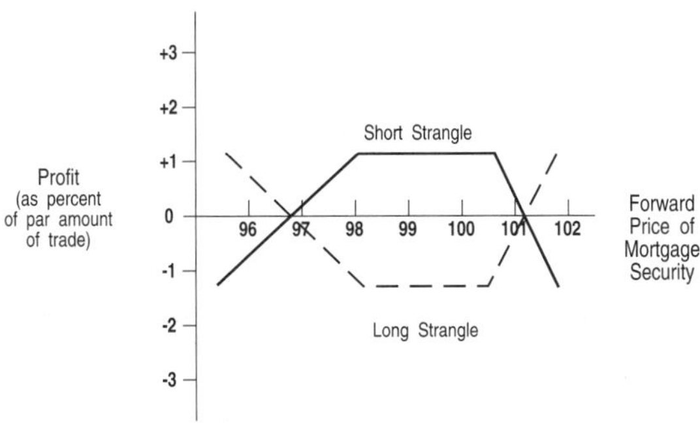

current market price. Because their strike prices are out-of-the-money, strangle buyers pay lower fees than do straddle buyers, but market prices must change more before they earn a profit. The trades are called "strangles" because the out-of-the-money strikes resemble a noose around the option seller that tightens when the market is volatile.

Figure 35.5 shows profits and losses from a strangle position. In this example, the put is struck at 98 for a fee of $^{20}/_{32}$, and the call is struck at 100 for a fee of $^{18}/_{32}$. The total outlay is $1^{6}/_{32}$, less than the straddle fees shown in Figure 35.4. The breakeven points are $96^{26}/_{32}$ and $101^{6}/_{32}$, somewhat outside the breakeven points for straddles. Like straddle users, strangle buyers expect volatile rates while sellers expect more stable markets. But strangle users are typically less confident about their expectations.

DIRECTIONAL STRATEGIES

Portfolio managers can use options trades to benefit from expectations that rates will move in a particular direction. Income strategies such as short calls, covered calls, and short puts all have a directional bias, producing a positive return only in certain interest rate environments. But options positions also can be combined to produce directional strategies with other risk/return profiles. Possible combinations include vertical, horizontal, and diagonal spreads. These strategies take their names from the way in which options quotations

Table 35.1—SS&TG Options Quotations
January 1, 19xx
(in points—32nds)

	Calls			*Puts*		
	Expiration Date			*Expiration Date*		
Strike Price	*Feb.*	*Mar.*	*Apr.*	*Feb.*	*Mar.*	*Apr.*
100	0-05	0-10	0-14	1-05	1-16	1-27
99	0-18	0-22	0-24	0-18	0-30	1-09
98	1-06	1-08	1-14	0-07	0-18	0-29

■ Vertical Spread ▨ Diagonal Spread □ Horizontal Spread

Vertical Spread – same expiration date, different strike prices
Horizontal Spread – different expiration dates, same strike price
Diagonal Spread – different expiration dates, different strike prices

for differing strike prices and expiration dates are sometimes presented in tabular format (see Table 35.1).

Vertical Spreads

Vertical spreads, also called price spreads, involve simultaneously buying and selling the same class of option (put or call) on the same security for the same expiration date but at different strike prices.

An example of a vertical spread is selling calls at the current forward market price (at-the-money) and buying calls at a strike price above the market (out-of-the-money). The fee received exceeds the fee paid, resulting in a small net cash inflow.

Like a short call position, this vertical spread trade is designed to be profitable in a stable or declining price environment and unprofitable when prices rise. However, because the trade also contains a long call position, the potential losses on a vertical spread from rising prices are capped. This particular spread trade benefits from declining prices, so it is called a "bear vertical spread."

Consider an investor who sells calls struck at 99 for 1 point and buys calls struck at 100 for $^{16}/_{32}$, resulting in a net inflow of $^{16}/_{32}$. Figure 35.6 shows the profit/loss profile of this vertical spread trade at expiration. The trade is profitable if the market price remains below $99^{16}/_{32}$. However, as the price rises above 99, the profit declines because the call at 99 will be exercised. If prices rise above 100, both calls will be exercised: the investor must sell the security at 99 but will exercise his call and buy the same security at 100. This 1 point loss is partially offset by the difference between fee income received and paid, so that the maximum loss is $^{16}/_{32}$ regardless of how high prices rise. The maximum gain is also $^{16}/_{32}$.

Vertical spread trades can be constructed using either puts or calls, to benefit from either bull or bear markets. They are used by portfolio managers who want to pursue a current income strategy, but who are less confident of their market expectations than are users of short calls or puts. Vertical spread trades can produce only limited profits, but they also limit the risks.

Horizontal Spreads

Horizontal or time spreads involve simultaneously buying and selling the same class of option (put or call) at the same strike price for different expiration dates (see Table 35.1). For example, on January 1, an investor may sell an at-the-money put for February expiration and buy an at-the-money put for March expiration.

Horizontal spread trades can be structured with various risk/return profiles, but they all have one thing in common: limited losses and gains. While both horizontal and vertical spreads produce limited gains and losses, horizontal spreads also require the investor to pair off (get rid of) the unexpired option when the first option expires, in order to lock in profits. The resulting high ratio of transactions costs to profits discourages most investors from entering into horizontal spread trades. Horizontal spread trades provide benefits to portfolio managers with highly specific risk/return objectives.

Diagonal Spreads

A diagonal spread is a cross between a vertical spread and a horizontal spread. The investor simultaneously purchases and sells either puts or calls on the same security for both different strike prices and different expiration dates (see Table 35.1). For instance, on January 1, an investor buys an at-the-money call for February expiration and sells a 1 point out-of-the-money call for March expiration.

Figure 35.6—Value of Vertical Spread Position at Expiration

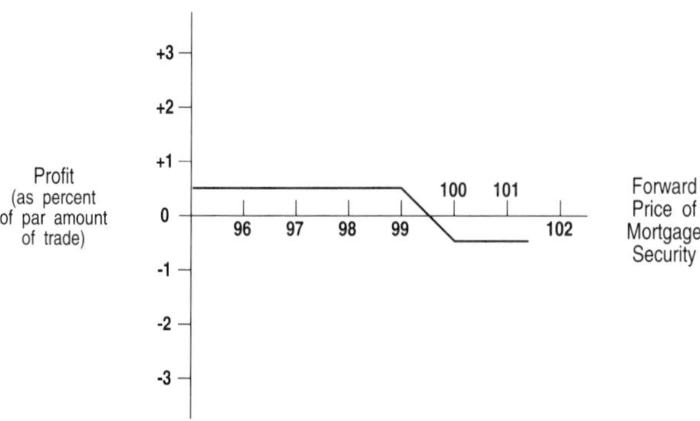

A variety of diagonal spread positions can be constructed for different desired risk/return characteristics and directional biases. For example, the investor can use puts instead of calls, set the strike price on the purchased option above that on the sold option, or sell rather than buy the option expiring first. In all, eight types of diagonal spread trades are possible.

Like horizontal spreads, diagonal spreads can produce only limited gains or losses, and require the investor to pair off the far option when the near option expires to avoid continued exposure. This can mean high transactions costs relative to possible profits.

TAKING ACTION

Investors should not make the decision to employ options strategies lightly. Selecting appropriate strategies and preparing for trading can be major tasks.

Understand the Existing Portfolio

Options strategies are most effective when undertaken within the context of the total portfolio. Investors must not only have specific objectives in mind (enhancing income, controlling interest rate risk) before selecting an options strategy; they must also know how their portfolio's value behaves under various interest rate scenarios. Knowing the risk/return characteristics of the existing portfolio is essential before using options to achieve investment objectives.

Obtain Authorization to Trade

Portfolio managers often need approval from higher management, the board of directors, or even shareholders before entering into options trades. This conservative approach is reasonable because certain types of options contain the potential for significant losses. Before they can obtain authorization, portfolio managers usually must demonstrate a thorough knowledge of how options strategies can help to attain investment goals.

Check Statutory, Regulatory, and Accounting Constraints

Short options transactions can expose firms to unlimited losses; long options positions allow them to leverage a small investment into a large securities position. These risks have led legislators and regulators to scrutinize options transactions. The resulting controls on options activity differ by industry among the various statutory and regulatory authorities. Options transactions also receive varying accounting treatments. Investors should examine applicable statutes, regulations, and accounting conventions before entering into options trades.

Set Up Dealer Relationships

A variety of dealers that trade mortgage securities, including Freddie Mac's own Securities Sales and Trading Group (SS&TG), also trade OTC options on these instruments. Portfolio managers who intend to buy options or to pair off (sell back) options previously written must exercise particular care in selecting trading partners. In the OTC market, there are no performance guarantees to protect the investor from default by the option seller. Integrity, experience, and resources are a must.

Monitor Positions

After executing options trades, investors should monitor positions periodically to see whether the positions are still meeting their investment objectives. In many instances, managers find it desirable to close out trades before the originally intended date either because profit objectives have been achieved or in order to limit losses on an unsuccessful trade.

Options on mortgage securities present portfolio managers with a wide range of new opportunities. They provide new ways to enhance return and to manage risk that are not available through investment in the underlying securities. In today's investment market, no contender can afford to overlook an instrument that may furnish the margin of success.

Chapter 36

Risk, Return, and Hedging of Fixed-Rate Mortgages

by Douglas T. Breeden,
Research Professor of Finance,
Fuqua School of Business, Duke University
and
Chairman of the Board,
Smith Breeden Associates

Mortgages comprise 31% of the U.S. credit market outstanding, compared to only 21% in U.S. Treasury and agency securities and 13% in corporate bonds. Bank loans, municipal bonds, and consumer credit each represent only 7% of the credit market. In recent years, the supply of new mortgage securities has been more than twice the supply of new corporate bonds issued. The mortgage market today is one of the most liquid markets in the world, despite the fact that only about one-third of total residential mortgages have been securitized (as of 1989).

Such observations demonstrate the importance of understanding the risks and returns of mortgage securities. Because many savings and loans have failed for lack of risk management of mortgage portfolios, it is also important to understand the hedging of mortgage securities. Hedging allows banking institutions to take risks they would otherwise consider unacceptable and pass those risks to other market participants who specialize in taking them.

The risk, return, and hedging aspects of mortgages are more complicated than for most fixed-income securities, because mortgages give the borrower the option to prepay the loan at par at any time during the life of the loan. While our understanding of risk, return, pricing, and hedging of securities with options has been propelled by the seminal work of Black and Scholes [1973] and the literature that has built upon that work, mortgages are much more complicated option-like securities than those dealt with by Black and Scholes.

Black and Scholes assume, for example, 1) that interest rates are constant, 2) that the option is "European" in that it could be exercised only on the final maturity date, 3) that the exercise price is known and fixed, and 4) that the returns on the underlying asset are normally distributed. Of course, the volatility of interest rates is the reason the prepayment option in a mortgage has value and is of interest. Furthermore, it may well be optimal for different people to exercise their prepayment options at different times, particularly as they have different effective costs of exercising their options. Finally, the underlying asset for the prepayment option is a bond, which certainly does not have normally distributed returns.

In this article, mortgages are viewed as far too complicated to value precisely and rigorously, even with the Black-Scholes model and the many improvements developed in the eighteen subsequent years. Given this view, my goal here is limited and data-oriented.

Data on interest rates, prepayment rates, and mortgage prices are used to develop risk and return properties and hedging methods that reflect the information in market prices. Assuming that market prices reflect the information of well-informed investors, mortgage prices for different coupons should reflect some of the most up-to-date values and models of the complicated prepayment options. The article uses both the cross section of mortgage prices by coupon and the time series of prices and prepayment rates to develop risk and return estimates and hedging strategies. It is shown that many of the risk functions inferred empirically do have characteristics that would be expected from the option pricing theory of Black and Scholes.

The flow of the paper is as follows. Section I examines mortgage payments and the prepayment option. Section II examines historical interest rate volatility and the yield spread between mortgages and Treasuries. Section III analyzes mortgage prepayment rates and the factors that move them. Section IV examines historical mortgage prices and their sensitivity to bond prices. Section V examines the market's implicit price elasticities or "effective durations" for different mortgage coupons and relates them to mortgage price volatility. Section VI develops effective dynamic hedging strategies for mortgages. Section VII presents data series on monthly rates of return for different mortgage coupons and summary statistics of risk and return for them. Section VIII summarizes the paper's principal results.

I. MORTGAGE PAYMENTS AND THE PREPAYMENT OPTION

Consider a borrower who takes out a standard thirty-year fixed-rate mortgage for $100,000 to buy a house worth $125,000. One can calculate that the mortgage must have level monthly payments of $952.32 to amortize the loan and reflect an annual interest rate of 11%, compounded monthly.

As this is a fixed-rate, fixed-payment loan, if market rates increase to 12%, the present value of the borrower's fixed payments declines to $92,583. A smaller debt is good for the borrower, which reflects the now below-market rate of 11%. On the other hand, if rates decrease to 10%, the present value of the borrower's payments increases to $108,518, reflecting the fact that the borrower's loan is now above the current market rate.

Table 36.1 shows the entire schedule of payments and their present values for three different mortgages with 9%, 11%, and 13% rates, discounted at current market rates from 7% to 18%.

A typical fixed-rate mortgage provides the borrower with the option to pay off the mortgage at the unpaid outstanding balance ($100,000 initially), usually with no prepayment penalty. Continuing with the 11% fixed-rate mortgage example, if rates decrease to 10%, the borrower's same monthly payments would amortize a new loan for $108,518, which could be obtained from another bank to pay off the old loan. By prepaying, the borrower pockets $8,518 in present value (8.52 "points" or % of par), less any refinancing costs not included in the rate (usually assumed to be two to five points).

The gross amounts of the refinancing gains from prepaying mortgages with 9%, 11%, and 13% coupons are also in Table 36.1. Note that the gains from refinancing and prepayment can be quite large; a 13% mortgage refinanced at 9%, for example, results in a $37,481 gain per $100,000 of loan balance, less refinancing costs.

Looking at the column labeled "Prepayment Profits" for the 11% mortgage, one can see that they are equal to a call option on the present value of the mortgage's fixed cash flows without prepayments, with an exercise price of par. The call option is "in the money" if rates have fallen below the fixed mortgage rate, and many models assume that the mortgage will be refinanced and prepaid. Thus, in theory, whenever the current market mortgage rate is below the fixed coupon rate (or far enough below to offset refinancing costs), the bank or mortgage investor will be paid off and receive $100,000 (or 100% par). If rates have risen above the mortgage's fixed rate, then the borrower is assumed to keep the mortgage outstanding, resulting in values below par for the bank or mortgage investor.

Thus, from the mortgage investor's point of view, the prepayment option is "heads (rate up) I lose, as my bond falls in value," and "tails (rates down) I don't win, as the mortgage is prepaid at par." This asymmetric situation (called "negative convexity" from its payoff graph's curvature) is not attractive unless there is compensation for this option risk. Insured mortgage investors are compensated in fact by a positive spread of about 1.25% above Treasury rates of comparable duration.

A mortgage investor's theoretical payoff pattern is shown in Figures 36.1 and 36.2. The investor's profits are identical to buying a straight long-term, fixed-rate bond that cannot be prepaid (which has interest rate risk) and shorting a call option on that bond to the borrower. Alternatively, and equivalently through the "put and call parity" relationship, the investor's position has the risk of investing in riskless short-term Treasury bills and having written a put option on the long-term, fixed-rate bond having the level payments promised on the mortgage. If rates decrease, the investor receives a certain amount (called at par), while if rates increase, the mortgage remains outstanding (put to the investor) at a loss in market value.

The values of prepayment options on mortgages with different coupons are very similar to Treasury bond options with different exercise prices (see Table 36.1). For example, the prepayment option on a 9%, thirty-year mortgage has

Table 36.1—Value of the Option to Prepay a $100,000 Mortgage

			Borrower's Fixed Mortgage Rate								
			9.00%			11.00%			13.00%		
Monthly Loan Payment			$804.62			$952.32			$1,106.20		
Current Mortgage Rate (%)	20-year T-Bond Yield (%)	T-Bond Futures Price	PV (Payment)	Prepayment Profit	T-Bond Call X = 105.14 Q = 0.84	PV (Payment)	Prepayment Profit	T-Bond Call X = 86.68 Q = 0.99	PV (Payment)	Prepayment Profit	T-Bond Call X = 72.82 Q = 1.16
7.00	5.50	130.10	120,941	20.94	20.94	143,141	43.14	43.14	166,270	66.27	66.27
8.00	6.50	116.66	109,657	9.66	9.66	129,786	29.79	29.79	150,757	50.76	50.72
9.00	7.50	105.14	100,000	0.00	0.00	118,357	18.36	18.34	137,481	37.48	37.39
10.00	8.50	95.23	91,687	0.00	0.00	108,518	8.52	8.50	126,052	26.05	25.93
11.00	9.50	86.68	84,490	0.00	0.00	100,000	0.00	0.00	116,158	16.16	16.03
12.00	10.50	79.27	78,224	0.00	0.00	92,583	0.00	0.00	107,543	7.54	7.46
13.00	11.50	72.82	72,738	0.00	0.00	86,090	0.00	0.00	100,000	0.00	0.00
14.00	12.50	67.19	67,908	0.00	0.00	80,374	0.00	0.00	93,360	0.00	0.00
15.00	13.50	62.25	63,634	0.00	0.00	75,316	0.00	0.00	87,485	0.00	0.00
16.00	14.50	57.90	59,834	0.00	0.00	70,818	0.00	0.00	82,260	0.00	0.00

Notes: X = Exercise Price.
Q = Quantity of Call Options Purchased.

Figure 36.1—Mortgage = Bond – Call Option

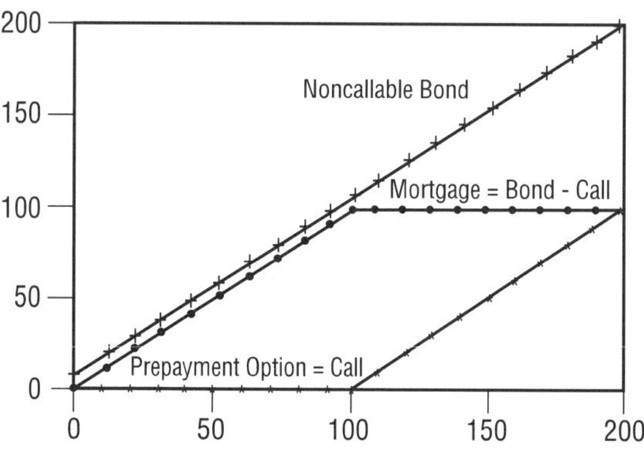

Figure 36.2—Mortgage = Riskless Bills – Put Option

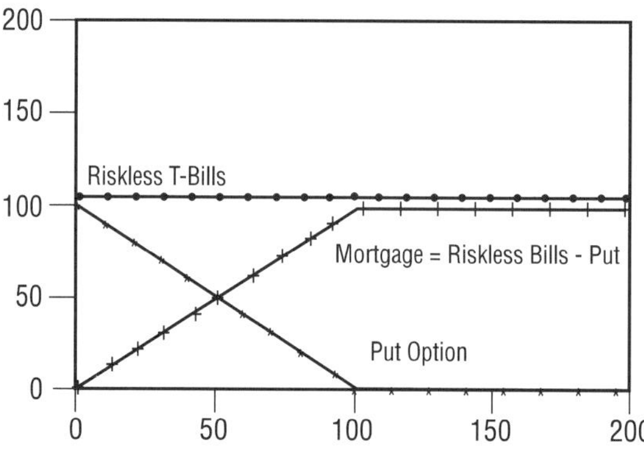

similar payoffs to those of 0.84 call options on twenty-year T-bond futures with an exercise price of 105.14. Payoffs on the prepayment options of 11% and 13% mortgages are likewise similar to those of 0.99 and 1.16 T-bond options with exercise prices of 86.68 and 72.82, respectively.

As simple as this analysis is, it is remarkably useful in understanding hedging and pricing for fixed-rate mortgages. To hedge these risks, we create offsetting positions through dynamic trading strategies or option purchases. A mortgage may be viewed either as long a bond and short a call, or just short a put. Thus, to hedge a mortgage security, one can either 1) short a straight bond and purchase or dynamically create a call option, or 2) purchase or dynamically create a put option. Whether a mortgage is priced properly depends upon whether the interest rate spread between the mortgage's yield and that on comparable risk noncallable bonds is too large or too small in relation to the costs of option purchase or option creation.

II. INTEREST RATE VOLATILITY AND THE MORTGAGE-TREASURY YIELD SPREAD

Most data sets on mortgage-backed securities (MBS) start in the mid-1980s, as that is when the MBS market grew most rapidly and when data became more generally available. Early work on hedging MBSs was done by Breeden and Giarla [1987], using data for the three and a half-year period from 1984 to mid-1987.

For this current article, data for the thirteen-year period from December 31, 1977, through December 31, 1990, were collected. The length of the period gives us more power to examine the effects of recession (1980, 1981–1982), rate volatility (1979–1982), and burnout on mortgage prepayments, pricing, and hedging (1988–1990).

Price data were obtained from the *Wall Street Journal* for the entire period. Prepayment data are from Salomon Brothers (monthly for 1983–1990) and from Drexel, Burnham, Lambert (annually for 1978–1982). The price data from the *Wall Street Journal* are known to contain several errors, so the data were carefully checked by examining the time series of price changes for the various coupons, as well as the time series of price spreads across coupons. Apparent errors in the data were corrected prior to the analysis. As the prices examined are for MBSs guaranteed by the Government National Mortgage Association (GNMA), carrying a "full faith and credit" guarantee of the U.S. government, credit risk is not a serious issue and is ignored throughout the article.

Interest rate volatility increased dramatically in 1979 when the Federal Reserve changed its monetary policy. Figure 36.3 shows the levels of both short-term and long-term interest rates for 1979–1991. Both short-term (three-month) and long-term (ten-year) rates exceeded 15% in 1981 and then dropped to as low as 5% and 7%, respectively. These huge interest rate movements caused correspondingly huge price movements in mortgages, Treasury bonds, and futures prices.

Note also that the slope of the yield curve changes quite significantly during the period examined. It was significantly downward-sloping in 1979, turns to steeply upward-sloping in 1983–1984, to downward-sloping in 1989, and back to a sharp upward slope in 1991. As McConnell and Singh [1991] have shown, the slope of the yield curve has significant implications for prepayment rates on adjustable-rate mortgages (ARMs) versus fixed-rate mortgages. It is plausible that the slope of the yield curve also affects prepayments on fixed-rate mortgages.

Figure 36.4 shows the spread in yields between current market rates for par GNMA mortgage securities and seven-year Treasury securities, which have similar price elasticity. Given that the securities have similar credit risks (none) and similar interest rate risks, spread fluctuations should reflect primarily the value of the prepayment option described in Section I. The borrower's prepayment option has greater value in times of greater rate volatility, and lenders and investors should require greater spreads of promised mortgage yields over Treasury yields at those times.

As interest rate volatility was greatest from 1979 to 1982 and in late 1985 to 1986, it is comforting that Figure 36.4 shows that mortgage-Treasury spreads are widest during those periods. Prior to late 1979 and from 1987–1990, rate volatility was comparatively low, which made the borrower's prepayment option less valuable and the equilibrium mortgage-Treasury spread low. Thus, the general pattern of movements is broadly consistent with our simple prepayment option analysis.

Figure 36.3—3-Month and 10-Year Treasury Rates: 1979 to May 1991

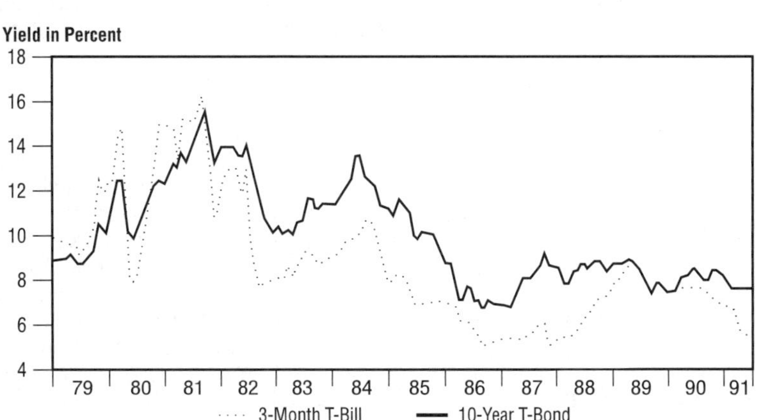

Figure 36.4—Par Mortgage Spread to 7-Year Treasury

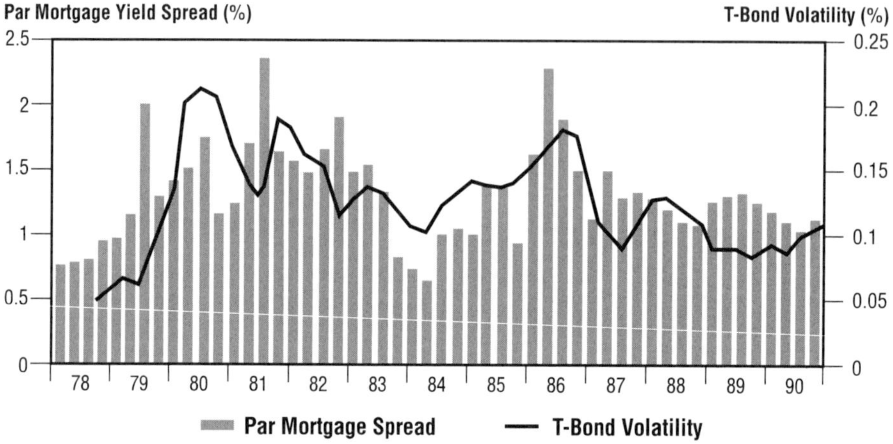

Par Mortgage Spread — T-Bond Volatility

T-Bond volatility is annualized and based upon the last 12 months' returns.

III. PREPAYMENT DATA AND ANALYSIS

Prepayment rates on fixed-rate mortgages respond primarily to several factors: 1) the mortgage's coupon rate in relation to current refinancing opportunities; 2) the age of the mortgage; 3) the season of the year; 4) the degree of "burnout"; and 5) the growth/recession state of the macroeconomy.

The effects of the major variables on prepayments are as follows. First, higher-coupon mortgages should have higher prepayment rates, as Table 36.1 shows that the benefit from prepayments is larger. Second, few people refinance immediately after they enter into a mortgage loan. As a mortgage ages, people become more mobile and more inclined to refinance, which leads to increases in prepayment rates. After about two years, FHA mortality series show that prepayments on par mortgages flatten out at about an annual prepayment rate of 6%, and the mortgages are viewed as well-seasoned.

Next, mobility and prepayments are related to weather for homebuilding and school year timing, both of which lead to increases in prepayments during the summer and decreases during the winter. Richard and Roll [1989] show that the longer mortgage rates have been below the mortgage's coupon rate, and the longer it has been optimal to refinance, the more the composition of the pool's borrowers changes toward those who, for whatever reason, tend to be less inclined to refinance. The slowing of the prepayment rate of a pool of mortgages as the quick payers depart is called the burnout effect.

Finally, economic growth affects job mobility and therefore prepayment rates, as mortgages are often prepaid when the borrower moves to another location. Slower economic growth means less mobility and slower prepayments. The tables and figures to follow illustrate all these effects.

Table 36.2 shows the annualized percentage paydowns from prepayments quarterly from 1978 to 1990 for GNMAs with coupons from 8% to 15%. Note that these prepayment rates are for mortgages with fixed maturities, so the time series reflect mortgages that are aging. In contrast to FNMA and FHLMC mortgage-backed securities, all the mortgages underlying a GNMA MBS have initial maturities of thirty years, so one can be assured that a thirty-year GNMA MBS that matures in 2010 was issued in 1980. Also note that no data exist for high-coupon mortgages prior to 1980, as rates had never before been high enough for those high-coupon MBSs to be issued!

Look at mortgages with coupons of 10% or higher that were recently issued, and the aging effect is apparent. Immediately after the mortgages were issued, prepayment rates were very low (usually <1%). Then, despite the very high interest rates of 1981–1982, prepayment rates increased on these new mortgages, while prepayments of seasoned discounts such as GNMA 8s and 9s slowed because of the very high interest rates.

The general sensitivity of prepayments to interest rate movements is also easy to see. When rates were high in 1981–1982, prepayments were low. When rates dropped sharply in 1985–1986, prepayment rates accelerated dramatically from the 5% to 10% range to as high as 45% on high

Figure 36.5—GNMA Seasonal Prepayment Multipliers: 1983–1990

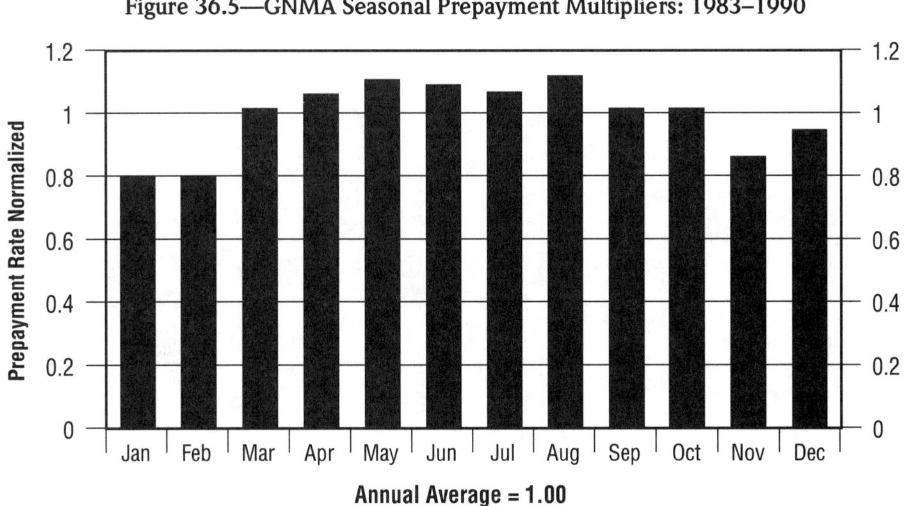

coupons. Subsequent to that 1986–1987 period of rapid prepayments, the burnout effect described becomes apparent. Despite the fact that interest rates generally remained low in the 1988–1990 period, prepayment rates on high-coupon mortgages dropped by half or more. The expected seasonal pattern of prepayments is shown in Figure 36.5, with prepayments lowest in the winter and highest in summer.

A problem with examining the risks of investments in mortgage-backed securities is that the volatile movements in interest rates often dominate the effects of other variables and lead to apparent non-stationarities in the relationships. For example, when GNMA 13s sold at a discount to par in 1981–1982, it was not optimal to prepay them. Yet during most of the remaining period they were premiums, and it was optimal to prepay. As will be shown, mortgage price volatilities should be and are very different in those different circumstances.

A simple transformation of the data that is used often in this paper (as it generally works very well) is to examine data series for investment strategies sorted by a given spread of the mortgage's coupon to the coupon of the current par mortgage. Thus, instead of examining the prepayment rates, risks, and returns of GNMA 13s, we often look at those series for the changing (but well-defined) set of mortgages that have coupons that are, say, 2% to 3% above the current par mortgage rate, i.e., "premium mortgages." This transformation mitigates the interest rate effect and allows for better examination of other effects.

Table 36.3 shows annual averages of prepayment rates for securities sorted by their spreads to the par mortgage rate. The higher prepayment rates of high coupons are apparent from examining this table, as is the burnout effect.

The annual growth rate of GNP, the number of housing starts, and the national unemployment rate are all displayed in Table 36.3 as indicators of macroeconomic performance and mobility. The recession periods of mid-1980 and late-1981 through 1982 have very low prepayment rates, even on seasoned discounts sorted so as to hold interest rates approximately constant. This shows the expected macroeconomic effect. Studies that start with data from the mid-1980s often cannot detect this effect, as their tests have little power because of the consistency of growth from 1983 through 1990. Studies that use older data that cover recessions typically find a strong macroeconomic effect, particularly related to housing starts.

Figure 36.6 graphs the relationship of prepayment rates by degree of premium or discount for the entire time period 1978–1990. Prepayments form an "S-curve" as they flatten out at both ends of the graph. For very high premiums, it is optimal for most people to refinance and prepay, and they are probably doing so with as much haste as ever, whether the rate saving is 3% or 5%. For deep discounts, it is not optimal for most borrowers to prepay, and such people are probably minimizing prepayments.

Still, there is always a base level of prepayments due to forced house sales, nuisance mortgage bal-

Table 36.2—GNMA Annualized Paydowns from Prepayments—Quarterly 1978–1990

Date	Par Mtg Yield (%)	3-Month Treasury (%)	10-Year Treasury (%)	Slope 10Yr–3M (%)	T-Bond Futures Price	8%	9%	10%	11%	12%	13%	14%	15%
						Mortgage Coupon — Annualized Percentage Paydown							
33178	8.73	6.65	8.12	1.47	95.94	6.4	6.7						
63078	9.33	7.21	8.59	1.38	93.00	6.4	6.7						
93078	9.32	8.07	8.50	0.43	93.31	6.4	6.7						
123178	10.13	9.60	9.12	–0.54	90.34	6.4	6.7						
33179	10.06	9.77	9.08	–0.69	90.19	7.1	2.2	0.1					
63079	9.88	9.25	8.76	–0.49	91.81	7.1	2.2	0.1					
93079	11.50	10.44	9.42	–1.02	87.78	7.1	2.2	0.1					
123179	11.67	12.53	10.31	–2.22	82.19	7.1	2.2	0.1	0.8				
33180	14.08	14.98	12.60	–2.38	67.94	3.4	2.2	0.7	0.8				
63080	11.39	8.18	9.98	1.80	81.19	3.4	2.2	0.7	0.8				
93080	13.57	11.89	11.83	–0.06	70.69	3.4	2.2	0.7	0.8				
123180	13.72	15.02	12.43	–2.59	71.38	3.4	2.2	0.7	0.8				
33181	14.57	13.00	13.10	0.10	67.06	1.4	1.3	1.2	1.4		0.7	0.2	0.4
63081	15.94	15.08	13.84	–1.24	64.38	1.4	1.3	1.2	1.4		0.7	0.2	0.4
93081	18.42	15.15	15.76	0.61	56.00	1.4	1.3	1.2	1.4		0.7	0.2	0.4
123181	15.95	11.54	13.93	2.39	61.91	1.4	1.3	1.2	1.4		0.7	0.2	0.4
33182	16.01	13.90	14.17	0.27	61.94	1.1	1.1	1.3	1.9		2.6	2.3	4.2
63082	16.14	13.32	14.32	1.00	60.69	1.1	1.1	1.3	1.9		2.6	2.3	4.2
93082	13.38	7.79	11.93	4.14	71.06	1.1	1.1	1.3	1.9		2.6	2.3	4.2
123182	12.21	8.13	10.31	2.18	76.63	1.3	1.6	1.5	2.1	0.4	3.5	4.2	19.8
33183	12.13	8.95	10.59	1.64	75.97	2.3	3.5	2.0	3.1	0.7	5.8	16.4	46.4
63083	12.49	9.04	10.89	1.85	74.44	3.3	5.2	2.7	4.0	1.1	9.1	22.3	35.7
93083	12.79	9.00	11.39	2.39	72.72	3.7	5.8	3.0	4.4	1.8	8.4	15.6	21.0
123183	12.69	9.26	11.76	2.50	70.03	2.8	4.4	2.4	3.6	1.7	7.4	12.3	19.9
33184	13.20	9.98	12.43	2.45	66.22	2.6	2.5	2.9	3.7	3.1	7.8	11.6	22.1

63084	14.52	10.26	13.83	3.57	59.63	3.5	2.8	3.2	4.3	4.1	8.9	16.1	19.8
93084	13.46	10.58	12.40	1.82	67.22	2.5	2.3	2.5	3.4	3.8	7.1	11.5	12.7
123184	12.45	8.08	11.45	3.37	71.06	2.3	2.0	2.4	3.3	3.6	6.6	9.5	14.3
33185	12.65	8.44	11.63	3.19	69.72	2.5	2.3	2.5	3.4	4.0	7.6	13.4	22.3
63085	11.40	7.01	10.15	3.14	77.06	3.5	3.0	3.1	4.2	5.7	9.6	17.9	24.0
93085	11.41	7.27	10.33	3.06	75.59	4.7	4.1	4.2	6.0	9.1	16.1	31.8	35.8
123185	9.76	7.24	8.98	1.74	85.22	4.7	4.6	4.3	5.7	9.6	17.1	30.7	30.8
33186	9.00	6.51	7.38	0.87	102.31	4.4	5.1	4.4	7.2	16.2	25.0	34.8	39.8
63086	9.58	6.13	7.42	1.29	99.56	7.3	7.3	7.0	14.7	38.1	41.0	50.4	41.5
93086	9.24	5.31	7.49	2.18	96.56	10.0	9.7	10.3	21.2	49.3	47.2	51.9	46.7
123186	8.61	5.79	7.25	1.46	98.19	9.6	9.0	10.4	21.9	43.3	41.8	45.2	37.5
33187	8.53	5.95	7.62	1.67	98.47	7.7	8.0	12.2	24.4	41.2	36.1	37.2	33.4
63087	9.75	5.86	8.37	2.51	91.50	10.6	10.2	16.1	29.4	42.9	35.6	40.6	37.5
93087	10.80	6.88	9.65	2.77	81.69	8.5	8.8	10.6	16.7	27.4	27.8	31.7	29.2
123187	10.01	5.84	8.86	3.02	87.97	6.4	7.2	8.0	11.2	18.8	19.1	22.3	22.4
33188	9.80	5.86	8.65	2.79	90.09	5.3	5.9	6.5	9.9	19.7	17.2	22.6	24.3
63088	9.90	6.74	8.80	2.06	88.75	7.9	8.5	10.6	15.3	27.5	24.9	29.0	26.2
93088	9.90	7.47	8.83	1.36	88.75	8.1	7.6	9.9	12.9	21.2	21.3	24.3	21.2
123188	10.34	8.36	9.13	0.77	89.13	6.8	7.9	8.3	10.7	18.8	17.0	21.6	19.6
33189	10.69	9.18	9.27	0.09	88.41	5.3	5.5	6.4	8.2	15.6	14.7	22.0	21.2
63089	9.51	8.24	8.08	–0.16	97.94	5.9	6.6	7.4	8.9	15.6	16.6	22.0	20.0
93089	9.80	8.15	8.28	0.13	95.84	7.1	6.3	9.1	11.6	19.1	16.1	20.4	20.7
123189	9.33	7.82	7.91	0.09	98.66	6.4	7.1	8.6	12.7	20.6	17.0	20.2	18.5
33190	9.92	8.03	8.63	0.60	91.88	5.7	6.2	6.9	10.9	18.2	14.6		17.8
63090	9.63	7.98	8.41	0.43	94.34	6.7	7.3	7.7	10.8	17.3	15.9		16.6
93090	9.77	7.35	8.81	1.46	89.38	6.9	7.2	8.0	10.2	16.4	13.5		13.5
123190	9.14	6.33	8.06	1.43	95.72	5.9	6.0	6.4	8.7	13.8	13.1		13.8

Source: 1979–1982: Drexel, Burnham, Lambert (annual), 1983–1990; Salomon Brothers (monthly). Prices and rates are end of quarter. Prepayment rates are averages for the quarter.

Table 36.3—Average Annual GNMA Prepayments by Coupon-Par Mortgage Rate

					Discounts										Premiums				
	Average	House	GNP	Unem-	–4.99	–3.99	–2.99	–1.99	–0.99	–0.49	0.00	0.50	1.00	1.50	2.00	2.50	3.00	4.00	5.00
	Par	Starts	Growth	ployment	–4.00	–3.00	–2.00	–1.00	–0.50	0.00	0.49	0.99	1.49	1.99	2.49	2.99	3.99	4.99	5.99
Year	Mortgage	(000)	(%)	(%)	Annualized Paydown from Prepayments (%)														
1978	9.14	2,020	5.3	6.1				7.7	8.0	8.9	6.7								
1979	10.65	1,745	2.5	5.8			3.9	4.1	1.0	0.3									
1980	12.98	1,292	–0.2	7.1		1.7	1.2	1.1	2.1	3.2	2.5	3.7	3.2	4.8	4.8				
1981	15.71	1,084	1.9	7.6	1.3	1.2	1.3	1.2	0.4	1.4	0.3								
1982	14.77	1,062	–2.5	9.7	1.5	2.4	2.4	2.7	3.4	2.1	3.4	3.5		4.8	4.2	12.0			
1983	12.52	1,703	3.6	9.6	3.7	3.6	2.2	3.4	3.9	4.5	7.1	10.3		19.8	18.9	40.7	37.3		
1984	13.27	1,750	6.8	7.5	2.5	2.7	3.2	4.9	7.2	6.9	11.2	10.2	12.7	15.7	15.9	16.0			
1985	11.64	1,742	3.4	7.2			3.4	3.7	4.1	5.4	6.5	8.6	11.1	14.0	18.8	25.1	26.3	26.8	30.8
1986	9.21	1,805	2.7	7.0					8.0	8.0	7.7	8.0	10.4	15.6	23.6	31.7	37.4	41.6	40.5
1987	9.50	1,621	3.4	6.2					8.6	9.9	12.1	16.0	18.6	23.6	28.8	27.2	30.2	32.3	34.1
1988	9.84	1,488	4.5	5.5				7.2	8.0	8.3	10.0	10.9	14.1	17.7	17.8	20.7	21.0	22.3	21.9
1989	9.84	1,376	2.5	5.3				6.5	6.8	7.5	8.2	9.7	11.8	13.2	15.3	18.2	17.6	19.9	19.7
1990	9.67	1,193	1.0	5.5				6.5	6.8	7.0	7.6	9.2	10.4	12.0	15.2	14.4	14.8	15.5	15.0
Averages																			
1978–1982		1,441	1.4	7.3	1.4	1.8	2.2	3.4	3.0	3.2	3.2	3.6	3.2	4.8	4.5	12.0			
1983–1987		1,724	4.0	7.5	3.1	3.2	2.9	4.0	6.3	6.9	8.9	10.6	13.2	17.7	21.2	28.1	32.8	33.6	35.1
1988–1990		1,352	2.7	5.4				6.7	7.2	7.6	8.6	9.9	12.1	14.3	16.1	17.7	17.8	19.2	18.8
1978–1990		1,529	2.7	6.9	2.3	2.3	2.5	4.5	5.2	5.6	6.9	9.0	11.5	14.1	16.3	22.9	26.4	26.4	27.0

Notes: GNP Growth is in real terms.
Economic data are from the U.S. Department of Commerce.

Figure 36.6—GNMA Prepayment Rates versus Coupon-Par: Average 1978–1990

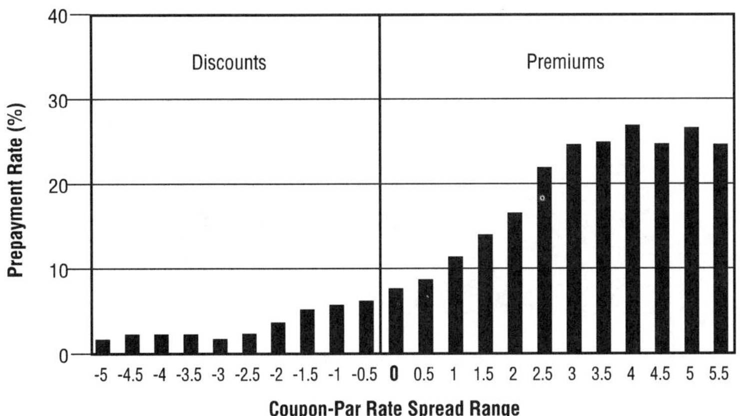

Bar 0 represents Coupon-Par spread between 0 and .49.

ance levels, refinancing against higher collateral values, and the actions of fiscally conservative borrowers who simply wish to reduce debt. Most of these effects are relatively insensitive to rates and form the flat base of minimal core prepayments.

Figures 36.7, 36.8, and 36.9 show average prepayment rate curves for three subperiods that are chosen to illustrate the major effects. The first subperiod, 1978–1982, has many new mortgages originated when rates surged from 9% to 16% during the period. Prepayments are generally low during this subperiod because of the lack of seasoning (aging) of these mortgages. During the 1983–1987 period, these same mortgages become well-seasoned, and the expected S-curve of prepayments is quite dramatic. Following those rapid paydowns, prepayment rates slow in the 1988–1990 period due to burnout effects.

Figure 36.10 displays clearly the change in the prepayment function for GNMA 13s pre- and post-burnout.

Figure 36.7—GNMA Prepayment Rates versus Coupon-Par: Average 1978–1982

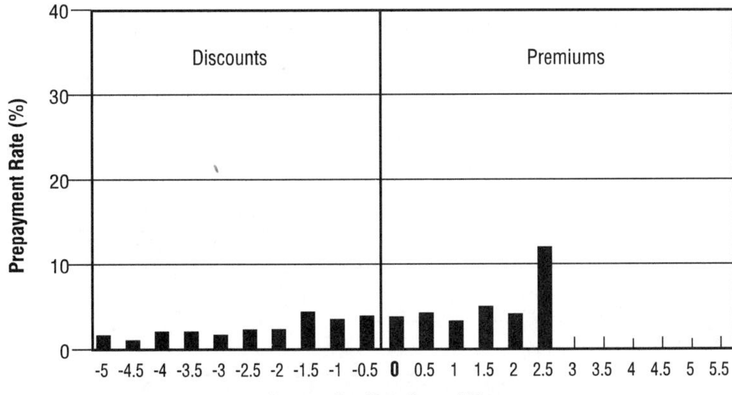

Bar 0 represents Coupon-Par spread between 0 and .49.

Figure 36.8—GNMA Prepayment Rates versus Coupon-Par: Average 1983–1987

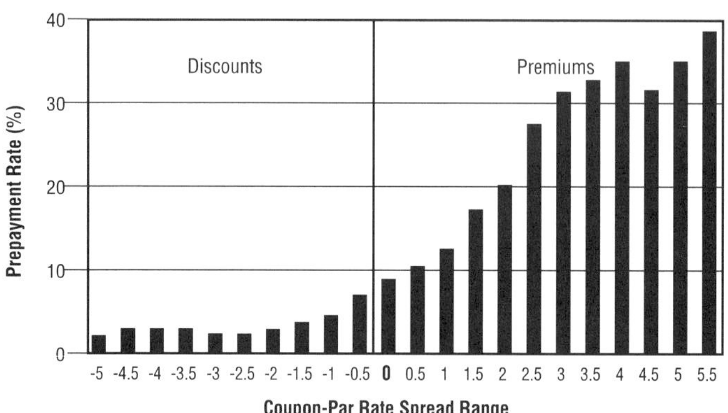

Bar 0 represents Coupon-Par spread between 0 and .49.

Figure 36.9—GNMA Prepayment Rates versus Coupon-Par: Average 1988–1990

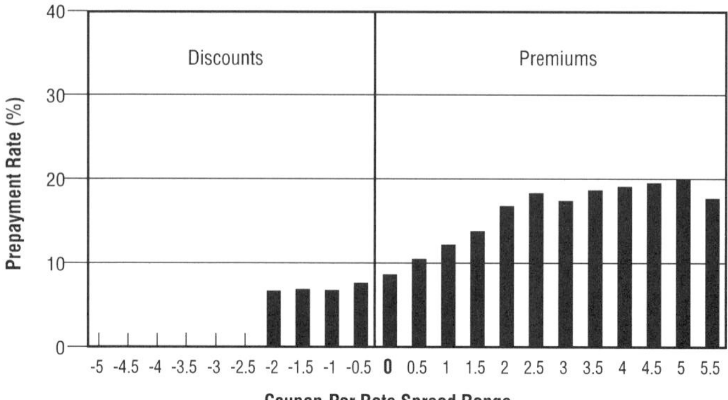

Bar 0 represents Coupon-Par spread between 0 and .49.

Figure 36.10—Prepayment Burnout of GNMA 13s

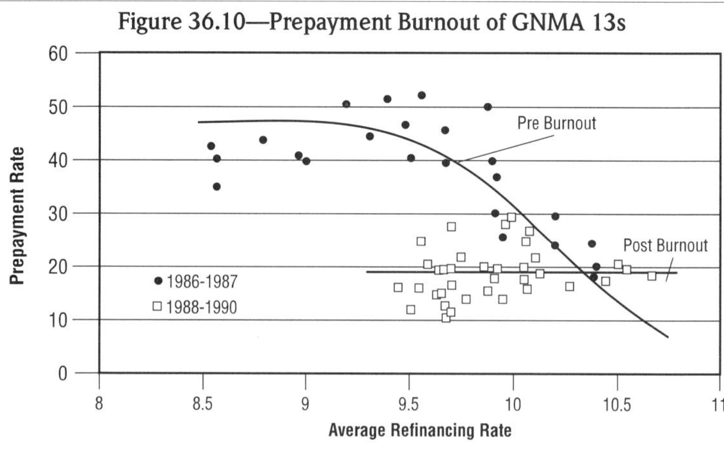

Monthly observations. Data are not seasonally adjusted.

IV. MORTGAGE PRICE CURVES

Here we analyze historical mortgage prices. End-of-month bid price data come from the *Wall Street Journal* for all coupons, including half coupons. Table 36.4 presents end-of-quarter prices (expressed as a percent of par) for mortgages with coupons ranging from 8% to 15%.

A number of observations can be made from Table 36.4. First, as interest rates increased from the 7.5% level at the end of 1977 to over 15% in September 1981, twenty-year Treasury bond futures prices dropped as expected from 99% to 56% of par. Prices for GNMA 8s dropped from 97 to 56 over the same period, moving very much in step with T-bond futures. From September 1981 to December 1990, rates fell back to the 8% level, the near-bond futures price increased to 96, and GNMA 8s increased to 94.

As we noted earlier, a mortgage is like a fixed-rate bond less a call option. As bond prices fell, the call option for GNMA 8s became almost worthless, so the GNMA 8s' price behavior should be very similar to that of long-term T-bonds. Looking across different coupons, one sees that all mortgage prices move up and down generally with T-bond futures prices and opposite movements in interest rates, reflecting their fixed rates.

To see the effect of the prepayment option, examine the movements of GNMA 13 prices in relation to T-bond futures prices. In contrast to the GNMA 8s, which were always discounts, the GNMA 13s sold for discounts to par in 1981, 1982, and 1984, but sold for premiums during all other years (when mortgage rates were below 13%). As interest rates increased from March 1981 to September 1981, T-bond futures dropped eleven points from 67 to 56, and GNMA 13s dropped fourteen points from 92 to 78. From then until the end of 1982, T-bond futures increased by twenty points to 76, and GNMA 13s increased by twenty-five points to 103.

Thus, during this period of high rates and discount prices, GNMA 13s were just as volatile as T-bond futures. As interest rates continued to drop from December 1982 to December 1986, however, and T-bond futures rose by twenty-two points from 76 to 98, GNMA 13s increased only by six points to 109. The reason for this limiting of price increases is the surge in GNMA 13 prepayments shown in Table 36.2, from 3% annually in 1982 to over 40% annually in late 1986.

According to Table 36.1, given no prepayments and a current mortgage rate of 9%, the value of the GNMA 13 would exceed 137% of par. The rapid prepayments that occurred in 1986 caused the GNMA 13s to sell for 109 rather than at the 137 price that would have occurred with no prepayments.

Not all borrowers prepay as soon as refinancing rates appear attractive, so mortgages do sell at prices significantly above par, "capping out" at about 110–115 according to the data in Table 36.4. Theoretical pricing models that derive mortgage prices that never significantly exceed par, because optimal prepayments are assumed, are not very realistic.

Figures 36.11 through 36.14 give historical relationships of GNMA 9s, 11s, 13s, and 15s to Treasury bond futures prices. The fits are statistically quite significant, with the high-coupon 15s having the least precise fit, i.e., the greatest "basis risk." The curvature (negative convexity) predicted by the option analysis in Figure 36.1 is increasingly evident as one moves to the high-coupon GNMA 11s, 13s, and 15s.

As Table 36.1 illustrates, these mortgages are effectively short call options on T-bond futures with different exercise prices. As these calls become in-the-money, the mortgage's price gains are limited substantially by significantly increased prepayments. The shapes of these curves are as anticipated in Section I, in that they resemble curves for riskless investments less put options with various exercise prices.

V. RISK ANALYSIS WITH IMPLIED MORTGAGE PRICE ELASTICITIES

The cross section of mortgage prices for different coupons can be used to find "implied price elasticities" or modified durations for mortgages. These implied price elasticities are useful as measures of risk and for the construction of hedges.

First, consider what an appropriate risk measure for a mortgage investment should be. For straight bonds, modified duration is extremely useful because of its close theoretical and practical relationship to price volatility. Unfortunately, for mortgages the standard calculation of modified duration is usually an incorrect and misleading measure of price sensitivity. This statement applies both to duration computed using scheduled cash flows without prepayments, as well as to calculations that base expected cash flows on a current forecast of future prepayment rates. The problem lies in the fact that the duration of cash flows changes systematically with interest rates as borrowers use the prepayment option to their benefit.

To see the potential error in using duration calculations for price volatility, consider the case

Table 36.4—GNMA Fixed-Rate Mortgage Prices

	Market Yields, Spreads, and Futures Prices						*GNMA Prices By Mortgage Coupon*							
	Par Mtg	*7-Year*	*Par Mtg-*	*3-Month*	*TED*	*T-Bond*	*8%*	*9%*	*10%*	*11%*	*12%*	*13%*	*14%*	*15%*
Date	*Yield*	*Treasury*	*Treasury*	*LIBOR*	*Spread*	*Futures*								
123177	*8.50%*	*7.61%*	*0.89%*	*7.31%*	*1.03%*	*99.50*	*96.88*	*103.44*						
33178	8.73	7.98	0.75	7.56	0.91	95.94	94.66	101.75						
63078	9.33	8.53	0.80	8.75	1.54	93.00	91.50	98.00						
93078	9.32	8.49	0.83	9.56	1.49	93.31	92.34	98.16						
123178	10.13	9.20	0.93	11.81	2.21	90.34	89.75	94.56						
33179	10.06	9.10	0.96	10.69	0.92	90.19	89.75	94.72						
63079	9.88	8.71	1.17	10.69	1.44	91.81	91.13	95.53						
93079	11.50	9.45	2.05	12.88	2.44	87.78	86.00	90.44						
123179	11.67	10.31	1.36	14.56	2.03	82.19	81.56	85.69	90.31	96.13				
33180	14.08	12.58	1.50	20.00	5.02	67.94	70.78	74.34	78.38	83.75				
63080	11.39	9.82	1.57	9.69	1.51	81.19	84.44	88.84	93.81	98.59				
93080	13.57	11.84	1.73	13.75	1.86	70.69	74.94	77.69	82.19	86.94				
123180	13.72	12.47	1.25	17.75	2.73	71.38	71.16	75.81	80.38	85.97				
33181	14.57	13.21	1.36	14.94	1.94	67.06	68.75	72.25	77.00	81.75		91.94		
63081	15.94	14.05	1.89	17.69	2.61	64.38	64.69	67.56	72.06	76.78		86.84	91.31	
93081	18.42	16.04	2.38	17.75	2.60	56.00	56.06	59.75	64.13	68.56		78.00	82.06	
123181	15.95	14.12	1.83	13.80	2.26	61.91	62.25	66.34	71.03	76.38		86.53	91.91	96.09
33182	16.01	14.36	1.65	15.30	1.40	61.94	62.75	67.25	71.72	76.75		86.84	91.56	95.06
63082	16.14	14.52	1.62	15.95	2.63	60.69	63.13	67.19	71.53	76.69		86.19	90.63	94.75
93082	13.38	11.66	1.72	11.05	3.26	71.06	73.63	78.25	82.91	88.59		98.63	101.47	104.22
123182	12.21	10.27	1.94	9.31	1.18	76.63	78.72	83.72	88.78	94.28		103.38	105.69	107.50
33183	12.13	10.51	1.62	9.63	0.68	75.97	80.16	85.13	89.53	94.53		103.34	105.47	105.91
63083	12.49	10.85	1.64	9.75	0.71	74.44	77.81	82.78	87.75	92.66		102.31	105.16	106.41
93083	12.79	11.34	1.45	9.56	0.56	72.72	76.69	81.09	86.06	91.06		101.03	105.13	107.41
123183	12.69	11.80	0.89	9.94	0.68	70.03	75.31	80.13	85.41	90.91	96.50	101.47	105.44	107.94

33184	13.20	12.39	0.81	10.81	0.83	66.22	72.63	77.28	82.47	88.22	93.84	98.97	104.16	107.44
63084	14.52	13.81	0.71	12.13	1.87	59.63	66.66	70.69	75.63	81.13	86.81	92.34	98.00	101.84
93084	13.46	12.50	0.96	11.50	0.92	67.22	72.16	76.66	81.41	87.50	93.12	98.16	102.41	105.53
123184	12.45	11.47	0.98	8.75	0.67	71.06	76.97	81.72	87.13	93.25	98.16	101.97	106.03	108.81
33185	12.65	11.68	0.97	9.06	0.62	69.72	76.63	80.81	85.94	91.56	96.56	101.63	106.25	108.69
63085	11.40	10.14	1.26	7.81	0.80	77.06	83.50	88.28	94.03	98.75	102.16	106.13	108.97	112.41
93085	11.41	10.17	1.24	8.06	0.79	75.59	83.88	88.28	93.16	97.88	102.88	106.84	109.63	111.69
123185	9.76	8.83	0.93	8.00	0.76	85.22	91.22	96.09	101.31	104.81	107.44	108.25	109.59	112.03
33186	9.00	7.32	1.68	7.44	0.93	102.31	95.72	100.00	104.22	106.91	108.25	108.34	108.81	114.06
63086	9.58	7.30	2.28	6.88	0.75	99.56	93.69	97.28	102.19	105.25	105.78	106.56	107.28	114.25
93086	9.24	7.30	1.94	6.13	0.82	96.56	95.41	98.72	104.28	107.25	107.91	108.47	109.06	113.44
123186	8.61	7.07	1.54	6.38	0.59	98.19	98.22	101.63	106.53	107.75	108.13	109.13	110.06	114.31
33187	8.53	7.40	1.13	6.63	0.68	98.47	97.31	102.19	106.69	107.84	108.91	110.06	112.53	115.00
63087	9.75	8.23	1.52	7.25	1.39	91.50	91.00	96.09	101.31	105.88	108.72	111.34	113.03	115.00
93087	10.80	9.45	1.35	8.31	1.43	81.69	83.78	89.38	95.41	101.19	106.38	109.44	112.00	114.00
123187	10.01	8.63	1.38	7.44	1.60	87.97	88.16	94.00	99.97	104.56	108.00	109.78	112.00	114.00
33188	9.80	8.45	1.35	6.94	1.08	90.09	89.31	95.97	101.00	107.91	110.31	111.94	114.13	115.00
63088	9.90	8.65	1.25	7.94	1.20	88.75	89.00	94.88	100.56	105.97	109.47	112.00	113.75	115.50
93088	9.90	8.73	1.17	8.75	1.28	88.75	89.13	94.94	100.53	105.19	108.25	110.31	113.41	114.63
123188	10.34	9.20	1.14	9.38	1.02	89.13	87.44	93.03	98.31	103.06	105.88	108.38	111.81	112.56
33189	10.69	9.36	1.33	10.31	1.13	88.41	86.25	91.59	96.72	101.25	104.25	107.91	110.69	111.22
63089	9.51	8.08	1.43	9.31	1.07	97.94	93.16	97.81	102.09	105.50	108.44	110.50	110.75	111.00
93089	9.80	8.35	1.45	9.19	1.04	95.84	92.13	96.69	100.94	104.47	108.84	110.16	111.25	111.38
123189	9.33	7.96	1.37	8.38	0.56	98.66	94.25	98.63	102.78	105.72	108.84	110.69	111.94	112.31
33190	9.92	8.69	1.23	8.50	0.47	91.88	90.66	95.69	100.38	104.06	107.50	109.38		
63090	9.63	8.45	1.18	8.38	0.40	94.34	92.13	97.09	101.72	105.13	108.13	111.00		
93090	9.77	8.70	1.07	8.31	0.96	89.38	90.63	96.06	101.22	105.25	109.13	111.94		
123190	9.14	7.98	1.16	7.63	1.00	95.72	94.38	99.41	103.56	106.94	111.50	113.50	115.03	116.53

Notes: Bid, % par
Price data from the *Wall Street Journal.*
The TED Spread is 3-month LIBOR minus the 3-month T-bill yield.
Yield for 3-month LIBOR and 3-month T-bill from Salomon Brothers.

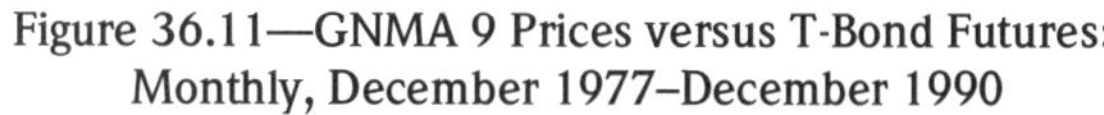
Figure 36.11—GNMA 9 Prices versus T-Bond Futures: Monthly, December 1977–December 1990

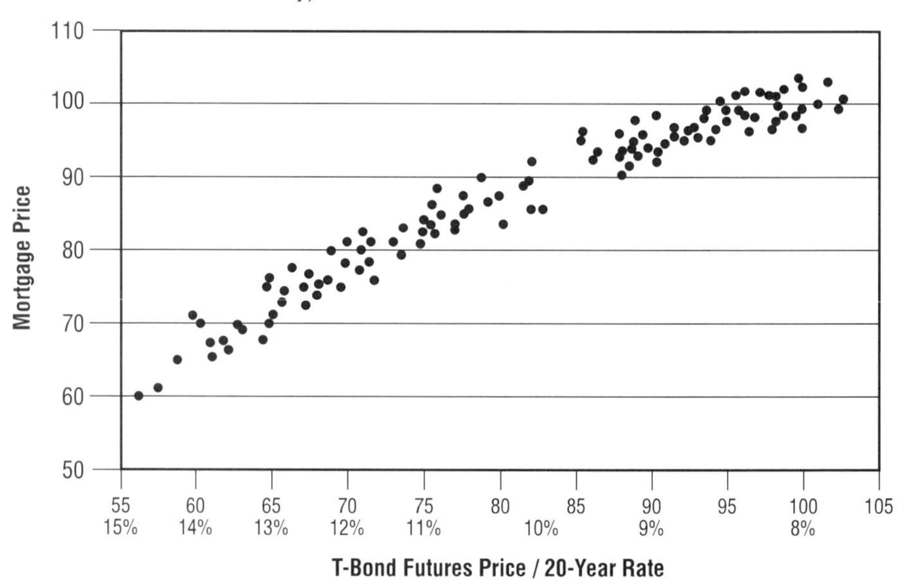

of a high-coupon mortgage security before it has been burned out, such as GNMA 13s at the middle of 1985. The prepayment rate at that time was about 10% to 15% annually. As the par mortgage rate was near 11.5%, the 13s were premiums by 1.5%. Looking at Figure 36.13's S-curve of the prepayment function at that time, one sees that mortgages in this premium range have the most sensitivity of prepayments to movements in interest rates.

Figure 36.12—GNMA 11 Prices versus T-Bond Futures: Monthly, October 1979–December 1990

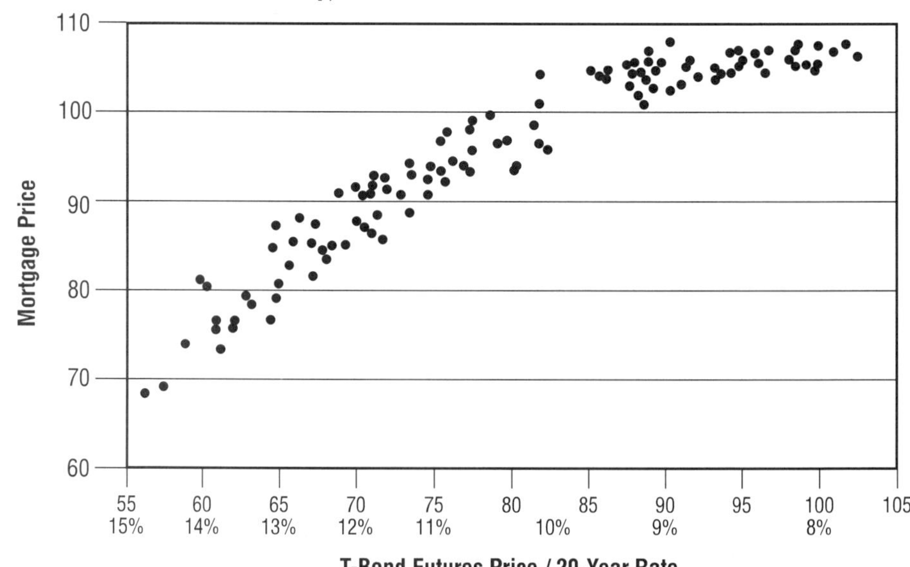

Figure 36.13—GNMA 13 Prices versus T-Bond Futures: Monthly, February 1981–December 1990

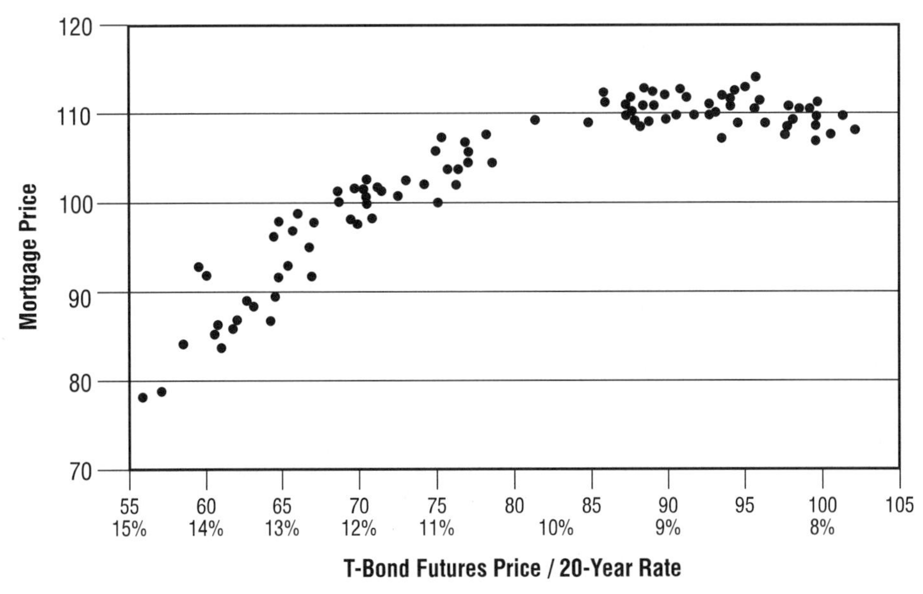

Duration computed at that time, based upon cash flow forecasts, would be in the four- to five-year range. The standard risk management usage of duration would imply that this mortgage moves 4% to 5% for 100-basis point moves up or down in rates. During the subsequent year (June 1985

Figure 36.14—GNMA 15 Prices versus T-Bond Futures: Monthly, October 1981–December 1990

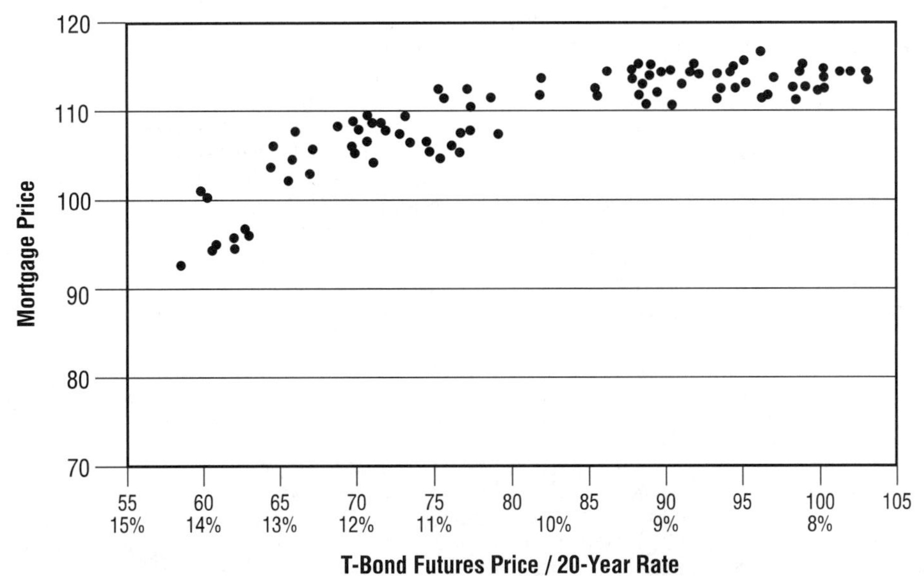

to June 1986), the par mortgage rate dropped by almost 200 basis points, so the duration-based estimate is that the GNMA 13 would increase in price by approximately 8% from 106 to 114. In actuality, the price increased only by 0.5% to 106.56.

Why did the GNMA 13s increase in price by such a small amount as rates fell sharply? As rates fell, prepayments accelerated sharply to the 40% level. Increased prepayments cause capital losses on paydowns of premiums, which largely offset the price benefit from discounting cash flows at the 200-basis point lower rates. Was this foreseeable, given the drop in rates by 200 basis points?

Although the extent of the prepayment increase was not easily predicted, rational models would all have shown some significant sensitivity of premium mortgage prepayments to rate moves. By using a prepayment *function* rather than a point estimate, one recognizes that for premium securities price moves upward are limited by prepayment increases. Similarly, price moves of premiums downward are also limited by reduced prepayments as rates increase. Thus, premiums have shorter "effective durations" and price elasticities due to the systematic prepayment effect. For discount mortgages, the same type of analysis gives the result that effective durations should be greater than standard computations, as price moves upward on discounts are enhanced by the capital gains of increased prepayments caused by lower rates.

Market participants are now well aware of the effects of changing prepayments on price volatility, although not many were in mid-1985. As the example demonstrates, correct understanding of the prepayment function and its price effect can be more important than interest rate moves in the prices of premium securities. One method for using market prices to capture that effect is to use a "roll-up, roll-down" approach (which can be justified as an approximation, given the homogeneity of option prices in the ratio of the underlying asset's price to the exercise price).

This approach simply estimates what the value of a GNMA 13 will be if rates decrease by 1% by using the current market price of the GNMA 14. As rates decrease by 1%, a GNMA 13 that has a coupon 1.5% over the old par mortgage rate will then have a 2.5% premium to the new rate. The GNMA 14s, however, have a premium of 2.5% over the old par rate. The price of the GNMA 14s presumably reflects the market's prepayment forecast for 2.5% premium securities, as well as its valuation of that option. Using the price of the 14s takes advantage of some of the market's knowledge. Correspondingly, for a % increase in rates, the GNMA 13 becomes an 0.5% premium to which the price of GNMA 12s currently responds.

Using the roll-up, roll-down approach on June 30, gives a price elasticity of 2.7% for the GNMA 13s rates move down by 1%, and a price elasticity of 3.9% rates move up by 1%. This is consistent with the adversely asymmetric payoff pattern (negative convexity) anticipated due to the prepayment option.

In December 1985, after rates had dropped sharply and prepayments had begun to accelerate, the GNMA 13 roll-up, roll-down elasticities were reduced to 1.2% and 0.8%, as the market began to feel the prepayment option's shortening of effective durations. These "implied price elasticities" from market prices would have provided much better volatility predictions in the subsequent year than would standard duration calculations.

Figures 36.15 through 36.17 give the monthly time series of implied elasticities based upon the price spreads of GNMA 9s and 8s, 11s and 10s, and 13s and 12s, respectively. Generally, these implied elasticities behave in sensible ways. In each graph, elasticities decrease as interest rates fall and bond prices increase, because prepayments increase and effective durations shorten. Furthermore, comparing the elasticities across graphs, one sees that implied elasticities for high coupons (premiums) are smaller than for low coupons (discounts). Certainly, that pattern of risk estimates is validated by subsequent price volatility, as we show later. Implied price elasticities are very useful in assessing subsequent price risk.[1]

The non-stationarities of mortgage price risks are striking in these implied price elasticity graphs. Seeing these, it just is not sensible to treat GNMA 13s or other coupons as if they have a well-defined,

1 This roll-up, roll-down approach for implied elasticities needs to be modified if the maturities of adjacent coupons differ substantially from that of the mortgage coupon considered. If rates jump 1%, a GNMA 13 with twenty years to maturity is treated as a GNMA 12, which has twenty-three years to maturity. The different years to maturity also reflect different seasoning and prepayments, which might be significant. For the coupons examined here (from 8% to 15%), a compensating weighted-average maturity (WAM) adjustment did not alter implied elasticities significantly. For GNMA 7 1/2s, however, the differences in WAMs and seasoning (versus the GNMA 8s) were significant. A use of implied elasticities involving GNMA 7 1/2s would be reasonable only after adjusting for the WAM differential.

Figure 36.15—Implied Elasticities: GNMA 9 and 8 Prices: Monthly, December 1977–December 1990

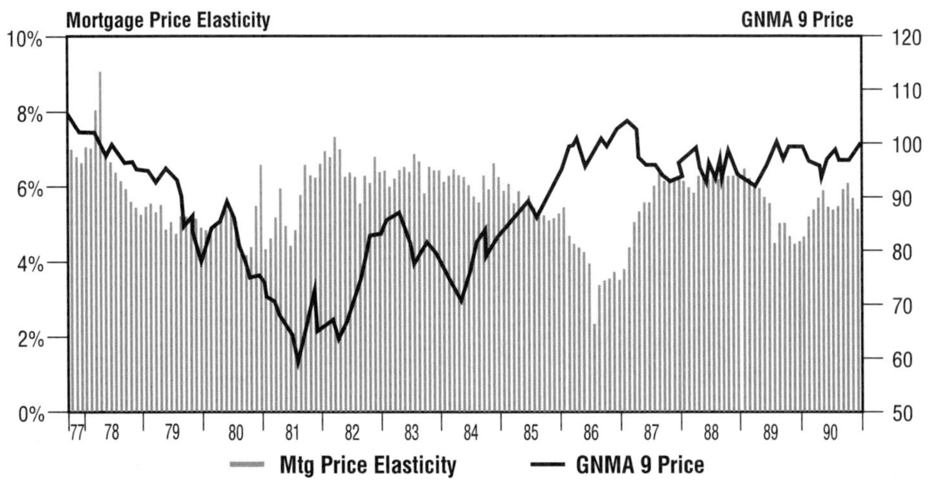

stationary risk profile that is valid for long periods of time. The risks in fact depend very much upon the level of interest rates, which affects whether the mortgage is a premium or a discount security, as well as the speed of prepayments.

To develop a more stationary risk profile for fixed-rate mortgage investments, the transformation is made to trading strategies that invest in mortgages with constant spreads to the par coupon. Thus, instead of considering a buy-and-hold strategy with GNMA 13s, consider a strategy of adjusting each month always to hold the mortgage coupon, that is, say, 1.5% over the par coupon. As rates increase (decrease), higher- (lower-) coupon mortgages are bought. Table 36.5 shows the time series of elasticities from these trading strategies, and Figures 36.18–36.20 present the results graphically.

Figure 36.16—Implied Elasticities: GNMA 11 and 10 Prices: Monthly, October 1979–December 1990

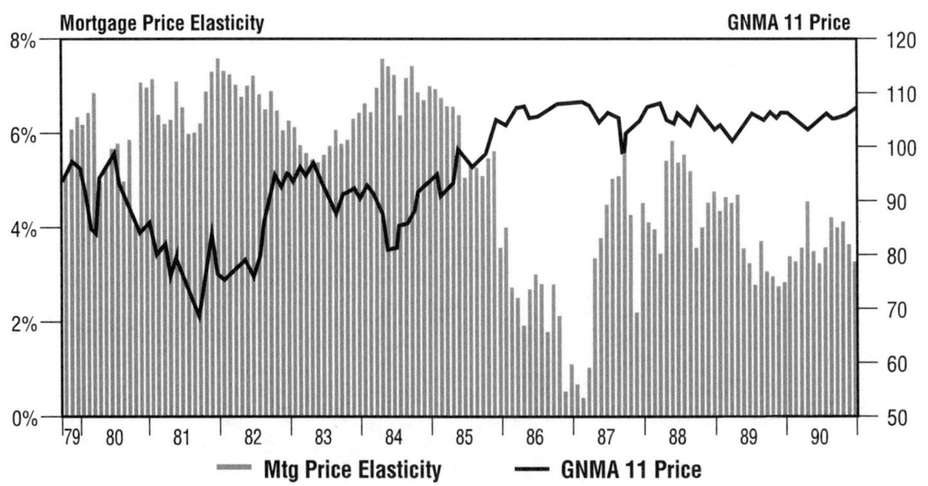

Figure 36.17—Implied Elasticities: GNMA 13 and 12.5 Prices: Monthly, February 1981–December 1990

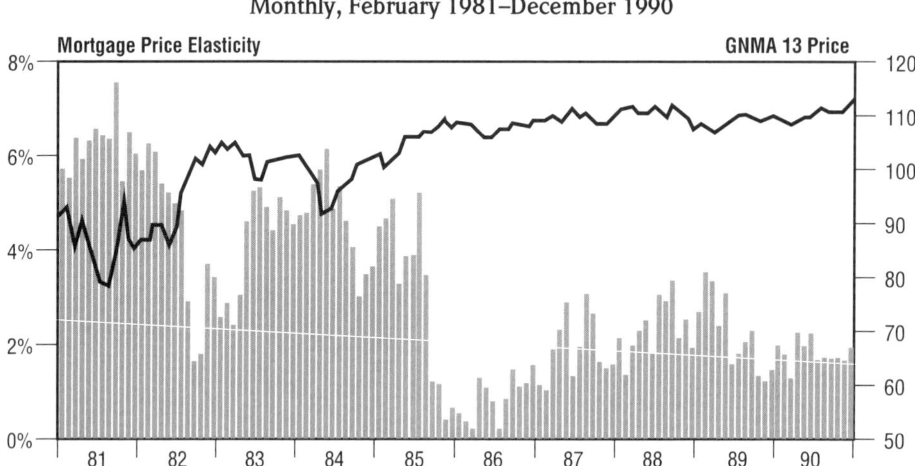

Figures 36.18 through 36.20 show that these strategies give much more stationary risk profiles than investing in constant-coupon mortgages. Figure 36.18 shows that the implied elasticities for investing in GNMAs with discounts of 1% or more from the par coupon are quite stable at approximately 6% for the thirteen-year period. Figure 36.19 shows that buying coupons 1% to 2% over par gives a relatively stable elasticity of 3.5%, and Figure 36.20 shows that 3% or greater premium investments have relatively stable elasticities near 1.5% or 2%. Thus, a stable risk strategy in fixed-rate mortgages can be constructed, but it does require dynamic adjustment of the portfolio's coupon mix.

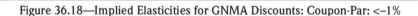

Figure 36.18—Implied Elasticities for GNMA Discounts: Coupon-Par: <–1%

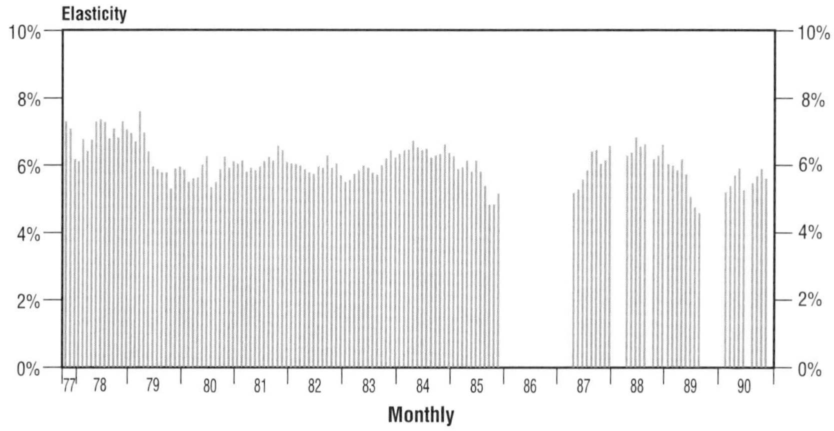

Figure 36.19—Implied Elasticities for GNMA Premiums: Coupon-Par: +1% to +2%

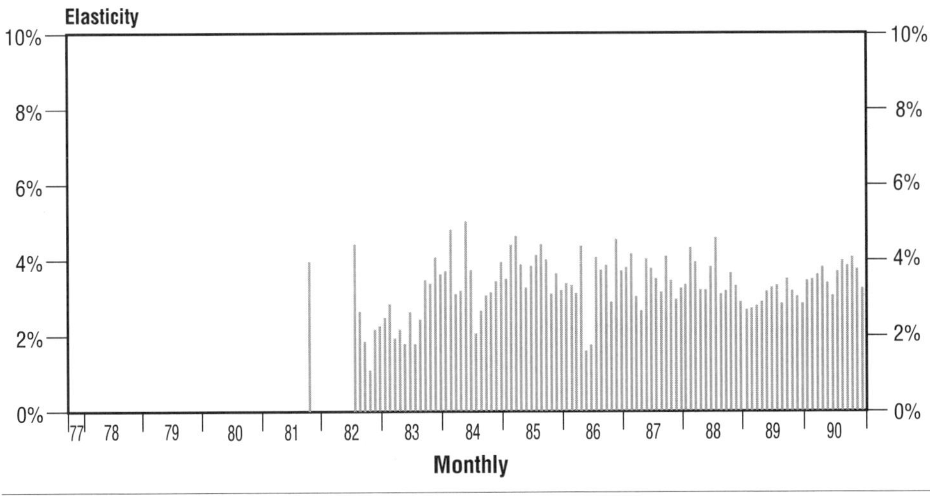

Figure 36.20—Implied Elasticities for GNMA High Premiums: Coupon-Par: >+3%

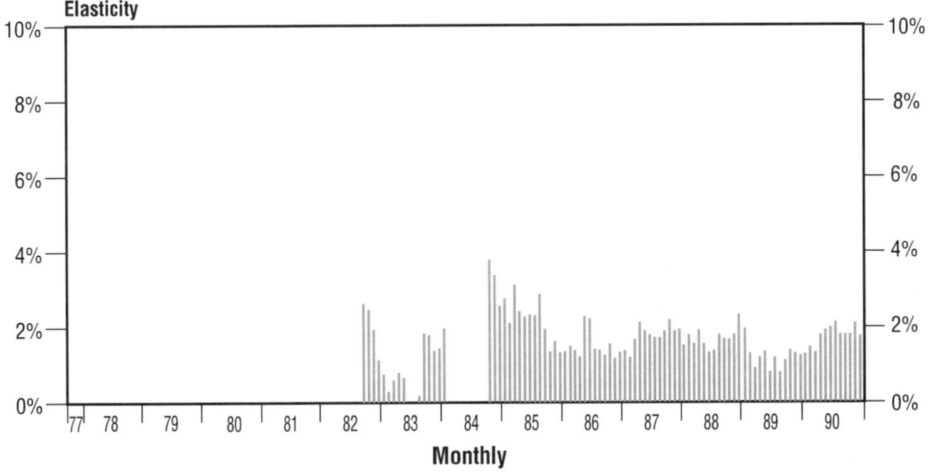

VI. DYNAMIC HEDGING STRATEGIES

Here we test simulated dynamic hedging strategies for mortgages using the implied elasticities from mortgage prices. For every month from January 1978 through December 1990, implied elasticities are computed for adjacent mortgage coupons. These elasticities are sorted by their spreads to the par mortgage coupon as in Table 36.5, typically with two coupons averaged in each bucket, e.g., 11.0s and 11.5s. To reduce the impact of price reporting errors on the results, the monthly elasticities for the last twelve months are averaged for each 1% coupon bucket and used in the construction of the hedges.

A separate dynamic hedging simulation is run for each mortgage coupon; every month its spread to the par coupon is computed, and its elasticity is estimated from the functions of Table 36.5. Based upon that elasticity and the current elasticity of the near twenty-year Treasury bond futures, the hedge position is computed, as well as its gain or loss during the next month. Adding the mortgage's coupon income, its gain or loss on principal paid down, and any capital gain or loss due to price

Table 36.5—Summary of Elasticities

		Monthly Cross-Sectional Simple Averages (%)						*12-Month Moving Averages (%)*					
	Par Mtg	*Discount*		*Premium*				*Discount*		*Premium*			
Date	*Yield*	*<–1%*	*0% to –1%*	*0% to +1%*	*1% to 2%*	*2% to 3%*	*> 3%*	*< –1%*	*–1% to 0%*	*0% to 1%*	*1% to 2%*	*2% to 3%*	*3% to 4%*
123177	8.50	7.2	6.9	6.8									
33178	8.73	6.2	7.6	7.5									
63078	9.33	6.4	7.3										
93078	9.32	7.4	6.3										
123178	10.13	6.7						6.8	7.0	7.7			
33179	10.06	7.0						6.9	6.6	8.6			
63079	9.88	7.0	5.1					7.1	6.0				
93079	11.50	5.9						6.8	5.6				
123179	11.67	5.3	6.4					6.5	5.7				
33180	14.08	5.9						6.2	5.8				
63080	11.39	5.7	5.1					5.8	5.6				
93080	13.57	5.4						5.8	5.7				
123180	13.72	6.3						5.9	5.1				
33181	14.57	6.0						5.9	5.1				
63081	15.94	5.9						6.0					
93081	18.42	6.1						6.0					
123181	15.95	6.6	4.6	4.3				6.1	4.8	4.2	4.0		
33182	16.01	6.0	5.2					6.1	4.8	4.2	4.0		
63082	16.14	5.9	4.8					6.1	4.7	4.5	4.0		
93082	13.38	5.9	5.5	3.7	2.7	4.3		6.1	4.7	4.4	3.7	4.3	
123182	12.21	6.1	4.4	5.3	2.2	1.7	2.0	6.1	4.7	4.3	2.5	2.7	2.3
33183	12.13	5.5	4.8	5.3	2.0	0.4	0.2	5.9	4.7	4.5	2.5	2.1	1.5
63083	12.49	6.0	4.9	5.4	2.8	1.2	0.6	5.9	4.8	4.6	2.4	1.9	1.2
93083	12.79	5.8	5.5	4.9	3.6	2.2	0.1	5.9	5.0	4.7	2.3	1.6	1.1
123183	12.69	6.4	5.7	4.9	3.7	2.4	1.4	5.9	5.2	5.0	2.8	1.6	0.9

33184	13.20	6.5	5.6	5.2	3.2	3.8		6.1	5.4	5.0	3.1	1.9	1.2
63084	14.52	6.6	6.2	3.9	3.8			6.3	5.7	4.8	3.6	2.3	1.4
93084	13.46	6.4	5.5	4.1	3.1	4.0		6.4	5.6	4.8	3.6	3.0	1.7
123184	12.45	6.6	5.2	4.8	3.9	2.6	2.5	6.5	5.5	4.6	3.5	3.3	2.6
33185	12.65	5.9	5.6	4.7	4.6	2.3	3.2	6.4	5.4	4.5	3.6	3.2	2.9
63085	11.40	6.2	5.0	3.2	3.8	2.7	2.4	6.3	5.1	4.4	3.5	2.9	2.7
93085	11.41	5.4	5.1	5.2	4.0	2.6	1.9	6.1	5.1	4.3	3.9	2.5	2.6
123185	9.76		5.2	5.6	3.3	1.6	1.3	5.8	5.2	4.6	3.9	2.3	2.2
33186	9.00		4.5	4.9	3.1	1.3	1.4	5.7	5.0	4.7	3.6	2.1	1.9
63086	9.58		4.3	5.2	1.8	0.4	2.2	5.5	5.1	5.0	3.4	1.7	1.8
93086	9.24		2.8	5.4	3.9	0.6	1.3	5.1	4.6	5.1	3.3	1.3	1.5
123186	8.61		2.7	3.5	3.8	0.6	1.3		3.9	4.9	3.4	1.0	1.5
33187	8.53		5.2	5.0	3.1	1.0	1.6		3.7	4.7	3.5	0.8	1.5
63087	9.90	5.6	5.5	5.3	3.8	2.2	1.9	5.4	4.0	4.7	3.7	1.2	1.5
93087	10.80	6.6	6.2	6.1	4.1	2.8	2.0	5.8	5.1	4.9	3.6	1.6	1.7
123187	10.01	6.6	6.3	5.4	3.3	1.9	1.9	6.0	5.9	5.3	3.5	2.0	1.8
33188	9.24		5.9	6.0	3.9	2.0	1.6	6.0	6.0	5.6	3.6	2.3	1.9
63088	9.90	6.7	6.3	5.8	4.6	2.7	1.4	6.4	6.2	5.7	3.7	2.4	1.8
93088	9.39		6.3	5.8	3.7	2.3	1.7	6.5	6.2	5.6	3.7	2.5	1.7
123188	10.34	6.4	5.6	5.0	2.7	2.2	2.3	6.6	6.1	5.5	3.6	2.5	1.7
33189	10.69	5.9	5.4	4.7	2.9	3.5	1.0	6.4	5.9	5.3	3.3	2.7	1.7
63089	9.51	5.0	4.7	4.3	3.3	2.2	0.8	6.2	5.6	5.0	3.1	2.7	1.5
93089	9.30		5.2	4.4	3.2	2.6	1.1	5.9	5.3	4.6	3.1	2.7	1.4
123189	9.33		4.5	4.2	2.9	2.9	1.3	5.6	4.9	4.4	3.0	2.9	1.2
33190	9.92	5.6	5.3	4.7	3.6	2.7	1.4	5.4	4.9	4.4	3.2	2.7	1.2
63090	9.63	5.4	5.1	4.7	3.0	3.0	2.0	5.3	4.9	4.4	3.3	2.9	1.4
93090	9.77	5.9	5.6	5.3	3.8	3.6	1.8	5.5	5.1	4.7	3.4	3.0	1.6
123190	9.14		5.2	4.3	3.3	4.2	1.8	5.5	5.3	4.8	3.6	3.2	1.8
Averages		6.10	5.37	4.99	3.37	2.32	1.58	6.06	5.29	4.95	3.40	2.34	1.72

Figure 36.21—Cumulative Investment Performance: GNMA 9s Value of $1 Unhedged and Hedged

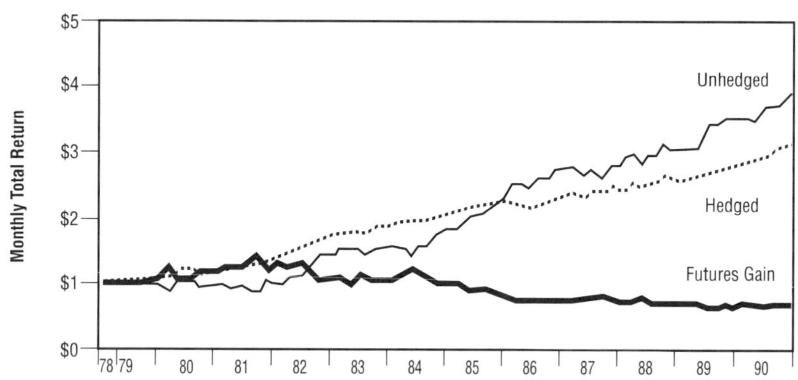

changes gives the total profit for the month, from which we compute the rate of return.

The performance of the hedges can be shown in several ways. First, the hedges are examined graphically according to three different perspectives, following which the statistical data are examined. Figure 36.21 graphs the cumulative total return on GNMA 9s, which were available for the entire period of 1979–1990 (losing one year to the moving average development of the elasticity function).

Graphs for the other coupons are very similar and are not shown. The pattern in all graphs shows that the hedging was successful, in that the return is more stable. At the same time, the hedge gives a lower return than the unhedged position, as interest rates generally fell during the simulation periods.

Hedge fluctuation due to basis risks is more apparent if the dominant uptrend is removed by examining excess returns. As most financing of mortgage securities is done through repurchase agreements ("repos") at rates near or below three-month LIBOR, excess returns over LIBOR were computed for each mortgage coupon. Figures 36.22 and 36.23 are representative of these results.

Figure 36.22—Cumulative Investment Performance: GNMA 9 Return in Excess of LIBOR

Figure 36.23—Cumulative Investment Performance: GNMA 13 Return in Excess of LIBOR

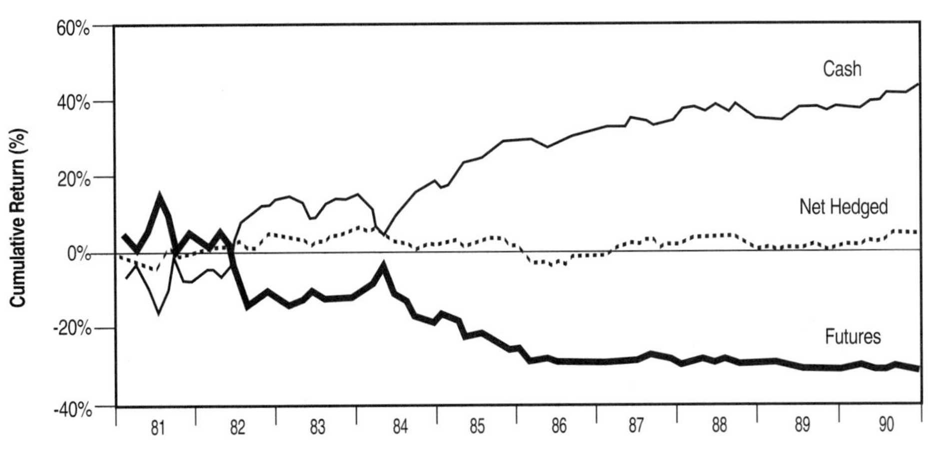

GNMA 8s and 9s, which were discounts in most of the period, generally earned a sub-LIBOR hedged return, while premiums such as GNMA 13s and GNMA 15s earned hedged returns in excess of LIBOR. In both Figures 36.22 and 36.23, the mirroring of futures gains and losses with cash gains and losses is apparent. With a hedge, when the cash profit is up, the futures hedge profit is down, and vice versa.

The "net hedged" return is much more stable than either futures or cash returns, and stays nearer the zero excess return line. As these returns are hedged to betas near zero, the equilibrium excess returns to the hedging strategies should on average be near zero.

Figures 36.24 and 36.25 clearly show the hedge effectiveness, as they give scatter plots of monthly and cumulative cash gains and losses versus corresponding futures gains and losses. The graphs for other coupons look quite similar to 36.24 and 36.25. Futures gains and losses of the hedges are approximately "equal but opposite," as the slopes are near 1.00. Comparing Figure 36.25 to 36.24, one sees the more precise fit over time as many monthly gain and loss fluctuations in the basis cancel out.

Figure 36.24—Monthly Hedge Performance: GNMA 13s Hedged with T-Bond Futures

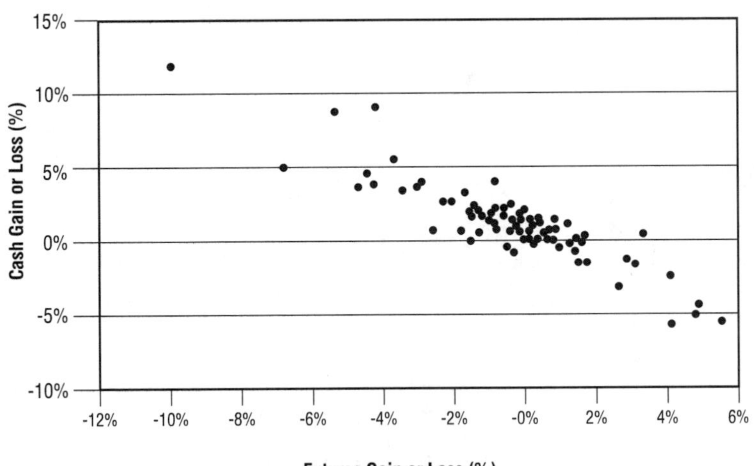

Figure 36.25—Cumulative Hedge Performance: GNMA 13s Hedged with T-Bond Futures

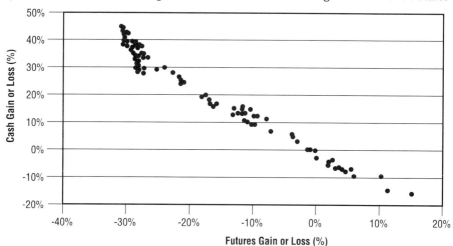

Another interesting way to view hedged returns is to graph their monthly gains and losses on the same scale as the unhedged returns. The hedged returns should show less volatility. Figures 36.26 and 36.27 show these graphs for GNMA 9s and 13s, respectively.

These figures show clearly the lower volatility of hedged monthly returns during the volatile interest rate period of 1979–1986. In the more recent period of relatively low interest rate volatility, the more volatile GNMA 9s show reduced volatility from hedging, but the GNMA 13s do not. During this recent period of lower rates, the GNMA 13s have sold for high premiums and have relatively little price volatility. As a result, the basis risk of the hedge is so great that the hedge effects little reduction in volatility. Thus, Figures 36.26 and 36.27 presage the different statistical results for the subperiods analyzed in the next section.

The most interesting features of these mortgage hedges are the dynamic option creation aspects. As shown in Section I, mortgages should have negative convexity due to the written prepayment options. Section III showed price graphs that verify

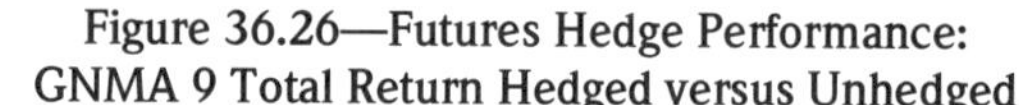

Figure 36.26—Futures Hedge Performance: GNMA 9 Total Return Hedged versus Unhedged

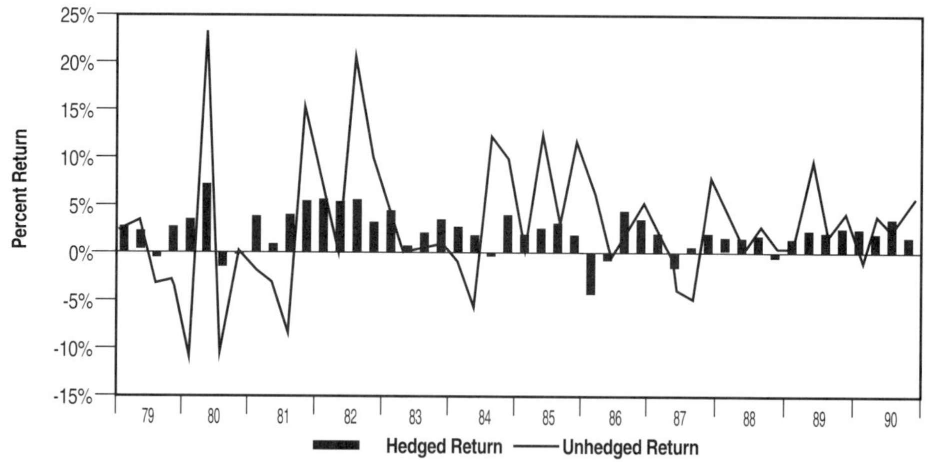

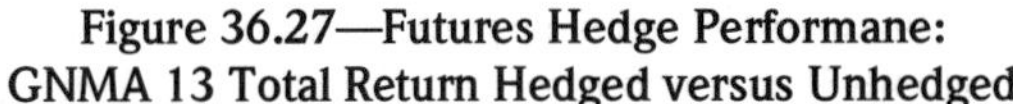

Figure 36.27—Futures Hedge Performane: GNMA 13 Total Return Hedged versus Unhedged

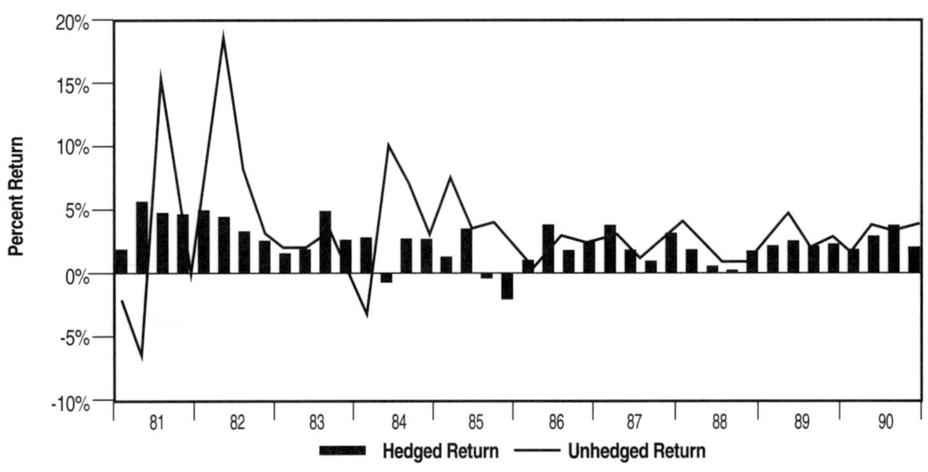

the presence of the expected curvature. Hedges for mortgages essentially create put options, as mortgage risks are analogous to those of written puts.

Figure 36.28 graphs the hedge elasticities for GNMA 13s versus Treasury bond prices. These elasticities summarize the dynamic trading strategy for GNMA 13s. When bond prices are high, elasticities (risks) are low, and hedge positions are low. When bond prices are low, prepayments slow, and the bond has a high elasticity and requires a large hedge position. Thus, the hedge sells short large amounts of T-bond futures at low prices and buys some of them back as prices increase (and rates fall).

The similarities to theoretical delta hedging curves of the option pricing literature are striking. This is the same type of trading strategy for creating a put option, as it should be. Graphs for other coupons trace out portions of that curve, with the portion depending upon whether the security was primarily a premium or a discount. GNMA 13s were both above and below par so they trace out the entire curve.

Figure 36.28—Dynamic Mortgage Hedges: GNMA 13 Elasticities versus T-Bond Futures

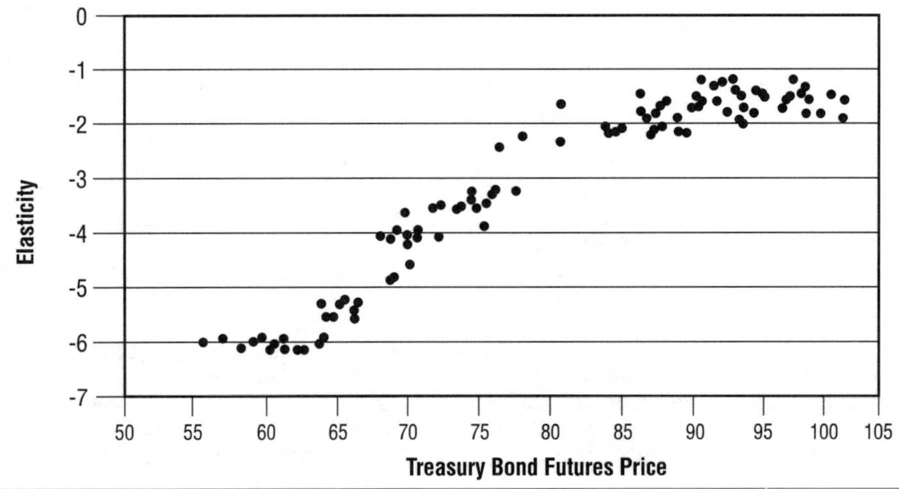

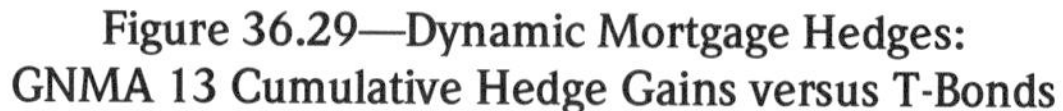
Figure 36.29—Dynamic Mortgage Hedges: GNMA 13 Cumulative Hedge Gains versus T-Bonds

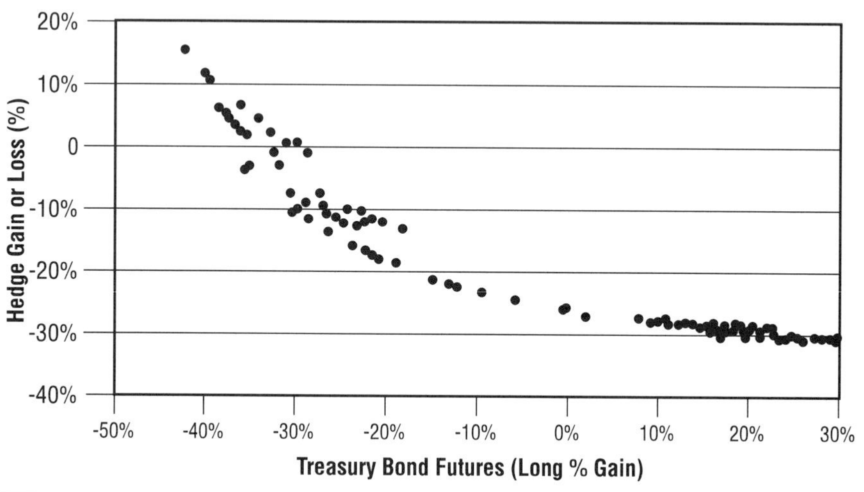

Another expected option-like feature is demonstrated in Figure 36.29. This plots the actual cumulative hedge profit versus Treasury bond futures prices. As the hedge creates a put option, the payoffs should be similar to the payoffs on a put option. Again, the dynamic hedge gives the expected payoff pattern, as the payoffs created have positive convexity that is a hedge for the negative convexity of the prepayment option. Graphs (not shown) of these cumulative payoffs for other coupons also resemble put options, with the strike prices varying with the mortgage's coupon, as expected.

Another important aspect of mortgage hedging and pricing is illustrated in Figure 36.29, as the curve drifts to the left as time passes. This normal pattern is attributable to the "whipsaw loss" or option creation cost present in any dynamic option replication. Whipsaw losses are incurred when the option creation strategy involves buying more contracts at higher prices and selling at lower prices, as put and call option creation strategies do. With that dynamic trading strategy, an increase in price followed by a return to the previous price results in a net loss from buying high and selling low, which is a whipsaw loss. As time passes, whipsaw losses accumulate. They are the inevitable costs of option creation.

Estimates of option creation costs are important in mortgage pricing, as they differ by coupon, are economically significant, and are the most complex part of a modern "option-adjusted spread" analysis. The extent of the loss is related more to the volatility of the trading position than to the general scale of it (which relates to the mortgage's elasticity). Thus, the whipsaw cost for a coupon is found by comparing its dynamic hedging returns to those of a constant hedge with the same average elasticity.

As that average elasticity is known only ex post, it could be viewed as one that assumes "perfect foresight." As the perfect foresight elasticity has the same overall interest rate exposure as the actual dynamic hedge, the difference in average return will be the loss due to the dynamic hedge adjustments about the average elasticity.

We have estimated whipsaw costs for each mortgage coupon for two major subperiods for which there were a meaningful amount of data by coupon, 1982–1986 and 1987–1990. Figure 36.30 shows the annualized excess returns of the perfect foresight hedges over those of the dynamic hedging strategies.

The amounts range from lows of ten to twenty-five basis points for deep discounts and very high premiums to 130 to 170 basis points for coupons between par and 3% premiums to par. As the amount of dynamic hedge adjustment can be seen from Table 36.5 (and Figure 36.28) to be greatest for coupons in that low premium range, the general shape of the whipsaw curve is sensible.

In terms of the usual option pricing nomenclature, whipsaw is caused by changes in the "delta hedge ratio." Changes in delta are sometimes called "gammas," which Cox and Rubinstein [1985, Chapter 5] show to be greatest for options

Figure 36.30—GNMA Mortgage Option Creation Costs: Sorted by Coupon - Par

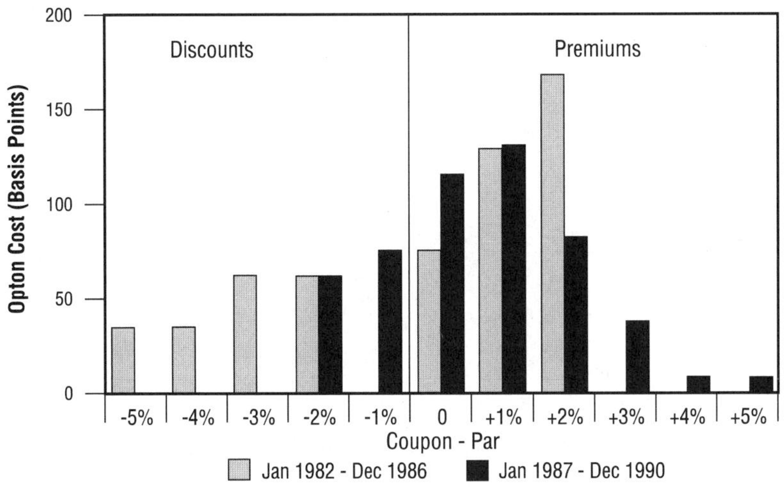

0 includes optiooons costs for coupons between 0 and 1% over par mtg coupon.

that are at the money. Low premium mortgages are mortgages whose prepayment options are at the money for many borrowers, as there are some costs to refinancing.

Note that whipsaw costs are lower in the more recent period of low volatility of interest rates, as expected. The general levels of whipsaw costs by coupon, in Figure 36.30, are of the same general magnitudes (but somewhat higher for the low premiums) as those assumed by many research firms today.

VII. STATISTICAL ANALYSIS OF MORTGAGE RISKS, RETURNS, AND HEDGES

This section compares hedged and unhedged returns on mortgages from 1979 to 1990 to Treasury returns of comparable duration, as well as to returns of major bond and stock indexes. Betas are presented for mortgages relative to the Salomon Brothers Mortgage Index, to twenty-year Treasury bond futures, and to the Standard & Poor's 500 stock price index.

Unfortunately, data are not available for all mortgage coupons for the entire period (see Table 36.4). GNMA 10s and 11s were introduced only in late 1979, after the surge in interest rates generated originations of those higher-rate mortgages. GNMA 13s, 14s, and 15s were introduced at various times during 1981; prior to that time mortgage interest rates had never been that high. An oddity is the fact that rates jumped so quickly in 1981 and 1982 that GNMA 12s were not issued in large enough amounts to be quoted in the *Wall Street Journal* until the end of 1983. Finally, GNMA 14s and 15s had prepaid so much that their prices became of extremely poor quality, and the *Wall Street Journal* stopped quoting their prices in March 1990.

Given this ragged data set, the analysis is performed for three subperiods: calendar years 1979–1981, 1982–1986, and 1987–1990. The first and second subperiods had generally very high and volatile rates; the more recent subperiod had lower rates and lower rate volatility.

Table 36.6 gives for each of the subperiods the means and standard deviations of monthly returns both hedged and unhedged on all GNMA coupons from 8% to 15%. For comparison purposes, we analyze Ibbotson Associates' series of "Intermediate-Term Government Bonds" and "Long-Term Government Bonds," as they represent total returns on bench mark five-year and twenty-year government bonds. Returns for the Salomon Brothers Mortgage Index, Standard & Poor's 500 stock price index, the Shearson Lehman Government/Corporate Index, three-month treasury bills, and three-month LIBOR are also shown.

During the 1979–1981 period, average mortgage returns unhedged and returns on other long-term bonds were lower than those on Treasury bills, as rates increased significantly during the period. Hedged returns on mortgages were much

Table 36.6—Mortgage and Bond Returns: Means and Standard Deviations (Monthly)

Long-Term Bonds and Stocks	*1979–1981*		*1982–1986*		*1987–1990*	
	Mean(%)	*Std Dev(%)*	*Mean(%)*	*Std Dev(%)*	*Mean(%)*	*Std Dev(%)*
5 -Year Treasury	0.52	3.32	1.33	1.77	0.65	1.39
20 -Year Treasury	0.04	5.28	1.71	3.70	0.64	2.71
Shearson Lehman Gov't/Corp	0.42	3.39	1.40	1.85	0.67	1.50
Standard & Poor's 500	1.21	4.39	1.61	4.23	1.09	5.52
Salomon Mortgage Index	0.16	4.80	1.62	2.36	0.78	1.52
GNMA 8 Unhedged	0.12	5.16	1.77	3.07	0.76	2.48
GNMA 9 Unhedged	0.15	5.05	1.74	2.96	0.79	2.25
GNMA 10 Unhedged	N/A	N/A	1.71	2.83	0.77	1.93
GNMA 11 Unhedged	N/A	N/A	1.61	2.67	0.80	1.29
GNMA 12 Unhedged	N/A	N/A	N/A	N/A	0.84	1.00
GNMA 13 Unhedged	N/A	N/A	1.42	2.03	0.88	0.71
GNMA 14 Unhedged	N/A	N/A	1.30	1.69	0.83*	0.54*
GNMA 15 Unhedged	N/A	N/A	1.26	1.48	0.79*	0.55*
Short-Term Bills and Hedges	*1979–1981*		*1982–1986*		*1987–1990*	
	Mean(%)	*Std Dev(%)*	*Mean(%)*	*Std Dev(%)*	*Mean(%)*	*Std Dev(%)*
Treasury Bills (3-month)	0.95	0.24	0.69	0.16	0.57	0.10
LIBOR (3-month)	1.17	0.25	0.81	0.20	0.68	0.08
GNMA 8 Unhedged	0.88	1.83	0.92	1.24	0.59	1.43
GNMA 9 Unhedged	0.92	1.62	0.91	1.18	0.61	1.36
GNMA 10 Unhedged	N/A	N/A	0.89	1.23	0.58	1.29
GNMA 11 Unhedged	N/A	N/A	0.87	1.14	0.62	0.86
GNMA 12 Unhedged	N/A	N/A	N/A	N/A	0.71	0.75
GNMA 13 Unhedged	N/A	N/A	0.83	1.07	0.81	0.67
GNMA 14 Unhedged	N/A	N/A	0.76	1.12	0.80*	0.65*
GNMA 15 Unhedged	N/A	N/A	0.75	1.10	0.76*	0.57*

* Data for GNMA 14s and 15s end in March 1990.

higher than unhedged returns, as the hedges provided protection for the fall in rates.

Comparing standard deviations across subperiods, we see that the 1979–1981 period had the highest volatility of returns and rates, with the ranking of returns reversed as rates fell in the 1982–1986 and 1987–1990 periods. In both of those periods, hedge losses reduced the returns on mortgages. In both 1982–1986 and 1987–1990, however, the hedged returns on mortgages exceeded those of Treasury bills. Unhedged returns in mortgages were similar to those of comparable duration Treasuries in the 1982–1986 period and exceeded them in the 1987–1990 period.

Next, let us examine Table 36.6 for the effectiveness of the dynamic hedging strategies in reducing risk. For GNMA 8s, 9s, 10s, and 11s, in all subperiods, the dynamically hedged returns are of substantially lower volatility than the unhedged returns. For the high coupons, hedges were very effective in reducing risk in the 1982–1986 period when rates were high and there was great rate volatility. In the 1987–1990 period, the dynamic hedges were not helpful in reducing the risks of high coupons. Their primary risks then were prepayment basis risks that are independent of (or very non-linear in) interest rates. During 1987–1990, elasticities for the high coupons were very small, so mortgage investors were aware of the limited usefulness of interest rate hedges for them.

In an alternative analysis of dynamic hedging, Table 36.7 shows the results of regressions of unhedged mortgage returns on the dynamic futures hedge returns. These results are compared to those for similar regressions on Treasury bond futures (excess) returns for a long position. Both of these regressions benefit from being able to fit the slope ex post. This is an advantage over the actual dynamic hedges, as they used only data available at the times the hedges were placed.

There are two interesting things to note about Table 36.7. First, the slopes in the dynamic futures hedge regressions should be approximately 1.00. They are for the discounts, but they are less than that for the high coupons, particularly during the 1987–1990 period. As futures hedge positions are chosen in advance, negative convexities of the mortgages will make the hedges seem too large ex post when rates decline. This is at least a partial explanation for slopes being less than 1.00 in the last two subperiods and greater than 1.00 in the first subperiod.

The slopes for the Treasury bond futures regressions give the estimated interest rate elasticities of the mortgages divided by the elasticity of the twenty-year Treasury bond contract. In each period, those estimates logically decline in each period for the higher coupons.

The second point may be more subtle, but it is of significant interest, as comparison displays the hedging advantage of dynamic adjustments. The period of greatest rate volatility for which there were many coupons is the second subperiod, 1982–1986. For mortgages hedged with a fixed slope (estimated ex post) in T-bond futures, the R-squareds range from 0.78 to 0.38.

Note that the dynamic mortgages constructed from the same Treasury bond futures returns, but with dynamically changing hedge ratios, show R-squareds improved to a range of 0.84 to 0.52. For the high-coupon mortgages, which went through significant changes in elasticities during that period, the improvement in hedge correlation is especially large.

Thus, in times of great rate volatility, dynamic hedging strategies significantly improve hedge correlation. In times of low rate volatility (e.g., 1987–1990), the dynamic hedging strategy does not improve upon a static hedging strategy.

The results of the same regression equations are also shown in Table 36.7 for the longest time period for which coupons from 8% to 15% were continuously available, November 1981 to March 1990. They show even more clearly the higher correlations of the dynamic hedging strategies than those of the static hedging strategies with the same hedge instrument.

Finally, Table 36.8 shows the betas, or return sensitivities, of mortgage returns on different coupons to movements in the Salomon Brothers Mortgage Index and to the Standard & Poor's 500 stock price index. As the Salomon index includes these mortgages, it is not surprising to see very strong relationships there. Furthermore, the higher betas for discounts than for premiums make intuitive sense and are consistent with the elasticity analyses.

What is more interesting is that the GNMA 8s and 9s have had recent increases in betas. This is partly because the index also includes premiums, which have had reduced elasticities as rates have fallen, and partly due to the growing weight on FNMA and FHLMC mortgage securities, which have lower elasticities.

The mortgage index regressions of Table 36.8 and the Treasury bond futures regressions of Table 36.7 give bond market betas for mortgages. Betas relative to the stock market are in the second panel of Table 36.8.

Stock market betas for mortgages move much like other bonds' betas move across the subperiods. During the 1979–1981 period and the 1982–

Table 36.7—Dynamic Hedge Effectiveness

	A: Dynamic Futures Hedges								*B: Treasury Bond Futures*							
	1979–1981		*1982–1986*		*1987–1990*		*Nov 81–Mar 90*		*1979–1981*		*1982–1986*		*1987–1990*		*Nov 81–Mar 90*	
	Slope	R^2	*Slope*	R^2	*Slope*	R^2	*Slope*	R^2	*Slope*	R^2	*Slope*	R^2	*Slope*	R^2	*Slope*	R^2
GNMA 8	–1.19	0.92	–0.94	0.84	–1.11	0.88	–1.03	0.87	0.92	0.91	0.64	0.78	0.68	0.90	0.71	0.83
GNMA 9	–1.17	0.93	–1.93	0.84	–1.03	0.86	–1.00	0.87	0.91	0.92	0.62	0.78	0.60	0.89	0.67	0.82
GNMA 10	N/A	N/A	–0.90	0.82	–0.95	0.80	–0.97	0.85	N/A	N/A	0.56	0.70	0.49	0.85	0.60	0.75
GNMA 11	N/A	N/A	–0.92	0.82	–0.82	0.64	–0.92	0.84	N/A	N/A	0.50	0.62	0.32	0.66	0.52	0.65
GNMA 12	N/A	N/A	N/A	N/A	–0.69	0.44	–0.78**	0.74**	N/A	N/A	N/A	N/A	0.18	0.45	0.26**	0.44**
GNMA 13	N/A	N/A	–0.82	0.75	–0.56	0.22	–0.89	0.80	N/A	N/A	0.32	0.44	0.10	0.21	0.33	0.45
GNMA 14	N/A	N/A	–0.75	0.63	–0.29*	0.07*	–0.83	0.73	N/A	N/A	0.24	0.34	0.05*	0.06*	0.26	0.36
GNMA 15	N/A	N/A	–0.70	0.52	–0.46*	0.20*	–0.83	0.67	N/A	N/A	0.22	0.38	0.08*	0.20*	0.24	0.40
Avg. Slope																
t-statistic =	20.5		14.3		9.6		17.0		19.2		9.9		10.0		12.4	

Notes: A: GNMA 8 Unhedged Return = a + b [GNMA 8 Dynamic Futures Hedge Gain %]
B: GNMA 8 Unhedged Return = a + b [Near Treasury Bond Futures Gain %]

* Data for GNMA 14s and 15s end in March 1990.
** Data for GNMA 12s cover only January 1984–December 1990.

Table 36.8—GNMA Mortgage Betas

	A: Salomon Mortgage Index						*,B: Standard & Poor's 500*					
	1979–1981		*1982–1986*		*1987–1990*		*1979–1981*		*1982–1986*		*1987–1990*	
Unhedged	*Beta*	*t(b)*	*Beta*	*t(b)*	*Beta*	*t(b)*	*Beta*	*t(b)*	*Beta*	*t(b)*	*Beta*	*t(b)*
GNMA 8	1.06	38.8	1.26	29.0	1.44	12.7	0.40	2.1	0.31	3.6	0.04	0.6
GNMA 9	1.05	49.7	1.21	27.5	1.28	11.7	0.41	2.2	0.31	3.7	0.03	0.6
GNMA 10	N/A	N/A	1.16	30.7	1.06	10.1	N/A	N/A	0.28	3.6	0.01	0.2
GNMA 11	N/A	N/A	1.08	25.6	0.72	10.6	N/A	N/A	0.26	3.4	0.03	0.9
GNMA 12	N/A	N/A	N/A	N/A	0.50	7.1	N/A	N/A	N/A	N/A	0.03	1.4
GNMA 13	N/A	N/A	0.78	17.0	0.27	4.9	N/A	N/A	0.16	2.7	0.03	1.9
GNMA 14	N/A	N/A	0.61	12.6	0.16*	3.2*	N/A	N/A	0.12	2.4	0.03*	1.8*
GNMA 15	N/A	N/A	0.49	9.7	0.21*	4.7*	N/A	N/A	0.15	3.6	0.02*	1.3*

* GNMA 14s & 15s only from January 1987 to March 1990.

1986 period, these betas are significantly positive in the 0.20 to 0.40 range, consistent with other studies. This is so because interest rates rose when the stock market dropped in the recession of 1980 and 1981–1982, and rates dropped when the stock market recovered during the growth years from late 1982 through 1986. In the 1987–1990 period, the stock market did well, while rates were relatively stable, leading to betas that were insignificantly different from zero.

VIII. SUMMARY

This article has presented the theoretical reasons for negative convexity of mortgages and showed that the data support the theory. A method that uses the market's implied price elasticities for risk analysis and hedging is found to be successful in constructing hedges of these very complicated securities. The dynamic nature of the hedging strategies inevitably generates whipsaw losses attributable to replication of the prepayment option. These losses, however, are reasonable in size and in pattern compared to those estimated by current mortgage researchers.

Returns on mortgages were examined for both hedged and unhedged positions, with average levels of returns found to exceed Treasury returns of comparable duration. Hedging simulations indicate that some hedged returns exceeded LIBOR financing costs, and some did not. The evidence presented here appears to be consistent with returns that are commensurate with mortgage risks. The methods for estimating whipsaw option replication costs and implied price elasticities for mortgages with changing risks, however, should help investors in their attempts to identify relative value in mortgage markets.

ENDNOTE

The author gratefully acknowledges the help of Michael Giarla, Campbell Harvey, Timothy Rowe, and especially research assistants, Michelle Rodgerson and Kathryn Waseleski.

REFERENCES

Asay, Michael R., France-Helene Guillaume, Ravi K. Mattu. "Duration and Convexity of Mortgage-Backed Securities," in Frank J. Fabozzi, ed., *The Handbook of Mortgage-Backed Securities*, 2nd edition. Chicago: Probus Publishing Co., 1987.

Black, Fischer, and Myron S. Scholes. "The Pricing of Options and Corporate Liabilities." *Journal of Political Economy* 81 (May-June 1973), pp. 637–659.

Breeden, Douglas T., and Michael J. Giarla. "Hedging Interest Rate Risks with Futures, Swaps and Options," in Frank J. Fabozzi, ed., *The Handbook of Mortgage-Backed Securities*, 2nd edition. Chicago: Probus Publishing Co., 1987.

Cox, John C., and Mark Rubenstein, *Options Markets*. Englewood Cliffs, NJ: Prentice-Hall, 1985.

Diller, Stanley. "Parametric Analysis of Fixed Income Securities: Options, Passthroughs, Convexity, and Asset/Liability Management." Goldman Sachs Financial Strategies Group, June 1984.

Dunn, Kenneth B., and John J. McConnell. "Valuation of GNMA Mortgage-Backed Securities." *Journal of Finance* 36 (June 1981), pp. 599–616.

Jacob, David P., and Alden L. Toevs. "An Analysis of the New Valuation, Duration and Convexity Models for Mortgage-Backed Securities." Morgan Stanley Fixed Income Analytical Research, January 1987.

McConnell, John J., and Manoj K. Singh. "Prepayments and the Valuation of Adjustable Rate Mortgage-Backed Securities." *Journal of Fixed Income* 1 (June 1991), pp. 21–35.

Richard, Scott F., and Richard Roll. "Prepayments on Fixed-Rate Mortgage-Backed Securities." *Journal of Portfolio Management* 15 (Spring 1989), pp. 73–82.

Salomon Brothers. "An Analytical Record of Yields and Yield Spreads." 1987.

____________. "Monthly Mortgage Securities Prepayment Profile." Monthly 1983–present.

Schwartz, Eduardo, and Walter Torous. "Prepayment and the Valuation of Mortgage-Backed Securities." *Journal of Finance* 44 (June 1989), pp. 375–392.

Stocks, Bonds, Bills, and Inflation 1991 Yearbook. Chicago: Ibbotson Associates, 1991.

Waldman, Michael, and Steven P. Baum. "The Historical Performance of Mortgage Securities: 1972–1980." Salomon Brothers Mortgage Research, August 1980.

Waldman, Michael, and Mark Gordon. "Evaluating the Option Features of Mortgage Securities." Salomon Brothers Mortgage Research, September 1986.

Part VI

The Securitization of Credit Cards

Chapter 37

Evaluating the Risk of Credit Card-Backed Securities

by Gregory C. Raab,
Neil Baron
and
Deborah W. Madden
Fitch Investors Service

INTRODUCTION

Not all credit card deals are created equal. Default rates on underlying credit card receivables are one of the variables that determine the credit risks inherent in any transaction. Other factors that influence credit quality include:

1. the effect of monthly card payment activity on default experience.
2. exposure to credit deterioration of a third-party credit enhancement provider or seller, and
3. the timing of principal repayment.

Various forms of credit enhancement techniques combined with innovative legal and financial structures have been used to substantially mitigate or eliminate credit concerns. Nevertheless, in Fitch's view there are clear quality graduations of credit strength and payment structures among these highly rated securities.

Most credit card transactions are of extremely high quality. It is difficult to precisely determine how an economic recession would affect the default experience on credit cards. However, most credit card transactions contain early repayment triggers sensitive to significant deteriorations in monthly cash flows from the underlying receivables. As such, a dramatic decline in the performance of the underlying receivables would trigger an amortization event causing an early payout of principal. However, amortization triggers should not be overly conservative to avoid an unnecessary repayment of investors' principal. This early warning trigger combined with the excess yield created by the receivables, enables many transactions to withstand default rates at significant multiples of historical experience.

The credit card backed securities sector will attract many large regional and money center banks to the market in the 1990s as they sell assets to improve capital positions. Demand for these securities will come from traditional structured investors as well as new entrants seeking high-quality assets with attractive yields. Fitch believes that in making investment decisions, investors should focus on the structural as well as the credit aspects of these securities. This report has been prepared to assist the investor in the decision-making process.

An example showing the difference between deal structures of the two biggest issuers is the Sears Credit Account Trust 1989-A issue, lowered to AA from AAA by Fitch, and Citicorp's National Credit Card Trust 1989-5 rated AAA by other agencies. While both are high quality securities, the credit and payment structures differ. Sears' level of losses on the credit card receivables has historically been less than Citicorp's. This is attributable to differences in marketing philosophies. However, this difference in loss experience is more than offset by Citicorp's high level of excess spread and a very fast monthly payment rate (MPR). Citicorp's higher level of excess spread enables it to withstand a greater increase in defaults on the underlying receivables before utilizing the credit enhancement than the Sears transaction. Furthermore, a high MPR would help retire the Citicorp issue more rapidly than the Sears issue should an amortization even be breached. Finally, from a legal perspective, the Citicorp structure is stronger than the one utilized by Sears. Both structures

Figure 37.1—ABS Volume by Collateral Type
1989: $25.5 Billion

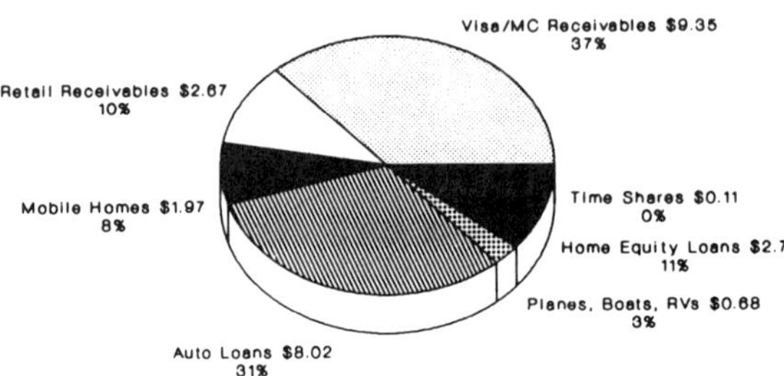

Source: Asset Sales Report

insulate the receivables from their respective sellers. However, since Sears' corporate family retains the risk of loss, via the retention of the subordinate certificates, a Sears bankruptcy might lead to a legal argument that could disrupt the flow of funds to investors in Sears' senior/subordinate transaction. While this legal challenge would most likely not succeed, thereby preserving the cash flow dedicated to investors, it is not as strong a structure as asset-backed securities without this risk. For this reason the Sears 89-A was lowered to AA from AAA when Sears senior debt was lowered to A from AA–. Table 37.1 is a checklist of the key structural considerations Fitch reviews when rating a credit card-backed transaction. (More detailed explanations are provided later in the text.)

CREDIT CARD ASSET-BACKED SECURITIES

The asset-backed securities (ABS) market has grown rapidly since the first ABS deal was structured in 1985. Asset securitization is the sale of rights to receive future cash flows from receivables in the form of securities placed with investors in the public or private markets.

To investors, they offer significantly higher yields than comparable Treasuries or similarly rated corporate debt. The average life of most ABSs ranges from one to five years. The average life of a security is the expected average time it will take to repay each dollar of principal. Asset-backed securities are structured to obtain an investment grade rating from Fitch.

Figure 37.2—ABS Volume by Year
$73.0 Billion as of Q1 1990

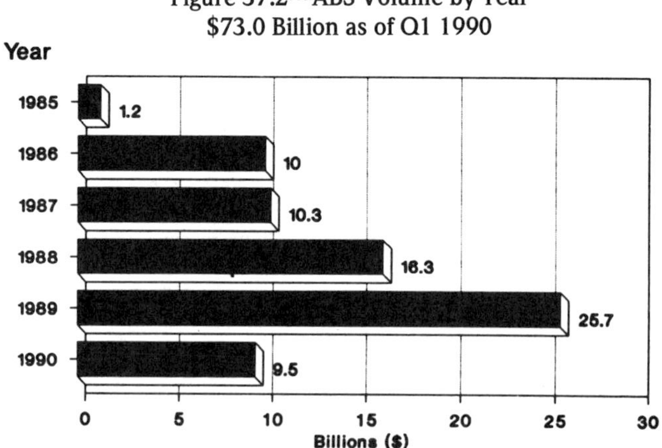

Source: Asset Sales Report

Table 37.1—Checklist for Investors

Risk exposure to credit card transactions:	*Example*	
	SEARS 89-A	*NCCT 89-5*
Seller	Sears	Citicorp
Decline in underwriting standards	Unlikely	Unlikely
Change in loanholder's contractual payment schedule or payment patterns*	Unlikely	Unlikely
Change in principal repayment to investors	Possible	Unlikely
Decrease in interest rates		
Contractual—for competitive reasons	Possible	Possible
Change in state usury laws	Unlikely	Possible
Increase in convenience usage	Unlikely	Possible
Rating downgrade of seller affecting rating of ABS transaction	Possible	N.A.
Servicer	Sears	Citicorp
Decline in collection standards	Unlikely	Unlikely
Bankruptcy	Unlikely	Remote
Disruption due to commingling of funds	Unlikely	Remote
Legal		
Disruption due to bankruptcy of seller	Unlikely	Remote
Credit Enhancement Provider	Senior/sub	Senior/sub
(LOC, Surety Bond or Guarantee)		
Rating downgrade of provider	N.A.	N.A.
Principal Funding Account	Amortizing	Soft bullet
Bankruptcy of GIC provider	N.A.	Unlikely
Bankruptcy of PFA hard bullet guarantor	N.A.	N.A.
Eligible Investments		
Seller CP—additional exposure to seller	Yes	Yes
Payment Structure		
Adequacy of amortization events (AE)	Strong	Strong
Speed of investor repayment after AE	16 months	9 months
Cushion available at amortization event	0%	1.70%

* In November 1988, Sears changed the minimum monthly payment calculation from 1/30 to 1/36 of the relevant balance.

The "Asset Sales Report" identifies $73 billion of asset-backed securities offered in the last five years. Over $9.3 billion was backed by credit cards in 1989. Other types of ABSs have been backed by loans secured by automobiles, trucks, boats, mobile homes, and equipment leases as well as home equity loans and high yield debt.

TYPES OF CREDIT CARDS

Credit cards are unsecured revolving debt obligations. In the event of a cardholder default, there is no collateral or asset for the lender to repossess, therefore limiting expected recoveries. Cardholders having difficulty making their loan payments usually pay their secured obligations first (i.e., mortgage and automobile loan). The principal repayment rates on each issuer's credit cards differ widely. The repayment rate will affect the performance of the portfolio as well as the expected speed of principal repayment to investors. Fitch reviews these factors when determining the level of credit enhancement consistent with a specific rating.

General Purpose Credit Cards

There are two types of general purpose credit cards: convenience cards and revolving credit lines. Convenience cards, such as American Express and Diners Club, require the repayment of the entire balance each month. Revolving credit lines, like VISA and MasterCard, require minimum monthly payments. All ABS credit card transactions to date have been backed by revolving credit lines.

Banks issue VISA and MasterCard credit cards, (which are used to purchase goods and services and to obtain cash advances) as members in worldwide VISA and MasterCard programs. Bank credit card finance charges typically include annual membership fees, merchant interchange fees (charged by creditors as partial compensation for credit risk, fraud losses, and partial receivables' funding) and other related fees. Interchange rates range from 1.0 percent to 1.85 percent of the transaction amount.

A significant number of cardholders are convenience users who pay the outstanding balance when the bill comes due. To increase credit usage, some issuers offer interest rate tiers in which higher outstanding balances incur lower interest rates. The interest rate spread between the lowest and highest tiers may be as high as 500 basis points. Banks also offer variable-rate credit cards with spreads of 300 to 825 basis points over the current prime or Treasury rates.

Premium credit cards, commonly referred to as 'Gold Cards,' extend higher credit limits and provide additional services. They are usually offered to good customers and higher income individuals who tend to be better credit risks.

Retail or Private Label Credit Cards

Credit cards are issued by retailers for use in affiliated outlets, such as Sears, Firestone, J.C. Penney, Montgomery Ward, and Macy's. Their usage will be directly related to the sale activity of the retailer. In addition to their own credit cards, retailers may accept other credit cards, limiting the usage of private label cards. Some retailers offer special credit card promotions to increase sales. In an ABS transaction this practice may increase the investors' credit risk if the new cardholders do not conform to acceptable underwriting standards.

An individual retailer's principal repayment rates may differ according to the various repayment programs it offers. For example, a retailer may offer longer repayment terms for "large ticket" items, such as major furnishings and appliances, than for other purchases.

In the event of a retailer's bankruptcy, the private label cardholders may not feel compelled to repay their unpaid balance. Bankruptcy may also cause experienced personnel to resign, and collection standards may be relaxed, further increasing credit card losses.

SEARS vs. CITICORP

Citicorp and Sears are the top two issuers of ABSs backed by credit card receivables. Both issuers actively use the senior/subordinate structure. The senior/subordinate structure utilized in Sears' Credit Account Trust transactions is unconventional compared to other credit card-backed issues. Sears, by indirectly holding the subordinate certificates, retains the risk of loss on the underlying receivables well in excess of historical loss performance. In the unlikely event of a Sears bankruptcy, creditors of Sears may claim that Sears' transfer of the receivables to the trust was not a sale but a pledge against the loans. If that challenge was successful, the flow of funds from cardholders to

**Table 37.2—Top 10 Credit Card ABS Issuers
As of Q1 1990**

Issuer	*$ (MM)*	*Issues*
Citibank N.A	9,562.0	14
Sears Roebuck & Co.	4,750.0	11
Maryland Bank, N.A.	3,500.0	7
First National Bank of Chicago	2,400.0	5
Chemical Bank	1,200.0	3
Security Pacific	750.0	1
J.C. Penney	600.0	2
Manufacturers Hanover	475.0	1
Chevy Chase Savings	450.0	2
National City Bank	350.0	1

Source: Asset Sales Report

certificate investors would be interrupted. While legal opinions have been given that a legal challenge would not be successful, this structure is weaker than structures used in other credit card-backed transactions. The Citibank senior/subordinate structure isolates the default risk in the subordinate certificates, and these certificates are sold in the public or private market. The selling of the subordinate certificates eliminates any recourse to the issuer (Citicorp) and therefore perfects the sales treatment of the securities. The top issuers of credit card securities include seven commercial banks, two retailers and one savings and loan. The primary motivation for these institutions to securitize include: improved capital ratios as well as developing alternative funding sources. Regional and money center banks are expected to actively use the ABS market to improve capitalization in the 1990s.

Transfer of Receivables

The servicer, typically the originator of the credit card receivables, sells or contributes specific credit card account balances (but not the accounts) to a separate trust or special purpose subsidiary. The trust conveys ownership of the underlying assets to investors through the sale of certificates. The receivables, which are removed from the books of the seller, become the assets of the trust.

Legal Issues

The legal structure of credit card transactions should assure that the seller's insolvency will not interrupt timely payment of principal and interest to investors. This insulation from the credit risk of the seller is more difficult to achieve for sellers subject to the United States Bankruptcy Code (the "Bankruptcy Code") than for banks and thrift institutions, which are not subject to the Bankruptcy Code.

When a seller retains a greater interest rate risk or default risk beyond the historical default rate on the assets transferred to the issuing trust, such transfer might be characterized as a pledge, instead of a sale. (Although there is meritorious argument against such characterization, legal precedent has been insufficient for legal counsel to opine that these transfers are sales.) If the transaction is characterized as a pledge, the investors would not own the assets; instead, they would be creditors of the seller, secured by a pledge of the assets. In such event, the bankruptcy of the seller is likely to result in a default on the certificates. Because banks and thrifts are not subject to the Bankruptcy Code, characterization as a pledge should not result in a default. Legal precedent and options of the FHLBB and FDIC, which should continue to have viability after the Financial Institutions Reform, Recovery and Enforcement Act of 1989, support this conclusion. Moreover, because banks and thrifts are less likely to retain risk of loss on the assets transferred (retention of risk of loss would keep the assets on their balance sheets for capital adequacy purposes), these transactions are probably characterized as sales. Although most pooling and servicing agreements of selling banks and thrifts generally provide for accelerated amortization of principal upon the seller's insolvency, such insolvency is attended by a prepayment and, therefore, reinvestment risk. These provisions are intended to protect investors (even though they pose such a reinvestment risk), and, as a result, their enforceability is important.

Accelerated amortization upon seller insolvency is accomplished by the distribution to investors of all pool collections, including collections on the seller's participation. Although counsel have been generally unable to opine on the enforceability of this provision in the event of the insolvency of a selling bank or thrift, there seems to be little or no incentive for a receiver of a failed bank or thrift to challenge this provision. While a successful challenge by a receiver would result in an earlier payment to the receiver (and a later payout to investor), such a result would not seem in the receiver's best interests in light of the high return on these assets and the fact that, due to the revolving nature of credit card accounts, later payments are not necessarily made on account of older and, therefore, less creditworthy balances. Moreover, the legal and accounting costs associated with an attempt to reallocate distributions of collections on an account-by-account basis would seem unwarranted by the benefits (if any) to the receiver. Moreover, the investors are likely to be paid out by the time the reallocation process would be complete. In informal discussions, the FDIC has generally concurred with this analysis.

There is concern, however, that a receiver might recharacterize these transactions as debt, accelerate them, and pay investors even earlier than is provided for in the pooling and servicing agreements. The FDIC's early payout of the RepublicBank, Delaware, credit card transaction is cited as a basis for this concern. However, that transaction involved the sale of notes which can be accelerated—not certificates of participation. The FDIC's acceleration of the RepublicBank transaction, therefore, is not much of an indication as to what a receiver might do in a certificate transaction.

This risk seems relatively low for several reasons. These transactions are most likely sales due to the absence of recourse against the selling bank or thrift. Moreover, the regulators have not accelerated the senior certificates issued by thrifts that have securitized assets (e.g., mortgages) by retaining subordinated participations and have been placed in conservatorship or receivership. Also, the short duration of the payout period after a credit card amortization event creates little or no incentive to accelerate.

The insolvency of a seller can also result in the loss of any trust funds held by the seller in a commingled account. More precisely, where the seller acts as servicer and deposits collections in its own account along with other funds of the seller, investors' claims to such collections could be no better than the claims of unsecured creditors. As a result, investors would have seller credit risk to the extent of collections held in a commingled account of the seller on the date of its insolvency.

To address this concern, recent transactions have provided that sellers must cease commingling collections if their short-term unsecured rating falls below F-1/A-1/P-1, as the case may be. Sellers that are unrated or rated below F-1/A-1/P-1 cannot commingle. Instead, all collections are deposited in an account of the certificate trustee either directly or within 24 to 48 hours of collection.

In some cases, the certificate trustee may lend collections to the seller so long as the seller's rating is at least F-1/A-1/P-1, or where the seller's obligation to repay such loan is guaranteed by an F-1/A-1/P-1 letter of credit. In the latter event, however, the rating of the certificates may be dependent on the rating of the letter of credit provider.

In summary, should a selling bank or thrift fail, proper structuring should preserve timely payment of principal and interest, including payment of collections that have not yet been distributed, and permit the enforcement of early amortization provisions.

Where a seller becomes subject to a proceeding under the Bankruptcy Code, characterization of the transfer as a pledge is likely to interrupt timely payment to investors, and the enforceability of provisions for early amortization is uncertain.

For example, suppose a seller deposits $145 million of credit card receivables in a trust, and the trust issues $100 million in participations to investors (in the form of certificates) and a $45 million participation back to the seller, $15 million of which is subordinated to the investors' participation. Also, suppose that the pooling and servicing agreement provides that upon the bankruptcy of the seller, all collections on the $145 million pool will be paid to investors until they are fully paid.

If the seller's transfer is characterized as a pledge (which is possible in light of the fact that the seller has retained default risk substantially in excess of the historic default rate), the investors will be secured creditors of the bankrupt seller and, as a result, are likely to suffer interruptions in payment of principal and interest on their certificates. Moreover, even in the absence of such characterization, the enforceability of the early amortization provision would be in doubt.

As a result, sellers subject to the Bankruptcy Code have created subsidiaries through which they affect these transactions. Sears, Roebuck & Co. ("Sears") transferred credit card receivables to its subsidiary, Sears Receivables Financing Group, Inc. ("SRFG"), which deposited the receivables in a trust that issued certificates of participation to investors and to SRFG. A portion of SRFG's participation was subordinated to the investors' participation.

Counsel opined that the transfer from Sears to SRFG was a true sale and that in the event of Sears' bankruptcy, SRFG would remain legally separate from (i.e., would not be substantively consolidated with) Sears.

Counsel did not opine that the transfer from SRFG to the trust was a sale, and disclosure was made to the effect that investors could suffer a default should SRFG become bankrupt for any reason, including as a result of a Sears' bankruptcy. This risk, however, was mitigated by (i) the relatively high credit rating of Sears, at the time AA; (ii) the belief, based on the structure of the transaction and legal opinions, that in the event of Sears' bankruptcy, SRFG would continue to survive with the pool intact and insulated from Sears' bankruptcy; (iii) the absence of any obligation or liability on the part of SRFG that would result in its insolvency (i.e., its special purpose nature) and (iv) opinions indicating that, should SRFG become bankrupt and the transfer to the trust be characterized as a pledge, investors would nevertheless be secured by a first priority perfected security interest in the pool and, therefore, not suffer ultimate loss.

Nevertheless, some concern was expressed that the creation and insertion of a subsidiary for, among other reasons, the purpose of retaining default risk on the assets might cause a court to look through the subsidiary and view Sears as both the seller and recourse provider. This was the primary reason the rating of Sears 89-A certificates were lowered to AA from AAA when Sears' senior debt was lowered to A from AA.

Figure 37.3—Investor and Seller Certificate Balance (During Revolving Period)*

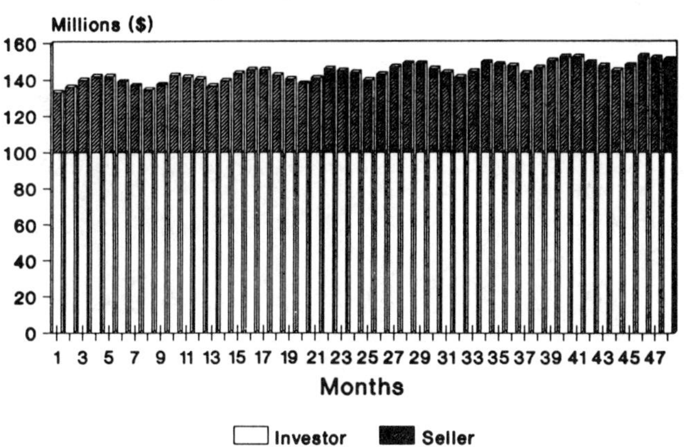

* The investor's principal balance remains fixed at $100 million during the revolving period while the seller's balance fluctuates between $33 and $53 million.

J.C. Penney & Co., Inc. affected a similar transaction through a subsidiary, JCP Receivables Inc. ("JCPR"). However, JCPR did not take back a subordinated participation but instead provided credit enhancement through a Credit Suisse letter of credit. For this reason, from a legal point of view, the rating of these certificates would not be dependent on J.C. Penney's rating.

INVESTOR PRINCIPAL PAYMENT STRUCTURES

The trust issues at least two types of certificates: the investor certificates and the seller certificate. The investor certificates, which typically represent 80 percent of the total receivables, are usually sold as a public offering. The outstanding balance of the seller's certificate is retained by the seller and is used as a buffer to offset the seasonal fluctuations in the outstanding credit card balances in the trust. Credit card balances are affected by the purchase and payment patterns of the cardholders and may fluctuate over time. However, the balance of a large pool of credit cards is fairly predictable over time. The seller's certificate reduces the risk of a premature reduction in the investors' outstanding principal balance, thereby maintaining the investors' balance at a fixed level for a stated term.

Non-Amortization Period

The investor certificates of an ABS generally have been structured to perform like a bond by offering an interest-only period followed by a bullet repayment of principal or rapid amortization. The interest-only period (also known as non-amortization period or revolving period) maintains the investors' principal balance at a fixed level for a specific period of time, usually two to five years. All principal payments are allocated to the seller and reinvested in new receivables.

Amortization Period

Slow pay structure. In a slow pay structure, the investors' percentage of the monthly principal collection is based on their prior month's percentage ownership in the receivable pool. The seller receives the remaining available monthly principal collections and the new receivables charges. As the investors' current percentage ownership in the pool decreases, the investors' monthly principal allocation percentage is also declining. The result is a relatively slow repayment of principal. When the investors' principal is repaid, the seller will own 100 percent of the entire pool. The slow pay method is not used due to the slow repayment of investors' principal.

Fast pay structure. In a fast pay structure, the investors' percentage of monthly principal collections remains fixed during the amortization period, based on the investors' percentage interest in the trust as of the last month of the non-amortization period. The seller receives the remaining available monthly principal collections and the new receivables charges. As the investors' percentage of the

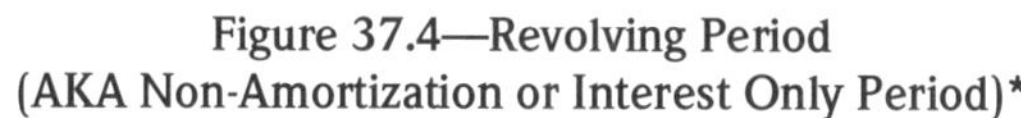

Figure 37.4—Revolving Period
(AKA Non-Amortization or Interest Only Period)*

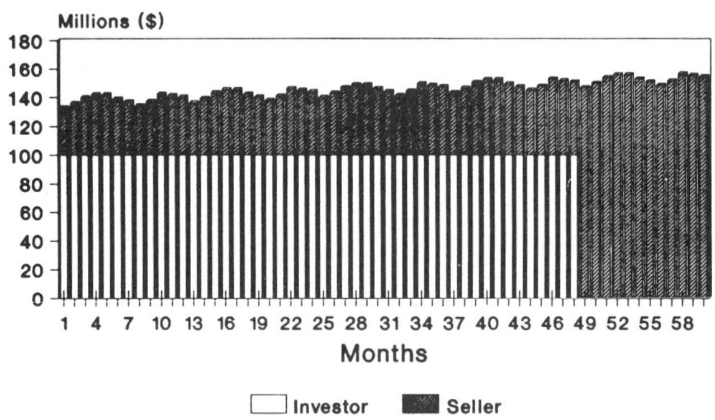

* The revolving period is followed by an amortization period which may repay the investor's principal using a variety of methods.

outstanding pool is decreasing, the investors are receiving a fixed percentage of the available monthly principal and therefore a faster repayment of principal. When the investors' principal is repaid the seller will own 100 percent of the entire pool. The fast pay method is regularly used as an allocation method to repay investors and also in conjunction with the controlled amortization method.

Controlled amortization structure. Another option is the controlled amortization method which allocates principal payments based on the fast pay method but subject to a maximum scheduled amount. Principal in excess of the controlled amortization amount will continue to be reinvested. This method provides a more predictable repayment schedule for the investors and helps reduce the risk associated with volatile payment rates. Controlled amortization is the most frequently used method of allocating principal to investors when a bullet repayment is not required.

Figure 37.5—Allocation of Principal—Slow Pay
(Amortization After Revolving Period)

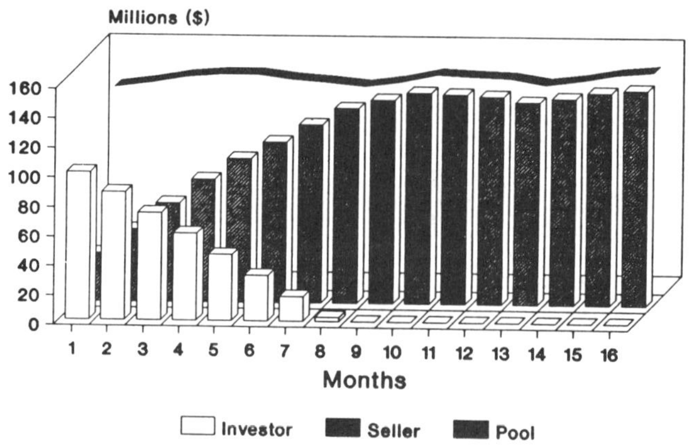

Table 37.3—Allocation of Principal Using The Slow Pay Method*

				Investor's Outstanding Balance				Seller's Outstanding Balance			
Month	Total Principal	Available Monthly Principal	New Charges	Principal Balance	Pct	Monthly Principal	Pct	Principal Balance	Pct	Monthly Principal	New Charges
1	133,000,000	17,733,333	20,733,333	100,000,000	75.19%	13,333,333	75.19%	33,000,000	24.81%	4,400,000	20,733,333
2	136,000,000	18,133,333	22,133,333	86,666,667	63.73%	11,555,556	63.73%	49,333,333	36.72%	6,577,778	22,133,333
3	140,000,000	18,666,667	20,666,667	75,111,111	53.65%	10,014,815	53.65%	64,888,889	46.35%	8,651,852	20,666,667
4	142,000,000	18,933,333	18,933,333	65,096,296	45.84%	8,679,506	45.84%	76,903,704	54.16%	10,253,827	18,933,333
5	142,000,000	18,933,333	15,933,333	56,416,790	39.73%	7,522,239	39.73%	85,583,210	60.27%	11,411,095	15,933,333
6	139,000,000	18,533,333	16,533,333	48,894,551	35.18%	6,519,274	35.18%	90,105,449	64.82%	12,014,060	16,533,333
7	137,000,000	18,266,667	15,766,667	42,375,278	30.93%	5,650,037	30.93%	94,624,722	69.07%	12,616,630	15,766,667
8	134,500,000	17,933,333	20,933,333	36,725,241	27.31%	4,896,699	27.31%	97,774,759	72.69%	13,036,635	20,933,333
9	137,500,000	18,333,333	23,333,333	31,828,542	23.15%	4,243,806	23.15%	105,671,458	76.85%	14,089,528	23,333,333
10	142,500,000	19,000,000	18,000,000	27,584,736	19.36%	3,677,965	19.36%	114,915,264	80.64%	15,322,035	18,000,000
11	141,500,000	18,866,667	17,866,667	23,906,772	16.90%	3,187,570	16.90%	117,593,228	83.10%	15,679,097	17,866,667
12	140,500,000	18,733,333	14,733,333	20,719,202	14.75%	2,762,560	14.75%	119,780,798	85.25%	15,970,773	14,733,333
13	136,500,000	18,200,000	21,200,000	17,956,642	13.16%	2,394,219	13.16%	118,543,358	86.84%	15,805,781	21,200,000
14	139,500,000	18,600,000	22,600,000	15,562,423	11.16%	2,074,990	11.16%	123,937,577	88.84%	16,525,010	22,600,000
15	143,500,000	19,133,333	19,133,333	13,487,433	9.40%	13,487,433	70.49%	130,012,567	90.60%	17,335,009	19,133,333
16	145,500,000	19,400,000	19,400,000	0	0.00%	0	00.00%	145,500,000	100.00%	19,400,000	19,400,000

* Using the slow pay method, the investors receive 75.19% the first month, 63.73% the second month, 52.17% in the third month etc. . . . The slow pay method would have repaid the investors in 15 months. The seller receives the remaining available monthly principal in addition to the new receivables charges. When the investor certificates are retired, the seller will own all of the outstanding balances.

Table 37.4—Allocation of Principal Fast Pay*

				Investor's Outstanding Balance				Seller's Outstanding Balance			
Month	Total Principal	Available Monthly Principal	New Charges	Principal Balance	Pct	Monthly Principal	Pct	Principal Balance	Pct	Monthly Principal	New Charges
1	133,000,000	17,733,333	20,733,333	100,000,000	75.19%	13,333,333	75.19%	33,000,000	24.81%	4,400,000	20,733,333
2	136,000,000	18,133,333	22,133,333	86,666,667	63.73%	13,634,085	75.19%	49,333,333	36.27%	4,499,248	22,133,333
3	140,000,000	18,666,667	20,666,667	73,032,581	52.17%	14,035,088	75.19%	66,967,419	47.83%	4,631,579	20,666,667
4	142,000,000	18,933,333	18,933,333	58,997,494	41.55%	14,235,589	75.19%	83,002,506	58.45%	4,697,744	18,933,333
5	142,000,000	18,933,333	15,933,333	44,761,905	31.52%	14,235,589	75.19%	97,238,095	68.48%	4,697,744	15,933,333
6	139,000,000	18,533,333	16,533,333	30,526,316	21.96%	13,934,837	75.19%	108,473,684	78.04%	4,598,496	16,533,333
7	137,000,000	18,266,667	15,766,667	16,591,479	12.11%	13,734,336	75.19%	120,408,521	87.89%	4,532,331	15,766,667
8	134,500,000	17,933,333	20,933,333	2,857,143	2.12%	2,857,143	15.93%	131,642,857	97.88%	4,449,624	20,933,333
9	137,500,000	18,333,333	23,333,333	0	0.00%	0	0.00%	137,500,000	100.00%	18,333,333	23,333,333
10	142,500,000	19,000,000	18,000,000	0	0.00%	0	0.00%	142,500,000	100.00%	19,000,000	18,000,000
11	141,500,000	18,866,667	17,866,667	0	0.00%	0	0.00%	141,500,000	100.00%	18,866,667	17,866,667
12	140,500,000	18,733,333	14,733,333	0	0.00%	0	0.00%	140,500,000	100.00%	18,733,333	14,733,333
13	136,500,000	18,200,000	21,200,000	0	0.00%	0	0.00%	136,500,000	100.00%	18,200,000	21,200,000
14	139,500,000	18,600,000	22,600,000	0	0.00%	0	0.00%	139,500,000	100.00%	18,600,000	22,600,000
15	143,500,000	19,133,333	19,133,333	0	0.00%	0	0.00%	143,500,000	100.00%	19,133,333	19,133,333
16	145,500,000	19,400,000	19,400,000	0	0.00%	0	0.00%	145,500,000	100.00%	19,400,000	19,400,000

* Table 37.4 demonstrates the advantage of using the fast pay method of principal allocation during the amortization period. Using the fast pay method, the investors receive 75.19% of the available principal each month and their principal is repaid in eight months versus the slow pay method which repaid the investors in 15 months. The seller receives the remaining available monthly principal in addition to the new receivables charges. When the investor certificates are retired, the seller will own all of the outstanding balances.

Figure 37.6—Allocation of Principal—Fast Pay (Amortization After Revolving Period)*

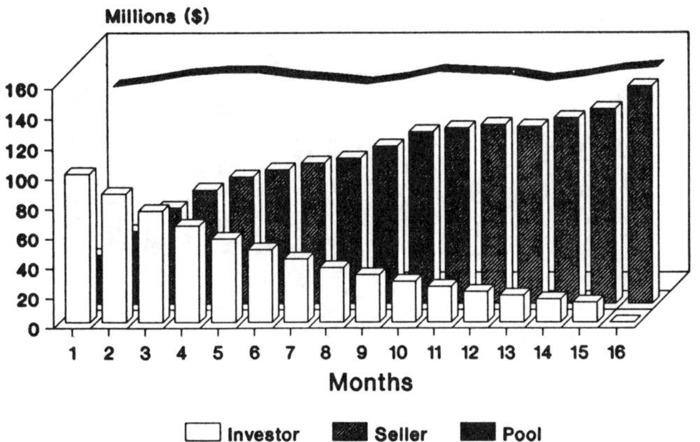

* Figure 37.6 graphically demonstrates the speed with which the investors are repaid using the fast pay method.

Table 37.5—Allocation of Principal Using a Controlled Amortization*

	INVESTOR'S OUTSTANDING BALANCE				
Month	*Principal Balance*	*Controlled Amortization Amount*	*Fast Pay Principal Allocation*	*Reinvested Principal*	*Seller Balance*
1	100,000,000	8,333,333	13,333,333	5,000,000	33,000,000
2	91,666,667	8,333,333	13,634,085	5,300,752	44,333,333
3	83,333,333	8,333,333	14,035,088	5,701,754	56,666,667
4	75,000,000	8,333,333	14,235,589	5,902,256	67,000,000
5	66,666,667	8,333,333	14,235,589	5,902,256	75,333,333
6	58,333,333	8,333,333	13,934,837	5,601,504	80,666,667
7	50,000,000	8,333,333	13,734,336	5,401,003	87,000,000
8	41,666,667	8,333,333	13,483,709	5,150,376	92,833,333
9	33,333,333	8,333,333	13,784,461	5,451,128	104,166,667
10	25,000,000	8,333,333	14,285,714	5,952,381	117,500,000
11	16,666,667	8,333,333	14,185,464	5,852,130	124,833,333
12	8,333,333	8,333,333	14,085,213	5,751,880	132,166,667
13	(0)	0	0	0	136,500,000
14	0	0	0	0	139,500,000
15	0	0	0	0	143,500,000
16	0	0	0	0	145,500,000

* The expected monthly principal allocation using the fast pay method ranges between $13,333,333 and $14,285,714. The controlled amortization amount is fixed at $8,333,333 (1/12 of original principal balance). Investors will receive a fixed payment of $8,333,333 per month for 12 months until the certificates are retired. The excess principal of $5,000,000 to $5,952,381 is reinvested in new receivables. This excess principal serves as a buffer that helps ensure the payment of the controlled amortization amount.

Figure 37.7—Controlled Amortization (Amortization After Revolving Period)*

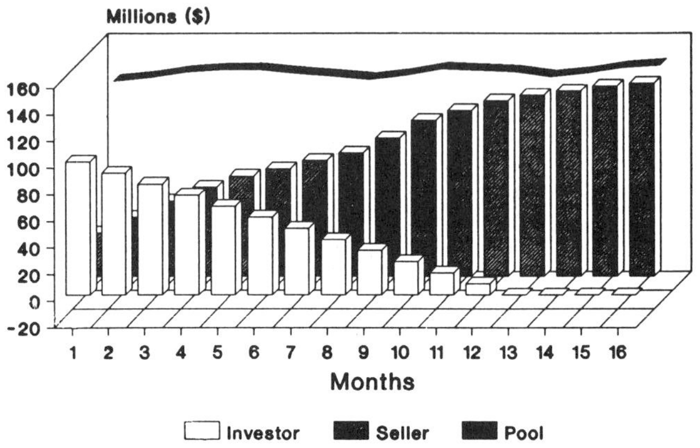

* Investors receive $8.33 million per month until the investor certificates are retired.

Principal Funding Account (PFA)

Principal collections, typically based on the controlled amortization method, are deposited into a PFA for a specific period of time (known as the accumulation period). The PFA earns interest at the certificate rate based on a guaranteed investment contract (GIC) with the PFA provider, typically a highly rated bank. The potential of the GIC provider's bankruptcy, although usually remote, may add interest rate risk, assuming the current market rates on the PFA balance (after the bankruptcy) cannot cover the investors' coupon payment. The accumulation period, which is transparent to investors, acts as an extension of the revolving period, paying interest only until the bullet maturity date. On the scheduled maturity date, which is the end of the accumulation period, the balance of the PFA is paid to the investors as a bullet payment.

Figure 37.8—Soft Bullet—Using PFA*

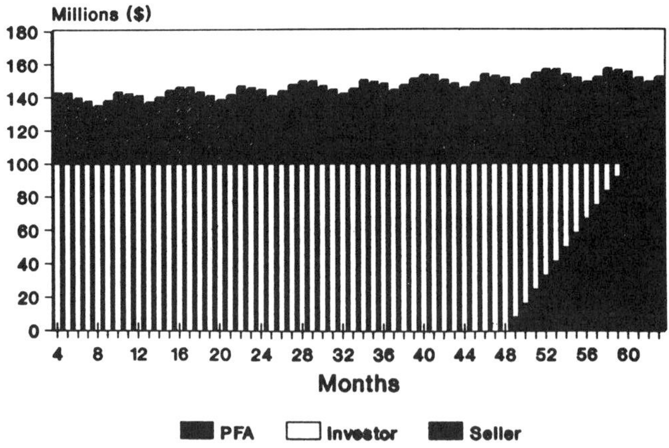

* This represents a 48-month revolving period, a 12-month accumulation (PFA) period, and a full execution of the bullet repayment in the 60th period.

Figure 37.9—Soft Bullet—Using PFA (Reduced MPR)*

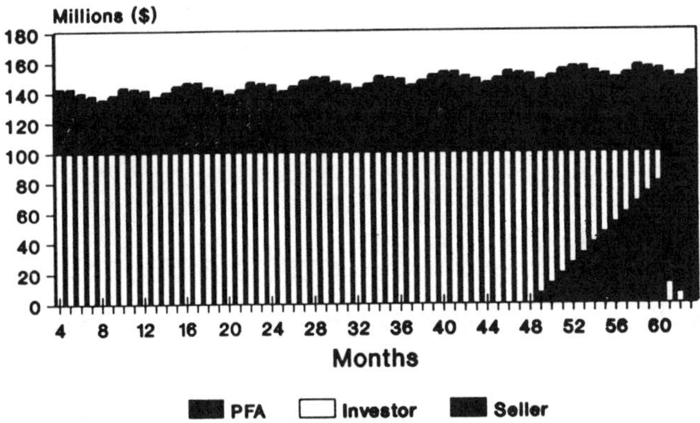

* This represents the same structure as Table 37.5, but the investors only receive a partial bullet repayment, due to insufficient funding of the PFA account, followed by 2 months of amortization in periods 61 and 62.

Bullet Maturity Mechanisms

The bullet maturity mechanism is advantageous for both the investors and the issuer. The investor significantly reduces the payment risk associated with volatile payment activity. The issuer is free to use the accounts to reissue a new security after the investor certificates are retired.

- *Soft Bullet*—On the stated maturity date, the PFA may not be fully funded due to a reduction in cardholder payment activity. If this occurs, investors would not be fully repaid by a single bullet payment; the current PFA balance would be distributed to investors with the remainder of the outstanding balance amortizing until the certificates are retired. The likelihood of a failure to execute the bullet repayment is fairly remote.
- *Hard Bullet*—If the PFA is not fully funded, a maturity guarantor or the PFA provider

Figure 37.10—Hard Bullet—Using PFA (Reduced MPR)*

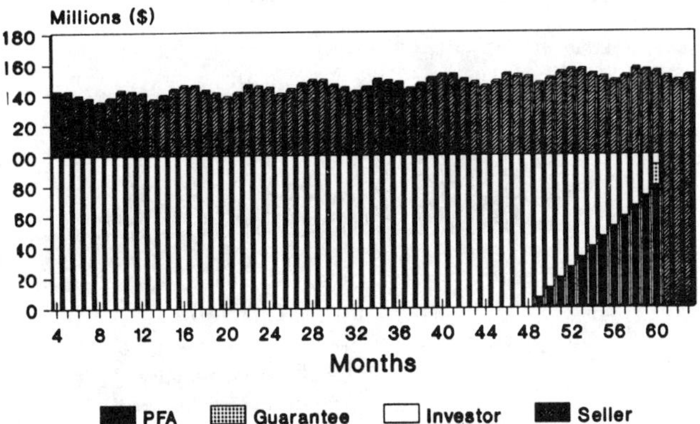

* The maturity guarantee is exercised in the 60th period (bullet maturity date) due to a reduction in the monthly payment rate (MPR) on the underlying receivables. The maturity guarantee would not be exercised if the MPR had continued as expected.

will guarantee the investors' principal bullet repayment up to a specific percentage of the initial offering. This virtually eliminates the prepayment risk associated with unpredictable timing of principal payments. In exchange for payment of the remaining portion of the bullet, the provider of the maturity guarantee receives interest on the outstanding balance at the investors' pass-through rate.

INTEREST PAYMENTS TO CERTIFICATE HOLDER

The yield on credit cards, which is high relative to other types of consumer loans, should cover the payment of investor interest in addition to the servicing fees and credit enhancement fees. The remaining yield, also known as excess spread, is available to protect the investor from losses on defaulted receivables.

During the non-amortization period, the investors will receive a fixed interest payment each month at the pass-through rate. Interest payments may be made monthly or semi-annually. After the non-amortization period the investor will receive principal repayment, based on a defined allocation method, and interest on the previous period's balance generated at the investor pass-through rate.

RETIREMENT OF CREDIT CARD ABS

Credit card transactions, unlike other amortizing ABSs, return to the balance sheet when the deal is retired. To continue to keep these assets off the issuer's books, issuers must continue to reissue new transactions. The volume of ABSs backed by credit cards will continue to increase as existing deals mature and are "reissued" and as new assets are securitized.

CREDIT ENHANCEMENT

Credit enhancement, which helps offset credit risk, prepayment risk and provides liquidity, is used to convert the cash flows from specific receivables into investment grade securities.

Without credit enhancement most credit card deals would probably be rated in the BB to BBB range on their own merit. To achieve a higher investment grade rating, credit enhancement is needed to insulate investors from the risk of uncertain timing of principal and interest payments and cardholder defaults. Fitch applies various stress tests on the cash flows from each portfolio, reviews the legal options, the quality of the servicer, and the originator's underwriting standards. Fitch then assigns a specific rating based on the level of credit enhancement provided. Credit enhancement may take any of the following forms:

Figure 37.11—Credit Card-Backed ABS Volume by Expected Maturity

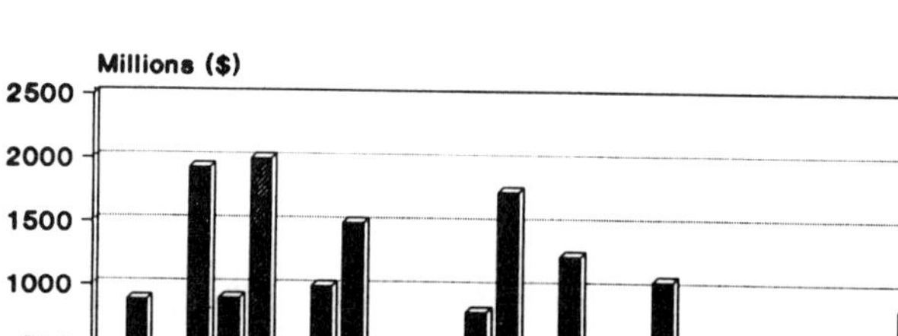
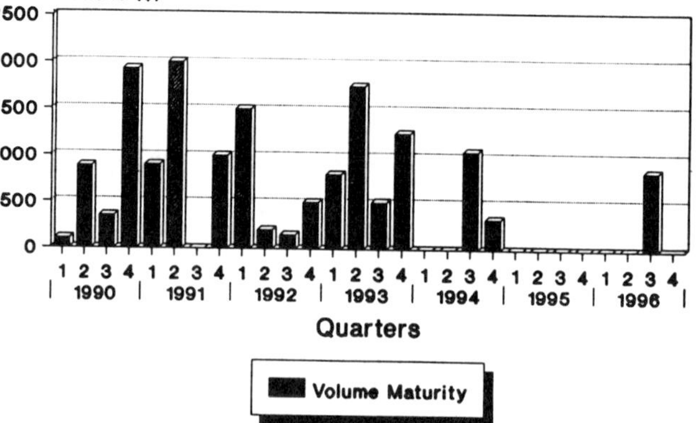

* In the 4th quarter of 1990 almost $2 billion of credit card ABSs will mature. As these deals mature, investors will receive $2 billion of cash from the repayment of principal which they will want to reinvest. The issuers will have $2 billion of credit card receivables back on their books that they will want to reissue as new securities.

Excess Cash Flow

The excess spread (yield) after paying the investors' interest, servicing fees, and credit enhancement fees may be available to protect the investor from losses on defaulted receivables. The expected excess spread is fairly high at approximately 700 to 800 basis points. (Example: A yield of 20 percent with an investor coupon of 10 percent and servicing fee of 2.50 percent would generate 750 basis points of excess yield.)

Irrevocable Letter of Credit (LOC)

A letter of credit provides a limited guarantee against cardholder defaults based on a percentage of the security's outstanding balance. LOC coverage on existing deals ranges from 5 percent to 30 percent, or a stated dollar amount. The LOC provider may require the seller to maintain a reserve or reimbursement account funded from excess cash flow on the underlying collateral. The reserve may also be funded by an initial deposit from the seller. This initial deposit is provided as a loan to the trust and is repaid in approximately one year from the monthly excess servicing. Draws against the LOC provider will reduce the available coverage amount and may be reimbursed from the reserve account or future excess servicing. There is some event risk in this structure because a downgrading of the LOC provider may affect the rating of the security.

Senior/Subordinate

A senior/subordinate structure offers two different types of ownership interest in the trust. The senior certificates receive credit enhancement from the issuance of a class of subordinate certificates. The subordinate investor, in a role similar to the LOC provider, absorbs losses due to cardholder defaults. Draws on the subordinate certificates may support the senior investors' monthly cash flows, and may be reimbursed from future excess servicing. Unreimbursed draws on the subordinate certificates are limited to the available subordination amount. The subordinate loss coverage typically ranges from 7 to 15 percent of the original outstanding principal balance. Principal payments to the subordinate investors may be withheld until the senior certificates are retired.

The senior/subordinate structure, when the seller does not retain the subordinate certificate, eliminates the event risk associated with a downgrading of the third-party credit enhancer thereby jeopardizing the rating of the ABS. Banks, to achieve sales treatment for regulatory and accounting purposes, are not permitted to retain any recourse to the investors and therefore must sell the subordinate certificates.

The senior/subordinate structure offers slightly lower costs eliminating or reducing the LOC fees. This savings is partially offset by wider spreads required to sell the subordinate certificates. The liquidity required to cover cardholder defaults for the senior certificates may be reduced, compared to an LOC which acts like a cash reserve, by the subordinate certificates' dependence on the monthly cash flow generated on the underlying collateral.

LOC on Subordinate Certificate

To sell the subordinate certificates issuers frequently obtain an LOC as credit enhancement.

Figure 37.12—Senior/Subordinate Structure (During Revolving Period)

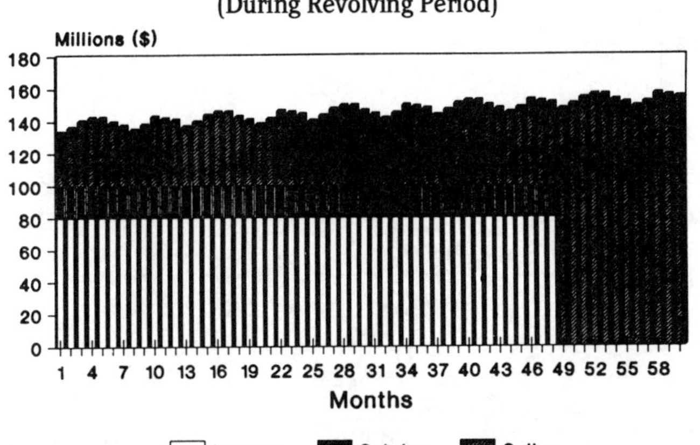

The amount of credit enhancement needed to achieve an investment grade rating is fairly high due to the default risk assumed from the senior investors.

Servicer Letter of Credit

A servicer letter of credit guarantees the trust's interest in the commingled funds. The servicer deposits the cardholders' monthly payments into a collection account and at the end of each month the available funds are distributed to the investors or are reinvested in new receivables. During this period, the account balances dedicated to the trust are commingled with accounts owned and/or collected by the servicer. A servicer's bankruptcy may endanger the investors' share of monthly collections. Without a servicer LOC, non-investment grade servicers may only be allowed to commingle funds for a short time (i.e., 1 to 2 days). A servicer LOC will allow the servicer to retain the collections for 30 days. Highly rated servicers may be allowed to commingle funds, without a servicer LOC, for 30 days. The servicer LOC also provides a source of liquidity for investors by advancing funds for delinquent loans.

AMORTIZATION EVENTS (Payout Event)

Volatility in the yield on the receivables and/or the credit card default experience (charge-offs) in the portfolio may cause the available cash flow to deteriorate. A significant decline in the pool's credit quality could jeopardize the timing and the ultimate repayment of investors' principal and interest. Early amortization events, which force an early retirement of the investors' certificates, provide additional credit protection by limiting the amount of portfolio deterioration during the non-amortization period.

Amortization triggers, based on the performance of the portfolio, are usually measured against changes in portfolio yield or default experience. Issuers are also structuring deals using a "base rate" which is sensitive to both increases in defaults and reductions in the portfolio yield (i.e., a simultaneous decrease in yield and an increase in default experience). The calculation of the base rate, which defines an amortization event, requires that the three-month average of the yield minus defaults must continue to be greater than the investor coupon plus the servicing fee and an excess servicing cushion. The cushion helps ensure that there will be excess cash available if the deal unwinds.

Conservative amortization events are an important ingredient in determining the appropriate credit support for a specific rating. However, amortization triggers should not be overly conservative so as to avoid an unnecessary amortization event and a subsequent early payout.

The monthly portfolio performance, especially during the revolving period, should be closely monitored to forecast potential amortization events.

Figure 37.13—Defaults versus Amortization Event Sears Credit Account Trusts*

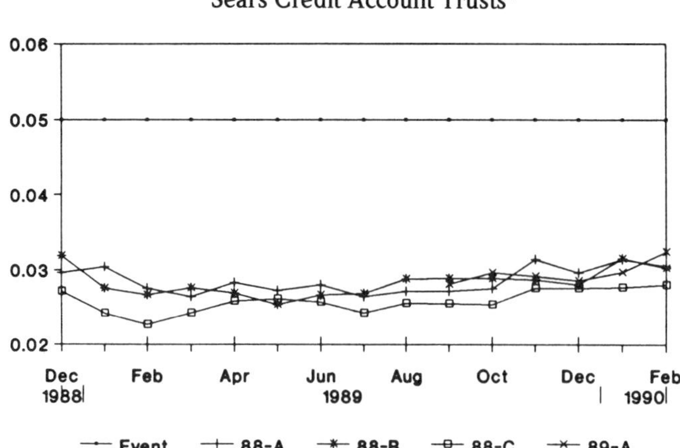

* Sears' default experience, on these four issues, has been relatively stable over the last 14 months. Defaults would have to nearly double for three consecutive months before an amortization event would occur.

Table 37.6—Examples of Early Amortization Events

Events affected by the performance of the portfolio:

	SEARS 89-A	*NCCT 89-5*
	Trigger at Issue	*Trigger at Issue*
1. Finance charges below	12.00% (17.88%)	N.A. (20.72)
2. Charge-offs above	5.00% (2.85%)	N.A. (4.65)
3. Base rate below	N.A.	13.95
Note the excess servicing cushion on each transaction after an amortization event:		
Investor coupon	(9.85%)	(9.45%)
Servicing	(2.00%)	(2.80%)
Excess cushion*	(0%)	(1.70%)

4. Three consecutive draws in the available subordination or letter of credit amount.
5. The seller's interest in the pool is reduced below a fixed level and the seller does not add new accounts.

Events affected by the performance of the seller:

6. Failure to make any payment/deposit or to observe or perform any other material covenants required in the pooling & servicing agreement.
7. Any representation or warranty which continues to be materially incorrect 60 days after written notification.
8. The filing of a petition for bankruptcy; or petitions seeking reorganization under any similar federal law.
9. Any order for relief entered by a court under federal bankruptcy laws unstayed for a period of 120 days.
10. Inability, for any reason, to transfer receivables to the trust.
11. The trust becoming an "investment company" under the Investment Company Act of 1984.
12. A servicer termination event—which includes:
    - A. Failure by the servicer to make any payment, transfer, or deposit as required by the pooling a servicing agreement.
    - B. Failure of the servicer to observe or perform any covenants or agreements related to the servicer in the pooling and servicing agreement.
    - C. Any incorrect representation, warranty, or certification made by the servicer having a material adverse effect on the investors.
    - D. Bankruptcy, insolvency, or receivership of the servicer.

* In Sears 89-A, if finance charges decrease while defaults increase, there may not be any excess cash available to offset a further deterioration of cash flow and draws may be made against the subordinate certificates. Citicorp uses a base rate of 13.95% which leaves 1.7% of excess cash available to offset additional losses before a draw against the subordinate certificate would be necessary.

REPURCHASE EVENTS AND ADDITIONAL ACCOUNTS

Additional accounts may be sold to the trust if the seller's interest goes below a specified level. The seller certificate reduces the yield on the portfolio and may also trigger an amortization event.

- *Convenience Usage*—The yield on the credit cards may also be effected by convenience usage. Cardholders who repay their entire balance every month are considered convenience users and incur no finance charges. The higher the convenience usage on a portfolio, the lower the expected yield.
- *Default Rate*—The default rates on credit cards are relatively high compared to ABS backed by other types of receivables. However, this is generally offset by much higher interest rates on the receivables. There are on expected recoveries on defaulted credit card accounts since they are unsecured, revolving debt obligations.
- *Payment Rate*—the monthly payment rate (MPR) is the ratio of cash (principal and

finance charges) received each month as a percentage of the outstanding balance. To determine the principal and interest components of the MPR:

1. The total monthly payment is the MPR times the outstanding balance (a MPR of 10 percent with an outstanding balance of $10,000 will result in $1,000 of total monthly payments).
2. The monthly interest generated is the APR times the outstanding balance (an APR of 12 percent on the $10,000 outstanding balance would yield $100 on monthly interest).
3. The monthly principal is the monthly payment of $1,000 minus the interest of $100, resulting in $900 of principal.

Effect of Payment Rate on Default Experience

A high MPR on a pool of loans will repay the investors' principal faster during the amortization period. The faster the investors' principal is repaid the less time there is for the pool to deteriorate. This reduces the default experience expected during the amortization period.

Credit card issuers have different philosophies in managing their portfolios. Some credit card pools experience fewer defaults but also generate lower yields and tend to have slower monthly payment rates. Other issuers trade off a high default rate for much higher APRs and they may have faster monthly payment rates. The MPR may also be affected by the demographic profile of the cardholders and/or the retailer's customers (for the private label cards). To demonstrate the impact of changes of MPR on default experience during the amortization period, Fitch has 'stressed' the expected default rates for the top two ABS issuers.

If the seller is unable to provide additional accounts, an amortization event occurs. Accounts may be removed or repurchased from the trust if the receivables are not in compliance with the pooling and servicing agreement.

PERFORMANCE STATISTICS

To determine the proper level of credit enhancement for each transaction, Fitch examines the performance of the credit card portfolio. To evaluate the risks associated with credit card structures, Fitch analyzes the primary elements connected with the performance of credit card loans: stated finance charge, convenience usage, the default rate and the payment rate.

- *Stated Finance Charge*—The annual percentage rate (APR) is assigned by the seller and can be modified at any time, although states restrict the maximum finance charge on credit cards.
- *Seasonality*—Issuers with wide seasonal swings in sales activity also have wide fluctuations in their credit card balances. Charge-offs, which are recorded several months after the initial billing, may be posted against a period of low sales volume with a small outstanding balance. This may cause wide fluctuations in the recorded default rates. An issuer with an annualized default rate of 2.0 percent may experience monthly fluctuation between 1.0 percent to 3.0 percent (annualized). Wide fluctuation in default experience may trigger an unnecessary amortization event. The default trigger should be measured against a three-month moving average to help offset these monthly fluctuations.

Charts Defined

Table 37.7 illustrates that an issuer with a high monthly payment rate could withstand a significantly higher level of defaults. For example, assuming the cardholders' monthly payment activity remains fairly stable, Citibank could withstand a 29.92 percent default rate, whereas Sears could only withstand a 17.30 percent default rate (Exhibits E and F).

Exhibits A and B illustrate the expected defaults that would be charged off during a fast pay allocation of a Sears and a Citibank portfolio. The Sears and Citibank trusts would incur $12.62 and $17.03, respectively, per $1,000 of credit card receivables during their projected paydown periods. Exhibits C and D illustrate the expected defaults if an amortization event was triggered by an increase in defaults. In this case, the Sears and Citibank trusts would incur defaults in amounts equal to $29.82 and $22.78 per $1,000, respectively. Exhibits E and F illustrate the expected defaults that the trust could incur if the cash reserve was depleted and no draws were made on the credit enhancement. The Sears and Citibank trust could withstand default in amounts equal to $102.96 and $109.60 per $1,000, respectively.

Table 37.7—Defaults vs. Paydown Method

A. SEARS AMORTIZATION SCHEDULE

Expected Performance

APR	17.59%	Inv Coupon	10.00%
MPR	8.58%	Servicing	2.00%
Default	2.12%	Excess Yield	3.47%

Mth	*Principal Balance Outstanding*	*Monthly Principal Payment*	*Monthly Defaults*
1	1000.00	71.14	1.77
2	928.86	72.18	1.64
3	856.67	73.24	1.51
4	783.43	74.32	1.38
5	709.12	75.41	1.25
6	633.71	76.51	1.12
7	557.20	77.63	0.98
8	479.57	78.77	0.85
9	400.80	79.93	0.71
10	320.87	81.10	0.57
11	239.77	82.29	0.42
12	157.49	83.49	0.28
13	74.00	74.00	0.13
Total		1,000.00	12.62

B. CITIBANK AMORTIZATION SCHEDULE

Expected Performance

APR	20.72%	Inv Coupon	10.00%
MPR	14.16%	Servicing	2.80%
Default	4.65%	Excess Yield	3.27%

Mth	*Principal Balance Outstanding*	*Monthly Principal Payment*	*Monthly Defaults*
1	1000.00	124.33	3.88
2	875.67	126.48	3.39
3	749.19	128.66	2.90
4	620.52	130.89	2.40
5	489.64	133.15	1.90
6	356.49	135.44	1.38
7	221.05	137.78	0.86
8	83.26	83.26	0.32
9			
10			
11			
12			
13			
Total		1,000.00	17.03

C. SEARS AMORTIZATION SCHEDULE

Using Amortization Events

APR	17.59%	Inv Coupon	10.00%
MPR	8.58%	Servicing	2.00%
Default	5.01%	Excess Yield	0.58%

Mth	*Principal Balance Outstanding*	*Monthly Principal Payment*	*Monthly Defaults*
1	1000.00	71.14	4.17
2	928.86	72.18	3.88
3	856.67	73.24	3.58
4	783.43	74.32	3.27
5	709.12	75.41	2.96
6	633.71	76.51	2.65
7	557.20	77.63	2.33
8	479.57	78.77	2.00
9	400.80	79.93	1.67
10	320.87	81.10	1.34
11	239.77	82.29	1.00
12	157.49	83.49	0.66
13	74.00	74.00	0.31
Total		1,000.00	29.82

D. CITIBANK AMORTIZATION SCHEDULE

Using Amortization Events

APR	20.72%	Inv Coupon	10.00%
MPR	14.16%	Servicing	2.80%
Default	6.22%	Excess Yield	1.70%

Mth	*Principal Balance Outstanding*	*Monthly Principal Payment*	*Monthly Defaults*
1	1000.00	124.33	5.18
2	875.67	126.48	4.54
3	749.19	128.66	3.88
4	620.52	130.89	3.22
5	489.64	133.15	2.54
6	356.49	135.44	1.84
7	221.05	137.78	1.15
8	83.26	83.26	0.43
9			
10			
11			
12			
13			
Total		1,000.00	22.78

Table 37.7 continued

E. SEARS AMORTIZATION SCHEDULE

	Using Amortization Events		
APR	17.59%	Inv Coupon	10.00%
MPR	8.58%	Servicing	2.00%
Default	17.30%	Excess Yield	–11.71%

Mth	*Principal Balance Outstanding*	*Monthly Principal Payment*	*Monthly Defaults*	*Default Rate*	*Reserve Account*
1	1000.00	71.14	14.42	17.30%	60.00
2	928.86	72.18	13.39	17.30%	50.94
3	856.67	73.24	12.35	17.30%	42.58
4	783.43	74.32	11.29	17.30%	34.93
5	709.12	75.41	10.22	17.30%	28.01
6	633.71	76.51	9.14	17.30%	21.83
7	557.20	77.63	8.03	17.30%	16.39
8	479.57	78.77	6.91	17.30%	11.71
9	400.80	79.93	5.78	17.30%	7.80
10	320.87	81.10	4.63	17.30%	4.67
11	239.77	82.29	3.46	17.30%	2.33
12	157.49	83.49	2.27	17.30%	0.79
13	74.00	74.00	1.07	17.30%	0.07
Total		1,000.00	102.96		

F. CITIBANK AMORTIZATION SCHEDULE

	Using Amortization Events		
APR	20.72%	Inv Coupon	10.00%
MPR	14.16%	Servicing	2.80%
Default	29.92%	Excess Yield	–22.00%

Mth	*Principal Balance Outstanding*	*Monthly Principal Payment*	*Monthly Defaults*	*Default Rate*	*Reserve Account*
1	1000.00	124.33	24.93	29.92%	60.00
2	875.67	126.48	21.83	29.92%	44.53
3	749.19	128.66	18.68	29.92%	31.29
4	620.52	130.89	15.47	29.92%	20.33
5	489.64	133.15	12.21	29.92%	11.68
6	356.49	135.44	8.89	29.92%	5.38
7	221.05	137.78	5.51	29.92%	1.48
8	83.26	83.26	2.08	29.92%	0.01
9					
10					
11					
12					
13					
Total		1,000.00	109.60		

POOL STATISTICS

The credit evaluation requires the review of the portfolio's statistics on delinquencies, charge-offs, recoveries, principal repayment schedules, collateral yield, and composition of accounts by age, balance, and credit limits. In addition Fitch reviews the issuer's credit underwriting and servicing standards.

Geographic Distribution

The loss experience in geographically well-diversified portfolios should be more stable than portfolios with state concentrations. The risk associated with future economic declines may be partially offset if the concentration is in a state with a diverse economic base.

SERVICER

The underwriting standards and servicing quality have a significant impact on the performance of the credit card receivables. Credit criteria reflect a seller's business philosophy. Some card issuers prefer to have more cards outstanding and are willing to take greater risks. These issuers usually charge a higher interest rate to offset the higher expected losses.

The card issuer assesses an applicant's willingness and ability to pay. A credit scoring model that incorporates the card issuer's historical performance and business strategy is used to evaluate each application. The total debt-to-income ratio and credit bureau reports are reviewed. Once the card is issued the servicing becomes important.

The large servicing operations benefit from economies of scale and have significant automated systems for billing and collecting account balances. These systems enable efficient allocation of employee time. The delinquencies and losses reflect both the underwriting and servicing. Lax servicing will result in higher delinquencies and losses. Since credit cards are unsecured debt usually having a revolving line of credit, the early identification and withdrawal of the credit limit on delinquent accounts will minimize losses.

On-site visits to the seller/servicer include a discussion of underwriting procedures and policies and an explanation of servicing capabilities. These meetings provide excellent information on management's commitment and depth of expertise.

Many servicers want the right to commingle collections on trust receivables with the servicer's own accounts. The rating of the servicer compared to the rating on the ABS is important because if the servicer enters bankruptcy the trust's collections held by the servicer may be lost. In cases where the servicer is not rated high enough to enable commingling of funds, the servicer may obtain a letter of credit to cover this risk.

Table 37.8—Servicer Evaluation

Outline of Servicer Review

I. Business Overview
- ♦ Company Organization
  - Management
  - Business Strategy
  - Marketing
- ♦ Core Markets
  - Competition in Region
- ♦ Relationship with Parent Company

II. Credit Underwriting
- ♦ Organization of Underwriting Dept.
- ♦ Background of Underwriters
- ♦ Credit Underwriting Policies and Procedures
- ♦ Collateral Valuation
- ♦ Documentation Requirements
- ♦ At The Same Underwriting Procedures Used for All the Pools

III. Servicer Operations
- ♦ Staffing
- ♦ Collections
  - Prepayments
  - Calculation of Delinquencies; How Are They Reported
  - Reports to Credit Bureaus; Which Ones Are Used
  - Recency of Payment Method Vs Contractual Obligation When Reporting Delinquencies; Which Method is Used
  - How Are Sold Receivables Reported
  - Writeoffs
  - Quality Control Scope and Frequency of Reviews
  - File Maintenance
  - Internal Audit, External
  - Management Information Systems
  - Tour of Facility

Chapter 38

Understanding Credit Card Subordinate Certificates

by William F. Wallace,
Morgan Stanley & Co.

EXECUTIVE SUMMARY

The increased popularity of credit cards in the United States during the past several years has led to a related rise in term credit card securitization as a means of funding for credit card issuers. Pressure on banks to achieve and/or maintain higher capital ratios, as well as to obtain the funding flexibility provided to both banks and retailers, has caused a greater volume of credit card securities to be issued. As securitization techniques have become more sophisticated and cost efficient, various methods of credit enhancement for investor certificates have been developed. This publication will focus on the senior/subordinate method and, in particular, describe the credit and cash flow timing profile of subordinate classes. While each subordinate class has unique structural characteristics, which are described in its prospectus or offering memorandum, substantial similarities exist that can simplify investment decisions for potential investors.

Given the current market environment, we believe that even at AA or A levels of credit support, significant loss protection exists for subordinate class investors. A breakeven analysis indicates that a combination of lengthy deterioration in a portfolio's excess spread and a severe slowdown in payment rates would be required before available credit support is exhausted. As a result, these subordinate class securities represent truly attractive instruments that can provide good value in today's market.

STRUCTURAL CONSIDERATIONS

Overview of Revolving Trust

The sale of more than $63.5 billion in publicly offered credit card securities has been made possible through the development and evolution of the credit card trust structure. In a credit card securitization, credit card accounts and the receivables that periodically arise in these accounts are sold to a trust, which funds the purchase of the receivables through the issuance of investor certificates. As the principal is paid on the receivables, the cash proceeds are reinvested in new receivables that are generated from the same or other accounts in the trust. This revolving process can be structured to continue for as long as the seller of the receivables desires, as long as the portfolio generates enough yield to support periodic losses, servicing costs, trust expenses and certificate interest costs. If this excess spread becomes negative, the revolving period stops and all principal is utilized as received

---

This chapter is based on or derived from information generally available to the public from soures we believe to be reliable. No representation is made that it is accurate or complete. Morgan Stanley & Co. Incorporated and others associated with it may have positions in, and may effect transactions in, securities and instruments of issuers mentioned herein and may also perform or seek to perform investment banking services for the issuers of such securities and instruments. The following has been prepared solely for information purposes and is not a solicitation of an offer to buy or sell any security or instrument or to participate in any trading strategy. Past results are not necessarily indicative of future results. Price and availability are subject to change without notice. To our readers worldwide: This publication has been issued by Morgan Stanley & Co. Incorporated, approved by Morgan Stanley International, a member of the Securities Association, and by Morgan Stanley Japan Ltd. The investments discussed or recommended may be unsuitable for certain private investors depending on their specific investment objectives and financial positions. We recommend that such investors obtain the advice of their Morgan Stanley International or Mortan Stanley Japan Ltd. representative about the investments concerned. Reprinted with permission.

Figure 38.1—Understanding Credit Card Subordinate Certificates Calculation of Excess Spread During Revolving Period

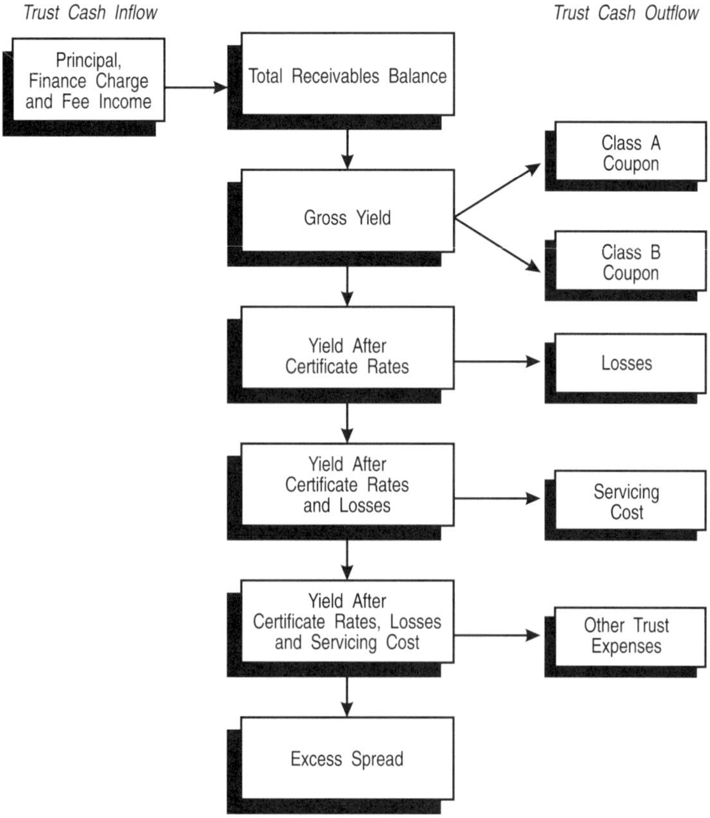

Source: Morgan Stanley

to pay the remaining certificate balance. The accelerated principal repayment is analogous to converting the structure to a pass-through. The revolving process is similar to an ongoing business, which is permitted to operate only if positive cash flow is generated (see Figure 38.1).

Glossary

Total receivables balance: Total balance of all receivables in the pool sold to the trust.

Investor Interest: Predetermined dollar amount of the Total Receivables Balance (e.g., $500 million). Comprised of Senior Class (Class A) and Subordinate Class (Class B).

Seller Interest: Portion of Total Receivables Balance necessary to absorb daily volatility. Calculated as the Total Receivables Balance minus the Investor Interest.

Gross Yield: Sum of annual percentage rate, annual, late, and overlimit fees, cash advance fees and interchange income (merchant discount).

Certificate Rate: Coupon on both the senior and subordinate classes of the Investor Interest.

Losses: Actual net losses (after recoveries, if applicable).

Servicing Cost: Compensation to the servicer for the cost of providing customer service and collections personnel excluding marketing expenses. Generally 2% to 2.5% per year.

Other Trust Expenses: Credit support, trustee, accounting and other ongoing expenses.

Excess Spread: Gross Yield less Certificate Rates, Losses, Servicing Costs and Other Trust Expenses.

Amortization Events (Triggers)

The rating agencies require a receivables pool to begin to self-liquidate upon the occurrence of an event that is perceived to create material credit risk to investors (an Amortization Event, or Trigger). The following are examples of Amortization Events:

- The inability of the trust to be self-supporting, as indicated by a negative excess spread
- An increase in losses to a certain percentage level, usually calculated on a three-month moving average
- A reduction in the amount still available from the Subordinate Amount (i.e., the dollar amount of credit enhancement)
- A reduction in the principal payment rate below a certain level
- The failure of the seller to add additional accounts to the pool when the Seller Interest falls below a minimum threshold of 7%–25% of the pool balance
- A material disruption in the ongoing business of the seller/servicer, as indicated by a receivership of bankruptcy filing
- A change in the legal characterization of the trust, such as qualifying as an investment company
- Other events, such as a breach of warranty or failure of the seller to make payments.

Once an early Amortization Event occurs, a Rapid Amortization principal repayment period commences. The rating agencies want a portfolio to liquidate as quickly as possible to minimize the potential damage to the Investor Interest from the effects of the actual Trigger or Amortization Event. There have been five term credit card issues that have hit early Amortization Events. In August 1988, a Republic Bank Delaware issue was redeemed after its parent went into receivership. In the summer of 1991, two Chevy Chase Savings Bank issues hit a three-month loss rate threshold and two Southeast Bank issues hit negative excess spread triggers. The Southeast Bank Credit Card Trusts 1990A and 1990B announced that payout events for each occurred at the end of June and July 1991, respectively. The payout event was the result of the average yield less losses on the receivables falling below the level required to cover transaction carrying costs, including the coupon, servicing fee and letter of credit (LOC) fee. The overall trust portfolio yield declined in combination with increased losses. For example, losses on 1990A moved from 4.46% in January 1991 to 6.83% in June 1991; losses on 1990B moved from 3.68% to 6.87% during the same period. Standard and Poor's (S&P) attributed some of this increased loss experience to a weakened Florida economy and a dramatic increase in collection personnel turnover during the fourth quarter of 1990. The Southeast Bank issues illustrate that rapid increases in losses can trigger repayment if yield does not increase or at least remain constant. However, the rating agencies confirmed that the existing cash flow from the receivables plus the LOC available to cover principal and interest shortfalls would continue to provide a AAA level of investor protection from principal losses, even though early principal repayment began as a result of an excess spread trigger. This phase is critical for subordinate class investors in senior/subordinate structures since it is the only time that a claim may be made by senior class investors on the subordinate principal cash flows.

RISKS TO SUBORDINATE CLASS INVESTORS

The subordinate class investors will not incur losses as long as there is credit support available to them. As a result, the key determinants of the magnitude of potential losses to subordinate class investors are:

- The portfolio payment rate subsequent to the Amortization Event
- The probability and potential severity of the portfolio's negative excess spread during the Amortization Period
- The ability of structural features and credit enhancement to absorb losses.

Pool Payment Rate

Payment rates are a function of both the minimum payment terms of the credit card issuer and the number of cardholders who actually revolve balances and incur finance charges (revolvers) versus those who pay in full every month (convenience users). The payment rates of selected major issuers are shown in Table 38.1.

The payment rate, defined as the monthly collections on the credit card accounts as a percentage of the receivables outstanding, has a significant impact on the allocation of losses from the receivables pool between the Investor Interest and Seller Interest. The faster investors are paid down, the lower their pro rata shares of losses on the pool will be in absolute terms. The rating agencies focus

Table 38.1—Selected Average Monthly Credit Card Payment Rates* In Percent

Issuer	1989	1990	1991
Citicorp	13.36	12.78	12.48
Discover Card	12.84	13.37	13.66
First Chicago	13.87	14.51	14.09
MBNA America Bank	14.86	14.55	13.94
Norwest	12.80	13.69	13.14
Sears	7.90	7.28	7.10

* Total payment rates include payments by cardholders of principal and interest.

Source: Most recent 1991 prospectus for each of the above issuers, Moody's, S&P

their analyses on the principal component of monthly collections, since it is this principal that will be used to fully pay down first the senior class portion, then the subordinate class portion, of the Investor Interest. As payment rates decline, there is a greater risk that the credit enhancement will be tapped to cover losses.

The purchase rate, defined as the amount of new cardholder charges available to be purchased or contributed to the trust, will affect the overall balance of the pool. Fluctuations in the purchase rate are caused by various economic and marketing factors. During recessions, for instance, when consumer credit demand is low, purchase rates tend to decline and credit card issuers often experience little or no growth in receivables balances. Purchase rates increase to reflect seasonal demand, especially at the end of the year during the Christmas shopping season, as well as in response to marketing programs initiated by credit card issuers (e.g., frequent flier mileage programs and programs that allow cardholders to select catalog merchandise depending upon their credit activity, etc.). If the purchase rate is lower than the payment rate, the receivables balance in the pool will drop, which could trigger an Amortization Event if the seller does not add new accounts to the trust. A continued low purchase rate subsequent to an Amortization Event could cause the Amortization Period to extend. Statistics have shown that a low purchase rate is not an immediate consequence of the recession, as demonstrated by VISA International's disclosure that charge volume was up by 16% in the second quarter of 1991 over the second quarter of 1990. Figure 38.2 indicates the relatively low likelihood of a cyclical decline in receivables balances as a consequence of the increasing trend in revolving consumer debt.

Figure 38.2—Growth in Revolving Consumer Credit 1985–September 1991

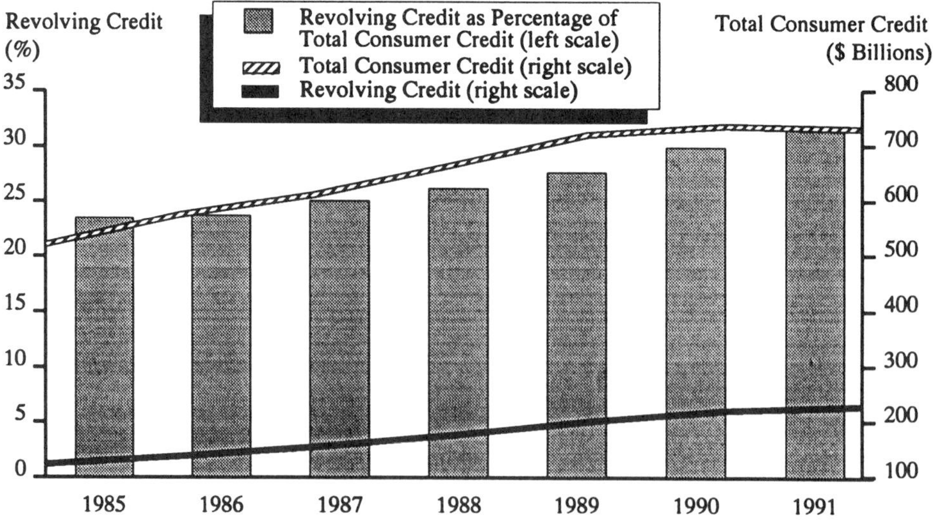

Source: Federal Reserve's G.19 statistical release of Consumer Installment Credit

Negative Excess Spread

Negative excess spread can result from various factors such as a flawed business strategy, (e.g., poorly defined target market), poor credit underwriting standards, recessionary pressures (e.g., personal bankruptcy filings) and a competitive squeeze on finance charge income, fees and interchange. For example, some credit card issuers target customers with large revolving balances and are comfortable with the higher loss potential for this type of borrower. Other issuers may target higher-quality borrowers who pay off balances more quickly and therefore do not generate either yields or losses but generate significant interchange income. Investors should evaluate the likelihood, if any, of a prolonged simultaneous deterioration in both yields and losses. Representative recent yields and losses are shown in Table 38.2.

Table 38.2—Selected Yield and Loss Statistics In Percent

Issuer	*Gross Yield*	*Losses*
Citicorp	20.05	6.59
Discover Card	18.41	4.29
MBNA America Bank	18.61	3.21
Norwest	20.34	3.99
Sears	18.21	3.44

Source: Most recent 1991 prospectus for each of the above issuers, Moody's, S&P

Credit Enhancement

The general motivation for an issuer of credit card-backed securities to use a senior/subordinate structure as opposed to a stand-alone LOC is to improve the pricing of the senior class of the Investor Interest. Investors have been concerned by the event/third-party risk of an Aaa/AAA-rated LOC provider and are attracted to the downgrade protection provided by both the senior/subordinate and cash collateral account structures. The introduction of the cash collateral account as credit enhancement in the spring of 1991 was well-received by investors and may also provide attractive economics to issuers as a method of credit enhancement.

The senior/subordinate structure normally involves multiple layers of credit protection to benefit the various parties involved in the transaction, beginning with the senior class investor's protection via the subordinate class. External credit enhancement, normally in the form of a partial LOC or cash collateral account large enough to achieve a A or AA rating, is provided to protect payments due the subordinate class investor. A spread account, funded by the excess of the yield on the receivables less coupon payments to investors, servicing and other trust expenses, builds up to a stated cap amount and is available solely for the benefit of the credit enhancement provider. Free cash flows on the entire Investor Interest, not just the subordinate class, are used to fund or replenish the spread account.

The level of credit enhancement and size of the subordinate class depend upon the desired rating for the senior and subordinate classes. The rating agencies generally require that either a cash collateral account or an LOC from an A-rated or higher bank cover 54% to 70% of the subordinate class principal balance in order for the subordinate class to qualify for an A rating. On the other hand, the first Discover Card subordinate class to be sold publicly in July 1991 was rated Aa1/AA and had a reserve account (a cash collateral spread account funded initially by a deposit from the seller/servicer and maintained at a given level by deposits from excess spread as necessary) that was initially 102.5% of the subordinate class balance. However, the more recent Discover Card 1991C and 1991D transactions in October 1991 featured an A2/A-rated subordinate class with a reserve account that initially covered 69.8% of the Class B principal but could build to 77% under certain circumstances.

To receive a subordinate class rating, the rating agencies employ a credit sizing methodology. The level of credit enhancement on the subordinate class is calculated as if the entire Investor Interest (senior and subordinate classes combined) was rated A or AA, as applicable. The subordinate class is then sized to obtain a AAA rating for the senior class. The rating agencies also determine the expiration date for the credit enhancement, which allows for a severe slowdown in the pool's payment and purchase rates in a stress scenario. This date will extend beyond the expected final payment date on the Class B certificates.

CASE STUDIES: CITIBANK AND DISCOVER CARD STRUCTURES

While all of the subordinate classes sold to date (Citibank, Colonial National Bank, Discover Card, Household and Signet) provide a significant credit protection against all but the most severely adverse performances, structural differences can create significant timing differences of cash flows to investors should a stress case scenario actually occur. These timing differences can result in quicker or slower repayment of the subordinate class principal. A detailed matrix of cash flow priorities for each structure is included in Appendix 1.

Although the detailed cash flows of each particular issue are complex, the sequence and priority of payment is generally a three-step process.

Step 1

If the senior class required amount (generally defined as certificate interest, servicing fee and charged-off principal including interest on past due certificate interest) exceeds the senior class finance charge collections and reinvestment income, the subordinate class collections (finance charges, principal or both, depending on the structure) are used to cover the deficiency. Subordinate class interest is paid from subordinate class and senior class excess finance charge collections.

Step 2

If subordinate class principal collections are applied to the senior class required amount or a shortfall still exists, the subordinate class ownership percentage shifts downward. Ownership percentage can be reinstated through future excess finance charge collections. Principal payments not used to pay the senior class required amount are used to pay senior class principal.

Step 3

Subordinate class interest shortfalls and unreimbursed ownership percentage shifts are reimbursed from excess finance charge collections and

Table 38.3—Summary of Credit Enhancement Features Discover Card and Citibank Subordinate Classes

	Discover Card	*Citibank*	*Comments*
• Rating	A2/A	A2/A	–
• Amount of Class B Credit Enhancement	69.8% initial 77% maximum	63.5%*	–
• Type of Credit Enhancement	Reserve (Cash Collateral) Account	Cash Collateral Account; Letter of Credit	–
• Class A Fully Paid Prior to Class B Principal Payout	Yes	Yes	Protects Class A
• Class B Interest Shifts if Significant Class A Shortfall	Yes	Yes	Protects Class A
• Fixing of Investor Principal Allocation as of End of Revolving Period	Yes	Yes	Protects Classes A and B
• Maximization of Investor Finance Charge Allocation as of End of Revolving Period	Yes	No	Protects Classes A and B
• Subordinate Amount Increase in Certain Events	Yes	No	Protects Classes A and B
• Subordination of Servicing	No	Yes	Protects Classes A and B
• Use of Excess Servicing to Reimburse Class B	At All Times	At All Times	Protects Classes A and B
• Use of Credit Enhancement to Reimburse Class B	Yes	Yes	Protects Class B
• Credit Enhancement Balance Does Not Decline in Proportion to Investor Interest**	Yes	Yes	Protects Class B

* Approximate; varies slightly from issue to issue.

** As compared to traditional securitization in which the credit enhancement generally declines in absolute terms as the pool principal balance amortizes.

Source: Morgan Stanley

credit enhancement (timing varies depending on the structure).

We have selected the A2/A-rated Discover Card structure issued in October 1991 and the A2/A-rated Citibank structure for comparison. The Citibank model was selected because of the relatively large volume issued. The Discover Card issue was selected because it has a different cash flow sequence than the Citibank structure. Table 38.3 provides an overview of the investor protection features of each issue.

Breakeven Analysis

To illustrate how unlikely the scenarios must be in order for the subordinate class investor to lose principal, we calculated breakeven scenarios by lowering finance charge rates 9 percentage points below current and historical finance charge yields for each structure (e.g., from 18% to 9% annually for the Discover Card and from 20% to 11% for Citibank), by assuming purchase rates equal to payment rates and by using current market financing rates. Summary model results are included in Appendix 2. We then determined the combination of the monthly principal payment and annualized principal loss rates required for the subordinate class investor to just avoid losing principal. The actual Discover Card and Citibank credit enhancement structures were used (see Table 38.4).

Table 38.4—Breakeven Loss Rate In Percent

Principal Payment Rate	*Discover Card*	*Citibank*
2	6.6	5.2
4	9.4	8.5
6	12.1	11.6
8	14.8	14.7
10	17.4	17.7

Source: Morgan Stanley

Both structures can withstand severe deterioration in yields, losses and payment rates before subordinate class investors would lose principal. For example, the principal payment rates in Table 38.4 can decline to as low as 2% (9–10 percentage points below historical averages) and only at loss

Figure 38.3—Subordinate Class Principal Loss Frontier Discover Card Trust 1991C

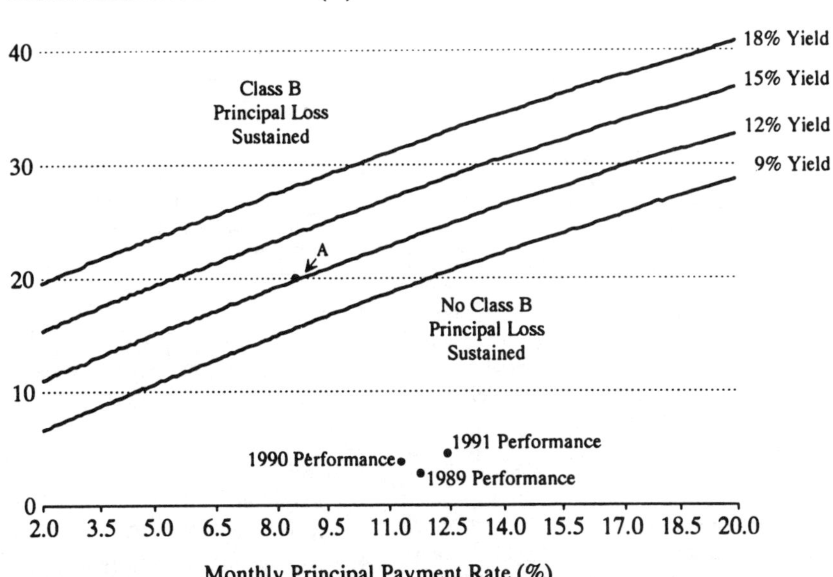

Source: Morgan Stanley

Figure 38.4—Subordinate Class Principal Loss Frontier
Standard Credit Card Master Trust 1

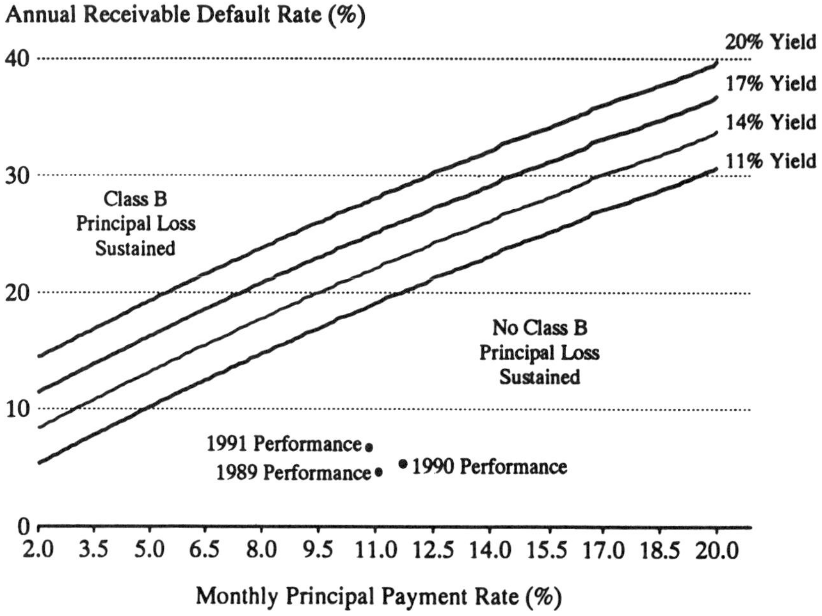

Annual Receivable Default Rate (%)

40, 30, 20, 10, 0

20% Yield
17% Yield
14% Yield
11% Yield

Class B Principal Loss Sustained

No Class B Principal Loss Sustained

1991 Performance
1989 Performance
1990 Performance

2.0 3.5 5.0 6.5 8.0 9.5 11.0 12.5 14.0 15.5 17.0 18.5 20.0

Monthly Principal Payment Rate (%)

rates higher than 6.6% for Discover Card and 5.2% for Citibank would a subordinate class investor lose principal.

For example, the Discover Card, at a yield of 12% and a principal payment rate of 8.7%, as indicated by Point A in Figure 38.3, would require a loss experience greater than 20% before a subordinate class investor would sustain losses. As shown in Figure 38.3, actual loss performance reported for 1989, 1990 and 1991 was 3.3%, 3.9% and 4.3%, respectively, far below the principal loss threshold.

At higher payment rates, the Citibank structure can withstand slightly higher losses since the subordinate class credit enhancement (e.g., either the LOC or cash collateral account) cannot be drawn upon to reimburse subordinate class investors for senior class losses that had caused a subordinate class draw in prior periods until the senior class has been fully paid.

Credit enhancement is accessed sooner in the Discover Card structure. Consequently, slightly lower subordinate class credit enhancement remains in the Discover Card structure to absorb subordinate class losses. On the other hand, the Discover Card structure performs slightly better at slower payment rates. See Appendix 1 for a detailed comparison of cash flow priorities in each structure.

Figures 38.3 and 38.4 illustrate the subordinate class principal loss frontiers (each modeling stress scenarios with differing yield assumptions). Investors should note that the results as illustrated in Appendix 2 are affected by:

- Absolute level of yield and losses
- Mix of yield, losses, coupon and servicing fee that determines excess spread (e.g., greater losses will result in faster prepayments, assuming all other factors are held constant)
- Principal payment rate
- Ratio of Investor Interest to receivables balance at the time of the Amortization Event
- Subordinate class as a percentage of senior class
- Credit enhancement as a percentage of subordinate class balance
- Credit enhancement expiration date
- Cause of the Amortization Event (e.g., bankruptcy)
- Purchase rate versus payment rate.

CONCLUSION

Subordinate classes of credit card securitizations are structured to provide a significant level of protection in all but the most severely stressed scenarios for losses and payment rates. Investors willing to take the time to understand the structural protection afforded in the various subordinate securities available will be rewarded with attractive yields. Morgan Stanley would be pleased to discuss the mechanics of each issue in more detail with interested investors. For further information, please contact Kenneth J. Bock at (212) 296-6450; Richard J. Watson at (212) 296-6544; or Kimberly L. Hirschman at (212) 296-6446.

Appendix 1

SOURCES AND USES OF FUNDS MATRICES

Figures 38.5, 38.6 and 38.7 illustrate the sources and uses of funds in order of application for the Discover Trust 1991C, 1991D and Standard Credit Card Master Trust. The examples of how to use these charts (Figures 38.5 and 38.6) should assist the reader in understanding how to compare the cash flows of these securities. The examples below illustrate the Discover Card model.

Figure 38.5—Sources of Funds

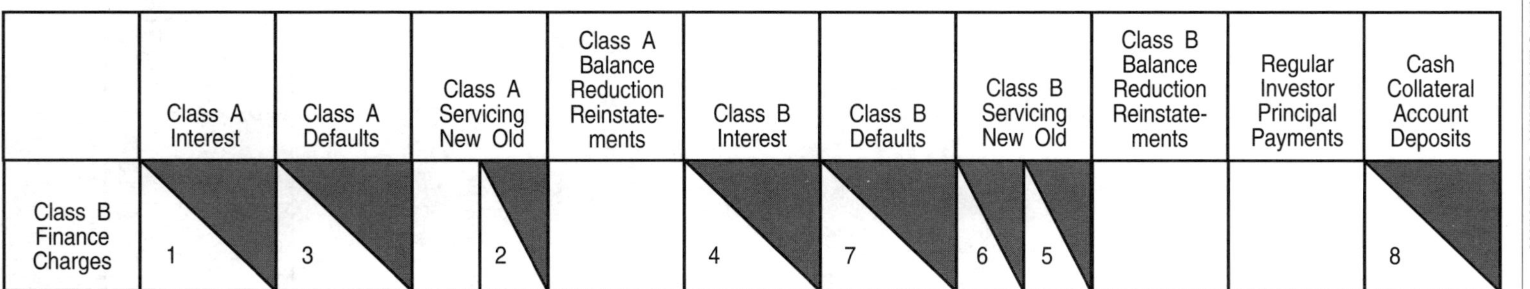

	Class A Interest	Class A Defaults	Class A Servicing New Old	Class A Balance Reduction Reinstatements	Class B Interest	Class B Defaults	Class B Servicing New Old	Class B Balance Reduction Reinstatements	Regular Investor Principal Payments	Cash Collateral Account Deposits
Class B Finance Charges	1	3	2		4	7	6 5			8

The Source of Funds (vertical axis) is applied or used in the following order for the purpose described along the horizontal axis.

Source: *Class B Finance Charges are applied in order to:*

1. Class A Interest
2. Unpaid Prior Period (Old) Class A Servicing
3. Class A Defaults
4. Class B Interest
5. Unpaid Prior Period (Old) Class B Servicing
6. Current Period (New) Class B Servicing
7. Class B Defaults
8. Cash Collateral Account Deposit

Note: For example, Class B Interest only has a claim on any remaining Class B Finance Charges after Class B Finance Charges have been used to fully pay Class A Interest, "Old" (past due) Class A Servicing and Class A Defaults.

Source: Morgan Stanley

Figure 38.6—Use of Funds

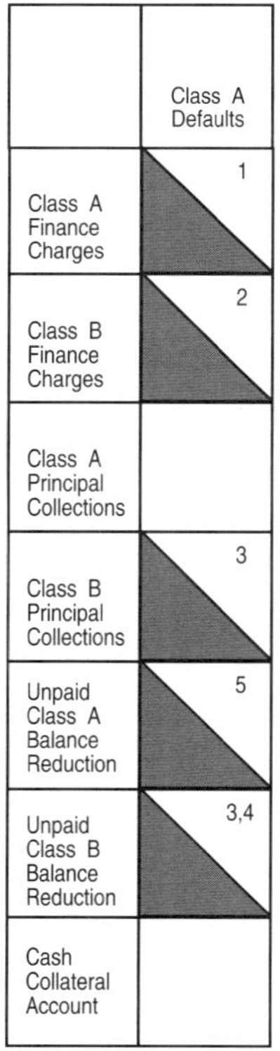

	Class A Defaults
Class A Finance Charges	1
Class B Finance Charges	2
Class A Principal Collections	
Class B Principal Collections	3
Unpaid Class A Balance Reduction	5
Unpaid Class B Balance Reduction	3,4
Cash Collateral Account	

The Uses of Funds (horizontal axis) draws upon the sources (vertical axis) in the following order:

Use: *Class A Defaults are drawn in order from:*

1. Class A Finance Charges
2. Class B Finance Charges
3. Class B Principal Collections

3,4. Unpaid Class B Balance Reduction

5. Unpaid Class A Balance Reduction

Note: For example, Class B Principal Collections are third in line to be used to cover Class A Defaults after Class A Finance Charges and Class B Finance Charges have either been depleted during the distribution period or were originally unavailable.

Source: Morgan Stanley

Figure 38.7—Discover Card Trust 1991C and 1991D Cash Flow Priority Schedule

Uses of Funds

(Each cell: upper right number / lower left number)

Sources of Funds	Class A Interest	Class A Defaults	Class A Servicing New	Class A Servicing Old	Class A Balance Reduction Reinstate-ments	Class B Interest	Class B Defaults	Class B Servicing New	Class B Servicing Old	Class B Balance Reduction Reinstate-ments	Regular Investor Principal Payments	Cash Collateral Account Deposits
Class A Finance Charges	1 / 1	1 / 4	1 / 3	1 / 2		2 / 5	2 / 7		2 / 6			1 / 8
Class B Finance Charges	2 / 1	2 / 3		2 / 2		1 / 4	1 / 7	1 / 6	1 / 5			2 / 8
Class A Principal Collections											1 / 1	
Class B Principal Collections	3 / 1	3 / 3		3 / 2							2 / 4	
Unpaid Class A Balance Reduction		5 / 1										
Unpaid Class B Balance Reduction	3 / 1	3,4 / 2					3 / 3					
Cash Collateral Account						3 / 1	4 / 3		3 / 2	1 / 4		

Note: The numbers in the upper right corners of the boxes indicate the order uses listed along the top draw upon the sources listed down the left side. The numbers in the lower left corners of the boxes indicate the order the sources listed on the left are applied to the uses listed along the top.

Source: Morgan Stanley

Figure 38.8—Standard Credit Card Master Trust Cash Flow Priority Schedule

Uses of Funds

Sources of Funds	Class A Interest	Class A Defaults	Class A Servicing	Class A Balance Reduction Reinstatements	Class B Interest	Class B Defaults	Class B Servicing	Class B Balance Reduction Reinstatements	Regular Investor Principal Payments	Cash Collateral Account Deposits
Class A Finance Charges	1 / 1	1 / 2	1 / 3	1 / 4	2 / 5	1 / 6		1 / 7		1 / 8
Class B Finance Charges	2 / 3	2 / 4		2 / 5	1 / 1	2 / 6	1 / 2	2 / 7		2 / 8
Class A Principal Collections									1 / 1	
Class B Principal Collections	3 / 1	3 / 2							2 / 3	
Unpaid Class A Balance Reduction		5 / 1								
Unpaid Class B Balance Reduction	3 / 1	3,4 / 2				3 / 3				
Cash Collateral Account					3 / 1	4 / 2		3 / 3		

Note: The numbers in the upper right corners of the boxes indicate the order uses listed along the top draw upon the sources listed down the left side. The numbers in the lower left corners of the boxes indicate the order the sources listed on the left are applied to the uses listed along the top.

Source: Morgan Stanley

Appendix 2

SUMMARY FINANCIAL MODEL CASH FLOWS

Figure 38.9—Summary Credit Card Certificate Cash Flows
Discover Card

505,474,592	Initial Pool Principal Balance
350,000,000	Initial Class A Investor Balance
35,000,000	Initial Class B Investor Balance
24,440,000	Initial Credit Enhancement Amount
26,950,000	Maximum Credit Enhancement Amount
35,000,000	Available Subordinate Amount
8.000%	Class A Pass-Through Rate
8.375%	Class B Pass-Through Rate

9.00%	Annual Finance Charge Collection Rate
5.00%	Monthly Principal Collection Rate
10.00%	Annual Net Charge-Off Rate
1	Charge-Off Starting Period
2.00%	Servicing Fee
0.00%	Reinvestment Rate

8.96	Class A Average Life
18	Class A Final Maturity
0	Class A Principal Loss
19.08	Class B Average Life
20	Class B Final Maturity
0	Class B Principal Loss
9.88	Investor Average Life

			Class A Percentage			Class B Percentage										
Period	Principal Receivable	Seller Balance	Fin	Prin	Net C/O	Fin	Prin	Net C/O	Class A Investor Balance	Class B Investor Balance	Class A Investor Charged-Off Amount	Total Principal Paid to Class A	Class B Investor Charged-Off Amount	Class B Principal Losses Reserve Draw	Total Principal Paid to Class B	Reserve Account Amount
0	505,474,592	120,474,592							350,000,000	35,000,000						
1	482,172,720	119,470,637	69.24	69.24	69.24	6.92	6.92%	6.92	327,702,083	35,000,000	2,916,667	22,297,917	2,964,063	2,964,063	0	24,440,000
2	459,218,053	118,475,048	72.59	69.24	67.96	7.26	6.92%	7.26	305,743,004	35,000,000	2,730,851	21,959,079	2,762,205	2,762,205	0	21,247,708
3	436,600,411	117,487,756	76.22	69.24	66.58	7.62	6.92%	7.62	284,112,654	35,000,000	2,547,858	21,630,350	2,576,213	2,576,213	0	18,182,899
4	414,309,808	116,508,592	80.16	69.24	65.07	8.02	6.92%	8.02	262,801,116	35,000,000	2,367,605	21,311,538	2,398,960	2,398,960	0	15,301,083
5	392,336,445	115,537,786	84.48	69.24	63.43	8.45	6.92%	8.45	241,798,659	35,000,000	2,190,009	21,002,457	1,958,729	1,958,729	0	12,599,519
6	370,670,704	114,574,971	89.21	69.24	61.63	8.92	6.92%	8.92	221,095,733	35,000,000	2,014,989	20,702,926	1,458,207	1,458,207	0	10,338,186
7	349,303,147	113,620,180	94.42	69.24	59.65	5.58	6.92%	9.44	200,682,968	35,000,000	1,842,464	20,415,766	1,219,732	1,219,732	0	8,577,375
8	328,224,507	112,673,345	100.00	69.24	57.45	0.00	6.92%	10.02	180,551,163	35,000,000	1,672,358	20,131,805	1,038,441	1,038,441	0	7,055,038
9	307,425,688	111,734,400	100.00	69.24	55.01	0.00	6.92%	10.66	160,691,288	35,000,000	1,504,593	19,859,875	859,683	859,683	0	5,713,994
10	286,897,756	110,803,280	100.00	69.24	52.27	0.00	6.92%	11.38	141,094,476	35,000,000	1,339,094	19,596,812	683,376	683,376	0	4,551,706
11	286,631,940	109,879,920	100.00	69.24	49.18	0.00	6.92%	12.20	121,752,020	35,000,000	1,175,787	19,342,456	509,439	509,439	0	3,565,726
12	246,619,623	108,964,254	100.00	69.24	45.66	0.00	6.92%	13.13	102,655,369	35,000,000	1,014,600	19,096,651	337,792	337,792	0	2,753,683
13	226,852,342	108,056,218	100.00	69.24	41.62	0.00	6.92%	14.19	83,796,124	35,000,000	855,461	18,859,245	291,667	291,667	0	2,113,287
14	207,321,783	107,155,750	100.00	69.24	36.94	0.00	6.92%	15.43	65,166,033	35,000,000	698,301	18,630,091	291,667	291,667	0	1,642,326
15	188,019,773	106,262,785	100.00	69.24	31.43	0.00	6.92%	16.88	46,756,988	35,000,000	543,050	18,409,045	291,667	196,749	0	1,338,668
16	168,938,283	105,377,262	100.00	69.24	24.87	0.00	6.92%	18.62	28,561,021	35,000,000	389,642	18,195,967	291,667	0	0	1,141,919
17	150,069,420	104,499,118	100.00	69.24	16.91	0.00	6.92%	20.72	10,570,302	35,000,000	238,009	17,990,720	291,667	0	0	1,166,762
18	131,405,422	103,628,292	100.00	69.24	7.04	0.00	6.92%	23.32	0	27,777,130	88,086	10,570,302	291,667	0	7,222,870	1,352,953
19	112,938,661	102,764,723	100.00	69.24	0.00	0.00	6.92%	21.14	0	10,173,938	0	0	231,476	0	17,603,192	1,698,651
20	101,908,350	101,908,350	100.00	69.24	0.00	0.00	6.92%	9.01	0	0	0	0	84,783	0	10,173,938	2,204,347

Source: Morgan Stanley

Figure 38.10—Summary Credit Card Certificate Cash Flows

Standard Credit Card Master Trust 1

700,000,000	Initial Principal Receivables Amount
500,000,000	Initital Class A Investor Balance
62,000,000	Initial Class B Investor Balance
39,340,000	Initial Credit Enhancement Amount
39,340,000	Maximum Credit Enhancement Amount
8.250%	Class A Pass-Through Rate
8.470%	Class B Pass-Through Rate

11.000%	Finance Charge Collection Rate
5.000%	Monthly Principal Collection Rate
10.000%	Annual Net Default Rate
1	Default Starting Period
2.000%	Servicing Fee
0.000%	Reinvestment Rate

9.64	Class A Average Life
19	Class A Final Maturity
0	Class A Principal Loss
19.39	Class B Average Life
20	Class B Final Maturity
0	Class B Principal Loss
10.72	Investor Average Life

Period	Principal Receivable	Seller Balance	Investor Principal Collection	Class A Fin Charge/ Default	Class B Fin Charge/ Default	Class A Invested Amount	Class B Unpaid Principal Balance	Class A Default Amount	Total Class A Principal Payment	Class B Default Amount	Class B Principal Loss Draw	Total Class B Principal Payment	Cash Collateral Account Amount
0	700,000,000	138,000,000				500,000,000	62,000,000						39,340,000
1	665,784,167	136,333,333	80.29%	71.43%	8.86%	471,003,881	62,000,000	4,166,667	28,996,119	516,667	0	0	39,340,000
2	632,115,289	134,710,164	80.29%	70.74%	8.78%	442,305,509	62,000,000	3,925,032	28,698,372	487,058	0	0	39,314,921
3	598,958,160	133,128,416	80.29%	69.97%	8.72%	413,902,215	62,000,000	3,685,879	28,403,294	459,163	0	0	39,266,216
4	566,385,686	131,586,058	80.29%	69.10%	8.67%	385,791,352	62,000,000	3,449,185	28,110,863	432,954	0	0	39,195,312
5	534,308,885	130,081,105	80.29%	68.11%	8.65%	357,970,296	62,000,000	3,214,928	27,821,055	408,402	0	0	39,103,612
6	502,746,884	128,611,617	80.29%	67.00%	8.66%	330,436,448	62,000,000	2,983,086	27,533,848	385,479	0	0	38,992,496
7	471,691,922	127,175,697	80.29%	65.73%	8.69%	303,187,229	62,000,000	2,753,637	27,249,219	364,157	0	0	38,863,320
8	441,136,343	125,771,491	80.29%	64.28%	8.76%	276,220,085	62,000,000	2,526,560	26,967,145	344,408	0	0	38,717,417
9	411,072,600	124,397,189	80.29%	62.62%	8.87%	249,532,481	62,000,000	2,301,834	26,687,604	326,206	0	0	38,556,098
10	381,493,248	123,051,021	80.29%	60.70%	9.04%	223,121,907	62,000,000	2,079,437	26,410,574	309,524	0	0	38,380,648
11	352,390,947	121,731,260	80.29%	58.49%	9.26%	196,985,874	62,000,000	1,859,349	26,136,033	294,336	0	0	38,192,334
12	323,758,460	120,436,218	80.29%	55.90%	9.56%	171,121,915	62,000,000	1,641,549	25,863,959	280,615	0	0	37,992,398
13	295,588,651	119,164,247	80.29%	52.85%	9.95%	145,527,584	62,000,000	1,426,016	25,594,331	268,336	0	0	37,782,062
14	267,874,481	117,913,738	80.29%	49.23%	10.45%	120,200,457	62,000,000	1,212,730	25,327,127	257,474	0	0	37,562,526
15	240,609,013	116,683,121	80.29%	44.87%	11.11%	95,138,130	62,000,000	1,001,670	25,062,327	248,002	0	0	37,334,967
16	213,785,405	115,470,864	80.29%	39.54%	11.96%	70,338,222	62,000,000	792,818	24,799,908	239,898	0	0	37,100,544
17	187,396,910	114,275,470	80.29%	32.90%	13.09%	45,798,371	62,000,000	586,152	24,539,851	233,136	0	0	36,860,394
18	161,436,879	113,095,483	80.29%	24.44%	14.58%	21,516,236	62,000,000	381,653	24,282,135	227,692	0	0	36,615,632
19	135,898,753	111,929,477	80.29%	13.33%	16.62%	0	23,969,276	179,302	21,516,236	223,543	35,520,221	2,510,503	847,135
20	110,796,988	110,796,988	80.29%	0.00%	17.64%	0	0	0	0	199,744	190,989	23,778,287	405,433

Source: Morgan Stanley

Index

A

AB Asesores, 256
ABS, *see* Asset-back security
ABSC, *see* Asset-backed
Accounting
  see Business
  constraints, 411
  costs, 205
  fees, 203
  issues, *see* Asset-backed finance
  policies, 206
  Standards Board (ASB), 87, 224, 240
    see Federal, Financial, International
  Standards Committee, 240
  treatment, 183
Accounts, *see* Funds and accounts
Accretion bonds, 394-395
Accrual, 244
  see Zero
  bonds, 61
Acquisitions, 10
ACT, *see* Advance
Actuarial analysis, 142
Adjustable-rate mortgage (ARM), 38, 68, 303, 342, 343, 351, 353, 366, 417
Administrator, 241, 242-243, 245
  exposure, 297
  performance risk, 170
Advance corporation tax (ACT), 244
Adverse selection, 4, 5
AFGI, *see* Association
Agency
  see U.S.
  cost reduction, 28
Agricultural equipment loan, 27
All-in-costs, 122, 371
  reduction, 114
Amax Coal, 78
AMBAC Indemnity Corp., 174, 179, 190, 192
American Express, 451
Amortization, 153, 163, 239, 295
  see Controlled, Mortgage, Non-amortization, Planned, Targeted
  event, 464, 465, 466, 473, 478
  period, 455-460
  schedule, 143, 391
  triggers, 449, 464, 473
AMS, *see* Australian
Annual percentage rate (APR), 466
Annuity, *see* Flexible, Single
Anti-branching laws, 10
APR, *see* Annual
Arbitrage, 63
  see Cost, Yield curve
  risk, 158
Argentaria, 256
ARM, *see* Adjustable
Arrangement fees, 271
Arrears, 100
  securitizations, 317-318
ASB, *see* Accounting
Asset, 29, 236-238, 245-247, 248, 251-252, 253-254, 255-256, 258-259, 260-261, 263
  see Commercial, Consumer, Corporate, Revenue, Risk, Securitized, Yield
  balance, 63
  bundling, 31
  cash flow, 78
  diversification, 6, 111
  duration, 23
  liability management, 85
  origination, 206
  originator, 200
  pool, 153, 159-160, 164, 219, 228
  portfolio, 46, 238
  risk, 154-156, 217
    analysis, 153, 161-162, 164-165
  selection criteria, 143
  transfer, 31, 236-237, 250
    tax issues, 252, 258-259, 261
  transferability, 236-237, 253-254, 255-256, 258, 260-261, 263
  types, 245-247, 248, 253-254, 255-256, 258, 260-261, 263
  value, *see* Investor
  yield, 158
Asset-backed bonds, 129, 218
Asset-backed commercial paper programs, 277-286
  overview, 279-280
  risk-based capital implications, 284-285
Asset-backed Euro commercial paper
  benefits, 289-290
  costs, 297-298
  disadvantages, 290
  risks/rewards, 289-298
Asset-backed finance, 217-221
  accounting issues, 223-226
Asset-backed instruments, 261, 279
Asset-backed securities, 46, 49, 56, 57, 78, 128, 136, 153, 154, 181, 192, 455, 463, 469
  see Credit card, Global, Insured, Subordinated
  market evolution, 30-31
  structure, 27-60
    introduction, 27-28
  trader risk control, 217-221

types, 217-218
Asset Backed Securities Corporation (ABSC), 9, 45
Asset-backed structure, 130
Asset Guaranty Reinsurance Co., 174
Asset securitization, 31, 40, 56-57, 85, 169, 235-264
  Belgium, 251-253
  consideration, 87-89
  credit risk analysis, 153-167
  France, 247-251
  future, 3-14
  Germany, 253-255
  Hong Kong, 263-264
  Italy, 258-260
  Japan, 260-263
  Scotland, 245-247
  Spain, 255-258
  United Kingdom, 235-245
Assignor, 250-251, 253, 255
Association of Certified Public Accountants, 261
Association of Financial Guaranty Insurors (AFGI), 187
At-the-money, 400, 410
AT&T, 72, 73, 217
Audits, 105
August Decree, 255, 256
Australian mortgage-backed securities, 337-340
Australian Mortgage Securities (AMS), 338
Automobile
  see National
  finance industry (U.S.), 109-126
    geographic concentration, 125-126
    legal vehicles, 119-121
    pricing, 122-123
    transaction size, 123-124
  installment
    contracts, 35
    loans, 27, 48, 51-52, 56
Automobile loans, 38, 87, 181-182
  European implications, 126
  receivables, 235
  securities, issuers, 112-118
    market share, 112-114
  securitization, 109-126
    objectives, 114-115
  securitization structures, 118-126

B

Back fee, 399
Backstop
  banks, 290, 293, 297
  facility, 290 292-294, 297
Bad and Doubtful Debts (B&DDs), 89
Balance, 367
  see Off-balance, On-balance, Receivables
  sheet, 118, 128, 145, 165, 200, 205, 223, 228, 240, 255, 274, 280
Banco Bilbao Vizcaya (BBV), 255, 256
Banco Commerciale, 258
Banco Santander, 255, 256
Banesto, 256
Bank(s), 3, 173, 174
  see Bankstop, Commercial, Senior
  credit, 278
  debt, 10
  European, *see* Securitization
  loan, 166, 277
  originators, 5
  structure, securitization, 11-14
  syndicate, 79
Bank Boston, 118
Bank breakup
  benefits/costs, 3-14
Bank for International Settlements (BIS), 199, 293, 342, 345, 350
  Committee, 84
  framework, 87, 89
Bank of America, 118
Bank of England, 85, 86, 200, 202, 203, 238-241, 252, 263, 309, 348
  requirements, 242
Bank of Spain, 256
Banker(s)
  see Investment, Mortgage, Nonbankers
  duty of confidentiality, 254
Banking
  organizations, incentives, 282-283
  structure, securitization, 11-14
Banking and Finance Commission, 252
Bankruptcy, 56, 63, 81, 104, 136, 137, 162, 256, 291, 297, 450
  see U.S.
  consolidation, 180
  law, 266
  Law, 262
  remote, 265
  risk, 8
  support arrangement, 55
Bankruptcy Act of 1898, 150
Barclays Bank PLC, 176
Base funding cost, 271
Basis
  points, 34, 123, 299, 302, 304, 312, 323, 326, 347, 350, 359, 369, 370, 378, 430, 452
  risk, 295, 425
  swaps, 295
Basle Accord, 112, 124
Basle Agreement, 84-85, 309
Basle Committee, 174, 199
Basle Conversions, 84
Basle rules, 313
Bausparkassen, 346
Bayerische Vereinsbank AG, 174
BBV, *see* Banco
BCCI, 202
Bear Stearns, 53, 63, 64
  Home Loans, 315
  Mortgage Securities, 315
Belgian Bankruptcy Act, 253
Belgian Stock Exchange, 252
Beneficiary, 246
Bid/bidder, 80
BIS, *see* Bank for International
Black and Scholes model, 413
Black period, 255, 256
Blocked account, 171
Blue Cross/Blue Shield, 164

BMW, 120, 121
Boat
installment loans, 27, 48
loan receivables, 153
Bond(s), 103, 244, 303
see Accretion, Accrual, Asset-backed, Collateralized, Companion, Corporate, Coupon, Eurobond, Fixed-rate, Junk, Mortgage, On-balance, Payment, Performance, Plain, Planned, Senior, Subordinated, Surety, Targeted, Tax-exempt, U.S. Treasury, Z, Zero
balance, 63
holders, 63
insurance, 65
issues, 144
portfolio, 185
principal, 61
Bonding, 23-24
Bonos de Titulizacion Hipotecaria, 256
Book value, 19
Borrowers, 4, 5, 11, 13, 14, 28, 289, 292, 294, 295, 297, 327, 339, 348, 355, 358, 414, 418, 425
costs, 289
defaults, 5
B Pieces, 363-373
Break-even
analysis, 471, 477-478
margin, 205
BSC, *see* Building
BSD, 85, 238
Bucket, 433
Building Societies, 305, 318, 348
Building Societies Act (1986), 239, 306
Building Societies Commission (BSC), 239, 318
Building Society, 306, 308
Built-in capital, 181, 184
Bullet
see Hard, Soft
maturity, 313-314
mechanisms, 461-462
payment, 138
Business
Accounting Council, 261
debt, 111
expansion, 201
strategy, 219
Buyers, 6

C

Caisee de Refinancement Hypothecaire (CRH), 346, 355
Callable
see Noncallable
debt, 353
Call, *see* Covered, Long, Naked, Short
Call option, 15, 19, 24, 301, 400, 405
Canada Mortgage and Housing Corporation (CMHC), 320, 322
Canadian Imperial Bank of Commerce (CIBC), 290, 291, 297, 309, 312, 317
Mortgage (CIBCM), 290, 291, 295, 297
Canadian MBS market, 320-321
see Prepayable
Canadian NHA MBS market, risks/opportunities, 319-335
Cap, 149, 295, 303
see Floor, Interest rate
Capital, 79, 84-85, 205, 206, 239, 243, 264, 277
see Asset-backed, Built-in, Equity, Return, Trading
adequacy, 140, 144, 185, 199-200, 313, 345
see Guarantor
standards, 342
amount, 10-11
costs, 7-11
see Marginal
loans held/sold, 7-9
debt markets, 78
gain/loss realization timing, 323
gains, 13, 16, 19
guidelines, 284, 285
losses, 6
market, 110, 153
ratios, 114, 199, 283
repayment, 218
Capital Guaranty Insurance Co., 174, 179
Capital Markets Assurance Co. (CapMac), 122, 174, 179
Capital Reinsurance Co., 174, 192
CapMac, *see* Capital Markets
Capping out, 425
Capstead Mortgage, 110
CARCO, *see* Chrysler
Caridad Mexican Copper Mine deal, 78-80
Cash
collateral, 69, 103, 121, 127, 172, 174, 202, 204, 475
deposit, 205
reinvestment risk, 106-107
reserve fund, 69
Cash flow, 4, 6, 15, 20, 22, 23, 45, 56, 57, 62, 63, 78, 99, 105, 143-148, 150, 154, 165, 169-171, 206, 217, 218, 221, 228, 230, 280, 315, 321, 323, 331, 376, 393, 463, 476, 487-489
see Asset, Pool
frequency, 322-323
increase, 62
insurance, 338
projections, 155
reinvestment, 333
risk, 4, 100, 135-152, 315
stability, 390, 391, 393
timing uncertainty, 319
variability, 386
variance, 6
CBO, *see* Collateralized
CD, *see* Certificate
Cedulas, 255
Central Bank of Mexico, 72
Cerro Colorado Copper Project, 80
Certificate
see Pass-through, Subordinate
yield, 472
Certificate holder, 147
see Senior, Subordinated
interest payments, 462

Certificate of deposit (CD), 6, 12, 19, 166, 278, 346
Certificate yield shortfall potential risk, 158
CFC, *see* Chrysler
Changing durations, 23
Charge-offs, 466
Chase Manhattan Bank, 110, 118
Chase Securities, 118
Chatsworth Funding, Inc., 190
Chattel paper, 119
Chemical Bank, 114, 130
Chevy Chase Savings Bank, 473
Chrysler Finance Corporation, 112, 115, 116, 118, 121, 124
  CARCO, 118
  CARCO Dealers Wholesale Trust, 122
  CFC, 112, 113
  Premier Auto Trust, 120
CIBC, *see* Canadian
CIBCM, *see* Canadian
Citibank, 68, 80, 190, 258, 466, 475-479
  Colombus Capital, 313
  Espana, 255, 256
Citicorp, 75, 110, 112, 114, 120, 124, 263, 449, 452-455
  National Credit Card Trust, 449
Citifin, 255, 256
Claim(s), *see* Securitized, Senior, Subordinated
Claim rejection risk, 165
Clawback, 243
CLO, *see* Collateralized
Closed-end fund, 21
Closing date, 80
CMHC, *see* Canada
CMO, *see* Collateralized
CMS, 313
CMT, *see* Constant
COB, *see* Commission
COFI, *see* Cost of Funds
Co-insurers, 11
Collar, *see* Prepayment
Collateral, 5, 40, 52, 150, 180, 182, 184, 369
  see Cash, Coupon, Fixed-rate, Mortgage
  account, 145
  coupon, 62
  pool, 49
  quality issues, 316-317
  trading, 61
Collateralization, *see* Cross, Overcollateralization
Collateralized bonds obligations (CBO), 154, 184
Collateralized loans/leases obligations (CLO), 154
Collateralized mortgage obligation (CMO), 4, 21-23, 30, 31, 33, 40, 42, 43, 45, 46, 48, 55, 56, 61, 62, 310, 375
  see Fitch, Subordinated
  issuer, 56
  structures, 61-62
  tranche, 57, 383-387
  tranche risk, 389-396
  volatility ratings, 383-388
Collection(s), 273
  process, 36
Colonial National Bank, 475
Comdisco, 159-162
  Receivables Trust, 159-160
Comision Nacional del Mercado de Valores, 256
Commercial
  see Uniform
  asset, 154, 155
  bank, 7, 12, 13, 82, 116, 191
    loan, 27, 203
  finance company, 82
  law, 266
  loan, 5, 111, 153
  mortgage, 13, 142, 185, 345
    loans, 27, 48, 52
Commercial paper (CP), 13, 89, 105, 106, 156-158, 312-313
  see Asset-backed, Euro, U.S.
  conduit financing, 313
  conduit structures, 229
  market, 105
    overview, 277-278
  rates, 89
  rollover, 265
  structure, 89
Commercial Union, 174
Commingling, 230
  risk, 162
Commission Bancaire, 249
Commission des Operations de Bourse (COB), 248, 249
Commitments, 284, 285
  see Zero
Commodity
  see Forward
  indexed loan, 79
  loan, 78
  markets, 75
  prices, 37
  price swap, 78
  securitization financing opportunities, 77-82
Common stock, 375
Companhia Vale do Rio Doce, 80
Companies Act
  (1985), 242
  (1989), 240
Companies Ordinance, 264
Companion
  bond, 389-391
  classes, 43-45
Company, *see* Companies, Intercompany
Competitive advantage, 199-201
Competitiveness, 85, 351
Computer
  installment loans, 27
  leases, 191
Comunidad de bienes, 256
Concentrations, elimination, 100-101
Connie Lee Insurance Co., 174
Conseil des Bourses de Valeurs, 250
Conservatorship, 139
CONSOB, *see* National Commission
Consolidation, 223
Constant maturity treasury (CMT) index, 303, 363, 371, 372

Constant prepayment rate (CPR), 311, 324, 329-331, 377, 379-381
Consumer, 12
  asset, 154, 155
  credit, 252
  Credit Act of 1974, 237, 241
  credit law, 259
  debt, 111
  law, 250
  loan, 4, 27, 241
  protection law, 264
  receivables, 154, 185
Consumption Tax Law Enforcement Order, 261
Contingency insurances, 133
Contingency risk
  management, 127-133
  transfer, 127-133
Contingent liability, 140
Contractual SPV, 252, 253
Control duration risk, 302-303
Controlled amortization, 138
  structure, 456-460
Convenience usage, 465
Convexity, 438
  risk, *see* Portfolio
Cooke ratios, 77
Copper price risk, 79
Corporate
  see Noncallable
  assets, 91, 153
  bonds, 186, 413
  loans, 235
  planning, 219
  Tax Law, 263
Cost(s), 271
  see Agency, Capital, Default, Rating, Servicing, Weighted
  arbitrage, 312
Cost of funds index (COFI), 68, 363, 370
Counterparty
  see Foreign, Swap
  approval, 220
  risks, 140, 149
Coupon, 431-433, 436, 439, 441, 460
  see Collateral
  paying bonds, 61
  paying collateral, 61
  rate, 34, 35, 57
Covenants, 5, 9, 154, 229-230
Coverage, 74
Covered call, 406-407
CP, *see* Commercial paper
CPR, *see* Constant
Credit, 74
  see Mortgage, Securitized, Structured, Tax, Third
  analysis, 135
  crunch, 77
  curve, 143, 145
  enhancer, 110, 128, 153, 202
  evaluation, 279
  extension, 4
  facility, 313
  intensive mortgage securities, 363-373
  loss, 11, 161, 172, 376
  protection, 273, 293
  protection structure, 173
  quality, 202, 218, 285, 292, 316, 317
  rating, 80, 107, 289
  regulation, 241-242, 250, 252-253, 262, 264
  safeguards, 282
  securitization, 6
  support, 63, 143-145, 148
  support levels, 142-143
  support provider, 149
  tranching, 62
  warranties, 223
Credit card, 229, 241
  asset-backed securities, 450-451
    retirement, 462
  balances, 290, 455
  certificates, 453
  debt, 203
  receivables, 27, 38-40, 48, 52, 55, 74, 87, 153, 154, 171, 191, 238, 243, 260, 280, 452, 454
    backed trust structure, 49-51
  securities, 453
  securitization, 449-489 structure, 136, 138
  subordinate certificates, 471-489
  transaction, 138, 453
  types, 451-452
Credit card-backed securities
  risk evaluation, 449-469
Credit enhancement, 40, 49, 51, 62, 102, 106, 109, 127, 144, 153, 159, 163-164, 169-177, 203, 204, 217, 218, 228, 249, 273-274, 281, 282, 291-292, 341, 356, 462-464, 475, 478
  see External
  fees, 271, 375
  level/type, 121-122
  providers, 173-174, 202, 291
  risk, 156-157, 169-171
    cover, 171-173
  structures, 315-316
Credit Foncier, 355
Credit Reinsurance Co., 174
Credit risk, 4, 6, 11-13, 83, 99-103, 135-152, 169-171, 202, 218, 220-221, 291-292, 337-340, 348, 350, 364-370, 375, 376, 381
  allocation, 348-351
    Denmark, 348-350
    France, 350
    Germany, 350-351
    United Kingdom, 351
  analysis, *see* Asset
  guarantees, 4
  guarantors, 4-5
  management, 127-133
  premium, 4
  transfer, 127-133
Credit Lyonnais, 53, 80
Credit Suisse, 30, 122, 174
Credit Union, 340
Creditwatch, 282
CRH, *see* Caisse
Cross-border
  reinsurance, 192

risk, 71-72
Cross-collateralization, 341, 348
Cross currency swaps, hedging, 294-295
Cross-hedge, 398
Cross-subsidies, 12
Crown Corporation, 320
Cures, 63
Currency
see Cross
conversions, 274
exchange risk, 78
hedging programs, 265
risk, 85, 170
risk protection, 149
swap counterparties, 135

D

Data protection, 250, 254, 259, 264
legislation, 252
Data Protection Act of 1984, 241
DBL, 123
Dealer
see National, Security
fees, 271
floorplan loan, 27
relations, 402, 411
Dean Witter, 118
Debentures, *see* Subordinated
Debt, 9, 20, 48, 55, 189, 199, 217, 246, 255, 346
see Bank, Business, Callable, Capital, Consumer, Credit card, Deposit, Foreign, Long-term, Non-insured, Senior, Short-term, Subordinated
equity instruments, 84
holders, *see* Securitization
instruments, 4, 109, 121
issuance, 277
service, 31
transfer, 248
Debt-to-income ratio, 469
Declining subordination, 148-149
Decree of 1989, 247, 248
Default, 21, 63, 273, 282, 310, 376, 451
see Borrower, Intermediary, Mortgage
cost, 364, 370
curve, 63
experience, payment rate effect, 466
hazards, 357-361
rate, 102, 364, 366, 465
Default risk, 23, 29, 36-40, 55, 369
reallocation, structures, 46-56
reduction, structures, 46-56
shift, 48-49
Delinquency, 21, 36, 37, 40, 48, 56, 63, 65, 100, 140, 146, 148, 155, 161, 230
data, 155-156
Delivery month, 80
Delta hedge ratio, 440
Demand deposits, 6, 158
Department
plans/strategies, 219
Deposit(s), 12, 13, 341, 346
see Certificates, Demand, Federal
debt, 7
embedded option effect, 19
funds, 8
insurance, 10, 12
intermediaries, 16, 17, 24
Depositary, 250
Depositors, 11, 12
Derecognition, 224
Deutsche Bank, 80, 122, 162
Developed housing finance systems
mortgage securitization, 341-356
DG Bank, 355
DIAC, 130
Diagonal spread, 410-411
Dilutions, 137, 266
Diners Club, 451
Directional strategies, 409-411
Disclosed reserves, 84
Disclosure, *see* Favorable
Discount
margin, 309
rate, 132
Discover
Card, 475-479
Trust, 481
Disintermediation, 106
Disposal proceeds, 243-244
Distribution
flexibility, 140
rights, *see* Oil
Diversification, 46, 161, 183
see Asset, Portfolio
benefits, 7
Dividends, 21, 244
Documentation risk, 218, 221
Donaldson Lufkind Jenrette, 116
Downgrade, 172, 174, 183
protection, 156, 182
risk, 158, 182, 296-297
Downside exposure, 224, 225
Drexel Burnham Lambert, 116, 417
Droit de partage, 249
Due diligence, 230
Duration, 299, 425, 430
see Control, Portfolio, Price
imbalance, 17
uncertainty, 320-323
Dynamic
hedges, 443
hedging strategies, 433-441

E

Eagle Star insurance, 291, 316
Eastbridge, 301
Capital Inc., 299
offshore fund, 302
philosophy, 299
EC, *see* European
ECI Adjustable Income Portfolio, N.V., 299
Economic risk, 218, 221
Economies of scale, 205
ECP, *see* MAES, Euro commercial

EEC, *see* European
EITF, 228
E-L, *see* Epargne
Elasticity, 432, 433, 439
    see Implied
Embedded options, *see* Deposit, Loan
Emerging economies, *see* International
Enhancement, 129
    see Credit, Return
Enhance Reinsurance Co., 174
Enron Corporation, 80
Epargne-Logement (E-L) plans, 346
Equipment leases, 27, 48, 111, 156, 161
Equipment loan, *see* Agricultural
Equitable assignment, 86
Equity, 9, 10, 48, 84, 199, 200, 205-206, 280
    see Debt
    capital, 7, 189, 204
    darling, 246
    exposure, 202
    loan, *see* Home
    tranche, 145
ERISA, 167
Escrow accounts, 75
Eurobonds, 244
Euro Commercial Paper (ECP), 89, 312
    see Asset-backed
Euro fixed-rate bond (FRB), 89
Euro fixed-rate note (FRN), 89
Euro MTN, 89
Euronotes, 80
European
    see Securitization
    Commission, 201
    Community (EC), 191, 199, 223, 225, 342, 345
        directives, 257
        First and Second Banking Directives, 201
        Solvency Ratio Directive, 242
    Economic Community (EEC), 124
    securitization, 203-204
    securitization market, 83
Euro-placement, 122
Event, *see* Amortization, Payout, Repurchase, Trigger
Event risk, 127, 128, 131, 137, 172, 218, 316
    premium, 132
Examiner guidance, 285-286
Excess spread, 473
    see Negative
Expiration
    see Term, Time
    date, 399, 407, 408, 410
External credit enhancement
    level setting, 103

F

Factoring company, 258
Facultative reinsurance, 189
FANMAC, *see* First Australian
Farm mortgages, 6
Farmer Mac
    obligations, 5
    poolers, 5
FASB, *see* Financial Accounting
Fast pay/slow pay structure, 147
Favorable disclosure treatment, 183
FCC, *see* Fonds
FCP, 251
FDIC, *see* Federal Deposit
Federal Accounting Standards Board, 200
Federal Banking Supervisory Authority, 254
Federal Deposit Insurance Act, 152
Federal Deposit Insurance Corporation, 8
    FDIC, 8, 10, 11, 14, 453
Federal Home Loan Bank Board, 68
    FHLBB, 68
Federal Home Loan Mortgage Corporation, 29
    FHLMC, 29-31, 35, 40, 46, 47, 51, 56, 57, 143, 279, 301, 341, 357, 361, 363, 375, 418, 443
Federal Housing Administration, 5, 341
    FHA, 5, 34, 46, 51, 110, 375, 418
Federal National Mortgage Association, 29, 110
    FNMA, 29-31, 34, 35, 40, 46, 51, 56, 110, 143, 279, 301, 302, 341, 342, 363, 418, 443
    guarantee, 43
    Guaranteed REMIC Pass-Through Certificate, 42
    REMIC trust, 43
Federal Reserve, 23, 112, 277, 285, 417
FEFTCL, *see* Foreign Exchange
FGI, *see* Financial
FGIC, *see* Financial
FHA, *see* Federal Housing
FHLBB, *see* Federal Home
FHLMC, *see* Federal Home
Finance, 74
    see Commercial, Developed, Monoline, Structured
    Act (1971), 237
    charge, 466
    companies, 191
    rates, 155
    sales comparison, 223
Financial Accounting Standards Board (FASB), 224
Financial guarantor, 181, 182
Financial guaranty
    insurance (FGI), 180
    reinsurance, 189-196
        market development, 190-192
Financial Guaranty Insurance Co. (FGIC), 174, 179
Financial Institutions Reform, Recovery, and Enforcement Act
    FIRREA (1989), 13, 152
Financial performance, 206
Financial Reporting Standard, 240
Financial risk, 99
Financial Security Assurance (FSA), 122, 174, 179, 181, 192, 312, 317
Financial Services Act of 1986, 241, 242
Financing
    see Commercial paper
    leases, 280
Firestone, 452
FIRREA, *see* Financial Institutions
First American Bank, 121
First Australian Mortgage Acceptance Corporation (FANMAC), 337-339
First Boston Corporation, 30, 115, 118, 121

Auto-Backed Securities Corp., 120
First-loss provider, 180, 182, 185
First Mortgage Securities, 310
First Security Bank of Utah, N.A., 162
Fitch, 376, 383, 449, 450, 462, 466
CMO model, 385-386, 385
CMO Volatility Ratings, 383, 389
indicated volatility, 397
scenario, 386-387
Fixed amount structure, 147-148
Fixed-rate
bonds (FRB), *see* Euro
collateral, 62
issues, 313-315
notes (FRN), 308-310, 312, 314
see Euro
Fixed-rate mortgage (FRM), 303, 342, 346, 353, 378
hedging, 413-446
return, 413-446
risk, 413-446
Flexible Premium Deferred Annuity (FPDA), 363
rate correlation, 370
Floaters, 382, 392-393
see Inverse
Floating-rate cost, 204
Floating-rate loan, 29
Floating-rate note, 203
see Inverse
classes, 56, 57-58
creation, 62
Floor, 62
cap, 79
subordination amount, 148
Floorplan
see Dealer
loan, 55
FNMA, *see* Federal National
Fondo de Titulizacion Hipotecaria, 255-257
Fonds Communs dde Creances (FCC), 191, 200, 248-250
Ford Credit Auto Loan Master Trust Series, 120
Ford Motor Credit Company, 58, 112, 118
Ford Credit, 113
New Master Trust, 124
Foreclosure, 36, 37, 140, 316, 376
rate, 367, 369
Foreign
exchange counterparty, 291
exchange risk, 71, 106
hedging, 294-295
Exchange and Foreign Trade Control Law (FEFTCL), 262
sovereign debt, 27
Forward
commodity price contract, 81
contract, 294
FPDA, *see* Flexible
Franchise, 11
Franchisee payment obligation, 27
Fraud, 12, 64, 65
FRB, *see* Fixed-rate
Front-end fees, 204
FRM, *see* Fixed-rate
FRN, *see* Fixed-rate
FSA, *see* Financial
Full principal, 172
Funding
see Base, Housing, Principal, Purchaser, Weighted
sources, 199
Funds
see Closed, Cost, Investment, Pension, Reserve, Sinking
access, 115
matrices, sources/uses, 481-486
Funds and accounts risk, 157-158
Future(s), 302
see U.S. Treasury
receivables, 73
FX costs, 89

G

GAAP, *see* Generally
Gain on sale/economics, 227-228
Gap/gapping, 115, 131
risk, 218, 221
Garn-St. Germain Act of 1982, 12
GECC, 120
GEM, 366
Generally Accepted Accounting Principles (GAAP), 228, 274, 275
General Electric
Capital Corporation, 56, 110
Capital Mortgage Service, 55, 56
General Motors Acceptance Corporation, 9, 30, 38, 46, 112
GMAC, 113, 115, 118, 121, 124
General purpose vehicle, 272
German Prospectus Act, 254
Gesellschaft mit beschrankter Haftung, 254
Gestora, 255, 256
Gewerbesteuer, 255
GIC, *see* Guaranteed
Gilt options, 315
Glass-Steagall Act, 10, 14
Global Advanced Technology Corp., 385
Global asset-backed securities market, bridges, 189-196
Global securitization, 111-112
GMAC, *see* General
GNMA, *see* Government
GNP, *see* Gross
Goldman Sachs, 75, 118
Goodwill, 84
Government National Mortgage Association, 30, 110, 191
GNMA, 30, 35, 46, 110, 191, 279, 301-303, 320, 341, 363, 375, 417-419, 423, 425, 428, 430-432, 436-439, 441, 443
GPM, *see* Graduated
Graduated Payment Mortgage (GPM), 366
Grantor trust, 120, 121
Great Depression, 63, 278
Gross national product (GNP), 419
Gross yield, 472
Grupo Sipi, 258
Guarantee(s), 55-56, 144, 285

see Federal National, Interest, Monoline, Parent, Performance, Prepayment, Third, U.S. agency
structures, 47-51
Guaranteed investment contract (GIC), 106, 130, 132, 149, 154, 173, 204, 296, 339, 460
Guarantors, 339
see Credit, Financial, Monoline
capital adequacy standards, 185-186
portfolio quality, 183
state regulatory standards, 186-187
underwriting standards, 184-185
Guaranty insurance, 183

H

Hard bullet, 461-462
structure, 138
Hazard
see Default
function estimation, 357, 360-361
models, 357
Health and Safety at Work Act (1974), 237
Health care receivables, 111
Hedge
see Delta, Dynamic, Mortgage
fluctuation, 436
ratio, 387
strategies, 407-408
Hedging, 15, 20, 79, 302, 394
see Cross, Currency, Dynamic, Fixed-rate, Foreign, Interest rate, Portfolio, Securitization
programs, 274-275
volatility changes, 23
Hell or high water clauses, 161
Hifin program, 289
Hipoteca mobilaria, 257
Hire purchase
agreements, 241
receivables, 203, 238, 243
HLIC, see Housing
HLT, 87
HMC, see Household
HMO, 164
Home
see Federal Home
builders, 20
equity loan, 27, 48, 52, 111, 154
Federal, 118
Home mortgage, 5
loan, 5
Hong Kong Shanghai Banking Corporation, 116
Horizontal spread, 410
Household, 475
Household mortgage, 203
Household Mortgage Corporation (HMC) PLC, 58, 83, 306, 313, 318
Housing
see Developed, Manufactured
funding, 342-348
Denmark, 345
France, 346
Germany, 346-347
United Kingdom, 347-348
Housing Loans Insurance Company (HLIC), 338
Hugoton Properties, 80

I

IAS, see International
IASC, see International
IF, see Inverse
IFIM Leasing, 130, 258
Implied
loss severity, 369
mortgage price elasticities, 425-433
Income Tax Law, 263
Incremental lending, 205
Indemnity
see Mortgage
limit, 132
policy, 127
Individual participants, benefits/costs, 11
Individual Retirement Account (IRA), 391
Industrial loan, 5, 111
Inflow/outflow, 147
Inland Revenue, 244
Ordinance, 264
Insolvency, 81, 139, 253, 255, 260, 262, 264
see Seller
Act (1986), 242, 247
considerations, 242-243, 247, 250, 259-260
remote, 242, 262, 264
Installment loan
see Automobile, Boat, Computer, Manufactured, Recreational, Truck
contract, 52
Installment sales contracts, 280
Institute of Chartered Accountants, 240
Institutions, see Issuing
Insurance, 23, 45, 55-56
see Bond, Cash flow, Contingency, Deposit, Federal Deposit, Guaranty, Monoline, Mortgage, Pool
companies, 3, 20, 82, 122
see Multiline
law (NY), 186
policy, 81
loan, 111
security structures, 47-51
underwriting, 4
Insured asset-backed securities, benefits, 181-183
monitoring, 182
surveillance, 182
Insured mortgage-backed securities, 376, 381, 382
Insured structures, 376-378
Insurer, 371
see Mortgage
tenure, 140
Intercompany sales, 266, 267, 272
Interest, 20, 53
see Certificate, Investor, Loan, Residual, Seller, Undivided
guarantee, 172
payment, 47, 305
principal payment, 61-62
savings, 205

structure shift, 53
Interest-only, 382, 393
payment (IO), 21, 23
securities, 45-46, 301
strips, 45-46, 56, 57, 62, 68
Interest rate, 21, 23, 78, 148, 149, 181, 204, 323, 393, 407
cap, 57, 316
exposure, 206
insensitivity, 347
mismatches, hedging, 295-296
sensitivity, 29
spike, 295
swap, 229, 244, 314
volatility, 15, 19, 23, 375, 416-418
Interest rate changes
effects, 16-20
exposure, 16
lender value response, 17-18
Interest rate risk, 6, 12, 15, 23, 24, 29, 30, 40, 78, 79, 85, 106, 170, 315, 347, 353, 375, 397, 414
see Retention
allocation, 351-353
Denmark, 351-353
France, 353
Germany, 353
United Kingdom, 353
exposure, 16
hedging incentive, 19-20
management, 15, 16
reallocation, structures, 56-58
reduction, 6-7, 114-115
Interest rate swaps, 56, 58
agreement, 87
Intermediary, 7, 15, 16, 19, 29, 78, 306, 342, 351
see Deposit
default risk, 345
Intermediation
see Disintermediation
services, 15-16
Internal reserve level, 102
International Accounting Standards (IAS)
Board, 200
Committee (IASC), 225
International securitization, emerging economies, 71-76
background, 71
In-the-money, 425
Inverse floater (IF), 62, 382, 393
Inverse floating-rate note, 56, 57-58
creation, 62
Investment(s), 157-158, 241, 268, 270, 271
see Guaranteed, Real Estate, Reinvestment
bank(s), 20
banker(s), 4, 5
company status, 244
fund, 82
tax credit, 20
trust, 82
Investors, 3, 4, 180, 217, 244, 251, 253, 346
see Portfolio, Protection, Subordinate
asset value, 142
base development, 308-309
benefits, 181
investor, 472
principal payment structures, 455-462
IO, *see* Interest-only
IRA, *see* Individual
Irrevocable
letter of credit, 463
standby letter of credit, 81
Issuer benefits, 182
Issuing institutions, 4-6
Italian Bankruptcy Law, 259
Italian Civil Code, 258
Italian Stock Exchange, 258

J

Jump Z bond, 395
Junior
note, 171
tranche, 7, 145
Junk bond, 111

K

Kommanditgesellschaft, 254
Kreditwesengesetz (Banking Act), 254

L

Labor, 74
La Caridad, *see* Caridad
Landesbanken, 342, 355
Law No.51/1991, 258, 259
Law of 1988, 247, 248, 250
Law of 1993, 248-250
Law of Property Act of 1925 (LPA), 236, 263
LDC, *see* Less
Leases, 155, 161
see Collateralized, Equipment, Finances, Operating
receivables, 203, 235, 243-244, 258
Legal
fees, 203, 271
risk, 71, 135-152, 275
transfer, 246
Lehman Brothers, 110
Lender
see Portfolio
credit function, 141-142
Less developed countries (LDCs), 77
Letter of credit (LOC), 9, 47, 49, 51, 56, 75, 127, 130, 132, 143-145, 147, 148, 156, 174, 180, 187, 273, 363, 454, 473, 475, 478
see Irrevocable, Servicer
Leverage, 62
Ley del Mercado de Valores, 257
Liability, 29, 61, 158, 225, 230, 237, 245, 296, 302, 348, 375
see Asset, Contingent, Tax
LIMEAN, 297
Limit structure, 219
Linked presentation, 224-225, 240
Liquidation, 294
proceeds, 53
surplus, 249

Liquidator, 128, 246
Liquidity, 4, 65, 78, 146-148, 158, 182, 299, 316, 318, 463
  backup line, 282
  coverage, 87
  enhancement, 273-274, 281
  facility, 132, 133, 156, 171, 282
  facility costs, 132
  fees, 271
  lines, 75, 204
  support, 149
Liquidity risk, 29-30, 40, 105, 170, 171, 218
  allocation, 353-355
    Denmark, 353
    France, 355
    Germany, 355
    United Kingdom, 355
  management, 127-133
  reduction, structures, 56
  transfer, 127-133
Listing restrictions, 242
Loan(s), 4, 155
  see Automobile, Bank, Capital, Collateralized, Commercial, Commodity, Consumer, Corporate, Dealer, Equipment, Equity, Floating, Home, Industrial, Installment, Insurance, Loan-to-value, Mortgage, Personal, Profit, Revolving, Senior, Student, Term, Time
  administration, 140
  amortization, structure, 52
  documentation, 206
  embedded option effect, 19
  facility, 273
  interest, 4
  loss, 50
  made/serviced (advantages), 3, 7
  origination, 351
  originators, 5
  pool, 4
  production, 139-140
  sales, 85
  transfers, 85-87
Loan-to-value (LTV), 350, 351, 359, 360
  loan, 351, 357, 359
  mortgage, 195
  ratio, 64, 155, 193, 195, 292, 348, 350, 357, 364
LOC, *see* Letter
Loi Dailly, 248
London Insurance, 191
London Interbank Offer Rate, 58
  see Mortgage-to-LIBOR
  LIBOR, 58, 62, 68, 80, 89, 91, 92, 118, 121, 204, 294, 295, 297, 306, 316, 348, 392, 393, 436, 437, 441, 446
  LIBOR-indexed MBS, 347
  LIBOR-Plus fund, risk management, 299-304
  LIBOR-Treasury spread risk management, 303-303
London Stock Exchange, 241, 242
Long call, 400
Long put, 398-399
Long-term debt rating scale, 165-166
Loss
  allocation, 190
  data, 155-156
  exposure, 193
  probability reduction, 101
LPA, *see* Law
LTV, *see* Loan-to-value
Luxembourg Stock Exchange, 241, 242

M

MAC, *see* Material
Mack Financial Corporation, 116, 118, 121
Mack Truck Receivables Corporation, 45
Macy's, 452
MAES ECP, 312
  No. 1 PLC, 289-298
  structure, 290-291
MAES Funding No. 2 PLC, 309
Management, 74, 139
  see Asset, London, Risk
  controls, 105
  fees, 271
  reports, 220
  structure, 206
  systems, 105
  time, 203
Manufactured housing installment loan, 27, 48, 52
Margin, 201, 309
  see Break-even, Discount
  Marginal
  capital cost, 10
  yield, 10
Marine Midland, 112, 114, 115-116, 118, 120, 123, 124
Market
  multifamily mortgage (MMUF), 321
  price, 408, 409
  risk, 218, 221, 384
  value, 19, 23
MasterCard, 452
Master trust, 120
Match-fund, 114
Matching requirements, 348
Material Adverse Change (MAC), 284
Maturity, 4, 155, 181, 258, 268, 319, 375, 387, 393, 394
  see Bullet, Constant, Very
  date, 138
  options, 19
  profile risk, 85
  structure, 4
MBIA, *see* Municipal
MBS, *see* Mortgage-backed
MCI, *see* Mortgage
Mechanical arrangements, 230
Medicare/Medicaid, 164-165
Medium Term Note (MTN), 107
  see Euro, U.S.
Merging laws, 10
Merrill Lynch, 118
  Asset-Backed Corporation (MLABC), 120-121
Mesa Limited Partners, 80
Mexcobre (Mexicana del Cobre), 79
Mezzanine

bonds, *see* Subordinated
tranche, 318
MFC, *see* Mortgage
MGIC, 190
MGICA, 337, 338
MGICA Securities Ltd. (MSL), 337
MIG, *see* Mortgage
Ministry of Finance (MOF), 260-262
Ministry of International Trade and Industry (MITI), 260-262
MIRAS, 236, 237, 245, 306
Mismatches, *see* Interest rate, Repayment
MITI, *see* Ministry of International
Mitigants, 74-75
MMOG, *see* Mortgage Manager
MMUF, *see* Market multifamily
Model Transaction Structure, 265-266
MOF, *see* Ministry of Finance
Monetary claim, 262
Money Lenders Law, 261
(1983), 262
Money Lenders Ordinance, 263
Money market
funds, 158
mutual funds, 12, 40
Monoline, 103, 127, 131, 192
financial guarantee companies, 174
financial guarantor role, 179-187
products, 179-181
strength assessment, 183-187
guarantees, 132
guarantors, 183
insurance companies, 173, 183
insured portfolio, 183
insurers, 130-131, 182, 183, 312
Monte Carlo simulation methods, 186
Montgomery Ward, 452
Monthly Payment Rate (MPR), 449, 465-466
Moody's, 5, 63, 186, 220, 290, 363, 376
Investor's Service, 186
Moral hazard, 4-6, 13, 14
Morgan Guaranty Trust Company, 45, 159, 162
Morgan, JP, 75, 297
Morgan Stanley, 123
Mortgage, 6, 33-35, 36-38, 105, 110, 169, 242, 243, 257
see Adjustable, Canadian, Collateralized, Commercial, Credit, Farm, Federal, Fixed-rate, Government, Graduated, Home, Household, Implied, Loan-to-value, On-balance, Pool, Premium, Prepayable, Primary, Real Estate, Remortgaging, Residential, Reviewable
bankers, 20
Banking Act, 200
bond, 165, 175, 341, 348
characteristics, 35
collateral, 376
Corporation, 191, 306
credit institution (MCI), 345, 348, 353
default application, 357-359
Funding Corporation (MFC), 312, 313
hedge, statistical analysis, 441-446
Indemnity Guarantee (MIG), 131, 132, 170, 173, 316
provider, 170-171
indemnity guaranty, 193
instruments, *see* Securitized
insurance, 337-340, 350
insurer, 338, 339
loan, 33, 37, 45, 255
see Commercial, Multifamily, Residential
loan production, 15-16
operation report description, 139-142
management/organization, 139
originator, 21
pass-through market, 145
pass-through security, 30, 51, 186
pass-throughs, 402
payments, 413-416
pool, 20, 42-44, 57, 87
indemnity policy, 176
insurance, 51, 189, 193
portfolio, 45, 46, 353, 375
prepayments, 19, 24
price curves, 425
rate, 34
return, statistical analysis, 441-446
risk, 357
statistical analysis, 441-446
Securities (No.2) PLC, 310
securities market, 136
see U.K.
securitization, 171, 297
see Developed Housing
securitization, elements, 15-25
introduction, 15
servicing rights, 154
types, 110, 366
yield, 132
Mortgage-backed instruments, 301
Mortgage-backed receivables, 252
Mortgage-backed securities (MBSs), 27, 29, 31, 40, 48, 52, 63, 110-112, 173, 175, 235, 279, 287-446
see Australian, Canadian, Insured, Non-prepayable, Prepayable, Residential, Senior, U.K.
payments, 46-47
Mortgage-backed transactions, 236-237
Mortgage Manager Obligation Guarantee (MMOG), 338
Mortgage Related Security (MRS), 397, 399, 401, 402
Mortgage-to-LIBOR yield spread, 347
Mortgage-Treasury
spread risk, monitoring, 304
yield spread, 416-418
MPR, *see* Monthly
MRS, *see* Mortgage Related
MSL, *see* MGICA
MTN, *see* Euro, Medium, U.S.
Multi-country securitization, 265-275
structure, 274
Multifamily mortgage
see Market
loans, 27, 142
Multiline, 131, 192
insurance company, 127, 173-174

Multioriginator program, 105
risk, 107-108
Multiple-seller vehicles, 272
Multi-tranche structures, 309-312
Municipal Bond Investors Assurance Corp. (MBIA), 174, 179, 190
Mutual funds, 22, 158
see Money
Mutual thrifts, 10

N

Naked call, 406, 407
Napoleonic Code, 223
National Association of Insurance Commissioners, 75
NAIC, 75
National Automobile Dealers Association Blue Book, 119
National Century Financial Enterprises (NCFE), 164
National Commission for Companies and the Stock Exchange, 259
CONSOB, 259
National Home Loans (NHL) Corporation PLC, 201, 306, 309-313, 317, 318
National Housing Act (NHA), *see* Canadian
National Mortgage Market Corporation Limited (NMMC), 337, 338
National Physicians Funding, 162-165
Health Care Receivables Funding Notes, 162-164
National Premier Financial Services (NPFS), 164, 165
National Securities Market Commission, 256, 257
NatWest, 313
Navistar, 116, 118, 120
NCFE, *see* National Century
Negative excess spread, 475
Neiretz Law (1990), 350
Net present value (NPV), 132
projects, 11
New South Wales Government, 338
New York Stock Exchange, 80
NHA, *see* National Housing
NHL, *see* National Home
Non-amortization period, 455
Nonbankers, 3
Noncallable corporates, 372
Non-compliance risk, 129
Noninsured debt, 7
Non-prepayable MBS, 321
Non-proportional reinsurance, 190, 192
Non-recourse funding, 78
Nonrecoverable losses, 147
Notarial fees, 256
Note, *see* Fixed-rate, Floating, Junior, Medium, Promissory, Senior, Subordinated
Notice to account debtors, 272
Novation, 86
NPFS, *see* National Premier
NPV, *see* Net

O

OAS, *see* Option
Obligation, 85, 243, 284, 291
see Collateralized, Farmer, Franchisee, On-sheet, Repurchase, Support
October 1987 stock market crash, 123, 347
OECD, 71-73, 112
Off-balance funding, 345
Off-balance sheet, 200, 201, 227, 238-241, 252, 254, 263, 270, 283, 292
accounting aspects, 240
finance, 289
financing, 342
legal aspects, 240-241
regulatory aspects, 238-240
treatment, 78, 224, 261, 270
Oil
distribution rights, 27
industry, 79
prices, 37
On-balance sheet, 201, 238-241
accounting aspects, 240
legal aspects, 240-241
mortgage bonds, 3345
obligations, 341
servicing, 140
regulatory aspects, 238-240
One-off structure, 249
Operating
Companies, 265-267, 272-275
leases, 280
Operational
control, 220
risk, 99, 103, 105-107
Operations, 74
Optimization, *see* Structured
Option(s), 397-403
see Call, Embedded, Gilt, Maturity, Over, Put, Split-fee, Strategic, U.S. Treasury
adjusted, 372
adjusted spread (OAS), 63, 315, 373, 385, 440
pricing, 319, 330-331
exercising, 402
premium, 406
trading strategies, 398-402
value, 400
Organization, 139
Originating pool, 100
Origination, 112, 141, 154-157, 164, 312, 316, 358, 359
see Asset, Loan
process, 363-364
Originators, 3-6, 100, 129-132, 141, 172, 203-205, 223, 224, 238, 240, 242, 245, 246, 255, 260, 262, 291, 341
see Asset, Bank, Loan, Mortgage, Multi-originator, Seller
recourse, 107
level setting, 101-102
reserve setting, 101-102
Orphan structure, 241
Osprey Mortgage Securities, 175-177, 191
OTC, *see* Over-the-counter
Out-of-the-money, 400, 408, 409
Out-of-the-money put, 399

Overcollateralization, 127, 130, 182, 149, 283, 291, 318
Overhead costs, 205
Over-the-counter (OTC)
market, 406
option, 399, 402, 405, 407
Owners trust, 120
Ownership
issues, 237
structure, 23-24

P

PAC, *see* Planned
Packager, 56
Packaging, 85
Pairoffs, 400
Paper, *see* Chattel, Commercial
Parent guarantee, 363
Paribas, 79
Pari passu, 293
Parity price, 328
Partial principal, 172
Participants, *see* Individual
Participation
certificate, 110
companies, incentives, 283
Participaciones Hipotecarias (PHs), 255-257
Pass-through, 146
see Mortgage
certificate, 159
format, 118
rate (PTR), 377, 378, 380, 462
securities, 217
structure, 47-48, 122, 249
Pay, *see* Fast
PAY, *see* Sequential
Payment, 154
see Bullet, Certificate, Franchisee, Graduated, Interest, Interest-only, Investor, Monthly, Mortgage, Mortgage-backed, Pool, Prepayment, Principal, Principal-only, Repayment
rate, *see* Default
risk, 71, 73, 79, 81
Payor risk analysis, 165
Pay-out event, 51, 464
Pay-through structure, 48
PE, *see* Price
Penn Square Bank debacle, 7
Penny, J.C., 452
Pension funds, 3, 41, 82
Performance, 314
see Administrator, Portfolio, Servicer, Third
bonds, 65, 81-82
guarantees, 63, 81, 173
information, 356
measures, 219
ratios, 283
risk, 71, 73-74, 79
statistics, 466-468
Personal loan, 87
Petrodollars, 77
PFA, *see* Principal
Pfandbriefe, 346
PH, *see* Participaciones
Philbro Energy Oil, Inc., 79, 80
Pipeline
analysis, 402
fallout, 397
Plain vanilla bond, 157
Planned amortization class bond, 43-45
band, 44
PAC, 46, 62, 382, 389-390
tranche, 310
Pledge, 230, 253, 257
deeds, 260
PMI, *see* Primary
PO, *see* Principal-only
Political risk, 74, 218
Pool, 9, 35, 101, 102, 128, 267, 268, 281, 282
see Asset, Collateral, Loan, Mortgage, Originating, Prepayable, Weighted
balance, 155
cash flow, 141
characteristics, 155
hazard insurance policy, 55
insurance, 171-173, 189, 315, 316, 363, 376
see Mortgage
policy, 47
insurer, 56, 129
mortgage insurance policies, 339
payment rate, 473-474
restructuring, 100-101
size, 132
statistics, 469
Poolers, 4-6
see Farmer
Portfolio, 5, 11, 12, 23, 27, 30, 43, 101, 102, 131, 140, 142, 155, 225, 227, 251-253, 262, 279, 292, 302, 305, 346, 367, 373
see Asset, Bond, Guarantor, Monoline, Mortgage, Senior
analysis, 142-143
diversification, 115
duration, 302
hedging, 57
investor, 110
lender, 110
low convexity risk, quantitative analysis, 299-302
manager, 57, 61, 405, 411
monitoring, 105
performance, 138-139, 143, 299, 316, 464
risk, 144
securitization, 100
selection, 207
strategy, 110
structuring, 105
yield, 302
Position, 411
Preferred stock, 84, 166, 375
rating scale, 165-166
Premium, 428, 438
see Credit, Event, Flexible, Option, Single, Transactions, Yield
mortgage, 419
Prenda, 257

Prepayable
  see Non-prepayable
  Canadian MBS, 321-323
  MBS, 319, 320
  pools, 326, 332
Prepayment, 4, 23, 35, 36, 44, 46, 62, 63, 147, 148, 295, 310, 320, 330, 331, 358, 363, 364, 378, 384
  see Constant, Mortgage, Public
  collars, 385, 391
  data/analysis, 418-424
  guarantees, 45
  macroeconomic models, 24
  option, 323-324, 413-416
  penalty, 33
  provisions, 155
  rates, 29, 35, 380, 418
    curves, 423
  risk, 4, 6, 28-29, 33-36, 42-44, 105-106, 229, 375, 377, 386
  risk reallocation, structures, 40-46
  risk reduction, 6-7
  speed, 44, 45, 386
Presentation, *see* Linked, Separate
Price
  see Implied, Market, Mortgage, Parity, Purchase, Strike
  appreciation, 299
  risk, 430
  sensitivity duration, 372
  stability, 390, 393
  volatility, 401, 438
Price to earnings (PE) ratio, 204
Pricing
  see Option
  implications, 359
  risk, 319
  UPP impact, 328
Primary Mortgage Insurance (PMI), 63
Prime rate, 278
Principal, 4, 20, 43, 53, 68, 369, 378, 379, 466
  see Bond, Full, Partial, Unscheduled
  Funding Account (PFA), 460, 461
  interest payment, 61-62
Principal-only, 393-394
  see Super
  payment (PO), 21, 23
  securities, 45-46
  strips, 45-46, 56, 57, 62, 376, 382
Profit, 245
Profitability, 199, 200, 205, 299
Profit extraction, 244-245
Profit/loss recognition, 223
Profit/profitability comparison, 89-95
Promissory notes, 261, 277
Property
  location, 366-367
  type/purpose, 366
  value decline, 367-369
Provider
  see Credit enhancement, First-loss, Mortgage
  risk analysis, 165
Proportional reinsurance, 190
Protection of Investors Ordinance, 263
Prudential Home, 110
Prudential Securities, 118, 120
PSA, *see* Public
PTR, *see* Pass-through
Public Securities Association (PSA), 398
  Standard Prepayment Model, 33, 34, 42-45
Purchase
  price (seller), 266-267
  rate, 136, 137, 475
Purchaser, funding, 271
Put option, 15, 439
  see Long, Out, Short, Synthetic

Q

Quality control, 139, 140
Quantitative analysis, *see* Portfolio
Quota-share, 190, 192

R

RAM, *see* Reverse
Ranking definitions, 140-141
Rating agency, 294
  approach, 185-187
  costs, 205, 271
  criteria, 377
  fees, 203
Real Estate Mortgage Investment Conduit, 42
  see Federal National
  REMIC, 42, 52, 55, 58, 61, 121, 148
  structures, 61-62
Real estate prices, 40
Receivables, 101, 136, 149, 207, 228, 229, 251-252, 254, 260, 265, 266, 268, 273, 279, 294, 296
  see Automobile loan, Consumer, Credit card, Future, Health, Hire, Lease, Mortgage-backed, Trade, Truck
  balance, 472
  elimination, 100
  transfer, 236-237, 250
  transferability, 245-247, 253-254, 255-256, 258, 260-261, 263
  trustee, 237
  types, 245-247, 253-254, 255-256, 258, 260-261, 263
  unit trust, 252
Recession, 35, 37
Recourse, 228-229
  see Originator
  risk, 228-229
Recoveries, 63
Recreational vehicle, 119
  installment loan, 27, 48
Redemption, 296, 311, 318
  rate, 132
Refinancing risk, 170, 173, 291, 292-294, 353
Registration tax, 252, 258
Regulation cost, 10-11
Regulation Q, 13
Regulatory
  issues, 254-255, 259
  risk, 218, 221

Reimbursement, 162
Reinsurance
see Cross-border, Facultative, Financial Guaranty, Non-proportional, Proportional, Treaty
forms, 190
methods, 189
slips, 189
Reinsurers, 195, 196, 316
Reinvestment, 296
see Cash, Cash flow
loss, 219
opportunities, 323
rate, 320, 332
risk, 170, 218-219, 296, 314, 319
REMIC, see Real Estate
Remortgaging, 194
Renault, 116, 130
Repayment, 318, 320, 321, 449
see Capital, Trigger
mismatches, 296
rate, 451
schedule, 456
Repo, see Repurchase
Reporting
procedures, 273
structure, 219
Repossession, 155, 161
Representations, 229-230
RepublicBank, 453, 473
Repurchase
agreement (repo), 302, 436
event, 465-466
obligation, 86
Reserve, see Internal, Originator
Reserve fund, 81, 144, 145
see Cash
structure, 53
Residential Funding Corporation, 110
Residential mortgage, 29, 154, 185, 248, 320
backed securities, 111
loans, 27, 35, 40, 48, 87, 235
Residual, 22
claimant, 21
holder, 62
interest, 268
tranche, 4
value, 23, 161
Resolution Trust Corporation (RTC), 63, 68, 139
Retailer, 137
Retention of interest rate risk, 229
Retirement, 16
Return, see Fixed-rate mortgage
Return enhancement, see Total
Return on capital employed (ROCE), 88, 89, 91, 92, 95
see Trading
Revenue assets, 243
Reverse annuity mortgage (RAM), 325-327, 331
Reviewable-rate mortgage (RRM), 342, 343
Revolving
corporate loan, 87
loan, structure, 55
personal overdraft, 87
trust, 471-472
Risk, 283
see Administrator, Arbitrage, Asset, Asset-backed, Bankruptcy, Basis, Cash, Cash flow, Certificate, Claim, Collateralized, Commingling, Control, Convexity, Copper, Counterparty, Credit, Cross-border, Credit, Currency, Default, Documentation, Downgrade, Economic, Event, Financial, Fixed-rate, Foreign, Funds, Gap, Interest, Intermediary, Legal, Liquidity, London, Market, Maturity, Mortgage, Multi, Non-compliance, Operational, Payment, Payor, Performance, Political, Portfolio, Prepayment, Price, Pricing, Provider, Recourse, Refinancing, Regulatory, Reinvestment, Retention, Securitization, Securitized, Servicer, Servicing, Special, Structuring, Subordinate, Swap, Third, Transaction, Trustee, Yield, Zero
allocation, 97-196
allocation structures, 46
analysis, 425-433
assessment, 9, 218-219
asset ratio, 87, 89, 205
aversion, 20
control, 6, 217-221
estimation, 6
evaluation, see Credit card-backed
exposure, 37
identification, 97-196
management, 85, 197-231
see London
market control, 329-330
principal classes, 28-29
profile change, 202
reallocation, 27-60
benefits, 31-33
reduction, 6-7, 27-60
retention arrangement, 228-229
syndication, 189
tolerance, 140
transfer, 78, 86
ROCE, see Return
Rochester Community Savings Bank, 122
Rollover, 278
see Commercial paper
RRM, see Reviewable
RTC, see Resolution
Ryland Mortgage, 110

S

Sales
see Installment, Intercompany, Seller
finance comparison, 223
Salomon, Inc., 191
Salomon Brothers, 75, 79, 80, 115, 118, 123, 306, 417, 441, 443
Savings & Loans (S&Ls), 64, 68
S curve, 418
Sears, Roebuck & Co., 110, 118, 147, 148, 449, 450, 452-455, 466
Credit Card Account Trust, 147, 452
Receivables Financing Group (SRFG), 454
Seasonal fluctuations, 75
Seasonality, 466

Seasoning, 34-35, 364
  see Weighted
SE Banken, *see* Skandinaviska
SEC, *see* Securities and Exchange
Secondary market, 30, 144, 182
  yield, 17
Secondary marketing, 139, 140
SECPAC, *see* Security
Securities and Exchange Commission (SEC), 167, 277-278
Securities and Exchange Law (1948), 261
Securities and Futures Commission, 264
Securities Investment Trusts, 261
Securitization, 47, 217, 279, 338-340
  see Arrears, Asset, Bank, Banking, Commodities, Credit, Credit card, European, Global, International, Mortgage, Multi-country, Portfolio
  asset selection, 202-203
  attractions, 84-85
  benefits/costs, 3-11
  contracts, 227
  debt holder expropriation, 9-10
  economic analysis, 204-206
  European view, 83-95
    introduction, 83-84
  evaluation, 199-215
    European view, 199-215
  future, 14
  hedging, 23-24
  practical aspects, 206-207
  process, 280-283
  prospects, 355-356
  rationale, 217
  reasons, 199-202
  regulatory considerations, 85-87
  strategy, 110
  trade-offs, 227-231
  transaction, 285
  transaction risk, 99-108
Securitized
  assets, risks, 33-40
  claim, pricing, 24
  credit, 3
  mortgages instruments, types, 20-22
Security/securities, 255, 257, 260
  see Asset-backed, Credit, Insurance, Interest-only, Global, Mortgage, Mortgage-backed, Pass-through, Principal-only, Public, Senior, Sequential, Structure, Subordinated, Value, Zero
  considerations, 243, 253, 262, 264
  dealer, 36
  funds, 299
  law(s), 252-253, 254-255, 257
  Pacific Securities Australia Limited (SECPAC), 337
  process, 363-364
  regulation, 241-242, 250, 252-253, 259, 262, 264
  Sales & Trading Group (SS&TG), 402
Security Pacific, 114, 121-122
Self-correcting mechanisms, 181, 184-185
Self-supporting structures, 145
Seller
  see Multiple
  bankruptcy, 136, 138, 150
  credit quality, 136
  insolvency, 138
  interest, 472
  rating impact, 136-138
  sales, 267-268
Seller/originator, 152
Seller/servicer, 109, 136, 152
Selling restrictions, 242
Senior
  see Super
  bank loan portfolio, 185
  bonds, 62
  certificate, 454
  certificate holder, 53
  claims, 21
  debt, 315, 375, 454
  management, 219
  mortgage-backed securities, 375-382
  notes, 171
  securities, 51-55
  structures, 65
  subordinated bond, 127
  subordinated leverage, 370
  subordinated pass-through, 146
  subordinated structures, 65, 121, 122, 171, 180, 315, 316, 363, 376-378, 381, 450, 452, 463
  tier, 121
  tranche, 4
Separate presentation, 225
Sequential
  payment bond (PAY), 391-392
  pay security, 42-43
Servicer, 138, 141, 154, 158, 367, 469
  see Seller
  credit quality, 138
  flexibility, 142
  letter of credit, 464
  performance risk, 158
  risk, 157
    analysis, 162, 165
Servicing, 112, 141, 155-156, 164, 463
  see Mortgage, On-balance
  arrangements, 230-231
  costs, 471, 472
  fees, 271, 375, 377
    adequacy, 229
  risks, 138-139
Set-off, 258, 261
Setting-off claims, 258
Settlement
  date, 398
  procedures, 273
SFAS, 228
SFK, *see* Svensk
SGIC, *see* State
Share, *see* Time
Shareholders, 14, 259
Shearson Lehman, 118, 441
Short call, 405-406, 409
Short put, 407, 409
Short-term debt rating scale, 166-167
SICAV, 251
Sidetur, 80

Signet, 475
Single Premium Deferred Annuity (SPDA), 363, 371-373
  rate correlation, 370-371
Sinking fund, 45
Skandinaviska Enskilda Banken, 176, 191
SMM, 324, 329, 330
Societe des Bourses Francaises, 31
Societe Generale de Belgique, 79
Society National Bank, 165
Soft bullet, 138, 461-462
Sogem, S.A., 79
Southeast Bank, 473
Sovereign, *see* Foreign
Spanish Securities Market Act, 257
SPC, *see* Special
SPDA, see Single
SPE, *see* Special
Special Purpose
  company, 203, 206, 261, 262
  Corporation (SPC), 48, 87, 150, 151
  entity (SPE), 120-121, 150, 279-286
  subsidiary, 453
  Vehicle (SPV), 80-82, 86, 99-102, 104-107, 169-173, 218, 223, 236-238, 240-246, 248, 251-256, 258-264, 312-314, 375, 376
    see Contractual, Statutory
    administration, 105
    consolidation, 225
    Japanese (SPVJ), 262, 263
    SPV Collateralized Mortgage Securities PLC, 309
Special Risk Services (SRS), 129, 131-133
Sperry Lease Finance Corporation, 30
Split-fee option, 399-400
Spread, 34, 123, 348, 350, 371, 431, 433
  see Diagonal, Excess, Horizontal, London, Mortgage, Mortgage-to-LIBOR, Mortgage-Treasury, Option, Vertical
SPV/SPVJ, *see* Special Purpose
SRFG, *see* Sears
SRS, *see* Special Risk
SS&TG, *see* Security
Stability testing, 387-388
Stamp duty, 248, 256-258
  Ordinance, 263
Standard Credit Card Master Trust, 481
Standard & Poor's (S&P), 5, 75, 135-151, 185, 186, 193, 220, 279, 282, 290, 291, 305, 338, 376, 441, 443
Standard Security, 246
State Guaranty Insurance Corp. of South Australia (SGIC), 192
Statutory
  assignment, 86
  SPV, 252
Sticky jump Z bonds, 395
Stochastic process, 63
Straddle, 408
Strangle, 409
Strategic
  options, 405-411
  planning, 85
Strike price, 398, 400, 406, 408
Strips, 21
  see Interest-only, Principal-only
Structural considerations, 248-250, 252, 254, 256-257, 259, 261-262, 263-264, 471-473
  accounting aspects, 249, 252, 254, 259, 261-262, 264
  legal aspects, 248-249, 252, 254, 256, 259, 261, 263
  regulatory aspects/constraints, 249-250, 252, 254, 256, 259, 261, 263-264
Structured finance, 166
  deals, 63-69
  introduction, 61
  law, 233-286
  optimization, 62-63
  techniques, 61-69
Structured securities, 135-152
Structured securitized credit, 3
Structuring
  see Portfolio
  expertise, 182-183
  fees, 203
Structuring risk, 99, 104
  legal issues, 104
  regulation, 104
  taxation, 104
Student loan, 111
Subordinate certificate, 463-464
  see Credit card
Subordinate class investors, risks, 473-475
Subordinated
  see Senior
  asset-backed securities, 51-55
  bonds, 128, 129, 132, 375
  certificate holder, 53
  claims, 21
  class, 369
  CMO class, 55-56
  debentures, 10
  debt, 84, 166, 225, 291, 375
  mezzanine bonds, 130
  notes, 133, 171
  securities, 121
  structures, 65
  tranche, 116, 145, 376, 377, 379, 382
  undivided interest, 267
Subordination, 138
  see Declining, Floor
  structures, 145-147
Subparticipation, 86
Subrogation, 251
Subsidies, *see* Cross
Substitution, 244, 310
  rights, 293, 295
Sun Alliance, 173, 191, 316
Super
  PO, 46
  senior, 66
Supply of Goods (Implied Terms) Act (1982), 237
Supply of Goods and Services Act of 1982, 237
Support obligation, 86
Surety, 144, 146, 156

bond, 47, 51
Surrender penalty, 371
Svensk Fastighetskredit (SFK), 175-176
Swap, 149, 302
see Basis, Commodity, Cross, Currency, Interest rate
counterparty, 158, 204
risk, 170
Swedish Export Credit Corporation, 176
Swiss Bank Corporation, 122
Synthetic put, 400, 407

T

TAC, *see* Targeted
Take or pay contract, 78
Targeted amortization class bonds, 43-45
TAC, 46, 62, 382, 390-391
TAURUS, 238
Tax, 149, 243-245, 250-251, 253-255, 257-258, 260, 264
see Advance, Corporate, Income, Investment, Registration, Structuring, Transfer, Value Added, Withholding
advice fees, 203
asymmetries, 28
leakage, 245
liability, 42
treatment, 183
Taxes Act (1988), 244
Tax-exempt bonds, 186
Telmex, 72-75
Term
authorization, 220
corporate loan, 87
Termination triggers, setting, 102
Term-to-expiration, 406
Texas Commerce Bank, 79
Third party, 251, 261, 279, 314
credit guarantee, 171
performance risk, 173
Third World, 217
Thrifts, 7, 110, 116
see Mutual
Thyssen, 80
Tiers, 84-85, 121, 167
see Senior
Time share loan, 27, 52
Time to expiration, 401-402
Titrisation, 200
Tokyo Stock Exchange, 262
Top-down analysis, 154
Total return enhancement, 331, 332-333
Trade
authorization, 402, 411
execution, 402
preparation, 402
receivables, 235, 280, 290, 292
tax, 254, 255
Trading
see Option
company status, 244
return on capital employed (TROCE), 89, 91
strategies, 431
Tranches, 4, 106, 290, 295, 314
see Collateralized, Equity, Junior, Mezzanine, Multi-tranche, Planned, Residual, Senior, Subordinated
assessment, 384
Tranching, *see* Credit
Transaction, 131, 137, 139, 158, 159, 172, 181, 182, 224, 229, 308
see Automobile, Credit card, Model, Mortgage-backed, Securitization
authorization, 220
economics, 89-95
control, 220
cost, 29, 36, 204, 411
reduction, 28
manager, 104
recording, 220
risk assessment, 297
Transactions-cost premium, 4
Transfer, 453
see Legal, Loan, Risk
tax, 257-258
tax issues, 237-238, 248
Treasury
see Constant, London, Mortgage, U.S.
management, 206
Treaty reinsurance, 189
Trigger, 149
see Amortization, Termination
event, 137
level, 74, 75
repayment, 473
Triple witching hour, 306
Truck
installment loan, 27
manufacturers, 116-118
Receivables Underlying Certificates (TRUCS), 118
TRUCS, *see* Truck
True sale, 151, 265-267, 272
Trust(s), 12, 246
see Credit card, Federal National, Grantor, Investment, Master, Owners, Receivables
Trustee, 63, 149, 154, 243, 245, 246, 291
see Receivable
expenses, 472
fee, 375
risk, 157
analysis, 162, 165
Trygg-Hansa Insurance Company, 173, 174, 176, 192

U

UAP, 173
UBS, *see* Union Bank
UCC, *see* Uniform
UL, *see* Universal
U.K. housing market, developments, 305-308
U.K. mortgage-backed securities, 192-196
U.K. mortgage securities market, developments, 305-318
Underwriter, 56, 109, 118, 367
Underwriting, 139-141

see Guarantor, Insurance
guidelines, 193
procedures, 366
standards, 366
Undivided interest, 265-268
see Subordinated
calculation, 268-271
UNI-Europe, 173
Uniform Commercial Code (UCC), 72, 119, 151
Union Bank of Switzerland (UBS), 80, 122, 174
Union Carbide, 289
Union Federal Savings Bank of Indianapolis, 123
Universal Life (UL)
rate correlation, 370-371
reset rates, 363
Unscheduled principal payment (UPP), 324-327
see Pricing
UPP, see Pricing, Unscheduled
U.S. agency guarantees, 46-47
U.S. Bankruptcy Code, 136, 150, 151, 453
U.S. Department of Housing and Urban Development (HUD), 110
U.S. Department of Labor, 167
U.S. Domestic CP, 89, 312-313
U.S. MTN, 89
U.S. Treasury, 4, 118, 122, 123, 302, 341, 384, 387, 450
bills, 17, 278, 441
bonds, 111
futures, 425, 433, 441, 443
options, 416
index, 68
rate, 371
yield, 348
yield curve, 303

V

VA, see Veteran's
VADM, see Very
Valeurs mobilieres, 250
Value Added Tax (VAT), 238, 245, 248, 252, 259, 263
Value sources, 1-95
security innovation, 28-33
VAT, see Value Added Tax
Vertical spread, 410
Very Accurately Defined Maturity (VADM), 391
Veterans Affairs, 46
Veterans' Administration (VA), 5, 51, 110, 375
Visa International, 73, 452, 474
Volatility, 20, 391, 400-401, 438, 464
see Collateralized, Hedging, Interest rate, Price
developments, 384-385
levels, 383
measurement, 387
rating (V-rating), 383
see Collateralized, Fitch
definitions, 395
strategies, 408-409
Volvo Auto Receivables, 12
V-rating, see Volatility

W

W-2 form, 64
WAL, see Weighted
WAM, see Wrap-around
Warranties, 223, 229-230, 242
Weighted average, 155, 323-325
cost of funding approach, 204
life (WAL), 33, 42, 387, 392
pool seasoning, 195
Weighting, see Zero risk
Western Financial Savings Bank, 116, 118, 126
Whipsaw
cost, 440, 441
loss, 440
Winterthur, 174
Withholding taxes, 78, 253, 255, 257, 263
World War II, 20, 278
Wrap-around mortgage (WAM), 325-327, 331
Write-offs, 228

Y

Yield, 50, 57, 88, 154, 162, 217, 268, 270, 299, 319, 371, 390, 391
see Asset, Certificate, Gross, Marginal, Mortgage, Mortgage-to-LIBOR, Mortgage-Treasury, Portfolio, Secondary, U.S.
on weighted risk assets (YOWRA), 88, 89, 92, 95
premium, 289
Yield curve, 319, 323, 331
advantage, 331
arbitrage, 61

Z

Z bond, 394-395
see Jump, Sticky
Zero coupon
accrual class, 42
bond, 203
security, 22
Zero loss
exposure, 130
standard, 184
Zero risk weighting, 86
Zero weighted commitments, 313
Zero weighting, 252

About the Publisher

PROBUS PUBLISHING COMPANY

Probus Publishing Company fills the informational needs of today's business professional by publishing authoritative, quality books on timely and relevant topics, including:

- Investing
- Futures/Options Trading
- Banking
- Finance
- Marketing and Sales
- Manufacturing and Project Management
- Personal Finance, Real Estate, Insurance and Estate Planning
- Entrepreneurship
- Management

Probus books are available at quantity discounts when purchased for business, educational or sales promotional use. For more information, please call the Director, Corporate/Institutional Sales at 1-800-998-4644, or write:

Director, Corporate/Institutional Sales
Probus Publishing Company
1925 N. Clybourn Avenue
Chicago, Illinois 60614
FAX (312) 868-6250